Communications in Computer and Information Science 1688

More information about this series at https://link.springer.com/bookseries/7899

Tran Khanh Dang · Josef Küng ·
Tai M. Chung (Eds.)

Future Data and Security Engineering

Big Data, Security and Privacy, Smart City
and Industry 4.0 Applications

9th International Conference, FDSE 2022
Ho Chi Minh City, Vietnam, November 23–25, 2022
Proceedings

 Springer

Editors
Tran Khanh Dang 🆔
Ho Chi Minh City University of Food
Industry
Ho Chi Minh City, Vietnam

Josef Küng
Johannes Kepler University of Linz
Linz, Austria

Tai M. Chung
Sungkyunkwan University
Seoul, Korea (Republic of)

ISSN 1865-0929   ISSN 1865-0937 (electronic)
Communications in Computer and Information Science
ISBN 978-981-19-8068-8   ISBN 978-981-19-8069-5 (eBook)
https://doi.org/10.1007/978-981-19-8069-5

This Springer imprint is published by the registered company Springer Nature Singapore Pte Ltd.
The registered company address is: 152 Beach Road, #21-01/04 Gateway East, Singapore 189721, Singapore

Preface

In CCIS volume 1688 we present the accepted contributions for the 9th International Conference on Future Data and Security Engineering (FDSE 2022). The conference took place during November 23–25, 2022, in the main campus of Ho Chi Minh City University of Food Industry (HUFI), Vietnam. Besides DBLP and other major indexing systems, the FDSE proceedings have also been indexed by Scopus and listed in the Conference Proceedings Citation Index (CPCI) of Thomson Reuters.

The annual FDSE conference is a premier forum designed for researchers, scientists, and practitioners interested in state-of-the-art and state-of-the-practice activities in data, information, knowledge, and security engineering to explore cutting-edge ideas, to present and exchange their research results and advanced data-intensive applications, and to discuss emerging issues on data, information, knowledge, and security engineering. At FDSE, researchers and practitioners are not only able to share research solutions to problems of today's data and security engineering themes but are also able to identify new issues and directions for future related research and development work.

The two-round call for papers resulted in the submission of 170 papers. A rigorous single blind peer-review process was applied to all of them. This resulted in 53 accepted papers (an acceptance rate of 31.2%) and four keynote speeches for CCIS volume 1688, which were presented at the conference. Every paper was reviewed by at least three members of the international Program Committee, who were carefully chosen based on their knowledge and competence. This careful process resulted in the high quality of the contributions published in this volume. The accepted papers were grouped into the following sessions:

- Invited Keynotes
- Big Data Analytics and Distributed Systems
- Security and Privacy Engineering
- Machine Learning and Artificial Intelligence for Security and Privacy
- Smart City and Industry 4.0 Applications
- Data Analytics and Healthcare Systems
- Short Papers: Security and Data Engineering

In addition to the papers selected by the Program Committee, nine internationally recognized scholars delivered keynote speeches:

- Dirk Draheim, Tallinn University of Technology, Estonia
- Václav Snášel, Technical University of Ostrava, Czech Republic
- Johann Eder, Alpen-Adria-Universität Klagenfurt, Austria
- Tai M. Chung, Sungkyunkwan University, South Korea
- Ahto Buldas, Tallinn University of Technology, Estonia
- Manuel Clavel, Vietnamese-German University, Vietnam, and University of Navarra, Spain

- Truyen Tran, Deakin University, Australia
- Josef Küng, Johannes Kepler University Linz, Austria
- Phan Thanh An, Ho Chi Minh City University of Technology, VNU-HCM, Vietnam

The success of FDSE 2022 was the result of the efforts of many people, to whom we would like to express our gratitude. First, we would like to thank all authors who submitted papers to FDSE 2022, especially the invited speakers for the keynotes. We would also like to thank the members of the committees and additional reviewers for their timely reviewing and lively participation in the subsequent discussion in order to select the high-quality papers published in this volume. Last but not least, we thank the Organizing Committee members and the host institute, HUFI, for their great support of FDSE 2022 even during the COVID-19 pandemic time.

November 2022   Tran Khanh Dang
                                                                        Josef Küng
                                                                    Tai M. Chung

Organization

Honorary Chair

Nguyen Xuan Hoan — Ho Chi Minh City University of Food Industry, Vietnam

Program Committee Chairs

Tran Khanh Dang — Ho Chi Minh City University of Food Industry, Vietnam
Josef Küng — Johannes Kepler University Linz, Austria
Tai M. Chung — Sungkyunkwan University, South Korea

Steering Committee

Artur Andrzejak — Heidelberg University, Germany
Manuel Clavel — Vietnamese-German University, Vietnam, and University of Navarra, Spain
Dirk Draheim — Tallinn University of Technology, Estonia
Johann Eder — Alpen-Adria-Universität Klagenfurt, Austria
Dinh Nho Hao — Institute of Mathematics, Vietnam Academy of Science and Technology, Vietnam
Dieter Kranzlmüller — Ludwig Maximilian University of Munich, Germany
Erich Neuhold — University of Vienna, Austria
Silvio Ranise — Fondazione Bruno Kessler, Italy
Makoto Takizawa — Hosei University, Japan
A Min Tjoa — TU Wien, Austria

Program Committee

Artur Andrzejak — Heidelberg University, Germany
Phan Thanh An — Ho Chi Minh City University of Technology, Vietnam
Pham The Bao — Saigon University, Vietnam
Hyunseung Choo — Sungkyunkwan University, South Korea
Manuel Clavel — Vietnamese-German University, Vietnam, and University of Navarra, Spain
H. K. Dai — Oklahoma State University, USA

Vitalian Danciu   Ludwig Maximilian University of Munich,
                                Germany
Quang-Vinh Dang   Industrial University of Ho Chi Minh City,
                                Vietnam
Nguyen Tuan Dang   Saigon University, Vietnam
Tran Tri Dang   RMIT University, Vietnam
Thanh-Nghi Do   Can Tho University, Vietnam
Thanh-Dang Diep   Ludwig Maximilian University of Munich,
                                Germany
Dirk Draheim   Tallinn University of Technology, Estonia
Johann Eder   Alpen-Adria-Universität Klagenfurt, Austria
Duc Tai Le   Sungkyunkwan University, South Korea
Ngo Duong Ha   Ho Chi Minh City University of Food Industry,
                                Vietnam
Trung Ha Le Hoai   University of Information Technology, Vietnam
Raju Halder   Indian Institute of Technology, Patna, India
Trung-Hieu Huynh   Industrial University of Ho Chi Minh City,
                                Vietnam
Kha-Tu Huynh   International University - VNU-HCM, Vietnam
Kien Huynh   Stony Brook University, USA
M-Tahar Kechadi   University College Dublin, Ireland
Nhien-An Le-Khac   University College Dublin, Ireland
Tomohiko Igasaki   Kumamoto University, Japan
Koichiro Ishibashi   University of Electro-Communications, Japan
Le Pham Tuyen   Kyunghee University, South Korea
Nguyen Thi Bich Ngan   Technical University of Ostrava, Czech Republic
Thien Khai Tran   Ho Chi Minh City University of Foreign
                                Languages and Information Technology,
                                Vietnam
Nguyen Le Hoang   Ritsumeikan University, Japan
Nguyen Van Sinh   International University - VNU-HCM, Vietnam
Ha Mai Tan   National Taiwan University, Taiwan
Hoang Duc Minh   National Physical Laboratory, UK
Nguyen Thai-Nghe   Can Tho University, Vietnam
Trung Viet Nguyen   Can Tho University of Technology, Vietnam
Long Nguyen Thanh   Ho Chi Minh City University of Food Industry,
                                Vietnam
An Khuong Nguyen   Ho Chi Minh City University of Technology,
                                Vietnam
Duy Ngoc Nguyen   Deakin University, Australia
Nguyen Van Thinh   Ho Chi Minh City University of Food Industry,
                                Vietnam

Thanh Binh Nguyen	Ho Chi Minh City University of Technology, Vietnam
Alex Norta	Tallinn University of Technology, Estonia
Eric Pardede	La Trobe University, Australia
Vinh Pham	Sungkyunkwan University, South Korea
Pham Nguyen Huy Phuong	Technical University of Ostrava, Czech Republic
Erik Sonnleitner	Johannes Kepler University Linz, Austria
Michel Toulouse	Hanoi University of Science and Technology, Vietnam
Tran Minh Quang	Ho Chi Minh City University of Technology, Vietnam
Le Hong Trang	Ho Chi Minh City University of Technology, Vietnam
Tran Van Hoai	Ho Chi Minh City University of Technology, Vietnam
Minh Truong	Ho Chi Minh City University of Technology, Vietnam
Takeshi Tsuchiya	Tokyo University of Science, Japan
Lam Son Le	Ho Chi Minh City University of Technology, Vietnam
Edgar Weippl	SBA Research, Austria
Kok-Seng Wong	VinUniversity, Vietnam
Wolfram Woess	Johannes Kepler University Linz, Austria

Local Organizing Committee

Tran Khanh Dang	Ho Chi Minh City University of Food Industry, Vietnam
La Hue Anh	Ho Chi Minh City University of Technology, Vietnam
Nguyen Le Hoang	Ritsumeikan University, Japan
Josef Küng	Johannes Kepler University Linz, Austria
Le Thi Hong Anh	Ho Chi Minh City University of Food Industry, Vietnam
Thai Doan Thanh	Ho Chi Minh City University of Food Industry, Vietnam
Trung-Hieu Huynh	Industrial University of Ho Chi Minh City, Vietnam
Nguyen Hai Binh	Ho Chi Minh City University of Food Industry, Vietnam
Tuan Phat Tran-Truong	Ho Chi Minh City University of Food Industry, Vietnam
Nguyen Van Tung	Ho Chi Minh City University of Food Industry, Vietnam

Additional Reviewers

Christopher Höllriegl
Viet Ngo
Xuan Tinh Chu
Tan Dat Trinh
Sang Vu
Thai Do
Manh-Tuan Nguyen
Hoang Xuan Bach
Huu Huong Xuan Nguyen

Tuan Phat Tran-Truong
Hadi Nowandish
Chibuzor Udokwu
Mohammad Mustafa Ibrahimy
Viet Hang Duong
Van Loi Cao
Ho Duc Dan
Vo Thi Hong Tuyet
The Cuong Nguyen

Host and Sponsors

Contents

Machine Learning and Artificial Intelligence for Security and Privacy

Smart City and Industry 4.0 Applications

Data Analytics and Healthcare Systems

Short Papers: Security and Data Engineering

Invited Keynotes

Towards a Foundation of Web3

Ahto Buldas[1,4], Dirk Draheim[2(✉)], Mike Gault[3], and Märt Saarepera[4]

[1] Centre for Digital Forensics and Cyber Security, Tallinn University of Technology,
Akadeemia tee 15a, 12618 Tallinn, Estonia
`ahto.buldas@taltech.ee`
[2] Information Systems Group, Tallinn University of Technology, Akadeemia tee 15a,
12618 Tallinn, Estonia
`dirk.draheim@taltech.ee`
[3] Guardtime, Avenue d'Ouchy 4, 1006 Lausanne, Switzerland
`mike.gault@guardtime.com`
[4] Guardtime, A. H. Tammsaare tee 60, 11316 Tallinn, Estonia
`{ahto.buldas,mart.saarepera}@guardtime.com`

Abstract. The Web3 vision takes blockchain disintermediation to a
next level by making it ubiquitous, encompassing not only payments
and financial services but also digital identities, data and business models. Recently, Web3 has gained massive attention by major analysts such
as Gartner, Forrester, Forbes Technology Council and the Harvard Business Review. Albeit the current enthusiasm about Web3, we are lost in
a state of confusion about what Web3 actually is – or could be. In this
paper, we take an engineering approach. We discuss a potential foundation of Web3 in terms of fundamental components, architectural principles and a Web3 design space. We conclude that, from an engineering
viewpoint, the Web3 can be characterized as the integration of digital
rights exchange into the (application layer) internet protocols. Finally,
on the basis of these findings, we discuss the Alphabill platform as a
Web3 enabling technology.

Keywords: Web3 · Blockchain · Decentralized finance · DeFi ·
Alphabill

1 Introduction

The Web3 vision takes blockchain disintermediation to a next level by making it ubiquitous, encompassing not only payments and financial services but
also digital identities, data and business models. Where the vision of a ubiquitous integration of emerging technology has become widely known as Internet of
Things (IoT), the Web3 narrative can be characterized as the *Web of Everything*,
and even more, the *Web of Everything and Everybody*, since the idea of being
"owned and operated by its users" [1] is the key ingredient of Web3. Although
Web3 is still in its infancy, it has gained massive attention by major analysts
such as Gartner [2], Forrester [3] and Forbes Technology Council [4] as well as the
Harvard Business Review [1,5,6], and the expectations are high towards Web3

© The Author(s) 2022
T. K. Dang et al. (Eds.): FDSE 2022, CCIS 1688, pp. 3–18, 2022.
https://doi.org/10.1007/978-981-19-8069-5_1

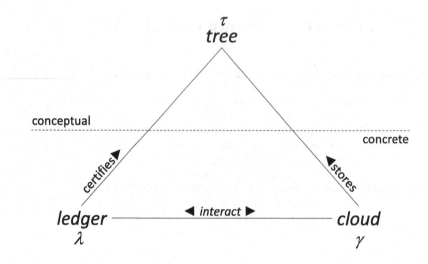

Fig. 1. Web3 fundamental components: tree, ledger and cloud.

being "our chance to make a better internet" [1]. In Table 1, we have summarized a series of Web3 characteristics that we find most significant for the current Web3 narrative[1] by comparing them to corresponding Web 2.0 characteristics.

Albeit the current enthusiasm about Web3, we are lost in a state of confusion. The Forbes technology article titles "Why Web3 Is So Confusing". The Forrester article is titled "Web3 Isn't Going To Fix The Shortcomings Of Today's Web". And when both the Gartner article [2] and the Harvard Business review article [5] are titled "What Is Web3?", they rather aim at giving an overview of the current Web3 narrative than answering the question. And, actually, since the Web3 does not yet exist, the question of 'what *is* Web3', can only be about overviewing its current narrative. Therefore, for an engineering research endeavor, the question to be asked has to be 'what *will be* Web3'?

In this paper, we discuss a potential foundation of Web3 in terms of fundamental components, architectural principles and a Web3 design space. We postulate that any implementation of Web3 can be explained in terms of three fundamental components, i.e., tree, ledger and cloud (Fig. 1) that adhere to a series of Web3 architectural principles and thus form the basis to elaborate the full Web3 design space.

In [9], we have contributed the architecture of the Alphabill platform – a platform for universal asset tokenization, transfer and exchange as a global medium of exchange. In this paper, we discuss Alphabill as an enabler for Web3 – in terms of the suggested Web3 foundation.

We proceed as follows. In Sect. 2, we provide an outline of the suggested Web3 foundation. In Sect. 3, we briefly sketch the Web3 design space. In Sect. 4, we discuss the Alphabill platform. We finish with a conclusion in Sect. 5.

---

[1] Not to be confused with Web 3.0 [7] (related to the Semantic Web [8]).

Table 1. Most significant Web3 characteristics – compared to Web 2.0.

	Web 2.0	Web3
Payments	Online bank transfers between accounts hosted by commercial banks; "digital payments in existing currencies – through Paypal and other »e-money«providers such as Alipay in China, or M-Pesa in Kenya" [10]; M1-money	Cryptocurrencies; direct payments between web users, without intermediaries; currency neither owned by central bank nor collateralized (being neither M0-, nor M1-money); (central bank digital currency [11] is usually not considered part of Web3)
Financial services	Financial services are not considered as part of Web 2.0 (although they might be made accessible through web-based e-commerce services)	Built-in DeFi [12–15]; financial services are considered integral part of Web3 (disrupting both commercial banking and investment banking)
Identity concepts	Public key infrastructure (including established routines of personal identity proofing [16]; also: cloud-based identity	Self-sovereign identity [17]
Data ownership	Data owned and utilized by companies	Data owned and utilized by users
Trust anchors	Authorities, companies	Peer-to-peer [18], consensus protocols
Protocol characteristics	Stateless (protocols connect siloed applications, protocols regulate the "transmission of data, not how data is stored" [19])	Stateful ("collectively maintained universal state for decentralized computing" [19])
Business models	Silicon Valley tech giants (Alphabet, Amazon, Meta); super-scaling e-commerce; social media/networks (commercialization of customer data)	Decentralized autonomous organization (DAO) [20]; also: genuine DeFi business models (decentralized payment services, decentralized fundraising, decentralized contracting) [14]
Use cases	(i) Usual narrative: content consumption (Web 1.0); content production (Web 2.0): social media/networks, collective intelligence systems [21]. (ii) Practically: business-to-customer (B2C) e-commerce (dotcom [22] and post-dotcom era); (iii) Despite SOA (Web services) [23], business-to-business (B2B) is rather not considered a Web 2.0 use case	All Web 2.0 use cases, however, disintermediated; disintermediated B2B is considered an integral part of Web3; non-fungible tokens (NFTs) [24,25] ("can represent real-world items like artwork and real estate" [26], "can also ... represent individuals' identities, property rights, and more" [26])

2   A Web3 Foundation

We postulate that any implementation of Web3 can be explained on the basis of three fundamental components, i.e., tree, ledger and cloud (abbreviated as $\tau + \lambda + \gamma$), see Fig. 1, that adhere to a series of Web3 architectural principles and thus form the basis to elaborate the full Web3 design space, compare with Table 2. We say that the Web3 fundamental components together with the Web3 architectural principles and the elaborated Web3 design space form the foundation of Web3.

Table 2. A Web3 foundation.

- Web3 Fundamental Components
  - *Tree.* Partitioned information tree. Each partition establishes its own language and rules. Access rights are an integral part of the tree.
  - *Ledger.* Provides certificates for Web3 information. Fully certified complete protocol Web3 log.
  - *Cloud.* Stores the full version history of the web tree.
- Web3 Architectural Principles
  - *Pervasive Digital Rights.* Web3 is about the integration of digital rights exchange into the (application layer) internet protocols.
  - *Data Abstraction Principle.* The Web3 state tree is manipulated and *only* manipulated through Web3 protocols.
  - *Web3 Livestream.* All Web3 protocol activities are recorded in the Web3 ledger.
  - *Maximizing Data Protection.* Data privacy/anonymity are protected maximally against *everybody* (in tension with data transparency required by *regulators*).
  - *Ultra Scalability.* Ledger transaction performance is the *sine-qua-non* precondition for the Web3 to be turned into reality.
- Web3 Design Space
  - *A Better Web*
  - *Amalgamation of Intranet and Internet*
    * *A Massive Enterprise Application Backbone*
    * *A Massive Devops Backbone*
  - *A Web of Everything*
    * *A Web of Manufacturing and Logistics*
    * *SDN, IoT and Blockchain*
  - *A Web of Everybody*
    * *Disintermediation*
    * *Governance*
    * *Collective Intelligence*

2.1   The Web3 Information Tree

The fundamental component τ represents the latest Web3 information as a tree[2]. The tree structure is extended to a graph structure by nodes that contain node addresses and are interpreted as references – as we are used to from hyperlinks [27] and transclusions [27,28]. Conceptually, the Web3 information is actually a graph. We stay in the tradition of modeling web information as a tree. We do not do so for the sake of tradition in its own right. It is the language-oriented stance of the tree approach that is beneficial for us, when we conceptualize an essential ingredient of Web3: each partition of Web3 defines its own domain-specific language. Furthermore, the tree approach allows for a convenient ad-hoc addressing scheme: paths in the tree[3].

– The tree τ is a child-ordered, node-colored tree.

Edges, child-ordering and node colors of τ are used to express information. We call the color of a node its *node information*. Depending on the context, we call the color a node also the *label* of the node (i.e., we use *node color*, *node information* and *node label* as interchangeable). We use the label l of a node v also to identify the sub tree σ that has v as a root, and call l also the *label of sub tree σ*. We understand τ as an abstract syntax tree that adheres to a context-free grammar that we call the *grammar of τ*[4,5]. We call the language that τ belongs to the *Web3 base language*, denoted by W (the grammar of τ is the grammar of W, and $\tau \in W$).

The Web3 tree τ is partitioned. A partition is a *sub tree* of τ. The purpose of a partition is to hold the information of a specific asset or a specific domain. The list of example partitions is sheer endless. Basically, all of the cryptocurrency-based platform visions seen during ICOs (initial coin offerings) in the last decade can be realized as partitions in Web3. Examples of partitions could be: a cryptocurrency, a real-estate tokenization platform [31] (ideally connected to the official cadastre; or even being the official cadastre), an e-procurement system for the public sector [32,33], a nation-wide healthcare information system [34], a business-to-business vending platform, a particular relational database of a certain company etc. Each partition owns a partition-specific language (that is used describe the content of the partition) and is governed by partition-specific rules.

Figure 2 illustrates an example Web3 tree τ. The topmost part of τ (in Fig. 2, consisting of labels of the form τx) realizes the addresses of the Web3 partitions. Figure 2 depicts three partitions having the addresses $\tau 1/partition$, $\tau 4/partition$, and $\tau 1/\tau 1.3/\tau 1.3.2/partition$. Actually, addresses of partitions are not special,

---

[2] Latest= at each point in time. Versioning comes in through the other fundamental components: cloud γ and ledger λ.

[3] Compare to X-Paths: https://www.w3.org/TR/xpath-31/.

[4] Abstract syntax trees are indeed child-ordered, node-colored trees.

[5] As suggested by the *integrated source code paradigm* [29,30], we overcome concrete syntax (we exclude concrete syntax from our considerations) and work with grammar and a direct utilization of its abstract syntax.

each node in the Web3 tree can be addressed, see the address of the node labeled l_3 in Fig. 2 as an example.

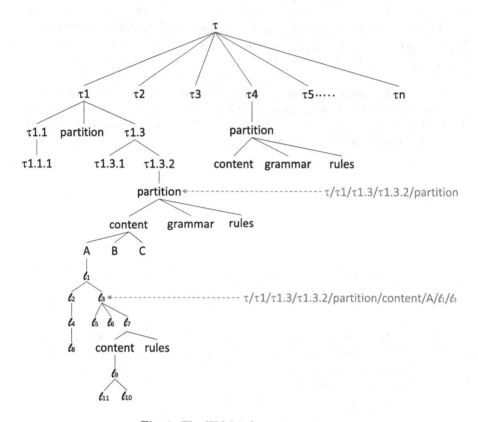

Fig. 2. The Web3 information tree τ.

The Web3 base language W contains a language for describing context-free grammars as a sub-language. Each partition has three child nodes: *content, grammar,* and *rules* (see Fig. 2). The grammar node contains a the grammar of the partition. All sub trees of the content node has to adhere to this grammar. Furthermore, W contains a programming language as sub language that allows for establishing rules for sub trees of τ. This programming language has the same intentions as Bitcoin's programming language Script and the smart contract [35] languages [36,37] of other blockchain technologies such as Ethereum's Solidity[6]. We call this sub language of W simply the Web3 programming language.

The rules node of a partition contains rules that are written in the Web3 programming language. A rule evaluates to true or false and can have side-effects upon its execution. The rules are triggered whenever the content of the partition is about to be changed by a Web3 protocol. Whenever a rule is violated (evaluates

---

[6] https://docs.soliditylang.org/en/v0.8.16/.

to false), the change is rejected. The rules of a partition are used to complete the partition's context-free grammar, i.e., they are used enforce needed context-sensitive properties of the partition. But the Web3 programming language allows for much more. It allows to access the full protocol history that is reflected in the Web3 ledger λ and, therefore, to access the full version history of τ – either directly via λ or indirectly via λ (via hash identifiers provided by λ) by accessing data stored in the cloud γ (γ and λ and options to distribute data over γ and λ will be described in Sect. 2.2).

Actually, the rule-based control of Web3 is much more fine-grained. Rules cannot be only added to partitions, but to any sub tree of τ, see sub tree l_7 in Fig. 2 for an example. The rules apply to all sub trees of the corresponding (sibling) content node.

Pervasive Digital Rights. In the Web3, digital rights are a pervasive concept. They are so essential for the Web3 vision that the Web3 can be even characterized in terms of them, i.e., as the integration of digital rights exchange into the (application layer) internet protocols. Digital rights express trusted, certified ownership of digital assets. Digital rights manifest in digital signatures of digital assets stored in the Web3 tree τ. Complex digital rights scenarios can be expressed with the Web3 programming language. The enforcement of digital rights is on a different page. Basic digital rights that are merely about consuming (accessing) digital assets might be enforced (ensured) technologically. However, in general, when digital rights are about re-use of digital assets, they need to be collateralized by appropriate regulations. With the Web3, the notion of digital rights itself seems to become generalized. They are not merely about the utilization of digital assets anymore, instead, they express rights in real-world assets (legal assets or physical assets). Again, such notion of digital rights need to collateralized by regulations. In this strand of Web3, regulations and institutions [38,39] need to co-evolve [40,41] with the emerging Web3. The Web3 need to anticipate (conceptually and technologically) such developments.

Access rights represent a basic form of digital rights. Similar to digital rights, access rights are an essential, integral part of the tree. Access right owners are identified via public cryptographic keys. We consider the access rights as part of the rules. Access rights can be established with the Web3 programming language, allowing for arbitrarily complex, dynamic access right management. Practically, we can assume that the Web3 defines an access rights language (that can itself be considered part of the Web3 programming language).

Eric Schmidt and Jared Cohen have explained the "future of identity" [42] in the "new digital age" [43] as follows: "The shift from having one's identity shaped off-line and projected online to an identity that is fashioned online and experienced off-line will have implications for citizens, states and companies as they navigate the new digital world." [42] We postulate that the Web3 principle of pervasive digital rights is of utmost significance for changing the concepts of online identities and identities.

2.2   The Ledger and the Cloud

The Web3 tree τ is a purely conceptual model. It explains the informational structure of the Web3 and, most importantly, introduces the notion of Web3 partition. The Web3 cloud γ and the Web3 ledger λ together provide the concrete realization of the Web3. The cloud γ stores the full version history of the Web3 tree γ. The Web3 ledger λ provides certificates for Web3 information. It is the fully certified complete protocol Web3 log. Occasionally, we therefore call the ledger λ also the Web3 *certification ledger*

The Web3 cloud and ledger can be implemented as overlay network to any internet protocol stack such as, of course, the TCP/IP protocol stack of today's Internet. The Web3 tree τ manifests merely through application-layer protocols that are kept free from any lower-layer concepts and, therefore, is independent of any changes to lower protocol layers. Today's dominating Web protocol *http* relies on IP addresses and is therefore intertwingled with the current Internet protocol stack at the Internet layer. DNS (Domain Name Service) is designed as an aftermath to *http*. The functioning of today's Web tree is anchored in trust into the centralized mechanism of IP address allocation – provided by the Internet organizations ICANN (Internet Corporation for Assigned Names and Numbers) and IANA (Internet Assigned Numbers Authority). Trust in today's Web tree is rooted in trust into ICANN and IANA. The Web3 tree τ can gain trust from the Web3 ledger λ in its role as the certification backbone of the Web3. Again, the ledger can be kept free from any lower-layer concepts. It is Web3 cloud component γ that needs to be related to a concrete internet protocol stack when it is realized.

Data Abstraction and Livestreaming. The concept of the Web3 ledger λ can be explained best through two architectural principles that go hand-in-hand with each other: the Web3 *data abstraction principle* and Web3 *livestreaming*. Data abstraction is a core software engineering principle [44]. In the context of the Web3 it means, that the Web3 tree γ is manipulated and *only* manipulated through a set of well-defined Web3 protocols. This is not so in the Web. From the beginning [45], the *http* protocol had a *post* method, which allows for adding new data to a Web server. Soon after [46], the *http* protocol was enriched by a *put* method that allows for updating a specific web resource. The point is that the *post* and the *put* method are rather seldomly used in practice. Instead, Web resources are manipulated by all kinds of means, i.e., direct writes to the file system, mitigated by a web content management system etc. This means that the complete log of Web protocol activities would not reflect at all the actual Web version history.

In our Web3 foundation, it is an architectural principle that all Web3 protocol activities are recorded in the Web3 ledger λ and we call this principle Web3 *livestreaming*. Of course, this principle makes only sense if the Web3 is always only manipulated through defined Web3 protocols – which is the essence of the Web3 *data abstraction principle*. We postulate, that the Web3 ledger λ is the only authoritative reference for Web3 content. As such is certified, becoming: the fully certified complete Web3 log.

Following the current state of the art, a natural candidate to implement the Web3 ledger λ is with today's blockchain technology [18,47–49]. The reason for this is the efficiency of the blockchain data structure. We can assume that verifying a signature is thousand times more costly than computing a hash [9], which leads to the concept of organizing the data in blocks, computing a Merkle tree per block and signing this tree (via its root hash). This efficiency argument holds independent of the concrete consensus mechanism of a blockchain or the question whether the blockchain is permissionless or permissioned etc.

There are two fundamental options to distribute Web3 data over the Web3 tree τ and the Web3 ledger λ:

– *Pure certification ledger.* No data is stored in the ledger λ. All Web3 data is stored (only) in cloud γ. A chunk of Web3 data δ that is exchanged via a Web3 protocols is represented in the ledger by a hash value h_δ. The hash value h_δ serves as identifier of δ, i.e., to retrieve δ from γ.
– *Certification/data ledger.* Some of the data that is exchanged via Web3 protocols are stored directly in the ledger λ.

Maximizing Data Protection. A reason for not storing data directly in the ledger is efficiency. This reason is independent of whether the ledger is public or not. If the ledger is public, a natural pattern (to maximize data protection) is to formulate Web3 (partition) rules only in terms of data stored in the ledger λ – the Web3 rules can now be called *ledger rules*. Then, assuming that the data in the cloud γ is not public (and effectively protected), only such data would be stored in the ledger that is needed in formulating Web3 (partition) rules. Storing clear data in the ledger does not automatically break anonymity.

Ultra Scalability. Ledger transaction performance is the *sine-qua-non* precondition for the Web3 to be turned into reality. We discuss ultra scalability as part of the Alphabill scenario discussion in Sect. 4.

3   On the Web3 Design Space

The Web3 is said to be "our chance to make a better internet" [1]. A "better Web" has been envisioned long before the Web. Already in 1960, Ted Nelson founded project Xanadu[7] [50,51] – the original hypertext [27] project. Today, more than 50 years later, the requirements that have been formulated for Xanadu (Table 3) read like a wish list for the "better internet" including: a document type system, transclusions [28], secure user identification, access rights management, data replication etc. Last but not least, a royalty mechanism and payment system for the consumption of digital assets was in the Xanadu list.

---

[7] https://xanadu.com.au.

Table 3. The original 17 rules of Ted Nelson's Xanadu.

1	Every Xanadu server is uniquely and securely identified
2	Every Xanadu server can be operated independently or in a network
3	Every user is uniquely and securely identified
4	Every user can search, retrieve, create and store documents
5	Every document can consist of any number of parts each of which may be of any data type
6	Every document can contain links of any type including virtual copies ("transclusions") to any other document in the system accessible to its owner
7	Links are visible and can be followed from all endpoints
8	Permission to link to a document is explicitly granted by the act of publication
9	Every document can contain a royalty mechanism at any desired degree of granularity to ensure payment on any portion accessed, including virtual copies ("transclusions") of all or part of the document
10	Every document is uniquely and securely identified
11	Every document can have secure access controls
12	Every document can be rapidly searched, stored and retrieved without user knowledge of where it is physically stored
13	Every document is automatically moved to physical storage appropriate to its frequency of access from any given location
14	Every document is automatically stored redundantly to maintain availability even in case of a disaster
15	Every Xanadu service provider can charge their users at any rate they choose for the storage, retrieval and publishing of documents
16	Every transaction is secure and auditable only by the parties to that transaction
17	The Xanadu client-server communication protocol is an openly published standard. Third-party software development and integration is encouraged

Analysing today's enterprise application landscape [52,53] leads to similar requirements in regard to crosscutting concerns. The fact that today's enterprise applications are implemented as web-based applications gives us an idea of another huge opportunity for Web3 that has been overlooked so far: the systematic *amalgamation of intranet and internet* (where we think of the intranet as a potential *enterprise application backbone* [52,53]. In the same vein, the Web3 can become a *massive Devops backbone*. The SUM (Single Underlying Model) of the orthographic modeling approach [54] can be integrated as partition into Web3 – enabling both CASE 2.0 as described in [55,56] and the model-driven organization as described in [57].

As the *Web of everything* the Web3 encompasses the Internet of Things (IoT). And as such, it becomes a *Web of manufacturing and logistics* [58–61]. The integration of SDN (software-defined networking), IoT and blockchain technology [62–64] will become a strand of research contributing to Web3.

As a *Web of everybody*, massive *disintermediation* is the standard narrative of the Web3. Disintermediation leads to re-shaped institutions [38,39,65] as well as entirely new institutions. As the societies' institutional architecture [40], governance needs to be re-thought and re-designed.

Collective intelligence (CI) [66] systems form an extremely important class of web-based applications with Wikipedia and Reddit being just two examples [21]. CI systems are natural candidates for Web3 partitions. CI systems will stay with us in the future and their importance will even steadily increase. For example, enterprises have started to understand the potential of CI for their endeavors [53] – take Blackrock's Aladdin[8] system and Genpact's Cora system[9] as (particularly important) examples.

4   The Alphabill Scenario

Recently [9], we have described the Alphabill platform and its architecture, see Fig. 3. Alphabill is a platform for universal asset tokenization, transfer and exchange as a global medium of exchange. Users of the Alphabill platform can launch arbitrarily many partitions on the platform. Alphabill is a partitioned, replicated, sharded blockchain. Each partition implements an individual token and corresponding transaction system. Alphabill partitions correspond to the notion of Web3 partitions in our Web3 foundation. The Alphabill platform provides the necessary protocols, languages, libraries and toolkits to implement partitions in such a way that they show robustness and unlimited scalability. Robustness is achieved through replication, i.e., highly redundant partitions. The ultra scalability is enabled by a novel electronic money scheme, the bill scheme [67,68]. Each Alphabill partition is sharded. Through its decomposability, the bill money scheme eliminates coordination efforts between shards. Coordination between partitions is achieved efficiently through a dedicated atomicity partition and a novel, three-phase commit protocol.

As a proof-of-concept, we have successfully delivered the bill-based blockchain technology KSI Cash [9,68–71]. The performance of the technology has been

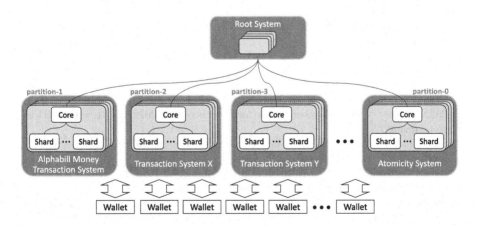

Fig. 3. The Alphabill platform.

---

[8] https://www.blackrock.com/aladdin.
[9] https://www.genpact.com/cora.

tested exhaustively, together with the European Central Bank, in order to assess the technological feasibility of a digital euro [9]. The tests achieved: (i) 15 thousand transactions per second, under simulation of realistic usage, with 100 million wallets, and (ii) up to 2 million payment orders per second, i.e., an equivalent of more than 300,000 transactions per second, in a laboratory setting with the central components of KSI Cash.

5   Conclusion

Too often, we think and talk about Web3 in terms of individual Web3 solutions (individual Web3 products, individual Web3 assets, individual Web3 business models etc.) – although Web3 is clearly a vision of a digital ecosystem, and, actually, a vision of the most encompassing digital ecosystem. In our opinion, it is unlikely that Web3 emerges – out of nothing – as a series of Web3 solutions (independent of how much venture capital might be pumped into such individual efforts). What we need in first place, is to shape and to provide excellent (ultra-useful, ultra-easy, ultra-robust, ultra-scalable[10]) infrastructure and tools to enable Web3 solutions. And, we are convinced, now is the time to do so. From an engineering perspective, Web3 is the integration of digital rights exchange into the (application layer) internet protocols. From a design perspective, we need to care more for the completeness of vision of Web3. With the Web3 foundation suggested in this paper, we hope to help with the completeness of vision of Web3.

References

1. Jin, L., Parrott, K.: Web3 is our chance to make a better Internet. Harvard Business Review 10 May (2022). https://hbr.org/2022/05/web3-is-our-chance-to-make-a-better-internet
2. Wiles, J.: What is Web3? Gartner, 15 February 2022. https://www.gartner.com/en/articles/what-is-web3
3. Bennett, M.: Web3 isn't going to fix the shortcomings of today's Web. Forrester, 10 May 2022. https://www.forrester.com/blogs/web3-isnt-going-to-fix-the-shortcomings-of-todays-web/
4. Platz, B.: Why Web3 is so confusing. Forbes Technology Council, 1 June 2022. https://www.forbes.com/sites/forbestechcouncil/2022/06/01/why-web3-is-so-confusing/
5. Stackpole, T.: What is Web3? Harvard Business Review 10 May (2022). https://hbr.org/2022/05/what-is-web3
6. Esber, J., Kominers, S.D.: Why build in Web3. Harvard Business Review 16 May (2022). https://hbr.org/2022/05/why-build-in-web3
7. Shannon, V.: A 'more revolutionary' Web. The New York Times 23 May (2006)
8. Berners-Lee, T., Hendler, J., Lassila, O.: The Semantic Web - a new form of Web content that is meaningful to computers will unleash a revolution of new possibilities. Scientific American 17 May (2001)

---

[10] Ultra-scalability is the sine-qua-none pre-condition for any Web3 vision to take of [9].

9. Buldas, A., et al.: An ultra-scalable blockchain platform for universal asset tokenization: design and implementation. IEEE Access **10**, 77284–77322 (2022). https://doi.org/10.1109/ACCESS.2022.3192837
10. Lagarde, C.: Central banking and Fintech - A brave new world? Bank of England Conference, London, 29 September (2017)
11. Fernández-Villaverde, J., Sanches, D., Schilling, L., Uhlig, H.: Central bank digital currency: central banking for all? Rev. Econ. Dyn. **41**, 225–242 (2021)
12. Grassi, L., Lanfranchi, D., Faes, A., Renga, F.M.: Do we still need financial intermediation? the case of decentralized finance - DeFi. Qualitative Research in Accounting & Management, pp. 1–22, February 2022
13. Zetzsche, D.A., Arner, D.W., Buckley, R.P.: Decentralized finance. J. Financ. Regulation **6**(2), 172–203 (2020)
14. Chen, Y., Bellavitis, C.: Blockchain disruption and decentralized finance: the rise of decentralized business models. J. Bus. Ventur. Insights **13**(e00151), 1–8 (2020)
15. Schär, F.: Decentralized finance: on blockchain- and smart contract-based financial markets. Federal Reserve Bank of St. Louis Rev. **103**(2), 153–174 (2021)
16. International Organization for Standardization: ISO 29003:2018 - Information technology - Security techniques - Identity proofing. ISO (2018)
17. Mühle, A., Grüner, A., Gayvoronskaya, T., Meinel, C.: A survey on essential components of a self-sovereign identity. Comput. Sci. Rev. **30**, 80–86 (2018)
18. Andy Oram (ed.): Peer to Peer: Harnessing the Power of Disruptive Technologies. O'Reilly (2001)
19. Voshmgir, S.: Token Economy - How the Web3 reinvents the Internet, 2nd edn. BlochainHub Berlin (2020)
20. Wang, S., Ding, W., Li, J., Yuan, Y., Ouyang, L., Wang, F.Y.: Decentralized autonomous organizations: Concept, model, and applications. IEEE Trans. Computat. Social Syst. **6**(5), 870–878 (2019)
21. Suran, S., Pattanaik, V., Draheim, D.: Frameworks for collective intelligence: a systematic literature review. ACM Comput. Surv. **52**(1), 1–36 (2020)
22. Stiglitz, J.E.: The Roaring Nineties: A New History of the World's Most Prosperous Decade. Norton, W. W (2004)
23. Draheim, D.: The service-oriented metaphor deciphered. J. Comput. Sci. Eng. **4**(4), 253–275 (2010)
24. Niforos, M.: The promising future of NFTs remains in a state of flux. Financial Times, 20 June 2022
25. Dowling, M.: Fertile LAND: pricing non-fungible tokens. Financ. Res. Lett. **44**(102096), 2–5 (2022)
26. Sharma, R.: What is a non-fungible token (NFT)? Investopedia, 22 June 2022
27. Nelson, T.H.: A file structure for the complex, the changing and the indeterminate. In: Proceedings of ACM'65 - the 20th ACM National Conference, pp. 84–100. ACM (1965)
28. Nelson, T.H.: The heart of connection: Hypermedia unified by transclusion. Commun. ACM **38**(8), 31–33 (1995)
29. Draheim, D., Weber, G.: The integrated source code paradigm. In: Draheim, D., Weber, G. (ed.) Form-Oriented Analysis, pp. 229–247. Springer, Heidelberg (2005). https://doi.org/10.1007/3-540-26893-6_12
30. Draheim, D., Weber, G.: Form-Oriented Analysis. Springer, Heidelberg (2005)

31. Lazuashvili, N., Norta, A., Draheim, D.: Integration of blockchain technology into a land registration system for immutable traceability: a casestudy of Georgia. In: Di Ciccio, C., Gabryelczyk, R., García-Bañuelos, L., Hernaus, T., Hull, R., Indihar Štemberger, M., Kő, A., Staples, M. (eds.) BPM 2019. LNBIP, vol. 361, pp. 219–233. Springer, Cham (2019). https://doi.org/10.1007/978-3-030-30429-4_15
32. Akaba, T.I., Norta, A., Udokwu, C., Draheim, D.: A framework for the adoption of blockchain-based e-procurement systems in the public sector. In: Hattingh, M., Matthee, M., Smuts, H., Pappas, I., Dwivedi, Y.K., Mäntymäki, M. (eds.) I3E 2020. LNCS, vol. 12066, pp. 3–14. Springer, Cham (2020). https://doi.org/10.1007/978-3-030-44999-5_1
33. Abodei, E., Norta, A., Azogu, I., Udokwu, C., Draheim, D.: Blockchain technology for enabling transparent and traceable government collaboration in public project processes of developing economies. In: Pappas, I.O., Mikalef, P., Dwivedi, Y.K., Jaccheri, L., Krogstie, J., Mäntymäki, M. (eds.) I3E 2019. LNCS, vol. 11701, pp. 464–475. Springer, Cham (2019). https://doi.org/10.1007/978-3-030-29374-1_38
34. Azogu, I., Norta, A., Draheim, D.: A framework for the adoption of blockchain technology in healthcare information management systems a case study of Nigeria. In: Proceedings of ICEGOV'2019: the 12th International Conference on Theory and Practice of Electronic Governance, pp. 310–316. ACM (2019)
35. Szabo, N.: Smart Contracts: Building Blocks for Digital Markets. Nick Szabo (1996)
36. Dwivedi, V.K., Pattanaik, V., Deval, V., Dixit, A., Norta, A., Draheim, D.: Legally enforceable smart-contract languages: a systematic literature review. ACM Comput. Surv. **54**(5), 1–34 (2021)
37. Dixit, A., Deval, V., Dwivedi, V., Norta, A., Draheim, D.: Towards user-centred and legally relevant smart-contract development: a systematic literature review. J. Ind. Inf. Integr. **26**(100314), 1–18 (2022)
38. Williamson, O.E.: Transaction cost economics: the governance of contractual relations. J. Law Econ. **22**(2), 233–261 (1979)
39. Williamson, O.E.: Transaction cost economics: How it works; where it is headed. De Economist **146**, 23–58 (1998)
40. Draheim, D., Krimmer, R., Tammet, T.: On state-level architecture of digital government ecosystems: from ICT-driven to data-centric. Special Issue in Memory of Roland Wagner. Trans. Large-Scale Data- Knowl.-Centered Syst. **48**, 165–195 (2021)
41. Buldas, A., Draheim, D., Nagumo, T., Vedeshin, A.: Blockchain technology: intrinsic technological and socio-economic barriers. In: Dang, T.K., Küng, J., Takizawa, M., Chung, T.M. (eds.) FDSE 2020. LNCS, vol. 12466, pp. 3–27. Springer, Cham (2020). https://doi.org/10.1007/978-3-030-63924-2_1
42. Schmidt, E., Cohen, J.: The future of identity, citizenship and reporting. In: Schmidt, E., Cohen, J.: The New Digital Age - Transforming Nations, Businesses, and Our Lives, pp. 32–81. Vintage Books, New York (2013)
43. Schmidt, E., Cohen, J.: The New Digital Age - Transforming Nations, Businesses, and Our Lives. Vintage Books, New York (2013)
44. Liskov, B., Zilles, S.: Programming with abstract data types. SIGPLAN Notices **9**(4), 50–59 (1974)
45. Berners-Lee, T., Fielding, R., Frystyk: Hypertext Transfer Protocol - HTTP/1.0. RFC 1945. Network Working Group (1996)
46. Fielding, R., et al.: Hypertext Transfer Protocol - HTTP/1.1. RFC 2616. Network Working Group (1999)
47. Nakamoto, S.: Bitcoin: a peer-to-peer electronic cash system (2008). Accessed 20 Apr 2022. https://bitcoin.org/bitcoin.pdf

48. Narayanan, A., Clark, J.: Bitcoin's academic pedigree. Commun. ACM **60**(12), 36–45 (2017)
49. Narayanan, A., Clark, J.: Bitcoin's academic pedigree. ACM Queue Mag. **15**(4), 1–30 (2017)
50. Nelson, T.H.: Literary Machines: The Report On, and Of, Project Xanadu Concerning Word Processing, Electronic Publishing, Hypertext, Thinkertoys, Tomorrow's Intellectual Revolution, and Certain Other Topics Including Knowledge. Mindful Press, Education and Freedom (1993)
51. Knowlton, K.: Ted Nelson's Xanadu. In: Dechow, D.R., Struppa, D.C. (eds.) Intertwingled - The Work and Influence of Ted Nelson. History of Computing, pp. 25–28. Springer (2015)
52. Draheim, D.: On the radical de- and re-construction of today's enterprise applications - CENTERIS'2019 Keynote. In: Proceedings of CENTERIS'2019 - the 10th International Conference on Enterprise Information Systems. Procedia Computer Science, vol. 164, pp. 120–122. Elsevier (2019)
53. Draheim, D.: Collective intelligence systems from an organizational perspective - iiWAS'2019 Keynote. In: Proceedings of iiWAS'2019 - the 21st International Conference on Information Integration and Web-based Applications & Services, pp. 3–4. ACM (2019)
54. Atkinson, C., Stoll, D.: Orthographic modeling environment. In: Fiadeiro, J.L., Inverardi, P. (eds.) FASE 2008. LNCS, vol. 4961, pp. 93–96. Springer, Heidelberg (2008). https://doi.org/10.1007/978-3-540-78743-3_7
55. Draheim, D.: Case 2.0 - On key success factors for cloud-aided software engineering. In: Proceedings of MDHPCL'12 - the 1st International Workshop on Model-Driven Engineering for High Performance and Cloud Computing, pp. 1–6. ACM Press (2012)
56. Atkinson, C., Draheim, D.: Cloud aided-software engineering - Evolving viable software systems through a web of views. In: Mahmood, Z., Saeed, S. (eds.) Software Engineering Frameworks for the Cloud Computing Paradigm, pp. 255–281. Springer, London (2013). https://doi.org/10.1007/978-1-4471-5031-2_12
57. Tunjic, C., Atkinson, C., Draheim, D.: Supporting the model-driven organization vision through deep, orthographic modeling. EMISAJ (Enterp. Model. Inf. Syst. Architectures J.) **13**, 1–39 (2018)
58. Siddiqui, S., Shah, S.A., Ahmad, I., Aneiba, A., Draheim, D., Dustdar, S.: Toward software-defined networking-based IoT frameworks: a systematic literature review, taxonomy, open challenges and prospects. IEEE Access **10**, 70850–70901 (2022)
59. Hameed, S., Shah, S.A., Saeed, Q.S., Siddiqui, S., Ali, I., Vedeshin, A., Draheim, D.: A scalable key and trust management solution for IoT sensors using SDN and blockchain technology. IEEE Sensors J. **21**(6), 8716–8733 (2021)
60. Shah, S.A., Seker, D.Z., Hameed, S., Draheim, D.: The rising role of big data analytics and IoT in disaster management: recent advances, taxonomy and prospects. IEEE Access **7**, 54595–54614 (2019)
61. Shah, S.A., Seker, D.Z., Rathore, M., Hameed, S., Yahia, S.B., Draheim, D.: Towards disaster resilient smart cities: can internet of things and big data analytics be the game changers? IEEE Access **7**, 91885–91903 (2019)
62. Vedeshin, A., Dogru, J.M.U., Liiv, I., Yahia, S.B., Draheim, D.: Smart cyberphysical system for pattern recognition of illegal 3D designs in 3D printing. In: Hamlich, M., Bellatreche, L., Mondal, A., Ordonez, C. (eds.) SADASC 2020. CCIS, vol. 1207, pp. 74–85. Springer, Cham (2020). https://doi.org/10.1007/978-3-030-45183-7_6

63. Vedeshin, A., Dogru, J.M., Liiv, I., Ben Yahia, S., Draheim, D.: A secure data infrastructure for personal manufacturing based on a novel key-less, byte-less encryption method. IEEE Access **8**, 40039–40056 (2020)
64. Vedeshin, A., Dogru, J.M.U., Liiv, I., Draheim, D., Ben Yahia, S.: A digital ecosystem for personal manufacturing: an architecture for a cloud-based distributed manufacturing operating system. In: Proceedings of MEDES'2019 - the 11th International Conference on Management of Digital EcoSystems, pp. 224–228. ACM (2019)
65. Koppenjan, J., Groenewegen, J.: Institutional design for complex technological systems. Int. J. Technol. Policy Manage. **5**(3), 240–257 (2005)
66. Malone, T.W., Bernstein, M.S.: Handbook of Collective Intelligence. MIT Press (2015)
67. Buldas, A., Saarepera, M., Steiner, J., Draheim, D.: A unifying theory of electronic money and payment systems. TechRxiv (2021). https://doi.org/10.36227/techrxiv.14994558.v1
68. Buldas, A., Saarepera, M., Steiner, J., Ilves, L., Olt, R., Meidla, T.: Formal Model of Money Schemes and their Implications for Central Bank Digital Currency. Eesti Pank, Guardtime (2021). Accessed 11 Mar 2022. https://haldus.eestipank.ee/sites/default/files/2021-12/EP-A_Formal_Model_of_Money_2021_eng.pdf
69. European Central Bank, Eesti Pank, Bank of Greece, Deutsche Bundesbank, Central Bank of Ireland, Banco de España, Latvijas Banka, Banca d'Italia, De Nederlandsche Bank: Work Stream 3: A New Solution - Blockchain & eID. July 2021. Accessed 28 Mar 2022. https://www.ecb.europa.eu/paym/digital_euro/investigation/profuse/shared/files/deexp/ecb.deexp211011_3.en.pdf [last accessed: 28 March 2022] https://haldus.eestipank.ee/sites/default/files/2021-07/Workstream3-ANewSolution-BlockchainandeID_1.pdf
70. Olt, R., Meidla, T., Ilves, L., Steiner, J.: Summary report: Results of the Eesti Pank - Guardtime CBDC Research. Eesti Pank, Guardtime, December 2021. Accessed 11 Mar 2022. https://haldus.eestipank.ee/sites/default/files/2021-12/EP-Guardtime_CBDC_Research_2021_eng.pdf
71. Eesti Pank: Eesti Pank ran an experiment to investigate the technological possibilities of a central bank digital currency based on blockchain, Eesti Pank, 13 December 2021. Accessed 11 Mar 2022. https://www.eestipank.ee/en/press/eesti-pank-ran-experiment-investigate-technological-possibilities-central-bank-digital-currency-13122021

In-Memory Computing Architectures for Big Data and Machine Learning Applications

Václav Snášel[1](✉), Tran Khanh Dang[2], Phuong N.H. Pham[2], Josef Küng[3], and Lingping Kong[1](✉)

[1] Faculty of Electrical Engineering and Computer Science, VSB-Technical University of Ostrava, Ostrava, Czech Republic
{vaclav.snasel,lingping.kong}@vsb.cz
[2] Faculty of Information Technology, Ho Chi Minh City University of Food Industry (HUFI), Ho Chi Minh City, Vietnam
{khanh,phuongpnh}@hufi.edu.vn
[3] Johannes Kepler University Linz, Linz, Austria
josef.kueng@jku.at

Abstract. Traditional computing hardware is working to meet the extensive computational load presented by the rapidly growing Machine Learning (ML) and Artificial Intelligence algorithms such as Deep Neural Networks and Big Data. In order to get hardware solutions to meet the low-latency and high-throughput computational needs of these algorithms, Non-Von Neumann computing architectures such as In-memory Computing (IMC) have been extensively researched and experimented with over the last five years. This study analyses and reviews works designed to accelerate Machine Learning task. We investigate different architectural aspects and directions and provide our comparative evaluations. We further discuss IMC research's challenges and limitations and present possible directions.

Keywords: In-memory computing · Machining learning · Deep neural network · In-memory accelerator

1 Introduction

Almost three quintillion bytes of data are created daily from every imaginable field that users can monitor digitally [1]. And the volumes are increasing even more thanks to modern technology [2]. Big data is extensive information analyzed for patterns and trends that offer valuable insights. And big data analytics is a thriving research spot in various domains [3], which include web and digital media, finance and fraud services, customer services, healthcare, agriculture, etc. ML, a subset of Artificial Intelligent, can improve the communication and cooperation between big data and the machine by the well-designed technique providing predictive analytics solutions. For example, ML performs a meaningful role in the computer vision domain [4] (e.g., pattern recognition, reconstruction,

T. K. Dang et al. (Eds.): FDSE 2022, CCIS 1688, pp. 19–33, 2022.
https://doi.org/10.1007/978-981-19-8069-5_2

classification, Object detection, tracking, Semantic and Instance Segmentation;), time-series data prediction [5], decision classification [6] domain by extracting crucial information from images [7]. For this purpose, researchers have dedicated much effort to designing well-performed algorithms to address those applications. AlexNet [8] was designed for image recognition and achieved a good performance. Following the idea of AlexNet, VGGNet [9] GoogLeNet/Inception [10,11] and NASNet [12] are designed to improve accuracy further Classification [13]. Later, inspired by the previous works, ResNet [14] successfully tailored deep neural networks (DNN, a branch of ML) with up to 152 layers. Subsequently, many programming function libraries are proposed to provide simple in-time interfaces to the task-specific application, such as OpenCV [15] for the computer vision, torch_geometric [16] for the graph neural networks (GNN) [17], etc.

Those applications-specific algorithms start by transforming the collected big data into a high-dimensional representation and then extracting potential features, which increases the data movement and energy consumption along with the increased training weights [18]. The underlying hardware with processors is expected to provide fast and efficient support for the task-customized model. A complementary metal-oxide-semiconductor (CMOS) [19] is an integrated circuit design on a printed circuit board, allowing data processing by a sequence of boolean logic operations executed in silicon. However, the increased computation needs for GNN and the exponential growth of data spreading challenge the performance of CMOS logic. Therefore, researchers borrow the idea of energy-efficient computing paradigms to tackle data-intensive from the human brain [20], which connects memory and computation, enabling low energy consumption. However, this connection disobeys the conventional computer architecture, where program computing carries out in central processing units, and data is fetched from memory (located on a physically separate chip) according to the von Neumann architecture. This memory, i.e., typically a dynamic random access memory (DRAM), leads to long latency and energy consumption for data-intensive missions [21].

1.1   The History of IMC

IMC is application scalable that allows users to expand the size of their in-memory CPU pool by adding more nodes to the cluster and upgrading the nodes with more cores, RAM, and computing power [22].

The evolution of IMC has gone through multiple times. Originally, IMC was born as a database catching in the late eighties and early nineties [23]. In this type, the most frequently accessed data were kept in the memory, so the users did not have to go and fetch it from storage every time. Though the technology had evolved to accommodate other caching shapes, database caching stood still as one of the prevailing service subjects for IMC. However, this cache system was primitive; users may lose their data without protection once the server crashes. Therefore, by the early 2000s, the demand for data organization with new elements, e.g., trades, dependability, distribution, and splitting of the load among servers in a cluster, promoted the development of an in-memory data grid. The data grid is a cache form that allows users to maintain data in memory across multiple optional servers, and it is capable of scaling and handling enormous complexity [24] well. Subsequently, the in-memory databases [25] arised in the late 2000s, a technology that was not as fast as the other in-memory technology. However, it brought a comfortable and familiar working style at that moment. Then these three primary usages, namely database caching, in-memory data grid, and in-memory databases for in-memory computing, evolved in various directions. For example, In-memory streaming [26], in-memory accelerators [27,28], and in-memory computing platforms [29]. In-memory streaming became prominent in the early 2010s s served as data processing on dynamic data. This streaming dealt with a tremendous amount of data, pushed the demand for in-memory technology to a new level. However, the quantity of data streaming would lead to the problem of fast power consumption of processing, and the hardware and software solutions to sustain that load were still challenging. One of the latest and most logical evolution is in-memory accelerators, which appeared in the early 2010s s with hands-on experience features for the average user. This easy-to-use and familiar paradigm for processing data was a crucial concern for in-memory computing development [30]. Ultimately, the in-memory computing platforms were built and allow us to deal with all other forms of computing.

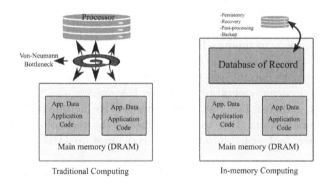

Fig. 1. Von Neumann bottleneck [31].

1.2 Tradition Architecture vs IMC

Comparisons between conventional architecture and the IMC are from two levels, computation metrics (or communication costs, e.g., latency, bandwidth, energy, and signal to noise ration (SNR)) and WL activation costs, BL/BLb swing.

In the conventional architecture, computation metrics scales differently depending on the required cycles in row-wise access, access-cycle delay, the bitlines (BL/BLb) capacitance, and maybe the column numbers. IMC operates one-time access on all rows; therefore, there is no scaling loss. However, due to the accumulation over the bit cells leading to an increased dynamic range, IMC has an SNR scaling cost. At the same time, the traditional architecture is not

Table 1. Comparison of the tradeoffs associated with memory accessing between conventional architecture and IMC; Consider accessing N bits of data from a $\sqrt{N} \times \sqrt{N}$ memory [32].

Metrics		Bandwidth	Latency	Energy	SNR
Conventional	Scale	Yes	Yes	Yes	No
	size	$N^{\frac{1}{2}}$	N	$N^{\frac{3}{2}}$	–
IMC	Scale	No	No	No	Yes
	size	–	–	–	$1/N^{\frac{1}{2}}$

able to scale the SNR due to the BL/BLb discharge requirement. The above comparison is listed in Table 1. From the secondary comparison level, IMC does not reduce the WL activation cost and prefers full swing, and conventional memory often exploits reduced swing. The advantage of IMC reflects in high energy and delay costs of moving data and accessing data from memory. The largest energy consumption on data movement between the memory and processing units causes the traditional architecture's bottleneck. Fig. 1 highlights the non-von Neumann MIC privilege, in which IMC does not separate between program execution and data storage [31,33].

Thanks to the advantage of IMC, e.g., optimizing latency for data/ program fetch, high computing parallelism, and scalability [34], IMC has emerged as one of the most profitable techniques for computing in the periphery of DNNs with big data. The basis of analogue computing follows the physical laws of memory circuits and memory-specific physical behavior [35]. A potential logic device state change/switch per operation increases the energy and time cost during computation for a digital IMC, which determines the lifetime of the circuit due to persistence constraints. Due to these reasons, the technology for designing high-performance, well-scalability, and low-consumption IMC processors is in desperate need.

This work provides a brief overview of big data and ML, along with classic ML techniques and its applications. Then we present IMC in terms of evolution and IMC types, followed by an introduction of the benefits of IMC compared to the traditional architecture. The architecture design and optimization overview is presented in Sect. 2 from three perspectives, the GPU, reduced precision and the hardware accelerator options. This review focuses on the basic architecture introduction, and it does not involve detailed hardware knowledge. Finally, we conclude the review in Sect. 3 with potential problems and future scope.

2   Hardware Design and Optimization Techniques

The increased demand for fully exploiting this IMC computing paradigm to the growth of the number and size of neural networks requires us to customize well-established optional architectures and provide novel methodologies for optimizing the data flow [37]. Meanwhile, the effort from researchers are also dedicated

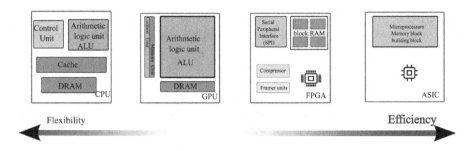

Fig. 2. Overview of ML hardware available today [36]

to the significant research towards customize computation process that are best suited for the underlying hardware [38].

A DNN [39] learns specific cognitive tasks that mimic the human brain's operation by connecting plastic synapses, called neurons. Each layer passes the input data through the neuron to the next layer, and the neurons perform multiply-accumulate operations. During this learning process, the weights of these neurons (interconnections) get updated via a supervised learning algorithm based on gradient descent [40]. Then, the final layer responds based on the error estimation, and the errors are back-propagated. The training steps involve extensive MVMs sequences, and the neuron weights are updated to reduce the error. One of the most substantial benefits of IMC is the capability to parallelize MVM procedures within a memory array. In order to optimize the training process and reduce the computation cost, there is a significant effort on the design of new hardware platform for neural network working load, based on various methods, e.g., reduced/mixed precision, hardware accelerator, and highly optimized dataflow.

Along with the tremendous progress in ML, the unsustainably demands of the energy and memory grow, bringing together the development of scalable processor and software systems such as Central Processing Units (CPU) and ML-specialized Graphical Processing Units (GPU), Application Specific Integrated Circuits (ASIC) [41] and Field Programmable Gate Arrays (FPGA) [42], targeting training the neural network/ML with massive training data or inference of the attributes for the new samples [43]. These hardware provide the primary underlying platform for the DNN/ML tasks and brings tremendous performance benefits. Four hardware types (CPU, GPU, FPGA, and ASIC) contribute to the specific applications deployed in the corresponding environment. The typical performance measurement on the hardware includes throughput (computational capacity), efficiency, and cost or data latency, etc. Comparatively, CPU and GPU are more flexible than FPGA and ASIC. In contrast, FPGA and ASIC achieve high efficiency as shown in Fig. 2.

CPU operates the calculation fast and possesses dynamic circuitry but is unsuitable for accessing extensive data. The integrated circuit microprocessors are the basis of the Modern CPUs, which host one or more CPUs on a single chip. GPU is probably the most popular hardware option for ML/DNN tasks, which involve extensive matrix-to-matrix multiplication, especially in convolution operations [44]. The users can program and reconfigure the hardware on FPGA through hardware descriptive language, which has become recognized by NN researchers due to the high performance and less power consumption [45]. Not only is the FPGA applied in the training task of ML, but the researcher also applies it for inference. FPGA is capable process massive amounts of data through the controlling data path, which frees the processor for other jobs and offers better real-time implementation [46]. Another advantage of FPGA is the possibility of customized design for an individual solution. This custom design directly defines fixed data trails on a series of blocks, such as data interface or precision provision. The users benefit from the dynamic FPGA, and various optimization paths can improve the overall performance of tasks. The reconfiguration of FPGA is widely used for ML task implementation, which leads to prototyping and density enhancement of two kinds with a different purposes [47]. Recently studies claim that FPGA has achieved more success in various domains than GPUs [48]. However, it is recognized that ASIC is more efficient on specific task than FPGA [49], which has the full self-design capability since ASIC is customized for a particular use rather than general-purpose specifications.

2.1   The GPU Option

GPUs are designed initially for accelerating graphics. GPU consumes silicon for building simple but many cores to maximize throughput instead of large caches and complex control logic [50]. Contrary to the CPU, which speeds up a single control flow, GPU focuses on expanding the Arithmetic logic unit (ALU), which can execute hundreds of billions of floating-point operations simultaneously, making them beneficial for ML/DNN tasks and gaming applications. The advantage of GPUs lies in the parallel architecture and its incredible development based on the continued increase in transistors due to Moore's law [51]. As a result, almost every 9 to 18 months, a new version of GPUs comes out and brings higher performance and benefits. However, the users must learn graphics application programming interfaces (APIs) or application conversion for programming the pipeline operations in abstract GPUs, which is difficult for general-purpose usage. The hardware GPU vendors are working on providing a platform that hides the GPU's existing architectures behind and brings graphic APIs with virtual machines in front of users, e.g. GPU programming language [52]. The users can quickly implement general task-specific programming and models through those environments, such as DirectX (Microsoft Direct-series Graphics APIs), Open Graphics Library (OpenGL) [53], Advanced Micro Devices (AMD) [54], Open Computing Language (OpenCL) and Computer Unified Device Architecture (CUDA) [55], etc. Furthermore, these APIs provide direct access to the underlying GPU architecture and enable a new notion of the GPU as an efficient ML/GNN task-specific acceleration unit. Finally, the processor-independent programming languages based on APIs make it possible for just-in-time compiling. Benefiting from the parallelism processing, a lot of research [56,57] implement their DNN application' experiments on GPU support hardware machines through API. Those APIs are for general-purpose computation on a graphics processor.

Nevertheless, GPU architecture is imperfect [58], with some disadvantages to the DNN-specific tasks. First, the GPU process single instruction, multiple data (SIMD) model, which allows all processing units to operate the same instruction. From this SIMD point, the DNN model that fits the SIMD map will perform well. Otherwise, the programs are not mapped well. GPU is driving toward a single program with multiple data model [59], while it does not guarantee performance improvement due to the control-flow instruction program. Secondly, the users are implementing the model with the APIs supporting virtual machines that hide the GPU architectures. This abstract and absence of detailed application may hamper exploiting the best performance out of the GPUs [58]. For example, the users would not know how to reuse the memory under the APIs without cache model visibility. Furthermore, 64-bit floating-point numbers are limited in the programmable parts of GPUs, where the CPUs support those primitive types. The new version of GPU will focus on that built-in support for various and higher floating-point numbers gradually [58]. Last but not least, GPU architecture contains several mini graphics processors, with their computation unit and local cache, which fit the matrix multiplication. Any other hybrid processes with complex computation will not guarantee the same high-speed execution.

2.2   Reduced Precision Option

The option of reduced/mixed precision is considered by the researcher. One direction is to use the traditional CMOS and optimize digital circuits for the reduced precision arithmetic in MVM operation. We can see those designs employed on GPUs [60] and custom ASICs (i.e., application-specific integrated circuits, such as TUPs [61] and IPUs [62]). In the meantime, some other researches that focuses on the extension with the mixed precision technique [63,64].

For example, Daisuke [65] presented 3-bits data representation without significant performance deterioration on classification task. In this work, they performed non-uniform distributions on the training weights and activation with base-2 logarithmic that surpasses fixed-point results and avoids overweight digital multipliers. In addition, sun et al. [66] presented a 4-bits precision training technique that has been aggressively scaled down half from 8-bits. In this work, they proposed an adaptive Gradient Scaling technique that addressed the problem, i.e., gradients' insufficient range and resolution, impact of quantization errors. Their techniques were employed on various applications such as speech, computer vision, and natural language processing [67] showing negligible accuracy lose while helping significant hardware acceleration. Furthermore, Xiao [68] focused on accelerating DNN training workloads by reducing the numerical precision with hybrid 8-bit floating point data representation. The previous works with 8-bit floating point format design were not applicable for the popular networks such as Transformer [69] and MobileNET [70] with non-negligible performance decrease due to the forward and backward precision requirements. This work [68] proposed a novel hybrid 8-bits data representation and enables the hardware for deploying the DNN model without accuracy loss.

In mixed precision computation design, the neural network performs imprecisely computation on the forward and backward propagation while the gradients need to be accumulated in high precision [71]. Nandakumar [72] presented a mixed-precision architecture that fused the computational memory and digital processing units. The previous memory unit was for summations operation and imprecise conductance updates. In contrast, the processing unit performed the high-precision accumulated weight updates. The proposed architecture achieved 97.73% classification accuracy on the MNIST [73] dataset using a PCM array on a multilayer perceptron.

2.3 Hardware Accelerator Option

IMC macro plays a function that allows the essential arithmetic operation. The effective logic control to utilize IMC macros is the business of microarchitecture. Considerable efforts are contributing to the hardware accelerator design tailored for DNN tasks or ML tasks [74], such as IBM Cognitive Chip [75], Diannao [76], ISAAC [77] and PipeLayer [78], etc. These architectures opt for optimization to facilitate data access and reduce computational costs. However, hardware accelerator techniques may conduct profitable energy efficiencies, but some accelerators often adapt exclusively to a single ML scenario (family) [79] or those accelerators are limited by the sophisticated training process to the DNN scenario. There are still limits and deficiencies to each of those architectures.

For example, ISAAC was a crossbar-based accelerator designed for CNN benchmarks, but this architecture did not consider weight updates and data dependency during the model's training. Moreover, the developed pipeline in ISAAC was only beneficial to the case when there was vast consecutive data in the system, which was limited by the updated weights during the batch data transition. LerGAN [80] was an architecture accelerator specialized for generative adversarial network [81] to address two problems, ineffectual computations and frequent off-chip memory access for exchanging intermediate data. The customized IMC dynamically reconfigured in-memory processing connections according to propagation dataflow and updating. LerGAN achieved at least 7x speedup over FPGA-based GAN-specific accelerator [82–84] GPU platform (unspecified GPU type in paper), and RRAM-based accelerator [85]. Diannao [76] performed 452 GOP/s for MVM operations in a small footprint of $3.02\,\mathrm{mm}^2$ and 485 mW, but it was limited by the memory bandwidth requirements of convolutional layers and task-specific layers. DaDianNao [86,87] improved the design of DaDianNao, addressing the transfer overhead problem on the circuit and time on a faster NFU and asynchronous communications. PipeLayer had achieved notable progress, improved the computation and energy costs corresponding to the CMOS-based accelerators. However, this achievement on training sacrificed the inference efficiency and caused probable pipeline bubbles. There were pieces of research that focused on fixing those deficiencies of

PipeLayer [78], such as Valavi [88] improved the pipelayer boom, AtomLayer [89] addressed the long latency, pipeline bubbles, and buffer overhead problems.

Diannao [76] optimized the energy consumption, speed, and memory performance, and the designed accelerator can perform 452 Giga fixed-point operations per second (GOP/s) in a small footprint of 3.02 mm^2 and 485 mW. Then following by DaDianNao, ShiDianNao [86] and PuDianNao [90] approaches. PuDian-Nao (65 nm process) performed up to 1056 GOP/s in 3.51 mm^2 area and only consumed 596 mW. It reached 1.20x faster and reduced the 128.41x energy than the NVIDIA K20M GPU (28 nm process). [77] designed ISAAC crossbar-based accelerator was organized in a hierarchy of chips/tiles/in situ multiply accumulators for the DNN [91] task, allowing data transmission through tiles within the chip. It also proposed a pipelined architecture enabling overlapping data access and computation. Furthermore, it defined a new encoding strategy and applied it to LFW Face Database problem [92]. PipeLayer [78] enhanced the execution of parallelism across Intra and inter-parallelism two levels. Further, this architecture removed the high-cost ADC/DAC components and replaced them with spiking-based input/write circuits. Meanwhile, it used a customized error backward and weight update process for training. AtomLayer [89] proposed an RRAM-based accelerator for improving training and inference efficiency. This design used the atomic layer to address long latency pipeline bubbles and on-chip buffer problems. In addition, it used unique filter mapping to manage energy consumption problems caused by layer switching and DRAM access. It benefited in power efficiency than ISSAC [77] and costed less than PipeLayer [78] in training.

SpiNNaker [93] optimized on speed and energy consumption, The design carried extensive very small packets. SpiNNaker used analog neuromorphic hardware optimizing communications infrastructure, with a multi-chip supercomputer possessing 20+ ARM9 cores per node. It aimed at a million-core engine qualified for modeling a billion neurons. Tiki-Taka [94] aimed at relaxing stringent hardware requirements. It proposed a coupled dynamical system that minimizes the unintentional implicit cost of the stochastic gradient process due to device asymmetry. This design performed parallel to the access memory and achieved low consumption and high speed. This improvement relaxed the material specification that resistive crossbar arrays can perform better than digital accelerators. TTv2 aimed at overcoming stringent symmetry requirement problem. TTv2 was an upgrade version of the Tiki-Taka algorithm. There were two improvements to the previous design. First, it decreased the device conductance states number to 100x. Second, it increased the noise tolerance by 100x to conductance modulations and 10x to MVM operation by the analog arrays. High resistance in a computational memory device benefits the memory currents from overall summation, which would also help reduce the parasitic voltage drop across the array rows/columns [35]. Meanwhile, the large read current for memory applications enables fast random readout and sense amplifiers' design. We investigate some research that put efforts on the IMC computation design towards the ML-specific task in recent years.

3   Conclusion and Future Scope

This work presents an overview of the IMC-based architecture for big data and ML tasks. First, we introduce IMC evolution and access memory techniques, then the benefits of IMC compared to the traditional architecture. Subsequently, we review three optimization paths for the IMC architecture to improve performance metrics, e.g., throughout, energy consumption, speed, and precision solution. This review shows that numerous efforts have contributed to developing well-designed IMC architecture and improving the application model. As a result, those proposed algorithms achieved tremendous success and progress in practice.

As we can see, ML algorithms are powerful tools for various application domains, while their implementation for big data needs to be accommodated on IMC architecture. Although general-purpose hardware (CPUs and GPUs) can supply explicit solutions, their energy efficiencies have limitations because of their excessive flexibility support. On the other hand, hardware accelerators (FPGA and ASCI) win on the energy efficiency aspect, but individual accelerator often adapts exclusively to a single ML approach (family). It is a well-known No-Free-Lunch theorem, implying that an ML strategy that performs well on one dataset may function poorly on another. This scene indicates that an accelerator may not always get consistent good accuracy. Regardless of the test accuracy, such an accelerator may fail another compatible problem once the ML task is altered or the user selects other ML algorithms [90]. On the other hand, unlike DNN, which shares similar MVM computational routines, there is notable diversity among existing ML approaches [95], making it challenging to develop a universal ML accelerator. This diversity comes from the problem that Different ML methods may differ significantly in their computational primitives and locality properties, such as XGboost and k-nearest neighbors, where the costs are from the decision and distance calculations, respectively.

From a long hardware evolution perspective, there is a risk of freezing computation in hardware [86]. As (1) hardware can rapidly grow with ML application progress, much presently evolves with technological advancement, (2) the improvement of one or two percentage accuracy up may not be worth adapting hardware each time for this purpose. (3) end users readily accept the software library's support for accessible design. And they determine between a challenging but high-speed "hardware library" and slow but flexible implementation. Nevertheless, no matter what execution the user prefers, the accuracy, speed, and memory size requirements are growing, requiring an efficient processing platform [96]. Hardware/Software collaboration heterogeneity design from hybrid platforms is an option for the researcher [83].

Acknowledgements. The authors gratefully acknowledge financial support DST/INT/Czech/P-12/2019, reg. no. LTAIN19176.

References

1. Hashiyana, V., Suresh, N., Sverdlik, W.: Big data: We're almost at infinity. In: 2017 IST-Africa Week Conference (IST-Africa), pp. 1–7. IEEE (2017)
2. Salkuti, S.R.: A survey of big data and machine learning. Int. J. Electr. Comput. Eng. (2088–8708) **10**(1) (2020)
3. Zhang, Y., Huang, T., Bompard, E.F.: Big data analytics in smart grids: a review. Energy Inform. **1**(1), 1–24 (2018). https://doi.org/10.1186/s42162-018-0007-5
4. Khan, A.I., Al-Habsi, S.: Machine learning in computer vision. Procedia Comput. Sci. **167**, 1444–1451 (2020)
5. Lim, B., Zohren, S.: Time-series forecasting with deep learning: a survey. Philosophical Trans. Roy. Soc. A **379**(2194), 20200209 (2021)
6. Chen, T., Guestrin, C.: Xgboost: a scalable tree boosting system. In: Proceedings of the 22nd ACM SIGKDD International Conference on Knowledge Discovery and Data Mining, pp. 785–794 (2016)
7. Khan, A.A., Laghari, A.A., Awan, S.A.: Machine learning in computer vision: a review. EAI Endorsed Trans. Scalable Inf. Syst. **8**(32), e4 (2021)
8. Krizhevsky, A., Sutskever, I., Hinton, G.E.: Imagenet classification with deep convolutional neural networks. Commun. ACM **60**(6), 84–90 (2017)
9. Simonyan, K., Zisserman, A.: Very deep convolutional networks for large-scale image recognition. arXiv preprint arXiv:1409.1556 (2014)
10. Szegedy, C., et al.: Going deeper with convolutions. In: Proceedings of the IEEE Conference on Computer Vision and Pattern Recognition, pp. 1–9 (2015)
11. Szegedy, C., Vanhoucke, V., Ioffe, S., Shlens, J., Wojna, Z.: Rethinking the inception architecture for computer vision. In Proceedings of the IEEE Conference on Computer Vision and Pattern Recognition, pp. 2818–2826 (2016)
12. Zoph, B., Vasudevan, V., Shlens, J., Le, Q.V.: Learning transferable architectures for scalable image recognition. In: Proceedings of the IEEE Conference on Computer Vision and Pattern Recognition, pp. 8697–8710 (2018)
13. Wang, W., Yang, Y., Wang, X., Wang, W., Li, J.: Development of convolutional neural network and its application in image classification: a survey. Optical Eng. **58**(4), 040901 (2019)
14. He, K., Zhang, X., Ren, S., Sun, J.: Deep residual learning for image recognition. In: Proceedings of the IEEE Conference on Computer Vision and Pattern Recognition, pp. 770–778 (2016)
15. Bradski, G.: The opencv library. Dr. Dobb's J. Softw. Tools Prof. Programmer **25**(11), 120–123 (2000)
16. Longa, A., Santin, G., Pellegrini, G.: Pyg, torch_geometric (2022). http://github.com/PyGithub/PyGithub. Accessed 24 Sept 2022
17. Wu, Z., Pan, S., Chen, F., Long, G., Zhang, C., Philip, S.Y.: A comprehensive survey on graph neural networks. IEEE Trans. Neural Networks Learn. Syst. **32**(1), 4–24 (2020)
18. Zhao, R., Luk, W., Niu, X., Shi, H., Wang, H.: Hardware acceleration for machine learning. In: 2017 IEEE Computer Society Annual Symposium on VLSI (ISVLSI), pp. 645–650. IEEE (2017)
19. Faggin, F., Mead, C.: Vlsi implementation of neural networks (1990)
20. Jesan, J.P., Lauro, D.M.: Human brain and neural network behavior: a comparison (2003)
21. Mijwel, M.M.: Artificial neural networks advantages and disadvantages. Retrieved from LinkedIn (2018) http://www.linkedin.com/pulse/artificial-neuralnetWork

22. Reuben, J.: Rediscovering majority logic in the post-cmos era: a perspective from in-memory computing. J. Low Power Electron. Appl. **10**(3), 28 (2020)
23. Lynham, J.: How have catch shares been allocated? Marine Policy **44**, 42–48 (2014)
24. Hoschek, W., Jaen-Martinez, J., Samar, A., Stockinger, H., Stockinger, K.: Data management in an international data grid project. In: Buyya, R., Baker, M. (eds.) GRID 2000. LNCS, vol. 1971, pp. 77–90. Springer, Heidelberg (2000). https://doi. org/10.1007/3-540-44444-0_8
25. Kabakus, A.T., Kara, R.: A performance evaluation of in-memory databases. J. King Saud Univ.-Comput. Inf. Sci. **29**(4), 520–525 (2017)
26. Rashed, M.R.H., Thijssen, S., Jha, S.K., Yao, F., Ewetz, R.: Stream: towards read-based in-memory computing for streaming based data processing. In: 2022 27th Asia and South Pacific Design Automation Conference (ASP-DAC), pp. 690–695. IEEE (2022)
27. Peng, X., Huang, S., Jiang, H., Lu, A., Yu, S.: Dnn+ neurosim v2. 0: an end-to-end benchmarking framework for compute-in-memory accelerators for on-chip training. IEEE Trans. Comput.-Aided Des. Integrated Circuits Syst. **40**(11), 2306–2319 (2020)
28. Angizi, S., He, Z., Fan, D.: Dima: a depthwise cnn in-memory accelerator. In: 2018 IEEE/ACM International Conference on Computer-Aided Design (ICCAD), pp. 1–8. IEEE (2018)
29. Ríos, C., et al.: In-memory computing on a photonic platform. Sci. Adv. **5**(2), eaau5759 (2019)
30. Zanotti, T., Puglisi, F.M., Pavan, P.: Reconfigurable smart in-memory computing platform supporting logic and binarized neural networks for low-power edge devices. IEEE J. Emerging Sel. Top. Circuits Syst. **10**(4), 478–487 (2020)
31. Agrawal, A., Jaiswal, A., Lee, C., Roy, K.: X-sram: enabling in-memory boolean computations in cmos static random access memories. IEEE Trans. Circuits Syst. I: Regular Papers **65**(12), 4219–4232 (2018)
32. Verma, N., et al.: In-memory computing: advances and prospects. IEEE Solid-State Circuits Mag. **11**(3), 43–55 (2019)
33. Wang, Y.: Design considerations for emerging memory and in-memory computing. In: VLSI 2020 Symposium on Technology and Circuits. Short Course 3(8) (2020)
34. Sebastian, A., Le Gallo, M., Khaddam-Aljameh, R., Eleftheriou, E.: Memory devices and applications for in-memory computing. Nature Nanotechnol. **15**(7), 529–544 (2020)
35. Ielmini, D., Pedretti, G.: Device and circuit architectures for in-memory computing. Adv. Intell. Syst. **2**(7), 2000040 (2020)
36. Jawandhiya, P.: Hardware design for machine learning. Int. J. Artif. Intell. Appl. **9**(1), 63–84 (2018)
37. Dazzi, M., Sebastian, A., Benini, L., Eleftheriou, E.: Accelerating inference of convolutional neural networks using in-memory computing. Front. Comput. Neurosci. **15**, 674154 (2021)
38. Saikia, J., Yin, S., Jiang, Z., Seok, M., Seo, J.: K-nearest neighbor hardware accelerator using in-memory computing sram. In: 2019 IEEE/ACM International Symposium on Low Power Electronics and Design (ISLPED), pp. 1–6. IEEE (2019)
39. Dietterich, T.G.: Machine-learning research. AI Mag. **18**(4), 97–97 (1997)
40. LeCun, Y., Bottou, L., Bengio, Y., Haffner, P.: Gradient-based learning applied to document recognition. Proc. IEEE **86**(11), 2278–2324 (1998)
41. Capra, M., Peloso, R., Masera, G., Roch, M.R., Martina, M.: Edge computing: a survey on the hardware requirements in the internet of things world. Future Internet **11**(4), 100 (2019)

42. Kim, J.-W., Kim, D.-S., Kim, S.-H., Shin, S.-M.: The firmware design and implementation scheme for c form-factor pluggable optical transceiver. Appl. Sci. **10**(6), 2143 (2020)
43. Freund, K.: A machine learning landscape: where amd, intel, nvidia, qualcomm and xilinx ai engines live. http://www.forbes.com/sites/moorinsights/2017/03/03, Forbes, 2022. Accessed 23 Sept 2022
44. Chmielewski, Ł, Weissbart, L.: On reverse engineering neural network implementation on GPU. In: Zhou, J., et al. (eds.) ACNS 2021. LNCS, vol. 12809, pp. 96–113. Springer, Cham (2021). https://doi.org/10.1007/978-3-030-81645-2_7
45. Zhang, C., Li, P., Sun, G., Guan, Y., Xiao, B., Cong, J.: Optimizing fpga-based accelerator design for deep convolutional neural networks. In: Proceedings of the 2015 ACM/SIGDA International Symposium on Field-Programmable Gate Arrays, pp. 161–170 (2015)
46. Jung, S., Kim, S.: Hardware implementation of a real-time neural network controller with a dsp and an fpga for nonlinear systems. IEEE Trans. Ind. Electron. **54**(1), 265–271 (2007)
47. Sahin, S., Becerikli, Y., Yazici, S.: Neural network implementation in hardware using FPGAs. In: King, I., Wang, J., Chan, L.-W., Wang, D.L. (eds.) ICONIP 2006. LNCS, vol. 4234, pp. 1105–1112. Springer, Heidelberg (2006). https://doi.org/10.1007/11893295_122
48. Nurvitadhi, E., Sim, J., Sheffield, D., Mishra, A., Krishnan, S., Marr, D.: Accelerating recurrent neural networks in analytics servers: Comparison of fpga, cpu, gpu, and asic. In: 2016 26th International Conference on Field Programmable Logic and Applications (FPL), pp. 1–4. IEEE (2016)
49. Boutros, A., Yazdanshenas, S., Betz, V.: You cannot improve what you do not measure: Fpga vs. asic efficiency gaps for convolutional neural network inference. ACM Trans. Reconfigurable Technol. Syst. (TRETS) **11**(3), 1–23 (2018)
50. Kerbl, B., Kenzel, M., Winter, M., Steinberger, M.: Cuda and applications to task-based programming (2022). http://cuda-tutorial.github.io/part2_22.pdf. Accessed 23 Sept 2022
51. Tarditi, D., Puri, S., Oglesby, J.: Accelerator: using data parallelism to program gpus for general-purpose uses. ACM SIGPLAN Not. **41**(11), 325–335 (2006)
52. Jang, H., Park, A., Jung, K.: Neural network implementation using cuda and openmp. In: 2008 Digital Image Computing: Techniques and Applications, pp. 155–161. IEEE (2008)
53. Silicon Graphics Khronos Group. Opengl (2022). http://www.opengl.org/. Accessed 23 Sept 2022
54. Advanced Micro Devices. Amd radeon graphics cards specifications (2022). http://www.amd.com/en/support/kb/faq/gpu-624. Accessed 23 Sept 2022
55. Nvidia. Cuda toolkit (2022). http://developer.nvidia.com/cuda-zone. Accessed 23 Sept 2022
56. Zhang, C., Song, D., Huang, C., Swami, A., Chawla, N.V.: Heterogeneous graph neural network. In: Proceedings of the 25th ACM SIGKDD International Conference on Knowledge Discovery & Data Mining, pp. 793–803 (2019)
57. Touvron, H., Cord, M., Sablayrolles, A., Synnaeve, G., Jégou, H.: Going deeper with image transformers. In: Proceedings of the IEEE/CVF International Conference on Computer Vision, pp. 32–42 (2021)
58. Osman, A.A.M.: Gpu computing taxonomy. In: Recent Progress in Parallel and Distributed Computing, IntechOpen (2017)
59. Ashu Rege. An introduction to modern gpu architecture (nvidia talk). http://download.nvidia.com/developer/cuda/seminar/TDCI_Arch.pdf

60. author. Nvidia, gpu (2022). http://www.nvidia.com/en-us/data-center/a100/. Accessed 21 Sept 2022
61. author. Googlecloud, tpu (2022). http://cloud.google.com/tpu/docs/bfloat16. Accessed 21 Sept 2022
62. author. Graphcore, ipu (2022). http://www.graphcore.ai/. Accessed 21 Sept 2022
63. Jia, X., et al.: Highly scalable deep learning training system with mixed-precision: training imagenet in four minutes. arXiv preprint arXiv:1807.11205 (2018)
64. Goncalo, R., Pedro, T., Nuno, R.: Positnn: training deep neural networks with mixed low-precision posit. In: IEEE International Conference on Acoustics, Speech and Signal Processing (ICASSP), pp. 7908–7912 (2021)
65. Miyashita, D., Lee, E.H., Murmann, B.: Convolutional neural networks using logarithmic data representation. arXiv preprint arXiv:1603.01025 (2016)
66. Sun, X.: Ultra-low precision 4-bit training of deep neural networks. Adv. Neural Inf. Process. Syst. **33**, 1796–1807 (2020)
67. Graves, A., Mohamed, A., Hinton, G.: Speech recognition with deep recurrent neural networks. In: 2013 IEEE International Conference on Acoustics, Speech and Signal Processing, pp. 6645–6649. IEEE (2013)
68. Sun, X., et al.: Hybrid 8-bit floating point (hfp8) training and inference for deep neural networks. In: Advances in Neural Information Processing Systems, 32 (2019)
69. Lin, T., Wang, Y., Liu, X., Qiu, X.: A survey of transformers. arXiv preprint arXiv:2106.04554 (2021)
70. Chen, Y., et al.: Mobile-former: bridging mobilenet and transformer. In: Proceedings of the IEEE/CVF Conference on Computer Vision and Pattern Recognition, pp. 5270–5279 (2022)
71. Sebastian, A., et al.: Computational memory-based inference and training of deep neural networks. In: 2019 Symposium on VLSI Technology, pp. T168–T169. IEEE (2019)
72. Nandakumar, S.R., et al.: Mixed-precision deep learning based on computational memory. Front. Neurosci. **14**, 406 (2020)
73. Yann, L., Corinna, C., Burges Christopher, J.C.: Mnist, dataset (2022). http://yann.lecun.com/exdb/mnist/. Accessed 21 Sept 2022
74. Wang, C., Gong, L., Qi, Yu., Li, X., Xie, Y., Zhou, X.: Dlau: a scalable deep learning accelerator unit on fpga. IEEE Trans. Comput.-Aided Des. Integr. Circuits Syst. **36**(3), 513–517 (2016)
75. Merolla, P., Arthur, J., Akopyan, F., Imam, N., Manohar, R., Modha, D.S.: A digital neurosynaptic core using embedded crossbar memory with 45pj per spike in 45 nm. In: 2011 IEEE Custom Integrated Circuits Conference (CICC), pp. 1–4. IEEE (2011)
76. Chen, T., et al.: Diannao: a small-footprint high-throughput accelerator for ubiquitous machine-learning. ACM SIGARCH Comput. Archit. News **42**(1), 269–284 (2014)
77. Shafiee, A., et al.: Isaac: a convolutional neural network accelerator with in-situ analog arithmetic in crossbars. ACM SIGARCH Comput. Archit. News **44**(3), 14–26 (2016)
78. Song, L., Qian, X., Li, H., Chen, Y.: Pipelayer: a pipelined reram-based accelerator for deep learning. In: 2017 IEEE International Symposium on High Performance Computer Architecture (HPCA), pp. 541–552. IEEE (2017)
79. Chen, Y., Chen, T., Zhiwei, X., Sun, N., Temam, O.: Diannao family: energy-efficient hardware accelerators for machine learning. Commun. ACM **59**(11), 105–112 (2016)

80. Mao, H., Song, M., Li, T., Dai, Y., Shu, J.: Lergan: a zero-free, low data movement and pim-based gan architecture. In: 2018 51st Annual IEEE/ACM International Symposium on Microarchitecture (MICRO), pp. 669–681. IEEE (2018)
81. Creswell, A., White, T., Dumoulin, V., Arulkumaran, K., Sengupta, B., Bharath, A.A.: Generative adversarial networks: an overview. IEEE Signal Process. Magazine **35**(1), 53–65 (2018)
82. Salami, B., Unsal, O.S., Kestelman, A.C.: Comprehensive evaluation of supply voltage underscaling in fpga on-chip memories. In: 2018 51st Annual IEEE/ACM International Symposium on Microarchitecture (MICRO), pp. 724–736. IEEE (2018)
83. Makrani, H.M., Sayadi, H., Mohsenin, T., Rafatirad, S., Sasan, A., Homayoun, H.: Xppe: cross-platform performance estimation of hardware accelerators using machine learning. In Proceedings of the 24th Asia and South Pacific Design Automation Conference, pp. 727–732 (2019)
84. Song, M., Zhang, J., Chen, H., Li, T.: Towards efficient microarchitectural design for accelerating unsupervised gan-based deep learning. In: 2018 IEEE International Symposium on High Performance Computer Architecture (HPCA), pp. 66–77. IEEE (2018)
85. Li, B., Song, L., Chen, F., Qian, X., Chen, Y., Li, H.H.: Reram-based accelerator for deep learning. In: 2018 Design, Automation & Test in Europe Conference & Exhibition (DATE), pp. 815–820. IEEE (2018)
86. Chen, Y., et al.: Dadiannao: a machine-learning supercomputer. In: 2014 47th Annual IEEE/ACM International Symposium on Microarchitecture, pp. 609–622. IEEE (2014)
87. Luo, T., et al.: Dadiannao: a neural network supercomputer. IEEE Trans. Comput. **66**(1), 73–88 (2016)
88. Korchagin, P.A., Letopolskiy, A.B., Teterina, I.A.: Results of research of working capability of refined pipelayer equipment. In: International Conference "Aviamechanical Engineering and Transport" (AVENT 2018), pp. 416–420. Atlantis Press (2018)
89. Qiao, X., Cao, X., Yang, H., Song, L., Li, H.: Atomlayer: a universal reram-based cnn accelerator with atomic layer computation. In: Proceedings of the 55th Annual Design Automation Conference, pp. 1–6 (2018)
90. Liu, D., et al.: Pudiannao: a polyvalent machine learning accelerator. ACM SIGARCH Comput. Archit. News **43**(1), 369–381 (2015)
91. O'Shea, K., Nash, R.: An introduction to convolutional neural networks. arXiv preprint arXiv:1511.08458 (2015)
92. Huang, G.B., Mattar, M., Berg, T., Learned-Miller, E.: Labeled faces in the wild: a database for studying face recognition in unconstrained environments. In: Workshop on faces in 'Real-Life' Images: Detection, Alignment, and Recognition (2008)
93. Furber, S.B., Galluppi, F., Temple, S., Plana, L.A.: The spinnaker project. Proc. IEEE **102**(5), 652–665 (2014)
94. Gokmen, T., Haensch, W.: Algorithm for training neural networks on resistive device arrays. Front. Neurosc. **14**, 103 (2020)
95. Wang, C., Gong, L., Li, X., Zhou, X.: A ubiquitous machine learning accelerator with automatic parallelization on fpga. IEEE Trans. Parallel Distrib. Syst. **31**(10), 2346–2359 (2020)
96. Yan, B., et al.: Resistive memory-based in-memory computing: from device and large-scale integration system perspectives. Adv. Intell. Syst. **1**(7), 1900068 (2019)

Secure and Efficient Implementation of Electronic Money

Ahto Buldas[1,3]([✉]), Dirk Draheim[2], and Märt Saarepera[3]

[1] Centre for Digital Forensics and Cyber Security, Tallinn University of Technology, Akadeemia tee 15a, 12618 Tallinn, Estonia
ahto.buldas@taltech.ee
[2] Information Systems Group, Tallinn University of Technology, Akadeemia tee 15a, 12618 Tallinn, Estonia
dirk.draheim@taltech.ee
[3] Guardtime, A. H. Tammsaare tee 60, 11316 Tallinn, Estonia
mart.saarepera@guardtime.com

Abstract. During the last years, central banks have discussed possible use of central bank digital currencies (CBDC) – electronic cash. Besides the financial and economic factors also the security and scalability of technical implementation of CBDC have been studied. Blockchain technology provides high level of security independent of the technical infrastructure and enables central banks to outsource most of the CBDC operations to the private sector while still having full control over the total amount of CBDC in circulation. Scalability of blockchain solutions depends on the possibility of decomposing (sharding) the blockchain. Electronic money and payments can be represented and organized in several ways, including accounts, bills/coins, and also unspent transaction outputs (UTXOs). We show how the representation of money and payments influences the existence of secure and decomposable blockchain implementations of electronic money. We show that the bill money scheme can be securely and efficiently implemented as sharded blockchains.

Keywords: Blockchain · Central bank digital currency · Electronic cash

1   Introduction

During the last years, central banks have discussed possible use of central bank digital currencies (CBDC) – electronic cash. Besides the financial and economic factors also the scalability and security of technical implementation of CBDC have been studied. Blockchain technology provides a high level of security independent of the technical infrastructure and enables central banks to outsource most of the CBDC operations to the private sector while still having full control over the total amount of CBDC in circulation. The security measures may depend on whether the blockchain solution is public (permissionless) or private (permissioned). Private blockchains are less costly but their security needs somewhat more care as some type of insider attacks have to be considered.

T. K. Dang et al. (Eds.): FDSE 2022, CCIS 1688, pp. 34–51, 2022.
https://doi.org/10.1007/978-981-19-8069-5_3

Scalability has been the biggest technical concern of using blockchain-based CBDC. Nation-wide deployment of electronic cash requires service rates of ten to hundred thousands transactions per second while blockchain money solutions like Bitcoin only offer the rate of few dozen transactions per second. The key of filling the scalability gap is the possibility of decomposing (sharding) the blockchain. The efficiency of decomposition highly depends on the need for inter-component communication. For example, whenever two accounts are in different components, paying from one account to another requires two simultaneous operations in both components: debiting one account and crediting the other. This is technically challenging as it requires solving the atomic commit problem (often called "two generals problem"), which has no deterministic time solutions if possible message loss is considered. On the other hand, if we imagine a single coin or bill given by one person to another, the only parameter that changes is the ownership of the coin/bill. Such operation is atomic by definition. Hence, if an electronic money solution uses coins and bills to represent money and is sharded so that some coins and bills belong to one shard and others to another shard, then every single coin payment is uni shard and does not require inter shard communication. We explain the implications of a general composition theory of money schemes [1] about how the possibility of efficient sharding depends on the choice of the money scheme (accounts, coins, etc.). One implication of the theory is that blockchain-based implementations of account money schemes are to hard efficiently and securely, while bill based money schemes have efficient and secure sharding mechanisms.

This work focuses on the security of sharded blockchain implementations of the bill money scheme considering that the blockchain is used in a permissioned and controlled scenario by the central bank. However, we consider the possibility that the central bank can outsource most of the service machinery to the private sector. The security of the solution is based on special types of lightweight user-initiated audit protocols that are executed during every payment. The goal of the audit procedure is to verify that each particular bill is properly used, i.e., all the ledger rules are fulfilled. We study two types of audit protocols:

1. Full audit – if successful, guarantees that the ledger rules are followed
2. Probabilistic audit – guarantees that any deviation from ledger rules will be detected very soon. The motivation behind probabilistic audit is that the communication complexity of the audit protocol is reduced.

The existence of communication-efficient probabilistic protocols seems to depend on the chosen money scheme and the blockchain certification scheme. We show that such protocols exist in the KSI-Cash CBDC solution [2] that is based on the bill money scheme, i.e. simulates the use of physical cash. It remains an open question if efficient probabilistic audit protocols exist for other money schemes.

In Sects. 2 and 3, we explain money schemes and the decomposability of payments. We formalize the implementation of money schemes and investigate their blockchain implementations in Sects. 4 and 5. In Sect. 6, we show that the bill scheme has atomic decompositions – and the account and UTXO schemes do not. In Sects. 7, 8 and 9, we discuss diverse security aspects of blockchain implementations. In Sects. 10 and 11, we describe KSI-Cash and its user side probabilistic audit. We finish the paper with the mentioned open research question in Sect. 12.

2 Money Schemes

A money scheme [1] describes the representational aspects of money and payments. Money can be represented as a set U of units and a value function $\nu : U \to \mathbb{N}$ that defines for each unit $u \in U$ its value $\nu(u) \in \mathbb{N}$, where N is the set of natural numbers. The units may be accounts, bills, UTXOs, etc. Payments represent the change of ownership of money and hence, it is also necessary to model the ownership. For that, a second function $\beta : U \to \mathbb{B}$ is introduced that assigns for each unit $u \in U$ its owner (bearer) $\beta(u) \in \mathbb{B}$, where $\mathbb{B}$ is the set of all potential bearers.

A triple $M = (U, \nu, \beta)$ is called a *money distribution* because it describes the units with their values and ownership. In such a model, we define the total amount of money as $\sigma(M) = \sum_{u \in U} \nu(u)$, and a money owned by a bearer $b \in \mathbb{B}$ by $\sigma(M, b) = \sum_{u \in \beta^{-1}(b)} \nu(u)$. Money distribution is only a static picture of money and does not distinguish different money schemes. What makes the most important technical difference between money schemes are the payments – transactions P that change the money distribution, but preserving the total amount of money.

Formally, a *money scheme* is a pair $(\mathcal{M}, \mathcal{P})$, where $\mathcal{M}$ is the set of all allowed money distributions and $\mathcal{P}$ is the set of all allowed payments – functions fof type $\mathcal{M} \to \mathcal{M}$. We make a natural and intuitive assumption that for every $M \in \mathcal{M}$, there exists a composition $P = P_1 \circ \ldots \circ P_k$ of payments $P_i \in \mathcal{P}$ such that $\sigma(P(M), b) = 0$, i.e. every bearer can always spend all the money he/she owns. This property is called *quasi completeness* in [1]. We also assume that in every money scheme $(\mathcal{M}, \mathcal{P})$, the identity function $1_{\mathcal{M}}$ defined by $1_{\mathcal{M}}(M) = M$ is a payment, i.e. $1_{\mathcal{M}} \in \mathcal{P}$.

Note that the set $\mathcal{P}$ of payments is not necessarily composition-closed, i.e. a composition $P = P_1 \circ P_2$ of payments $P_1, P_2 \in \mathcal{P}$ is not always a payment. From practical implementation view-point, payments represent transactions that are initiated by payment orders sent to the money and payment system by its users. If two users send their payment orders P_1, P_2 to the system, then the money and payment system does not necessarily accept "composite" payment orders the execution of which is equivalent to applying $P_1 \circ P_2$ to the current money distribution.

In account money schemes, payments change the values $\nu(u)$ and $\nu(v)$ of two units (accounts) $u, v \in U$ so that in the resulting money distribution $P(M) = (U', \nu', \beta')$ we have $U' = U$ (no accounts are created or deleted), $\beta' = \beta$ (ownership of accounts stays the same), and $\nu'(u) + \nu'(v) = \nu(u) + \nu(v)$ (total amount of money does not change).

In bill money schemes, payments change only the ownership $\beta(u)$ of a unit u, i.e. in the resulting money distribution $P(M) = (U', \nu', \beta')$ we have $U' = U$ (no bills are created or deleted), $\nu' = \nu$ (the nominal values of the bills stays the same), but it may be that $\beta'(u) \neq \beta(u)$.

In UTXO money schemes, payments delete a set $u_1, \ldots, u_m$ of units and create a set $v_1, \ldots, v_k$ units so that $\nu(u_1) + \ldots + \nu(u_m) = \nu'(v_1) + \ldots + \nu'(v_k)$.

3   Payments and Their Descriptional Complexity

In this section, we describe and categorise all possible types of payments and show how payments can be algebraically decomposed to irreducible payments.

If the current money distribution is $M = (U, \nu, \beta)$, then every payment P can be characterised by three subsets U^-, U^+, U^0 of U.

- U^-: the set of units that P deletes.
- U^+: the set of units that P creates.
- U^0: the set of units u the parameters $\nu(u), \beta(u)$ of which are changed by P.

To completely characterise P, it is also necessary to define the parameters of the newly created units in U^+ and the way how exactly P changes the parameters of the units in U^0, but for the purpose of this section such details are unnecessary.

The *descriptional complexity* $\|P\|$ of P is the sum of the sizes of U^-, U^+, U^0, i.e. $\|P\| = |U^-| + |U^+| + |U^0|$. The *input complexity* $\|P\|_{\mathsf{in}}$ of P is the sum of the sizes of U^-, U^0, i.e. $\|P\|_{\mathsf{in}} = |U^-| + |U^0|$. For $P = 1_{\mathcal{M}}$, we have $\|P\| = \|P\|_{\mathsf{in}} = 0$. In the following, we present three more examples of the complexities of payments:

- *Single bill transfer:* A payment P that changes the bearer of a single unit u and does nothing else. In this case, $\|P\| = \|P\|_{\mathsf{in}} = 1$.
- *Account payment:* A payment P that changes the values n_1, n_2 of two units u_1 and u_2 to n_1', n_2' so that $n_1' + n_2' = n_1 + n_2$. In this case, $\|P\| = \|P\|_{\mathsf{in}} = 2$.
- *UTXO payment:* A payment P that deletes units $u_1, \ldots, u_k$ with values $n_1, \ldots, n_k$ and creates units $u_1', \ldots, u_\ell'$ with values $n_1', \ldots, n_\ell'$ so that $n_1' + \ldots + n_\ell' = n_1 + \ldots + n_k$. In this case, $\|P\| = k + \ell$ and $\|P\|_{\mathsf{in}} = k$.

A payment P is *composition-irreducible* if there exist no payments P_1, P_2 with $\|P_1\| < \|P\|$, $\|P_2\| < \|P\|$ such that $P = P_1 \circ P_2$. Clearly, every payment is a composition of composition-irreducible payments. It can be shown [1] that there are the following composition-irreducible payments P with $\|P\| \leq 2$:

- *Zero creation* – creates a unit with value 0, i.e. $\|P\| = 1$ and $\|P\|_{\mathsf{in}} = 0$.
- *Zero deletion* – deletes a unit with value 0, i.e. $\|P\| = 1$ and $\|P\|_{\mathsf{in}} = 1$.
- *Single unit transfer* – changes the bearer of one unit, i.e. $\|P\| = \|P\|_{\mathsf{in}} = 1$.
- *Transfer with recreation* – deletes a unit and creates a new unit with the same value, i.e. $\|P\| = 2$ and $\|P\|_{\mathsf{in}} = 1$.
- *Two unit split* – creates a new unit and changes the parameters of a unit, i.e. $\|P\| = 2$ and $\|P\|_{\mathsf{in}} = 1$.
- *Two-unit swap* – changes the values and possibly bearers of two units, i.e. $\|P\| = \|P\|_{\mathsf{in}} = 2$.
- *Two unit join* – deletes a unit and changes the parameters of a unit, i.e. $\|P\| = \|P\|_{\mathsf{in}} = 2$.

It can also be shown that every payment P is a composition of payments with $\|P\| \leq 2$, and hence, these seven payment types together with the identity payment are the only existing composition-irreducible payments.

4   Money Scheme Implementations by Transition Systems

Money schemes are special cases of *transition systems*. Every transition system is a pair (S, T), where S is the set of states and T is a set of *state transitions* (functions of type $S \to S$) that contains the identity transition 1_S defined by $1_S(s) = s$ for every $s \in S$. Transition systems are equivalent to *state machines* and in this paper we refer to them simply as *machines*. This is motivated by modelling machine-implementations of money schemes.

Definition 1 (Implementation). A transition system (S, T) *implements a money scheme* $(\mathcal{M}, \mathcal{P})$ if (Fig. 1):

1. There is an interpretation map $\pi : S \to \mathcal{M}$, i.e. every state s of the machine is interpreted as a money distribution $M = \pi(s)$.
2. For every payment $P \in \mathcal{P}$ and every state $s \in S$ interpreted as a money distribution $M \in \mathcal{M}$ (i.e. $\pi(s) = M$) there exists a transition $t \in T$ such that the state $s' = t(s)$ is interpreted as the money distribution $P(M)$, i.e. $\pi(s') = \pi(t(s)) = P(\pi(s)) = P(M)$.

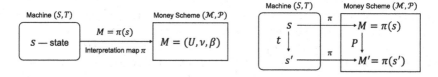

Fig. 1. Implementation of a money scheme by a transition system (machine).

A *decomposition* of a money scheme is an implementation of the money scheme with two machines, formally defined as follows:

Definition 2 (Decomposition). Transition systems $(S_1, T_1), (S_2, T_2)$ *decompose a money scheme* $(\mathcal{M}, \mathcal{P})$ if:

1. There is an interpretation map $\pi : S_1 \times S_2 \to \mathcal{M}$, i.e. every pair of states $s_1 \in S_1, s_2 \in S_2$ of the machines is interpreted as a money distribution $M = \pi(s_1, s_2)$ (Fig. 2, left).
2. For every payment $P \in \mathcal{P}$ and every pair of states state $s_1 \in S_1, s_2 \in S_2$ interpreted as a money distribution $M \in \mathcal{M}$ (i.e. $\pi(s_1, s_2) = M$) there exist transitions $t_1 \in T_1, t_2 \in T_2$ such that the pair of states $s'_1 = t_1(s_1), s'_2 = t_2(s_2)$ is interpreted as the money distribution $P(M)$, i.e. (Fig. 2, right)

$$\pi(s'_1, s'_2) = \pi(t_1(s_1), t_2(s_2)) = P(\pi(s_1, s_2)) = P(M).$$

Decomposition of a money scheme can also be defined as implementation of the money scheme by the *direct product* of the machines $(S_1, T_1), (S_2, T_2)$, which is defined as a machine (S, T), where $S = S_1 \times S_2$ and $T = T_1 \times T_2$ and for every $t = (t_1, t_2) \in T_1 \times T_2$ and $s = (s_1, s_2)$ the new state $s' = t(s)$ is defined by $t(s) = (t_1(s_1), t_2(s_2))$.

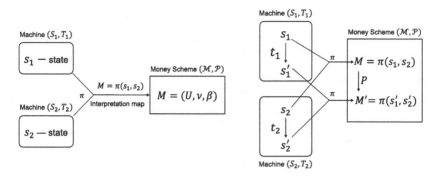

Fig. 2. Decomposition of a money scheme.

5 Blockchain Implementations of Money Schemes

By an *evolution* of a transition system (S, T) is a sequence

$$(s_0, \tau_0; (t_1, \tau_1), (t_2, \tau_2), \ldots, (t_m, \tau_m)),$$

where $s_0 \in S$ is the *initial state*, $t_1, t_2, \ldots, t_m \in T$ are transitions, and $\tau_0 < \tau_1 < \tau_2 < \ldots < \tau_m$ are real numbers interpreted as timestamps. The *final state* s' of the evolution is defined by $s' = t_m(t_{m-1}(\ldots t_1(s_0) \ldots))$. Intuitively, evolution is a description of the execution of the transition system in time.

For security-critical transition systems such as money schemes it is vital to store the evolution and protect its integrity with cryptography. Therefore, *certificates* $C_0, C_1, C_2, \ldots, C_m$ to the evolution, so that the certified evolution

$$(s_0, \tau_0, C_0; (t_1, \tau_1, C_1), (t_2, \tau_2, C_2), \ldots, (t_m, \tau_m, C_m))$$

cannot be maliciously modified without making it cryptographically inconsistent. The certificates also prove the *uniqueness* of the certified evolution, i.e. it must convince the verifiers that there exist no alternative versions of the evolution.

What is also important for the verifiers is whether they see the whole evolution that includes all transition that have been executed so far, i.e. if verification happens at time τ, then also the fact that no transitions happened in between τ_m and τ. This suggests a certification scheme, where transitions of the evolution are certified in batches (blocks) in a pre-determined time schedule and the certified evolution being in the form:

$$(s_0, \tau_0, C_0; (B_1, \tau_1, C_1), (B_2, \tau_2, C_2), \ldots, (B_m, \tau_m, C_m)) \tag{1}$$

where every block B_i represents a composition $t_i^1 \circ \ldots \circ t_i^{m_i}$ of transitions. Note that some blocks B_i may be empty and in this case, they represent the identity transition 1_S. Certified data structures in the form of (1) are called *blockchains*.

Blockchain implementation of a transition system (S, T) is a network of machines called a *blockchain node* that consists of three machines (Fig. 3):

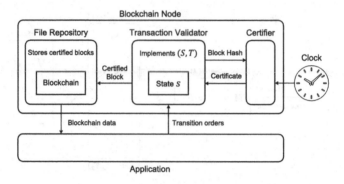

Fig. 3. Blockchain node.

- *File repository* – stores certified blocks and, on request, provides applications with blockchain data.
- *Certifier* – regularly (based on clock) creates block certificates based on a cryptographic hash of the block.
- *Transaction validator* – receives transition orders from applications, verifies them using the current state $s \in S$, combines transactions to blocks, obtains certificates from the certifier, and sends certified blocks to the file repository.

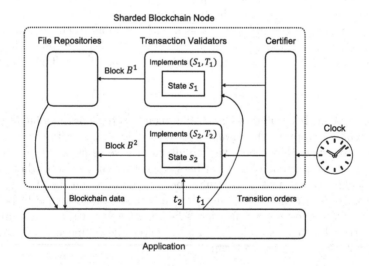

Fig. 4. Sharded blockchain node.

A blockchain implementation of a composed money scheme with two transition systems (S_1, T_1) and (S_2, T_2) is a network of machines called a *sharded blockchain node* (Fig. 4). It has two independent transaction validators that implement (S_1, T_1) and (S_2, T_2) and produce sub-blocks B^1 and B^2, respectively. It also has two file repositories, and a common certifier for both blocks. The blockchain produced by the first transaction validator is in the form:

$$(s_0^1, \tau_0, \varPi_0^1, C_0; (B_1^1, \tau_1, \varPi_1^1, C_1), (B_2^1, \tau_2, \varPi_2^1, C_2), \ldots, (B_m^1, \tau_m, \varPi_m^1, C_m)),$$

where $\varPi_i^1$ denotes additional information (usually in the form of a hash chain) that helps to verify the blockchain against the certificate C_i. Analogously, the blockchain produced by the second transaction validator is in the form:

$$(s_0^2, \tau_0, \varPi_0^2, C_0; (B_1^2, \tau_1, \varPi_1^2, C_1), (B_2^2, \tau_2, \varPi_2^2, C_2), \ldots, (B_m^2, \tau_m, \varPi_m^2, C_m)).$$

For executing a payment P, two transaction orders t_1, t_2 has to be sent to the two transaction validators (Fig. 4) and the validators include these transactions to the blocks B^1 and B^2, respectively.

6   Atomic Decomposition of a Money Scheme

As the blocks have to be produced based on a fixed time schedule, there is a limited time for the validators to decide whether to include t_1 and t_2 to the blocks B^1 and B^2. Considering possible message loss and network delays between the transaction validators and applications, it is always possible that only one of the transactions t_1, t_2 is received in time (considering the block creation schedule).

It is known that there exist no deterministic time protocols (executed between transaction validators) which ensure that either $t_1 \in B^1$ and $t_2 \in B^2$, or $t_1 \notin B^1$ and $t_2 \notin B^2$. Such a communication problem is often called the *two generals problem*. Therefore, it is possible that $t_1 \in B^1$ but $t_2 \notin B^2$ and vice versa. In transition system terms, instead of executing (t_1, t_2), either $(t_1, 1)$ or $(1, t_2)$ is executed in the implementing machines.

If $(S_1, T_1), (S_2, T_2)$ represent a decomposition of a money scheme $(\mathcal{M}, \mathcal{P})$ and such errors cannot in principle be avoided, we can only ask how the partial transactions $(t_1, 1), (1, t_2)$ are interpreted in the money scheme as changes of the money distribution. Do they preserve total money? Are they payments, i.e. elements of $\mathcal{P}$? If the current states are $s_1 \in S_1$ and $s_2 \in S_2$ and money distribution is $M = \pi(s_1, s_2)$, then $P(M) = \pi(t_1(s_1), t_2(s_2))$. The money distribution after applying the erroneous pair $(t_1, 1)$ is $M_1 = \pi(t_1(s_1), s_2)$ and after applying $(1, t_2)$, the resulting money distribution is $M_2 = \pi(s_1, t_2(s_2))$. It is intuitive and natural to require that:

1. There are payments $P_1, P_2 \in \mathcal{P}$ such that $P_1(M) = M_1$ and $P_1(M) = M_1$.
2. If the money $\sigma(M, b)$ of a bearer b is reduced by P, i.e. if $\sigma(M, b) > \sigma(P(M), b)$, then P_1 and P_2 do not reduce $\sigma(M, b)$ more than P, i.e.:

$$\sigma(M, b) - \sigma(P(M), b) \geq \sigma(M, b) - \sigma(M_1, b),$$
$$\sigma(M, b) - \sigma(P(M), b) \geq \sigma(M, b) - \sigma(M_2, b).$$

3. If the money $\sigma(M,b)$ of a bearer b is raised by P, i.e. if $\sigma(M,b) < \sigma(P(M),b)$, then P_1 and P_2 do not raise $\sigma(M,b)$ more than P, i.e.:

$$\sigma(P(M),b) - \sigma(M,b) \geq \sigma(M_1,b) - \sigma(M,b),$$
$$\sigma(P(M),b) - \sigma(M,b) \geq \sigma(M_2,b) - \sigma(M,b).$$

4. If the money $\sigma(M,b)$ of a bearer b is not changed by P, i.e. if $\sigma(M,b) = \sigma(P(M),b)$, then also P_1 and P_2 do not change $\sigma(M,b)$, i.e. $\sigma(M_1,b) = \sigma(M,b)$ and $\sigma(M_2,b) - \sigma(M,b)$.

If a decomposition of a money scheme $(\mathcal{M}, \mathcal{P})$ has such properties, then such a decomposition is said to be *atomic*. It can be shown [1] that atomic decomposition of a money scheme has the following properties:

- $(S_1,T_1),(S_2,T_2)$ can be interpreted as money schemes $(\mathcal{M},\mathcal{P}_1)$ and $(\mathcal{M},\mathcal{P}_2)$ where the elements of $\mathcal{P}_1$ contains payments that correspond to transaction pairs $(t_1,1)$ and $\mathcal{P}_2$ contains payments that correspond to pairs $(1,t_2)$.
- Money $\sigma_1(M,b)$ of a bearer b in (S_1,T_1) is defined as the largest amount of money b can pay with a a sequence of transactions of type $(t_1,1)$.
- Money $\sigma_2(M,b)$ of a bearer b in (S_2,T_2) is defined as the largest amount of money b can pay with a a sequence of transactions of type $(1,t_2)$.
- $\sigma_1(M,b) + \sigma_2(M,b) = \sigma(M,b)$
- The total amount σ_1 of money in $(\mathcal{M},\mathcal{P}_1)$ and the total amount σ_2 of money in $(\mathcal{M},\mathcal{P}_2)$ are invariant and $\sigma_1 + \sigma_2 = \sigma(M)$. There is no transfer of value from $(\mathcal{M},\mathcal{P}_1)$ to σ_2 of money in $(\mathcal{M},\mathcal{P}_2)$ and vice versa.

For example, there is no atomic decomposition of an account scheme such that (S_1,T_1) handles one subset of accounts and (S_2,T_2) handles other accounts, because there is no possibility to pay from an account handled by (S_1,T_1) to an account handled by (S_2,T_2). Otherwise, the values σ_1 and σ_2 would change.

From a bit more general viewpoint, we define *unitwise decompositions* as those decompositions where there is a rule that divides the set U of the existing units into two non-intersecting subsets U_1 and U_2 so that:

- Every $P \in \mathcal{P}_1$ acts only on U_1 and does not delete, create, or change the parameters of the units of U_2.
- Every $P \in \mathcal{P}_2$ acts only on U_2 and does not delete, create, or change the parameters of the units of U_1.

It can be shown that if $\mathcal{P}$ contains composition-irreducible payments P with $\|P\|_{\text{in}} = 2$ with input units in two different components, then $(\mathcal{M},\mathcal{P})$ is not unitwise atomically decomposable. Note that the newly created units can always be chosen in the same component, and hence, the input complexity $\|P\|_{\text{in}}$ (and not $\|P\|$) is critical for unitwise atomic decomposability. Some implications:

- The account money scheme has no unitwise atomic decompositions, because it implements two-unit swap.
- The UTXO money scheme has no unitwise atomic decompositions, because it implements two-unit join.

- The bill money scheme has unitwise atomic decompositions, as single bill payments have complexity $\|P\|_{\text{in}} = 1$ and can be executed in parallel.

Moreover, the bill money scheme enables *total unitwise atomic decomposability* where every bill u is maintained in a separate machine and in the blockchain setting in a separate transaction validator that produces the blockchain (ledger) of the bill u in the form:

$$(s_0^u, \tau_0, \Pi_0^u, C_0; (B_1^u, \tau_1, \Pi_1^u, C_1), (B_2^u, \tau_2, \Pi_2^u, C_2), \ldots, (B_m^u, \tau_m, \Pi_m^u, C_m)),$$

where B_i^u is either empty or contains a single payment P_i^u, and Π_i^u denotes additional information (usually in the form of a hash chain) that helps to verify the blockchain against the certificate C_i.

7 Security of Blockchain Implementations

In the so called *permissionless* blockchain systems new blocks are verified by thousands of nodes and erroneous blocks in the certified blockchain can be considered as almost impossible. However, permissionless systems tend to be more costly to manage and to have larger CO2 traces compared to *permissioned* blockchain systems where the number of redundant nodes is much smaller.

Hence, it is probably more efficient to implement Central Bank Digital Currency (CBDC) as a permissioned blockchain system, where new blocks are verified by just a few nodes. However, in this case, due to potential internal threats, erroneous blocks in the blockchain should be considered a possibility.

In the blockchain node (Fig. 3), the transaction validator together with the file repository are modelled as an adversarial entity that may deviate from ledger rules. Misbehavior of a node may be caused by internal attacks by malicious employees of system operators who may also be owners of money.

The practical goal of an attacker is to buy some goods by using falsified electronic cash, so that such a deception remains undetected for certain time sufficient for the attacker to escape. We assume *covert adversaries* [3,4] that are considered successful only if their malicious behaviour remains undetected at least for some time. The Certifier (Fig. 3) is guaranteed to create a unique block certificate C_n for every block number n. Adversary has no control over the Certifier that is assumed to be controlled by the central bank.

We assume that a bill payment scheme is used in the CBDC blockchain solution, where every bill u has a bill ledger. At every payment with u, an *audit protocol* is executed to verify that the bill is properly used, i.e. all the ledger rules are fulfilled. In the sequel, we study two types of audit protocols:

1. *Full audit* – guarantees that the ledger rules are followed.
2. *Probabilistic audit* – guarantees that any deviation from ledger rules will be detected very soon with high probability.

8   Rules of a Bill Ledger

Let U be the set of all bills and $\beta_0 : U \to B$ be a function that defines the initial owner $\beta_0(u)$ of every bill $u \in U$. We assume that both U and β_0 are verifiably certified by Central Bank and cannot be altered by other parties. Every payment order is in the form $P^u = \langle \iota, b, \lambda, s \rangle$, where ι is a unique identifier of u, $b \in B$ is the payee identifier, λ is a unique identifier of the payment order, and s is a signature of the payer. Every block B_n^u of the bill ledger

$$(s_0^u, \tau_0, \Pi_0^u, C_0; (B_1^u, \tau_1, \Pi_1^u, C_1), (B_2^u, \tau_2, \Pi_2^u, C_2), \ldots, (B_m^u, \tau_m, \Pi_m^u, C_m)),$$

is either empty, or contains a payment order $P_n^u = \langle \iota, b, \lambda, s \rangle$, where:

1. $\lambda = H(\iota, \beta_0(u))$ and s is the signature of $\beta_0(u)$ if P_n^u is the first payment with u, where $H : \{0,1\}^* \to \{0,1\}^k$ is a cryptographic hash function.
2. $\lambda = H(P_{n'}^u)$ and s is the signature of b' if $P_{n'}^u = \langle \iota, b', \lambda', s' \rangle$ is the payment order contained in the *last non-empty block* $B_{n'}^u$ in the sequence $B_1^u, \ldots, B_{n-1}^u$.

Hence, the blocks $B_{n'+1}^u, B_{n'+2}^u, \ldots, B_{n-2}^u, B_{n-1}^u$ must be empty. The collision-resistance of H guarantees that λ is unique for every payment order.

The certificate C_n contains the block hash r_n and there is a function F^H that uses H as an oracle such that $F^H(u; B_n^u, \Pi_n^u) = r_n$, and If $R^u \neq \underline{R}^u$ and $F^H(u; B^u, \Pi^u) = F^H(u; \underline{B}^u, \underline{\Pi}^u)$, then the computations of F^H contain either an H-collision, or an H-pre-image of 0^k – a bitstring X such that $H(X) = 0^k$. Both are assumed to be infeasible to find for practical hash functions.

9   User Side Full Audit

The main idea behind the full audit is that every user who has received u with a payment $P_{n'}^u$ and later, at block $n > n'$, uses u in a payment P_n^u, verifies that the blocks $B_{n'+1}^u, B_{n'+2}^u, \ldots, B_{n-1}^u$ are empty (Fig. 5).

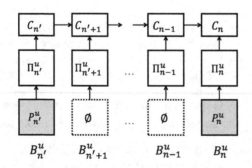

Fig. 5. User side full audit.

9.1   Full Audit Protocol

Assume that a user has a bill u paid to her with a payment order $P_{n'}^u$ at block n', and that the user's wallet already contains the certificates $C_0, \ldots, C_{n'}$ that were already verified, the block $B_{n'}^u$, and the proof $\Pi_{n'}^u$ which also has been verified.

In a block $n > n'$, the user creates a block B_n^u with a new payment order $P_n^u = \langle \iota, b, \lambda, s \rangle$, where $\lambda = H(P_{n'}^u)$ and sends it to the transaction validator. User then executes the following *full audit protocol*:

1. User requests $C_{n'+1}, \ldots, C_n$ and $\Pi_{n'+1}^u, \ldots, \Pi_n^u$ from the file repository.
2. User verifies $C_{n'+1}, \ldots, C_n$.
3. User verifies $\Pi_{n'+1}^u, \ldots, \Pi_n^u$, assuming that $B_{n'+1}^u, \ldots, B_{n-1}^u$ are empty, i.e. for every $i \in \{n'+1, \ldots, n-1\}$ the user extracts the block hashes x_i from C_i and checks that $F^H(u; \emptyset, \Pi_i^u) = r_n$.

9.2   Security of the Full Audit

Ledger rules violation means inserting a block $\overline{B}_i^u = \{P_i^u\}$ to the ledger, where P_i^u does not properly follow $P_{n'}^u$, e.g. is not signed by $P_{n'}^u.b$. If the full audit at n also verifies, then $F^H(u; B_i^u, \Pi_i^u) = r_n = F^H(u; \underline{B}_i^u, \underline{\Pi}_i^u)$ and there is a collision for H or an X such that $H(X) = 0^k$ (Fig. 6).

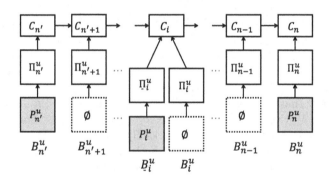

Fig. 6. Ledger rules violation leads to a hash collision.

9.3   Communication Complexity of the Full Audit

Let N be the total number of bills. The size of a proof is $k \cdot \log_2 N$ bits. As we need $n - n'$ proofs during the audit, the total number of bits communicated is $(n - n') \cdot k \cdot \log_2 N$ which may be impractical if $n \gg n'$. Using the probabilistic audit enables to reduce the communication complexity. The idea is that we check a random d-element subset of $B_{n'+1}^u, B_{n'+2}^u, \ldots, B_{n-1}^u$. In the general case, with the bill ledger certification scheme that we described, such an audit is inefficient because the detection probability δ of one single illegal block is about $\frac{d}{n-n'}$ which means that for a high δ the number d of detected blocks must be close to $n - n'$. We show that proper ledger certification schemes enable to keep d small.

10   KSI-Cash Bill Ledger

In this section, we describe the bill ledger certification scheme of the KSI-Cash CBDC solution [2] enables efficient probabilistic audit protocols with d being a fixed constant that only depends on the required detection probability and not on the length $n - n'$ of the auditing interval.

10.1   Hash Chains

By a hash chain c we mean a (possibly empty) list $\langle (b_1, y_1), (b_2, y_2), \ldots, (b_\ell, y_\ell) \rangle$, where $b_i \in \{0, 1\}$ and $y_i \in \{0, 1\}^k$ for every $i \in \{1, \ldots, \ell\}$. The bitstring $b_1 b_2 \ldots b_\ell$ is called the shape of c. Every hash chain can be viewed as a function $c : \{0, 1\}^k \to \{0, 1\}^k$ defined as follows:

1. $\langle \rangle(x) = x$ for every $x \in \{0, 1\}^k$, where $\langle \rangle$ is the empty list

2. $\langle c \| (b, y) \rangle(x) = \begin{cases} H(c(x), y) & \text{if } b = 0 \\ H(y, c(x)) & \text{if } b = 1 \end{cases}$,   where $\langle c \| (b, y) \rangle$ denotes the list

   obtained from c by adding (b, y) as the last element.

10.2   The Idea of Probabilistic Audit

For every block B_n^u, we define the *ledger hash* x_n that is a function of the previous ledger hash x_{n-1} and the block B_n^u. If $B_n^u = \emptyset$, then $x_{n+1} = x_n$. Hence, if $B_{n'}^u = \{P_{n'}^u\}$ is the last non-empty block of u, and the current block number is $n - 1$, then $x_{n-1} = x_{n-2} = \ldots = x_{n'}$ if ledger is correctly formed. We say that the empty blocks $n' + 1, \ldots, n - 1$ are *consistent* with $B_{n'}^u$.

Assume now that an illegal block $B_i^u = \{P_i^u\}$ with $n' < i < n - 1$ is added to the ledger (Fig. 7) with $P_i^u.\lambda \neq H(P_{n'}^u)$, i.e. P_i^u "double-spends" the bill u. Then $x_i \neq x_{n'}$ and hence, each of the empty blocks $B_{i+1}^u, B_{i+2}^u, \ldots, B_{n-1}^u$ is either consistent with $B_{n'}^u$ or with B_i^u, but not with both. The empty blocks that are consistent with $B_{n'}^u$ are called *black* blocks, and the empty blocks that are consistent with B_i^u are called *white* blocks. Hence, each of the blocks $B_{i+1}^u, B_{i+2}^u, \ldots, B_{n-1}^u$ is either black or white (Fig. 7).

The next payment P_n^u with u in the block $B_n^u = \{P_n^u\}$ may either refer back to $B_{n'}^u$ (i.e. $P_n^u.\lambda = H(P_{n'}^u)$) or to B_i^u (i.e. $P_n^u.\lambda = H(P_i^u)$). In the former case, during the audit protocol the blocks $B_{i+1}^u, B_{i+2}^u, \ldots, B_{n-1}^u$ must be shown to be black, and in the latter case these blocks must be shown to be white. For randomly chosen $j \leftarrow \{i + 1, \ldots, n - 1\}$, either

- The probability that B_j^u is consistent with B_i^u is $\leq \frac{1}{2}$
- The probability that B_j^u is consistent with $B_{n'}^u$ is $\leq \frac{1}{2}$

and hence, an audit with one randomly selected block B_j^u in at least one of the two cases succeeds with probability not larger than $\frac{1}{2}$.

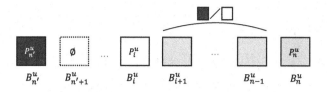

Fig. 7. Blocks of an inconsistent bill ledger.

10.3 Proofs and Ledger Hashes in KSI-Cash

For every $n > 0$, a proof Π_n^u is a pair (x_{n-1}^u, c_n^u), where x_i^u is a ledger hash computed by the rules:

1. $x_0^u = 0$
2. $x_i^u = h_0(x_{i-1}^u, h_D(R_i^u))$, where:
   - $h_D(X) = H(X)$ if $X \neq \emptyset$, and $h_D(X) = 0$ if $X = \emptyset$
   - $h_0(x, y) = H(x, y)$ if $y \neq 0$, and $h_0(x, y) = 0$ if $y = 0$

and c_n^u is a hash chain with the shape special to u from x_n to the block hash r_n in C_n, i.e. $c_n^u(x_n) = r_n$. The function F_H is defined as follows:

$$F^H(u; B, (x, c)) = c(h_0(x, h_D(B))).$$

Lemma 1 guarantees that two different non-empty blocks $B_{n'}^u$ and $B_{n''}^u$ must have different ledger hashes. If $n' < n'' < j$, then the ledger hash x_j cannot equal to both $x_{n'}$ and $x_{n''}$ and then by Lemma 2 (proved in [5]) , if the block B_j^u is consistent with both $B_{n'}^u$ and $B_{n''}^u$, we have a collision for H.

Lemma 1. If $\emptyset \neq B_{n'}^u \neq B_{n''}^u \neq \emptyset$, then either $x_{n'}^u \neq x_{n''}^u$, or we have an explicit H-collision or a bitstring X such that $H(X) = 0$.

Proof. If $x_{n'}^u = x_{n''}^u$, then by definition $h_0(x', h_D(B_{n'}^u)) = h_0(x'', h_D(B_{n''}^u))$ for some $x', x'' \in \{0,1\}^k$, which by $B_{n'}^u \neq \emptyset$ and $B_{n''}^u \neq \emptyset$ implies $h_0(x', H(B_{n'}^u)) = h_0(x'', H(B_{n''}^u))$. If $H(B_{n'}^u) = 0$ or $H(B_{n''}^u) = 0$, then we can take $X = B_{n'}^u$ or $X = H(B_{n''}^u)$ and have $H(X) = 0$. If $H(B_{n'}^u) \neq 0 \neq H(B_{n''}^u)$, then by definition of h_0, we have $H(x', H(B_{n'}^u)) = H(x'', H(B_{n''}^u))$ and because of $B_{n'}^u \neq B_{n''}^u$, we have a collision for H. □

Lemma 2. If $c^u, \underline{c}^u$ are two hash chains with the same u-specific shape, and $c^u(x_{n'}^u) = \underline{c}^u(x_{n''}^u)$ and $x_{n'}^u \neq x_{n''}^u$, then we have an explicit H-collision.

Proof. Let $c^u = \langle (b_1, y_1), \ldots, (b_\ell, y_\ell) \rangle$ and $\underline{c}^u = \langle (b_1, y_1'), \ldots, (b_\ell, y_\ell') \rangle$ be two hash chains of the same shape. We use induction on ℓ. If $\ell = 0$, then $c^u = \langle \rangle = \underline{c}^u$ and for every $x_{n'}^u \neq x_{n''}^u$, we have $c^u(x_{n'}^u) = x_{n'}^u \neq x_{n''}^u = \underline{c}^u(x_{n''}^u)$ and hence, the induction basis trivially holds. Assume now that the statement holds for the chains of length $\ell - 1$, for example, for the chains $c = \langle (b_1, y_1), \ldots, (b_{\ell-1}, y_{\ell-1}) \rangle$

and $c' = \langle(b_1, y'_1), \ldots, (b_{\ell-1}, y_{\ell-1})\rangle$. Hence, $c^u = \langle c \| (b_\ell, y_\ell)\rangle$ and $\underline{c}^u = \langle c' \| (b_\ell, y'_\ell)\rangle$. If $b_\ell = 1$, then it follows from $c^u(x^u_{n'}) = \underline{c}^u(x^u_{n''})$ that

$$H(y_\ell, c(x^u_{n'})) = H(y'_\ell, c'(x^u_{n''})). \tag{2}$$

If $c(x^u_{n'}) \neq c'(x^u_{n''})$, then (2) represents a collision for H. If $c(x^u_{n'}) = c'(x^u_{n''})$, we apply the induction hypothesis to imply that the computations $c(x^u_{n'})$, $c'(x^u_{n''})$ contain an H-collision. The proof for the case $b_\ell = 0$ is similar. $\qquad\square$

11   User Side Probabilistic Audit in KSI-Cash

User has a bill u paid to her with a payment order $P^u_{n'}$ at block n'. We assume that user wallet contains the certificates $C_0, \ldots, C_{n'}$ that were already verified, the block $B^u_{n'}$, and the proof $\Pi^u_{n'}$, that have also been verified. In a block $n > n'$, the user creates a block B^u_n with a new payment order $P^u_n = \langle \iota, b, \lambda, s\rangle$, where $\lambda = H(P^u_{n'})$, sends it to the transaction validator, and initiates the next protocol:

Probabilistic Audit Protocol:

1. The user requests and verifies the certificates $C_{n'+1}, \ldots, C_n$.
2. The user generates d random numbers $n_1, \ldots, n_d \in \{n'+1, \ldots, n-1\}$.
3. The user requests $\Pi^u_{n_1} = (x'_{n_1}, c^u_{n_1}), \ldots, \Pi^u_{n_d} = (x'_{n_d}, c^u_{n_d})$ and checks that $x'_{n_1} = \ldots = x'_{n_d} = x^u_{n'}$, and $c^u_{n_1}(x^u_{n'}) = r_{n_1}, \ldots, c^u_{n_d}(x^u_{n'}) = r_{n_d}$.

11.1   Simplistic Security Analysis

Let the ledger be inconsistent already at block $B^u_{n'}$ and there are black blocks and white blocks that are inconsistent with each other (Fig. 8). Therefore:

- If the fraction of white blocks between n' and n is $\leq \frac{1}{2}$, and the payment P^u_n is "white" ($P^u_n.\lambda = H(P^u_i)$), then the audit succeeds with probability $\leq 2^{-d}$.
- If the fraction of black blocks between n' and n is $\leq \frac{1}{2}$, and P^u_n is "black" ($P^u_n.\lambda = H(P^u_{n'})$), then the audit succeeds with probability $\leq 2^{-d}$.

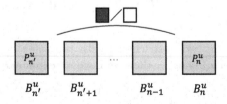

Fig. 8. Security argument for probabilistic audit.

This analysis is precise only if the two blocks $B^u_{n'}, B^u_{n''}$ are very close, i.e. $n' \approx n''$. In a more realistic scenario, adversary may choose suitable block numbers, for example, by delaying the execution of transactions, in order to make the success probability of probabilistic audit as high as possible. In the next section, we analyze such a possibility and show that such manipulation is not possible considering the properties of practical money systems.

11.2   Security: Alternating Payments Case

First, consider a scenario, where the adversary has to execute black payments and white payments alternatively as shown in Fig. 9. Assume that the bill u have paid to two different honest users b and b' at block n_0 and n_1, respectively. We assume that the payment to b is already an illegal transaction, i.e. from the block n_0 and further, the later blocks (and their certificates) may be consistent with only one branch of the bill ledger. The blocks consistent with the payment to b are said to be *black*, and the blocks consistent with the payment to b' are said to be *white*.

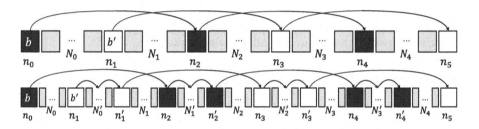

Fig. 9. Alternating attack and general attack.

Later at block n_2, the user b pays u to another user, at block n_3 the user b' pays u to another user, and at block n_4 the bill u is being paid again. We assume that the adversary can choose the blocks n_1, n_2, n_3, n_4 in an appropriate way in order to hide the inconsistency of the ledger from probabilistic audit.

We assume that there are $N_0 = n_1 - n_0 - 1$ between the payments to b and b'. Analogously, let $N_1 = n_2 - n_1 - 1$, $N_2 = n_3 - n_2 - 1$, and $N_3 = n_4 - n_3 - 1$ (Fig. 9, upper). Note that all these blocks depicted as grey are either black or white. The color of these blocks can be chosen by the adversary. When the payment is made at the block n_2, the adversary is interested that most of the $N_0 + N_1$ grey blocks are black, because the payment at n_2 is checked to be consistent with the black branch. When the payment is made at n_3, the adversary is interested that most of the $N_1 + N_2$ blocks are white, and for the payment at n_4, most of the $N_2 + N_3$ should be black again.

In the general case, the adversary has to execute black and white payments in arbitrary order (Fig. 9, lower), that before the payment that continues the black block at n_0 is made at the block n_2, some payments continue the white block at n_1 and the last such payment happens at the block n_1'. We assume that the number of blocks between n_1 and n_1' is N_0'. It may be that none of such payments happen and then $n_1' = n_1$ and $N_0' = 0$, and hence, we have the alternating attack. Analogously, we assume that some payments may continue the black block at n_2 and the last such payment happens at the block n_2', etc.

Say the adversary wants that any of the probabilistic test with d samples should succeed with probability $1 - \delta$. This means that every single-sample test must succeed with probability $1 - \epsilon$, where $(1 - \epsilon)^d = (1 - \delta)$. For small values of ϵ and δ they are related linearly: $\epsilon \approx \frac{\delta}{d}$. We can show that in the general case:

$$n_{k+1} - n_0 > N_0 + N_0' + N_1 + N_1' + \ldots + N_{k-1} + N_{k-1}' + N_k$$

$$\geq \left(\frac{1 - \epsilon}{\epsilon}\right)^{k-1} (N_1 + N_1') - \left[\frac{1 - \epsilon}{\epsilon} + \ldots + \left(\frac{1 - \epsilon}{\epsilon}\right)^{k-2}\right] (N_0 + N_0'),$$

and hence, the required delays between payments must grow exponentially, that is clearly not realistic to enforce by adversaries in practice.

12   Probabilistic Audit for Account Money Schemes?

We cannot just copy the idea of probabilistic audit from bill ledgers, because of very different ledger rules. Even if the total amount of money is controlled by the Central Bank (via count-certified trees [6], etc.), there is always "money on the fly" – payer account debited but payee account not yet credited. The amount of "money on the fly" gives attackers room for illegal transactions that are hard to detect "on-line". It would be an interesting research question whether there exist efficient probabilistic audit protocols for account money schemes.

References

1. Buldas, A., Saarepera, M., Steiner, J., Draheim, D.: A unifying theory of electronic money and payment systems. TechRxiv (2021). https://doi.org/10.36227/techrxiv. 14994558
2. Buldas, A., Draheim, D., Gault, M., Laanoja, R., Nagumo, T., Saarepera, M., Shah, S., Simm, J., Steiner, J., Tammet, T., Truu, A.: An ultra-scalable blockchain platform for universal asset tokenization: design and implementation. IEEE Access **10**, 77284–77322 (2022)
3. Aumann, Y., Lindell, Y.: Security against covert adversaries: efficient protocols for realistic adversaries. In: Vadhan, S.P. (ed.) TCC 2007. LNCS, vol. 4392, pp. 137–156. Springer, Heidelberg (2007). https://doi.org/10.1007/978-3-540-70936-7_8
4. Aumann, Y., Lindell, Y.: Security against covert adversaries: efficient protocols for realistic adversaries. J. Cryptol. **23**(2), 281–343 (2007)

5. Buldas, A., Niitsoo, M.: Optimally tight security proofs for hash-then-publish time-stamping. In: Steinfeld, R., Hawkes, P. (eds.) ACISP 2010. LNCS, vol. 6168, pp. 318–335. Springer, Heidelberg (2010). https://doi.org/10.1007/978-3-642-14081-5_20

6. Buldas, A., Laur, S.: Knowledge-binding commitments with applications in time-stamping. In: Okamoto, T., Wang, X. (eds.) PKC 2007. LNCS, vol. 4450, pp. 150–165. Springer, Heidelberg (2007). https://doi.org/10.1007/978-3-540-71677-8_11

Managing the Quality of Data and Metadata for Biobanks

Johann Eder[✉] and Volodymyr A. Shekhovtsov

Universität Klagenfurt, Universitätsstraße 65-67, 9020 Klagenfurt am Wörthersee,
Austria
{johann.eder,volodymyr.shekhovtsov}@aau.at

Abstract. Medical research requires biological material and data of
documented trustworthy quality for delivering relevant and reproducible
results. The management of the quality of biological samples for medical research received high attention in recent years resulting in well-
documented and audited standard operating procedures and standards
for the documentation of various quality characteristics. We need similar
efforts to establish systems, policies, and procedures for assuring well-
documented quality characteristics of data and metadata. We review the
typical data and metadata characteristics and point to precise definitions
of these properties. We present and discuss the requirements for managing these qualities and propose a process and the necessary activities for
biobanks to establish such a holistic system for data quality management.
The complex nature of biobanks as data producers, data providers, data
mediators, and data repositories dealing with data from various sources
and the highly sensitive nature of personal health data makes them a
most interesting use case for data quality management, supporting both
known and unknown future demands.

Keywords: Data quality · Metadata quality · Biobank · Quality
management · Medical data

1 Introduction

Each data item has some quality. The challenges are knowing this quality and
achieving the quality necessary for the intended usage of data: making decisions,
gaining information and knowledge, processing it together with other data, etc.
The required data quality and the reliable documentation of data quality do
not happen by chance but they can only be achieved by careful management of
data quality, and of all processes that influence data quality [3,4,14,15,30]. We
discuss here the management of data quality for the use case of biobanks and
medical data. The domains of biobanks and medical research are challenging
domains for data quality due to the significance of data quality for the results of

This work has been supported by the Austrian Bundesministerium für Bildung, Wis-
senschaft und Forschung within the project BBMRI.AT (GZ 10.470/0010-V/3c/2018).

medical research and the complex organization of biobanks as data producers, data repositories, data mediators, and data providers. The documented quality of data is of utmost importance to achieve reliable and reproducible results in medical studies. The data in biobanks comes from different sources, and the biobanks also produce some data. Biobanks have to serve both the usage of data known in advance and the usage of data in studies not known at the time the data is collected and prepared.

Biobanks are essential infrastructures for biomedical research. They collect biological material like tissue, blood, etc., and conserve and store it to provide this material for medical studies. In recent years, biobanks have been very successful in establishing quality management for biological specimens so that they can provide material possessing established quality characteristics [5,6] and standards for the documentation of these qualities [20,22]. Biobanks also provide data associated with the samples, collecting the data from various sources with ever-increasing demand and supply of data. Therefore, we argue that it is necessary to establish a concept for a *quality management system for biobank data*, too:

- Low reproducibility of medical studies has potentially dangerous consequences for any developments based on these studies, such as developing new drugs or medical procedures and is at least a waste of resources.
- To achieve high reproducibility, medical research needs both biomaterial and the associated data of high or at least known quality, because reproducibility depends on the reliability of conclusions based on research results, which, in turn, highly depends on the quality of data available for studies.
- Achieving high-quality of data is not possible without establishing well-defined standard operating procedures for data quality management, and increasing personnel awareness of the importance of such procedures, and the data quality itself.
- In particular, such procedures are necessary because, without them, the resulting quality will only depend on the abilities and the personal preferences of the persons responsible for data collection and the actual quality characteristics of the available data will be undocumented.

The recognition of the need for data management in biobanks grows in acceptance [13,23,28], and it is increasingly recognized that integrated documentation of both the biological samples and the data accompanying it is necessary [16,35]. Precise characterizations of data quality for biobanking are only recently investigated in depth ([30,31]. These characterizations build the necessary basis for developing concepts, policies, processes, and systems for a data quality management infrastructure for biobanks in an adequate way. In this paper, we contribute to this endeavor and provide the necessary background for establishing such an infrastructure, in particular, the concepts of data item and metadata quality for biobanks, and a set of data item and metadata quality characteristics as well as all the activities needed for holistic management of data quality.

2   Data in Biobanks

Biobanks are collections of biological material (samples) such as tissue, blood, or other bodily fluids, cell cultures, etc., accompanied by *data* [9,17,23,26]. Biobank data [1,30] represent a set of collected facts about the physical samples stored in the biobank. Such data contain facts about the samples themselves (such as freezing, history, ischemia time), about the persons the samples originate from (e.g., health record, lifestyle), prescribed therapies and drugs. Data is collected by humans (e.g. amnesia, lifestyle, pathologists report) or through equipment such as in laboratory (e.g. cholesterin level), or radiological equipment, etc.(e.g. , X-ray images). Typically, data is interpreted and summarized by humans creating various forms of medical reports.

The data describes *data subjects* (general categories to which the data belongs, such as patient, disease, or drug data), originates from *data sources* (human sources, laboratory sources, etc.), and is stored and represented according to *data formats* (textual data, image, or video data).

2.1   Organizing Biobank Data

In [14,30] we proposed to represent biobank data as values of *data item attributes* forming *biobank data items* (most often corresponding to physical samples) belonging to *biobank collections* which, in turn, belong to *biobanks*.

Biobank data consists of *biobank data items* composed of *data item attributes* and their values. Samples and their annotating data are organized in collections. To include samples and data in a biobank, the informed consent of the owner, i.e., the donor of data and material, is necessary. Samples and data are only available for researchers after careful examination of the intended medical study and whether the usage is covered by the informed consent. Therefore, metadata [14,31] is used to describe the content of biobanks and their collections for researchers without violating the privacy requirements of the donors of data and samples.

2.2   Roles of Biobanks in Data Management

Biobanks have different roles in the management of the data associated with the samples.

- **Data producers.** Biobanks produce data, in particular, data about the handling of the biological samples, above all the documentation of quality characteristics of the samples, e.g., the process from sample harvesting to storing, the standard operating procedures applied, etc. [7]
- **Data repository.** Biobanks receive data from various sources (health care, medical studies, lab data) and store them for usage to support the selection of samples satisfying requirements for a medical study and to provide data sets for medical research.

- **Data providers.** The premiere mission of biobanks is to provide samples and data for medical research projects. As data providers, biobanks support researchers in the selection of relevant cases, which involves passing enough information that researchers can decide whether the biobanks is able to provide data in such a quality that it is useful for intended research projects. Data and quality data are also necessary for the selection of biological samples qualifying to be used in a medical study [10].
- **Data mediators.** Biobanks might not store data themselves or are not entitled to store such data but may refer to data stored in other information systems (e.g., health records, laboratory information systems, *omics data, etc.). In this role, biobanks mediate between the data owners and data managers and the researchers needing the data to accompany the samples.

All these different roles pose different requirements, different challenges and also different possibilities for the management of data and metadata qualities which we will discuss in more detail after defining the basic characteristics constituting data item quality and metadata quality.

2.3 Data Item Quality in Biobanks

We start from the most general definition of data item quality. As the data in biobanks always serve specific goals (e.g., it can provide additional information related to physical samples) and it can do it to a different degree of success. It is natural to assume that the data of high quality serves its goals better than low-quality data. Based on that, data item quality in biobanks can be defined as *degree of success for the biobank data in achieving its goals*.

We define a structure of data item quality as a set of data item quality characteristics where each characteristic is accompanied by corresponding data item quality metrics quantifying this characteristic. The definition of a data item quality metric includes the technique for calculating its value for a specific data item or a biobank artifact (such as collection) on different levels of aggregation.

In this paper, we limit ourselves to the definitions of the data item quality characteristics and the informal descriptions of their most important metrics. We refer to [30] for the detailed treatment of the data item quality for biobanks.

2.4 Data Item Quality Characteristics

This section describes specific data item quality characteristics that form a concept for data item quality in biobanks. For this, following [30], we selected the following seven characteristics: *data item completeness, accuracy, reliability, consistency, timeliness, precision,* and *provenance*.

Data Item Completeness. This characteristic [19, 21] is defined as *the degree of presence for the required data item attribute values in a biobank sample or a collection*. It reflects the need to collect all necessary data. Sufficient data item completeness contributes to high quality.

It is possible to define the following data item completeness metrics, among others: *sample completeness* as a ratio of a number of instantiated attributes for a sample to a number of attributes declared for a collection, *sample-based collection completeness* as an average of sample completeness values for all samples in a collection, and *attribute-scoped collection completeness* as a degree of value presence for a specific attribute in a collection. An example of attribute-scoped collection completeness is a degree of value presence for the body mass index (BMI) attribute in a collection calculated as a ratio of the number of BMI values present in a collection to the number of samples in a collection (assuming that every sample can contain a BMI value).

Data Item Accuracy. This characteristics [25] can be defined as either *syntactic accuracy*, which is *a degree of correspondence between data item attribute values and their domains*, or as *indirect accuracy based on the accuracy of the context of the data item attribute values* (e.g., their data collection method). It reflects the need to represent the real world truthfully. Low accuracy means the data is vague, not precise enough, or plainly incorrect (not corresponding to reality). High-quality data is accurate.

Correspondingly, *syntactic accuracy metrics* measure the degree of correspondence between the data items and the constraints related to a given domain, whereas *indirect accuracy metrics* reflect the accuracy of the context elements associated with the data, in particular, the data collection method. For the latter metrics, the context quality has to be calculated first, and the quality of the data item has to be derived from that quality. An example of the data item attribute value violating the domain constraint can be the negative value recorded for the patient age attribute. In this case, the attribute-scoped collection accuracy can be calculated as the ratio of the number of negative patient age values to the total number of samples in a collection.

Data Item Reliability. This characteristic is defined as *indirect reliability based on the reliability of the context of the data item attribute values* (e.g., their source or data collection method). Low reliability means that the biobank data cannot be trusted, so its quality is low. For example, the reliability of the data about the cause of death is much higher if a trained pathologist provided it than if it was attributed to a general practitioner.

Similarly to data item accuracy metrics, *indirect data item reliability metrics* is defined based on the reliability metrics defined for data sources or diagnostic methods used for data collection. For the cause of death data item attribute, the attribute-scoped collection reliability can be calculated as the average of its data source reliability values recorded for all samples in a collection.

Data Item Consistency. This characteristic is defined as *a reverse degree of variability with respect to the data source or collection method*. This means, for example, that the biobank data is more consistent if it was collected by a smaller number of methods or comes from a smaller number of sources. It reflects the need for uniformly collected and, therefore, coherent data. Sufficient consistency contributes to high data item quality.

On the sample level, the possible metric can be a *sample consistency degree based on the total number of methods* calculated as a reverse ratio of the number of methods used to collect attribute values for a sample to the total number of such methods for its collection. It is also possible to take into account the number of values collected by the methods. An example of such a metric on the collection level can be a *collection consistency degree based on the most frequently applied method* calculated as the ratio of the number of values collected by the most frequently used method to the total number of collected values in a collection.

Data Item Timeliness. This characteristic is defined as *the length of time between the change in a real-world state and the time when the data reflects that change.* It reflects the need for the data to represent actual real-world states. Good quality data is current, so its timeliness is high.

The sample-level metric for measuring data item timeliness can be defined as *the reverse distance of time between creating the sample and adding the value of a specific data item attribute for this sample.* An example of low timeliness is the case when collecting BMI value for a person is done two years after collecting the blood sample: such situations are usually unacceptable.

Data Item Precision. This characteristic is defined as *the degree of category resolution for the values of categorical data attributes and the number of significant digits - for the values of numeric data attributes.* An example of the degree of category resolution can be the number of used categories. For example, having just three categories for blood pressure (high, average, and low) is not precise and negatively contributes to quality.

On the sample level, it is possible to define *the average precision degree based on the total number of categories* metric calculated as an average of the number of categories used for the attribute values for a sample.

Data Item Provenance. This characteristic [16, 34, 35] is defined as *the completeness of the information about the data item collection method or source.* For data with low provenance, it is not possible or difficult to understand where it comes from or how it was collected.

Data item provenance metrics can be defined as *a degree of method information instantiation for a sample* calculated as a ratio of a number of instantiated collection methods for the attributes to a total number of attributes declared for a collection to which the sample belongs or as an *attribute-scoped collection-level source provenance* calculated as a ratio of the number of samples containing the data source information for the value of a specific data item attribute to the total number of samples in a collection. An example of the latter metric is a collection-level source provenance for the BMI data item attribute.

3   Metadata in Biobanks

We follow [27] in defining the metadata as "*the information that provides the context and additional information about the domain data or conditions on the usage of data.*" In biobanks, metadata as the additional information about the domain data can refer to the values of the biobank data item quality metrics (*quality metadata*) or to the semantic descriptions of the data items necessary to understand the data (*content* or *semantic metadata*). We will primarily deal with the quality metadata further in this paper. The metadata differs from data in purpose and usage, but not in format or structure, so it can be considered the data itself: "data that provides information about other data" [29].

3.1   Biobank Metadata Motivation and Goals

There are two main problems with the biobank data which make introducing biobank metadata necessary (we first discussed these problems in [14] and provided their detailed treatment in [31]):

1. A significant percentage of data served by a biobank comes from external sources, so it acts as a data broker for this external data and has to provide appropriate descriptions for such data.
2. In biobanks, the direct search within the data by the researchers can be problematic due to privacy and other reasons.

Establishing biobank metadata can help in solving these problems as follows. For the first problem, such metadata can include the descriptions of the external data. For the second problem, the biobank metadata can be searched in place of the original data to find collections with specific properties or help decide if the discovered collections can be used for an intended study.

Based on the above, again following [14], it is possible to distinguish the following main goals for the biobank metadata [31]:

1. to support the biobank in describing the external data;
2. to support the researchers in their search for biobank collections without direct access to sample data;
3. to support the researchers in their decisions if the specific biobank collection (possibly a part of the search results) is relevant or not.

We will deal with both the second and third goals further in this paper, as these are the goals mostly relevant for quality metadata.

3.2   Metadata Quality in Biobanks

We start from the most general definition of metadata quality. As the biobank metadata serves specific goals (out of the list introduced in the previous section) and can do it to various degrees of success, we can state that the metadata of high quality serves its purpose well, whereas low-quality metadata does the opposite. Based on that, metadata quality in biobanks can be defined as a *degree of success for the biobank metadata in achieving its goals.*

The following examples illustrate the quality of the biobank metadata:

1. The biobank samples are accompanied by the metadata, which stores the probability for the sample data to be collected with the same analytical method. This is an example of the method consistency metadata defined on the sample level. It makes it possible to search for the biobank samples possessing specific consistency values, so it addresses the second metadata goal. Suppose the values of this metadata uniquely identify most of the samples in a collection. In that case, it supports search better than the metadata containing values which are mostly the same for all samples. As a result, it can be stated that the quality of the method consistency metadata is higher for this collection.

2. The biobank states that the BMI data is only defined for a certain percentage of the samples in a collection, and these percentage values are stored with collections. This is the example of BMI data attribute completeness metadata defined on the collection level. Such metadata makes it possible to decide on the relevance of the collection for the research dealing with BMI data, so it addresses the third metadata goal. If such completeness values are missing for most collections in a biobank, the above decisions are not well supported there. As a result, it can be stated that the quality of the BMI completeness metadata is low for this biobank.

We define the structure of metadata quality as a set of metadata quality characteristics where each characteristic is accompanied by metadata quality metrics quantifying this characteristic. The definition of a metadata quality metric includes the technique for calculating a metric value for a metadata element or a biobank artifact (such as collection) on different levels of aggregation.

In this paper, we limit ourselves to the definitions of the metadata quality characteristics and the informal descriptions of some of their metrics. We refer to [31] for the detailed treatment of the metadata quality for biobanks.

3.3 Metadata Quality Characteristics

In this section, we describe specific metadata quality characteristics. For this, following [31], we selected nine characteristics: *metadata accuracy, completeness, coverage, consistency, timeliness, provenance, reliability, conformance to expectations*, and *accessibility.*

Metadata Accuracy. This characteristic is defined as *a degree of correspondence of the metadata values to their domains* (syntactic metadata accuracy). It reflects the need for the metadata to be accurate. High-accuracy metadata supports the search better as the data item values corresponding to the artifacts found when searching within accurate metadata values are more likely to conform to the provided search criteria; it also supports decisions based on the found artifacts better as these decisions are more accurately based on the data item values corresponding to the artifacts.

Correspondingly, metadata accuracy metrics measure *the degree of correspondence between the metadata values and the constraints related to a given domain.* An example of the domain constraint served well by such a metric is the non-negativity constraint for the data item reliability value domain. The resulting *data item reliability accuracy metric* on the collection level is calculated as a ratio of the number of negative data item reliability values to the total number of data item reliability values recorded for a collection, over all its data item attributes and all samples.

Metadata Completeness. This characteristic is defined as *the degree of presence of the metadata connected to data item values.* It reflects the need to supplement all data items with the corresponding metadata. More complete metadata supports the search within metadata values better as more metadata values correspond to artifacts, so these artifacts are more likely to be found; it also supports decisions based on the found artifacts better as these decisions are supported with more metadata values.

The metadata completeness metrics can be defined on the sample level as a *ratio of a total number of instantiated sample-level metadata values to a total number of all metadata values declared for a sample.* It can also be defined on the collection level calculated as *a degree of metadata value presence for a specific data item attribute in a collection.* An example could be the degree of presence of all metadata values (for all defined data item quality characteristics) for the patient age data item attribute for a specific collection (patient age timeliness, patient age provenance, etc., taken together).

Metadata Coverage. This characteristic is related to metadata completeness and is defined either as *a degree of presence of attributes holding non-empty metadata values* or *a degree of diversity for the values of metadata attributes.* In the latter case, it can define which number or which percentage of allowed metadata values for a certain attribute is present for a collection. Metadata with broader coverage supports the search within metadata values better as more diverse metadata values correspond to artifacts, so these artifacts are more likely to be found by specifying various search criteria; it also supports decisions based on the found artifacts better as these decisions are supported with richer data values, allowing for better judgment.

Correspondingly, the metadata coverage metrics can be defined as *the relative number of metadata attributes for which the values are present for a collection* or as *the relative number of diverse metadata values for a collection metadata attribute.* An example for the latter metric could be the ratio of the diverse values present for the data item consistency metric calculated over all attributes for all samples in a collection to the total number of possible values for the data item consistency domain.

Metadata Consistency. This characteristic is defined as *the reverse degree of variability with respect to the metadata standard or source*. It reflects the need for the metadata to be consistent, e.g., corresponding to the same standard. Highly consistent metadata supports the search within metadata values better as more metadata values are likely to match the consistent search criteria, and there is less possibility that the specific criteria will match only some consistent subset of the data; it also supports decisions based on the found artifacts better as these decisions are supported with unambiguous and conflict-free data.

A collection-level consistency metric can be calculated as *a relative number of values instantiating a specific metadata attribute belonging to a biobank collection conforming to the most frequently applied standard*. An example of this metric is the ratio of the number of data item reliability values conforming to the most frequently used data item reliability standard to the total number of reliability values recorded for a collection.

Metadata Timeliness. This characteristic is defined as *a degree of proximity between the time of a change in a data item and the time when the metadata reflects that change*. It reflects the need for the metadata to reflect the real state of the data items. Highly timely metadata supports the search within metadata values better as the search is more likely to return relevant and current collections; it also supports decisions based on the found artifacts better as these decisions are supported with current data.

Metadata timeliness metrics are based on *the reverse distance of time between creating the data attribute value and its supplementing metadata values*. A collection-level metadata timeliness metric can e.g. be calculated as an aggregation of all relative reverse distance values calculated for a specific data item attribute combined with all metadata attributes for all samples in a collection. An example of this metric is the average of the normalized reverse distances of time between storing data item attribute values and recording their reliability values over all data item attributes within all samples in a collection, where the normalization means calculating a ratio of the current data item reliability-related distance to the maximal distance of this kind found in a collection.

Metadata Provenance. This characteristic is defined as *completeness with respect to the metadata standard, collection method, or source*. It characterizes the degree of linking between the metadata sources and standards on the one side and the metadata values on the other. In this section, we will only consider provenance with respect to the metadata standard. High-provenance metadata supports the search within metadata values better as the search is more likely to return trusted information; it also supports decisions based on the found artifacts better as these decisions are supported with data that can be trusted. For low-provenance metadata, it is not possible or difficult to understand where it comes from and what standard it conforms to.

Metadata provenance metrics can, e.g., be defined on the sample level as *a percentage of sample's metadata attributes possessing information about stan-*

dards, or on the collection level as *a degree of standard information presence for a specific data item attribute in a collection*. An example of the latter metric is the degree of presence of standard information values for all defined data item quality characteristics for the BMI data item attribute for a collection (BMI timeliness standard, BMI reliability standard, etc., taken together).

Metadata Reliability. This characteristic is defined as an *indirect metadata reliability based on the reliability of the context of the metadata attribute values* (e.g., their source or data collection method). For example, the reliability of the metadata provided by the biobank itself can be higher than the metadata from external sources. Highly reliable metadata supports the search within metadata values better as it is more likely to return information that can be trusted; it also supports decisions based on the found artifacts better as these decisions are supported with data that can be trusted.

It is possible to define *indirect metadata reliability metrics* based on the reliability metrics defined for data sources or diagnostic methods used for metadata collection. For example, for the data item precision metadata attribute, the attribute-scoped collection reliability can be calculated as the average of its source reliability values recorded for all samples in a collection.

Metadata Conformance to Expectations. This characteristic is defined as *the ability for the metadata to support achieving its goals,* namely to support the search and the ability to make decisions based on found artifacts. Here we will treat it in the narrower sense as *the ability for the metadata to support finding the requested data-item level artifacts* (e.g., collections). Metadata that conforms to expectations better supports the search based on metadata values better.

Metadata Accessibility. This characteristic is defined as *the degree of ability for the metadata value to be available when necessary or to be found when requested.* It reflects the need for the metadata itself to be accessible (it can be inaccessible e.g. due to privacy restrictions). In this, it differs from conformance to expectations reflecting the need for the corresponding data item-level artifact to be found. Highly accessible metadata (which is easier to find) supports the search within metadata values better as the search is more likely to return requested metadata elements; it also supports decisions based on the found artifacts better as these decisions are supported with data that is easier to access.

Accessibility metrics can be defined, e.g., on a collection level as *a degree of metadata value accessibility for a specific data item attribute in a particular collection* calculated as a ratio of the number of accessible metadata values defined for all the values of a specific data item attribute within a collection to the total number of metadata values of this kind. For example, it could characterize the accessibility of metadata elements (storing the values for all defined data item quality metrics) for the patient age data item attribute for a collection (age reliability, age provenance, etc., taken together).

4   A Concept for a Data Quality Management System

Achieving high levels of data quality characteristics requires quality control procedures and quality management activities that have to be implemented as a part of a holistic data quality management system. This section presents activities for biobanks to establish a quality management system and discusses data quality strategies.

To address common data quality problems (from missing values to failing to represent ontological changes [11]), we propose to extend the standard operating procedures (SOPs) for handling the materials to guarantee the quality of the data recorded together with the materials in the same way as they are extended to guarantee the quality of the materials themselves. Sections 4.2 and 4.3 introduce quality control procedures and quality management activities which can be referred to in such extended SOPs.

4.1   Quality Characteristics for Source Documents

The set of necessary characteristics for source documents can be abbreviated as ALCOA [36] - the document should be:

1. *attributable*, information of its origin (responsible party);
2. *legible* i.e., possible to understand;
3. *contemporaneous* i.e., containing most recent data;
4. *original* i.e., not a first or second-level copy;
5. *accurate* i.e., reflecting the truth about the real world.

Achieving high levels for these characteristics is one of the goals for quality control procedures and quality management activities presented below.

4.2   Procedures for Data Quality Control

A data quality management system, according to [24], has to include the set of procedures to control the quality of the associated data. A set of procedures of this kind to be implemented by biobanks is shown below.

Defining the Desired Quality Characteristics and Their Values. It is necessary to start with the description of the quality characteristics and their levels (values) available in the data sources and the list of requirements on which quality characteristic and which its level is desired. All this has to be defined across different quality dimensions (characteristics).

Reviewing the Data Management Process. After defining the desired quality characteristics, it is necessary to look at the whole process [16,34,35]: (1) starting from the original data source (which is always the real world) measured by means of some equipment or through our senses; (2) continuing with a first representation of what we observe in the real world; (3) going through all steps of the process until its final step when the data ends in a database.

Providing for the Attributability of Data Items. The most important quality characteristic, which must be defined for each data item, is its attributability i.e., the availability of the information about the person who made the first recording of the data. It is a specific kind of data item provenance introduced in Sect. 2.4. This information describes who is responsible for the data in a way which reveals the whole data production chain, so it is possible to go back along this chain if it is necessary to trace the origin of data.

Defining Quality Evaluation and Measurement Activities. After providing for attributability of the data, the next task after defining the quality is to define the ways of evaluating and measuring the quality.

4.3   Data Quality Management Activities

The processes defined as a part of the quality management system contain a whole range of data quality activities to improve and sustain data quality.

Quality Requirements Acquisition. This is a process of defining and documenting the quality requirements for data. In the course of such acquisition, the opinions of stakeholders (biobank administrators and prospective medical researchers) are taken into account, and the user requirements collected from stakeholders are converted into system specifications appropriate for establishing data collection procedures helping in reaching the required data quality levels. A major difficulty for biobanks is that data is also collected for future research projects, where the necessary quality characteristics are not yet known. Here it is advisable to collect and analyze the current best practices and the requirements in current projects.

Data Measurement. This is the process of measuring the data to determine the degree to which it meets the collected requirements. This activity involves various measurement procedures, specific for different quality characteristics, such as completeness measurement, which checks if the whole set of attributes for the specific data items is present in the whole volume of data.

Root Cause Processing. This activity involves identifying and remediating the root causes of data quality issues. Such data quality bottlenecks are important and have to be addressed early. They can be found by comparing the results of the measurements with the threshold values specified in quality requirements.

Data Quality Monitoring. Monitoring has to be performed continuously to help in sustaining the quality [15]. In the process of such monitoring, data measurement and root cause processing steps are repeated, i.e., the measurements are performed on the specific data items or the collections of data, the results of these measurements are checked against the quality requirements, and the possible quality issues are identified and resolved.

Cooperating with Business Process and Technology Owners. The goal of such cooperation is to improve the production, storage, and use of the data belonging to the organization. Business process owners can help understand the processes for which they are responsible, find and resolve the problematic issues in these processes that negatively affect data quality, and find possible ways for process improvement. The technology owners can help understand which techniques and tools can be used to address data quality issues and which technical measures (including possible hardware or software acquisitions) can be necessary to improve the data quality.

Complex and large organizations like medical universities with associated hospitals have complex business processes within and between different organizational units [12] with different roles, goals, and obligations. It is a major challenge to motivate and organize the preparation of data from general routine health care and medical studies for secondary use in future research projects, including documenting the quality characteristics of these data sets.

Supporting the Quality Culture. This activity involves advocating for and modeling a culture committed to quality among the biobank personnel. Such quality culture includes a common understanding of the importance of data quality, the awareness of the possible quality problems, as well as the existing techniques and tools addressing quality issues. This quality culture should also extend to the organizations and personnel collecting and delivering data outside of the perimeter of the biobank organization, e.g., health care professionals responsible for patient treatment rather than research. The establishment of incentive systems for rewarding quality conscience is frequently helpful.

Out of the above activities, the assessment of the condition (current state) of the data and the ongoing measurement of that condition is central to the purpose of the data quality program.

4.4   Data Quality Management for the Different Roles of Biobanks

As outlined in Sect. 2, biobanks have different roles in the management of data for medical research, and in each role, the necessary activities are different.

As data producers, biobanks are responsible for managing data quality from source to sink. Biobanks primarily produce data about sample harvesting, fixation, storage, and delivery. This handling of the biological samples is typically guided by standard operating procedures developed to standardize the quality of the stored biological matter. These procedures document the provenance of the material and produce sample quality data. In turn, controlling the quality of these data requires the inclusion of data quality management into these standard operating procedures. For this production of data, all the activities outlined in the previous section are relevant and have to be implemented.

In the role of data repositories, biobanks have to ensure to properly assess the quality of the data handed over to them for long-term archiving. This involves, in particular, reviewing the data quality management of the data producers, measuring the data quality, and monitoring the data quality, particularly in cases of continuing data delivery.

In the role of data providers, biobanks have to carefully collect and analyze the data quality requirements of the researchers requesting material and data. It is the ultimate guiding aim for biobanks to satisfy these requirements. Therefore these requirements have to be continuously monitored and are the input for all the other data quality management activities. On the other hand, biobanks have to provide not only data and samples for researchers but also information about the quality characteristics of the available data. Sufficient information about the data quality has to be offered to researchers requiring sufficient quality of the metadata used for the search for material and data meeting the needs for performing intended studies. If only anonymized data can be delivered, then it is necessary to understand the data quality implications of the anonymization procedures, respectively perform the anonymization in such a way that the information loss and the loss of data quality are minimized [33].

As data mediators, biobanks also establish communication about data quality requirements between the researchers and the data providers. On the one hand, the collection of data quality requirements has to be communicated to the organizations or organizational units producing and storing the data in the selection of data providers for specific purposes. On the other hand, biobanks have to assess the data quality and its documentation by the data providers and have to make this information available to the requesters, such that they can make an informed decision on which data to use for their purposes.

Respecting these different roles, biobanks have to establish a data and metadata quality strategy to be able to manage data quality issues effectively and efficiently. In defining the possible data quality strategy for biobanks, we refer to [8] addressing data quality strategies in general, while [2,18,32] focus on the medical domain in particular. According to [8], the data quality strategy is a "cluster of decisions centered on organizational data quality goals that determine the data processes to improve, solutions to implement, and people to engage". Such a strategy is then the basis for implementing data management in a holistic way: by clarifying data quality goals, selecting and developing appropriate tools and procedures, defining business processes and standard operating procedures, establishing management structures, defining job profiles, training all involved staff in the required skills, and last but not least, establishing a culture which values the strive for quality.

5   Conclusions

The reproducibility of scientific studies based on biobank data is the overarching goal for the data management and data quality management activities in biobanks, as proposed in this paper. For supporting scientific studies with data, it is necessary to know about the quality of that data. The quality characteristics are inherent to data, i.e., data always have qualities) - the question is how to be aware of these qualities. For example, while each data item possesses some precision and some reliability, it is not always possible to know how precise or imprecise, how reliable a specific data item is. The quality of data can typically not be seen by just inspecting the data. Therefore a data quality management process has to be established to generate and communicate the necessary documentation of quality characteristics over the whole lifecycle of the data.

The *quality of the data quality documentation* helps researchers to decide whether it is possible to use the specific material or the specific data set for some research project. Awareness of data quality and reliable documentation of data quality characteristics is also necessary if data from different sources have to be combined, for example, in multi-center studies.

The frequently cited "garbage in, garbage out" principle for data quality in biobanks means: if it is not possible to know the quality of input in scientific studies, it will also not be possible to know the quality of their output. The proposed data quality management system helps in preventing data of unknown or questionable quality from being used in medical studies, ultimately improving the quality of their outputs, the correctness and reliability of their findings, and their reproducibility in studies with data of comparable quality.

References

1. ASQ Quality Glossary. https://asq.org/quality-resources/quality-glossary/d
2. Guidance on a data quality framework for health and social care. Health Information and Quality Authority, Dublin (2018)
3. Batini, C., Cappiello, C., Francalanci, C., Maurino, A.: Methodologies for data quality assessment and improvement. ACM Comput. Surv. (CSUR) **41**(3), 1–52 (2009)
4. Batini, C., Pernici, B.: Data quality management and evolution of information systems. In: IFIP World Computer Congress, TC 8, pp. 51–62. Springer (2006). https://doi.org/10.1007/978-0-387-34732-5_5
5. Betsou, F.: Quality assurance and quality control in biobanking. In: Biobanking of Human Biospecimens, pp. 23–49. Springer (2017). https://doi.org/10.1007/978-3-319-55120-3_2
6. Dollé, L., Bekaert, S.: High-quality biobanks: pivotal assets for reproducibility of OMICS-data in biomedical translational research. Proteomics **19**(21–22), 1800485 (2019)
7. Doucet, M., et al.: Quality matters: 2016 annual conference of the national infrastructures for biobanking. Biopreserv. Biobank. **15**(3), 270–276 (2017)
8. Dravis, F.: Data quality strategy: a step-by-step approach. In: ICIQ (2004)
9. Eder, J., Dabringer, C., Schicho, M., Stark, K.: Information systems for federated biobanks. In: Transactions on Large-Scale Data-and Knowledge-Centered Systems I, pp. 156–190. Springer (2009). https://doi.org/10.1007/978-3-642-03722-1_7
10. Eder, J., Gottweis, H., Zatloukal, K.: It solutions for privacy protection in biobanking. Public Health Genom. **15**(5), 254–262 (2012)
11. Eder, J., Koncilia, C.: Modelling changes in ontologies. In: OTM International Conference On the Move to Meaningful Internet Systems, pp. 662–673. Springer (2004). https://doi.org/10.1007/978-3-540-30470-8_77

12. Eder, J., Lehmann, M., Tahamtan, A.: Choreographies as federations of choreographies and orchestrations. In: International Conference on Conceptual Modeling, pp. 183–192. Springer (2006). https://doi.org/10.1007/11908883_22
13. Eder, J., Shekhovtsov, V.A.: Data Quality for Medical Data Lakelands. In: International Conference on Future Data and Security Engineering, pp. 28–43. Springer (2020). https://doi.org/10.1007/978-3-030-63924-2_2
14. Eder, J., Shekhovtsov, V.A.: Data quality for federated medical data lakes. Int. J. Web Inf. Syst. **17**(5), 407–426 (2021). https://doi.org/10.1108/IJWIS-03-2021-0026
15. Gassman, J.J., Owen, W.W., Kuntz, T.E., Martin, J.P., Amoroso, W.P.: Data quality assurance, monitoring, and reporting. Controll. Clin. Trials **16**(2), 104–136 (1995)
16. Holub, P., Wittner, R., et al.: Towards a Common Standard for Data and Specimen Provenance in Life Sciences, July 2021. https://doi.org/10.5281/zenodo.5093125, preprint
17. Karimi-Busheri, F., Rasouli-Nia, A.: Integration, networking, and global biobanking in the age of new biology. In: Biobanking in the 21st Century. Springer (2015). https://doi.org/10.1007/978-3-319-20579-3_1
18. Kerr, K., Norris, T.: The development of a healthcare data quality framework and strategy. In: ICIQ, pp. 218–233 (2004)
19. Király, P., Büchler, M.: Measuring completeness as metadata quality metric in Europeana. In: 2018 IEEE International Conference on Big Data (Big Data), pp. 2711–2720. IEEE (2018)
20. Lehmann, S., et al.: Standard preanalytical coding for Biospecimens: review and implementation of the sample PREanalytical code (SPREC). Biopreserv. Biobank. **10**(4), 366–374 (2012)
21. Margaritopoulos, M., Margaritopoulos, T., Mavridis, I., Manitsaris, A.: Quantifying and measuring metadata completeness. J. Am. Soc. Inf. Sci. Technol. **63**(4), 724–737 (2012)
22. Moore, H.M., Kelly, A.B., Jewell, S.D., et al.: Biospecimen reporting for improved study quality (BRISQ). J. Proteome Res. **10**(8), 3429–3438 (2011)
23. Müller, H., Dagher, G., Loibner, M., Stumptner, C., Kungl, P., Zatloukal, K.: Biobanks for life sciences and personalized medicine: importance of standardization, biosafety, biosecurity, and data management. Current Opin. Biotechnol. **65**, 45–51 (2020)
24. Zozus, M.N., Kahn, M.G., Weiskopf, N.G.: Data quality in clinical research. In: Clinical Research Informatics, 2nd Ed., pp. 213–248. Springer (2019)
25. Olson, J.E.: Data Quality: The Accuracy Dimension. Morgan Kaufmann, Burlington (2003)
26. Quinlan, P.R., Gardner, S., Groves, M., Emes, R., Garibaldi, J.: A data-centric strategy for modern biobanking. In: Biobanking in the 21st Century, pp. 165–169. Springer (2015). https://doi.org/10.1007/978-3-319-20579-3_13
27. Radulovic, F., Mihindukulasooriya, N., García-Castro, R., Gómez-Pérez, A.: A comprehensive quality model for Linked Data. Semant. Web **9**(1), 3–24 (2018)
28. Ranasinghe, S., Pichler, H., Eder, J.: Report on data quality in biobanks: problems, issues, state-of-the-art. arXiv:1812.10423 (2018)
29. Riley, J.: Understanding metadata. Washington DC, United States: National Information Standards Organization 23 (2017)
30. Shekhovtsov, V.A., Eder, J.: Data item quality for biobanks. Trans. Large-Scale Data Knowl.-Centered Syst. **L**, 77–115 (2021). https://doi.org/10.1007/978-3-662-64553-6_5

31. Shekhovtsov, V.A., Eder, J.: Metadata quality for biobanks. Appl. Sci. **12**(19), 9578 (2022). https://doi.org/10.3390/app12199578
32. Slone, J.P.: Information quality strategy: an empirical investigation of the relationship between information quality improvements and organizational outcomes. Ph.D. thesis, Capella University (2006)
33. Stark, K., Eder, J., Zatloukal, K.: Priority-based k-anonymity accomplished by weighted generalisation structures. In: International Conference on Data Warehousing and Knowledge Discovery, pp. 394–404. Springer (2006). https://doi.org/10.1007/11823728_38
34. Stark, K., Koncilia, C., Schulte, J., Schikuta, E., Eder, J.: Incorporating data provenance in a medical CSCW system. In: International Conference on Database and Expert Systems Applications, pp. 315–322. Springer (2010)
35. Wittner, R., et al.: Lightweight distributed provenance model for complex real-world environments. Scient. Data **9**(1), 1–19 (2022)
36. Woollen, S.W.: Data Quality and the Origin of ALCOA. Newsletter of the Southern Regional Chapter Society of Quality Assurance, Summer (2010)

Big Data Analytics and Distributed Systems

Towards a Privacy, Secured and Distributed Clinical Data Warehouse Architecture

Ranul Deelaka Thantilage[1,2](✉) , Nhien-An Le-Khac[1](✉) ,
and M-Tahar Kechadi[1,2]

[1] School of Computer Science, University College Dublin, Dublin, Ireland
ranul.thantilage@ucdconnect.ie, {an.lekhac,tahar.kechadi}@ucd.ie
[2] Insight Centre for Data Analytics, Dublin, Ireland
https://www.insight-centre.org/, https://www.ucd.ie/

Abstract. Reputed organisations are always prompting Data Warehouses (DWs), which are essential for storing and mining their historical datasets. When it comes to the healthcare industry, DWs are becoming ever so imperative, as efficient storage for medical data is vital for one's health while mining it and seeking new insights. While clinical datasets are very complex, their timely integration and analysis are crucial to providing excellent care for patients. This research aims to provide an efficient data warehousing solution with multiple privacy and security measures integrated by design. Securing the data at all stages: during data input, exploration, pre-processing, selection, analysis, and presentation, is very challenging. This research explores data security from a holistic perspective and possible distributed analysis mechanisms while streamlining data sharing between healthcare centres to increase efficiency and better patient treatments. This study also considers security and privacy issues at all stages of the data warehousing process (data lifecycle) to ensure its correct handling and use. We focus on distributed clinical data warehouse architectures. We also describe the main requirements of a clinical data warehouse for the whole data lifecycle, Data Capture, Acquisition Management, Archiving, Sharing, Reporting, Analysis, and Privacy and Security. The proposed architecture is evaluated considering existing state-of-the-art concerning data analysis and sharing capabilities while ensuring data security and privacy.

Keywords: Data warehouse · Clinical data · Cardiology · Architectures · Data security · Data privacy · Clinical data warehouse requirements

This project is part of the Eastern Corridor Medical Engineering centre (ECME). It is supported by the EU INTERREG VA Programme, managed by the Special EU Programmes Body (SEUPB).

T. K. Dang et al. (Eds.): FDSE 2022, CCIS 1688, pp. 73–87, 2022.
https://doi.org/10.1007/978-981-19-8069-5_5

1   Introduction

It is imperative to perform healthcare analytics on data collected from multiple sources. Data analytics will help identify different trends and patterns for improvised healthcare behaviour. In addition, it will help forecast future drug usage patterns, measure healthcare centre efficiency, and analyse decisions and results of doctors and clinical staff. Moreover, it will aid in better healthcare treatment for patients while increasing the accuracy of treatments and minimizing costs where possible. Healthcare data is complex and collected from various heterogeneous sources. As per the current healthcare standards [x], [20], a clinical data warehouse would need to store a wide variety of data. For example, image files of digital tests and blood reports will be just additions on top of the general patient information and medical history. Especially in the healthcare industry, the technology updates as soon as new research brings up varying digital tests to make treatment much more efficient. These new additions would mean new data types for the DW. Therefore, a key concern would be that the DW architecture should be future-proof to support different data types from varying sources, which are constantly evolving.

Flexibility, scalability, data integration, and software system compatibility are all addressed by current state-of-the-art healthcare data warehousing solutions. Recent healthcare research projects have focused on building GDPR [22] compliant data gathering techniques in the form of a consent management system. However, these systems lack the integration of privacy and security by design for clinical data warehouses. Even though some frameworks have suggested interesting techniques for data security and privacy, they are not always efficient. They need high-end computing power, which is not always available during some critical times of care.

The main research objective is to integrate privacy and security in clinical DW while ensuring data quality and value are not lost during the data transition to secure forms. To summarise, healthcare big data warehouse architecture should integrate security and privacy by design. Data safety and privacy, as well as the capacity to share, analyse and extract meaningful insights to enhance healthcare research and practices, are the main goals of building a healthy clinical DW. In this paper, we propose a distributed clinical DW architecture to tackle the aforementioned security and privacy concerns while ensuring data sharing and availability at critical healthcare timelines. Identifying stakeholders and their requirements is crucial to help develop privacy-by-design and security-by-design clinical DW architecture. It will support efficient data sharing and analysis of healthcare data.

The paper is organised as follows. We discuss related work on DW security and privacy in Sect. 2. In Sect. 3, we showcase the system requirements of a clinical DW and the data flow of the proposed DW architecture. Section 4 proposes privacy and security preserving clinical DW architecture. Section 5 discusses the data processing, privacy, and security components of the system. In Sect. 6, we evaluate the proposed architecture. We include and give some future directions in Sect. 7.

2   Related Work

DWs are a desirable target since they hold the healthcare institute's most valuable assets. The healthcare industry has been substantially affected by the digital revolution. Many aspects of our life are made easier by big data, however, electronic health records (EHRs) include some of the most important knowledge and sensitive patient information. In 2018, around 500 data breaches resulted in the exposure of over 15 million patient healthcare records. Halfway through the next year, the figure had risen to 25 million records according to Davis of Health IT Security [5]. There are several ways to ensure data security. Similar to other computing security principles DW security also follows the CIA principle of Confidentiality, Integrity, and Availability.

Several solutions have been proposed and implemented to prevent such breaches and attacks to happen in distributed big data warehouses. Sebaa et al. [17] have proposed a Hadoop-based architecture and conceptual data model for a medical data warehouse but they have not looked at security or privacy solutions. Using the Advanced Encryption Standard (AES) and the One-Time Pad (OTP) encryption technique, a secure data warehouse architecture is proposed by Gupta et al. [7]. The proposed architecture does not look into privacy-preserving or healthcare-specific DWs. Shahid et al. [18] propose a three-layered big data warehouse architecture. Data access control, secure storage, and data anonymisation are developed in the architecture. They do not have a secure emergency authentication mechanism for sharing critical clinical data. Mia et al. [13] propose a privacy-preserving clinical DW architecture. By combining three data sources, they create a prototype with a whole pipeline from data gathering through analytics. They do not look at emergency data authentication or sharing of critical data. The key properties of these existing solutions were taken into account and further enhanced when developing the proposed clinical DW architecture.

Blockchain has become a key and revolutionary concept in data security and hence integrating it into healthcare data warehousing will give many benefits. Secure Views protect data from unauthorized user access. It shields users from potentially seeing information from data records that have been filtered by the view. De-identification, a type of dynamic data masking, refers to severing the connection between the data and the person with whom it was originally linked. Data anonymisation is a technique to protect data privacy that maintains the data but conceals the source, by removing personally identifying information like names, social security numbers, and addresses from data sets.

2.1   Blockchain

According to Crosby et al. [4] a blockchain is a distributed database of records, or public ledger, of all transactions or digital events that have been completed and shared among participants. Each transaction in the public ledger is double-checked by a majority of the system's members. Haleem et al. [8] show the four main taxonomy of blockchain systems. Public blockchains provide a fully decentralized network, while private blockchains are restricted to a single entity. A consortium blockchain is a permissioned network and public only to a specific group, while hybrid blockchains combine the benefits of both private and public blockchains. In this study, the authors discuss blockchain technology and its major benefits in healthcare, as well as fourteen key uses of blockchain in healthcare. It is critical to ensure that a health blockchain is "fit-for-purpose." This notion serves as the foundation of the study by Mackey et al. [12], which includes perspectives from a diverse set of practitioners at the vanguard of blockchain conception, development, and deployment. If implemented successfully blockchain would be an ideal solution for security issues such as ransomware attacks, and data breaches. Blockchain-integrated healthcare applications are still in their development, and more effort in terms of technical discovery and research is required. It would be inefficient and costly to store huge documents on the blockchain, such as complete electronic medical records or genetic data sets. In addition, querying data within a blockchain is challenging, restricting clinical, statistical, and research applications. Hence further research should be conducted on how to efficiently use blockchain technology within implementations of minimal data processing resources as the base of a new generation of health information exchange.

2.2 Secure Views

Secured views are designed to aid data scientists in inspecting and understanding the dataset from several angles while keeping patient-sensitive data hidden. When views are particularly specified for data privacy limiting access to sensitive data that should not be disclosed to all users, they should be declared as secure views. Views built only for query convenience, such as views developed to ease queries for which users do not need to comprehend the underlying data format, should not be utilized as secure views may take longer to perform than non-secure views. Shahid et al. [18] break down into three types of secured views; statistical view giving measurements for characteristics that are automatically calculated, such as standard deviations, domain ranges, and value statistics, and anonymised view providing a comprehensive view of shared datasets protected by several techniques, and anatomized view providing both broad and detailed views of quasi-identifiers. Murphy [14] looks into an approach where data is frequently exported into a user-friendly data mart. This also restricts the number of patients a client may see (secure views), which is significant from the standpoint of patient privacy. Kalio et al. [9] discuss a framework for data warehouse security and privacy that uses a hybrid method. To allow secure viewing, the system uses three layers of authentication, and the user must be a registered user. The result set of a query constructed on top of one or more tables is referred to as a view. Views do not retain data; nevertheless, view requirements are evaluated during runtime, and the result is displayed to the user. Secure views are more complicated queries that need more processing power. In addition, a single view becoming compromised can lead to a data breach expanding to all users using that particular secure view.

2.3 De-identification

De-identification masks the true identity of data owners, by deleting all fields that might directly identify a person. Individuals are named using a new random identifier when the data is de-identified and shared. In some circumstances, keeping the relationship between the old and new IDs is needed to update de-identified data. The de-identification procedure can be achieved in two ways, according to the Privacy Rule of the Health Insurance Portability and Accountability Act (HIPAA) [21]. They are Expert Determination and the Safe Harbor Method. De-identification and anonymisation go hand in hand. It's frequently mistaken with de-identification and used interchangeably. Although both anonymisation and de-identification attempt to safeguard the privacy of the data subject, they are conceptually distinct. Shukla et al. [19] describes a method for de-identifying electronic healthcare data that uses chained hashing to generate short-lived pseudonyms to reduce the impact of inference attacks, as well as a re-identification strategy that emphasizes information self-determination. Kayaalp [10] looks into modes of de-identification in terms of clinical data, and breaks into 08 distinct modes. Repository-wide batch de-identification, on-demand cohort-specific de-identification, on-demand de-identification of query results, de-identification with patient and provider identifiers, scientist-involved de-identification, patient-involved de-identification, physician-involved de-identification, and online de-identification by honest brokers. Rahmani et al. [15] use a novel bio-inspired algorithm based on the natural phenomenon of apoptotic cells in the human body to solve the challenge of concealing sensitive clinical data in big data warehouses. De-identification can be accomplished in a variety of ways. The effectiveness of the de-identification process is dependent not only on the automatic de-identification systems' ability but also on the users of de-identification systems.

2.4 Anonymisation

Anonymisation is the process of deleting or encrypting identifiers that link an individual to stored data to secure private or sensitive information. The individually identifiable message is relayed via a data anonymisation procedure, which maintains the data but hides the source. Data anonymisation techniques include masking, pseudonymization, generalization, swapping, perturbation, and synthetic data. Santos et al. [16] present a transparent data masking method for numerical values in DWs based on the mathematical modulus operator that may be employed without requiring changes to the user application or source code. Existing pseudonymization models rely on external trusted third parties, making de-pseudonymization a multistage process requiring an additional interpersonal connection, which might result in significant delays in patient treatment. Hence, Aamot et al. [1] suggest an improved technique based on an asymmetric encryption scheme that separates the pseudonymization and de-pseudonymization tasks. Kumar et al. [11] studies dynamic data masking and aid to analyse the level of security needed for real-time applications. A realistic categorization module for a built-in data masking architecture is proposed by Ali et al. [2]. The suggested module would identify sensitive data and choose the optimum masking format to increase data privacy and security at rest. By mapping sensitive data characteristics with the appropriate irreversible or reversible masking techniques, this module allows sensitive data attributes to be securely utilized and conforms with privacy regulatory standards inside the healthcare data warehouse. Anonymisation too has its limitations. As shown by Guerra-Balboa et al. [6] although structural concepts can give high-value data in general, they are vulnerable to vulnerabilities such as background knowledge and attribute-linkage attacks. According to Chen et al. [3] standard k-anonymity approaches cannot adequately safeguard a data set with significant sequential correlation. Healthcare data warehouses contain location-based data in some instances, these approaches are challenged with data sets with sparse or short trajectories, as trajectories might have minimal overlap, resulting in inescapable data and value loss. Further constraints mentioned in related work include the distinction between synthetic and anonymised data, as well as the loss of data quality in some cases.

3 System Modelling

3.1 Requirements of Clinical DWs

Clinical DWs have varying requirements based on their stakeholders. The advent of numerous new forms of organizations, such as physician medical groups and medical research institutions, has resulted from the growth of Big Data. There are an increasing number of stakeholders offering diverse medical services, and their resource input and behavioural engagement have varying implications on the services they provide. Stakeholders in the healthcare industry have a significant impact on the industry's trajectory. By studying the literature, and analyzing the requirement of users and stakeholders such as healthcare organizations, patients, doctors, clinical staff, administrators, researchers, and regulatory organizations, this research identified the requirements of a clinical DW architecture which was further summarized in 05 categories as shown below.

01 - Data Capture Requirements. Clinical data is available in varying file formats (image files, video files, document files, etc.), both open source, and proprietary. Therefore it is a must for the DW to support import from *multiple data types*. In healthcare centres, varying digital devices can be found. Radiography, cardiology, ultrasound, etc. A DW warehouse should support the data import/export from/to *multiple devices*. Doctors tend to write notes on observations done on a patient, these *clinical notes* should be imported to the DW. Data capture should be supported from *non-standard* and *legacy devices*.

02 - Acquisition Management Requirements. Incorrect data might pose serious health risks for patients and place a major burden on practitioners, leading to fraud, misbehaviour, poor treatment, and data theft. Hence *maintaining record integrity* is a must. *Metadata tagging* would allow faster query time and make sure the DW is efficient. *Data ownership tagging* and usage rights would ensure proper governance and user authorization during access. *Dynamic data normalizing* will be helpful for records with continuous numerical values. *Cloud access* will aid in maintaining ease of access to the system globally. *Interoperability between clinical data standards (HL7, DICOM, etc.)* will facilitate smooth information transfer between health information systems.

03 - Archive Requirements. To reap the benefits of EHR breakthroughs, a healthcare data transfer plan that encourages a scalable health information system with *system migration capabilities* is essential. A tiered approach to data management with *multi-tier storage* with *standards based archiving* will ensure that all information about a patient is available within conventional clinical processes. In addition, *disaster management and data recovery* plan with backups are essential for healthcare institutes as downtime should be minimized.

04 - Sharing, Reporting and Analysis Requirements. Specific *data views based on job role* would ensure only necessary data is available and in easy to access form that is already preferred by the user. *Side-by-side comparison* of reports for physicians will aid in identifying differences in one or more reports and understanding the disease's progress. *Geo-location-based disease analysis* is important in understanding disease risk factors, incidence, and consequences, according to spatial epidemiology. *Restricting and alert if allergic drug diagnosed* can prevent life-threatening mistakes. *Drug side effect-based and community-based disease analysis* can aid in for better treatments.

05 - Security and Privacy Requirements. *Data anonymisation* safeguards a patient's right to privacy while also helping to prevent data breaches and identity theft. *User access control* is a critical component of data security because it maintains user rights so that legitimate users may only access data in the system that corresponds to their rights. *Encryption in data transport and data storage* is one of the most helpful data protection solutions. Even if attackers obtain access to the data, healthcare providers can make it more difficult for them to read patient information by encrypting data in transit and at rest.

3.2 Data Flow of Proposed Architecture

The DW will be protected with an IDPL, Intrusion Detection, and Prevention Layer. This layer will ensure the data warehouse is not attacked by hackers and other unauthorized users for attacks such as denial of service. At the stage of data input, all users are authenticated. Data input will then be funnelled through the MSIL, Malicious Software Identification Layer. This layer will scan all input files and ensure no malicious software or codes are entered into the data warehouse.

Next, the data will be transported through encrypted channels to the processing area. At this stage data will be cleaned, modelled, meta-data added, and standardized. User IDs and other personal identifiers of the data will pass through a de-identification phase and then all data will be funnelled through the anonymisation layer. Technologies such as blockchain can be utilized in this layer to further secure the data. The anonymised data will then be encrypted and passed to the data marts for storage. Each data mart is linked with the central demographic data mart where all demographic data is stored.

At the level of data analysis or presentation, the data is first passed through a data filtration layer, which ensures to filter and release of data that is only intended for the specific user. All users have to pass through the previously mentioned IDPL and the user authentication layer before gaining access. In the architecture, each user or user group is defined with an anonymity level as shown below.

1. **Anonymity Level 01:** Full Access to own records. This level of anonymity is assigned to patients so that they could have access to any of their records. The data will be decrypted and de-anonymised.
2. **Anonymity Level 02:** Full Access to specific users' data. This level of anonymity is assigned to doctors so that they have access to all necessary data of the patients they treat. The data will be decrypted and de-anonymised.
3. **Anonymity Level 03:** Limited Access to specific users' data. This level of anonymity is assigned to nurses so that they have access to only the necessary data of the patients they are assigned with. The data will be decrypted and de-anonymised.
4. **Anonymity Level 04:** Limited Access to specific anonymised data. This level of anonymity is assigned to clinical researchers and other staff who are authorized to access data that are anonymised and given consent by the data owner. The data will be decrypted but not de-anonymised.

The data warehouse has a specific data access mechanism granted by patient consent to access specific sets of their data for globally recognized emergency treatment centres. This will be similar to a Digital Emergency Medical Card (DEMC). For example, the allergies of a patient, critical conditions, specific surgery details, and other necessities of a patient will be made available here. An emergency can occur in any part of the World, at this stage, it is unsure if the patient will be responsive or unresponsive. Hence a new mechanism of secure three-factor user authorization is proposed to enable access to this data. Emergency Treatment Units (ETUs) globally can pre-register with the platform. The individual can enter their travel plan to the platform which will ensure that the ETUs in the area have access to the DEMC. In addition, a patient-related access control such as; a smart card, bio-metric or similar authentication mechanism can authenticate access on behalf of the individual even at times when he/she is unresponsive. This would ensure the relevant critical medical information is accessible throughout their journeys, at times of emergencies and this mechanism will be a breakthrough feature in the proposed clinical data warehouse framework. A usual data warehouse focuses on secure data storage and efficient analysis, but when it comes to a clinical data warehouse it is essential to aid in efficient treatments and improving healthcare. Stored and secured data, if not possible to be accessed during a patient's last breath, to save his/her (the data owner's) life, might be the most secure storage solution but would be an inefficient technology in an industry such as healthcare. The proposed architecture solves this critical issue in clinical data warehousing.

4 System Architecture

The proposed clinical data warehouse adopts a distributed big data architecture as clinical data is distributed in its nature and contains both structured and unstructured data. Clinical data is stored on various platforms in the healthcare industry. Each of these follows different formats, some even following proprietary formats. Therefore, it is a must for the proposed data warehouse to allow cross-platform standardization. These include interoperability with clinical data standards such as HL7, and DICOM. As most individuals travel the World nowadays, their clinical records should be given access at any given time from any geographic location. Therefore, it is most efficient to use a cloud-based data warehouse ensuring easy access to medical records globally. Rather than a healthcare centre governing the data, each individual should be given ownership to govern their own clinical data. This ensures that the patient itself can choose which data to be shared and when. Anonymous data can be made available for research and analysis purposes and patients can electronically provide consent to anonymise and use their data for research and analysis purposes.

To achieve this the architecture shown in Fig. 1 ensures to enforce data protection at all stages of the data life-cycle; data input, processing, storage, and analysis or presentation. Section 5 explains each component of the DW architecture in terms of data, security, and privacy.

5 Data, Security and Privacy Components

Even though data security and data privacy are connected, they serve different goals and require separate countermeasures. Confidentiality, integrity, availability, and non-repudiation are all goals of data security. In other words, data security ensures that only authorized people have access to data. While the primary goal of data privacy is to prevent shared data from revealing sensitive information about data owners. Data privacy rules govern this obligation. Due to the importance of the quality of shared data, privacy preservation is a difficult issue. The proposed DW architecture ensures data security and data privacy by using the following components.

Central Data Components

- **Data Processing Layer.** This is a key layer of the DW that takes care of functions such as data cleaning, data modelling, adding meta-data, and data standardization. These are key components of any DW.
- **Data Marts.** It is these data marts that collectively form the distributed cloud DW-based encrypted system. Each data mart is linked with the demographic data mart which stores all individual identifier-related data.

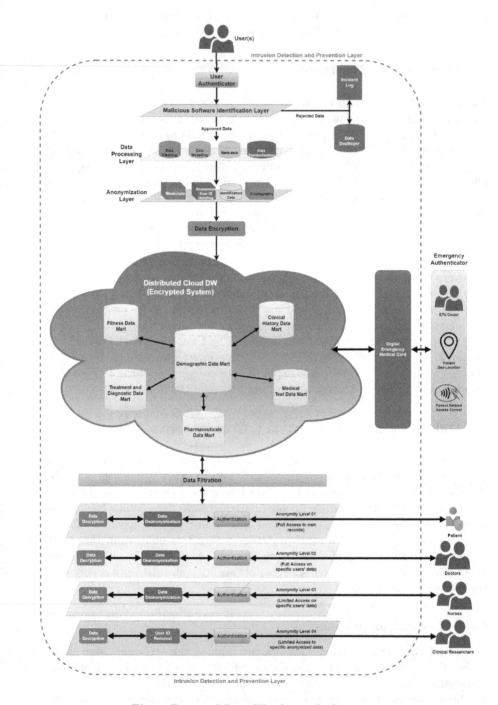

Fig. 1. Proposed Data Warehouse Architecture.

- **Digital Emergency Medical Card.** This is a key component that facilitates the treatment of patients that undergo accidents and other emergencies. This is a collection of all data that should be accessed by an emergency treatment centre.

Data Security Components

- **User Authenticator.** This ensures that only authorized users are given access to the DW.
- **Malicious Software Identification Layer.** This component runs a malware scan on all files that are entered into the DW to ensure there are no malware attacks.
- **Incident Logs.** Any data detected as malware is logged on the incident log with information about the user/IP address which entered the data.
- **Data Destroyer.** Data identified as malware are destroyed/removed using this component
- **Data Encryptor/Decryptor.** The encryptor interface has methods for performing typical encryption, random number generation, and hashing operations on data content. The decryptor restores the original form of the encrypted data.
- **Encrypted Data Transport Channels.** In addition to content encryption, transport encryption ensures all data transport channels are secure from third-party attacks.
- **Emergency Authentication.** This ensures the digital emergency medical card, when accessing at a time patient is non-responsive by only passing three levels of authentication, ETU doctor, patient geo-location, and patient-related access control like a smart card.
- **Intrusion Detection and Prevention Layer.** This is the process of monitoring and eliminating events in the DW regarding malicious software and cyber attacks.

Data Privacy Components

- **Anonymisation Layer.** The anonymisation layer is the key layer concerning data privacy control of the DW. This uses technology such as blockchain, anonymising user IDs, de-identification, and performing other cryptographic operations to ensure data privacy.
- **Anonymity Level based De-anonymisation.** As each user is granted access based on anonymity levels, this component ensures that only the relevant data is de-anonymised for the respective user.
- **Data Filtration.** This layer ensures only relevant data can be accessed as per the authorization given to each user.
- **Anonymity Level based Secure Views.** Each user is given their own secure view based on the anonymity level assigned by using this component.

6   Evaluation

In terms of evaluating the proposed architecture, we will use a case study to showcase how the proposed system would be an effective solution in the health-care industry.

Person X is a patient with a critical heart condition, that requires special attention during any surgery performed. In addition, X has severe allergic reactions to some drugs. X is from Europe and travels on a tour to a different continent. X meets with an accident, is found unconscious, and gets airlifted to the nearest hospital. The doctors diagnose that his condition is critical and needs to undergo immediate surgery.

If X's medical data were not available to be accessed by the doctors at the emergency treatment centre as most typical clinical data warehouses do not facilitate secure data sharing, but rather are kept within the healthcare facility, the doctors would not be aware of the critical heart condition of X nor his allergies. A higher possibility is doctors start the open surgery immediately but with a lower success rate as the previous critical heart conditions would come as a surprise. Similarly, if an allergy-based drug is diagnosed not knowing it can be life-threatening. Therefore, the chances of survival for X might be reduced. This would be the case with a general clinical data warehouse.

The proposed architecture is equipped with an emergency authenticator component that specializes in rapid multi-factor authentication to access critical data for global emergency treatment centres. Hence the doctors would have access to the necessary data of X which can be carefully reviewed before the surgery. Therefore, the clinical staff and doctors would be aware of the current conditions and allergies and allow them to prepare as necessary for a successful surgery without surprises.

The clinical DW architecture that is being presented would guarantee that the necessary and urgent medical information is available during the patient's travels and in an emergency. This mechanism will be a ground-breaking feature. When it comes to a clinical data warehouse, it is crucial to support effective therapies and enhance healthcare. Unlike a typical data warehouse, which focuses on secure data storage and efficient analysis. The most secure data storage option might not be suitable in a sector like healthcare if the data would not be able to be retrieved during a patient's final breath to save his or her (the data owner's) life. The suggested architecture includes a specialized data access mechanism and emergency authorization system to address this important clinical data warehousing problem.

Table 1 shows the feature-wise comparison of the proposed clinical DW architecture with existing state-of-the-art. The feature list was developed based on the identified key requirement of clinical DWs and their stakeholders.

The Table 1 further proves that the proposed clinical DW architecture addresses all the privacy and security requirements of healthcare data.

In terms of security, the intrusion detection, and prevention layer, user & emergency authenticator, malicious software identification layer, and encryption ensures security-by-design DW architecture. Privacy is assured by a separate

Table 1. Feature comparison with existing DW architectures.

Features	[17]	[7]	[18]	[13]	Ours
Healthcare specific DW architecture	✓	✗	✓	✓	✓
Intrusion detection & prevention	✗	✗	✗	✗	✓
Malicious software identification	✗	✗	✗	✗	✓
De-identification of patient data	✗	✗	✓	✓	✓
Secure data encryption	✗	✓	✓	✓	✓
Data authentication for emergency treatment	✗	✗	✗	✗	✓
Anonymity level based secure views	✗	✗	✓	✗	✓

anonymisation layer that integrates blockchain, anonymous user IDs, and the de-identification of data. In addition, secure anonymity level-based views are added to ensure a privacy-by-design DW architecture.

The DW architecture proposed is of a distributed system and supports the naturally distributed nature of clinical data sets. Data mart distribution is based on the identified categorization of clinical data sets such as demographic data, medical test data, pharmaceutical data, etc. Data sharing and analysis components of the DW are made possible by having specific secure views based on the needs and requirements of the particular researcher. In addition, the emergency authenticator component facilitates a multi-factor geo-location-based authentication to release critical data for emergency treatment centres at times when the client or patient is unresponsive. The deployment of the system can be cloud-based which would add ease in access from healthcare-related institutes globally and aid in facilitating central cloud access for heterogeneous clinical data from multiple sources.

7   Discussion and Conclusion

Clinical data is distributed in nature itself. Therefore, according to identified requirements of clinical data warehousing distributed storage is a must. Distribution of the data can happen from different perspectives, e.g. sensitivity of data, location of a healthcare facility, etc. Clinical data happens to be both in the form of structured and unstructured data of multiple formats. Additionally, support for multiple schemas would be necessary. Therefore, the data warehouse architecture should support high-end privacy of the data, high scalability, high traceability, and data distribution.

Clinical data would need specific security and privacy measures to be taken. It would be an added challenge to efficiently distribute the data as most data is kept solely by different healthcare centres/facilities. A streamlined process would need to be adapted to better facilitate data sharing across facilities for efficient treatments. Therefore, automated data anonymisation is essential while ensuring privacy and cross-compatibility of the data. To recapitulate, healthcare big data warehouse architecture should be built which integrates security and privacy by design. Data safety and privacy, as well as the capacity to analyze and extract meaningful insights to enhance healthcare research and practices, are the major goals of building a healthy healthcare data warehouse.

The architecture developed was formulated focusing on the key components of data security and data privacy. A data component known as the 'Digital Emergency Medical Card' and a privacy and security component known as the 'Emergency Authenticator' was added to the data warehouse architecture. This ensures access to crucial medical data for doctors at emergency treatment centres globally. This access is granted using three levels of authentication, doctor user authentication, patient geo-location, and patient-related access control like a smart card. Security in all stages: data input, processing, transport, storage, and analysis was assessed, in developing a privacy-by-design clinical data warehousing architecture.

A prototype of the proposed architecture will be further developed in future works. It will then be tested based on the key identified features to ensure it meets the outlined requirements of a clinical DW architecture. Furthermore, we will enhance the proposed framework to increase scalability.

References

1. Aamot, H., Kohl, C.D., Richter, D., Knaup-Gregori, P.: Pseudonymization of patient identifiers for translational research. BMC Med. Inform. Dec. Mak. **13**(1), 1 (2013). https://doi.org/10.1186/1472-6947-13-75, BMC Medical Informatics and Decision Making
2. Ali, O., Ouda, A.: A classification module in data masking framework for Business Intelligence platform in healthcare. In: 7th IEEE Annual Information Technology, Electronics and Mobile Communication Conference, IEEE IEMCON 2016, December 2016. https://doi.org/10.1109/IEMCON.2016.7746327
3. Chen, R., Fung, B.C., Mohammed, N., Desai, B.C., Wang, K.: Privacy-preserving trajectory data publishing by local suppression. Inf. Sci. Inform. Comput. Sci. Intell. Syst. Appl. Int. J. **231**, 83–97 (2013). https://doi.org/10.1016/J.INS.2011.07.035
4. Crosby, M., Nachiappan, Pattanayak, P., Verma, S., Kalyanaraman, V.: Blockchain Technology. Technical report (2015). http://www.blockchaintechnologies.com/blockchain-definition
5. David, J.: The 10 Biggest Healthcare Data Breaches of 2019, So Far (2019). https://healthitsecurity.com/news/the-10-biggest-healthcare-data-breaches-of-2019-so-far
6. Guerra-balboa, P., Pascual, M., Parra-arnau, J., Forn, J., Strufe, T.: Anonymizing Trajectory Data : Limitations and Opportunities (2013)
7. Gupta, S., Jain, S., Agarwal, M.: DWSA: A secure data warehouse architecture for encrypting data using AES and OTP encryption technique. Adv. Intell. Syst. Comput. **742**, 505–514 (2019). https://doi.org/10.1007/978-981-13-0589-4_47/COVER, https://link.springer.com/chapter/10.1007/978-981-13-0589-4_47
8. Haleem, A., Javaid, M., Singh, R.P., Suman, R., Rab, S.: Blockchain technology applications in healthcare: an overview. Int. J. Intell. Netw. **2**(May), 130–139 (2021). https://doi.org/10.1016/j.ijin.2021.09.005

9. Kalio, Q.P., Nwiabu, N.D.: A framework for securing data warehouse using hybrid approach. Int. J. Comput. Sci. Math. Theory **5**(1), 44–55 (2019). https://www.iiardpub.org
10. Kayaalp, M.: Modes of De-identification Modes of De-identification, April, 2018
11. Kumar, G.K.R., Rabi, B.J.D., Manjunath, T.N.: A study on dynamic data masking with its trends and implications. Int. J. Comput. Appl. **38**(6), 19–24 (2012). https://doi.org/10.5120/4612-6828
12. Mackey, T.K., Kuo, T.T., Gummadi, B., Clauson, K.A., Church, G., Grishin, D., Obbad, K., Barkovich, R., Palombini, M.: 'Fit-for-purpose?' - challenges and opportunities for applications of blockchain technology in the future of healthcare. BMC Med. **17**(1), 1–17 (2019). https://doi.org/10.1186/s12916-019-1296-7
13. Mia, M.R., Hoque, A.S.M.L., Khan, S.I., Ahamed, S.I.: A privacy-preserving national clinical data warehouse: architecture and analysis. Smart Health **23**(2021), 100238 (2022). https://doi.org/10.1016/j.smhl.2021.100238
14. Murphy, S.: Data Warehousing for Clinical Research, pp. 679–684. Springer, US, Boston, MA (2009). https://doi.org/10.1007/978-0-387-39940-9_120
15. Rahmani, A., Amine, A., Hamou, R.M.: De-identification of health data in big data using a novel bio-inspired apoptosis algorithm. Int. J. Organ. Collective Intell. **5**(3), 1–15 (2015). https://doi.org/10.4018/ijoci.2015070101
16. Santos, R.J., Bernardino, J., Vieira, M.: A data masking technique for data warehouses. In: ACM International Conference Proceeding Series, May 2014, pp. 61–69 (2011). https://doi.org/10.1145/2076623.2076632
17. Sebaa, A., Chikh, F., Nouicer, A., Tari, A.K.: Medical big data warehouse: architecture and system design, a case study: improving healthcare resources distribution. J. Med. Syst. **42**(4), 1–16 (2018). https://doi.org/10.1007/s10916-018-0894-9
18. Shahid, A., Nguyen, T.A.N., Kechadi, M.T.: Big data warehouse for healthcare-sensitive data applications. Sensors **21**(7) (2021). https://doi.org/10.3390/s21072353
19. Shukla, A., Sahni, M.K., Aggarwal, S., Rai, B.K.: Real-time De-identification of Healthcare Data, April 2018 (2018)
20. Sravanthi, K., Reddy, T.S.: Applications of big data in various fields. Int. J. Comput. Sci. Inf. Technol. **06** (2015). https://www.ijcsit.com
21. US Department of Health and Human Services: Health Insurance Portability and Accountability Act of 1996 (HIPAA)—CDC (1996). https://www.cdc.gov/phlp/publications/topic/hipaa.html
22. Wolford, B.: What is GDPR, the EU's new data protection law? - GDPR.eu. https://gdpr.eu/what-is-gdpr/

Improving the Storage Utilization of 0-Complete Trees as Index Structures

H. K. Dai[1]([⊠]) and K. Furusawa[2]

[1] Computer Science Department, Oklahoma State University, Stillwater,
OK 74078, USA
dai@cs.okstate.edu
[2] Department of Computer Science, University of North Dakota, Grand Forks,
ND 58202, USA

Abstract. A compact 0-complete tree is an indexing mechanism that can be effectively used for large databases with long and variable-size keys. Compared to B-trees, compact 0-complete trees eliminate search values from secondary indices altogether. They are replaced with small surrogates whose typical eight-bit length will be adequate for most practical key lengths. Hence the secondary indices are simply hierarchical collections of (surrogate, pointer)-pairs. However, the overall storage performance of a compact 0-complete tree structure suffers from its dependency on the distribution of keys. We present a structural modification of 0-complete trees coupled with retrieval and maintenance algorithms that improve their storage utilization by reducing page-underfilling. This is achieved by introducing the notion of a sequence set that is analogous to that of B^+-trees.

Keywords: Index structure · B-tree · 0-complete tree

1 Introduction

B-trees provide a general and practical solution to the problem of indexing large files [1]. Their effectiveness and widespread use as index structures, are a consequence of their support of relatively fast and balanced access, good storage utilization (at least 50%), gradual expansion and shrinking, ordered sequential access to data items, insurance against the catastrophic behavior, and ease of implementation. Comparing B-tree retrieval to extendible hashing techniques [2], the former does not depend on storage of data in particular locations. Consequently, B-trees can be used to support secondary access paths. B-trees naturally tend to be the method of choice, since they provide both satisfactory primary and good secondary access to data sets.

However, unlike extensible hashing or compact 0-complete trees, B-tree index structures must duplicate the indexed attribute values of the keys. The replication of many secondary index values results in an index structure whose size may exceed that of the database itself. The inclusion of search values within pages of

T. K. Dang et al. (Eds.): FDSE 2022, CCIS 1688, pp. 88–102, 2022.
https://doi.org/10.1007/978-981-19-8069-5_6

B-trees may significantly decrease the branching factor of the page, and increase tree-depth and retrieval time.

Compact 0-complete trees are introduced in [5], and are studied and analyzed in [7–9], and [6]. These index structures eliminate search values from secondary indices altogether: they are replaced with small surrogates whose typical eight-bit length will be adequate for most practical key lengths. Hence the secondary indices are simply hierarchical collections of (surrogate, pointer)-pairs. This organization reduces the size of the secondary index structure by 50–80% and increases the branching factor of the trees, thus providing a reduced number of disk accesses per exact-match query.

Although compact 0-complete trees provide an attractive alternative, there are two shortcomings which the other commonly used index structures such as B-tree do not have:

1. Page-underfilling after split, and
2. Empty nodes inserted at the leaf-level.

The cause of the two problems is that the overall performance of a compact 0-complete tree structure heavily depends on the key distribution and could possibly create many underfilled pages and empty leaf-nodes. Although the expected storage utilization in compact 0-complete trees is much better compared to B-trees and prefix B-trees, some particular non-uniformly distributed data could seriously degrade storage utilization. The empirical study in [5] demonstrates that a compact 0-complete tree structure behaves as theoretically predicted when input record keys are uniformly distributed over the key space.

Although compact 0-complete trees analytically outperform other commonly used index structures such as B-trees and prefix B-trees, the above-mentioned shortcomings could be a barrier in practice since real key distributions tend to be rather skewed. It is a well-known fact that for B-trees and prefix B-trees, index size and storage utilization are independent from the key distribution. That is, storage utilization for B-trees is guaranteed to be at least 50% for all key distributions.

The search algorithm for compact 0-complete trees is independent of key type and key length since all keys in index pages are treated as a sequence of digits and encoded by a $\log_2 M$-bit surrogate, where M is the maximum key length. Thus the same implementation can be used regardless of whether the keys are character strings, integers, reals, or their combinations. However, a tradeoff to make the implementation work efficiently is that all keys are recommended to be filtered to eliminate unnecessary 1-bits so that the number of empty leaf-entries is minimized. Unfortunately, studying each key distribution in bits and implementing such a filter could be more work for implementers than just modifying the implementation to fit in each key type.

In our study we modify the retrieval and maintenance algorithms for and improve the performance of compact 0-complete trees. The main results of the study are:

1. Providing maintenance algorithms that reduce underfilling of index pages after splitting, and

2. Introducing the notion of a sequence set to further minimize index size.

Note that it is not difficult to modify the maintenance algorithms so that an overfilled index page after insertion is split exactly in half. But that may also cause unwanted side-effects such as the appearance of empty entries in the upper layers of compact 0-complete trees. Unfortunately, the tighter the index range to choose for a splitting point, the more is the chance that many empty entries are inserted in index pages. Therefore the goal of our modification is to reduce page-underfilling by setting up an index range to make sure the index close to the beginning, or close to the end, will not be chosen as a splitting point.

The sequence set is based on the idea of grouping the records into blocks and then maintaining the blocks, as records are added and deleted. The purpose of the index is to guide us to the block in the sequence set that contains the record, if it exists in the sequence set at all. Note that the index set itself does not contain data, it contains only information about where to find the data.

By introducing the sequence set, the size of the index structure is further minimized, and at the same time, it is possible to select the splitting point to manipulate the number of empty nodes inserted in the leaves of the index tree. If a splitting algorithm that is similar to the original compact 0-complete tree is used, the number of dummy nodes in the index structure can be reduced. However, the tradeoff is a higher chance of underfilled index and sequence set blocks, and that is certainly not a good choice. Therefore the splitting algorithm for the sequence set has the same principle as the one for index pages above.

2   0-Complete Trees: An Overview

We will in this section introduce a variant of binary tries, called a 0-complete tree, which will serve as the conceptual index structure that mirrors the actual retrieval structure, and will study its compact representation—the practical index structure. Then we will examine maintenance operations on compact 0-complete trees: searching, insertion, and deletion, and comment on the performance and storage utilization of compact 0-trees as index structures.

A *binary trie* structure can be transformed into a compact 0-tree, which is a compact multi-way search tree. A *trie* [4] is a multi-branching edge-labeled tree in which data items to be retrieved are stored at its leaves. Retrieval is achieved by successively comparing symbols in the search key with edge labels and following the indicated path to the desired leaf.

A binary trie is a trie structure with binary edge-labels—every edge is labeled with either 0 or 1. In a binary trie T, a node v is called a *0-node* (*1-node*) if the in-edge of v is labeled by 0 (respectively, 1). The *discriminator* of a node v is the string $D_v \in \{0,1\}^*$ such that $D_v = xy$ where x labels the path from the root of T to v, and $y = 0^{depth(T)-length(x)}$.

A *0-complete tree* is a binary trie T such that (1) the sibling of every 0-leaf must be present in T, and (2) the number of 1-nodes in T is one less than the number of leaves in T.

A *complete binary tree* is a binary tree in which every node has either 0 or 2 immediate descendants. It was proved in [9] that every complete binary tree satisfies the two conditions for the 0-completeness.

The nodes in a 0-complete tree T can be topologically ordered by the common pre-order traversal of the tree. The immediate successors of leaves in the pre-order traversal of T are called *bounding nodes* in T. We note that a 0-complete tree T with N leaves has $N - 1$ bounding nodes, which are precisely the 1-nodes in T.

Discriminators and bounding nodes in a 0-complete tree T can be used to establish a partition of the *key space*, in which each *key interval* corresponds to each leaf in T. Denote by:

$$u_1, v_1, \ldots, u_2, v_2, \ldots, u_{N-1}, v_{N-1}, \ldots, u_N$$

the pre-order traversal of a 0-complete tree T with N leaves, where u_i's are leaves and v_i's are bounding nodes in T.

The key space is partitioned as:

$$[D_{u_1}, D_{v_1}), [D_{u_2}, D_{v_2}), \ldots, [D_{u_N}, 1^{depth(T)})$$

Observe that $D_{v_1} = D_{u_2}, D_{v_2} = D_{u_3}, \ldots, D_{v_{N-1}} = D_{u_N}$.

The significance of the bounding nodes is two-fold: (1) knowledge of the discriminators of bounding nodes is sufficient to identify the appropriate key interval of any data item with any given key, using a B-tree-like search operation, and (2) knowledge of the depths of bounding nodes can be used to compute the partition (key intervals) of the key space as follows.

Let M denote the (maximum) key length. Let D_i denote the discriminator of the ith bounding node in the pre-order traversal of a 0-complete tree of N leaves, where $i = 1, 2, \ldots, N - 1$ ($D_0 = 0^M$, and $D_N = 1^M$). Assuming knowledge of the depth sequence:

$$(d_i \mid d_i \text{ is the depth of the } i^{\text{th}} \text{ bounding node})_{i=1}^{N-1},$$

then the term D_i in the sequence $(D_i)_{i=1}^{N-1}$ can be computed inductively (hence the key intervals):

> algorithm *compute_discriminators*
>> set the d_i^{th} bit in D_{i-1} to 1
>>> set all subsequent (lower-order) bits in D_{i-1} to 0
>> end *compute_discriminators*

A compact representation of a 0-complete tree T, called a C_0-tree, is a hierarchical structure of index nodes (index pages). Each index page corresponds to a 0-complete subtree T' of T and contains the sequence of ordered pairs (depth$_i$, pointer$_i$), where (1) the ith bounding node in the pre-order traversal of T' is denoted by u_i, (2) depth$_i$ denotes the depth of u_i, and (3) pointer$_i$ points to the index page for the 0-complete subtree of T' rooted at u_i, or to the leaf page preceding u_i.

The 0-complete tree for an indexed file serves as a conceptual index structure, whereas the C_0-tree for the underlying 0-complete tree serves as a practical index structure for the file organization.

Retrieval, insertion, and deletion operations depend on the search operation for a given search key. A naive algorithm for the search operation on compact 0-complete trees, based on applying the algorithm *compute_discriminators* on the depth sequence in an index page of the C_0-tree, is to compute the partition of key intervals and choose the appropriate key interval for continuing search. This approach suffers the inefficiency of the recurrence in the algorithm *compute_discriminators*.

A more efficient implementation of the search operation reduces to comparisons of small integers, regardless of the key length or key type. In this algorithm, an array of increasing 1-bit positions in the search key is first computed, and then those positions are compared with the depth field of the index page one by one. Thus, the key comparison time for any access is significantly reduced.

For the insertion operation of a key K, the binary search tree property of the conceptual 0-complete tree T yields the appropriate leaf for key insertion. To preserve the 0-completeness of the conceptual tree, it may be necessary to prolong the path from $root(T)$ to the leaf of insertion by adding empty ("dummy") 0-leaves to distinguish K from an existing key in T.

Reflecting the practical compact C_0-representation onto its conceptual 0-complete model, the insertion operation can be described informally below:

1. Locate the appropriate index page (data page) in the C_0-tree by invoking the search operation on the search key K.
2. Compute the depth of the data page in the conceptual 0-complete tree.
3. Based on the depth of the data page and comparing K with keys in the data page, decide if K should be inserted before/after the insertion location (some number of dummy (depth, pointer)-pairs may be inserted simultaneously to preserve the 0-completeness of the conceptual tree).
4. The insertions in step 3 may cause an overfilled condition in the index page. To correct this overfilled condition, perform a "minimal" splitting of the overfilled index page into two index pages. A minimal splitting finds the (depth, pointer)-pair (other than the last) in the original index page I that has the minimum depth, d_{min}. Let d_{last} denote the depth component of the last (depth, pointer)-pair. The original index page I is split immediately following the "minimal"-pair into two index pages I_0 and I_1.
   If the split index page I was the root index page in the C_0-tree, then a new root index page must be created with a sequence of two (depth, pointer)-pairs: (d_{min}, I_0) and (d_{last}, I_1). If the split index page I was not the root of the C_0-tree, then it was referenced by a (depth, pointer)-pair, (d_{last}, I). This pair is replaced by a sequence of two (depth, pointer)-pairs: (d_{min}, I_0) and (d_{last}, I_1). This splitting and promotion may result additional index-page splittings at upper levels.

Note that with minimal splitting there is no guarantee of even splitting as with B-trees. A variant of the minimal partitioning algorithm, "optimized" splitting (see [5]), can minimize some of the potential effects of skewed key sequences. In optimized splitting, the index page splits right after the entry that is as close to the middle as possible with depth less than all the depths of its predecessors. Although this splitting option does not prevent page-underfilling altogether, it is a much closer approximation of even splitting. The key idea of the optimized splitting algorithm is analogous to that of the minimal partitioning algorithm with slight modifications. Henceforth only optimized splitting is used in this article for discussions.

Deletion/concatenation is essentially the reverse of insertion/splitting, and is described informally below.

1. Locate the appropriate index page in the C_0-tree by invoking the search operation on the search key.
2. Delete the corresponding (depth, pointer)-pair from the index page (some dummy (depth, pointer)-pairs may be deleted simultaneously to preserve the 0-completeness of the conceptual tree).
3. The deletions in step 2 may cause an underfilled condition in the index page, which can be corrected by performing a concatenation of two index pages. Like splitting, it can propagate upward through the C_0-tree. Just as splitting promotes a (depth, pointer)-pair, concatenation must involve demotion of (depth, pointer)-pairs. This can cause underfilling in the parent index page and may eventually cause the deallocation of the root index page.

The small, fixed-size surrogates (the depth-components of (depth, pointer)-pairs in index pages) replacing the keys in the tree-like index structure yields significant space efficiency: (1) increasing the branching factor of index pages, and (2) decreasing the depth of the index structure (hence the number of accesses).

The expected storage utilization of a C_0-tree is $\ln 2$ (≈ 0.693), as in the case of B-trees [10]. However, due to the presence of dummy (depth, pointer)-pairs, the number, L, of index pages at the lowest level of the tree exceeds the actual number, N, of records. For random keys, this value asymptotically tends to

$$L = N(\log_2 e + 1)/2 \approx 1.221\,N.$$

The number of dummy (depth, pointer)-pairs is

$$D = N(\log_2 e - 1)/2 \approx 0.221\,N,$$

so that $(\log_2 e - 1)/(\log_2 e + 1) \approx 0.181$ (about 18%) of (depth, pointer)-pairs at the lowest tree level will be nil, just to ensure consistency with an underlying 0-complete tree.

3   Structural Modification of 0-Complete Trees

In this section, we develop a structural modification of 0-complete trees by (1) designing an index-page splitting algorithm that reduces page-underfilling,

(2) introducing the notion of a sequence set, and (3) providing semantic changes in parallel to the structural changes on 0-complete trees.

Note that, due to the space limitation of this article, we present only the motivations and key ideas for the structural modification of 0-complete trees coupled with retrieval and maintenance algorithms. Their algorithmic details and implementations are provided in the full version of this article.

3.1   Index-Page Splitting Algorithm

The basic idea of optimized splitting in the original 0-complete tree [5] is that the depth of the splitting point must be the minimum of all the depths in the first page after the split, and the index that is the closest to the middle of the page is chosen as long as the first condition is met. A problem arises if entries with minimum depths appear near the beginning of index pages. The example depicted in Figs. 1 and 2 illustrates this problem.

depth	record-pointer	record
1	$\longrightarrow$	00000000
3	$\longrightarrow$	10010001
4	$\longrightarrow$	10101000
2	$\longrightarrow$	10110000
3	$\longrightarrow$	11000100
4	$\longrightarrow$	11100001
0	$\longrightarrow$	11110001

Fig. 1. An index page before splitting in an original 0-complete tree.

depth	page-pointer	page		
1	$\longrightarrow$	depth	record-pointer	record
		1	$\longrightarrow$	00000000
0	$\longrightarrow$	depth	record-pointer	record
		3	$\longrightarrow$	10010001
		4	$\longrightarrow$	10101000
		2	$\longrightarrow$	10110000
		3	$\longrightarrow$	11000100
		4	$\longrightarrow$	11100001
		0	$\longrightarrow$	11110001

Fig. 2. An index page after splitting in an original 0-complete tree.

In Fig. 1, the minimum depth (=1) occurs at the first entry, hence the page is underfilled after a split (see Fig. 2).

The worst case occurs when all the minimum depths happen to be at the beginning of the page in increasing order when overfilling occurs in a leaf index page. The problem is that more than one dummy node may be inserted in increasing order for a single insertion – the index page might split again and again until the last page is no longer overfilled. Under uniform key distribution, those underfilled pages are expected to be filled eventually. However those pages may not be filled under some skewed key distribution, such as keys always starting with a 1-bit. The scenario is shown in Figs. 3 and 4.

depth	record-pointer	record
1	$\xrightarrow{nil}$	
2	$\longrightarrow$	10000001
3	$\longrightarrow$	11000101
8	$\longrightarrow$	11100000
7	$\longrightarrow$	11100001
4	$\longrightarrow$	11100010
$\vdots$		
0	$\longrightarrow$	11111100

Fig. 3. An index page before (worst-case) splitting in an original 0-complete tree.

depth	page-pointer	page
1	$\longrightarrow$	depth record-pointer record 1 $\xrightarrow{nil}$
2	$\longrightarrow$	depth record-pointer record 2 $\longrightarrow$ 10000001
3	$\longrightarrow$	depth record-pointer record depth record-pointer record 3 $\longrightarrow$ 11000101
0	$\longrightarrow$	depth record-pointer record 8 $\longrightarrow$ 11100000 7 $\longrightarrow$ 11100001 4 $\longrightarrow$ 11100010 $\vdots$ 0 $\longrightarrow$ 11111100

Fig. 4. An index page after (worst-case) splitting in an original 0-complete tree.

The worst-case behavior elicited by the example in Fig. 3 is summarized in Fig. 4. After the first splitting, the first page contains only one entry (with depth

= 1), and the second page is still overfilled. Therefore the second page splits, again resulting into two pages, and so on. Moreover if all the keys start with a 1-bit, no other entry will be inserted into the first page (depth = 1, pointer = nil).

The key idea of our modified index-page splitting algorithm is to choose a splitting index point with the minimum depth within a certain range to prevent underfilling of pages. It also simplifies the implementation by guaranteeing index page splitting into no more than two pages.

Note that it is not difficult to modify the original splitting algorithm so that an overfilled index page is split exactly in half. But that may also cause unwanted side-effects such as the appearance of dummies in the upper layers of C_0-trees. Unfortunately, the tighter the index range to choose for a splitting point, the more is the chance that many dummies are inserted in index pages. Therefore

depth	page-pointer	page		
1	$\xrightarrow{nil}$			
		depth	record-pointer	record
		1	$\longrightarrow$	00000000
2	$\longrightarrow$	3	$\longrightarrow$	10010001
		4	$\longrightarrow$	10101000
		2	$\longrightarrow$	10110000
		depth	record-pointer	record
		3	$\longrightarrow$	11000100
0	$\longrightarrow$	4	$\longrightarrow$	11100001
		0	$\longrightarrow$	11110001

Fig. 5. The index page in Fig. 1 after modified splitting.

depth	page-pointer	page		
1	$\xrightarrow{nil}$			
2	$\xrightarrow{nil}$			
3	$\xrightarrow{nil}$			
		depth	record-pointer	record
		1	$\xrightarrow{nil}$	
		2	$\longrightarrow$	10000001
4	$\longrightarrow$	3	$\longrightarrow$	11000101
		8	$\longrightarrow$	11100000
		7	$\longrightarrow$	11100001
		4	$\longrightarrow$	11100010
		depth	record-pointer	record
0	$\longrightarrow$	$\vdots$		
		0	$\longrightarrow$	11111100

Fig. 6. The index page in Fig. 3 after modified splitting.

the goal of our modification is to prevent page-underfilling by selecting an index range that is not close to the beginning, or close to the ending of the index page. Figures 5 and 6 illustrate the modified splitting algorithm on the examples from Figs. 1 and 3, respectively. Details about insertion of nil-pointers in upper layers of C_0-trees are provided in the full version of this article.

In both Figs. 5 and 6, the splitting point is chosen closer to the middle, and dummy nodes are inserted in the upper layer of index pages instead. In Fig. 6, the leaf page is split only once since the second page after splitting is not overfilled.

3.2   Sequence Set Blocks

The sequence set [3] is based on the idea of grouping the records into blocks and then maintaining the blocks as records are added and deleted. The purpose of the index is to guide us to the block in the sequence set that contains the record. Note that the index set itself does not contain data, it contains only information about where to find the data. B^+-trees and prefix B^+-trees are examples of similar modifications of B-trees, with prefix B-trees using sequence set blocks. The advantage is a smaller index structure and fast sequential access.

With a sequence set, the number of the dummy entries in the leaves of index pages depends on how we select splitting points from the sequence set blocks. Figures 7 and 8 show examples with the original and modified 0-complete tree structures. In Fig. 8, all the dummy nodes are eliminated by using the sequence set.

In an original 0-complete tree where we have no control over key distribution, we can not reduce dummy entries since the conceptual 0-complete tree structure is fixed with the keys inserted in a given order. By using a sequence set, we can manipulate dummy entries in the upper level (leaves of the index structure). For example, by choosing the index with the minimum depth from a sequence set block (the minimum-depth computation runs in linear time – by comparing consecutive entries), the number of the dummy nodes can be minimized. However, the tradeoff is a higher chance of the underfilling of sequence set blocks, and that

depth	record-pointer	record
1	$\xrightarrow{nil}$	
2	$\xrightarrow{nil}$	
3	$\xrightarrow{nil}$	
4	$\xrightarrow{nil}$	
5	$\xrightarrow{nil}$	
6	$\xrightarrow{nil}$	
7	$\xrightarrow{nil}$	
8	$\longrightarrow$	11111110
0	$\longrightarrow$	11111111

Fig. 7. A leaf index page in an original 0-complete tree.

depth block-pointer sequence set block

		record
0	$\longrightarrow$	11111110
		11111111

Fig. 8. A leaf index page and a sequence set in a modified 0-complete tree.

is certainly not a good choice. Therefore the splitting algorithm for the sequence set blocks has the same principle as the one for index pages. Considering the leaf block in the example depicted in Fig. 9, Figs. 10 and 11 show the results of applying the minimum-depth splitting algorithm (minimizing dummy nodes but possibly causing underfilled sequence set blocks) and the even-splitting algorithm (partitioning evenly but possibly creating dummy nodes) to the sequence set block, respectively. Details about splitting algorithms are provided in the full version of this article.

depth block-pointer sequence set block

		record
		00000000
		00001111
		10000001
0	$\longrightarrow$	11110000
		11111000
		11111001
		11111011
		11111111

Fig. 9. A leaf index page and a sequence set block before splitting in a modified 0-complete tree.

depth block-pointer sequence set block

		depth	record
1	$\longrightarrow$	5	00000000
		1	00001111
		depth	record
		2	10000001
		5	11110000
0	$\longrightarrow$	8	11111000
		7	11111001
		6	11111011
		–	11111111

Fig. 10. A leaf index page and a sequence set block after minimum-depth splitting.

depth block-pointer sequence set block

depth	block-pointer		
1	$\xrightarrow{nil}$		
2	$\xrightarrow{nil}$		
3	$\xrightarrow{nil}$		
4	$\xrightarrow{nil}$		

		depth	record
		5	00000000
5	$\longrightarrow$	1	00001111
		2	10000001
		5	11110000

		depth	record
		8	11111000
0	$\longrightarrow$	7	11111001
		6	11111011
		–	11111111

Fig. 11. A leaf index page and a sequence set block after even splitting.

In Fig. 10, the splitting point with the minimum depth is chosen (index = 1, depth = 1), so no dummy entry is inserted in the leaf of the index page. However, this causes underfilling of the first sequence set block after the split. On the other hand, the overfilled block is split exactly in half in Fig. 11. The depth of the splitting point is five since the fifth digit (instead of the first digit as in Fig. 10) is the first different digit between the two keys 11110000 and 11111000. Dummy entries (depth = 1, 2, 3, and 4) are placed in the index page as a side-effect.

3.3 Semantic Changes

So far, the structural changes made from the original 0-complete tree are:

1. Entries with nil-pointers appear not only in the leaves of the index page but also in upper levels of the index structure.
2. The purpose of the index set is to provide access to the correct sequence set block that includes keys and the records.

Note that some semantics are also changed along with the structural changes above. In the original 0-complete tree structure, each entry presents a certain key range (that is computed by the depth) and an entry with a nil-pointer simply means that no key is in that range. On the other hand, in the modified index-page splitting algorithm, an entry with a nil-pointer does not represent any key range, and keys in that range are found at nearest entry below which has non-nil-pointer. An example is given in Fig. 12.

index page 1
key range: [00000000, 11111111]

depth	page-pointer	page
1	$\xrightarrow{nil}$	

index page 2
key range: [00000000, 11000000)

		implied key range
depth	block-pointer	of sequence set block
1	$\xrightarrow{nil}$	
3	$\longrightarrow$	[00000000, 10100000)
5	$\xrightarrow{nil}$	
6	$\longrightarrow$	[10100000, 10101100)
4	$\longrightarrow$	[10101100, 10110000)
2	$\longrightarrow$	[10110000, 11000000)

(depth page-pointer **2** $\longrightarrow$)

index page 3
key range: [11000000, 11111111]

		implied key range
depth	block-pointer	of sequence set block
3	$\longrightarrow$	[11000000, 11100000)
4	$\xrightarrow{nil}$	
5	$\longrightarrow$	[11100000, 11111000)
0	$\longrightarrow$	[11111000, 11111111]

(depth page-pointer **0** $\longrightarrow$)

Fig. 12. A complete modified 0-complete tree structure.

In original 0-complete trees, the third entry in index page two (depth = 5, nil-pointer) means that no key belongs to the range [10100000, 10101000). In the modified index-page splitting algorithm, an entry with a nil-pointer does not represent any range and the search procedure must go down in an index page until it finds an entry with a non-nil-pointer. Therefore the search procedure stops at the fourth entry (depth = 6, non-nil-pointer), where the range [10100000, 10101000) is a subrange of [10100000, 10101100).

The same analysis is obtained for upper layers of the index structure. The first entry in index page one (depth = 1, nil-pointer) does not represent any range and the range [00000000, 10000000) implied by that entry is found at the next entry (depth = 2, non-nil-pointer) as a subrange of [00000000, 11000000). There is no entry with a nil-pointer in the upper layer of the index page in the original 0-complete tree.

There are some similarities between C'-Trees [5] and the modified 0-complete tree structure developed in this paper. In a C'-Tree, the leaves of the index structure contain depth-pointer pairs, which point to data blocks containing sequential records.

Note that C'-trees do not strictly follow the property of the original 0-complete trees. In a C'-tree, a key that belongs to a missing 1-leaf can be stored in the immediately preceding leaf page (according to the pre-order traversal) as long as space is available. However, a new page must be created for a key that belongs to a 0-leaf with a nil-pointer, which is not the case for the modified 0-complete tree structure.

The empirical study in [5] shows that a C′-tree, when compared to the original 0-complete tree, would yield better retrieval performance only for small records whose length is at most 20 bytes because of the storage overhead caused by underfilled blocks. In the modified 0-complete trees, underfilled blocks are further reduced.

4   Concluding Remarks

The modified 0-complete tree index structure coupled with retrieval and maintenance algorithms presented here reduces the number of underfilled index pages caused by a non-uniform key distribution. A side-effect of the modification may be the existence of dummy nodes in upper layers of index pages, whereas for original 0-complete-trees, dummy nodes exist only in the leaves. The size of the index structure is expected to be greatly reduced by introducing a sequence set. A smaller index structure reduces the number of disk accesses. The introduction of a sequence set in an index structure facilitates a fast sequential access of the keys.

Algorithmic details and implementations of the modified retrieval and maintenance algorithms for searching, insertion, and deletion are presented in the full version of this article.

Future directions for research include the worst-case and expected-case analyses and comparisons for the original and the modified 0-complete tree structures. The expected-case behavior of the original 0-complete trees is detailed in [5]. Simulations of different index structures including 0-complete trees, modified 0-complete trees, B-trees, and prefix B-trees may also be of interest. However, the outcome may heavily depend on key distributions that may not be realistic.

So far 0-complete trees are not widely used in practical applications. The Q_0-tree [8] is a variation of the 0-complete tree, which attempts to accommodate the 0-complete tree structure to spatial databases. We hope that this research eliminates the worst-case scenario caused by non-uniform key distributions and encourages the application of this novel index structure to various fields.

References

1. Comer, D.: The ubiquitous B-tree. ACM Comput. Surv. **11**(2), 121–137 (1979)
2. Fagin, R., Nievergelt, J., Pippenger, N., Strong, H.R.: Extendible hashing – a fast access method for dynamic files. ACM Trans. Database Syst. **4**(3), 315–344 (1979)
3. Folk, M.J., Zoellick, B.: File Structures, 2nd edn. Addison-Wesley, Reading (1992)
4. Fredkin, E.: Many-way information retrieval. Commun. ACM **3**, 490–500 (1960)
5. Orlandic, R.: Design, analysis and applications of compact 0-complete trees. Ph.D. thesis, Department of Computer Science, University of Virginia (1989)
6. Orlandic, R., Mahmoud, H.M.: Storage overhead of O-trees, B-trees and prefix B-trees: a comparative analysis. Int. J. Found. Comput. Sci. **7**(3), 209–226 (1996)

7. Orlandic, R., Pfaltz, J.L.: Compact 0-complete trees. In: Proceedings of the Four-teenth Conference on Very Large Databases, pp. 372–381. Association for Computing Machinery and IEEE Computer Society, August 1988

8. Orlandic, R., Pfaltz, J.L.: Q_0-tree: a dynamic structure for accessing spatial objects with arbitrary shapes. Institute for Parallel Computation, University of Virginia, Technical Report IPC-TR-91-010. December 1991

9. Orlandic, R., Pfaltz, J.L.: Compact 0-complete trees: a new method for searching large files. Institute for Parallel Computation, University of Virginia, Technical Report IPC-TR-88-001, January 1988

10. Yao, A.: On random 2–3 trees. Acta Informatica $9(2)$, 159–170 (1978)

Implement the Data Conversion System by Using α-Lightweight Coreset for Validation Process

Nguyen Le Hoang[1], Tran Khanh Dang[2(✉)], and Thai San Dang[3]

[1] Ritsumeikan University, Kyoto, Japan
[2] Ho Chi Minh City University of Food Industry, Ho Chi Minh City, Vietnam
`khanh@hufi.edu.vn`
[3] Ho Chi Minh City University of Technology, Ho Chi Minh City, Vietnam

Abstract. In recent years, data have been created and stored in different places with various formats and types. This causes a lot of difficulties for data analysis and data mining which can make profits for every aspect of social applications based on these valuable data. In order to overcome this problem, data conversion is a crucial step that we have to build for linking and merging different data resources into a unified data store. This paper implements a complete data conversion system based on the elastic data conversion framework. In addition, we also apply the α-Lightweight Coreset for the data validation process of this system.

Keywords: Data conversion · Coreset · Data integration system · Data transformation · Data sampling

1 Introduction

The rapidly successful evolution of computing has allowed pocket-size machines, so-called smartphones, to exchange information effectively in real-time with terabyte-sized memory and hyper-performance CPU servers, which led humans to become more and more involved, dependent to be exact, in various forms of computation systems. In consequence, data volume and value rise as time goes by, plus computation use cases and contexts also get complicated along with such increasing development of technology. As the role of engineers or managers in the software industry, we may find ourselves in some of those situations where the tasks require data to be linked or merged from various resources. For example, the needs to be able to access and process data in real-time of the multiple IoT devices in one specific system, data analysis tasks require getting data from many different sources to make more long-term, effective decisions... these are just a few amongst many situations in real life that can only be settled if data from various resources could somehow connect to each other. To make real the solutions for those situations, data migration is the non-trivial step that we have to face and overcome.

Data migration could be described as a process that converts and transforms data from different database systems (different formats); then, in the larger

T. K. Dang et al. (Eds.): FDSE 2022, CCIS 1688, pp. 103–118, 2022.
https://doi.org/10.1007/978-981-19-8069-5_7

picture, the data can be unified into a set of the unified dataset that we could easily use for a variety of purposes. A few examples to clarify: In the United States, transport agencies and departments rely on large amounts of data, which can be extracted from the black bus boxes and the cameras on the road, to get a comprehensive yet in-depth view of the traffic situation of a city. When combining these datasets with population data such as population density or distribution, the management agencies, and related departments would be able to make appropriate decisions and, even further than that, publish policies about traffic flow, reconstruct or establish traffic infrastructure, and navigate traffic to avoid traffic jams. The problem is that departments often store data with completely different formats and database systems. Hence, data migration is an indispensable step in the integration, analysis, and decision-making process.

However, the data migration process is complex, and achieving the desired result is not always possible. This process usually requires the specific dedication of engineers to comprehend and manually correct the schema of the target dataset in each source to solve issues such as data model semantic or data representation ambiguity... The problems are more and more challenging when the big data nature takes into account when data types are not only heterogeneous but the data's volume is also produced continuously with enormous mass. Here arises the question: how can we make the migration process so that it can handle a large amount of data with different variety of data types and still be reasonably fast? As with almost any conformity performance optimizing tasks, we break the whole thing down into atomic-sized pieces, then desperately look at any corners and ask repeatedly, "could we cut short this?".

Also, a reminder that we are dealing with datasets not only significant in volume and size but also massive in variety and velocity. Consequently, the demand to look for more reasonable methods becomes necessary. The standard approach is that instead of facing the problem as a whole, which is a large dataset, we could find the answer from the smaller subset of the targeting data. This result is subsequently used as the baseline for finding the actual solution for the original dataset; so, to have "the best" final output, we have to find "the best" coreset, which is the subset that must be small enough for effectively reducing computational complexity but must keep all representative characteristics of original data.

This paper implements a complete data conversion system based on the elastic data conversion framework in [5]. In addition, we also apply the α-Lightweight Coreset [11] for the data validation process of this system. The rest of this paper is organized as follows, some related works and research will be mentioned in Sect. 2, while our proposed and implemented system will be in Sect. 3. We do some experiments and evaluations in Sect. 4. The summary and conclusion will be in Sect. 5.

2   Related Works

2.1   Data Conversion

Due to the need for a data conversion system, since 2010, there have been a lot of research and proposed methods such as the iWay Big Data Integrator by Information Builders[1] that provides a modern approach to the conversion, integration, and management of data based on the Hadoop platform. The SQL Server Integration Services (SSIS)[2] products by Microsoft Corporation, which also has services to extract and transform data from various data sources such as XML files, and load the data into one or more data storages. Furthermore, Talend[3] also provides tools for big data integration and transformation solutions. However, these tools transform data directly through user interaction without the standard conversion data specification.

In 2013, a data transformation system based on a community contribution model was proposed by Ivan et al. [8]. In this system, the publicdata.eu portal includes all shared data from many different organizations of various formats. The system will make initial mappings, then let the community contribute by creating new mappings, re-editing existing mappings, transforming the data, and using the data. The accuracy in data conversion will improve over time with the contribution of the community (Fig. 1).

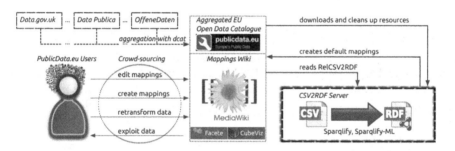

Fig. 1. Data transformation system based on a community contribution model [8].

In 2015, Rocha et al. proposed a method to support the migration of data from relational databases RDBMS to NoSQL [17]. This framework includes two main modules: the data migration module, which is responsible for automatically identifying all elements from the original relational databases (e.g., tables, properties, relationships, indexes, etc.), then creates equivalent structures using the NoSQL data model and the data mapping module which consists of an abstract class, designed as an interface between the application and the DBMS.

---

[1] https://www.tibco.com.

[2] https://docs.microsoft.com/en-us/sql/integration-services/sql-server-integration-services.

[3] https://www.talend.com/.

In 2017, a semi-automatic tool for converting ecological data was developed by Hyeonjeong et al. [12]. For gathering data in different formats from various research organizations and institutes specializing in an environment in Korea and then converting to a shared standard ecological dataset. (Fig. 2). This tool consists of 4 parts: the data file & protocol selection part for selecting data and the corresponding protocol, the species selection part for choosing which species in the data to be converted, and the attribute mapping part for mapping attributes from source data to normalized attributes defined in the protocol and the data standardization part for converting mapped data to a shared standard. However, this tool currently only supports data sources stored in **.csv** format and only converts data for a few species from the original data.

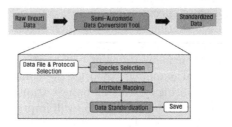

Fig. 2. Semi-automatic tool for converting ecological data in Korea [12].

Also, in 2017, by using a process engineering transformation tool, Milan et al. proposed a model integrating with the data transformation toolkit AutomationML (AML), an open standard XML-based data format for storage and exchange of technical information of the plant [16]. Although the model can work well, the process's input is stored only in the AML standard (Fig. 3).

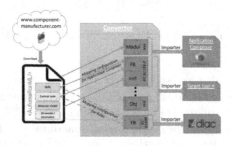

Fig. 3. Factory integration through the use of the data transformation toolkit for AutomationML [16].

In 2017, Luis et al. developed a data conversion framework to support energy simulation [15]. This framework aims to convert data into different formats to enable communication and interaction among different systems in an automated environment. This approach designs an intermediate component defined as the Interoperability Specification to enforce reciprocal interaction between two different data formats. Figure 4 illustrates the architecture of the interactive implementation.

Fig. 4. Data conversion framework to support energy simulation [15].

In 2020, Dang et al. proposed an elastic data conversion framework for a smart city open data integration system [5]. The framework was organized with multiple modules such as the I/O, data validation, schema detection, data conversion, and data storage. (cf. Figure 5). This model was then implemented and evaluated with MySQL and MongoDB. Even though the performances showed some promising results [6], the system lacked the data validation process.

In 2021, Ta et al. made some comparisons among different models, and the results showed that the intermediate data conversion model with JSON as the intermediate data type would be a good realistic application [19].

2.2 Coresets and α-Lightweight Coresets

Data sampling is one of the most popular options used in machine learning and data mining. The critical idea of data sampling is that instead of solving problems on the complete data with large-scale size, we can find the answer for the subset of this data; this result is then used as the baseline for finding the actual solution for the original data set. This idea motivates the data scientists to the *coreset*, which is defined as the most relevant subset that can be used to represent the whole data set. The term *coreset* was first used by Agarwal et al. in 2004 [1] in a problem about geometric approximation, then was employed by Har-Peled et al. in finding subsets for k-median and k-means clustering [9]. Since then, this term has been widely used, and various *coreset constructions* have been investigated to solve many big-data-related problems.

Many coreset construction algorithms have been proposed in recent years, such as Feldman et al. for high dimensional subspace and PCA and projective clustering [7]; Bachem et al. for non-parametric estimation [2] and k-clustering [3]; Lucic et al. for mixture models [14], etc. There are some coreset

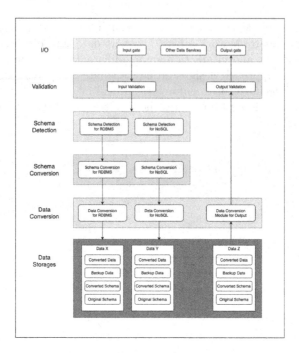

Fig. 5. Elastic data conversion framework for data integration system [5].

based on the Farthest-First-Traversal (FFT) algorithm, such as ProTraS in by Ros et al. [18], and another FFT-based coreset construction by Le et al. [13]. Hoang et al. compared these techniques in [10]. Compared to data sampling-based coresets, it is shown that even though FFT-based coresets have higher accuracy, they need a lot of runtimes. Therefore, in this paper, we will apply the α - *lightweight coreset* [11], a data sampling-based coreset, for the data validation process of the data conversion system. The definition of α-*lightweight coreset* can be stated as follows:

α-**Lightweight Coresets** [11]: *Given problem ϕ on data set $X \subset \mathbb{R}^d$ with solution $\phi_X(Q)$ for any $Q \subset \mathbb{R}^d$. Let $\varepsilon > 0$ and μ_X be mean of X. The subset $C \subset X$ is a lightweight coreset of X:*

$$|\phi_X(Q) - \phi_C(Q)| \leq \alpha\varepsilon\phi_X(Q) + (1 - \alpha)\varepsilon\phi_X(\{\mu_X\}) \tag{1}$$

- The $\alpha\varepsilon\phi_X(Q)$ term allows the approximation error to scale with the quantization error and constitutes the multiplicative part.
- The $(1 - \alpha)\varepsilon\phi_X(\{\mu_X\})$ term scales with the variance of the data and corresponds to the additive approximation error term that is invariant of the scale of the data.
- The value of α can be considered as *an adjustable parameter* for the α - *lightweight coreset*.

In [11], the authors have shown that as we decrease ε, the actual cost of the optimal solution obtained on α - *lightweight coresets* approaches the actual cost of the optimal solution on the complete data set in an additive manner. The α - lightweight coreset construction is based on the importance of sampling and is given in Algorithm 1.

Algorithm 1. α - Lightweight Coreset Construction [11]

Require: Set of data points X, the value of α coreset size m
Ensure: the α - lightweight coreset C
1: $\mu \leftarrow$ mean of X
2: **for all** $x \in X$ **do**
3:    $p(x) \leftarrow \frac{1}{2\alpha+1} \frac{1}{|X|} + \frac{2\alpha}{2\alpha+1} \frac{d(x,\mu)^2}{\sum_{x' \in X} d(x',\mu)^2}$
4: **end for**
5: $C \leftarrow$ sample points from where each point is sampled with probability and has weight $w_x = \frac{1}{m.q(x)}$
6: **return** the α - lightweight coreset C

Similar to the original paper of α - *lightweight coreset*, we set $\alpha = \frac{3}{4}$, the probability distribution $p(x)$ in Algorithm 1 will be as follows:

$$p(x) = \frac{2}{5} \frac{1}{|X|} + \frac{3}{5} \frac{d(x,\mu)^2}{\sum_{x' \in X} d(x',\mu)^2} \qquad (2)$$

3 Implementation

3.1 System Overview

In this implementation, the system's target will be converting data sets from MySQL to MongoDB. The working flow of the system is shown in Fig. 6 It has to satisfy these requirements:

1. The system should migrate data from the source database (MySQL) to the target database (MongoDB) successfully. Columns and rows should remain the same, and data types should automatically match the data type mapping from MySQL to MongoDB.
2. For the validation process, the system should be able to find the optimal subset, log the validation errors and send the report to users.
3. In detail, the system will receive the input and create the output as follows:
   - Input: the system will receive the MySQL backup file (.sql file extension) from users through CKAN UI.
   - Output: the system will generate the MongoDB compressed backup file (.gz file extension) and the validation report (.xlsx file extension); these files will be uploaded to CKAN UI.

The system contains six components as follows:

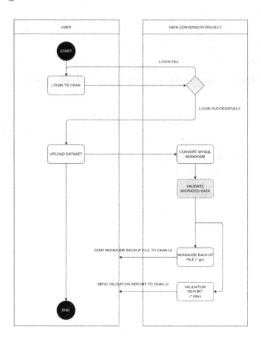

Fig. 6. Work flow of the system.

1. I/O: this component will be in charge of the input and output processes of the system and will communicate with the user through an intuitive interface.
2. Data Stores: saving and storing data of the system. For each input data, the data stores will protect the backup data (original data set and original data schema) and converted data (converted data set and converted schema).
3. Schema Detection: when new data is input, this component will detect and recognize the structure and schema of this data. The schema detection component must be able to handle both structured data and NoSQL data.
4. Schema Conversion: this module will convert the detected schema into the target data formats. This step requires the schema conversion module to understand and recognize the original schema's meanings.
5. Data Conversion: this will create a mapping for converting each original data record to the target data format. Then, this component is responsible for transforming the data according to the schema outlined in the previous step. Therefore, this process is only active when the schema-related modules have finished. The input of this component is the extracted schema, converted by the schema conversion and the original user data. The output is the data after conversion.
6. Validation: checking the input to ensure the data is convertible and validating the correctness of output before sending it to users. For example, the input data must be in some convertible formats, or the output data is similar to the original data.

3.2   Supporting Tools

1. CKAN stack[4]: We use CKAN stack as a UI component, the gateway for the user to interact with the data conversion backend system. A user gives input and receives the output:
   - Input: User will upload MySQL backup file.
   - Output: data conversion backend system will upload MongoDB backup file and validation report.
2. SchemaCrawler[5]: free database schema discovery and comprehension tool. It has a good mix of useful features for data governance. We can search for database schema objects using regular expressions and output the schema and data in a readable text format. After restoring successfully from the user's MySQL backup file, the backend system will use a schema crawler to crawl the MySQL database; the output will be schema information stored in JSON format.
3. Redis Cache[6]: Redis is an open source (BSD licensed), in-memory data structure store used as a database, cache, message broker, and streaming engine. We can utilize Redis with many memorization strategies:
   - Store schema information data-frame, which is constructed by pandas.
   - Store error indices after comparing two subsets at the validation process.
4. Apache Airflow[7]: We use airflow as a task executor. With airflow, we can determine which task will run before, after, or simultaneously by declaring DAG (Directed Acyclic Graph) without touching pythonic asynchronous programming too much.
5. Docker[8]: Docker is an open platform for developing, shipping, and running applications. Docker lets us separate our applications from our infrastructure to deliver software quickly. Moreover, we can manage our infrastructure the same way we collect our applications.
6. PostgreSQL[9]: We uses PostgreSQL to store the validation logging records and create user report. The logging module mainly involves the pre-defined class model (object with specific properties and methods) called logger, a log factory, and creating log records for the validation module. On the other hand, PostgreSQL is an object-relational database system, which provides a good interface with the object environment from the backend and leads to better performance when working with an object-oriented model like logger than any other database management.

---

[4] https://ckan.org.
[5] https://www.schemacrawler.com.
[6] https://redis.io.
[7] https://airflow.apache.org.
[8] https://www.docker.com.
[9] https://www.postgresql.org.

3.3   System Architecture

The sequence diagram (Fig. 7 (left)) of the system is described as follows:

1. The user sends to system backup MySQL file
2. The system restores the MySQL database with the user's uploaded file
3. The system extracts schemas from the MySQL database
4. The system stores the extracted schemas in the MongoDB database
5. The system then fetches records from the MySQL database
6. The system converts the fetched records into MongoDB records
7. The system stores converted data in the MongoDB database
8. The system fetches MySQL data table-by-table
9. The system then finds indices within the fetched data from step 8 by α-*lightweight coreset* method table-by-table
10. The system fetches data from MySQL with the chosen indices from step 9
11. The system fetches data from MongoDB with the chosen indices
12. The system compares row by row the fetched data from step 10 and step 11
13. While processing step 12, the system writes a log record to the validation logs database (PostgreSQL)
14. The system loads backup data from MongoDB
15. The system fetches log records from the validation logs database
16. The system sends users a MongoDB backup file from step 14
17. The system sends users validation logs report from step 15

3.4   Data Conversion Process

The data conversion process is shown in Fig. 7 (right) and is implemented as follows:

1. First, the user uploads a MySQL backup file to CKAN UI.
2. The upload action triggers data conversion backend to the backup file.
3. The data conversion backend then restores the whole MySQL database with the downloaded file
4. The backend then uses SchemaCrawler to extract the schema from the restored MySQL database. The schema contains all database information such as table names, column names, column data types... Schema could be in various formats such as plain text, JSON, YAML, etc. We chose to extract schema in JSON format for convenience for later steps.
5. The extracted schema from step 4 is stored in the MongoDB database as a document named "_schema".
6. The backend system gets the list of table names from the schema. It iterates through each table name and fetches a chunk of records from the MySQL database (in this project, I set the chunk-size is to 1000 records).
7. After fetching a chunk of records, the backend system converts the MySQL records into MongoDB records with the below data type mapping table.

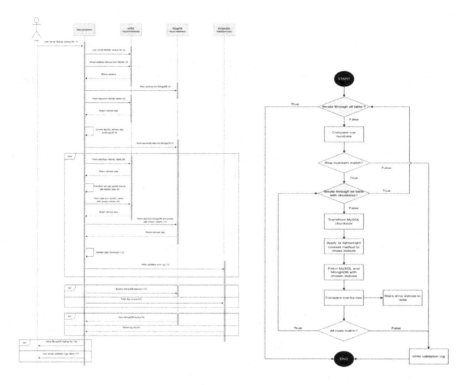

Fig. 7. Sequence Diagram (left) and Data Validation Process (right).

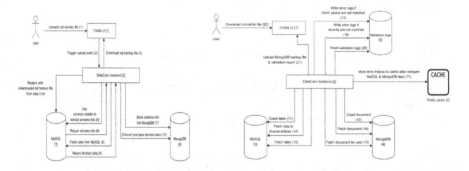

Fig. 8. Data Conversion Process (left) and Data Validation Process (right).

3.5   Data Validation Process

Formally, the usual way to implement the validation module is that we load the whole or parts of the dataset from the source database and its migrated counterpart from the target database into RAM, then compare them row by row to find errors then log error results into a report file and send to the user. However, this process will cost a lot of resources for big data sets. Instead, we just need to find the smaller subsets that still have all representative characteristics of the original dataset and then compare it row by row with its transformed counterpart from the target database.

So, the question is, how do we find the smaller subset that still has all representative characteristics of the original dataset? We will apply α-*lightweight coreset* to find the indices of the significant subset, look up both the source database (MySQL) and Target database (MongoDB) to get the corresponding records, and then compare those records with each other for the validation.

The validation process is shown in Fig. 8 (right) and is described as follows:

1. First, the system will get the list of MySQL table names from the schema. It will iterate through each table name.
2. The system counts the number of records in the specific table and the number of records in the corresponding MongoDB document and compares two values; if they are not matched: the system will write validation error logs to Validation logs data (PostgreSQL) and skip to next table if they are matched: the system will go to next step.
3. The system fetches a chunk of records (chunk-size: 1000 records) from the MySQL database and loads them into pandas data-frame.
4. The system transforms the fetched data frame into a whole new data-frame base on data types.
5. The system uses a newly transformed data frame to choose indices (apply α-*lightweight coreset* method). The number of indices to be chosen will be pre-determined by the user.
6. The system uses chosen index list from the previous step to fetch records from MongoDB and MySQL simultaneously.
7. The system compares the two fetched data sets from the previous step and write error indices to Redis with the corresponding table name as key.
8. The system also writes the validation error logs to Validation logs data (PostgreSQL).
9. After iterating through all chunks of records, the system will loop through the next table.
10. After iterating through all tables, the system will export the backup data from MongoDB and make a report (.xlsx file) from the validation logs database (PostgreSQL).
11. The system uploads MongoDB backup data and the report to CKAN UI.

Table 1. Experimental Data sets.

Table name	Total rows	Total columns	Description	Test type
Homer	20,000	18	Consisting of nearly all kinds of MySQL data types	General testing performance
Kierkegaard	34,000	7	Consisting of only *float*, *double* and *decimal* data types	Validating number data type performance
Nietzsche	18,000	11	Consisting of *varchar*, *char*, *test*, *varbinary*, *binary*, *blob*	Validating character and binary data type performance

Table 2. Experimental Results.

Error rate	Actual errors	Sample size	Uniform sampling average found errors	α-lightweight coresets average found errors
0.2%	4,000	2,000	398.54	376.53
0.2%	4,000	4,000	796.65	754.62
0.2%	4,000	6,000	1195.11	1129.91
0.25%	5,000	2,000	496.96	504.79
0.25%	5,000	4,000	993.22	1007.29
0.25%	5,000	6,000	1490.01	1510.35
0.3%	6,000	2,000	602.48	595.37
0.3%	6,000	4,000	1202.73	1191.8
0.3%	6,000	6,000	1802.76	1783.53

4 Evaluation

The performances of data conversion have shown some promising results in [6]. We focus on the data validation process in this evaluation by using the α-*lightweight coresets*. The experimental data sets[10] is described in Table 1.

The test shows how applying the α-*lightweight coresets* method could boost the validation process. Instead of checking all data rows, the system will choose the fraction of the whole dataset for the comparison; then, if there are errors, we can divide the number of mistakes by the sample percentage value to estimate the actual number of errors. The experiment will test whether or not the α-*lightweight coresets* method is better than the uniform random.

Below we describe how the experiment is conducted:

1. Create test data and insert them into MySQL. The data size for this test is fixed at 20,000 rows.

---

[10] These datasets can be accessed at https://www.kaggle.com/datasets/sanius/ckanext-mysql2mongodb.

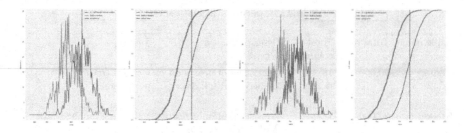

Fig. 9. Actual error = 4000 with sample size = 4000 (left) and sample size = 6000 (right).

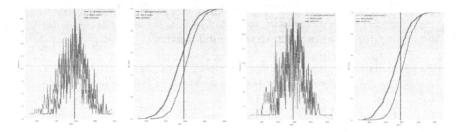

Fig. 10. Actual error = 5000 with sample size = 4000 (left) and sample size = 6000 (right).

2. Use the data conversion module of this project to convert MySQL data to MongoDB.
3. Corrupt MongoDB document by updating random data to different columns, the number of updated rows is the actual errors value, which is pre-determined by each experiment's iteration. In our experiment, the actual errors values are: 4,000 (0.2% of the whole data), 5,000 (0.25% of the whole data), and 6,000 (0.3% of the whole data).
4. Set the sample size (percentage of several indices to be chosen) to be in the range 0.1% to 0.3% of the whole data
5. Test for two cases (with random algorithm and with α-*lightweight coresets* algorithm) with each sample size value.
6. With each sample size and each algorithm, we run the test for 1000 times, log the number of found errors for each time. Test results include means, standard deviation, and variance based on the number of errors found.

The results are shown in Table 2 while Figs. 9, 10, 11 and 12 are illustrated the normal distribution of actual errors found in each scenario. As we can see, when comparing with uniform sampling random, in most cases, especially when the sample size value is low, the α-*lightweight coresets* algorithm can detect errors better.

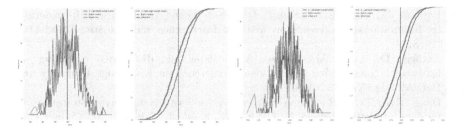

Fig. 11. Actual error = 6000 with sample size = 2000 (left) and sample size = 4000 (right).

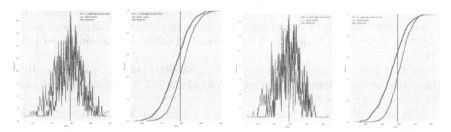

Fig. 12. Actual error = 6000 with sample size = 6000 (left) and sample size = 8000 (right).

5   Conclusions

In general, in this paper, based on the framework in [5] and using multiple supporting tools, we have implemented a complete data conversion system, especially for converting MySQL data to MongoDB data. Furthermore, by using the *α-lightweight coresets* algorithm [11], we proposed a fast and accurate method for the data validation process.

For future development, we will improve our system by decoupling the codebase by deprecating CKAN, separating the frontend and backend, then optimizing Apache Airflow and applying it as a task orchestrator instead of a task executor. Furthermore, we re-implement the codebase (backend) with asynchronous Python so that we could use modern asynchronous task executor frameworks such as Celery for the project, and we will extend our system with other database systems.

References

1. Agarwal, P.K., Procopiuc, C.M., Varadarajan, K.R.: Approximating extent measures of points. J. ACM (JACM) **51**(4), 606–635 (2004)
2. Bachem, O., Lucic, M., Krause, A.: Coresets for nonparametric estimation - the case of DP-means. In: International Conference on Machine Learning (ICML) (2015)

3. Bachem, O., Lucic, M., Lattanzi, S.: One-shot coresets: the case of k-clustering. In: International Conference on Artificial Intelligence and Statistics (AISTATS) (2018)
4. Bachem, O., Lucic, M., Krause, A.: Scalable and distributed clustering via lightweight coresets. In: International Conference on Knowledge Discovery and Data Mining (KDD) (2018)
5. Dang, T.K., Ta, M.H., Hoang Nguyen, L.: An elastic data conversion framework for data integration system. In: Dang, T.K., Küng, J., Takizawa, M., Chung, T.M. (eds.) FDSE 2020. CCIS, vol. 1306, pp. 35–50. Springer, Singapore (2020). https://doi.org/10.1007/978-981-33-4370-2_3
6. Dang, T.K., Ly, H.D., Ta, M.H., Hoang, N.L.: An elastic data conversion framework - a case study for MySQL and MongoDB. SN Comput. Sci. **2**, 4 (2021)
7. Feldman, D., Schmidt, M., Sohler, C.: Turning big data into tiny data: constant-size coresets for k-means, PCA and projective clustering. In: Symposium on Discrete Algorithms (SODA), Society for Industrial and Applied Mathematics pages 1434–1453 (2013)
8. Ivan, E., Claus, S., Michael, M., Soeren, A.: CSV2RDF: user-driven CSV to RDF mass conversion framework. In: Proceedings of the 9th International Conference on Semantic Systems (2013)
9. Har-Peled, S. Kushal, A.: Smaller coresets for k-median and k-means clustering. In: ACM Symposium on Computational Geometry (SoCG), pp. 126–134 (2005)
10. Hoang, N.L., Le, H.T., Dang, T.K.: A comparative study of the some methods used in constructing coresets for clustering large datasets. SN Comput. Sci. **1**, 215 (2020)
11. Hoang, N.L., Dang, T.K.: Alpha lightweight coreset for k-means clustering. In: The 16th International Conference on Ubiquitous Information Management and Communication (2022)
12. Hyeonjeong, L., Hoseok, J., Miyoung, S., Ohseok, K.: Developing a semi-automatic data conversion tool for Korean ecological data standardization. J. Ecol. Environ. **41**(11), 1–7 (2017)
13. Le, H.T., Hoang, N.L., Dang, T.K.: A farthest first traversal based sampling algorithm for k-clustering. In: The 14th International Conference on Ubiquitous Information Management and Communication (2020)
14. Lucic, M., Faulkner, M., Krause, A.: "training mixture models at scale via coresets. J. Mach. Learn. (JMLR) **18**, 5885–5909 (2017)
15. Luis, P., et al.: Interoperability: a data conversion framework to support energy simulation. Proceedings **1**(7), 695 (2017). ISSN: 2504-3900
16. Milan, V., Benjamin, B., Amil, G., Alois, Z.: Towards an integrated plant engineering process using a data conversion tool for AutomationML. In: IEEE International Conference on Industrial Technology, pp. 1205–1210 (2017)
17. Rocha, L., Vale, F., Cirilo, E., Barbosa, D., Mourão, F.: A framework for migrating relational datasets to NoSQL. Procedia Comput. Sci. **51**, 2593–2602 (2015)
18. Ros, F., Guillaume, S.: ProTraS: a probabilistic traversing sampling algorithm. Expert Syst. Appl. **105**, 65–76 (2018)
19. Ta, M.H., Dang, T.K., Hoang, N.L.: Intermediate data format for the elastic data conversion framework. In: The 15th International Conference on Ubiquitous Information Management and Communication (2021)

Content Selection Methods Using User Interest Prediction Based on Similarities of Web Activities

Takeshi Tsuchiya[1,2]([✉]), Rika Misawa[2], Ryuichi Mochizuki[2], Hiroo Hirose[2], Tetsuyasu Yamada[2], Yoshito Yamamoto[3], Hiroshi Ichikawa[4], and Quang Tran Minh[5,6]

[1] Institute for Data Science Education, Tokyo International University, Kawagoe, Japan
[2] Suwa University of Science, Nagano, Japan
ttsuchi@tiu.ac.jp, {tsuchiya,hirose}@rs.sus.ac.jp
[3] Tokyo University of Science, Shinjuku City, Japan
yama@rs.tus.ac.jp
[4] Otsuma Women's University, Chiyoda City, Japan
ichikawa.h@otsuma.ac.jp
[5] Faculty of Computer Science and Engineering, Ho Chi Minh City University of Technology, 268 Ly Thuong Kiet, District 10, Ho Chi Minh City, Vietnam
quangtran@hcmut.edu.vn
[6] Vietnam National University Ho Chi Minh City, Linh Trung Ward, Thu Duc District, Ho Chi Minh City, Vietnam

Abstract. This research predicts the current user's interests based on the characteristics of the user's recently acquired web activities and uses it for content selection. In conventional research, user interests are predicted using cookies for identifying individuals on a web service, and are obtained from the similarity of behavior patterns between current and previous users. In this case, the web advertising company can acquire information including personal information such as web activities, acquired contents on the web service, and inputted information.

The proposed approach analyzes the characteristics of web content acquired by users for each web service, constructs a combinable feature model named fog model, and then combines these models by adapting to the user's activities. The combined fog model can be considered a feature model learned from the characteristics of the user's interests. Then, from the candidate contents, the most likely content to be output from this fog model is chosen. Thus, information adapted to the user's interests can be selected and provided. The results of the evaluation to show that the proposed method is effective for approximately 57% users.

Keywords: Users' interest · Web targetting · Distributed learning

T. K. Dang et al. (Eds.): FDSE 2022, CCIS 1688, pp. 119–130, 2022.
https://doi.org/10.1007/978-981-19-8069-5_8

1 Introduction

Recently, web services have begun display web links and web advertisements with information relating to the displayed web content and the previously acquired information by the user. Users' data are not limited to a single web service domain but are collected and analyzed across several web domains, significantly improving the prediction accuracy of users' interest analysis [1].

User activity data include information related to the web activities of users, such as search words entering the web, contents leaving the web, time spent on web sites, and URLs of domains from which users enter and exit the web. Multiple sets of these data can be connected to obtain an overall understanding of the user's web activities, and they can be used as the target of analysis. Therefore, they contain highly private personal information that may be used to identify individuals and track the details of their web activities [2]. This information is acquired not only by the web service providers and users but also by third parties, such as web advertising companies, through the use of cookies. Third parties utilize the information for targeting advertising services and other purposes. Nevertheless, there are a certain number of malicious companies, and they may cause the leakage of personal information such as credit card information. Furthermore, the global trend is to protect highly private information in compliance with the General Data Protection Regulation, and third-party cookies are being eliminated [3].

Federated learning of cohorts (FLOC) [4] is currently proposed as a method to address the issue of user privacy. This method sends a user's browsing URL history via a browser and assigns a classification ID to each of the user's characteristic tendencies. As a result, it provides functions similar to conventional services, such as the distribution of web advertisements and the provision of interest information relevant to the classification's features. Nevertheless, this method collects information and send it to a third party that provides web browsers in the same way as the conventional method that uses cookies. This means that this method does not essentially solve the above problem.

This study does not use any user information acquired across web services by assigning cookies or session IDs. We propose a method for predicting interest based on the characteristics of information acquired from web content by users. The data are not transferred from one service to another, and combinable machine learning feature models named fog models are constructed and shared to indicate their features in the web service. To predict a user's interest, these fog models are combined according to the user's web activity to create a fog model that indicates the characteristics of the user's most recent interest information. The fog models are all converted into numerical values and exclude personal information, so we consider that private information is not a problem even if the fog models are shared among web services.

The authors have previously proposed a distributed machine learning platform for combining arbitrary fog models without accumulating training data [1]. The fog model can construct feature models with groups of nodes of arbitrary scales. Our approach in [1] shows that combining these fog models enables the use of machine learning-derived features without directly learning the data. Figure 1 shows an outline of the fog computing environment and the combined fog model in the previous research.

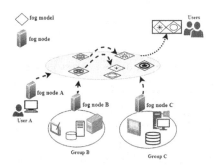

Fig. 1. Combination of distributed fog models.

2 Related Research and Approaches

This section describes related research and explains the approach take in this paper to address the research issues raised in related publications.

2.1 Related Research

Research [7] is a study that targets users' interest prediction similar way to this paper. Different from the current approach, this study collects the web activity logs of all users on a single server.

Particularly, this paper accumulates all web activities for each user. This enables the analysis of users' short-term interest information using the most recent data, as well as analysis of users' essential interests using data accumulated over a long-term period. This means that a flexible feature model can be constructed by varying the time covered by the data. However, the system is designed in such a way that users' personal data is managed on the memory network and accessible via application programing interfaces (APIs), meaning that historical information, including personal information, is shared among web services and users. As a result, it does not resolve the issues highlited in this paper.

A study [8] proposed a method for predicting users' interests based on their web activities, which is similar to the method proposed in this paper. The authors consider the user's activities as the surface expressions of the user's interest. Thus, it is shown to be possible to predict the essence of the user's interest by modeling the evolution of interest. In other words, data such as web activities are just the results provided by the interest and are used to demonstrate the

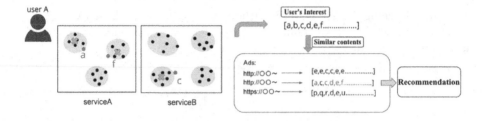

Fig. 2. Outline of user's interest prediction.

validity of the analysis. Since the evolutionary model is important, large-scale data acquisition itself does not occur, as in this paper and in [7]. The main focus is on the analysis of users' interests using the evolutionary model. Thus, in terms of approach and purpose, this method is positioned as different research from the proposed method. Furthermore, the effectiveness of the method can be discussed by comparing the results of our proposed method.

In addressing the issues of FLOC [4] described in Sect.1, Google has newly proposed 'Topics' [9]. It does not send the user's web activities, but the browser automatically extracts topics of interest from the user's activities. The extracted topics are limited to the user, web services, and web advertisements. This method is proposed to solve the current privacy issues by allowing users to choose whether to show or hide the topics they wish to share and by not displaying information on topics related to their privacy. Data analysis by the browser alone limits the extracted topic information to only the genres and classifications of the activities. Thus, the accuracy of analysis is limited compared to conventional methods that use web server activities and content. Our proposed method uses feature models trained on the same data as the conventional methods in the document, and it is expected to be more accurate.

2.2   Approach to Issues

Conventional research, including our approach in [1] calculates the similarity of a user's web activities and their characteristics to those of previous users. They are predicted based on these similarity patterns.

The method proposed in this paper focuses on the features of acquired contents from web services. Then, the features of the most recently acquired content are used to extract information about the user's current interests, and a similar content is selected. Specifically, users acquire the combinable feature model named fog model, which indicates the features of acquired content and combines these models based on their web activities to construct a fog model for each user. Then, using this model, the user can choose the content most similar to the user's interests, as shown in Fig. 2. The user data acquired by each web service is not shared with third-party services and users, and only the feature model using statistics derived from these data is shared.

3   Interest Prediction

This section first describes a method for constructing a fog model using the characteristics of the content acquired by the web service. Then, the user combines these models so that they are consistent across the user's web activities.

3.1   Features of Web Content

Current web services are composed of various contents, each with a different in scale. Thus, the users reach their target contents through search engines, hyperlinks from the main page, or external hyperlinks, depending on their interests and needs at the time. Each web content acquired by a user contains the user's interests.

Features of web content are determined by the included words; frequency of occurrence, location, and word order in the content text. In this paper, using the PV-DM of Doc2Vec [16], a natural language analysis method, is used for vectorization, and each feature is converted into a numerical value. From the similarity of the vectors, multiple clusters of web content can be formed for each web service, as shown in Fig. 3. Contents classified into the same cluster have similar characteristics to the contents acquired by the user, and users acquiring contents in the same cluster have similar interests.

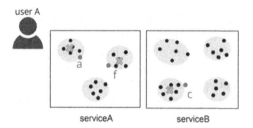

Fig. 3. Clusters in the web service.

3.2   Combination of Features

A fog model was constructed for each cluster. This model incorporates interest information acquired from web services by users. These models were combined using a method proposed in our previous research [1]. This study has clarified that combining multiple feature models (fog models) enables us to acquire the characteristics without directly learning the data, and it performs similarly to the conventional feature models learned from the accumulated data. Thus, it is expected that feature models including users' interest characteristics can be constructed by combining feature models without sharing data among web services.

The fog model in this paper uses word2vec to learn the frequency, location, and word order of words in the target text data [15], and constructs a fog model as a vector of higher dimensions for each cluster. Combining them entails averaging their dimensions, which are expressed as high-dimensional vectors. In other words, combining them necessitates that each dimension of the feature model has the same meaning. If each feature model exists in a different vector space, the averaging of dimensions by combining and comparison of dimensions among feature models is meaningless. As a result, it is necessary to use the same word statistics for the vectorization of web content without data accumulation. Feature models constructed using common statistical information can be combined. This feature model is combinable and is defined as a fog model in this research.

The same statistical information for text data is used in the construction of clusters. Because the statistical information is solely for contents in the same cluster, there was no need to consider the synchronization of the statistical information among clusters. The statistical information on words necessary for the construction of fog models contains all distributed data and must be used for all fog models. This paper prioritizes the convenience of implementation. Therefore, a word dictionary for constructing fog models is prepared in advance from web content and candidate web advertisements, and word statistics are generated as word corpus information from this information and shared among fog nodes.

3.3   Use of the Fog Model

The goal of our proposed method is to provide information and display the web content that is closest to the user's interests. In each case, the candidate contents most similar to the prediction are selected from the fog model that combined the user's web activities. For this purpose, candidate web content is also vectorized with the same dimensional space, and the same statistical information are used as clusters. The feature models are constructed using statistical information, assuming that each candidate web content is an output. The user's interests are selected on the basis of the similarity between the acquired feature model and the fog model constructed from the user's web activities. These are then displayed as web content and web advertisements.

4   Implementation

This section describes an implementation of the proposal method for displaying web advertisements. Table 1 shows the implementation.

4.1   Clustering of Web Contents Features

Each web service extracts and vectrorizes statistical information from all of its content. In this implementation, web content is analyzed using the PV-DM of Doc2Vec [16], and the contents are vectorized.

Table 1. Implementation.

Item	Specification
Platform	Python 3.9.3
Doc2Vec [16]	Gensim 3.8.3
X-means	Pyclustering 0.10.1.2
Machine learning tools	Scikit Learn 0.24.2

These vectors are clustered based on their similarity. The clustering is done using X-means [17]. The number of clusters cannot be estimated in advance since it is expected to vary greatly depending on the web content and the statistical information to be used. The use of X-means allow the number of clusters into some clusters that are appropriate for the web content depending on its characteristics. Newly added web content will belong to the cluster with the closest content.

Each divided cluster analyzes the content and constructs a feature model. The model was constructed using the occurrence information of words used as a dictionary and bag of words (BoW) [18]. This method does not consider the order of words. Furthermore, it is less accurate than the PV-DM described above. Nevertheless, clusters consisting of similar content already include the words indicating the features, so it can classify web content, and it is easy to construct fog models with lightweight processing. The method is used in the current implementation because it is feasible to classify web content. Using this method, a fog model is constructed for each cluster of web services as a unit. If there are performance issues, we can consider other methods.

4.2   Selection of Fog Models

Fog models constructed in clusters are acquired in tandem with the web activities of the target users. Then, these constructed models are combined. As this is an evaluation implementation, the constructed fog models are stored in the location specified for each web service. We intend to construct the system as a software infrastructure that can retrieve the models from arbitrary locations via an API.

5   Evaluation

The performance of the implemented proposed method in advertising targeting is compared with conventional methods using user data acquired from the current web service.

5.1   User Data

The data used for the evaluation are log data from targeted advertisements delivered by a certain web advertisement provider through multiple web services.

These data are derived through attribute analysis of the user's web activities and are delivered as web advertisements. Following that, click on it, which is regarded as data enabling them to determine whether the advertisements delivered matched the interests of the users and are appropriate.

Table 2 shows the details of the data. This evaluation targets 235 user data for which the web service activities can be retrieved and the web content is available, and it delivers web advertisements appropriate for each user. The word information used as a dictionary for the fog models in each cluster is constructed from approximately 2500 contents and more than hundred candidate web advertisements (cosmetics, fashion goods) in each cluster for delivery.

Table 2. Evaluation data.

Item	Specification
term	2021/06/06 – 2021/06/12
Type of data	Delivered & clicked advertisement
Active user	235
Number of prepared web services	About 500 services
Number of web contents per servie	Maximum 10000 web contents
Candidate of advertisement	800
Dictionary data	2500 contents and above ad

5.2 Evaluation Scenario

This evaluation applies the proposed method to the data shown in Table 2. The proposed method acquires and combines the fog models from the clusters belonging to each user's activities. The advertisements to be delivered to users are determined by the similarity between the fog model and the feature model, the outcome of which is a candidate web advertisement. The current implementation selects the top 10 advertisements with the highest similarity between the feature models.

Compared with the conventional method, the evaluation uses personal identification based on cookies [2]. The conventional method classifies user attributes (gender, age, orientation, etc.) based on web activities, and decides which advertisements to deliver. As mentioned above, the data are from the successful delivery of an advertisement by the conventional method (the delivered advertisements are clicked), and the effectiveness of the proposed method is demonstrated by evaluating its similarity to the web advertisement delivered. This evaluation focuses on the similarity between the advertisements selected using the proposed method and the delivered advertisements.

5.3   Results and Discussion

Figure 4 shows the results of the evaluation. The cos similarity between the top 10 web advertisements selected using the proposed method and those selected using the conventional method is evaluated. The graph shows the average of the similarity. The average cos similarity for the target users is 0.52, and the graph shows that most of the users fall within the range of $0.5 \leq$ cos similarity ≤ 0.8. Angle θ is the angle between two vectors, one proposed and one conventional. The value of θ is $36° < \theta$ and the value of $\theta \leq 60°$ can be obtained. Ideally, the angle θ should be close to $0°$, but the currently proposed method has a certain level of performance compared to the conventional method. Although insufficient, the proposed method shows the trend of content similarity. Furthermore, the proposed method does not identify individuals, which is currently under discussion; hence, it cannot improve the performance of the conventional method. Therefore, it will be critical to further improve the performance of the method to get closer to the conventional method.

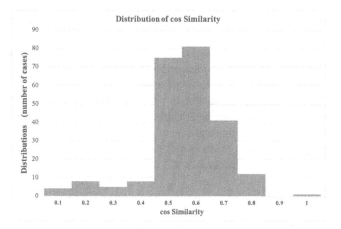

Fig. 4. Similarity of the proposed and current manner.

When checking individual cases, it is possible to observe both the cases where web advertisements are irrelevant to the user's web activities and the cases where the user's interests are precisely targeted. It is necessary to analyze what causes these cases. Currently, data with only one web service activity and data with only one cluster of web services are excluded as they are deemed incapable of appropriate evaluation. It is also possible that the BoW based fog model for each cluster can not detect content features due to the inadequacy of the word dictionary. These factors may have resulted in a significant performance decrease compared with the conventional method. Since there are individual cases in which appropriate web advertisements can be selected, the proposed method itself does not have a problem; rather, it depends on the cluster classification of web services and the performance of BoW based fog model. Therefore, it is necessary to analyze the contents of each web service and to have appropriate dictionary data for BoW. Although BoW is adopted in this paper because of implementation issues, it is necessary to consider other methods if sufficient performance cannot be obtained. In this case, we plan to consider using PV-BoW and PV-DM of Doc2Vec, which were partially used in this paper.

This evaluation does not cover a sufficient number of users. It is necessary to evaluate the generality of the proposed method by increasing the number of target users in the future.

5.4   Future Works

The web service content is updated daily, and target information is expanded daily. Additionally, the word dictionary used to construct the fog model will not only increase in terms of the word count but will also be frequently modified and revised. Thus, if the system is incapable of updating and learning additional information from the dictionary, it can not accomplish its goals before the method is used. In response to this problem, models, such as BERT [13] have been developed that employ a feature model that has been previously trained on a large amount of data, as well as additional training. This method targets a large amount of data in advance and does not require routine updating of information. In the future, we will consider using large amounts of data in advance to construct fog models. We will consider whether this method can handle frequent information updates and modifications.

The method proposed in this paper should be clustered by web service. It does not consider differences in the categories of web services or the confidentiality of information. In the future, it is necessary to have a flexible system that adapts to the characteristics of the information.

6   Conclusion

This paper proposed a method for predicting a user's interests from the acquired contents of web advertisements. We evaluated the proposed method for web advertisements. The evaluation results indicate that the proposed method is effective to a certain level. The proposed method does not require personal information, which is a recent issue. Thus, we believe it can be expected to be applied to real world applications with further performance improvement.

Acknowledgement. This research was partially supported by the Ministry of Education, Science, Sports and Culture, Grant-in Aid for Scientific Research (C), 2021–2023 21K11850, Takeshi TSUCHIYA.

References

1. Tsuchiya, T., Mochizuki, R., Hirose, H., Yamada, T., Koyanagi, K., Tran, M.Q.: Distributed Data Platform for Machine Learning Using the Fog Computing Model. SN Comput. Sci. 1(3), 164 (2020)

2. Bonomi, Flavio, Milito, Rodolfo, Natarajan, Preethi, Zhu, Jiang: Fog computing: a platform for internet of things and analytics. In: Bessis, Nik, Dobre, Ciprian (eds.) Big Data and Internet of Things: A Roadmap for Smart Environments. SCI, vol. 546, pp. 169–186. Springer, Cham (2014). https://doi.org/10.1007/978-3-319-05029-4_7

3. Laperdrix, P., Bielova, N., Baudry, B., Avoine, G.: Browser fingerprinting: a survey. CoRR arXiv:1905.01051 (2019)

4. https://github.com/WICG/floc

5. Mikolov, T., Chen, K., Corrado, G., Dean, J.: Efficient estimation of word representations in vector space. CoRR, Vol. abs/1301.3781 (2013)

6. McMahan, H.B., Moore, E., Ramage, D., Hampson, S., Arcas, B.A.: Communication-efficient learning of deep networks from decentralized data. In: Proceedings of the 20th International Conference on Artificial Intelligence and Statistics, JMLR: W&CP vol. 54, pp. 169–186 (2014)

7. Ren, K., et al.: Lifelong sequential modeling with personalized memorization for user response prediction. In: Proceedings 42nd International ACM SIGIR Conference on Research and Development in Information Retrieval, pp. 565–574 (2019)

8. Zhou, G., et al.: Deep interest evolution network for click-through rate prediction. In: AAAI (2019)

9. Topics API for Privacy Sandbox. https://blog.google/products/chrome/get-know-new-topics-api-privacy-sandbox/

10. Tsuchiya, Takeshi, Mochizuki, Ryuichi, Hirose, Hiroo, Yamada, Tetsuyasu, Koyanagi, Keiichi, Minh, Quang Tran: Selective combination and management of distributed machine learning models. In: Dang, Tran Khanh, Küng, Josef, Chung, Tai M.., Takizawa, Makoto (eds.) FDSE 2021. LNCS, vol. 13076, pp. 113–124. Springer, Cham (2021). https://doi.org/10.1007/978-3-030-91387-8_8

11. Bonomi, Flavio, Milito, Rodolfo, Natarajan, Preethi, Zhu, Jiang: Fog computing: a platform for internet of things and analytics. In: Bessis, Nik, Dobre, Ciprian (eds.) Big Data and Internet of Things: A Roadmap for Smart Environments. SCI, vol. 546, pp. 169–186. Springer, Cham (2014). https://doi.org/10.1007/978-3-319-05029-4_7

12. Guttman, A.:. R-trees: a dynamic index structure for spatial searching. In: ACM, vol. 14. no. 2 (1984)

13. Devlin, J., Chang, M.-W., Lee, K., Toutanova, K.: BERT: pre-training of deep bidirectional transformers for language understanding. arXiv:1810.04805 (2018)

14. Zhou, X., Huang, S., Zheng, Z.: RPD: a distance function between word embeddings. In: Proceedings of 58th The Association for Computational Linguistics, pp. 42–50 (2020)

15. Mikolov, T., Chen, K., Corrado, G., Dean, J.: Efficient estimation of word representations in vector space. CoRR, vol. abs/1301.3781 (2013)

16. Le, Q., Mikolov, T.: Distributed representations of sentences and documents. In: Proceedings of the 31st International Conference on Machine Learning. In: PMLR 32(2), 1188–1196 (2014)

17. Pelleg, D., Moore, A.: X-means: extending k-means with efficient estimation of the number of clusters. In: Proceedings of the Seventeenth International Conference on Machine Learning (ICML 2000). Accessed 16 Aug 2016

18. Harris, Z.S.: Distributional structure. Word 10(2–3), 146–162 (1954)

19. Agirre, E., Alfonseca, E., Hall, K., Kravalova, J., Paşca, M., Soroa, A.: A study on similarity and relatedness using distributional and wordnet-based approaches. In: Proceedings of Human Language Technologies: the North American Chapter of the Association for Computational Linguistics, pp. 19–27. Boulder (2009)

20. https://nodejs.org/en/
21. https://www.python.org/
22. https://radimrehurek.com/gensim/
23. Erickson, N., et al.: AutoGluon-tabular: robust and accurate AutoML for structured data. arXiv preprint arXiv:2003.06505 (2020)

ImageNet Challenging Classification with the Raspberry Pis: A Federated Learning Algorithm of Local Stochastic Gradient Descent Models

Thanh-Nghi Do[1,2]($\boxtimes$) and Minh-Thu Tran-Nguyen[1,2]

[1] College of Information Technology, Can Tho University, 92000 Cantho, Vietnam
{dtnghi,tnmthu}@ctu.edu.vn
[2] UMI UMMISCO 209 (IRD/UPMC), Sorbonne University, Pierre and Marie Curie University - Paris 6, Paris, France

Abstract. In this paper, we propose the federated learning algorithm of local stochastic gradient descent (SGD) models at edge devices (i.e. Raspberry Pis) to classify large ImageNet dataset having 1,281,167 images with 1,000 classes. The full very large training dataset is divided into subsets which are stored in local Raspberry Pis. And then, the federated learning algorithm uses Raspberry Pis to train in the incremental and parallel way local SGD models from their own subset without exchanging data. The incremental local SGD tailored on Raspberry Pi sequentially loads small data blocks of its own local training subset to learn local SGD models. In which, the local SGD algorithm uses $k$means to split the data block into k partitions and then it learns in the parallel way SGD models in each data partition to classify the data locally. The numerical test results on Imagenet dataset show that our federated learning algorithm of local SGD models with 4 Raspberry Pis (Broadcom BCM2711, Quad core Cortex-A72 (ARM v8) 64-bit SoC @ 1.5 GHz, 4 GB RAM) is faster than the state-of-the-art linear SVM run on a PC (Intel(R) Core i7–4790 CPU, 3.6 GHz, 4 cores, 32 GB RAM) with the competitive classification accuracy.

Keywords: ImageNet classification · Federated learning · Incremental local SGD · Raspberry Pi

1 Introduction

The most challenge in the computer vision community is the classification of ImageNet dataset [5,6] with more than 14 million images for 21,841 classes, due to the large scale number of images and classes. The efficient image classification algorithms allow to find what we are looking for in very large amount of images produced by internet users. The image classification task automatically categorizes the image into one of predefined classes. It consists of two key stages: the feature extraction and the machine learning scheme.

© The Author(s), under exclusive license to Springer Nature Singapore Pte Ltd. 2022
T. K. Dang et al. (Eds.): FDSE 2022, CCIS 1688, pp. 131–144, 2022.
https://doi.org/10.1007/978-981-19-8069-5_9

The classical approaches [1,7,9,12,13,25,33,37,42] proposed to use popular handcrafted features such as the scale-invariant feature transform (SIFT [26,27]), the bag-of-words model (BoW) and then to train Support Vector Machines (SVM [40]) to classify images. Recent convolutional neural networks (CNN [24]), deep neural networks including VGG19 [36], ResNet50 [17], Inception v3 [38], Xception [4], EfficientNet [39] aim to learn visual features from images and the classifier in an unified algorithm to efficiently classify images. These deep networks achieve the prediction correctness more over 70% for ImageNet challenging dataset.

For handling the classification task of ImageNet challenge, we propose to use the pre-trained deep learning network EfficientNet [39] without the top layer (i.e. softmax), to extract invariant features from images of ImageNet dataset. After that, we develop the new federated learning algorithm of local SGD models at the Raspberry Pis to classify ImageNet dataset. Firstly, the full very large training ImageNet dataset is divided into subsets which are stored in local Raspberry Pis. And then, the federated learning algorithm of local SGD models uses Raspberry Pis to train in the incremental and parallel way local SGD models from their own subset without exchanging data. To overcome the main memory limit, the incremental local SGD tailored on the Raspberry Pi sequentially loads small data blocks of local training subset to learn local SGD models. In which, the local SGD algorithm uses $k$means [28] to split the training data block into k data partitions and then it learns in the parallel way SGD models in each data partition to classify the data locally. The numerical test results on ImageNet dataset show that our federated learning algorithm of local SGD models with 4 Raspberry Pis (Broadcom BCM2711, Quad core Cortex-A72 (ARM v8) 64-bit SoC @ 1.5 GHz, 4 GB RAM) is faster than the state-of-the-art linear SVM such as LIBLINEAR [14] run on a PC (Intel(R) Core i7-4790 CPU, 3.6 GHz, 4 cores and 32 GB RAM) with the competitive classification accuracy. The federated learning algorithm of local SGD models on 4 Raspberry Pis takes 18 min to classify ImageNet dataset having 1,281,167 images in 1280 deep features into 1,000 classes with an accuracy of 88.07%.

The remainder of this paper is organized as follows. Section 2 briefly presents the federated learning algorithm of local SGD models. Section 3 shows the experimental results before conclusions and future works presented in Sect. 4.

2 Federated Learning of Local Stochastic Gradient Descent Models

Let us consider a classification task with the dataset $D = [X, Y]$ consisting of m datapoints $X = \{x_1, x_2, \ldots, x_m\}$ in the n-dimensional input space R^n, having corresponding labels $Y = \{y_1, y_2, \ldots, y_m\}$ being $\{cl_1, cl_2, \ldots, cl_p\}$.

2.1 Stochastic Gradient Descent

The stochastic gradient descent (SGD) algorithm tries to find p separating planes for p classes (denoted by normal vectors $w_1, w_2, \ldots, w_p \in R^n$) in which the plane w_i separates the class cl_i from the rest. This is accomplished through the unconstrained problem (1).

$$\min \ \Psi(w_p, [X, Y]) = \frac{\lambda}{2}\|w_p\|^2 + \frac{1}{m}\sum_{i=1}^{m} L(w_p, [x_i, y_i]) \tag{1}$$

where the errors are measured by $L(w_p, [x_i, y_i]) = max\{0, 1 - y_i(w_p.x_i)\}$ and a positive constant λ is to control the regularization strength ($\|w_p\|^2$).

Studies in [2,35] illustrate that the SGD algorithm solves the unconstrained problem (1) by updating w on T epochs with a learning rate η. For each epoch t, the SGD uses a single datapoint (x_i, y_i) randomly in the mini batch B_i to compute the sub-gradient $\nabla_t \Psi(w_p, [x_i, y_i])$ and update w_p as follows:

$$w_p = w_p - \eta \nabla_t \Psi(w_p, [x_i, y_i]) \tag{2}$$

The SGD is a simple yet efficient algorithm for large-scale learning due to the computational complexity corresponding to $O(mnp)$ (linear in the number of training datapoints m).

In recent last years, it rises powerful, low-cost embedded devices. For example, the Raspberry Pi 4 (Broadcom BCM2711, Quad core Cortex-A72 (ARM v8) 64-bit SoC @ 1.5 GHz, 4 GB RAM) is only 55 USD. This leads an increasingly popular choice for machine learning and IoT projects, as illustration in [21–23,30], image classification on IoT edge devices [29], MobileNet family tailored for Raspberry Pi [15], running AlexNet on Raspberry Pi [18].

Nevertheless, it is intractable to train the SGD models with the Raspberry Pi for ImageNet challenging problem having 1,281,167 images with 1,000 classes since it requires at least 16 GB RAM for loading the training dataset and the high computational cost.

Our federated learning algorithm of local SGD models at Raspberry Pis aims to reduce the training time and the required main memory for classifying such very large dataset ImageNet.

2.2 Federated Learning of Local SGD Models

The federated learning as illustrated in [20] is to train the decentralized machine learning model (e.g. deep neural networks) across multiple edge devices (e.g. smartphones or Internet of Things - IoT devices), while keeping the training data locally without exchanging data with other devices [16,19,43].

Our federated learning algorithm of local SGD models (denoted by FL-lSGD) uses Raspberry Pis to train the shared classification model. As showed in Fig. 1, the full training dataset is divided into v subsets which are locally stored in Raspberry Pis. The shared global classification model in the server includes

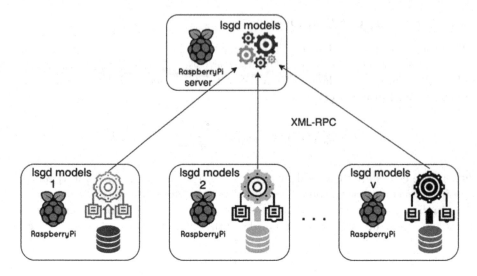

Fig. 1. Federated learning of local SGDs.

local SGD models which are learned from local training subset at the Raspberry Pi without exchanging training data. The communication used in the federated learning algorithm is XML-RPC protocol[1].

At the Raspberry Pi, our proposed local SGD algorithm (denoted by kSGD in Fig. 2) uses $k$means [28] to plit the training data block into k partitions and then it learns local SGD models in data partitions in parallel way on multi-core computers.

Algorithms 1 and 2 describe the k local SGD learning stage and prediction, respectively. *Code line 5* in Algorithm 1 parallelizes the training task of local SGD models with the shared-memory parallel programming in C on multi-core computers.

The k local SGD algorithm not only reduces the training complexity of the full SGD and but also allows to parallelize the training task of k local SGD models on multi-core computers.

Let us to illustrate the complexity of the k local SGD algorithm. Splitting the full training dataset with m datapoints in n dimensions and p classes into k balanced clusters leads the cluster size being about $\frac{m}{k}$ and the number of classes in a cluster scaling $\frac{p\omega}{k} < p$. The training complexity of a local SGD[2] is $O(\frac{m}{k}n\frac{p\omega}{k})$. Therefore, the complexity of parallel training k local SGD models on a P-core processor is $O(\frac{m}{Pk}\omega np)$. This illustrates that parallel learning k local SGD models is $\frac{Pk}{\omega}$ times faster than the global SGD training ($O(mnp)$).

---

[1] XML-RPC created in 1998 by Dave Winer of UserLand Software and Microsoft, is a remote procedure call (RPC) protocol which uses XML to encode its calls and HTTP protocol to exchange information between computers.

[2] It must be noted that the complexity does not include the minibatch k-means [34] used to partition the full dataset.

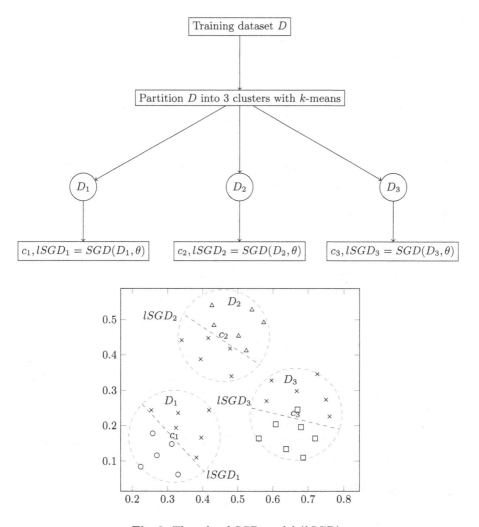

Fig. 2. Three local SGD model (kSGD).

Studies in [3, 10, 41] point out the trade-off between the capacity of the local learning algorithm and the complexity. The large value of k reduces significant training time of kSGD and making a very low generalization capacity. The small value of k improves the generalization capacity but also increasing the training time.

Algorithm 1: k local SGD algorithm (kSGD)

---

    input :
            training dataset D
            number of local models k
            parameters of SGD θ
    output:
            kSGD-model (k local SGD models)

1   **begin**
2   /*k-means performs the data clustering on D;*/
3   creating k clusters denoted by $D_1, D_2, \ldots, D_k$ and
4   their corresponding centers $c_1, c_2, \ldots, c_k$
5   #pragma omp parallel for
6   **for** $i \leftarrow 1$ **to** k **do**
7   /*learning a local SGD model from D_i;*/
8          $SGD_i = SGD(D_i, \theta)$
9   **end**
10   return kSGD-model $= \{(c_1, SGD_1), (c_2, SGD_2), \ldots, (c_k, SGD_k)\}$
11   **end**

To overcome the main memory limit of the Raspberry Pi, we propose to train local SGD models in the incremental fashion. The local training subset D tailored on the Raspberry Pi is split into T small blocks $\{D_1, D_2, \ldots, D_T\}$. The incremental local SGD (denoted by Inc-klSGD in Algorithm 3) sequentially loads data block D_t to learn local SGD models.

Finally, the federated learning algorithm collects via XML-RPC protocol vT local SGD models trained by Raspberry Pis to form the shared global classification model (denoted by FL-lSGD model $= \{kSGD_1, kSGD_2, \ldots, kSGD_{vT}\}$). The federated learning algorithm of local SGD models can be explained by training an ensemble of local SGD models.

The prediction of a new datapoint x (in Algorithm 4) is the majority vote among classification results $\hat{y}_1, \hat{y}_2, \ldots, \hat{y}_{vT}\}$ obtained by vT kSGD models.

3 Experimental Results

We are interested in the assessment of the federated learning algorithm of local SGD models (FL-lSGD) with the Raspberry Pis for classifying ImageNet challenging dataset. Therefore, it needs to evaluate the performance in terms of training time, demanded memory size and classification correctness.

Algorithm 2: Prediction of a new individual x with kSGD model

---

input :
> a new datapoint x
> kSGD-model $= \{(c_1, SGD_1), (c_2, SGD_2), \ldots, (c_k, SGD_k)\}$

output:
> predicted class $\hat{y}$

1 **begin**
2 | /* find the closest cluster based on the distance between x and cluster
   | centers $c_1, c_2, \ldots, c_k$ */
3 | $c_{NN} = \arg\min_c \ distance(x, c)$
4 | /* the class of x is predicted by the local SGD model SGD_{NN}
   | corresponding to c_{NN} */
5 | $\hat{y} = predict(x, SGD_{NN})$
6 | return predicted class $\hat{y}$
7 **end**

Algorithm 3: Incremental k local SGD (Inc-kSGD)

---

input :
> training dataset $D = \{D_1, D_2, \ldots, D_T\}$
> number of local models k
> parameters of SGD θ

output:
> inc-kSGD-model (ensemble of kSGD models)

1 **begin**
2 | **for** $t \leftarrow 1$ **to** T **do**
3 | | Loading data block D_t
4 | | $kSGD_t = kSGD(D_t, k, \theta)$
5 | **end**
6 | return inc-kSGD-model $= \{kSGD_1, kSGD_2, \ldots, kSGD_T\}$
7 **end**

Algorithm 4: Prediction of a new individual x with FL-lSGD model

---

    input :

        a new datapoint x

        FL-lSGD model $= \{kSGD_1, kSGD_2, \dots, kSGD_{vT}\}$

    output:

        predicted class $\hat{y}$

1 **begin**

2   **for** $t \leftarrow 1$ **to** vT **do**

3          $\hat{y}_t = predict(x, kSGD_t)$

4   **end**

5      $\hat{y} = $ majority-vote$\{\hat{y}_1, \hat{y}_2, \dots, \hat{y}_{vT}\}$

6   return predicted class $\hat{y}$

7 **end**

3.1 Software Programs

We implemented the FL-lSGD in Python using library Scikit-learn [32]. The full SGD algorithm is already implemented in Scikit-learn. We would like to compare with the best state-of-the-art linear SVM algorithm, LIBLINEAR [14] implemented in C/C++ (the parallel version on multi-core computers with OpenMP [31]) and the full SGD algorithm.

Our FL-lSGD algorithm trains the ensemble of local SGD models with 4 Raspberry Pis (RPis) Raspbian Bulleyes, Broadcom BCM2711, Quad core Cortex-A72 (ARM v8) 64-bit SoC @ 1.5 GHz, 4 GB RAM. LIBLINEAR, full SGD learn classification models on a machine (PC) Linux Fedora 32, Intel(R) Core i7–4790 CPU, 3.6 GHz, 4 cores and 32 GB main memory.

3.2 ImageNet Challenging Dataset

Experimental results are evaluated on ImageNet challenging ILSVRC2012 dataset [5,6] with 1,281,167 images and 1,000 classes which is the most popular visual classification benchmark [4–9,11–13,17,36,38,42].

We propose to use pre-trained EfficientNet [39] described in Fig. 3 to extract 1,280 invariant features from images (getting the last **GA pool** layer).

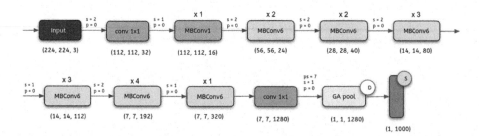

Fig. 3. Architecture of EfficientNet.

ImageNet dataset is randomly divided into training set (1,024,933 images) and testing set (256,234 images) with random guess 0.1% due to 1,000 classes.

3.3   Tuning Parameter

For training linear SVM models, it needs to tune the positive constant C in SVM algorithms for keeping the trade-off between the margin size and the errors. We use the cross-validation (hold-out) protocol to find-out the best value $C = 100,000$. LIBLINEAR uses L2-regularized Logistic Regression that is very closed to the softmax classifier used in deep learning networks, i.e. EfficientNet [39].

For the federated learning of local SGD models (FL-lSGD), the full training dataset is divided into 4 subsets which are stored in 4 Raspberry Pis. Therefore, a Raspberry Pi contains 256,233 images. Furthermore, the local SGD algorithm at the Raspberry Pi trains local SGD models in the incremental fashion with the training block size being 128,116. The Raspberry Pi needs about 1 GB RAM for learning local SGD models.

The parameter k local SGD models (number of clusters) of kSGD is set to 300 so that each cluster has about 500 datapoints. The idea gives a trade-off between the generalization capacity and the computational cost. Furthermore, the number of epochs and learning rate eta of SGD are 50 and 0.0001, respectively.

Due to the Raspberry Pi 4 (Broadcom BCM2711, Quad core Cortex-A72) and the PC (Intel(R) Core i7-4790 CPU, 4 cores) used in the experimental setup, the number of threads is setting to 8 for all training tasks.

3.4   Classification Results

We obtain classification results of FL-lSVM, kSVM and LIBLINEAR in Table 1, Figs. 4 and 5. The fastest training algorithm is in bold-faced and the second one is in italic. The same presentation format is accorded to performance in terms of classification accuracy, demanded memory size.

Given the differences in implementation, including the programming language (C++ versus Python), computer (PC Intel(R) Core i7-4790 CPU, 4 cores, 32 GB RAM versus Raspberry Pi 4 Broadcom BCM2711, Quad core Cortex-A72, 4 GB RAM), the comparison of training time is not really fair. But our FL-lSGD algorithm achieves interesting results.

Table 1. Overall classification accuracy.

No.	Algorithm	Language	Machine	Required memsize (GB)	Time (min)	Accuracy (%)
1	FL-lSGD	Python	4 RPis	1	**18.01**	88.07
2	Full-SGD	Python	PC	*20*	*151.30*	**88.81**
3	LIBLINEAR	C/C++	PC	*20*	2,980.25	*88.21*

Our FL-*l*SGD with 4 Raspberry Pis classifies ImageNet dataset in 18.01 minutes with 88.07% accuracy. The full SGD using the PC achieves 88.81% accuracy with 151.30 minutes in the training time. LIBLINEAR with the PC takes 2,980.25 minutes for training the classification model with 88.21% accuracy.

In the comparison of training time among algorithms, we can see that the FL-*l*SGD with 4 Raspberry Pis is fastest training algorithm. Our FL-*l*SGD with 4 Raspberry Pis is 165.57, 4.68 times faster than LIBLINEAR and the full SGD with the PC, respectively. The full SGD is 19.70 times faster than LIBLINEAR.

In term of demanded memory size, the FL-*l*SGD training algorithm requires about 1 GB RAM against at least 20 GB RAM being used by the full SGD and LIBLINEAR.

In terms of overall accuracy, the full SGD achieves the highest accuracy of 88.81%. Followed which LIBLINEAR gives the accuracy of 88.21%. The FL-*l*SGD has the competitive classification correctness of 88.07%. The comparison, algorithm by algorithm, shows that the superiority of LIBLINEAR and the full SGD on FL-*l*SGD corresponds to 0.14% and 0.74%, respectively.

The good performance of FL-*l*SGD algorithm is achieved by reducing the training complexity, the required main memory and parallelizing the training task of k local SGD models on multi-core computers.

The classification results show that our FL-*l*SGD algorithm is efficient for handling such large-scale multi-class datasets with Raspberry Pis.

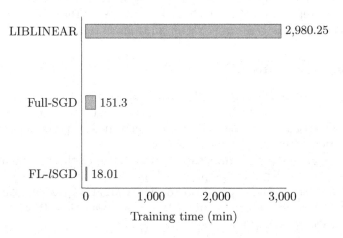

Fig. 4. Training time (min).

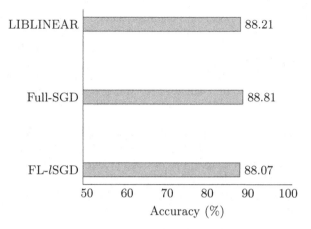

Fig. 5. Overall classification accuracy.

4   Conclusion and Future Works

We have presented the new federated learning algorithm of local SGDs, called FL-lGD at the Raspberry Pis to deal with ImageNet challenge having 1,281,167 images with 1,000 classes. An ensemble of local SGD models in FL-lSGD are learned from local training subset at the Raspberry Pi without exchanging training data. Furthermore, the algorithm sequentially loads small data blocks of the local training subset to learn local SGD models. In which, it splits the data block into k partitions using $k$means algorithm and then it learns in the parallel way SGD models in each data partition to classify the data locally. The numerical test results on ImageNet challenging dataset show that our FL-lSGD algorithm with 4 Raspberry Pis is respectively 165.57 and 4.68 times faster than the state-of-the-art LIBLINEAR, the full SGD on the PC, with a competitive accuracy of 88.07%.

In the near future, we will develop the federated learning algorithms of local SGD models at various edge devices. In addition, we will study the weighted combination of local SGD models in the classification to improve the accuracy.

Acknowledgments. This work has received support from the College of Information Technology, Can Tho University. We would like to thank very much the Big Data and Mobile Computing Laboratory.

References

1. Bosch, A., Zisserman, A., Munoz, X.: Scene classification via pLSA. In: Proceedings of the European Conference on Computer Vision, pp. 517–530 (2006)
2. Bottou, L., Bousquet, O.: The tradeoffs of large scale learning. In: Platt, J., Koller, D., Singer, Y., Roweis, S. (eds.) Advances in Neural Information Processing Systems, vol. 20, pp. 161–168. NIPS Foundation. www.books.nips.cc (2008)

3. Bottou, L., Vapnik, V.: Local learning algorithms. Neural Comput. **4**(6), 888–900 (1992)
4. Chollet, F.: Xception: deep learning with depthwise separable convolutions. arXiv:1610.02357 (2016)
5. Deng, J., Berg, A.C., Li, K., Fei-Fei, L.: What does classifying more than 10,000 image categories tell us? In: Daniilidis, K., Maragos, P., Paragios, N. (eds.) ECCV 2010. LNCS, vol. 6315, pp. 71–84. Springer, Heidelberg (2010). https://doi.org/10.1007/978-3-642-15555-0_6
6. Deng, J., Dong, W., Socher, R., Li, L.J., Li, K., Li, F.F.: Imagenet: a large-scale hierarchical image database. In: IEEE Computer Society Conference on Computer Vision and Pattern Recognition, pp. 248–255 (2009)
7. Do, T.-N.: Parallel multiclass stochastic gradient descent algorithms for classifying million images with very-high-dimensional signatures into thousands classes. Vietnam J. Comput. Sci. **1**(2), 107–115 (2014). https://doi.org/10.1007/s40595-013-0013-2
8. Do, T.-N.: Multi-class bagged proximal support vector machines for the imageNet challenging problem. In: Dang, T.K., Küng, J., Chung, T.M., Takizawa, M. (eds.) FDSE 2021. LNCS, vol. 13076, pp. 99–112. Springer, Cham (2021). https://doi.org/10.1007/978-3-030-91387-8_7
9. Do, T., Poulet, F.: Parallel multiclass logistic regression for classifying large scale image datasets. In: Advanced Computational Methods for Knowledge Engineering - Proceedings of 3rd International Conference on Computer Science, Applied Mathematics and Applications - ICCSAMA 2015, Metz, France, 11–13 May 2015, pp. 255–266 (2015)
10. Do, T.-N., Poulet, F.: Parallel learning of local SVM algorithms for classifying large datasets. In: Hameurlain, A., Küng, J., Wagner, R., Dang, T.K., Thoai, N. (eds.) Transactions on Large-Scale Data- and Knowledge-Centered Systems XXXI. LNCS, vol. 10140, pp. 67–93. Springer, Heidelberg (2017). https://doi.org/10.1007/978-3-662-54173-9_4
11. Do, T.-N., Le Thi, H.A.: Training support vector machines for dealing with the imageNet challenging problem. In: Le Thi, H.A., Pham Dinh, T., Le, H.M. (eds.) MCO 2021. LNNS, vol. 363, pp. 235–246. Springer, Cham (2022). https://doi.org/10.1007/978-3-030-92666-3_20
12. Do, T., Tran-Nguyen, M.: Incremental parallel support vector machines for classifying large-scale multi-class image datasets. In: Future Data and Security Engineering - Third International Conference, FDSE 2016, Can Tho City, Vietnam, 23–25 Nov 2016, Proceedings, pp. 20–39 (2016)
13. Doan, T., Do, T., Poulet, F.: Large scale classifiers for visual classification tasks. Multimedia Tools Appl. **74**(4), 1199–1224 (2015)
14. Fan, R.E., Chang, K.W., Hsieh, C.J., Wang, X.R., Lin, C.J.: LIBLINEAR: a library for large linear classification. J. Mach. Learn. Res. **9**(4), 1871–1874 (2008)
15. Glegola, W., Karpus, A., Przybylek, A.: Mobilenet family tailored for raspberry pi. In: Watróbski, J., Salabun, W., Toro, C., Zanni-Merk, C., Howlett, R.J., Jain, L.C. (eds.) Knowledge-Based and Intelligent Information & Engineering Systems: Proceedings of the 25th International Conference KES-2021, Virtual Event / Szczecin, Poland, 8–10 Sept 2021. Procedia Computer Science, vol. 192, pp. 2249–2258. Elsevier (2021)
16. He, C., Annavaram, M., Avestimehr, S.: Group knowledge transfer: federated learning of large CNNs at the edge. In: Larochelle, H., Ranzato, M., Hadsell, R., Balcan, M., Lin, H. (eds.) Advances in Neural Information Processing Systems 33: Annual

Conference on Neural Information Processing Systems 2020, NeurIPS 2020, 6–12 Dec 2020, virtual (2020)

17. He, K., Zhang, X., Ren, S., Sun, J.: Deep residual learning for image recognition. arXiv:1512.03385 (2015)

18. Iodice, G.M.: Running alexNet on raspberry pi with compute library (2018)

19. Kairouz, P., et al.: Advances and open problems in federated learning. Found. Trends Mach. Learn. **14**(1–2), 1–210 (2021)

20. Konečný, J., McMahan, B., Ramage, D.: Federated optimization: distributed optimization beyond the datacenter. arXiv:1511.03575 (2015)

21. Koul, A., Ganju, S., Kasam, M.: Practical Deep Learning for Cloud, Mobile, and Edge. O'Reilly Media Inc, CA, USA (2019)

22. Kulkarni, S.A., Gurupur, V.P., Fernandes, S.L.: Introduction to IoT with Machine Learning and Image Processing using Raspberry Pi. Chapman and Hall/CRC, NY, USA (2020)

23. Kurniawan, A.: IoT Projects with NVIDIA Jetson Nano. Apress, Berkeley, CA (2021). https://doi.org/10.1007/978-1-4842-6452-2

24. LeCun, Y., Bottou, L., Bengio, Y., Haffner, P.: Gradient-based learning applied to document recognition. In: Proceedings of the IEEE, vol. 86, pp. 2278–2324 (1998)

25. Li, F., Perona, P.: A bayesian hierarchical model for learning natural scene categories. In: 2005 IEEE Computer Society Conference on Computer Vision and Pattern Recognition (CVPR 2005), 20–26 June 2005, San Diego, CA, USA. pp. 524–531 (2005)

26. Lowe, D.: Object recognition from local scale invariant features. In: Proceedings of the 7th International Conference on Computer Vision, pp. 1150–1157 (1999)

27. Lowe, D.: Distinctive image features from scale invariant keypoints. Int. J. Comput. Vis. **60**, 91–110 (2004). https://doi.org/10.1023/B:VISI.0000029664.99615.94

28. MacQueen, J.: Some methods for classification and analysis of multivariate observations. Berkeley Symp. Math. Statist. Prob. Univ. California Press **1**, 281–297 (1967)

29. Magid, S.A., Petrini, F., Dezfouli, B.: Image classification on IoT edge devices: profiling and modeling. Clust. Comput. **23**(2), 1025–1043 (2020)

30. Norris, D.J.: Machine Learning with the Raspberry Pi. Apress, Berkeley, CA (2020). https://doi.org/10.1007/978-1-4842-5174-4

31. OpenMP Architecture Review Board: OpenMP application program interface version 3.0 (2008). www.openmp.org/mp-documents/spec30.pdf

32. Pedregosa, F., et al.: Scikit-learn: machine learning in Python. J. Mach. Learn. Res. **12**, 2825–2830 (2011)

33. Perronnin, F., Sánchez, J., Liu, Y.: Large-scale image categorization with explicit data embedding. In: IEEE Computer Society Conference on Computer Vision and Pattern Recognition, pp. 2297–2304 (2010)

34. Sculley, D.: Web-scale k-means clustering. In: Proceedings of the 19th International Conference on World Wide Web. p. 1177–1178. WWW 2010, Association for Computing Machinery, New York, NY, USA (2010). https://doi.org/10.1145/1772690.1772862

35. Shalev-Shwartz, S., Singer, Y., Srebro, N.: Pegasos: Primal estimated sub-gradient solver for SVM. In: Proceedings of the Twenty-Fourth International Conference Machine Learning, pp. 807–814. ACM (2007)

36. Simonyan, K., Zisserman, A.: Very deep convolutional networks for large-scale image recognition. arXiv:1409.1556 (2014)

37. Sivic, J., Zisserman, A.: Video google: a text retrieval approach to object matching in videos. In: 9th IEEE International Conference on Computer Vision (ICCV 2003), 14–17 October 2003, Nice, France, pp. 1470–1477 (2003)
38. Szegedy, C., Vanhoucke, V., Ioffe, S., Shlens, J., Wojna, Z.: Rethinking the inception architecture for computer vision. arXiv:1512.00567 (2015)
39. Tan, M., Le, Q.V.: Efficientnetv2: smaller models and faster training (2021)
40. Vapnik, V.N.: The Nature of Statistical Learning Theory. Springer-Verlag (1995). https://doi.org/10.1007/978-1-4757-3264-1
41. Vapnik, V., Bottou, L.: Local algorithms for pattern recognition and dependencies estimation. Neural Comput. 5(6), 893–909 (1993)
42. Wu, J.: Power mean SVM for large scale visual classification. In: IEEE Computer Society Conference on Computer Vision and Pattern Recognition, pp. 2344–2351 (2012)
43. Zhang, T., Gao, L., He, C., Zhang, M., Krishnamachari, B., Avestimehr, A.S.: Federated learning for the internet of things: applications, challenges, and opportunities. IEEE Internet Things Mag. 5(1), 24–29 (2022)

Covid-19 Detection Based on Lung Lesion Signs in Big Data Processing Environment

Thuong-Cang Phan[1](✉)[iD], Anh-Cang Phan[2][iD], Thi-Kim-Ngan Tran[2], and Thanh-Ngoan Trieu[1,3][iD]

[1] Can Tho University, Can Tho city, Vietnam
{ptcang,ttngoan}@cit.ctu.edu.vn
[2] Vinh Long University Of Technology Education,
Vinh Long, Vinh Long province, Vietnam
{cangpa,nganttk}@vlute.edu.vn
[3] University of Brest, Brest, France

Abstract. The world is going through a global health crisis known as the Covid-19 pandemic. Currently, the outbreak is still evolving in a complicated way with a high spreading speed and new variants appearing constantly. RT-PCR test is preferred to test a patient infected with Covid-19. However, this method depends on many factors such as the time of specimen collection and preservation procedure. The cost to perform the RT-PCR test is quite high and requires a system of specialized machinery for sample analysis. Using deep learning techniques on medial images provides promising results with high accuracy with recent technological advancements. In this study, we propose a deep learning method based on CasCade R-CNN ResNet-101 and CasCade R-CNN EfficientNet in a big data processing environment that accelerates the detection of Covid-19 infections on chest X-rays. Chest X-ray can quickly be performed in most medical facilities and provides important information in detecting suspected Covid-19 cases in an inexpensive way. Experimental results show that the classification of lung lesions infected with Covid-19 has an accuracy of 96% and mAP of 99%. This method effectively supports doctors to have more basis to identify patients infected with Covid-19 for timely treatment.

Keywords: Covid-19 · Lung lesions · X-rays · ResNet-101 · EfficientNet · Cascade R-CNN

1 Introduction

Since December 2019, SARS-CoV-2 is a new strain of coronavirus that has been identified as the cause of an acute respiratory infection epidemic namely Covid-19 in Wuhan (Hubei, China) [8]. On March 11, 2020, the World Health Organization declared Covid-19 a global pandemic. Patients with Covid-19 have diverse

T. K. Dang et al. (Eds.): FDSE 2022, CCIS 1688, pp. 145–160, 2022.
https://doi.org/10.1007/978-981-19-8069-5_10

clinical manifestations and complications such as pneumonia, respiratory failure, acute respiratory distress syndrome, and multiple organ failure. With a huge amount of infected people, it is necessary to build a tool to support rapid disease diagnosis for doctors. X-ray imaging equipment is easily available in most hospitals and it can be used as an important diagnostic tool for Covid-19. Doctors give the prescription to take chest X-rays of suspected patients being infected with Covid-19. Based on the X-rays received, doctors will detect the initial signs of suspected cases of infection. However, the X-rays of Covid-19 are similar to the X-rays of other viral pneumonia, thus it is difficult to distinguish patients with Covid-19 from patients with other viral pneumonia. Therefore, the application of deep learning techniques in the analysis and identification of medical images with high reliability will assist doctors in quickly diagnosing Covid-19 in high workload conditions.

Ramsey M. Wehbe et al. [16] presented DeepCOVID-XR, a deep learning AI algorithm, to detect Covid-19 by analyzing frontal chest radiographs. It is an ensemble of convolutional neural networks developed for the detection of Covid-19 on chest X-rays. The testing dataset included 2,214 images (1,192 of Covid-19 positive) from a single hold-out institution. The results showed that DeepCOVID-XR provided an accuracy of 83% with an AUC (Area under the ROC Curve) of 0.9. Amit Kumar Das et al. [6] proposed a deep neural network-based solution that can detect Covid-19 patients using chest X-rays. The three models used in this study are DenseNet201, ResNet50-V2, and Inception-V3. The dataset includes 538 images of Covid-19 patients and 468 images of non-Covid-19 patients. This proposed approach gave a classification accuracy of 91.62%. Saleh Albahli and Waleed Albattah [1] developed automated models for early detection of Covid-19 on chest X-ray images using InceptionNet-V3, Inception-ResNetV2, and NASNetlarge. The results showed that the InceptionNet-V3 gave the highest accuracy of 98.63% (with data augmentation) and 99.02% (without data augmentation). Duran-Lopez et al. [7] proposed to diagnose and locate Covid-19 in chest X-ray images using a custom CNN to extract relevant features and distinguish between Covid-19 and normal cases. The experiments were conducted with a 5-fold cross-validation scheme achieving an average accuracy of 94.43% and an AUC of 0.988. Gonçalo Marques et al. [12] proposed to use EfficientNet architecture and 10-fold stratified cross-validation for classification using images from Covid-19, pneumonia, and normal patients. The results show an average precision value of 97.54% and an average recall value of 96.69%. The F1-score for this multi-class classification was 97.11%. Ali Abbasian Ardakani et al. [3] proposed a method to diagnose Covid-19 using computed tomography images. The study used ten complex neural networks to identify Covid-19 infections. Out of all ten convolutional neural networks, the best performing was ResNet-101 and Xception. ResNet-101 and Xception were able to distinguish Covid-19 from non-Covid-19 cases with an AUC of 0.994. However, the sensitivity of ResNet-101 was 100%. It can be considered a highly sensitive model for Covid-19 diagnosis.

These related works detect Covid-19 from X-ray or CT images using deep learning models. However, to the best of our knowledge, there is not any study considering the training and testing time of the models in a parallel and distributed environment. The processing time is necessary to be considered since the analysis and identification of medical images need to support doctors in high workload conditions in a fast manner. In this study, we propose a deep learning algorithm based on CasCade R-CNN with the backbones of ResNet-101 and EfficientNet in a big data processing environment that accelerates the detection of Covid-19 infections based on chest X-rays. Chest X-ray can quickly be performed in most medical facilities and provides important information in detecting suspected Covid-19 cases in an inexpensive way. We provide the experimental results to compare, evaluate the accuracy, loss, and training time of the network models of four scenarios on a single-computer processing environment and on a distributed environment. The rest of the paper is presented as follows. Section 2 presents the basic theoretical background used in this study. Section 3 details the proposed method using deep neural networks for the detection of Covid-19 disease. Section 4 presents the experiments and evaluates the experimental results. Finally, we draw conclusions in Sect. 5.

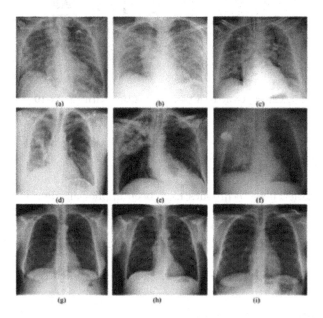

Fig. 1. Chest X-rays with COVID-19 infection (a-c), Chest X-rays with pneumonia (d-f), Normal chest X-rays (g-i) [5].

2   Background

2.1   Covid-19 Lung Damage on X-rays

Chest X-ray images are often prescribed to diagnose lung lesions. Figure 1 presents chest radiographs of Covid-19, pneumonia, and normal patients. The typical lung damage caused by Covid-19 that can be seen on X-rays is multi-focal bilateral, peripheral opacities with rounded morphology and lower lung-predominant distribution [11]. The indeterminate appearance of Covid-19 on chest X-rays is lung damage unilateral, central, or upper lung predominant distribution with the absence of typical findings. The atypical appearance of Covid-19 is pneumothorax or pleural effusion, pulmonary edema, lobar consolidation, solitary lung nodule, or mass diffuse tiny nodules.

Figure 2 presents chest radiographs of an elderly male patient from Wuhan, China. These are the three chest radiographs selected from the daily chest radiographs of this patient. The consolidation in the lower right region on day 0 extended into day 4 with new consolidation changes in the right midzone periphery and perihilar region. This midzone change improved on day 7 radiographs.

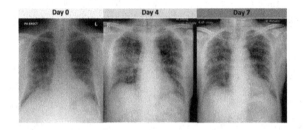

Fig. 2. Chest X-ray of a patient positive with Covid-19 [13].

2.2   Deep Neural Networks

Currently, deep learning techniques have been applied in almost all fields with outstanding advantages such as high accuracy and can be applied to different types of datasets. In this study, we use two deep neural networks, ResNet-101 and EfficientNet, for feature extraction and CasCade R-CNN for classification to detect the presence of lung infections on X-ray images. Detailed descriptions of network architectures and their advantages are presented below.

2.2.1   ResNet

ResNet [9] becomes the most commonly used architecture at the moment after winning the ImageNet Large Scale Visual Recognition Competition (ILSVRC 2015). The architecture needs fewer parameters but gives high efficiency by using skip connections. Skip connections keep information from being lost by connecting the previous layer to the next layer and skipping some intermediate layers. ResNet includes four different architectures, which are 34, 50, 101, and 152 layers. The ResNet-101 achieved quite good performance thus we chose to use ResNet-101 in our experiments. The architecture of ResNet-101 is presented in Fig 3.

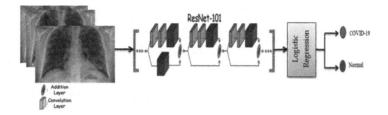

Fig. 3. ResNet-101 network architecture.

2.2.2 EfficientNet

The EfficientNet [15] was presented by Mingxing Tan and Quoc V. Le in the International Conference on Machine Learning, 2019. The authors studied model scaling and determined that a careful balance of depth, width, and resolution can lead to better performance. They proposed a scaling method that uniformly scales all dimensions using an effective compound coefficient, unlike conventional practice that arbitrarily scales these dimensions. The proposed method made sense since the depth of the networks and the number of channels needs to be suitable for the size of the input image. The EfficientNet architecture is presented in Fig. 4.

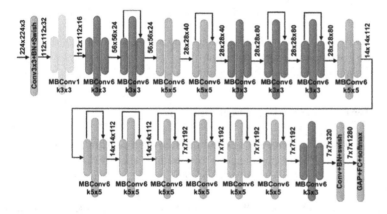

Fig. 4. EfficientNet network architecture [2].

2.2.3 Cascade R-CNN

Cascade R-CNN [4] is a multi-stage object detection architecture consisting of a sequence of detectors trained with increasing IoU thresholds. The detectors are trained stage by stage that the output of a detector is used for training the next detector. Resampling of progressively improved hypotheses minimizes the overfitting issue by ensuring that all detectors have a positive set of examples of equal size. The Cascade R-CNN architecture (Fig. 5) is motivated by the observation that the output IoU of a regressor is almost invariably better than the input IoU.

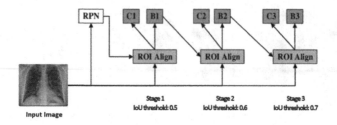

Fig. 5. Cascade R-CNN network architecture.

2.3   Evaluation Metrics

2.3.1   Loss Value

The loss value determines how much the prediction results differ from the actual labels to be predicted. This method measures the model performance that is low if the loss is high (the model does not do a good job) and vice versa. In this study, the binary cross entropy is used to calculate the loss value as presented in Eq. 1.

$$Loss = -\frac{1}{O} \sum_{i=1}^{O} y_i.log\hat{y}_i + (1 - y_i).log(1 - \hat{y}_i) \qquad (1)$$

where:

- $\hat{y}_i$: is the ith scalar value in the model output
- y_i: is the corresponding target value
- O: is the number of scalar values in the model output

2.3.2   Mean Average Precision (mAP)

Mean average precision (mAP) is a commonly used method in multi-class classification problems. This is a measure to evaluate the average accuracy over all classes of classification network models. The mAP measure is calculated after obtaining the AP (average precision). The AP (average precision) metric [14] is a measure of accuracy across all classes performing an 11-point interpolation to summarize the shape of the Precision x Recall curve.

2.3.3   AUC - Area Under the ROC Curve

The receiver operating characteristic curve (ROC) represents the classification performance of all classification thresholds. Basically, the curve plots two parameters, i.e., true positive rate and false positive rate. The area under the ROC curve (AUC) can be interpreted as the expected true positive rate averaged over all false positive rates ranging in values between 0 and 1 and the higher the AUC, the better the model is.

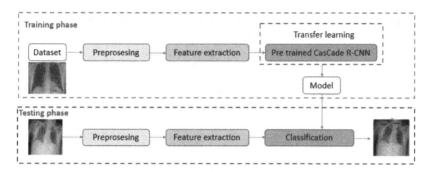

Fig. 6. Proposed model to detect Covid-19 based on lung lesions.

3   Proposed Method

The method of detecting lung injury caused by Covid-19 based on deep neural networks is implemented in a big data processing environment for fast and accurate diagnosis support. The general model of the proposed method is presented in Fig. 6. We use two deep neural networks, ResNet-101 and EfficientNet, for feature extraction and CasCade R-CNN for classification to detect the presence of lung infections on X-ray images. The CasCade R-CNN is pre-trained with the transfer learning approach to help the learning process faster and solve the problem of limiting training datasets.

In the pre-processing stage, we use cutout to randomly cut rectangular regions in the training images to reduce neuron activation by a certain amount. After using cutout, we use dropout to ignore some randomly selected neurons during the training process. The results after pre-processing are shown in Fig. 7.

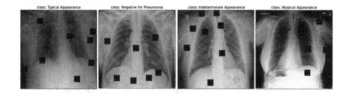

Fig. 7. Results after the pre-processing stage.

We proceed the training phase in a single computing node and on a Spark cluster to compare and evaluate the training time. Spark applications run as a collection of independent processes on a cluster, coordinated by the SparkContext in the driver program on the cluster manager (Fig. 8). The manager node is responsible for the configuration of the cluster, while the worker nodes perform the learning tasks submitted to them through a driver program along with an initial dataset. The manager computes the average weights to provide a global average parameter (W) of the network and the workers are responsible for training. Each worker updates its the local weights (W_i) to the manager and receives the average weights (W) when the averaging is executed.

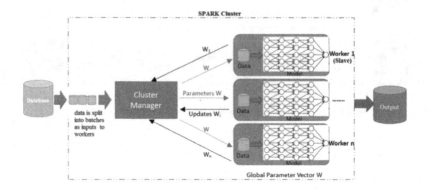

Fig. 8. Illustration of the training and extracting features in a Spark cluster.

The input dataset is divided into two parts (Train set 80% and test set 20%). In the Spark environment, feature vectors are extracted and converted into pipeline to prepare for the training process. Mini-batches from the pipeline are transferred to the computing workers. In each training step (epoch) the training parameters are synchronized to the parameter server through Data Shards. The parameter server aggregates and creates a central network model to evaluate the loss value, thereby adjusting the learning rate for the next learning step in the workers.

In the testing phase, the image after feature extraction will be passed through the trained model for automatic detection of lung lesions with bounding boxes and accuracy percentage.

4   Experiments

4.1   Dataset Description and Installation Environment

The SIIM-FISABIO-RSNA Covid-19 dataset [10] was curated by an international team of 22 radiologists consisting of 6,334 X-rays, with each case labeled as typical (3,007 images - 47%), indeterminate (1,736 images - 27%), atypical (1,108 images - 18%), and negative appearance of pneumonia (483 images - 8%). The dataset is divided into two subsets for training and testing with a ratio of 80:20. The experiments run on the same Kaggle environment with a computing configuration of 13 GB RAM and Tensor processing units TPU v3-8. The library that supports training network models is Keras.

The experiments will be conducted under two types of environment: single computing environment and parallel processing environment.

– **Single:** Processing in a single computer on Kaggle's platform with Xeon CPU, 16 GB RAM , and Nvidia Tesla P100 GPU. The library that supports network training is Tensorflow GPU 1.15.

– **Parallel:** Processing in a Spark cluster with one master and two workers. The master node has a configuration of CPU 4 GB 2 cores and the workers have a configuration of CPU 8 GB 2 cores. The library that supports network training is BigDL 0.12.

4.2 Scenarios and Parameters

We conduct the experiments with 4 scenarios and the training parameters as presented in Table 1. The suitable selection of model parameters plays an important role in helping the network models have high accuracy. The four scenarios allow us to evaluate the network models in 2 different processing environments. The input image size is 512×512px.

Table 1. Scenarios and the training parameters.

Sce	Environment	Training network	Feature extraction	Learning rate	Batch size	Num. classes	Num. steps	IoU
1	Single	CasCade R-CNN	EfficientNet	1e–4	18	4	50	0.5
2	Single	CasCade R-CNN	ResNet-101	1e–4	18	4	50	0.5
3	Parallel	CasCade R-CNN	EfficientNet	2.5e–4	4	4	50	0.5
4	Parallel	CasCade R-CNN	ResNet-101	2.5e–4	4	4	50	0.5

4.3 Results

The network models will be evaluated based on loss value, AUC, and mAP.

4.3.1 Loss Value

Figure 9 shows the loss values of the first two scenarios. As can be seen that in the first stage of the training process, the loss value tends to decrease rapidly and becomes stable in the next training steps. This shows that the extracted features are learned more effectively after a long training process. After 50 epochs, the loss is no longer improved, we stop the training process with the loss value of

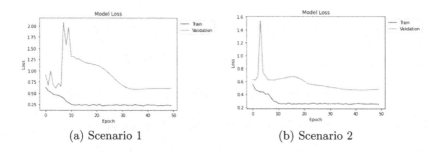

(a) Scenario 1   (b) Scenario 2

Fig. 9. Loss of scenarios 1 and 2.

scenarios 1 and 2 being 0.3276 and 0.2391, respectively. Thus, it can be concluded that the dataset in this study is more effective than the network model in scenario 2.

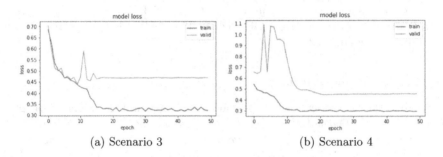

(a) Scenario 3   (b) Scenario 4

Fig. 10. Loss of scenarios 3 and 4 on a cluster of 2 workers.

Figure 10 shows the loss values of scenarios 3 and 4 on a Spark cluster of 2 workers, which are 0.3315 and 0.2951, respectively. As can be seen that the loss value of scenario 4 is smaller than that of scenario 3. The training process in a parallel computing environment will help to reduce the training time. However, when the number of workers increases, the loss value also increases. Scenario 3 has a loss value of 0.336 on a cluster of 8 workers and scenario 4 has a loss value of 0.3032 on the same cluster. This proves that when increasing the number of workers, the loss also increases, causing errors in the data synthesis process.

4.3.2   AUC

Figure 11 shows the performance of two scenarios 1 and 2 according to the AUC. As can be seen that in the first few steps of scenario 1, the AUC is lower than that of scenario 2, but in the later learning steps, both scenarios have an AUC of above 90%. The AUC of scenarios 1 and 2 are 0.9298 and 0.9689, respectively.

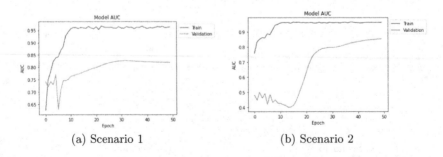

(a) Scenario 1   (b) Scenario 2

Fig. 11. AUC of scenarios 1 and 2.

Figure 12 shows the AUC of scenarios 3 and 4, respectively. The accuracy is unstable in the first 20 steps and then gradually improves in the next learning steps. The instability comes from unsuitable data and computation division in a cluster, leading to errors in the synthesis of training parameters. After a few training steps, the loss value and accuracy have gradually stabilized.

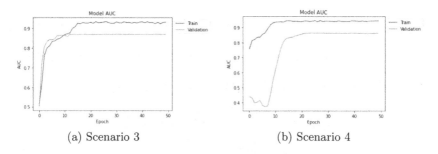

(a) Scenario 3   (b) Scenario 4

Fig. 12. AUC of scenarios 3 and 4 on a cluster of 2 workers.

The average AUC of the four scenarios is presented in Fig. 13. The AUC decreases when increasing the number of workers although the training time decreases. The EfficientNet model in scenario 3 has a lower AUC than that of ResNet-101 in scenario 4 but the value is relatively stable (almost unchanged with a different number of workers). The EfficientNet model in scenario 3 has a fewer number of layers and parameters thus when processing is distributed, the amount of input data decreases, which reduces the AUC. The ResNet-101 model in scenario4 has more layers and parameters than scenario 3. It helps the model in scenario 4 to have a higher AUC than that of scenario 3 and the AUC decreases when increasing the number of workers.

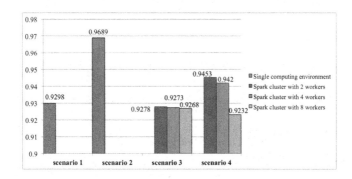

Fig. 13. Average AUC of four scenarios.

4.3.3   AP and mAP

Figure 14 is the AP values of the four scenarios on each class. The AP measures in scenarios 3 and 4 are lower than those in scenarios 1 and 2. The Typical appearance class has the highest AP compared to the other 3 classes. The Intermediate appearance class is the class with the lowest AP across all 4 scenarios.

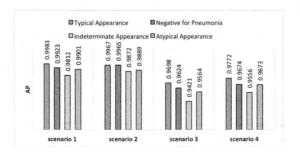

Fig. 14. AP of four scenarios on 4 classes.

The mAP values of the four scenarios are presented in Fig. 15. The mAP in scenarios 3 and 4 (parallel environment with 2 workers) are lower than those of scenarios 1 and 2 (single computer environment). The difference comes from errors arising in the process of transmitting and receiving data via the network in a computing cluster. It is inevitable that a packet transmits an error or erroneous data, which leads to the synthesis of training parameters or the creation of an intermediate network model that is not continuous, which takes more time for the synthesis process.

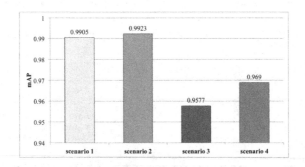

Fig. 15. mAP of four scenarios.

4.3.4   Training Time

The training time of the four scenarios is shown in Fig. 16. The EfficientNet model in scenario 1 has a much longer training time of 28,299 s than the ResNet-101 model in scenario 2 of 10,500 s. It is nearly 3 times longer than the training time of scenario 2. Although the ResNet-101 model in scenario 2 has more parameters than EfficientNet in scenario 1, it requires 2.3 times less memory and runs nearly 3 times faster on TPU and GPU. The number of parameters does not determine the memory consumption because memory is often governed by the size of the activations. The EfficientNet has large activations that cause more memory consumption.

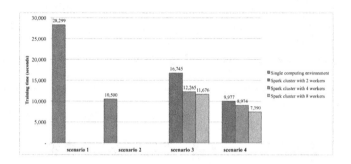

Fig. 16. Training time of four scenarios.

The training time of the network models has a large difference between a different numbers of workers (scenarios 3 and 4). In scenario 3, the training time is 32% faster on a cluster of 2 workers and 44% faster on a cluster of 4 workers in comparison with scenario 4. The parallel processing method in the Apache Spark environment provides faster training time, which proves the benefits of applying the parallel computing model.

4.3.5   Testing Time

Figure 17 is the processing time of the models on the test dataset in the Spark environment. A clear difference in the processing time can be seen between the Cascade R-CNN EfficientNet in scenario 3 and Cascade R-CNN ResNet-101 in scenario 4. The model in scenario 4 limits the Vanishing Gradient. If the number of epochs is too small, the network may not give good results. The training

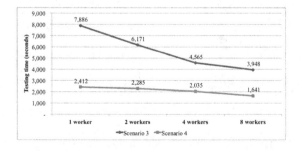

Fig. 17. Testing time of scenarios 3 and 4.

time will be long if the number of epochs is too big, leading to the problem of convergence and not getting good results. In addition, the network also increases the depth of layers to help extract more features.

4.3.6   Classification Results

The experimental dataset includes 1,263 images belonging to the SIIM-FISABIO-RSNA dataset, of which 583 images are labeled as Covid-19-infected. The accuracy of EfficientNet and ResNet-101 models in the testing phase are 0.9268 and 0.9420, respectively, with the average time for the test dataset being 5,643 s and 2,094 s. Figure 18 shows the illustrations of classification results using CasCade R-CNN.

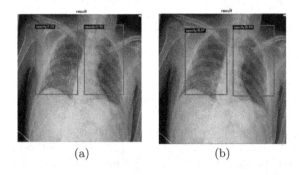

Fig. 18. Illustrations of classification results using Cascade R-CNN.

In these results, it is possible to localize the location of the lung-damaged areas, but it is not possible to determine the most severe area that needs to be treated. We applied GradCam heat map to reveal the most severe area of lung lesions. The illustration of GradCam heat map on X-rays is presented in Fig. 19.

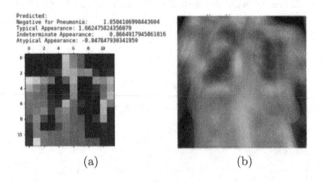

Fig. 19. Illustration of GradCam heat map on X-rays.

4.4   Comparison

We provide a comparison with some recent methods as shown in Table 2.

Table 2. Comparison with recent methods.

Authors	Method	Accuracy
Wehbe et al. [16]	DeepCOVID-XR: An Artificial Intelligence Algorithm to Detect Covid-19 on Chest Radiographs Trained and Tested on a Large U.S. Clinical Data Set	83%
Das et al. [6]	Automatic COVID-19 detection from X-ray images using ensemble learning with convolutional neural network	91.62%
Albahli and Albattah [1]	Detection of coronavirus disease from X-ray images using deep learning and transfer learning algorithms	98.63%
Duran-Lopez et al. [7]	COVID-XNet: A custom deep learning system to diagnose and locate COVID-19 in chest X-ray images	94.43%
Marques et al. [12]	Automated medical diagnosis of COVID-19 through EfficientNet convolutional neural network	96.69%
Ardakani et al. [3]	Application of deep learning technique to manage COVID-19 in routine clinical practice using CT images: Results of 10 convolutional neural networks	99.51%
Scenario 1	Cascade R-CNN EfficientNet on Single-computer environment	92.98%
Scenario 2	Cascade R-CNN ResNet-101 on Single-computer environment	96.89%
Scenario 3	Cascade R-CNN EfficientNet on Spark environment	92.68%
Scenario 4	Cascade R-CNN ResNet-101 on Spark environment	92.32%

5   Conclusion

Covid-19 is perhaps one of the most dangerous epidemics currently. The outbreak is still evolving in a complicated way with the appearance of new variants. RT-PCR test is prescribed to test a Covid-19 infected person but this method is costly. Thus, the use of chest X-rays can be a solution to help reducing cost and X-rays can quickly be performed in most medical facilities. In this work, we propose an approach using deep neural networks to detect the appearance of Covid-19 on chest X-rays in a big data processing environment that accelerates the detection. The method helps to classify the area of lung damage caused by Covid-19 to effectively support doctors in diagnosis. CasCade R-CNN is used in combination with two feature extraction models, EfficientNet and ResNet-101, in a single computing environment and parallel processing environment to compare and evaluate the suitable model for the problem. The experimental results provide high accuracy of 96% and an mAP of 99%. The CasCade R-CNN is pretrained to reuse the data features learned from other datasets. When processing in a cluster, an increase in the number of workers will cause an increase in the loss values and a reduction in the accuracy since the training parameter aggregation rise the error rate when working on many workers. However, it is inevitable that parallel computing saves processing time, especially in high-workload environments like hospitals. The processing in the Apache Spark environment reduces the training time by about 44% when working on a 4-worker cluster. The advantage of deploying large computational problems on Apache Spark is helping to save time on training, detecting, and localizing the injury area. The application of pre-trained CasCade R-CNN on public data sources increases the diagnostic and predictive performance of the model. This can effectively assist radiologists in diagnosing infected people in helping against the COVID-19 outbreak. The possible direction in the near future is to provide a survey on several effective networks for the problem of Covid-19 detection in particular and lung disease detection in general.

References

1. Albahli, S., Albattah, W.: Detection of coronavirus disease from x-ray images using deep learning and transfer learning algorithms. J. Xray Sci. Technol. **28**(5), 841–850 (2020)
2. Alhichri, H., Alswayed, A.S., Bazi, Y., Ammour, N., Alajlan, N.A.: Classification of remote sensing images using efficientnet-B3 CNN model with attention. IEEE access **9**, 14078–14094 (2021)
3. Ardakani, A.A., Kanafi, A.R., Acharya, U.R., Khadem, N., Mohammadi, A.: Application of deep learning technique to manage COVID-19 in routine clinical practice using CT images: results of 10 convolutional neural networks. Comput. Biol. Med. **121**, 103795 (2020)
4. Cai, Z., Vasconcelos, N.: Cascade R-CNN: delving into high quality object detection. In: Proceedings of the IEEE conference on computer vision and pattern recognition, pp. 6154–6162 (2018)
5. Chandra, T.B., Verma, K., Singh, B.K., Jain, D., Netam, S.S.: Coronavirus disease (COVID-19) detection in chest x-ray images using majority voting based classifier ensemble. Expert Syst. Appl. **165**, 113909 (2021)
6. Das, A.K., Ghosh, S., Thunder, S., Dutta, R., Agarwal, S., Chakrabarti, A.: Automatic COVID-19 detection from x-ray images using ensemble learning with convolutional neural network. Pattern Anal. Appl. **24**(3), 1111–1124 (2021)
7. Duran-Lopez, L., Dominguez-Morales, J.P., Corral-Jaime, J., Vicente-Diaz, S., Linares-Barranco, A.: COVID-XNet: a custom deep learning system to diagnose and locate COVID-19 in chest x-ray images. Appl. Sci. **10**(16), 5683 (2020)
8. Guan, W.J., et al.: Clinical characteristics of coronavirus disease 2019 in china. New England J. Med. **382**(18), 1708–1720 (2020)
9. He, K., Zhang, X., Ren, S., Sun, J.: Deep residual learning for image recognition. In: Proceedings of the IEEE conference on computer vision and pattern recognition, pp. 770–778 (2016)
10. Lakhani, P., et al.: The 2021 SIIM-FISABIO-RSNA machine learning COVID-19 challenge: annotation and standard exam classification of COVID-19 chest radiographs (2021)
11. Litmanovich, D.E., Chung, M., Kirkbride, R.R., Kicska, G., Kanne, J.P.: Review of chest radiograph findings of COVID-19 pneumonia and suggested reporting language. J. Thorac. Imaging **35**(6), 354–360 (2020)
12. Marques, G., Agarwal, D., de la Torre Díez, I.: Automated medical diagnosis of COVID-19 through efficientNet convolutional neural network. Appl. Soft Comput. **96**, 106691 (2020)
13. Ng, M.Y., et al.: Imaging profile of the COVID-19 infection: radiologic findings and literature review. Radiol. Cardiothorac. Imag. **2**(1), e200034 (2020)
14. Salton, G., McGill, M.J.: Introduction to modern information retrieval. Mcgraw-hill (1983)
15. Tan, M., Le, Q.: Efficientnet: rethinking model scaling for convolutional neural networks. In: International Conference on Machine Learning, pp. 6105–6114. PMLR (2019)
16. Wehbe, R.M., et al.: DeepCOVID-XR: an artificial intelligence algorithm to detect COVID-19 on chest radiographs trained and tested on a large us clinical data set. Radiology **299**(1), E167 (2021)

Predicting Loan Repayment Using a Hybrid of Genetic Algorithms, Logistic Regression, and Artificial Neural Networks

Pham Thanh Binh and Nguyen Dinh Thuan[✉]

University of Information Technology, VNU-HCM, Ho Chi Minh City, Vietnam
binhpt.15@grad.uit.edu.vn, thuannd@uit.edu.vn

Abstract. Loans are important products of financial institutions and banks. All institutions are trying to find effective business strategies to convince more customers to apply for a loan. However, some customers are unable to repay the loan after their application is approved. Therefore, many financial institutions and banks have considered some events when approving a loan. Determining whether a borrower can repay a loan is difficult. If the Financial institution, the Bank is too strict, there will be fewer approved loans, which means less profit. But if the approval is too loose, they will approve loans that default. The Machine learning classification algorithms are applied to predict loan default: Logistic Regression, Decision Tree, and Artificial Neural Networks. Accuracy, precision, recall, and ROC curve are used to evaluate the models and the results compared. We use feature selection techniques and propose models of Ensemble learning that are Logistic Regression with Decision Tree, and Logistic Regression with Decision Tree. We achieve the highest accuracy of 84.68% using the Logistic Regression with Decision Tree ensemble learning model.

Keywords: Loan repayment prediction · Logistic regression · Decision tree · Genetic algorithm · Ensemble learning

1 Introduction

Financial institutions and banks use credit scoring models to assess the risk of default. The models generate a score that predicts default, making lending decisions easier. The development of a loan repayment prediction model is time-consuming. These models are also fixed and are not easily developed with changing customer behaviour to predict default more accurately. Machine Learning approaches can help improve customer default prediction accuracy. The dataset used in this paper was from www.lendingclub.com. The dataset includes 37,066 loans between January 2018 and September 2020. In this study, we consider the problem of choosing predictor variables in the classification problem. Based on the factors gathered during the loan repayment process, the classification objective is to predict whether the borrower will be able to repay the loan or not. The method includes steps of data collection, data preprocessing, data analysis, and model building by applying Logistic Regression, Decision Tree, and Genetic Algorithm,

© The Author(s), under exclusive license to Springer Nature Singapore Pte Ltd. 2022
T. K. Dang et al. (Eds.): FDSE 2022, CCIS 1688, pp. 161–175, 2022.
https://doi.org/10.1007/978-981-19-8069-5_11

and we propose the method of feature selection and ensemble learning model is Logistic Regression with Decision Tree, Logistic Regression with Artificial Neural Networks Loan repayment prediction.

2 Related Works

In this paper, we look at different papers that have been used to predict defaults.

Wang et al. present a study that uses 4000 records and 21 attributes to build and evaluate a classifier predictive model. Four algorithms are used in this paper: Classic SVM, Backpropagation Neural Network, C4.5, and R SVM. The results show that the prediction accuracy of R SVM is better than other methods [1].

Reddy and Kavitha [2] use a neural network through attribute relevance analysis in the test class defaulter. Hassan and Abraham [3] used a bank dataset with 1000 cases with 24 numeric attributes to develop and compare models generated from different training algorithms, and conjugate gradient backpropagation. Scaling, and the Levenberg-Marquardt algorithm and secure one-step reverse propagation (SCG, LM, and OSS). Research shows that the slowest algorithm is OSS and the best algorithm is LM because it has the largest R.

Hamid and Ahmed [4] propose a classification model for the application of loans using three algorithms; J48, Bayesian network, and Naive Bayes classifier. They use the Weka app for deployment and testing. The results show that J48 has the best accuracy of 78.378%. Turkson et al. [5] applied 15 different types of machine learning algorithms to predict customer creditworthiness. Testing shows that, in addition to the nearest Centroid and Gaussian Naive Bayes. Each of these algorithms achieves accuracy rates from 76% to over 80%.

The Odegua recommends using an Extreme Gradient Bo boost algorithm called XGBoost to predict loan defaults. The prediction is based on loan data from a bank with a dataset containing 4368 samples and 10 attributes from both the loan application and applicant demographics. The location and age of the customer are the two most important characteristics that affect a loan's likelihood of default. The XGBoost model has an accuracy of 79%, accuracy (97%), recall (79%), and an F1 score (87%) [6]. Hybrid classifier and default prediction using a real data set of 132,029 cases from an international bank using AdaBoost, XGBoost, random forest, multilayer perception, and K-Nearest neighbours.

Mohammad et al. present a study on loan prediction by building logistic regression with a sigmoid function model and analyzing the problem of predicting defaulters. A logistic regression model is built and different performance measures are calculated. Models were compared based on performance measures of sensitivity and specificity. The best case accuracy obtained was 81.1%. The researchers concluded that the logistic regression method effectively detects the right target customers to grant loans [7].

3 Models

3.1 Logistic Regression

The classification models all seek to determine the boundary that divides groups between data. In Logistic regression, we also look for such a division boundary to solve the binary classification problem between two groups 0 and 1. In linear regression, we rely on a hypothetical regression function $h_w(x) = w^T x$ to predict the continuous target variable y. Because the value y can be out of range [0, 1], in Logistic Regression a function is needed that projects the predicted value on the probability space within the interval [0, 1] and at the same time creates nonlinearity for the regression equation to help it there is a better dividing line between two groups. That is the Sigmoid function or Logistic function that we will learn below [8].

Sigmoid Function

The logistic regression model is a continuation of the idea of linear regression into classification problems. From the output of the linear function, we feed the Sigmoid function to find the probability distribution of data. Note that the Sigmoid function is only used in the binary classification problem. For the classification problem of more than two labels, the Softmax function (to be explored in later chapters) is a generalized form of the Sigmoid function that will be used. The Sigmoid function is a nonlinear transform function based on the formula Eq. (1).

$$\sigma(t) = \frac{1}{1 + \exp(-t)} \tag{1}$$

The logistic—noted $\sigma(.)$—is a sigmoid function (i.e., S-shaped) that wrong form a number between 0 and 1.

3.2 Decision Tree

The decision tree in the diagram above is also called a binary decision tree because a question has only two options, True or False. We have some concepts related to decision trees:

Root node: The node at the top of the decision tree. All alternatives originate from this node.
Parent node: A node that can branch down to other nodes below. The underlying node is called a child node.
Child nodes: These are nodes where the parent node exists.
A Leaf node: The final node of a decision. Here we get the forecast result. The leaf node is in the last position so there will be no child nodes.
A Non-leaf node: Nodes other than leaf nodes.

From the above decision tree diagram, we see a decision tree composed of nodes and edges. At each node, a yes/no question is asked of an input variable. Depending on the answer, you will next turn to the True or False branch. Continue doing the same branching recursively until the answer is obtained at the last node [9].

3.3 Artificial Neural Networks (ANN)

A neural network, also known as an Artificial Neural Network, is a network that uses complex mathematical models to process information. They are based on the activity pattern of neurons and synapses in the human brain. Similar to the human brain, an artificial neural network connects simple nodes, also known as neurons. And such a set of nodes forms a network of nodes, hence the name artificial neural network. Similar to the human brain, in an artificial neural network, a series of algorithms are used to identify and recognize relationships in data sets. Artificial neural networks are used across a variety of technologies and applications such as video games, computer vision, speech recognition, social network filtering, automatic translation, and medical diagnostics. Surprisingly, neural networks are used for traditional and creative activities, like painting and art. The three main components of a neural network include: The input layer represents the input data. The hidden layer represents the intermediate nodes that divide the input space into regions with (soft) boundaries. It takes a set of weighted inputs and produces the wrong form through an activation function. The output layer represents the output of the neural network [12].

4   Hybrid Methodology

4.1   Ensemble Learning

Voting

A voting ensemble is an ensemble machine learning model that combines the predictions from multiple other models.

It is a technique that may be used to improve model performance, ideally achieving better performance than any single model used in the ensemble.

A voting ensemble works by combining the predictions from multiple models. It can be used for classification or regression. In the case of regression, this involves calculating the average of the predictions from the models. In the case of classification, the predictions for each label are summed and the label with the majority vote is predicted.

Regression Voting Ensemble: Predictions are the average of contributing models.

Classification Voting Ensemble: Predictions are the majority vote of contributing models.

There are two approaches to the majority vote prediction for classification; they are hard voting and soft voting.

Hard Voting. Predict the class with the largest sum of votes from models.

Soft Voting. Predict the class with the largest summed probability from models.

4.2   Suggestion Model

Voting Classifier

Majority Vote-based Ensemble Classifier:

Step 1: input data from column 1 to column 13 are independent variables, and output data from column 14 is the dependent variable.

Step 2: Data Preprocessing

Data cleaning: remove data missing value.
Handling Text and Categorical Attributes
Split Data into Training, Validation, and Testing Dataset
Feature Selection
Feature Scaling

Step 3: Apply 3 classifiers: Logistic Regression, Decision Tree, and Artificial Neural Networks to the training data.
Step 4: Predict the result of testing data, and compare the performance of the 3 classifiers.
Step 5: Performing Majority Voting for every observation.
Step 6: Compare the performance of the Majority Voting with the Logistic Regression, Decision Tree, and Genetic Algorithm classifiers.

The steps involved in the methodology are graphically represented below in Fig. 1

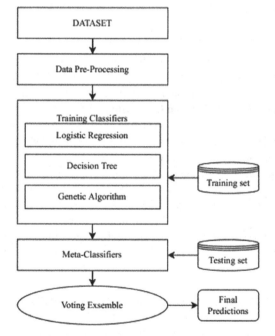

Fig. 1. Voting ensemble classifier

In this paper, we use Classification Voting Ensemble and Hard Voting. We develop voting ensembles in the Logistic Regression and Decision Tree model, Logistic Regression and Artificial Neural Networks model, in there, Logistic Regression and Decision Tree model we collect the highest Precision rate of 89.74% and ROC rate of 80.66% (Table 3).

5   Experiment

5.1   Dataset: Feature Analysis

In this paper, the dataset got from www.lendingclub.com. The dataset includes 37,066 loans between January 2018 and September 2020. Table 1 shows the 5 rows of the dataset.

Table 1. First five rows of the dataset.

credit_policy	purpose	int_rate	installment	log_annual_inc	dti	fico	days_with_cr_line	revol_bal	revol_util	inq_last_6mths	delinq_2yrs	pub_rec	not_fully_paid
1	credit_card	0.143	498.35	150000	15.7	694	37865	19748	0.674	3	5	0	0
1	home_improvement	0.11	870.29	55000	30.13	734	35947	11898	0.476	2	1	0	0
1	credit_card	0.088	785.32	165000	16.11	694	36373	20681	0.567	0	0	0	0
1	credit_card	0.17	285.03	40000	32.07	744	40269	8514	0.226	2	0	0	0
1	debt_consolidation	0.088	570.81	36000	23.73	714	38565	7555	0.256	1	0	0	1

- credit_policy: 1 if the customer meets the credit underwriting criteria of Lending-Club.com, and 0 otherwise.
- purpose: The purpose of the loan such as credit card, debt consolidation, etc.
- int_rate: The interest rate of the loan (proportion).
- installment: The monthly installments ($) owed by the borrower if the loan is funded.
- log_annual_inc: The natural log of the annual income of the borrower.
- dti: The debt-to-income ratio of the borrower.
- fico: The FICO credit score of the borrower.
- days_with_cr_line: The number of days the borrower has had a credit line.
- revol_bal: The borrower's revolving balance.
- revol_util: The borrower's revolving line utilization rate.
- inq_last_6mths: The borrower's number of inquiries by creditors in the last 6 months.
- delinq_2yrs: The number of times the borrower had been 30 + days past due on a payment in the past 2 years.
- pub_rec: The borrower's number of derogatory public records.
- not_fully_paid: indicates whether the loan was not paid back in full (the borrower either defaulted or the borrower was deemed unlikely to pay it back).

5.2   Data Preprocessing

Data Cleaning
Machine Learning algorithms cannot predict missing features, We can see that the dti, revol_util, inq_last_6mths, and delinq_2yrs attribute has missing values, so let's fix this, so we have three options to take care of missing values.

We have three options [8]:

```
[>  <class 'pandas.core.frame.DataFrame'>
    RangeIndex: 37066 entries, 0 to 37065
    Data columns (total 14 columns):
     #   Column            Non-Null Count  Dtype
    ---  ------            --------------  -----
     0   credit_policy     37066 non-null  int64
     1   purpose           37066 non-null  object
     2   int_rate          37066 non-null  float64
     3   installment       37066 non-null  float64
     4   log_annual_inc    37066 non-null  float64
     5   dti               36966 non-null  float64
     6   fico              37066 non-null  int64
     7   days_with_cr_line 37066 non-null  int64
     8   revol_bal         37066 non-null  int64
     9   revol_util        37054 non-null  float64
     10  inq_last_6mths    37066 non-null  int64
     11  delinq_2yrs       37032 non-null  float64
     12  pub_rec           37066 non-null  int64
     13  not_fully_paid    37066 non-null  int64
    dtypes: float64(6), int64(7), object(1)
    memory usage: 4.0+ MB
```

Fig. 2. Data cleaning

– Get rid of the corresponding attribute.
– Get rid of the whole attribute.
– Set the values to some value (zero, the mean, the median, etc.).

   In this paper, we choose option 1, to get rid of the corresponding attribute of the missing values in the training set. Figure 3 description of data cleaning.

Handling Text and Categorical Attributes.
In the dataset, we see the attribute 'purpose', let's fix this attribute, a common solution is to create one binary attribute per category: one attribute equal to 1 when the category is "all_other"(and 0 otherwise), another attribute equal to 1 when the category is "credit_card" (and 0 otherwise), another attribute equal to 1 when the category is "debt_consolidation" (and 0 otherwise), and so on [8] (see Fig. 4).

credit_card	debt_consolidation	educational	home_improvement	major_purchase	small_business
0	1	0	0	0	0
1	0	0	0	0	0
0	1	0	0	0	0
0	1	0	0	0	0
1	0	0	0	0	0

Fig. 3. Handling text and categorical attributes

Split Data into Training, Validation, and Testing Dataset
Loan Repayment data mentioned above will be divided into 2 parts: 70% of the time points used for training and 30% of the remaining will be used for testing in the case of all models.

Feature Selection
In this paper, we use the Genetic Algorithms (GAs) technique for feature selection, Genetic algorithms are a computer science technique for solving combinatorial optimization problems. GAs are based on evolutionary adaptations of biological populations based on Darwin's theory. It employs the principles of heredity, mutation, natural

selection, and crossover. GAs use some genetic terminology such as chromosome, population (Population), and Gene. Chromosomes are made up of Genes (represented by a linear sequence). Each gene carries some characteristics and has a certain position in the chromosome. Each chromosome represents a solution to the problem. In this article, I will explain the concepts of parallelism with programming in a specific problem. GAs are used for difficult problems, and have been successfully applied to some problems such as planning, control systems, travelling people problems, etc., Fig. 5.

The algorithm will be performed through the following steps:

Population initialization: Randomly generate a population of n individuals (where n is the solution to the problem).
Evaluation: Estimate the fitness of each individual.
Stop condition: Check the condition to end the algorithm.
Selection: Select two parents from the old population according to their fitness (the higher the fitness, the more likely it is to be selected).
Crossover: With a chosen probability, crossover two parents to create a new individual.
Mutation: With a selected mutation probability, transform the new individual.

Select result: If the stopping condition is satisfied, the algorithm terminates and chooses the best solution for the current population.
We have the overall diagram:

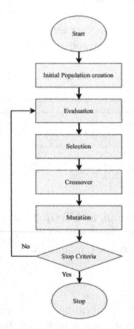

Fig. 4. How the genetic algorithm works

Feature Scaling

We apply technology feature scaling in the data processing is data normalization. Machine Learning algorithms do not work well when the input features have different values. Min-max normalization (also known as normalization) is the simplest method: the values are shifted and scaled so that they are between 0 and 1. We do this by subtracting the smallest value and dividing it by the largest and smallest values [8].

There are two common ways to get all attributes to have the same scale: min-max scaling and standardization.

In this paper, we choose min-max scaling.

$$x' = \frac{x - min(x)}{(x) - min(x)} \tag{2}$$

0.491807	1.268411	0.035292	1.071630	1.004770	0.498436	0.391567	0.162603	1.829279	0.714583	0.300395	0.238926	0.386843	1.193412	0.193019	0.260663	0.221177	0.262183
2.033318	0.158325	0.296288	0.323093	0.102024	0.286378	0.003432	0.285254	0.384146	1.087817	0.300395	0.238926	0.386843	0.837934	0.193019	3.836369	0.221177	0.262183
0.491807	1.229304	0.460964	0.118105	0.926396	0.944057	0.542356	0.072044	0.128309	0.263983	0.300395	0.238926	2.585025	0.837934	0.193019	0.260663	0.221177	0.262183
0.491807	0.479074	0.413384	0.364756	1.685458	0.629572	0.326793	0.254474	0.294258	0.263983	1.484679	0.238926	0.386843	0.837934	5.180638	0.260663	0.221177	0.262183
2.033318	0.831126	0.873532	0.601936	1.370512	1.416386	0.518787	0.252099	0.843961	0.637217	0.300395	0.238926	0.386843	1.193412	0.193019	0.260663	0.221177	0.262183
0.491807	0.547435	0.230648	0.583476	0.732509	0.367301	0.164245	0.050795	1.189687	0.263983	1.484679	0.238926	0.386843	0.837934	0.193019	0.260663	0.221177	3.814134
2.033318	1.976220	0.234153	0.060315	2.157150	1.022979	0.338752	0.216476	0.543180	1.989018	1.484679	0.238926	2.585025	0.837934	0.193019	0.260663	0.221177	0.262183

5.3 Performance Measures

Measuring Accuracy Using Cross-Validation

The K-fold cross-validation method is to randomly divide 3 separate subsets called folds, then train and evaluate the model three times, each time with a different fold to evaluate. Evaluate and train the remaining folds.

Confusion Matrix

The confusion matrix is a technique to evaluate the performance of the model in the classification problem. A confusion matrix is a matrix that represents the amount of data that belongs to a class and predicts which class the data belongs to [8].

True Positive (TP): there are 7147 records in the Positive class, the model classifies the records in the Positive class (correct prediction). True Negative (TN): there are 2230 records in the Negative class, the model classifies the records in the Negative class (correct prediction). False Positive (FP): is the record in the Negative class, but the model classifies 888 records in the Positive class (false prediction) → wrong type 1. False Negative (FN): is the record in the Positive class, but the model classifies 811 records in the Negative class (false prediction) → wrong type 2, see Fig. 6.

Precision

The precision determines that of the records classified by the model into the Positive class, how many records belong to the Positive class. The closer the Precision value

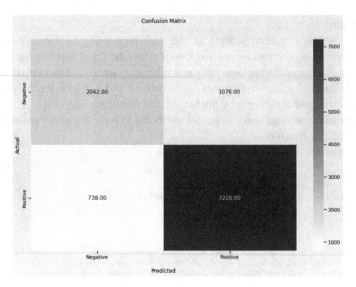

Fig. 5. Confusion matrix

is to 1, the more accurate the model is. The higher the precision, the more accurately classified records are in Eq. (3) [8].

$$precision = \frac{TP}{TP + FP} \tag{3}$$

TP is the number of true positives, and FP is the number of false positives.

Recall

Recall determines how many records actually in the Positive class are correctly classified by the model into the Positive class. The closer the Recall value is to 1, the more accurate the model is. The higher the recall, the more correct information is not missed in Eq. (4) [8].

$$recall = \frac{TP}{TP + FN} \tag{4}$$

FN is of course the number of false negatives.

F1-Score

It is often convenient to combine precision and recall into a single metric called the F1 score, in particular, if you need a simple way to compare two classifiers. The F1 score is the harmonic mean of Precision and Recall in Eq. (5). Whereas the regular mean treats all values equally, the harmonic mean gives much more weight to low values. As a result, the classifier will only get a high F1 score if both recall and precision are high [8].

$$F_1 = \frac{2}{\frac{1}{precision} + \frac{1}{recall}} = 2 \times \frac{precision \times recall}{precision + recall} = \frac{TP}{TP + \frac{FN+FP}{2}} \tag{5}$$

The ROC Curve

ROC (receiver operating characteristic) curve is a commonly used method for precise toxicity measurement used with classification problems, the ROC curve plots the true positive rate (TPR), another name for Recall, according to the false positive rate (FPR), FPR is the proportion of negative samples that are falsely classified as positive and is equal to 1-TNR (true negative rate). TNR is the proportion of negative samples that are correctly classified, also known as specificity [8].

One way to compare classifiers is to measure the area under the curve (AUC). A perfect classifier will have a ROC AUC equal to 1, whereas a purely random classifier will have a ROC AUC equal to 0.5.

5.4 Predicting Loan Repayment

Logistic Regression

Logistic regression is commonly used to estimate the probability that a sample of data belongs to a particular class (for example, the probability that an email is spam). If the estimated probability for a class is greater than 50%, then the model predicts that this sample belongs to that class (called the positive class, labelled "1"); otherwise, the prediction model does not belong to that class (i.e., it is in the negative class, labelled as "0"). So here is a binary classifier [11]. Below is the Cost Function for Logistic Regression with Ridge Penalty, see Table 2, Table 3.

$$\mathcal{L}_{\text{ridge}}(\beta; \lambda) = \|Y - X\beta\|_2^2 + \lambda\|\beta\|_2^2 = \sum_{i=1}^{n}\left(Y_i - \sum_{j=1}^{p}X_{ij}\beta_j\right)^2 + \lambda\sum_{j=1}^{p}\beta_j^2 \quad (6)$$

This loss function is the traditional sum-of-squares augmented with a penalty. The particular form of the penalty, $\lambda\|\beta\|_2^2$ referred to as the ridge penalty and λ as the penalty parameter.

Decision Tree

Use Classification and Regression Tree (CART) to train Decision Trees. First, the algorithm will divide the training set into two subsets according to the feature k and threshold t_k. The algorithm will search for pair (k, t_k) and generate subsets, Eq. (7) is the cost function that needs to be minimized.

$$J(k, t_k) = \frac{m_{\text{left}}}{m}G_{\text{left}} + \frac{m_{\text{right}}}{m}G_{\text{right}} \quad (7)$$

Where $\begin{cases} G_{\text{left}}_{\text{right}} & \text{measure the doping of the left/right subset} \\ \frac{m_{\text{left}}}{\text{right}} & \text{is the number of samples in the left/right subsets} \end{cases}$

By default, Gini doping is used, but the entropy phase can also be selected by assigning the criterion hyperparameter to "entropy". The concept of entropy comes from thermodynamics. It's a measure of the chaos of molecules: entropy approaches zero when the molecules are stationary and ordered. Entropy is often used as a measure of doping [9].

Artificial Neural Networks
Build an Artificial Neural Network (ANN) model by default using the Scikit-learning package and use the accuracy score, precision, recall, confusion matrix, and ROC the see the model's accuracy on the loan dataset, see Table 2 and, Table 3.

Model Comparison

Table 2. Genetic algorithm

Model	Accuracy	Precision	Recall	F1-score	ROC
Genetic Algorithm + Logistic Regression	0.75686	0.75801	0.97185	0.85172	0.59
Genetic Algorithm + Decision Tree	0.84697	0.88742	0.90136	0.89433	0.80475
Genetic Algorithm + Artificial Neural Networks	0.84381	0.8818	0.90374	0.89264	0.79729

Table 3. Ensemble learning - voting

Model	Accuracy	Precision	Recall	F1-score	ROC
Logistic Regression + Decision Tree	0.84688	0.8974	0.90123	0.89426	0.80669
Logistic Regression + Artificial Neural Networks	0.83371	0.8798	0.91563	0. 90254	0.80234

The results of the selected models: the method of combining the genetic algorithm with the logistic regression model, the genetic algorithm with the decision tree model, the genetic algorithm with the artificial neural network, and classifier models. Voting types will be compared. Table 2 is the value for Precision, Recall, and ROC curves for selected models. The highest accuracy was 88.74%, Recall 90.13% and AUC score was 80.47%. Table 3 Logistic regression with Decision Trees had an accuracy score of 84.68% and the highest ROC rate of 80.66%. Therefore, in our analysis, the Decision Tree model is preferred among the selected model. In Table 3, we used the techniques of voting ensemble learning, we can see an ensemble between the Logistic Regression with Decision Tree model has the value Precision, Recall, F1-Score, AUC-Score is better (Fig. 7).

Receiver Operating Characteristic – Voting:

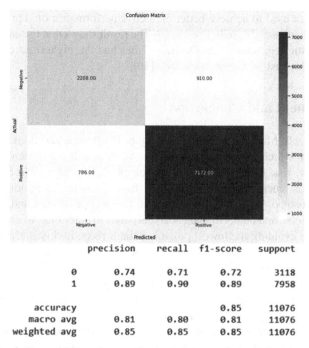

```
               precision    recall  f1-score   support

           0       0.74      0.71      0.72      3118
           1       0.89      0.90      0.89      7958

    accuracy                           0.85     11076
   macro avg       0.81      0.80      0.81     11076
weighted avg       0.85      0.85      0.85     11076
```

Fig. 6. Ensemble learning - voting logistic regression and decision tree

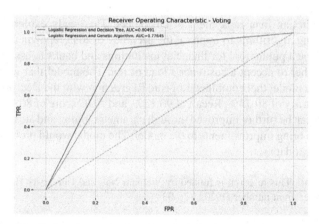

Fig. 7. Receiver operating characteristics for voting ensemble

There are Two Main Reasons to use the Ensemble Learning Model, that is:
Performance: An ensemble can make better predictions and achieve better performance than any single contributing model.

Robustness: An ensemble reduces the spread or dispersion of the predictions and model performance.

Ensembles are used to achieve better predictive performance on a predictive modelling problem than a single predictive model. The result shows that the ensemble learning model Logistic regression with Decision Trees had the highest accuracy score of 84.68% and the highest ROC rate of 80.66% [10].

6 Enhancement and Conclusion

Regarding the use of Machine Learning techniques in Finance, and Banking to achieve high profits, from which we see increasing interest. Research is conducted in the areas of credit scoring, risk management, and default prediction using Machine Learning methodology. Customers who can make loans from financial institutions, Banks and now can make loans directly on mobile devices. It is an opportunity and challenge for financial institutions, and banks to make loan decisions to determine whether customers can repay or not, avoiding the lowest possible default risks. In this study, I proposed a method of ensemble learning to improve the accuracy of predicting whether customers are likely to repay the loan or not? This helps to better understand customer behaviors to improve the prediction of customers' ability to repay loans and avoid default for financial institutions, and banks. The study also explores and understands the properties of loan data that contribute to default risk. Data analysis shows the correlation between the attributes to select the appropriate attributes to train the Machine Learning model. The testing and training data set is applied to Machine Learning algorithms to identify and find an algorithm with the best results. Indicators to evaluate the accuracy of the Machine Learning model include confusion matrix, precision, and recall, which were applied for predicting loan repayment of customers. This study explores the use of Machine Learning algorithms to improve the accuracy of loan repayment predictions. The model will be a public tool for financial institutions and banks to assess credit risk and decide whether to accept a customer's loan or not. The model that worked best in the study was the model that combined Logistic Regression with the Decision Tree with the highest Accuracy of 89.74%, Recall of 90.12%, and AUC score of 80.66%. This is a good result and can be further improved through parameter tuning and attribute selection methods that can bring improvements to the model. The model would probably be better if doing a different data set.

Acknowledgement. This research is funded by Vietnam National University HoChiMinh City (VNU-HCM) under grant number DS2022-26-03.

References

1. Wang, B., Liu, Y., Hao, Y., Liu, S.: Defaults assessment of mortgage loan with rough set and SVM. In: 2007 International Conference on Computational Intelligence and Security (CIS 2007), pp. 981–985. IEEE (2007)
2. Reddy, M.J., Kavitha, B.: Neural networks for prediction of loan default using attribute relevance analysis. In: 2010 International Conference on Signal Acquisition and Processing, pp. 274–277. IEEE (2010)

3. Hassan, A.K.I., Abraham, A.: Modeling consumer loan default prediction using Neural Network. In: 2013 International Conference on Computing, Electrical and Electronic Engineering (ICCEEE), pp. 239–243. IEEE (2013)
4. Hamid, A.J., Ahmed, T.M.: Developing prediction model of loan risk in banks using data mining. Mach. Learn. Appl. An Int. J. **3**(1), 1–9 (2016)
5. Turkson, R.E., Baagyere, E.Y., Wenya, G.E.: A machine learning approach for predicting bank credit worthiness. In: 2016 Third International Conference on Artificial Intelligence and Pattern Recognition (AIPR), pp. 1–7. IEEE (2016)
6. Odegua, R.: Predicting bank loan default with extreme gradient boosting. arXiv preprint arXiv:2002.02011 (2020)
7. Sheikh, M.A., Goel, A.K., Kumar, T.: An approach for prediction of loan approval using machine learning algorithm. In: 2020 International Conference on Electronics and Sustainable Communication Systems (ICESC), pp. 490–494. IEEE (2020)
8. Aurélien, G.: Hands-on Machine Learning with Scikit-Learn, Keras, and TensorFlow (2019)
9. Jason, B.: Machine Learning Algorithms from Scratch with Python (2016)
10. Jason, B.: Ensemble Learning Algorithms with Python Make Better Predictions with Bagging, Boosting, and Stacking (2021)
11. Natasha, A., Prastyo, D.D., Suhartono. Credit scoring to classify consumer loans using machine learning. In: AIP Conference Proceedings (2019)
12. Jason, B.: Deep Learning with Python Tap The Power of TensorFlow and Theano with Keras (2016)

Performance Evaluation of Regular Decomposition and Benchmark Clustering Methods

Laura Haryo and Reza Pulungan[✉] [ID]

Department of Computer Science and Electronics, Faculty of Mathematics
and Natural Sciences, Universitas Gadjah Mada, Yogyakarta, Indonesia
pulungan@ugm.ac.id

Abstract. This study compares three benchmark clustering methods—
mini batch k-means, DBSCAN, and spectral clustering—with regular
decomposition (RD), a new method developed for large graph data. RD
is first converted so that applicable to numerical data without graph
structure by changing the input into a distance matrix and the output
into cluster labels. The results indicate that mini batch k-means has the
best overall performance in terms of accuracy, time, and space consumption. RD and spectral clustering have competitive adjusted Rand index
(ARI), even though their time and space consumption is considerable
and can reach 2 and 30 times greater than mini batch k-means when
applied to the artificial datasets. On the other hand, DBSCAN produces
ARI as low as 0% in most default cases but increases up to 100% in
almost all experiments of the artificial datasets after varying the parameters. DBSCAN's accuracy, time, and space consumption, however, are
still worse than mini batch k-means.

Keywords: Performance evaluation · Regular decomposition ·
Spectral clustering · Mini batch k-means · DBSCAN

1 Introduction

Clustering is an unsupervised machine learning technique for grouping unlabeled data into clusters. It was used in data profiling [1] to detect duplication
of text within a single paragraph and in data processing for wind power forecasting to solve the problems of uncertain cluster numbers and initial cluster
centers [15]. It has also been applied to electric load clustering, later used for
consumer segmentation to obtain consumption categories and detect abnormal
power consumption, such as power theft and fraud [16].

Many clustering methods have been developed with the primary aim of finding clusters in datasets with a large number of samples. This paper focuses
mainly on a comparative analysis of some leading clustering methods, motivated
by their popularity in the data mining field. Two clustering methods that perform well on large datasets are mini batch k-means and DBSCAN [13]. Another

T. K. Dang et al. (Eds.): FDSE 2022, CCIS 1688, pp. 176–191, 2022.
https://doi.org/10.1007/978-981-19-8069-5_12

method currently emerging for large datasets is spectral clustering, with good accuracy but high time complexity.

In addition to the three methods, regular decomposition (RD) is a new method developed by Pehkonen and Reittu [7] to find the prominent distribution patterns in peer-to-peer systems. Reittu et al. [11] analyzed the performance of RD and concluded that it was suitable for large graphs and was better than spectral clustering for medium-sized graphs. Other studies also indicated that RD achieves good results in large graph datasets [3,4,8–10]. However, most RD research is on datasets with graph and time series features, never on datasets without graph structure. Since RD can potentially have good results in large datasets, this study applies RD to non-graph datasets and then compare it with the benchmark methods.

2 Preliminaries

2.1 Regular Decomposition

Regular decomposition (RD), shown in Algorithms 1 and 2, is a method that uses a graph model with a distance matrix as input. Therefore, a dataset must first be converted into a distance matrix D, a dissimilarity matrix obtained from the similarity matrix computed using the Gaussian method as in spectral clustering. Given samples x_i and x_j, their similarity is defined by:

$$s(x_i, x_j) = e^{-\|x_i - x_j\|^2 \gamma}, \tag{1}$$

where $\gamma = 1/F$ and F is the number of features. An entry d_{ij} of the distance matrix D is then given by:

$$d_{ij} = 1 - s(x_i, x_j). \tag{2}$$

Algorithm 1: Regular Decomposition [10]

Data: Distance matrix $D \in \mathbb{Z}_+^{m \times n}$, integers $k, t_{\max}, toi_{\max}$
Result: Partition matrix $R^* \in \{0,1\}^{n \times k}$
$L_{\min} \leftarrow \infty$;
for $s \in \{1, \ldots, t_{\max}\}$ **do**
    $R \leftarrow$ random $(n \times k)$ partition matrix;
    for $t \in \{1, \ldots, toi_{\max}\}$ **do**
      | $R \leftarrow$ LocalUpdate(R, D);
    $L \leftarrow L(R) = \sum\limits_{i=1}^{m} \sum\limits_{j=1}^{n} \sum\limits_{v=1}^{k} r_{jv} \cdot \left(\hat{\Lambda}_{iv} - d_{ij} \log \hat{\Lambda}_{iv} \right)$;
    if $L < L_{\min}$ **then**
      | $R^* \leftarrow R$;
      | $L_{\min} \leftarrow L$;

Algorithm 2: Function LocalUpdate() [10]

Data: Partition matrix $R \in \{0,1\}^{n \times k}$, distance matrix $D \in \mathbb{Z}_+^{m \times n}$
Result: Partition matrix $R \in \{0,1\}^{n \times k}$

for $v \in \{1, \ldots, k\}$ **do**
    $n_v \leftarrow \sum_{j=1}^{n} r_{jv}$;
    for $i \in \{1, \ldots, m\}$ **do**
        $\hat{\Lambda}_{iv} \leftarrow \sum_{j=1}^{n} \frac{d_{ij} r_{jv}}{n_v}$;
    for $j \in \{1, \ldots, n\}$ **do**
        s $\ell_{jv} \leftarrow \sum_{j=i}^{m} \left(\hat{\Lambda}_{iv} - d_{ij} \log \hat{\Lambda}_{iv} \right)$;
for $j \in \{1, \ldots, n\}$ **do**
    $Z_j \leftarrow \underset{v \in [k]}{\arg\min} \, \ell_{jv}$;
    for $v \in \{1, \ldots, k\}$ **do**
        $r_{jv} \leftarrow 1(Z_j = v)$;

Regular decomposition partitions a graph of n nodes into k disjoint non-empty sets, such that they have minimal stochastic fluctuations in terms of the average distance matrix Λ. RD first initializes the objective function L and matrix R by a random n-by-k partition matrix. Subsequently, RD updates R based on D using an expectation-maximization-like algorithm (i.e., function LocalUpdate() in Algorithm 2). The objective function L is then updated with a maximum likelihood estimation of $(\hat{\Lambda}, R)$ by minimizing the function $L(R)$, where $\hat{\Lambda}$ is the optimum of Λ. The result is matrix R^*, namely the partition matrix R obtained when the objective function L is minimum.

Since the resulting R^* is still a partition matrix, it is then converted to cluster labels. The default value of $t_{\max}$ is set to 10 to reduce the computation time and give conditions similar to spectral clustering, where the default number of times the k-means algorithm is invoked with different centroid seeds is also 10.

2.2   Spectral Clustering

Spectral clustering is also a method that uses the graph model [6]. Spectral clustering represents data points as nodes and relations between data points as edges. Here, data clustering boils down to finding a graph partition, by making the weights between different clusters as small as possible and the total weight between edges in the same cluster as large as possible. Spectral clustering is one of the most recent and popular graph-based methods because, with good accuracy, it can handle data with large dimensions [19].

2.3   Mini Batch k-Means

Mini batch k-means [14] is a method that uses the partitioning model [19], where data clusters are formed by partitioning, namely clustering and dividing the samples into blocks, each with a centroid closest to all its sample points [19]. The simplest partitioning model is k-means [5], which updates the centroid in each iteration until it reaches a convergent value with full batch optimization. Mini batch k-means is the development of k-means, where the optimization method of k-means is replaced with a set of mini batches to reduce the high computation time; a common problem in big data.

2.4   DBSCAN

Density-Based Spatial Clustering of Applications with Noise (DBSCAN) [19] is a method that uses the density model. The density model has criteria for forming clusters, namely that data with a high-density area are put in the same cluster [19]. DBSCAN is the first density-model method, which firstly looks for high-density areas by determining core points, $i.e.$, points with high-density neighbors [2]. A core point is then linked with its neighbors to form a cluster.

3   Methodology

3.1   Artificial Datasets

The artificial datasets are created using Scikit-Learn's `make_classification` and `make_blobs` [13]. They generate normally-distributed random n-class classification problems and isotropic Gaussian blobs, respectively. The parameters used in constructing the artificial datasets are [12]:

1. the number of samples $N \in \{1000, 5000, 10000\}$,
2. the number of clusters $K \in \{2, 5, 10\}$,
3. the number of features $F \in \{2, 5, 10\}$, and
4. the clusters' standard deviation $S \in \{0.5, 1, 2\}$ (only on `make_blobs` datasets).

These artificial datasets will be analyzed based on each parameter. The `make_classification` datasets are assumed to have informative but without repetitive or redundant features. The total number of the `make_blobs` dataset variations is 135. Because a `make_classification` dataset must have no more than 2^F clusters, datasets with two features cannot be formed if they have 5 or 10 clusters. The total number of `make_classification` datasets constructed is 39. Hence, the total number of artificial datasets is 174. No artificial dataset has missing data, noise, inconsistencies, and outliers.

The names of `make_blobs` and `make_classification` datasets begin with B and CL, respectively. The datasets are named as follows:

$$Ba_1Na_2Ka_3Fa_4S \quad \text{and} \quad CLa_1Na_2Ka_3F,$$

where a_1, a_2, and a_3 are the number of samples, clusters, and features, respectively, and a_4 is the standard deviation of the clusters. For instance, a `make_classification` dataset constructed with $N = 1000$, $K = 2$, and $F = 2$ is named CL1kN2K2F, and the set of `make_blobs` datasets whose clusters' standard deviation is 1 is denoted by B1S.

3.2 Benchmark Datasets

Three benchmark datasets are used in this study, specified in Table 1. All datasets are subjected to a simple preprocessing by deleting missing data, merging data-frames, naming columns, and converting categorical features to numerical ones. No removal of noise, inconsistencies, and outliers is done in order to determine how well the methods perform in dealing with these factors.

Table 1. Benchmark datasets [18]

Dataset	N	K	F
HEPMASS	10,500,000	2	27
KDD Cup 1999	4,898,430	23	41
Poker Hand	1,025,008	10	10

3.3 Evaluation Methods

The performance of the clustering methods is evaluated based on their accuracy, time, and space consumption. The accuracy is measured using the adjusted Rand index (ARI). By evaluating all pairs of samples and counting pairings allocated in the same or different clusters in the anticipated and true clusterings, the Rand index (RI) determines a similarity measure between two clusterings. The RI score is then *adjusted for chance* to create the ARI score, with the range of $[-1, 1]$. Each dataset is executed five times, and the average measure and its standard deviation (SD) are calculated from each execution's result. The maximum accuracy is recorded together with the associated time and space consumption, obtained using Python modules `time` and `tracemalloc`.

3.4 Analysis Methods

Using Default Parameters. The first stage is to analyze the clustering methods using each method's provided default parameters to find out their performance when there are no specific settings, a situation common for non-expert users. Analysis of the artificial datasets based on the four parameters proceeds descriptively and with statistical inference, while that of the benchmark datasets is done only descriptively. The statistical inference uses a t-test to determine whether the two population averages of the datasets are the same based on the two sample averages obtained from the evaluation results. The t-test requires that the two samples are independent and normally distributed. They should be independent since the two samples are generated using different parameters. They must also be normally distributed because the population of each artificially constructed dataset is normally distributed. The central limit theorem is then satisfied: if the sample size is less than 30 and normally distributed, then the sample mean is also normally distributed and equal to the population mean, and the sample standard deviation is equal to the standard error [17].

There are two different ways of conducting the t-test depending on the homogeneity of the population variance. Before the t-test, an F-test is first performed to determine whether the two population variances are the same based on the two existing sample variances. The details of the t-test and F-test are provided in Table 2. In the t-test, if the population means are different, the better one can be determined by inspecting the confidence interval of the average difference.

Table 2. The statistical inference guide

Steps	F-test	t-test
Hypothesis	$H_0 : \sigma_1^2 = \sigma_2^2;$ $H_1 : \sigma_1^2 \neq \sigma_2^2$	$H_0 : \mu_1 - \mu_2 = 0; H_1 : \mu_1 - \mu_2 \neq 0$
Significance level	$\alpha = 0.05$	
Test statistic	$F = \left(\frac{s_1}{s_2}\right)^2$	If $\sigma_1^2 = \sigma_2^2$: $t = \frac{\bar{x}_1 - \bar{x}_2}{\sqrt{s_p^2\left(\frac{1}{n_1} + \frac{1}{n_2}\right)}}$ with $s_p = \frac{(n_1-1)s_1^2 + (n_2-1)s_2^2}{n_1+n_2-2}$ If $\sigma_1^2 \neq \sigma_2^2$: $t = \frac{\bar{x}_1 - \bar{x}_2}{\sqrt{\frac{s_1^2}{n_1} + \frac{s_2^2}{n_2}}}$
Critical region	H_0 is rejected if **p-value** $< \alpha$	
	H_0 is rejected if $F > F_{n_1-1; n_2-1; \frac{\alpha}{2}}$ or $F < \frac{1}{F_{n_2-1; n_1-1; \frac{\alpha}{2}}}.$	If $\sigma_1^2 = \sigma_2^2$: H_0 is rejected if $t > t_{n_1+n_2-2; \frac{\alpha}{2}}$ or $t < -t_{n_1+n_2-2; \frac{\alpha}{2}}$ If $\sigma_1^2 \neq \sigma_2^2$: H_0 is rejected if $t > t_{k; \frac{\alpha}{2}}$ or $t < -t_{k; \frac{\alpha}{2}}$ with $k = \frac{\left(\frac{s_1^2}{n_1} + \frac{s_2^2}{n_2}\right)^2}{\frac{\left(\frac{s_1^2}{n_1}\right)^2}{n_1-1} + \frac{\left(\frac{s_2^2}{n_2}\right)^2}{n_2-1}}$
Conclusion	H_0 is rejected or not rejected	

One-Dimensional Analysis. The second stage is to analyze the methods by varying one of the parameters while the others remain default to determine the effects of each parameter on the methods. The parameters of the clustering methods to vary are specified in Table 3. The artificial datasets used in this analysis are sampled for simplicity since a large variety of parameters is required. In this stage, for each parameter P, we examine the ARI improvement rate of each method, in terms of the average ($\langle R \rangle$) and maximum (max R), defined by:

$$\langle R \rangle = \frac{1}{n_P} \sum_x \left(\Gamma(x) - \Gamma_d\right) \quad \text{and} \quad \max R = \max_x \left(\Gamma(x) - \Gamma_d\right), \qquad (3)$$

where $\Gamma(x)$ is the average of measure R when the value of parameter P is x, Γ_d is the average of measure R when P is set to its default value, and n_P is the number of all varied values of parameter P.

Table 3. The parameters of the clustering methods to vary [11,13]

Method	Parameter	Type	Notes
RD	k	int	The dimension of the projection subspace
	tmax	int	The number of optimization rounds
	toimax	int	The maximum number of optimization cycles
Spectral clustering	n_clusters	int	The dimension of the projection subspace
	gamma	float	The kernel coefficient of RBF
Mini batch k-means	n_clusters	int	The number of centroids to generate
	max_iter	int	The maximum number of iterations
	batch_size	int	The size of the mini batches
DBSCAN	eps	float	The maximum distance to be considered neighbors
	min_samples	int	The total weight to be considered core points

Multi-dimensional Analysis. The third stage is to analyze the methods by simultaneously varying all parameters randomly to determine the maximum accuracy achievable for RD and the three benchmark methods and the sensitivity of these methods to parameter variations. For each input parameter P of the clustering methods, 50 variations are generated according to a uniform distribution from an interval $[P_{\min}, P_{\max}]$, obtained from the one-dimensional analysis [12].

The artificial datasets used are the same as in the one-dimensional analysis. In contrast, only the KDD Cup 1999 is used for the benchmark dataset, which is again sampled to reduce evaluation time. In addition to the ARI improvement rates, the **p-value** is inspected, namely the probability that the results obtained in the multi-dimensional analysis are greater than those with default parameters.

4   Results and Analysis

4.1   Using Default Parameters

Number of Samples. Figure 1 shows that varying $N \in \{1000, 5000, 10000\}$ produces only minor effects on the methods' average accuracy. On make_blobs datasets, all methods achieve a max ARI above 83.0%, and DBSCAN has the worst average ARI ($\langle \text{ARI} \rangle$). The time for RD and spectral clustering to compute the max ARI is 1–229 s, far above other methods, which is less than 1 s. Spectral clustering's time consumption (11–591 s) is higher than RD's (less than 13 s) due to the high standard error mean. The space needed for computing the max ARI is 15–437 kB, with mini batch k-means requiring the least.

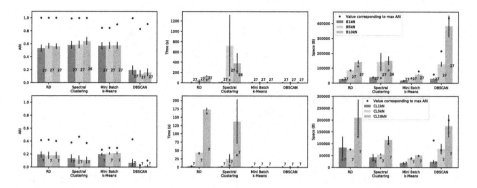

Fig. 1. The average performance of the clustering methods when (top) make_blobs and (bottom) make_classification datasets are varied based on the number of samples using default parameters.

On make_classification datasets, RD and mini batch k-means achieve the highest ⟨ARI⟩, while DBSCAN still has the lowest. Experiments show that DBSCAN reaches a max ARI of 2.8% and 10.0% for 1000 and 5000 samples, respectively, while others reach 26.6–46.6%. The time for RD to compute the max ARI is 2–162 s; for spectral clustering, 1–36 s; for other methods, less than 0.2 s. The required space for computing the max ARI is 15–200 kB, with mini batch k-means' tending to be lower. Since in subsequent analyses, the artificial datasets consistently produce a trend of higher time consumption for RD or spectral clustering and lower space consumption for mini batch k-means, this will not be elaborated on further but only presented in figures.

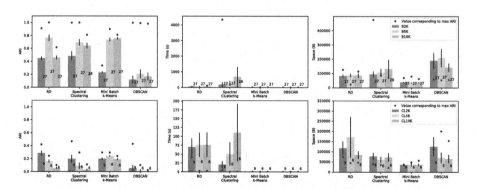

Fig. 2. The average performance of the clustering methods when (top) make_blobs and (bottom) make_classification datasets are varied based on the number of clusters using default parameters.

Number of Custers. Varying $K \in \{2, 5, 10\}$ also has minor effects on the methods' ⟨ARI⟩, as shown in Fig. 2. RD and spectral clustering obtain the best

⟨ARI⟩ on B2K and B5K, while mini batch k-means is better on B5K and B10K. DBSCAN achieves the lowest ⟨ARI⟩ on the three make_blobs datasets but has the highest overall max ARI in all datasets, ranging from 98.3 to 99.6%. On make_classification datasets, mini batch k-means produces the best ⟨ARI⟩ on the three datasets, while DBSCAN obtains the worst. The highest max ARI on CL2K and CL5K is achieved by spectral clustering at 46.6% and 29.4%, respectively, while on CL10K is achieved by mini batch k-means at 24.0%.

Number of Features. The t-tests indicate that varying $F \in \{2, 5, 10\}$ has insignificant effects on the methods' ⟨ARI⟩, as shown in Fig. 3. DBSCAN produces the worst ⟨ARI⟩ on all make_blobs datasets. RD has a better ⟨ARI⟩ than other methods on B2F. RD achieves the best overall max ARI in the experiments, 99.9% and above. Although DBSCAN gets an ARI of 0.0% on B10F, its max ARI on B2F and B5F is 90.6% and above. When applied to CL2F, all methods obtain relatively similar ⟨ARI⟩. However, on CL5F and CL10F, DBSCAN has the worst ⟨ARI⟩. DBSCAN also gets an ARI of 0.0% on CL10F. RD has the best ⟨ARI⟩ on CL10F and has a better overall ⟨ARI⟩ ranging from 24.8 to 41.8%. The max ARI achieved by mini batch k-means is stable in the 26.6 to 29.4% range.

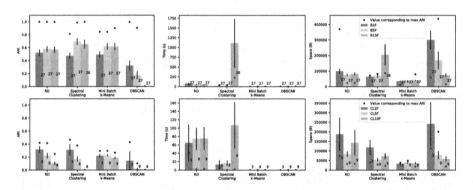

Fig. 3. The average performance of the clustering methods when (top) make_blobs and (bottom) make_classification datasets are varied based on the number of features using default parameters.

Standard Deviation of the Clusters. Figure 4 shows that varying the clusters' standard deviation also has insignificant effects on the methods' ⟨ARI⟩. DBSCAN gets the lowest ⟨ARI⟩ on B0.5S, B1S, and B2S, while spectral clustering and mini batch k-means get the best ⟨ARI⟩ on B2S. Although RD reaches 100% max ARI on B0.5S and B1S, it has a worse 66.1% max ARI on B2S. Spectral clustering and mini batch k-means get a max ARI of 84.2–99.9% on B0.5S, B1S, and B2S.

Benchmark Datasets. Figure 5 depicts the clustering methods' performance using default parameters on HEPMASS, KDD Cup 1999, and Poker Hand

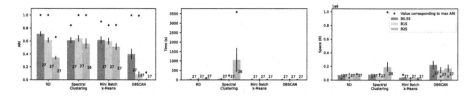

Fig. 4. The average performance of the clustering methods when make_blobs datasets are varied based on the standard deviation of the clusters using default parameters.

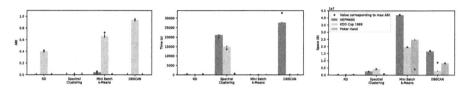

Fig. 5. The average performance of the clustering methods using default parameters on HEPMASS (RD & spectral clustering $N = 15000$, mini batch k-means $N = 10500000$, and DBSCAN $N = 1700000$), KDD Cup 1999 (RD & spectral clustering $N = 5000$ and $K = 11$, mini batch k-means $N = 4898430$ and $K = 23$, and DBSCAN $N = 100000$ and $K = 6$), and Poker Hand datasets (RD & spectral clustering $N = 15000$, mini batch k-means $N = 1025008$, and DBSCAN $N = 1025008$).

datasets. Mini batch k-means gets an $\langle$ARI$\rangle$ of 4.4% and a max ARI of 5.5%, the highest among others. It can process the entire HEPMASS dataset of 10.5 million samples with much less time and space than other methods. It is 7.7 h faster than DBSCAN (which processes a sample 6 times smaller) while needing only 26 kB more space. On the same sample size, RD needs much less time and space than spectral clustering; 12 and 62 times smaller, respectively. This result and the previous analysis of artificial datasets indicate that for the best time and space consumption, the order of methods is mini batch k-means, DBSCAN, RD, and spectral clustering. RD, spectral clustering, and DBSCAN on the sampled HEPMASS have an $\langle$ARI$\rangle$ and max ARI of no more than 0.006%.

Mini batch k-means obtains an $\langle$ARI$\rangle$ of 66.4% with a max ARI of 72.2% processing the entire KDD Cup 1999 dataset of size 4898430. DBSCAN reaches an $\langle$ARI$\rangle$ and max ARI of 94.4% with 100000 samples. RD and spectral clustering get a max ARI of only 40.7% and 0.0%, respectively, on a much smaller sample size. All clustering methods perform similarly when dealing with the Poker Hand dataset; all achieve a low $\langle$ARI$\rangle$, close to 0%.

4.2   One-Dimensional Analysis

Number of Samples. When applied to B5K5F1S and varied by one parameter (RD tmax, spectral clustering n_clusters, mini batch k-means n_clusters, and DBSCAN eps), all methods can obtain a max ARI of 90.0–100%. Although k has the biggest impact on RD's max ARI, it decreases the $\langle$ARI$\rangle$. In spectral clustering, **gamma** has a significant impact, although not as big as **n_clusters**. When varying $N \in \{1000, 5000, 10000\}$ on CL5K5F, most effects are mainly caused by the same parameters. RD improves by varying **k**, except on the 1000-sample dataset. In all other experiments, RD gets a higher $\langle ARI \rangle$ by increasing **tmax** and **toimax**. Spectral clustering on the 5000-sample dataset achieves the best max ARI with **gamma**, DBSCAN on the 10,000-sample dataset with **min_samples**, but the decrease with **eps** is greater than the increase with **min_samples**. The order of methods for the best max ARI is spectral clustering, mini batch k-means, RD, and DBSCAN, with the highest max ARI of 34.2–42.1%.

Number of Clusters. Varying $K \in \{2, 5, 10\}$ on B1kN5F1S, **k** has the most effect on RD's max ARI, although it decreases when $K = 5$ since the default setting already achieves 100%. Parameters affecting the other methods the most are still **n_cluster** and **eps**. All methods get the best max ARI of 93–100%, except RD gets 80.3% when $K = 2$ and spectral clustering gets 85.8% when $K = 10$. When applied to CL1kN5F, the same parameters still have the most significant impact on the max ARI, except that spectral clustering is most affected by **gamma** when $K = 5$. Although RD is more affected by **k** when $K = 5$, its max ARI decreases but is higher when **tmax** is varied. All methods show a sizable downward trend in the highest max ARI obtained from the cluster number variation, with the highest max ARI ranges of 94.5–97.6%, 24.5–36.6%, and 3.9–19.8%, respectively. RD and DBSCAN get the worst max ARI, while spectral clustering achieves the best except when $K = 10$, which is achieved by mini batch k-means.

Number of Features. When varying $F \in \{2, 5, 10\}$ on B1kN5K1S, parameters with the most effect on max ARI are still **k**, **n_clusters**, and **eps**, although RD always produces decreasing max R and DBSCAN decreasing only when $F = 2$. All methods get stable max ARI of 87.6–100%. Since CL1kN5K contains only $F \in \{5, 10\}$, the trend of the highest max ARI cannot be concluded. Spectral clustering gets the highest max ARI from **gamma** variation, while other methods are from the same parameters as the previous result. The order of methods for the best max ARI is spectral clustering, mini batch k-means, RD, and DBSCAN, with max ARI of 1.5–48.1% and RD showing negative max S when $F = 5$.

Standard Deviation of the Clusters. The result of varying $S \in \{0.5, 1, 2\}$ on B1kN5K5F reveals a decreasing trend of the highest max ARI. RD gets a negative max **k** when $S \in \{0.5, 1\}$. All methods obtain a max ARI of 92.2–100%, except for RD and DBSCAN, 61.8% and 41.9%, respectively when $S = 2$. Spectral clustering achieves the largest max **gamma** when $S = 2$ and the largest max **n_clusters** in other cases. Mini batch k-means and DBSCAN achieve the highest max **n_clusters** and max **eps**, respectively.

Benchmark Datasets. The highest max ARI achieved by the methods on HEP-MASS, KDD Cup 1999, and Poker Hand datasets is only 8.6%, indicating the minimal effect of varying one parameter on the benchmark datasets' max ARI.

4.3   Multi-dimensional Analysis

Number of Samples. Figure 6 shows that on B5K5F1S, all methods get a max ARI of 93.4–100%. DBSCAN achieves a p-value of 100% in all three variations, max ARI of 99.5–100%, and ⟨ARI⟩ of 69.8–76.4%, indicating that DBSCAN always produces better ARI after the variation, even though the default input is 0%. The p-value achieved by mini batch k-means is stable with a stable default maximum, while that of RD and spectral clustering increases according to the decreasing default maximum, which is still below 50.0% except for spectral clustering at the 10000 samples 64.4%. However, the default p-value of these three methods is already 79.2% and above. The figure also indicates that all methods tend to get stable max ARI on CL5K5F. Spectral clustering achieves a better max ARI although it is still only in 25.4–47.2%. Its p-value is also relatively high at 56.5–68.5%, and its max ARI is the highest among the methods. Although RD has a p-value of 74.9% when $K = 5000$, it still has worse max ARI than spectral clustering. Lastly, mini batch k-means has a maximum p-value of only 41.4%, while DBSCAN gets the lowest max ARI among the methods.

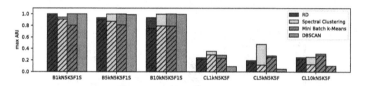

Fig. 6. The method's max ARI on B5K5F1S and CL5K5F ($N \in \{1000, 5000, 10000\}$). The patterned regions indicate the performance when using default parameters.

Number of Clusters. Figure 7 indicates that when applied to B1kN5K1S, all methods' max ARI is stable at 94.1–100%. DBSCAN achieves a p-value of 100% with all max ARI of 100%. RD, spectral clustering, and mini batch k-means obtain a p-value below 22.2% on the 5-cluster sample, but in the range of 52.4–96.0% on samples with 2 and 10 clusters, except for RD, which is 34.9% when $K = 2$. The figure also shows that the max ARI has a decreasing trend with increasing numbers of clusters of CL1kN5F in all four methods. RD, spectral clustering, and mini batch k-means obtain similar overall max ARI. However, spectral clustering gets the best p-value in the 56.4–78.9% range. DBSCAN always gets a 100% p-value, but its max ARI is still lower than the previous two methods.

Number of Features. Figure 8 indicates that when applied to B1kN5K1S, the max ARI increases slightly as the number of features increases. All methods produce a max ARI in the 87.6%–100% range. DBSCAN always gets a decrease in ⟨ARI⟩ and a 0.0% p-value on the 2-feature sample, while in other cases, the p-value and max ARI are at 100%. However, with default parameters, DBSCAN already

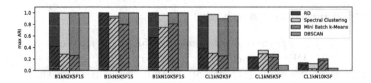

Fig. 7. The methods' max ARI on B1kN5F1S and CL1kN5F ($K \in \{2, 5, 10\}$). The patterned regions indicate the performance when using default parameters.

reaches 99.1% on the 2-feature case. RD, spectral clustering, and mini batch k-means produce a `p-value` of no more than 42.0%, and the max ARI is similar, although mini batch k-means tends to have a higher max ARI. Since there are only two samples in CL1kN5K, the general effects of varying the number of features cannot be ascertained, although they show a downward trend in all four methods. DBSCAN achieves a 100% `p-value` even though its highest max ARI is only 9.0%. The highest `p-value` of RD is only 19.6%, with its highest max ARI at only 10.8%. Spectral clustering gets a higher `p-value` and max ARI than RD and mini batch k-means, at 56.5–99.7% and 35.3–39.2%, respectively.

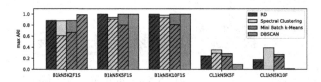

Fig. 8. The methods' max ARI on B1kN5K1S and CL1kN5K ($F \in \{2, 5, 10\}$). The patterned regions show the performance when using default parameters.

Standard Deviation of Clusters. Figure 9 (left) shows that spectral clustering and mini batch k-means achieve a stable max ARI as the clusters' standard deviation increases, consistently at 94.1% and above, with a `p-value` of 4.8–27.7%. RD and DBSCAN produce a decreasing max ARI when $S = 2$, at 54.0% and 70.0%, respectively. DBSCAN obtains a 100% `p-value` and 100% max ARI under the conditions, except when $S = 2$ at 70%. In contrast, under the conditions, RD gets a p-value and max ARI of no more than 16.0% and 6.6%, respectively.

Benchmark Datasets. Figure 9 (right) indicates that DBSCAN still achieves the best max ARI, reaching 96.7% with a `p-value` of 69.4% on KDD Cup 1999 dataset. Mini batch k-means has a max ARI of 74.1% with a sample size 40 times larger than DBSCAN, although its `p-value` is only 5.7%. RD and spectral clustering obtain a 100% `p-value` but with a max ARI of only 43.6% and 0.7%.

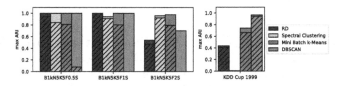

Fig. 9. The methods' max ARI on (left) B1kN5K5F ($S \in \{0.5, 1, 2\}$), and (right) KDD Cup 1999 (RD & spectral clustering with $N = 2000$ and $K = 9$, mini batch k-means with $N = 4898430$ and $K = 23$, and DBSCAN with $N = 100000$ and $K = 6$). The patterned regions indicate the performance when using default parameters.

4.4   Discussion

Stability. When the methods are run twice with different random initializations, they are expected to produce similar clusters. DBSCAN's accuracy remains consistent throughout runs. The three other methods, however, have an average ARI standard deviation of 1–4% on the artificial datasets.

Intuitive Parameters. Parameters must be intuitive to set correctly without knowing much about the data. The number of clusters is the critical parameter in RD, spectral clustering, and mini batch k-means. The methods' accuracy can decrease drastically if it is not known or incorrectly estimated. Spectral clustering's accuracy is also significantly affected by **gamma**, while DBSCAN' is mainly affected by **eps**, which is not explicit in the actual use. The one-dimensional analysis indicates that the difference in the ARI of these parameters can reach 80%.

Performance. The order of methods for the best time and space consumption is mini batch k-means, DBSCAN, RD, and spectral clustering. Using default parameters on the artificial datasets, the effect of varying N, K, F, and S on the $\langle$ARI$\rangle$ is minor. DBSCAN gets the worst $\langle$ARI$\rangle$ with 0% on 55 artificial datasets and at least 80% on 9 datasets. Other methods get an overall similar $\langle$ARI$\rangle$. Mini batch k-means achieves a max ARI of 72% on the entire KDD Cup 1999 dataset, DBSCAN 94% (with $N = 100000$ and $K = 6$), whereas RD and spectral clustering only 41% and 0%, respectively (with $N = 5000$ and $K = 11$).

The multi-dimensional analysis reveals a decreasing trend of max ARI with the increasing number of CL1kN5F clusters in all four methods. Other datasets produce a stable max ARI, except for RD and DBSCAN on datasets with $S = 2$, where the max ARI decreases. In almost all cases, DBSCAN's **p-value** reaches 100% because the previous default value is 0%. On **make_blobs** datasets, all methods have a stable max ARI of 94% and above, except when $S = 2$. Except on CL1kN2K5F, all methods achieve a max ARI of no more than 40% on **make_classification** datasets, where DBSCAN gets the lowest max ARI while spectral clustering and mini batch k-means always get higher. No significant changes in the max ARI occur on the KDD Cup 1999 dataset.

Limitations. Some limitations of this study that can be improved are as follows:

1. No gamma variation in RD. Experiments indicate that gamma has a significant impact on spectral clustering's accuracy. RD may have similar results.
2. Too limited dataset variations. Analyses of artificial datasets do not exhibit clear upward or downward trends. This may be remedied by adding variations, for example, by setting $F \in \{2, 5, 10, 20, 50\}$, and similarly with other parameters. Adding more artificial datasets with other distributions or benchmark datasets may produce clear-cut results, thus allowing us to arrive at definite trend conclusions.

5   Conclusion

Mini batch k-means achieves the best overall results, from accuracy to time and space consumption. Although spectral clustering has competitive ARI results on artificial datasets with default and multi-dimensional parameters, its time and space consumption is at least 2 and 30 times smaller, respectively. Mini batch k-means gets a 74% max ARI on the whole KDD Cup 1999 dataset, compared to spectral clustering's 1% on a 2449-time smaller dataset sampled from it.

If the number of optimization iterations is increased, RD is relatively competitive with spectral clustering in terms of ARI. However, its time and space requirement will be prohibitively larger than spectral clustering. On KDD Cup 1999, RD gets a 44% max ARI with the same samples as spectral clustering.

The analysis results using default parameters indicate that the order of methods for the best time and space consumption is mini batch k-means, DBSCAN, RD, and spectral clustering. Although DBSCAN produces very low measures at default parameters, some with only 0%, most p-value in the multi-dimensional analysis reaches 100%, with a max ARI of 100% in most make_blobs datasets. Its max ARI on KDD Cup 1999 of 100000 samples also reaches 97%.

Acknowledgements. This work is partially supported by Hibah Penelitian Fakultas Dana Masyarakat Tahun Anggaran 2022, Faculty of Mathematics and Natural Sciences, Universitas Gadjah Mada.

References

1. Dwiandriani, F., Kusumasari, T.F., Hasibuan, M.A.: Fingerprint clustering algorithm for data profiling using Pentaho data integration. In: 2nd ICITISEE, pp. 359–363 (2017). https://doi.org/10.1109/ICITISEE.2017.8285528
2. Ester, M., Kriegel, H.P., Sander, J., Xu, X.: A density-based algorithm for discovering clusters in large spatial databases with noise. In: KDD1996, pp. 226–231. AAAI Press (1996). https://dl.acm.org/doi/10.5555/3001460.3001507
3. Helistö, N., Kiviluoma, J., Reittu, H.: Selection of representative slices for generation expansion planning using regular decomposition. Energy **211**, 118585 (2020). https://doi.org/10.1016/j.energy.2020.118585

4. Kuusela, P., Norros, I., Reittu, H., Piira, K.: Hierarchical multiplicative model for characterizing residential electricity consumption. J. Energy Eng. **144**(3) (2018). https://doi.org/10.1061/(ASCE)EY.1943-7897.0000532
5. MacQueen, J.: Some methods for classification and analysis of multivariate observations. In: 5th Berkeley Symposium on Mathematical Statistics and Probability. vol. 1: Statistics, pp. 281–297 (1967)
6. Ng, A.Y., Jordan, M.I., Weiss, Y.: On spectral clustering: Analysis and an algorithm. In: NIPS'01, pp. 849–856. MIT Press (2001). https://dl.acm.org/doi/10.5555/2980539.2980649
7. Pehkonen, V., Reittu, H.: Szemerédi-type clustering of peer-to-peer streaming system. In: Cnet 2011, pp. 23–30. ITC (2011). https://dl.acm.org/doi/10.5555/2043527.2043531
8. Reittu, H., Bazsó, F., Norros, I.: Regular decomposition: an information and graph theoretic approach to stochastic block models. CoRR abs/1704.07114 (2017). http://arxiv.org/abs/1704.07114
9. Reittu, Hannu, Bazsó, Fülöp., Weiss, Robert: Regular decomposition of multivariate time series and other matrices. In: Fränti, Pasi, Brown, Gavin, Loog, Marco, Escolano, Francisco, Pelillo, Marcello (eds.) S+SSPR 2014. LNCS, vol. 8621, pp. 424–433. Springer, Heidelberg (2014). https://doi.org/10.1007/978-3-662-44415-3_43
10. Reittu, H., Leskela, L., Raty, T., Fiorucci, M.: Analysis of large sparse graphs using regular decomposition of graph distance matrices. In: IEEE Big Data 2018, pp. 3784–3792 (2018). https://doi.org/10.1109/BigData.2018.8622118
11. Reittu, H., Norros, I., Räty, T., Bolla, M., Bazsó, F.: Regular decomposition of large graphs: foundation of a sampling approach to stochastic block model fitting. Data Sci. Eng. **4**(1), 44–60 (2019). https://doi.org/10.1007/s41019-019-0084-x
12. Rodriguez, M.Z., et al.: Clustering algorithms: A comparative approach. PLoS ONE **14**(1), 1–34 (2019). https://doi.org/10.1371/journal.pone.0210236
13. Scikit-Learn Modules: Clustering. https://scikit-learn.org/stable/modules/clustering.html. Accessed 25 Mar 2021
14. Sculley, D.: Web-scale k-means clustering. In: WWW 2010, pp. 1177–1178. ACM (2010). https://doi.org/10.1145/1772690.1772862
15. Shi, H., et al.: An improved fuzzy c-means soft clustering based on density peak for wind power forecasting data processing. In: 2020 AEEES, pp. 801–804 (2020). https://doi.org/10.1109/AEEES48850.2020.9121374
16. Si, C., Xu, S., Wan, C., Chen, D., Cui, W., Zhao, J.: Electric load clustering in smart grid: Methodologies, applications, and future trends. J. Mod. Power Syst. Clean Energy **9**(2), 237–252 (2021). https://doi.org/10.35833/MPCE.2020.000472
17. Triola, M.F., Goodman, W.M., Law, R., Labute, G.: Elementary Statistics. Pearson/Addison-Wesley Reading (2006)
18. UCI Machine Learning Repository: UCI machine learning repository: Data sets. https://archive.ics.uci.edu/ml/datasets.php. Accessed 31 May 2021
19. Xu, D., Tian, Y.: A comprehensive survey of clustering algorithms. Ann. Data Sci. **2**(2), 165–193 (2015). https://doi.org/10.1007/s40745-015-0040-1

Security and Privacy Engineering

Authentication of Luxury Products – Identifying Key Requirements from a Seller and Consumer Perspective

Robert Zimmermann[1]([⊠]), Chibuzor Udokwu[1], Ricarda Kompp[1], Patrick Brandtner[1], and Alex Norta[2,3]

[1] University of Applied Sciences Upper Austria, 4400 Steyr, Austria
{robert.zimmermann,Chibuzor.Udokwu,Ricarda.Kompp,
Patrick.Brandtner}@fh-steyr.at
[2] Tallinn University, Tallinn, Estonia
alex.norta.phd@ieee.org
[3] Dymaxion OU, Tallinn, Estonia

Abstract. Luxury products are expensive goods of high quality that are produced in limited quantities. Unsurprisingly, the problem of counterfeiting is especially high for such products, causing various issues for sellers and consumers. Therefore, product authentication represents an important endeavor. While traditional approaches such as expert-based product authentication are reliable but expensive, consumer-based approaches are cheaper but significantly more error-prone. Hence, the development of efficient approaches that also consider the advantages of modern technologies, such as e.g., blockchains, provide a high potential for improving the status-quo. The current paper applies a mixed-method approach and reports about a quantitative survey in combination with expert interviews to identify the main requirements and preferences from consumer and seller perspective. Results show that the knowledge of authentication methods is unevenly distributed between experts and consumers. While both consumers and experts are aware of traditional, serial number-based approaches, blockchain-enabled ways of product authentication are only known by experts. However, both groups tend to prefer digital ways of authentication and agree that sellers, followed by producers, and lastly consumers are responsible for ensuring authentic products. Consumers desire many additional features for product authentication than experts. Most desired features include tracking the sales history via e.g., the blockchain or online directories, the traceability of ownership, or the possibility to conduct home tests for consumers. The results of the paper provide researchers and practitioners with a requirement base for developing novel authentication approaches.

Keywords: Luxury · Product authentication · Authentication requirements · Blockchain · Mixed method · NFT · Logistics · Trust

1   Introduction

Luxury goods are defined as goods that are of the best quality, most expensive, and/or produced in limited quantities [1]. Unsurprisingly, luxury products are prone to be counterfeited. Counterfeit luxury products can cost sellers and consumers a significant amount of money if they are not identified correctly [2]. Thus, several techniques have been established to ensure the authenticity of luxury products. Nevertheless, the authentication of luxury products can be costly and time-consuming as in most cases the thorough authentication of luxury products requires highly skilled specialists who need to be familiar not only with the specific authentication methods but also explicit characteristics of the luxury product being authenticated [3]. In contrast, some authentication methods can be used by consumers, requiring less time while producing only minor costs (e.g., [3–5]). Yet, these authentication methods can lead to uncertain results as these methods are not able to completely mimic the work of luxury product authentication specialists [6]. Due to this imbalance in access to authentication methods, it is crucial to determine which specific requirements sellers and consumers have when authenticating luxury products. As such, this paper contributes to the luxury product authentication literature by illuminating the features most requested for authenticating luxury products by sellers and consumers. Consequently, the following research questions are raised:

RQ1: Which methods for authenticating luxury products are known by sellers and consumers?
RQ2: What are the most requested features when authenticating luxury products from a seller and consumer perspective?

The paper is structured the following way. Following this introduction, Sect. 2 presents a literature review of previous studies dealing with the authentication of luxury products to provide the background of our study. Section 3 provides the methodology of this paper giving insights into how the data used in this study were collected. Consequently, Sect. 4 provides an analysis of the collected data and corresponding results. In Sect. 5 the results are discussed, and the research questions are answered. Closing, Sect. 6 provides a conclusion of the paper, limitations of our approach, and an outlook for future research.

2   Background

To gain an overview of previous studies dealing with the authentication of luxury products, a literature review was conducted in February 2022. Following vom Brocke et al. [7], the literature review focuses on research outcomes and applications, with the goal to summarize and integrate findings from literature, taking a neutral perspective for scholars specialized in authenticating luxury products. The literature search was conducted using the Scopus database applying the following search string.

TITLE-ABS-KEY (Luxury AND ("Fraud" OR "Counterfeit" OR "Authentication" OR "Authenticate"))

The literature review revealed 232 papers that were further screened for studies including, case studies, expert interviews, consumer surveys, or literature reviews containing relevant information about the authentication of luxury products to focus on studies presenting practical knowledge and knowledge summaries. This reduced the number of papers to a total of 15. The main findings of these papers, in terms of authenticating luxury products, can be found in Table 1.

Table 1. Literature review summary.

Source	Type of study	Main finding*
[1]	Conceptual LR	Combating counterfeits is an under-researched topic disregarding the needs of the industry
[8]	Empirical CS	The combination of neural networks can result in superior identification of fake products
[6]	Empirical EI	Blockchain technology is a solution for disintermediation, traceability, and transparency in the luxury goods sector
[9]	Empirical CS	Demonstration of a novel type of security label based on down-conversion photoluminescence from erbium-doped silicon
[10]	Empirical CS	When the cost difference for authentication services is small (large), platform(s) should adopt blockchain (manual) services
[11]	Conceptual LR	Effective authentication of luxury products must be addressed by the demand-, supply-, and legal side simultaneously
[12]	Empirical CS	Blockchain technology can be used as a tamper-proof information exchange mechanism
[13]	Empirical CS	Developed two detection systems, which led to more than 4,400 counterfeit online shops being taken down
[14]	Empirical CS	Block-chain solution to improve the performance of luxury product authentication
[15]	Empirical CS	Demonstration of tamper-proof holographic structures using laser direct writing
[16]	Empirical SV	As counterfeits have come remarkably close to the originals, brands should find new, creative ways to socially authenticate purchases for their customers
[4]	Empirical CS	Prototype of an RFID-based anti-counterfeiting security system
[5]	Empirical CS	A smartphone-based anti-counterfeiting system using 2D barcodes and public key cryptography should be applied using QR-codes
[17]	Empirical CS	Counterfeiter websites are different from authorized retailers in many key attributes
[3]	Empirical CS	Prototype of a mobile RFID-based self-validation system

Notes: * Regarding the authentication of luxury products; Literature Review (LR); Case Study (CS); Survey (SV); Expert Interview (EI).

Looking at these previous approaches, we discover that twelve of the 15 studies propose better authentication methods for luxury products. Among these papers, a slight focus on blockchain solutions is observable as four of the twelve papers propose blockchain solutions. Even though most papers found focus on improving authentication methods, the most recent literature review by [1] concludes that combating counterfeits is an under-researched topic disregarding the needs of the industry. Still, this is also in line with the found literature review conducted by [11], which summarizes that effective authentication of luxury products must be addressed by the demand-, supply-, and legal side simultaneously. Nevertheless, in view of the increasing quality of counterfeit products the survey of [16] suggests that authenticating luxury products with tools and techniques might not be possible in the future and thus, proposes brands to develop new creative ways to socially authenticate purchases for their customers.

In summary, we show that no previous study points out which methods are currently known and used by sellers and consumers, and which key features sellers and consumers require from these methods to authenticate luxury products. Thus, this study focuses on filling this research gap.

3 Method

To illuminate which authentication methods are known to sellers and consumers, and the key features these groups require when using them, a mixed method study combining an expert interview and a consumer survey was conducted. Mixed method approaches represent a combination of qualitative and quantitative methods and allow for a triangulation of data from different sources to extract new findings and modes of analysis [18, 19]. Such approaches produce insights into various phenomena of interest that are not fully understood using either a quantitative or a qualitative method only and have successfully been applied in a variety of settings [20–23]. More precisely, we combine qualitative expert interviews with a quantitative survey to include both deep and detailed expert knowledge and enrich it with the broader, quantitative consumer perspective. In the following subsections, we present detailed information about the conducted expert interviews (3.1) and consumer survey (3.2).

3.1 Expert Interview

An expert interview was conducted to gather in-depth knowledge about the currently known methods for authenticating luxury products from a seller's perspective. In this regard, expert interviews have shown to be well suited to collect insights regarding specific domain knowledge, which is difficult to uncover with survey-based methods only [24, 25].

For expert identification and selection, two main approaches can be applied: random selection and information-oriented selection [26]. In accordance with the aim of our study and the clearly focused domain of luxury product authentication, we chose an information-oriented sampling approach. Based on this structured selection procedure, we recruited 8 sellers of luxury products with multiple years of experience of authenticating luxury products. More detailed information about the experts can be found in Table 2.

The data collection procedure of our expert interview follows four distinctive steps: i) introduction questions collect details about the expert and ensure the expert status, ii) a semi-structured interview to ensure a free flow of the interview but also keep the interview focused on the topic of authenticating luxury products, iii) audio and video recordings as a basis for the transcription of the interviews, and iv) the generation of interview transcripts for further analysis [27, 28].

We analyzed the expert interviews by structuring the interview transcripts and applying cross-interview comparison to identify commonalities and differences between the expert opinions [29].

The interview comprises 16 questions, divided into three main topics: information about the sold/owned luxury products (5 questions), awareness of authentication methods (4 questions), and assessment of authentication methods (7 questions), enabling us to address the outlined research questions.

Table 2. Expert Interview participants.

No	Experience	Industry	Relevant expertise
1	>10 years	E-commerce for luxury watches	Journalist/blogger/lecturer
2	>20 years	Watches and jewelry store	Owner of a watch-making company
3	>8 years	E-commerce for luxury watches	Head of logistics
4	>10 years	Traditional fashion store	Upper management
5	>20 years	Watches and jewelry store	Upper management/Watchmaker
6	>6 years	Watches and jewelry store	Company owner
7	>10 years	Watches and jewelry store	Company owner
8	>7 years	Watches and jewelry store	Company owner

3.2 Consumer Survey

A consumer survey was conducted (30.06.–01.07.2022) using the same (though adapted) questions from the expert interview to gather in-depth knowledge about currently known methods for authenticating luxury products from a consumer perspective. Still, to reduce the complexity of the consumer survey we took the answers from the semi-structured expert interviews and used them as multiple-choice options for the consumer survey.

Participants were recruited using the crowdsourcing provider Clickworker.com. Clickworker.com ensures a high level of participant qualification by performing, ID checks, testing of writing and language qualifications, and a constant evaluation of their members' response patterns [30].

In total, 248 participants were recruited from the German-speaking area (Germany, Austria, and Switzerland). A demographic overview and background information of the participants is shown in Table 3. No abnormalities or biases were observed.

To compare the answers from experts with the answers from consumers we applied a Qualitative Comparative Analysis (QCA) based approach following [31] to summarize the received answers from both groups, allowing us to highlight differences in the knowledge and requirements in respect to luxury product authentication methods.

Table 3. Demographics and background information.

	N	%		N	%
Age (Ø = 37.88; σ = 11.57)			*Which luxury products do you own?*		
Gender			Watches	138	56%
Male	135	54%	Jewelry	129	52%
Female	111	45%	Accessories	140	56%
PNA	2	1%	Other	22	9%
Net household income (per month in EUR)			*Which luxury products would you resell?*		
<3000	104	42%	Watches	74	54%*
3001–5000	73	29%	Jewelry	58	45%*
5001€ – 7000€	37	15%	Accessories	66	47%*
7001€ – 9000€	5	2%	Other	9	41%*
PNA	29	12%	None	94	38%
Education			*Which luxury products did you buy used?*		
High School	79	31.5%	Watches	34	25%*
Bachelor	133	54%	Jewelry	19	15%*
Master or PhD	35	14%	Accessories	31	22%*
PNA	1	0.5%	Other	0	0%*

What is the average price of your luxury products?

	<500€	501€–1000€	1001€–1500€	1501€–2000€	>2000€
Watches	54	44	14	11	15
Jewelry	55	30	21	10	13
Accessories	88	32	19	2	0
Other	5	5	4	4	4

How long do you keep your luxury products?

	<1 y	<5 y	<10 y	>10 y	Depends
Watches	10	32	8	11	13
Jewelry	14	7	10	10	17
Accessories	12	34	10	1	9
Other	0	4	1	1	3

Notes: *Based on owners of respective luxury products; Prefer not to answer (PNA).

4   Results

The results of our expert interview and consumer survey regarding the awareness of sellers and consumers about authentication methods are displayed in Table 4. The features desired from sellers and consumers for future authentication methods are displayed in Table 5.

Looking at Table 4, it becomes evident that the knowledge about authentication methods is unevenly distributed between experts and consumers. While most people in both groups are familiar with manual, visual, or auditory inspection of abnormalities, and the verification via serial number, the rest of the features are far less known. Especially, verification via blockchain is a method mostly known by experts and not by consumers. We observe that, experts display a higher knowledge of authentication methods than consumers. It should be noted, as consumers were given multiple choice questions, which originated from the answers extracted from the expert interviews, their ad hoc knowledge might even be lower.

Table 4. Awareness authentication methods.

Which methods do you know for authenticating luxury products?	Experts		Consumers	
	N	%	N	%
Manual, visual, or auditory inspection for abnormalities	7	88%	126	51%
Verification of serial number	7	88%	136	55%
Material testing	3	38%	99	40%
Checking for special labels	1	13%	85	34%
Warranty card verification	3	38%	96	39%
QR code verification	3	38%	34	14%
GIA certificate check	2	25%	28	11%
Checking for laser engravings	1	13%	56	23%
Verification via NFC chip	1	13%	18	7%
Verification via Blockchain (NFT)	4	50%	13	5%
Video tutorials	1	13%	30	12%
RFID verification	1	13%	17	7%
None	N/A	N/A	11	4%

Note: Colors indicate number of mentions (green more mentions, red less mentions)

Looking at Table 5, it becomes apparent that consumers desire more features for authenticating luxury products than experts. Both groups agree that the independent verification of serial numbers in an online directory and the traceability of the sales history are desirable features. Similarly, they agree that the traceability of ownership, home test for consumers, high-resolution images on the internet, and a digital service book are less important. In contrast, expert regard certificates for a successful authentication, fast authenticity verification, and uniform procedures for authenticating luxury products far less important than consumers.

Concerning the question if analog or digital authentication methods would be preferable, consumers and experts mostly agree that digital methods would be the preferred way. Still, only one expert prefers analog authentication while more experts than consumers prefer a combination of both methods. Similarly, experts and consumers agree that sellers, followed by producers, followed by consumers are responsible for authenticating resold luxury products. They differ in the perception of who should pay for additional authentication services as follows. While consumers see mostly sellers and producers as responsible for such payments, experts see this responsibility as more evenly distributed with a strong focus on consumers.

Experts rate the ability to identify products via the blockchain (mean = 3.875; p = < 0.009) and the ability to transfer product ownership via the blockchain (mean = 3.75; p = < 0.015) significantly less than consumers (mean = 2.75; 2.73). The most important ability for both groups is to track the sales history of a product via the blockchain, and the least important ability is to sell luxury products using cryptocurrencies. In these cases, the perception of importance does not significantly differ between experts and consumers.

Table 5. Desired features for authenticating luxury products.

Which features/ capabilities would you like to see for luxury product authentication?				
	Experts		Consumers	
	N	%	N	%
Certificate of authenticity for successful authenticity verification	1	13%	115	46%
Fast authenticity verification	1	13%	107	43%
Uniform procedures for authenticity verification	1	13%	105	42%
Independent verification of a serial number in an online directory	4	50%	102	41%
Traceability of sales history	4	50%	101	41%
Traceability of ownership	2	25%	72	29%
Consumer home test for authenticity verification	2	25%	59	24%
High-resolution images of the original on the Internet	1	13%	58	23%
Digital service book	2	25%	39	16%
Would you prefer digital or analog authentication?				
Analog	1	13%	82	33%
Digital	4	50%	114	46%
Both in Combination	3	38%	52	21%
Who should be responsible for verifying the authenticity of resold products?				
Seller	7	88%	217	88%
Consumer	3	38%	77	31%
Producer	4	50%	120	48%
Who should pay for additional authentication services?				
Seller	4	50%	131	53%
Consumer	5	63%	24	10%
Producer	3	38%	93	38%
How would you rate the importance of these features?				
The ability to:		**Mean**	**Mean**	**p***
identify products via the blockchain		3.875	2.75	<0.009
transfer ownership of luxury products via the blockchain		3.75	2.73	<0.015
sell used luxury products with cryptocurrencies		2.25	2.05	0.650
track the sales history of luxury products via the blockchain		4.5	3.73	0.054

Notes: *Two-tailed independent t-test; Colors indicate number of mentions (green more mentions, red less mentions)

5 Discussion

In regard to RQ I, our results highlight that overall, consumers have an average knowledge of authentication methods at best. While they are familiar with manual, visual, or auditory inspection of abnormalities, and the verification via serial numbers, more modern features (e.g., QR codes, NFC chips, RFID, NFT) are only known by experts.

This reveals an interesting contradiction. As stated by [16] future counterfeits might be indistinguishable for consumers and thus brands should work on social authentication processes for luxury products. Yet, our research shows that consumers possess little knowledge about authentication processes in general. Thus, it might be a more suitable solution to first educate consumers in terms of authenticating luxury products before abandoning authentication methods at all. This would also be in line with the findings of [11], suggesting that only addressing the demand-, supply-, and legal side simultaneously is the most effective authentication way of authenticating luxury products. This might be a particularly difficult endeavor, as stated by [1], combating counterfeits is still an under-researched topic disregarding the needs of the industry. This observation also surfaces in our research. Since from the twelve papers suggesting new authentication methods, only six (blockchain [6, 12, 14], RFID [3, 4], QR-codes [5]) are known by experts. It becomes apparent that for an effective alignment of consumers, producers, and sellers, more efforts must be placed on educating these stakeholders on the needs and possibilities of each other.

Regarding RQII, it became evident that consumers wish for reliable authentication certificates, a fast authentication process, and uniform authentication processes. As stated before, the proper authentication of luxury products is a timely and cost-intensive procedure [3], which can produce high financial damage if done incorrectly [2]. Thus, it can be argued that consumers request features to reduce the costs and uncertainty of the authentication processes. For similar reasons, consumers might also request an independent verification of serial numbers in online directories and the traceability of sales history. These are also features which are most requested by sellers. Still, sellers (including consumers who want to resell products) might have different reasons for requesting a verification. In fact, sellers in most countries face significant legal issues when selling counterfeited products (e.g., Germany: up to 10.000€ fine and three years of prison) even if sold unintentionally [32]. Thus, they require a high amount of certainty regarding the result of an authentication process. Consequently, it could be argued that the requested features help sellers to enable a more secure authentication process. The remaining features (traceability of ownership, consumer home test for authenticity verification, high-resolution images of the original product on the internet, and a digital service book) were not highly requested by sellers and consumers. Thus, all these features would add an additional layer of work to the already complex process of authenticating luxury products. Therefore, they would contrast the will of sellers and consumers to reduce the complexity of the process, highlighted by [3, 5, 13]. In general, sellers and consumers agree that future authentication services should be mostly digital. This is also reflected in the conducted literature review as only two [9, 15] of the twelve papers comprising new authentication methods presented purely analog, and four [3–5, 8] papers hybrid verification methods. A probable reason for this might be the high hopes that are placed on digital technologies to decrease the complexity of processes in general. Also, sellers and consumers agree that overall, sellers should be responsible to verify the authenticity of luxury products. This indicates that the current status quo of the authentication process is acceptable for the involved stakeholders. Yet, this attitude might be counterproductive regarding the necessity of unifying the demand-, supply-, and legal side in order to ensure an effective authentication of luxury products as pointed out by [11]. Lastly, sellers and consumers disagree on who should pay for additional authentication services. As pointed out before, the authentication of luxury products is very cost intensive. Consequently, it is only reasonable to assume that neither group would be willing to increase these costs even further.

Reflecting on the performed literature review and the opinion of experts it became apparent that blockchain technology is a preferred direction of future authentication services. This ties in with the observations in our study that the traceability of product history and ownership is an important feature that is desired by both sellers and consumers of luxury products. Furthermore, QR-codes represents the preferred method for representing and verifying the authenticity of luxury products. Blockchain provides the possibility of storing a digital representation of luxury products and provides a traceable verification of the history and ownership of luxury products. For instance, physical luxury products encoded in QR codes can be stored on the blockchain as a non-fungible token (NFT), thus providing a unique digital representation of the luxury product [33]. A traceable product history and ownership can be achieved with blockchain-based digital signatures providing a verifiable timestamp of the transfer of ownership between two consumers and between sellers and consumers [34].

The NFT minting for preventing counterfeit product trading does not suffice by itself. We depict in Fig. 1 a thought experiment that reveals the shortcomings about the online trade of a luxury watch that involves the minting of an NFT. The goal of minting a luxury-watch assigned NFT is to establish a sense of identity authentication that assures the buyer the luxury watch is not a counterfeit product.

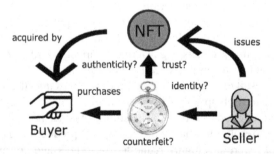

Fig. 1. Conceptual running case for online trading a luxury watch with included NFT minting

Merely minting an NFT does not resolve the issues of identity authentication of the luxury watch seller in Fig. 1. The buyer is still confronted with the problem of the credibility of the minted NFT and the issue of legitimate ownership transfer if the online trade is carried out involving the NFT. The seller may also mint several NFTs that reference the underlying asset of the same luxury watch to fraudulent repeat sales.

As a mitigation option, certainly the genesis NFT-minting phase can be complemented with multi-factor challenge-set self-sovereign identity authentication (MFSSIA) [35].

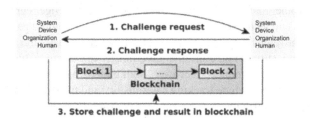

Fig. 2. The MFSSIA lifecycle for challenge-response management [36]

Briefly, in Fig. 2, the MFSSIA lifecycle depictions show the variability in terms of identity authentication. Thus, the issuer of challenges and respective responder can either be a system, device such as for IoT, an organization, or human. By storing first the challenge set on a blockchain and the corresponding responses too, immutable traceability is achieved for the life cycle. A subsequent evaluation of the responses yields either as a result that the identity authentication for a specific context is successful, or the responses are not satisfactory to culminate in a termination of a trade. Mapped to the thought experiment in Fig. 1, the challenge sets issued in support of the NFT printing could hypothetically first result in a self-sovereign identity authentication of the buyer and seller, the organization of the seller, and the ownership title for the luxury watch in that the seller possesses a purchasing invoice that is authenticated digitally.

Although experts rank blockchain and its related technologies high for achieving digital authentication of luxury products, consumers rank them lower. This could imply that experts, in contrast to consumers, are aware of the potential of blockchain-related technologies in ensuring a tamper-proof system of information storage. Still, blockchain-based applications that enable users of luxury products to independently verify product authenticity are currently not available for consumers, thus possibly reducing their knowledge and interest in them. Currently, common blockchain applications are mainly used in decentralized finance [37, 38]. As shown by the conducted literature review, studies have provided solutions for applying blockchain for authenticating luxury products along the supply chain (e.g., [6, 12, 14]).

6 Conclusion

In the current paper, we applied a mixed-method approach, combining qualitative (expert interviews) and quantitative (survey) methods. Regarding RQ1, an overview of authentication methods known by sellers and consumers could be derived (see Table 4). It became apparent that consumers only have limited knowledge about digital luxury product authentication methods. Regarding RQ2, the most requested features when authenticating luxury products from seller and consumer perspective could be identified (see Table 5). It became apparent that consumers request features to ensure a secure authentication process and features to reduce the complexity of the entire process. In contrast, experts mostly request features to ensure a more secure authentication process only.

In addition, we identified the main requirements in the context of luxury product authentication from consumer, sellers, and producer perspective. The results on the one hand show a high level of agreement regarding the responsibility for ensuring authentic products. On the other hand, there are different levels of knowledge regarding authentication approaches and technologies and disagreement on who should pay for additional authentication approaches. Experts agreed that the blockchain may offer a high potential for product authentication while consumers are mostly not aware of blockchain-based authentication for luxury products. However, both experts and consumers agreed that the most desired features include tracking sales history and traceability of ownership.

In summary, the contribution of our paper is twofold. First, we expand the body of luxury product authentication literature by providing a unique view on the most requested features when authenticating luxury products from seller and consumer perspective. Second, our work provides future research endeavors with a plethora of starting points. On the one hand, the development of novel and innovative authentication approaches based on technologies as, e.g., the blockchain, can build on the identified requirements and are hence provided with an ideal starting base. On the other hand, the identified important and less important features may also be used to further develop or adapt existing solutions from practitioners' point of view. Future research may also be conducted with a focus on additional countries or specific types of luxury products to provide further details for the identified requirements. Especially, it would be interesting to analyze the differences in product authentication requirements between different categories and value ranges of luxury products and compare e.g., watches with jewelry and cars or works of art. Broadening sample sizes for additional countries and comparing such results with our results would also increase the generalizability of results and identification of cultural differences in authentication requirements.

A limitation of the current paper might be the relatively small number of experts participating in the expert interviews. However, by applying the information-oriented, structured sampling approach presented in Sect. 3, we ensure the selection of actual experts with high levels of domain knowledge. This careful selection allows for generating qualitative results, with high internal validity [24, 39].

Acknowledgement. This research is partly sponsored by Robonomics Grant Program and the Government of Upper Austria as part of the excellence network for logistics Logistikum.Retail.

References

1. Sharma, A., Soni, M., Borah, S.B., Haque, T.: From silos to synergies: a systematic review of luxury in marketing research. J. Bus. Res. **139**, 893–907 (2022). https://doi.org/10.1016/j.jbusres.2021.09.007
2. Singh, D.P., Kastanakis, M.N., Paul, J., Felix, R.: Non-deceptive counterfeit purchase behavior of luxury fashion products. J. Consum. Behav **20**, 1078–1091 (2021). https://doi.org/10.1002/cb.1917
3. Ting, S.L., Tsang, A.H.C.: A two-factor authentication system using radio frequency identification and watermarking technology. Comput. Ind. **64**, 268–279 (2013). https://doi.org/10.1016/j.compind.2012.11.002

4. Ma, T., Zhang, H., Qian, J., Liu, S., Zhang, X., Ma, X.: The design of brand cosmetics anti-counterfeiting system based on RFID technology. In: 2015 International Conference on Network and Information Systems for Computers, pp. 184–189. IEEE (2015). https://doi.org/10.1109/ICNISC.2015.36

5. Rana, A., Ciardulli, A.: Enabling consumers to self-verify authenticity of products. In: The 9th International Conference for Internet Technology and Secured Transactions (ICITST-2014), pp. 254–255. IEEE (2014). https://doi.org/10.1109/ICITST.2014.7038816

6. de Boissieu, E., Kondrateva, G., Baudier, P., Ammi, C.: The use of blockchain in the luxury industry: supply chains and the traceability of goods. J. Enterp. Inform. Mange. 34, 1318–1338 (2021). https://doi.org/10.1108/JEIM-11-2020-0471

7. Brocke, J.v., Simons, A., Niehaves, B., Reimer, K.: Reconstructing the giant. on the importance of rigour in documenting the literature search process. In: ECIS 2009 Proceedings, vol. 161 (2009)

8. Peng, J., Zou, B., Zhu, C.: Combining external attention GAN with deep convolutional neural networks for real–fake identification of luxury handbags. Vis. Comput. 26, 357 (2021). https://doi.org/10.1007/s00371-021-02378-x

9. Larin, A.O., et al.: Luminescent erbium-doped silicon thin films for advanced anti-counterfeit labels. Adv. Mater. 33(16), 2005886 (2021). https://doi.org/10.1002/adma.202005886

10. Li, G., Fan, Z.-P., Wu, X.-Y.: The choice strategy of authentication technology for luxury e-commerce platforms in the Blockchain Era. IEEE Trans. Eng. Manag. 1–14 (2022). https://doi.org/10.1109/TEM.2021.3076606

11. Amaral, N.B.: What can be done to address luxury counterfeiting? an integrative review of tactics and strategies. J. Brand Manag. 27, 691–709 (2020). https://doi.org/10.1057/s41262-020-00206-6

12. Juma, H., Shaalan, K., Kamel, I.: Customs-based blockchain solution for exportation protection. In: Shen, H., Sang, Y. (eds.) PAAP 2019. CCIS, vol. 1163, pp. 405–416. Springer, Singapore (2020). https://doi.org/10.1007/978-981-15-2767-8_36

13. Wabeke, T., Moura, G.C.M., Franken, N., Hesselman, C.: Counterfighting counterfeit: detecting and taking down fraudulent webshops at a ccTLD. In: Sperotto, A., Dainotti, A., Stiller, B. (eds.) PAM 2020. LNCS, vol. 12048, pp. 158–174. Springer, Cham (2020). https://doi.org/10.1007/978-3-030-44081-7_10

14. Chia-Yu, W., Shin-Fu, S., Sheng-Ming, W.: Applying block-chain technology for commodity authenticity. In: 2019 IEEE International Conference on Consumer Electronics – Taiwan (ICCE-TW), pp. 1–2. IEEE (2019). https://doi.org/10.1109/ICCE-TW46550.2019.8991933

15. Wlodarczyk, K.L., Ardron, M., Weston, N.J., Hand, D.P.: Holographic watermarks and steganographic markings for combating the counterfeiting practices of high-value metal products. J. Mater. Process. Technol. 264, 328–335 (2019). https://doi.org/10.1016/j.jmatprotec.2018.09.020

16. Randhawa, P., Calantone, R.J., Voorhees, C.M.: The pursuit of counterfeited luxury: an examination of the negative side effects of close consumer–brand connections. J. Bus. Res. 68, 2395–2403 (2015). https://doi.org/10.1016/j.jbusres.2015.02.022

17. Wilson, J.M., Fenoff, R.: Distinguishing counterfeit from authentic product retailers in the virtual marketplace. Int. Crim. Justice Rev. 24, 39–58 (2014). https://doi.org/10.1177/1057567714527390

18. Kaplan, B., Duchon, D.: Combining qualitative and quantitative methods in information systems research: a case study. MIS Quart. 12, 571–586 (1988)

19. Brandtner, P.: Design and evaluation of a process model for the early stages of product innovation. In: New Waves in Innovation Management Research-Ispim Insights: Series in Innovation Studies, pp. 149–162 (2017)

20. Venkatesh, V., Brown, S.A., Bala, H.: Bridging the qualitative-quantitative divide: guidelines for conducting mixed methods research in information systems. MIS Quart. **37**, 21–54 (2013). https://doi.org/10.25300/MISQ/2013/37.1.02

21. Brandtner, P., Helfert, M.: Multi-media and web-based evaluation of design artifacts-syntactic, semantic and pragmatic quality of process models. Syst., Signs Actions: An Int. J. Inform. Technol., Action, Commun. Workpractices **11**, 54–78 (2018)

22. Andreas, A., Patrick, B., Petra, G., Andreas, H.: Search engine optimization meets e-business – a theory-based evaluation: findability and usability as key success factors. In: Proceedings of the International Conference on Data Communication Networking, e-Business and Optical Communication Systems, pp. 237–250 (2012)

23. Udokwu, C., Darbanian, F., Falatouri, T.N., Brandtner, P.: Evaluating technique for capturing customer satisfaction data in retail supply chain. In: 2020 The 4th International Conference on E-commerce, E-Business and E-Government, pp. 89–95. ACM, New York, NY, USA (2020). https://doi.org/10.1145/3409929.3414743

24. Brandtner, P., Udokwu, C., Darbanian, F., Falatouri, T.: Applications of big data analytics in supply chain management: findings from expert interviews. In: 2021 The 4th International Conference on Computers in Management and Business, pp. 77–82. ACM, New York, NY, USA (2021)

25. Döringer, S.: 'The problem-centred expert interview'. Combining qualitative interviewing approaches for investigating implicit expert knowledge. Int. J. Soc. Res. Methodol. **24**(3), 265–278 (2020). https://doi.org/10.1080/13645579.2020.1766777

26. Kellermayr-Scheucher, M., Hörandner, L., Brandtner, P.: Digitalization at the point-of-sale in grocery retail - state of the art of smart shelf technology and application scenarios. Procedia Comput. Sci. **196**, 77–84 (2022). https://doi.org/10.1016/j.procs.2021.11.075

27. Kurz, A., Stockhammer, C., Fuchs, S., Meinhard, D.: Das problemzentrierte interview. In: Buber, R., Holzmüller, H.H. (eds.) Qualitative Marktforschung, pp. 463–475. Gabler, Wiesbaden (2007). https://doi.org/10.1007/978-3-8349-9258-1_29

28. Brandtner, P., Mates, M.: Artificial intelligence in strategic foresight – current practices and future application potentials. In: Proceedings of the 2021 12th International Conference on E-business, Management and Economics (ICEME 2021), pp. 75–81 (2021)

29. Albers, S., Klapper, D., Konradt, U., Walter, A., Wolf, J. (eds.): Methodik der empirischen Forschung. Gabler Verlag, Wiesbaden (2009). https://doi.org/10.1007/978-3-322-96406-9

30. Clickworker.Com: Our Clickworker community (2022). https://www.clickworker.com/cli ckworker-crowd/

31. Mayring, P., et al.: Qualitative content analysis. A companion to qualitative research, vol. 1, pp. 159–176 (2004)

32. Markengesetz - § 143. MarkenG (2021)

33. Colicev, A.: How can non-fungible tokens bring value to brands. Int. J. Res. Mark. **78**, 120 (2022). https://doi.org/10.1016/j.ijresmar.2022.07.003

34. Thompson, S.: The preservation of digital signatures on the blockchain. See Also **2017**(3), (2017). https://doi.org/10.14288/sa.v0i3.188841

35. Norta, A., Kormiltsyn, A., Udokwu, U., Dwivedi, V., Aroh, S., Nikolajev, I. (eds.) A Blockchain Implementation for Configurable Multi-Factor Challenge-Set Self-Sovereign Identity Authentication. Zenodo (2022). https://doi.org/10.5281/zenodo.6810583

36. Leiding, B., Cap, C.H., Mundt, T., Rashidibajgan, S.: Authcoin: Validation and Authentication in Decentralized Networks. arXiv:1609.04955 [cs.CR] (2016)

37. Chen, Y., Bellavitis, C.: Blockchain disruption and decentralized finance: the rise of decentralized business models. J. Bus. Ventur. Insights **13**, e00151 (2020). https://doi.org/10.1016/j.jbvi.2019.e00151

38. Udokwu, C., Kormiltsyn, A., Thangalimodzi, K., Norta, A.: The state of the art for Blockchain-enabled smart-contract applications in the organization. In: 2018 Ivannikov Ispras Open Conference (ISPRAS), pp. 137–144. IEEE (2018). https://doi.org/10.1109/ISPRAS.2018.00029

39. Flyvbjerg, B.: Five misunderstandings about case-study research. Qual. Inq. **12**, 219–245 (2006). https://doi.org/10.1177/1077800405284363

Analysis of a New Practical SPN-Based Scheme in the Luby-Rackoff Model

Cuong Nguyen[(⊠)], Anh Nguyen, Long Nguyen, Phong Trieu, and Lai Tran

Institute of Cryptography Science and Technology, Government Information Security Committee, Hanoi, Vietnam
nguyenbuicuong@bcy.gov.vn

Abstract. Many modern block cipher schemes are constructed based on substitution-permutation networks (SPNs). Their provable security is often evaluated by idealizing S-boxes as underlying primitives (public or secret). This limits the security bound to the domain-size of the S-boxes, and it will not make much sense when this size is small. In this paper, we propose an SPN-based scheme, namely FLC, to achieve provable security in the Luby-Rackoff model in which the round functions are underlying primitives and secret. Concretely, the 3-round FLC scheme is pseudorandom, while the 5-round FLC scheme is super pseudorandom. Both of these results are capped at birthday-bound security up to $O(2^{\frac{w}{2}})$, when w is the size of the round functions. These are the best results for SPN-based schemes in the Luby-Rackoff model.

Keywords: Block cipher · Substitution-permutation networks · Practical security · Luby-rackoff model · Pseudorandom · Super pseudorandom

1 Introduction

Scheme plays an important role in constructing a secure block cipher. There are some well-known schemes, such as SPN, Feistel, and Lai-Massey. Their security is usually assessed by the pseudorandomness and the super pseudorandomness properties proposed by Luby-Rackoff [12]. In this model, a pseudorandom (resp. super pseudorandom) scheme ensures that there are no computationally unbounded distinguishers making a bounded number of queries that can determine whether the given scheme is a perfect random function (resp., permutation). According to [8,22], indistinguishability from a perfect random function (permutation) is one of the strongest security notions that we can expect from a block cipher. In order to analyse these security properties, the "H-coefficient technique" is one of the most effective methods. It was introduced in 1990 by Patarin in [20] and was systematized by himself in [21]. In 2017, Nachef et al. [17] extended this technique for some different variants when they studied different cryptographic attacks, including known-plaintext attacks (KPAs), nonadaptive chosen-plaintext attacks (NCPAs), adaptive chosen-plaintext attacks (CPAs), and adaptive chosen-plaintext and ciphertext attacks (CCAs).

© The Author(s), under exclusive license to Springer Nature Singapore Pte Ltd. 2022
T. K. Dang et al. (Eds.): FDSE 2022, CCIS 1688, pp. 210–224, 2022.
https://doi.org/10.1007/978-981-19-8069-5_14

1.1 Related Works

In 1988, Luby and Rackoff [12] gave the first formal definitions of the pseudo-randomness and the super pseudorandomness for block ciphers based on "ideal primitive" round functions. Then they proved that the 3-round Feistel is pseudorandom, and the 4-round Feistel is super pseudorandom (see [12]) up to $2^{\frac{w}{2}}$ queries, where w is the size of the round functions. There were the same results in the Lai-Massey scheme [23]. Moreover, evaluations of the pseudorandomness and tight bounds (beyond birthday bound) for some general forms of these schemes were evaluated in [8,10,13,14,16].

In 1999, Naor et al. [18] revisited the Luby-Rackoff model and presented the result for what can be viewed as the first evaluation for a non-linear, 1-round SPN. Then, the analysis of SPN continued to be developed both in terms of the security model and the tight bounds. Dodis et al. [5] consider SPN as the combination of S-boxes S and a non-cryptographic permutation P, where S is "secret" or "public".

SPNs with Secret S-boxes: [11] showed that the 3-round SPN, used in Serpent block cipher with a fixed bit-oriented permutation layer, is secure against non-adaptive adversaries. However, the security bound is $O(2^{\frac{n}{4}})$, where n is the size of the ideal primitives (here, the size of the S-boxes). Then, [15] analysed a number of candidates with SPN structure. They show that the 2-round linear SPNs with the "zero-freeness" linear permutation layer (meaning that all entries in the matrix representations of the linear permutation layers and their inverses shall be non-zero) are secure against chosen-plaintext attacks. Based on this secure building block cipher, the authors gave several instances for the internal components to achieve security against differential and linear cryptanalysis. Alternatively, the EME structure [9] can be considered a 2-round nonlinear-SPN scheme with block ciphers acting as the secret S-box. The structure achieves the security of super pseudorandomness. An EME variant with linear mixing [4] is a 2-round linear-SPN scheme. Then, this variant only achieves pseudorandom security when the linear mixing layer is also "zero-free" and does not achieve super pseudorandom security due to distinguishing attacks in [4].

SPNs with Public S-boxes: the adversary can query on this primitive. When the permutation P is linear and "zero-free", the results of [5] showed that the 3-round SPNs are secure up to $2^{\frac{n}{2}}$ queries, and then [7] claimed that the 4-round SPNs are secure up to $2^{\frac{2n}{3}}$ queries, where n is the size of S-boxes. Moreover, [5] showed that 1-round SPN is secure when P is keyed blockwise universal permutation.

Thus, to prove security for SPNs, the results in [5,7,15] require a common condition that the linear permutation layer is "zero-free". However, this constraint will affect the effective implementation of block ciphers when the block size is large (i.e., more than 128-bit). According to our survey of popular SPN-based block ciphers, only Kuznyechik [6] has a linear layer that satisfies this condition. However, the performance is not up to expectations compared to other block ciphers such as AES [3], Kalyna [19], ... In addition, Serpent [11] can achieve the provable security with the linear layer that does not satisfy "zero-freeness", but its security bound is limited by bit-oriented linear layers and simple proof tools.

1.2   Our Contributions

The paper aims to propose a specific cipher scheme that ensures theoretical security. We propose a concrete SPN-based scheme named FLC. The FLC scheme combines the w-bit round functions f (ideal primitives) and a fixed w-bit-oriented linear permutation LC (Linear Combination) to construct a $4w$-bit permutation. To the best of our knowledge, it is a new scheme. Then, we concentrate on analysing the provable security of FLC in the model of [11,15]. It is the main result of this paper. Concretely, FLC is secure up to $O(2^{\frac{w}{2}})$ queries in the Luby-Rackoff model where the round functions f are secret primitives. Remark that if FLC is considered to be a linear SPN with the round functions f being S-boxes, the security of FLC is not implied in [5,7,15] because the permutation LC has zero entries in matrix representation. Our results are much better than those in [11,15]. For example, when block size is of 128 bits, the security bound of FLC is 2^{16} compared to 2^4 in [15] and 2^1 in [11]. Moreover, we also pointed out some limitations of our approach based on Patarin's H-coefficient technique when evaluating the super pseudorandomness and improving the security bound of the 3-round FLC.

1.3   Outline

This paper is organized as follows: Sect. 2 introduces some basic definitions and the Luby-Rackoff model. In Sect. 3, we describe the FLC scheme. Finally, Sect. 4 presents our results regarding the FLC scheme's pseudorandomness and super pseudorandomness.

2   Preliminaries

2.1   Notation

Through this paper, we use the following notations: I_n denotes the set $\mathbb{Z}_2^n$, I_w^t is the product of t sets I_w. $F_{n,m}$ denotes the set of functions from I_n to I_m. P_n denotes the set of permutations on I_n. $\oplus$ denotes the exclusive OR of strings.

2.2   The Luby-Rackoff Model

In order to analyse the results of the paper in detail, in this section, we recall the Luby-Rackoff model which is used to determine whether a given function is taken at uniform or another distribution. Note that we are not trying to expand on the theoretical aspect but instead focus on analysing the proposed scheme in order to provide a secure and efficient structure that can be used for a concrete block cipher proposal. First, we will go over some basic concepts [22].

Definition 1 *(Definition 6, [22])*. *Let $n, m > 1$. A pseudorandom distinguisher is a deterministic algorithm $\mathcal{A}$ with unbounded (but finite) computation capabilities, which given a function $F : I_n \to I_m$ can query it by asking values $x \in I_n$ of which it obtains the image $y = F(x)$. Depending on the answers $y \in I_m$ it obtains, $\mathcal{A}$ outputs either 0 or 1.*

In this context, pseudorandom distinguishers are allowed to make adaptively chosen encryption queries (p.45, [22]). Moreover, $\mathcal{A}^F = 1$ and $\mathcal{A}^F = 0$ denote, respectively, the algorithm $\mathcal{A}$ output 1 and 0.

A random function of $F_{n,m}$ is defined as a random variable f of $F_{n,m}$ and can be viewed as a probability distribution $(\Pr[f = \phi])_{\phi \in F_{n,m}}$ over $F_{n,m}$. A random function (resp. permutation) is a function (resp. permutation) that is randomly chosen from $F_{n,m}$ (resp. P_n) with a fixed probability. Thus, we have a perfect random function (resp. permutation) $f^* \in F_{n,m}$ (resp. $c^* \in P_n$) where f^* is a random function (resp. permutation) is randomly chosen from $F_{n,m}$ (resp. P_n) with uniform probability.

Next, we define the advantage of a distinguisher $\mathcal{A}$ in distinguishing a random function F from a perfect random function F^*:

Definition 2 *(Definition 7, [22])*. *Let F be a random function, F^* be a perfect random function. The advantage of pseudorandom distinguisher $\mathcal{A}$ in distinguishing F from F^* is:*

$$\mathrm{Adv}_{\mathcal{A}}(F, F^*) := |\Pr[\mathcal{A}^F = 1] - \Pr[\mathcal{A}^{F^*} = 1]|.$$

The pseudorandom distinguisher is allowed to make only encryption queries, whereas the super pseudorandom distinguisher is allowed to make both encryption and decryption queries.

Definition 3 *(Definition 8, [22])*. *Let $n > 1$. A super pseudorandom is a deterministic algorithm $\mathcal{A}$ with unbounded (but finite) computation capabilities, which can query a given permutation $C \in P_n$ by providing it with values $x \in I_n$ of which it obtains to its choosing either the image $y = C(x)$ or the inverse image $y = C^{-1}(x)$. Depending on the answers $y \in I_n$, $\mathcal{A}$ outputs either 0 or 1.*

The advantage of a super pseudorandom distinguisher in distinguishing a random permutation C from a perfect random permutation C^* is similar to the case of pseudorandom distinguishers. In this paper, the random functions we want to distinguish from the perfect random ones are built by embedding perfect random functions $f_1^*, \ldots, f_t^*$ into a structure ϕ. The domain and range of $f_1^*, \ldots, f_t^*$ have variable size, which are smaller than the size of the domain and range of $\phi(f_1^*, \ldots, f_t^*)$. Such structure ϕ is sometimes called a function (or permutation) generator. Then, we have the formal definition of the pseudorandomness of a function (or permutation) generator with the range size n as follows:

Definition 4 *(Definition 9, [22])*. *A function generator ϕ is pseudorandom if for all polynomials $P(n), Q(n)$, there is an integer n_0 such that: $\forall n \geq n_0$, for all pseudorandom distinguishers $\mathcal{A}$ allowed to make $q \leq Q(n)$ queries:*

$$\mathrm{Adv}_{\mathcal{A}}(\phi(f_1^*, \ldots, f_t^*), F^*) \leq \frac{1}{P(n)}.$$

Super pseudorandom permutation generators are defined similarly with respect to super pseudorandom distinguishers.

H-coefficient Technique. We present two theorems of Patarin [22]) that are used to prove the pseudorandomness and super pseudorandomness of block ciphers.

We denote $\mathcal{X}$ as a subset of I_n^d to obtain all d-tuples $X = (x_1, \ldots, x_d), x_i \in I_n$ such that $x_i \neq x_j$ with $\forall 1 \leq i < j \leq d$.

Theorem 1 (Theorem 11, [22]). *Let $F \in F_{n,m}$ be a random function; let $F^* \in F_{n,m}$ be a perfect random function. Let d be an integer. If there exists a subset $\mathcal{Y} \subset I_m^d$ and two positive real numbers ϵ_1 and ϵ_2 such that:*

1) $|\mathcal{Y}| \geq (1 - \epsilon_1) \cdot |I_m|^d$

2) $\forall X \in \mathcal{X} \subset I_n^d, \forall Y \in \mathcal{Y} : \Pr[F(X) = Y] \geq (1 - \epsilon_2) \cdot \frac{1}{|I_m|^d}$.

Then, for any pseudorandom distinguisher $\mathcal{A}$ using d encryption queries

$$\mathrm{Adv}_{\mathcal{A}}(F, F^*) \leq \epsilon_1 + \epsilon_2.$$

Theorem 2 (Theorem 12, [22]). *Let $C \in P_n$ be a random permutation; let $C^* \in P_n$ be a perfect random permutation. Let d be an integer and $\epsilon > 0$. If $\forall X, Y \in \mathcal{X}$ such that:*

$$\Pr[C(X) = Y] \leq (1 - \epsilon) \cdot \frac{1}{|I_n|^d}.$$

Then for any super pseudorandom distinguisher $\mathcal{A}$ allowed to make d encryption or decryption queries

$$\mathrm{Adv}_{\mathcal{A}}(C, C^*) \leq \epsilon + \frac{d(d-1)}{2 \cdot 2^n}.$$

3   The FLC Scheme

This section proposes a scheme used to construct a $4w$-bit permutation from w-bit permutations. We call this scheme the FLC scheme (Four Leaf Clover scheme). In addition to the meaning that stands for the phrase "Four Leaf Clover", i.e., a structure in the sense of "luck" that achieves theoretically and practically provable security, the scheme is also a combination of a "cryptographic" function f with a "non-cryptographic" layer LC which has good implementation properties. The function f is computed based on four different round functions f_0, f_1, f_2, f_3 of w-bit size, and the permutation LC is oriented word w-bit processing to increase implementation efficiency. Concretely, with the input $X = (x^0, x^1, x^2, x^3) \in I_{4w}$ where $x_i \in I_w, \forall i \in \{0, 1, 2, 3\}$, the transformations are defined as follows:

$$f : I_{4w} \to I_{4w}$$
$$(x^0, x^1, x^2, x^3) \mapsto (f_0(x^0), f_1(x^1), f_2(x^2), f_3(x^3)) \tag{1}$$

and

$$LC : I_{4w} \rightarrow I_{4w}$$
$$(x^0, x^1, x^2, x^3) \mapsto (x^1 \oplus x^2 \oplus x^3, x^0 \oplus x^2 \oplus x^3, x^0 \oplus x^1 \oplus x^3, x^0 \oplus x^1 \oplus x^2) \quad (2)$$

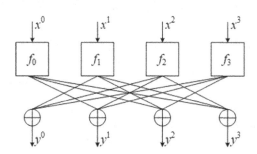

Fig. 1. 1-round FLC scheme.

The LC layer has an representing involutive binary matrix on I_w as:

$$\begin{pmatrix} 0\ 1\ 1\ 1 \\ 1\ 0\ 1\ 1 \\ 1\ 1\ 0\ 1 \\ 1\ 1\ 1\ 0 \end{pmatrix}$$

The particular form of this linear transform has also been used in part of the linear layer of Midori based on several considerations regarding both practical security and efficient implementation [1]. Then, the FLC scheme allows getting a base $4w$-bit permutation from the w bit permutations. Concretely, with input $X = (x^0, x^1, x^2, x^3) \in I_{4w}$ and output $Y = (y^0, y^1, y^2, y^3) \in I_{4w}$, the base permutation for the scheme is defined as follows:

$$F(f_0, f_1, f_2, f_3)((x^0, x^1, x^2, x^3)) = LC(f(x^0, x^1, x^2, x^3)) = (y^0, y^1, y^2, y^3),$$

such that

$$\begin{cases} y^0 = f_1(x^1) \oplus f_2(x^2) \oplus f_3(x^3) \\ y^1 = f_0(x^0) \oplus f_2(x^2) \oplus f_3(x^3) \\ y^2 = f_0(x^0) \oplus f_1(x^1) \oplus f_3(x^3) \\ y^3 = f_0(x^0) \oplus f_1(x^1) \oplus f_2(x^2) \end{cases}$$

where $f_i \in P_w$ and $x^i, y^i \in I_w$ with $\forall i \in \{0, 1, 2, 3\}$.

Then, *the r-round permutation of FLC scheme* is the composition of the r base permutations F. This $4w$-bit permutation is constructed by $4r$ permutations $f_0^1, f_1^1, f_2^1, f_3^1, \ldots, f_0^r, f_1^r, f_2^r, f_3^r \in P_w$ as follows:

$$\mathcal{F}^{(r)}(f_0^1, f_1^1, f_2^1, f_3^1, \ldots, f_0^r, f_1^r, f_2^r, f_3^r) = F(f_0^r, f_1^r, f_2^r, f_3^r) \circ \cdots \circ F(f_0^1, f_1^1, f_2^1, f_3^1).$$

4   The Provable Security of FLC in Luby-Rackoff Model

4.1   Analysis of the Pseudorandomness

Firstly, we present pseudorandom distinguishers for the 1-round and 2-round FLC schemes.

For the 1-round FLC scheme. Let $\mathcal{A}_1$ be a distinguisher that operates as follows:

1. $\mathcal{A}_1$ chooses two values $x = (x^0, x^1, x^2, x^3)$ and $x' = (x^{0'}, x^1, x^2, x^3)$.
2. $\mathcal{A}_1$ queries the oracle to obtain $y = (y^0, y^1, y^2, y^3)$ and $y' = (y^{0'}, y^{1'}, y^{2'}, y^{3'})$.
3. $\mathcal{A}_1$ checks whether $y^0 = y^{0'}$.
4. If $y^0 = y^{0'}$ then $\mathcal{A}_1$ returns 1; otherwise, returns 0.

Let p_1^* and p_1 be the probability that $\mathcal{A}_1$ returns 1 when the oracle is a perfect random permutation and the 1-round FLC scheme, respectively. Then, $p_1^* = 2^{-w}$ and $p_1 = 1$ because $y^0 = f_1^1(x^1) \oplus f_2^1(x^2) \oplus f_3^1(x^3) = y^{0'}$. Thus, the advantage of the pseudorandom distinguisher of A_1 is:

$$\mathrm{Adv}_{\mathcal{A}_1}(\mathcal{F}^{(1)}(f_0^1, f_1^1, f_2^1, f_3^1), F^*) = 1 - 2^{-w}.$$

For the 2-round FLC scheme. Let $\mathcal{A}_2$ be a distinguisher that operates as follows:

1. $\mathcal{A}_2$ choose two values $x = (x^0, x^1, x^2, x^3)$ and $x' = (x^{0'}, x^1, x^2, x^3)$.
2. $\mathcal{A}_2$ queries the oracle to obtain $y = (y^0, y^1, y^2, y^3)$ and $y' = (y^{0'}, y^{1'}, y^{2'}, y^{3'})$.
3. $\mathcal{A}_2$ checks whether $y^1 \oplus y^2 \oplus y^3 = y^{1'} \oplus y^{2'} \oplus y^{3'}$.
4. If $y^1 \oplus y^2 \oplus y^3 = y^{1'} \oplus y^{2'} \oplus y^{3'}$ then $\mathcal{A}_2$ returns 1; otherwise, it returns 0.

Let p_2^* and p_2 be the probability that $\mathcal{A}_2$ returns 1 when the oracle is a perfect random permutation and the 2-round FLC scheme, respectively. Then, $p_2^* = 2^{-w}$ and $p_2 = 1$ because $y^1 \oplus y^2 \oplus y^3 = f_0^2(f_1^1(x^1) \oplus f_2^1(x^2) \oplus f_3^1(x^3)) = y^{1'} \oplus y^{2'} \oplus y^{3'}$. Thus, the advantage of the pseudorandom distinguisher of A_2 is:

$$\mathrm{Adv}_{\mathcal{A}_2}(\mathcal{F}^{(2)}(f_0^1, f_1^1, f_2^1, f_3^1, f_0^2, f_1^2, f_2^2, f_3^2), F^*) = 1 - 2^{-w}.$$

Next, the pseudorandomness of the 3-round FLC scheme is presented in the following result:

Theorem 3. *Let 12 perfect random permutations $f_0^1, f_1^1, \ldots, f_2^3, f_3^3 \in P_w$. $C = \mathcal{F}^{(3)}(f_0^1, f_1^1, \ldots, f_2^3, f_3^3) \in P_{4w}$ is the 3-round FLC scheme, and $F^* \in P_{4w}$ is a perfect random permutation. For any pseudorandom distinguisher $\mathcal{A}$ allowed to make at most d encryption queries, we have*

$$\mathrm{Adv}_{\mathcal{A}}(C, F^*) \leq 5d(d-1)2^{-w+1}.$$

Proof. To prove this result, we use Theorem 1 of the H-coefficient technique. We denote $\mathcal{X}$ as a subset of I_{4w}^d that contains all d-tuples $X = (x_1, \ldots, x_d)$, $x_i = (x_i^0, x_i^1, x_i^2, x_i^3) \in I_{4w}$ such that $x_i \neq x_j$ with $\forall 1 \leq i < j \leq d$.

Step 1. Constructing the set $\mathcal{Y}$ and evaluating its cardinality.

Let $\mathcal{Y} \subset I_{4w}^d$ be the set of all $Y = (y_1, \ldots, y_d)$ where $y_i = (y_i^0, y_i^1, y_i^2, y_i^3) \in I_{4w}$ such that the values $\Delta y_i^{r,s,t} := y_i^r \oplus y_i^s \oplus y_i^t$ are pairwise different from any 3-tuples (r, s, t) where $0 \leq r < s < t \leq 3$. We will evaluate the cardinality of the set $\mathcal{Y}$. We have

$$|\mathcal{Y}| = |I_{4w}|^d \cdot (1 - \Pr[\exists 1 \leq i < j \leq d, \exists 0 \leq r < s < t \leq 3 : \Delta y_i^{r,s,t} = \Delta y_j^{r,s,t}])$$

$$\geq |I_{4w}|^d \cdot (1 - \sum_{1 \leq i < j \leq d; 0 \leq r < s < t \leq 3} \Pr[\Delta y_i^{r,s,t} = \Delta y_j^{r,s,t}])$$

$$= |I_{4w}|^d \cdot (1 - 4 \cdot \frac{d(d-1)}{2} \cdot 2^{-w}).$$

Thus, we put $\epsilon_1 = d(d-1) \cdot 2^{-w+1}$.

Step 2. $\forall X \in \mathcal{X}, \forall Y \in \mathcal{Y}$, we now establish the following probability

$$\Pr[C(X) = Y] = \Pr[C(x_i) = y_i; i \in \{1, \ldots, d\}].$$

We note that, throughout this proof, all probabilities are considered in the conditions $X \in \mathcal{X}$, and $Y \in \mathcal{Y}$. First, we represent the event $\{C(x_i) = y_i; i \in \{1, \ldots, d\}\}$ in another way that is easy to compute. We let U_i, V_i, W_i denote the values after the first, second, and final rounds of the 3-round FLC scheme with an input x_i. Then, the event $\{C(x_i) = y_i\}$ is the event $\{W_i = y_i\}$, illustrated by Fig. 2. On the other hand, we have the event $\{W_i = y_i\}$ is equivalent to

$$\begin{cases} y_i^0 \oplus y_i^1 \oplus y_i^2 = f_3^3(V_i^3) \\ y_i^0 \oplus y_i^1 \oplus y_i^3 = f_2^3(V_i^2) \\ y_i^0 \oplus y_i^2 \oplus y_i^3 = f_1^3(V_i^1) \\ y_i^1 \oplus y_i^2 \oplus y_i^3 = f_0^3(V_i^0) \end{cases} \tag{3}$$

Let A be the event $\{W_i = y_i, i \in \{1, \ldots, d\}\}$; and B be the event: for any $s \in \{0, 1, 2, 3\}$ then $V_i^s \neq V_j^s$ where $1 \leq i < j \leq d$. Then,

$$\Pr[A] \geq \Pr[A, B] = \Pr[A|B] \cdot \Pr[B]$$
$$= \Pr[A|B] \cdot (1 - \Pr[\overline{B}]).$$

Next, we will evaluate $\Pr[A|B]$ and $\Pr[\overline{B}]$.

For the probability $\Pr[A|B]$, we can easily prove that

$$\Pr[A|B] = \left(\frac{1}{2^w} \cdot \frac{1}{2^w - 1} \cdot \ldots \cdot \frac{1}{2^w - d + 1}\right)^4 = \frac{1}{(2^w(2^w - 1) \ldots (2^w - d + 1))^4}.$$

Next, we will establish the probability $1 - \Pr[\overline{B}]$. We have

$$\Pr[\overline{B}] = \Pr[\exists i < j \in \{1, \ldots, d\}, \exists s \in \{0, 1, 2, 3\} : V_i^s = V_j^s]$$
$$\leq \frac{d(d-1)}{2} \cdot 4 \cdot \max_{i < j; s} \Pr[V_i^s = V_j^s].$$

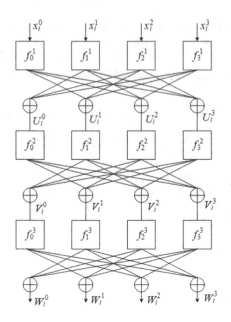

Fig. 2. The 3-round FLC.

Since we can reason similarly for all values of s, we only need to bound $\Pr[V_i^0 = V_j^0]$. We fix a pair (i, j) where $i < j$. We have the event $\{V_i^0 = V_j^0\}$ is equivalent to

$$e_{ij} = \{f_1^2(U_i^1) \oplus f_2^2(U_i^2) \oplus f_3^2(U_i^3) = f_1^2(U_j^1) \oplus f_2^2(U_j^2) \oplus f_3^2(U_j^3)\}.$$

Because $x_i \neq x_j$, there exists $r \in \{0, 1, 2, 3\}$ such that $x_i^r \neq x_j^r$. For $t \neq r$ and $t \in \{1, 2, 3\}$, we have

$$\Pr[e_{ij}] = \Pr[e_{ij}|U_j^t \neq U_i^t]\Pr[U_j^t \neq U_i^t] + \Pr[e_{ij}|U_j^t = U_i^t]\Pr[U_j^t = U_i^t]$$
$$\leq \Pr[e_{ij}|U_j^t \neq U_i^t] + \Pr[U_j^t = U_i^t].$$

We will establish the two probabilities $\Pr[e_{ij}|U_j^t \neq U_i^t]$ and $\Pr[U_j^t = U_i^t]$. For the first probability, we have

$$\Pr[e_{ij}|U_j^t \neq U_i^t] = \Pr[f_1^2(U_i^1) \oplus f_2^2(U_i^2) \oplus f_3^2(U_i^3) = f_1^2(U_j^1) \oplus f_2^2(U_j^2) \oplus f_3^2(U_j^3)|U_j^t \neq U_i^t].$$

Because $t \in \{1, 2, 3\}$, we only need to consider the case $t = 1$. The other case is the same. We have

$$\Pr[f_1^2(U_i^1) \oplus f_2^2(U_i^2) \oplus f_3^2(U_i^3) = f_1^2(U_j^1) \oplus f_2^2(U_j^2) \oplus f_3^2(U_j^3)|U_j^1 \neq U_i^1]$$
$$= \Pr[f_1^2(U_j^1) = f_1^2(U_i^1) \oplus f_2^2(U_i^2) \oplus f_3^2(U_i^3) \oplus f_2^2(U_j^2) \oplus f_3^2(U_j^3)|U_j^1 \neq U_i^1].$$

Put $\Delta = f_2^2(U_i^2) \oplus f_3^2(U_i^3) \oplus f_2^2(U_j^2) \oplus f_3^2(U_j^3)$. We have

$$\Pr[f_1^2(U_j^1) = f_1^2(U_i^1) \oplus \Delta | U_j^1 \neq U_i^1]$$
$$= \Pr[f_1^2(U_j^1) = f_1^2(U_i^1) | U_j^1 \neq U_i^1] \cdot \Pr[\Delta = 0]$$
$$+ \sum_{k \in I_w \setminus \{0\}} \Pr[f_1^2(U_j^1) = f_1^2(U_i^1) \oplus k | U_j^1 \neq U_i^1] \cdot \Pr[\Delta = k]$$
$$= \sum_{k \in I_w \setminus \{0\}} \Pr[f_1^2(U_j^1) = f_1^2(U_i^1) \oplus k | U_j^1 \neq U_i^1] \cdot \Pr[\Delta = k]$$
$$= \frac{1}{2^w - 1} \cdot \sum_{k \in I_w \setminus \{0\}} \Pr[\Delta = k] = \frac{1}{2^w - 1}(1 - \Pr[\Delta = 0]) \leq \frac{1}{2^{w-1}}.$$

Therefore, we have

$$\Pr[e_{ij} | U_j^t \neq U_i^t] \leq \frac{1}{2^{w-1}}.$$

For the second probability $\Pr[U_j^t = U_i^t]$ with the condition $x_j^r \neq x_i^r$ and $t \neq r$, we have

$$\Pr[U_i^t = U_j^t]$$
$$= \Pr[f_1^{t_1}(x_i^{t_1}) \oplus f_1^{t_2}(x_i^{t_2}) \oplus f_1^{t_3}(x_i^{t_3}) = f_1^{t_1}(x_j^{t_1}) \oplus f_1^{t_2}(x_j^{t_2}) \oplus f_1^{t_3}(x_j^{t_3})]$$

where $t_1 < t_2 < t_3$ and $t_i \in \{0, 1, 2, 3\} \setminus \{t\}$. Because $x_j^r \neq x_i^r$ and $t \neq r$, there exists $l \in \{1, 2, 3\}$ such that $x_j^{t_l} \neq x_i^{t_l}$. Thus, using the same method as above, we have

$$\Pr[U_i^t = U_j^t] \leq \frac{1}{2^{w-1}}.$$

From the two above statements, we have

$$\Pr[e_{ij}] \leq 2 \cdot 2^{-w+1}.$$

Thus,

$$1 - \Pr[\overline{B}] \geq 1 - \frac{d(d-1)}{2} \cdot 4 \cdot 2 \cdot 2^{-w+1}.$$

Therefore, we have

$$\Pr[C(x_i) = y_i; i \in \{1, \ldots, d\}] \geq \frac{(1 - d(d-1)2^{-w+3})}{(2^w(2^w - 1) \ldots (2^w - d + 1))^4}. \tag{4}$$

This means that

$$\Pr[C(X) = Y] \cdot |I_{4w}|^d \geq \frac{|I_{4w}|^d \cdot (1 - d(d-1)2^{-w+3})}{(2^w(2^w - 1) \ldots (2^w - d + 1))^4}$$
$$\geq (1 - d(d-1)2^{-w+3}).$$

We put $\epsilon_2 = d(d-1)2^{-w+3}$.
Using Theorem 1 with $\epsilon_1 = d(d-1)2^{-w+1}$ and $\epsilon_2 = d(d-1)2^{-w+3}$, we have

$$\mathrm{Adv}_{\mathcal{A}}(C, F^*) \leq 5d(d-1)2^{-w+1}.$$

The proof is complete.∎

4.2   Analysis of the Super Pseudorandomness

In this subsection, we will show that the 5-round FLC scheme is super pseudorandom.

Theorem 4. *Let 20 perfect random permutations $f_0^1, f_1^1, \ldots, f_2^5, f_3^5 \in P_w$. $D = \mathcal{F}^{(5)}(f_0^1, f_1^1, \ldots, f_2^5, f_3^5) \in P_{4w}$ is the 5-round FLC scheme, and $F^* \in P_{4w}$ is a perfect random permutation. For any super pseudorandom distinguisher $\mathcal{A}$ allowed to make at most d encryption and decryption queries, we have*

$$\text{Adv}_{\mathcal{A}}(D, F^*) \leq d(d-1)2^{-w+4} + d(d-1)2^{-4w-1}.$$

Proof. To prove this result, we use Theorem 2 of the H-coefficient technique. We denote $\mathcal{X}$ as a subset of I_{4w}^d that obtains all d-tuples $X = (x_1, \ldots, x_d), x_i = (x_i^0, x_i^1, x_i^2, x_i^3) \in I_{4w}$ such that $x_i \neq x_j$ with $\forall 1 \leq i < j \leq d$. $\forall X, Y \in \mathcal{X}$, we evaluate

$$\Pr[D(X) = Y] = \Pr[D(x_i) = y_i; i \in \{1, \ldots, d\}].$$

We will do this by using probability (4).
First, we put $C = \mathcal{F}^{(3)}(f_0^1, f_1^1, f_2^1, f_3^1, \ldots, f_0^3, f_1^3, f_2^3, f_3^3)$ as the 3-round FLC scheme. The event $D(x_i) = y_i$ is equivalent to

$$\begin{cases} C(x_i)^0 = (f_0^4)^{-1}(z_i^1 \oplus z_i^2 \oplus z_i^3) = g_0^4(\Delta z_i^{1,2,3}) \\ C(x_i)^1 = (f_1^4)^{-1}(z_i^0 \oplus z_i^2 \oplus z_i^3) = g_1^4(\Delta z_i^{0,2,3}) \\ C(x_i)^2 = (f_2^4)^{-1}(z_i^0 \oplus z_i^1 \oplus z_i^3) = g_2^4(\Delta z_i^{0,1,3}) \\ C(x_i)^3 = (f_3^4)^{-1}(z_i^0 \oplus z_i^1 \oplus z_i^2) = g_3^4(\Delta z_i^{0,1,2}) \end{cases}$$

where $z_i^0 = g_0^5(\Delta y_i^{1,2,3}), z_i^1 = g_1^5(\Delta y_i^{0,2,3}), z_i^2 = g_2^5(\Delta y_i^{0,1,3}), z_i^3 = g_3^5(\Delta y_i^{0,1,2}), g_s^4 = (f_s^4)^{-1}$ and $g_s^5 = (f_s^5)^{-1}$ for $s \in \{0, 1, 2, 3\}$ and $\Delta y_i^{r,s,t} = y_i^r \oplus y_i^s \oplus y_i^t$, see Fig. 3.

Put $a_i = (a_i^0, a_i^1, a_i^2, a_i^3) = (g_0^4(\Delta z_i^{1,2,3}), g_1^4(\Delta z_i^{0,2,3}), g_2^4(\Delta z_i^{0,1,3}), g_3^4(\Delta z_i^{0,1,2}))$. Let A be the event: $D(x_i) = y_i$ with $\forall i \in \{1, \ldots, d\}$. Then, A is equivalent to the event B: $C(x_i) = a_i$ with $\forall i \in \{1, \ldots, d\}$.
Let E be the event: the values $\Delta a_i^{r,s,t}$ are pairwise different for any (r, s, t), where $0 \leq r < s < t \leq 3$.
We have

$$\Pr[A] = \Pr[B] \geq \Pr[B, E] = \Pr[B|E] \cdot \Pr[E] = \Pr[B|E] \cdot (1 - \Pr[\overline{E}]).$$

Next, we establish $\Pr[B|E]$ and $\Pr[\overline{E}]$.
For the first probability, it is the probability (4). We have

$$\Pr[B|E] \geq \frac{(1 - d(d-1)2^{-w+3})}{(2^w(2^w - 1) \ldots (2^w - d + 1))^4}.$$

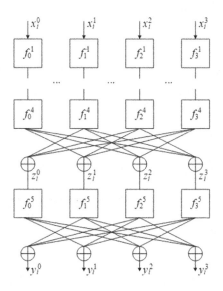

Fig. 3. The 5-round FLC.

For the second probability, we have

$$\Pr[\overline{E}] = \Pr[\exists i < j \in \{1,\ldots,d\}, \exists r < s < t \in \{0,1,2,3\} : \Delta a_i^{r,s,t} = \Delta a_j^{r,s,t}]$$

$$\leq 4 \cdot \frac{d(d-1)}{2} \max_{i<j;r<s<t} \Pr[\Delta a_i^{r,s,t} = \Delta a_j^{r,s,t}].$$

Now, we evaluate the probability $\Pr[\Delta a_i^{r,s,t} = \Delta a_j^{r,s,t}]$ with $(r,s,t) = (0,1,2)$. For the other cases of (r,s,t), we have the same results. We put e_{ij} as the event $\Delta a_i^{0,1,2} = \Delta a_j^{0,1,2}$ which is equivalent to $a_i^0 \oplus a_i^1 \oplus a_i^2 = a_j^0 \oplus a_j^1 \oplus a_j^2$ or $g_0^4(\Delta z_i^{1,2,3}) \oplus g_1^4(\Delta z_i^{0,2,3}) \oplus g_2^4(\Delta z_i^{0,1,3}) = g_0^4(\Delta z_j^{1,2,3}) \oplus g_1^4(\Delta z_j^{0,2,3}) \oplus g_2^4(\Delta z_j^{0,1,3})$. On the other hand, because $y_i \neq y_j$, there exists a 3-tuple (r^*,s^*,t^*) such that $\Delta y_i^{r^*,s^*,t^*} \neq \Delta y_j^{r^*,s^*,t^*}$.

Next, we consider two cases $(r^*,s^*,t^*) = (1,2,3)$ and $(r^*,s^*,t^*) \neq (1,2,3)$. By the similar method in the proof of Theorem 3 we have $\Pr[e_{ij}] \leq 2^{-w+2}$ for both case. Therefore,

$$\Pr[\overline{E}] \leq 4 \cdot \frac{d(d-1)}{2} \cdot 2^{-w+2}.$$

From the above arguments,

$$\Pr[D(x_i) = y_i; i] \geq \frac{(1 - d(d-1)2^{-w+3})(1 - d(d-1)2^{-w+3})}{(2^w(2^w-1)\ldots(2^w-d+1))^4}$$

$$\geq \frac{(1 - d(d-1)2^{-w+4})}{(2^w(2^w-1)\ldots(2^w-d+1))^4}.$$

This means that $\forall X, Y \in \mathcal{X}$,

$$\Pr[D(X) = Y] \cdot |I_{4w}|^d \geq \frac{|I_{4w}|^d \cdot (1 - d(d-1)2^{-w+4})}{(2^w(2^w-1)\dots(2^w-d+1))^4}.$$

Using Theorem 2 with $\epsilon = d(d-1)2^{-w+4}$, we have

$$\mathrm{Adv}_{\mathcal{A}}(D, F^*) \leq d(d-1)2^{-w+4} + d(d-1)2^{-4w-1}.$$

The proof is complete. ∎

4.3 Some Discussions

In the following, we discuss some limitations encountered in applying our approach. In particular, we show our approach cannot apply to prove super pseudorandomness of 3-round version; and to present some issues for analysing the 4-round version.

The Super Pseudorandomness of the 3-Round FLC. There exit $x_1 = (a, a, a, b_1), x_2 = (a, a, a, b_2)$ and $y_1 = (u, v_1, v_1, v_1), y_2 = (u, v_2, v_2, v_2)$ such that $\Pr[C(x_1) = y_1, C(x_2) = y_2] = 0$ where C is the 3-round FLC scheme and $a, b_1, b_2, u, v_1, v_2 \in I_w$, $b_1 \neq b_2$, $v_1 \neq v_2$. It means that we cannot use our approach to evaluate the super pseudorandomness for the 3-round FLC scheme.

The Super Pseudorandomness of the 4-Round FLC. Because of the same reasons as above, we cannot apply the techniques using in Theorem 4 to evaluate the super pseudorandomness for the 4-round FLC scheme.

Moreover, we have also considered an improvement proof of Theorem 3. We expand the set $\mathcal{Y} \subset I_{4w}^d$, which will include all $Y = (y_1, \dots, y_d)$ where $y_i = (y_i^0, y_i^1, y_i^2, y_i^3) \in I_{4w}$, such that for each pair $i, j \in \{1, \dots, d\}$ there exists at most one 3-tuple (r, s, t) for which $0 \leq r, s, t \leq 3$ are pairwise different, and satisfies $\Delta y_i^{r,s,t} = \Delta y_j^{r,s,t}$. Our purpose is to be able to get the super pseudorandomness for the 4-round FLC scheme by using our proof idea in Theorem 4.

To prove the pseudorandomness for the 3-round FLC scheme with the "new" set $\mathcal{Y} \subset I_{4w}^d$, we use the recurrence method. We need to evaluate the probability of event A that $W_i = y_i$, $\forall i \in \{1, \dots, d\}$. Let A_k be the event that $W_i = y_i$, $\forall i \in \{1, \dots, k\}$ (we can see that event A is event A_d). We have,

$$\Pr[A_k] = \Pr[(W_k = y_k) \cap A_{k-1}] = \Pr[A_{k-1}] \cdot \Pr[W_k = y_k | A_{k-1}].$$

Therefore, if we can evaluate the probability $\Pr[W_k = y_k | A_{k-1}]$, the relationship between $\Pr[A_k]$ and $\Pr[A_{k-1}]$ will be obtained. However, to compute this probability, for each $i \in \{1, \dots, k-1\}$ we have to evaluate the probability $\Pr[V_i^u = V_k^u | A_{k-1}]$ instead of the probability $\Pr[V_i^u = V_k^u]$ as in Theorem 3. The difficulty is that the probability of event $V_i^u = V_k^u$ may be affected by event A_{k-1} because the attacker is adaptive. This is our issue to evaluate the probability $\Pr[V_i^u = V_k^u | A_{k-1}]$. In other words, the super pseudorandomness for the 4-round FLC scheme is still our open problem.

The Practical of FLC. From the FLC scheme, we can completely construct a block cipher. In which, the round function is designed based on the permutation F of FLC, constructed by four functions f_0, f_1, f_2, f_3. Then, we specify the cryptographic components for f_0, f_1, f_2, f_3. For example, these permutations are defined based on a basis function f_w including the key XOR layer and the nonlinear layer S including S-boxes to ensure confusion and the linear transform layer D between w-bit states to ensure the diffusion. We receive a block cipher with block size $4w$, from the w-bit permutations. Another important note is that the FLC-based block cipher will perfectly match the optimal implementations on the w-bit platform using the same lookup technique as the AES block cipher. In particular, 256-bit block size case will be very suitable for the common 64-bit platform.

5 Conclusion

In this paper, we analyse the pseudorandomness and super pseudorandomness of the FLC scheme in Sect. 4. Concretely, the 3-round FLC is pseudorandom, and the 5-round FLC is super pseudorandom. We also present distinguishers attacking the pseudorandomness of the 1-round and the 2-round FLC scheme. However, we have not been able to improve our results yet due to the limitations of using our approach. To solve this, we may need another approach for applying the coefficient H, such as an approach in [2]. Moreover, considering the provable security of FLC in the quantum random oracle model is a challenging open problem. In addition, in order to construct a complete block cipher, we need to consider the practical security against cryptanalytic approaches and the implementation of FLC with chosen cryptographic components.

References

1. Banik, S., Bogdanov, A., Isobe, T., Shibutani, K., Hiwatari, H., Akishita, T., Regazzoni, F.: Midori: a block cipher for low energy. In: Iwata, T., Cheon, J.H. (eds.) ASIACRYPT 2015. LNCS, vol. 9453, pp. 411–436. Springer, Heidelberg (2015). https://doi.org/10.1007/978-3-662-48800-3_17
2. Chen, S., Steinberger, J.: Tight security bounds for key-alternating ciphers. In: Nguyen, P.Q., Oswald, E. (eds.) EUROCRYPT 2014. LNCS, vol. 8441, pp. 327–350. Springer, Heidelberg (2014). https://doi.org/10.1007/978-3-642-55220-5_19
3. Daemen, J., Rijmen, V.: The Design of Rijndael, vol. 2. Springer, Berlin (2002). https://doi.org/10.1007/978-3-662-04722-4
4. Datta, N., Nandi, M.: Characterization of EME with linear mixing. In: Yoshida, M., Mouri, K. (eds.) IWSEC 2014. LNCS, vol. 8639, pp. 221–239. Springer, Cham (2014). https://doi.org/10.1007/978-3-319-09843-2_17
5. Dodis, Y., Katz, J., Steinberger, J., Thiruvengadam, A., Zhang, Z.: Provable security of substitution-permutation networks. Cryptology ePrint Archive (2017)
6. Dolmatov, V.: Gost r 34.12-2015: Block cipher" kuznyechik". Tech. rep. (2016)
7. Gao, Y., Guo, C., Wang, M., Wang, W., Wen, J.: Beyond-birthday-bound security for 4-round linear substitution-permutation networks. IACR Trans. Symmet. Cryptol. **2020**, 305–326 (2020)

8. Gilbert, H., Minier, M.: New results on the pseudorandomness of some blockcipher constructions. In: Matsui, M. (ed.) FSE 2001. LNCS, vol. 2355, pp. 248–266. Springer, Heidelberg (2002). https://doi.org/10.1007/3-540-45473-X_21

9. Halevi, S., Rogaway, P.: A tweakable enciphering mode. In: Boneh, D. (ed.) CRYPTO 2003. LNCS, vol. 2729, pp. 482–499. Springer, Heidelberg (2003). https://doi.org/10.1007/978-3-540-45146-4_28

10. Hoang, V.T., Rogaway, P.: On generalized feistel networks. In: Rabin, T. (ed.) CRYPTO 2010. LNCS, vol. 6223, pp. 613–630. Springer, Heidelberg (2010). https://doi.org/10.1007/978-3-642-14623-7_33

11. Iwata, T., Kurosawa, K.: On the pseudorandomness of the AES finalists - RC6 and serpent. In: Goos, G., Hartmanis, J., van Leeuwen, J., Schneier, B. (eds.) FSE 2000. LNCS, vol. 1978, pp. 231–243. Springer, Heidelberg (2001). https://doi.org/10.1007/3-540-44706-7_16

12. Luby, M., Rackoff, C.: How to construct pseudorandom permutations from pseudorandom functions. SIAM J. Comput. **17**(2), 373–386 (1988)

13. Luo, Y., Lai, X., Gong, Z.: Pseudorandomness analysis of the (extended) lai-massey scheme. Inf. Process. Lett. **111**(2), 90–96 (2010)

14. Luo, Y., Lai, X., Hu, J.: The pseudorandomness of many-round LAI-Massey scheme. J. Inf. Sci. Eng. **31**(3), 1085–1096 (2015)

15. Miles, E., Viola, E.: Substitution-permutation networks, pseudorandom functions, and natural proofs. J. ACM (JACM) **62**(6), 1–29 (2015)

16. Moriai, S., Vaudenay, S.: On the Pseudorandomness of top-level schemes of block ciphers. In: Okamoto, T. (ed.) ASIACRYPT 2000. LNCS, vol. 1976, pp. 289–302. Springer, Heidelberg (2000). https://doi.org/10.1007/3-540-44448-3_22

17. Nachef, V., Patarin, J., Volte, E.: Feistel Ciphers. Springer, Cham (2017). https://doi.org/10.1007/978-3-319-49530-9

18. Naor, M., Reingold, O.: On the construction of pseudorandom permutations: Luby-Rackoff revisited. J. Cryptol. **12**(1), 29–66 (1999)

19. Oliynykov, R., et al.: A new encryption standard of ukraine: The kalyna block cipher. Cryptology ePrint Archive (2015)

20. Patarin, J.: Pseudorandom permutations based on the D.E.S. scheme. In: Cohen, G., Charpin, P. (eds.) EUROCODE 1990. LNCS, vol. 514, pp. 193–204. Springer, Heidelberg (1991). https://doi.org/10.1007/3-540-54303-1_131

21. Patarin, J.: The coefficients H technique. In: Avanzi, R.M., Keliher, L., Sica, F. (eds.) SAC 2008. LNCS, vol. 5381, pp. 328–345. Springer, Heidelberg (2009). https://doi.org/10.1007/978-3-642-04159-4_21

22. Piret, G.F., et al.: Block ciphers: security proofs, cryptanalysis, design, and fault attacks. Ph.D. thesis, Catholic University of Louvain, Louvain-la-Neuve, Belgium (2005)

23. Vaudenay, S.: On the Lai-Massey scheme. In: Lam, K.-Y., Okamoto, E., Xing, C. (eds.) ASIACRYPT 1999. LNCS, vol. 1716, pp. 8–19. Springer, Heidelberg (1999). https://doi.org/10.1007/978-3-540-48000-6_2

Authorization and Access Control for Different Database Models: Requirements and Current State of the Art

Aya Mohamed[1,2]([⊠]), Dagmar Auer[1,2], Daniel Hofer[1,2], and Josef Küng[1,2]

[1] Institute for Application-Oriented Knowledge Processing (FAW), Johannes Kepler University (JKU), Linz, Austria
{aya.mohamed,dagmar.auer,daniel.hofer,josef.kueng}@jku.at

[2] LIT Secure and Correct Systems Lab (SCSL), Linz Institute of Technology (LIT), Johannes Kepler University (JKU), Linz, Austria

Abstract. Traditional SQL-based data stores have been the market leaders for decades. However, they have drawbacks with today's massive and highly connected data due to their low flexibility in terms of data structures. NoSQL database models (i.e., key-value, column, document, and graph) are designed for unstructured data in large quantities. However, they currently lack fine-grained dynamic security support, with respect to authorization and access control, in contrast to relational database management systems. We define advanced authorization and access control requirements which are applicable for any database model regardless of the application and access control scenario. According to our discussion on existing access control features versus the requirements in the context of each database model, we conclude whether the requirements are satisfied or not, and provide a corresponding overview.

Keywords: Authorization · Access control · Requirements · Relational database model · NoSQL database models

1 Introduction

Today, NoSQL databases are increasingly used in business and security-critical domains, especially due to their ability to deal with big interconnected data [30]. Although NoSQL database systems have many advantages including scalability and availability, security features, especially authorization and access control to protect sensitive information, were not the primary focus and are not yet considered. Our initial motivation for addressing security issues in this context comes from our research on knowledge graphs, which rely on NoSQL data stores.

Authorization and access control are recognized as the most important security issues in big data [26]. Authorization is the specification of access rights in terms of who (subject) can perform which action on what (resource). Access control is crucial for internal as well as external security in enterprise systems to regulate and check the flow of information. It prevents access to data by unauthorized users.

T. K. Dang et al. (Eds.): FDSE 2022, CCIS 1688, pp. 225–239, 2022.
https://doi.org/10.1007/978-981-19-8069-5_15

In fact, there is no general solution that applies to all database models. This is because each database model has different access control requirements to protect information based on the kind of data (i.e., structured, semi-structured, or unstructured) regardless the underlying data store. Besides, the fine-grained access control (FGAC) solutions developed in the relational database management system (RDBMS) cannot be reused in non-relational data stores due to the schemaless nature of many NoSQL models.

The objective of this work is to guide researchers and practitioners in identifying authorization and access control requirements, features, and limitations of the selected database model. In this literature work, we aim to answer the following research questions:

RQ1 What are the general requirements to apply fine-grained dynamic authorization and access control in databases?

RQ2 Do these general requirements vary with the database model?

RQ3 Which requirements are satisfied by each database model?

RQ4 Are these requirements applicable to typical application scenarios for the various database systems with different models?

The remainder of this paper is organized as follows. We give an overview of related work in Sect. 2. In Sect. 3, we identify the general access control requirements used throughout this work. Furthermore, we discuss the relational and NoSQL database models (i.e., key-value, column, document, and graph) in Sects. 4 to 8 respectively. For each of these models, we give an overview followed by a discussion of the authorization and access control requirements ending with the features that are either supported in databases or published in research works. We then provide an overall discussion in Sect. 9. The paper concludes with a summary in Sect. 10.

2   Related Work

There are currently many survey works in the literature addressing the topic of security in databases, especially the NoSQL database management systems (DBMSs). For example, the work in Sicari et al. [25] is one of the very recent literature researches discussing security and privacy in the context of NoSQL database models selecting one for each category, i.e., Redis, Cassandra, MongoDB, and Neo4j for key-value, column, document, and graph respectively. They compare their security features and considerations with respect to encryption, authentication, authorization, and auditing. They also provide an overview of the RDBMS and compare it with the NoSQL in terms of schema, redundancy, atomicity, consistency, isolation, durability, scalability, and query language.

In Alotaibi et al. [3], access control models in different NoSQL databases are reviewed highlighting the lack of fine-grained access control. Dindoliwala and Morena [13] surveyed several NoSQL databases (i.e., MongoDB, Cassandra, GemStone, db4o, and Objectivity/DB) comparing the existing authentication, authorization, auditing, and data encryption features.

Moreover, the work presented in Zahid et al. [29] performs an assessment to evaluate the security of sharded NoSQL stores in Cassandra, MongoDB, CouchDB, Redis, and HBase. The assessment criteria are authentication, access control, secure configurations, data encryption, and auditing. The security features of the same databases are analyzed again in Dadapeer and Adarsh [12] along with defining the main security issues in NoSQL database.

In Sahafizadeh and Nematbakhsh [23], more NoSQL stores (i.e., HyperTable, Voldemort, DynamoDB, and Neo4j) are included in the comparison besides the five DBMSs used in [12, 29]. For each database, a summary of whether the defined security features are supported or not is provided.

However, these works have a broader focus on security-related features with little consideration for authorization and access control. Furthermore, they select the popular NoSQL stores to compare and analyze the existing features. On the contrary, we focus on the database model rather than a specific DBMS.

3 Authorization and Access Control Requirements

Access control systems have to consider specific requirements to provide fine-grained dynamic access control, e.g., *attribute-based access control (ABAC)*. In this section, we define five authorization and access control requirements below.

R1 Authorization policies can be described at different levels of the data model hierarchy.

R2 Fine-grained authorization policies can be defined and enforced based on content.

R3 Custom authorization policies can be defined.

R4 Authorization is supported at different layers.

R5 Context information can be specified in authorization policies.

The significance of requirement *R1* originates from the demand to directly access data at different granularity levels in applications, i.e., from sets of data objects to portions of a single one. Thus, concise authorizations specification and mechanisms to control access at varying granularity levels of data are needed [5].

The requirement *R2* concerns the ability to formulate content-based access rules for specific parts of the data storing unit in a database model. For instance, a document is the unit of storing data in document-oriented databases consisting of fields with keys and values. In this case, only fields satisfying certain criteria specified in the authorization policy should be accessed. Defining and enforcing fine-grained authorization policies in NoSQL data stores is challenging due to the schema-free structure such that different data are stored in one huge database.

Requirement *R3* is about defining rules with custom attributes, roles, or labels based on the implemented access control model rather than only using the built-in ones. Regarding requirement *R4*, the access control system should also be able to support external authorization. External authorization is about specifying and enforcing the authorization policy independent of the application and the underlying DBMS. Generally, external authorization can be handled either in the application, which is not scalable and hard to maintain, or using policy languages like the *eXtensible Access Control Markup Language (XACML)* as an external decision-making and enforcement mechanism.

In requirement *R5*, the context information in the authorization policy is associated with not only subject users requesting access, but also the resources to be accessed. Context-aware authorization policy addresses the dynamic varying user privileges affected by the frequent changes of context. Although the database model has no impact on the user context (e.g., time, location, and history), not all the database systems, especially non-relational ones, support context-based authorization policies and access control.

The identified requirements are not only implemented differently, but also the definition could vary from one database model to another due to the nature of the data stored in these systems, query language, and structure of the data model. For instance, the data model hierarchy, fine-grained level, and resource context are not the same for all database models. Requirements *R1*, *R2*, and *R5* are also identified as access control requirements for the access control model proposed in Kulkarni [16]. We additionally discuss the proposed requirements in the context of each database model along with the existing access control features in the upcoming sections.

4   Relational Data

The first relational database management system (RDBMS) evolved in the 1970s and is based on the rigid scientific fundamentals of the relational data model developed by Edgar F. Codd [30]. Figure 1 shows the relational model hierarchy. The data are stored in tables, also referred to as relations. The table columns and rows are called attributes and tuples respectively. The relation has a schema (i.e., metadata) which defines the attribute names along with their data type in addition to the instances representing the tuples at a given instant. The RDBMS relies on static schemas for controlling data type to maintain data integrity and evaluates each change to avoid introducing errors or maintenance issues. Furthermore, it supports only structured data and is managed by the common declarative query language *SQL*.

Access control approaches have been developed in relational systems ever since the first products emerged. In SQL'89, *discretionary access control (DAC)* is applied such that the relation creator in an SQL database becomes its owner. However, SQL'89 lacks control over who can create relations. The owner can then give access privileges (i.e., *SELECT*, *INSERT*, and *DELETE*) to other users using the *grant* operation in SQL which applies to base relations and views. The *DROP* relation privilege is not supported in SQL'89, but included in IBM DB2. In addition, the missing revoke operation is provided in SQL'92 to take away the previously granted privileges with the option of cascading revocation to revoke all the grants based on the revoked privilege. In general, DAC is prone to *Trojan Horse* attacks even if the relation access is strictly controlled. For instance, a user with *SELECT* privilege can violate these controls by creating a copy of the

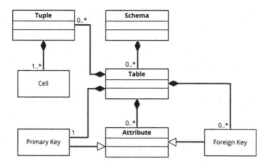

Fig. 1. Relational database model

relation. Another problem is related to access rights management such that the privileges for performing a particular task have to be explicitly granted to each user or group of users [24].

On the other hand, *mandatory access control (MAC)* is based on security labels associated with each data item and each user. Labels on data items and users are called security classification and clearance respectively. In relational databases, security classifications can be assigned to data at different levels of granularity. Assigning labels to entire relations or columns are coarse-grained. The finest granularity is at the tuple or element level. Nevertheless, secret data can be leaked using devious means of communication, i.e., covert channels [24].

Concerning the content-based fine-grained access control in requirement *R2*, there are two categories of enforcement mechanisms in the literature: view-based and query rewriting [9]. In view-based mechanisms, the resource authorized views are derived according to the specified authorization policy. Then, the access is granted to these views rather than the original data resource. On the other hand, the query rewriting enforcement approach intercepts the query submitted for execution to apply the authorization policy criteria.

In Bertino et al. [4], an access control model for relational databases supporting permission delegation and negative authorization is proposed. Moreover, *Oracle Virtual Private Database (VPD)* [7] enforces access control at the row level by appending the expressed content-based and context-based conditions in the authorization policy to the where clause of the SQL query. A FGAC at the cell level is introduced LeFevre et al. [17] using dynamically generated views nullifying the unauthorized cells. Last but not least, Agrawal et al. [2] proposed a language supporting grant command specification at the cell level [9].

The existing authorization and access control mechanisms are advanced and satisfy all the requirements. However, as the performance of relational databases degrades with joins, locks and impedance mismatch, non-relational databases emerged with various data storage models to address these limitations and handle large amounts of data [13]. In the following sections, we will explain each of the NoSQL models in detail.

5   Key-Value Data

The key-value model uses a hash table, and is the simplest one among all NoSQL models. It is powerful and efficient in storing schema-less data in the form of data values associated to keys which are used as indexes for quickly finding values in large data sets [3]. Data can be either stored as rows like structured data or JSON objects. *Redis*[1] and *Accumulo* are examples of native key-value databases.

Redis is an advanced open source data store where each key-value is a pair of binary strings for managing different types of binary data (e.g., XML documents, images, arrays, and bytes). It provides hashes to store and query the database objects. In Accumulo, data is stored in a distributed sorted map. The keys are logically divided into a row key to uniquely identify the row, a column, and an automatically generated timestamp used for versioning [19]. Each column is further divided into a family (i.e., the logical grouping of the key), a qualifier as a more specific key attribute, and a visibility tag which stores a logical combination of security labels.

According to the key-value model represented in Fig. 2, the hierarchy consists of a collection of records identified by their unique keys (cp. *R1*). Regarding requirement *R2*, the finest granularity in this model is the value of a particular key. If the value is an object with attributed values in the form of key-value pairs, access control should be applied at the field level.

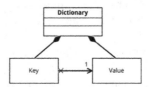

Fig. 2. Key-value database model

The Accumulo database applies fine-grained access control at the cell level such that security labels are assigned to key-value pairs as a new element to the key called *Column Visibility*. If these labels are satisfied at query time, the respective key and value will be included in the response of the user access request. On the contrary, Redis does not implement any access control mechanism [25]. The work in Moreno et al. [19] proposed a model design to describe who can access the values of specific data cells in a key-value database system. The labels may define rules for an access matrix, role-based access control (RBAC), or multilevel models.

---

[1] https://redis.io.

When matching the requirements in Sect. 3 with the available access control features, we find that the requirement *R1* is satisfied because the model hierarchy is simple (i.e., a table and key-value entries). Requirement *R2* is not satisfied for this model as the access to the fine-grained element is based on its security label or the assigned role rather than the content. We consider the key-value database model satisfying requirement *R3* because at least one database system has the option to specify custom authorization policies. For instance, custom security labels can be specified in the column visibility or each value during writing to Accumulo. Finally, no demonstration cases are presented for external authorization and context-based policy in key-value databases so far.

6   Column-Oriented Data

The column-oriented database is also referred to as column-family store. It is considered as an evolution of key-value stores where data are also represented as hash maps, but with more than one indexing level [1]. The meta model for column-oriented databases is illustrated in Fig. 3. Each column consists of a key and a value. The column-family is a set of rows equivalent to a table in the relational databases. A set of column-family is defined as a key space. This model is typically used in data mining and web applications because of its ability to deal with massive data and complex datasets in distributed systems. However, it is less flexible than key-value and document-oriented models because of the column-family that must define a schema at the application level. Examples of column-oriented databases are *Cassandra*[2] and *HBase*.

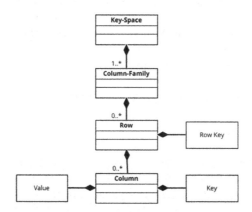

Fig. 3. Column-oriented database model

According to the column-oriented database model and requirement *R1*, authorization policies should specify constraints at the level of key space, column-family, row, and column. For requirement *R2*, FGAC should allow to limit access to a specific column values within a row.

---

[2] https://cassandra.apache.org.

Cassandra supports RBAC at the key space or column-family level according to the user role(s) and privileges. It also uses the GRANT/REVOKE security paradigm to manage permissions on database resources, which are assigned to roles [13]. The resource could be key space, role, table, index, or function. In Cassandra, access control at the object level is not available [12]. HBase enforces authorization using access control list (ACL). Kulkarni [16] proposed a fine-grained key-value access control (K-VAC) model where authorization policies can be specified at the level of column-family, key space, column, or row. However, this model is implemented as a library and restricted to specific databases, i.e., Cassandra and HBase.

Based on the research works and available access control features in column databases, it is possible to specify custom authorization policies at different levels (refer to *R3*). Additionally, the work in Kulkarni [16] claims to enforce content-based FGAC. It also provides three examples to apply context-based access control (*R5*) by describing user location and time of the day in the authorization policy. Since existing policy languages have no direct support for column-oriented data structures, this database model fails to meet requirement *R4*.

7   Document-Based Data

The document-based database model is the most commonly used NoSQL data model as it can manage structured, semi-structured (e.g., XML files), and unstructured (i.e., text) data. In this model, data is stored as schema-less documents with one or more fields as key-value pairs or nested documents as depicted in Fig. 4. Documents are analogous to records in the RDBMS and the term collection is equivalent to table, but without a pre-defined schema. Each document is identified by a unique key which is not only used to manipulate (i.e., insert, delete, and update) document data, but also for linking different documents. For fast data retrieval, indexing on specified fields can be added. Document data stores are typically used for blog software and content management systems due to their flexibility, high performance, and horizontal scalability. Examples are *MongoDB* and *Couchbase*.

MongoDB is a distributed general-purpose database that stores data in the form of JSON documents without schema definition. It has collections as an additional organization level for grouping similar documents and provides its own query language, i.e., *MongoDB Query Language (MQL)*. MongoDB is the first ranked NoSQL database due to its strengths including the support of all indexing techniques in relational databases for data sorting and faster searching [25].

The finest granularity in this database model is at the level of document fields (cp. *R1*), however, authorization policies should consider the rest of the hierarchy including document, collection, and up to the database level. Field-level policies control access to fields of a document with any structure level including a field of a document field (i.e., nested document) or an element of an array of fields.

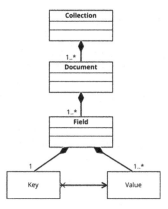

Fig. 4. Document-based database model

Document data stores support *role-based access control (RBAC)*. Couchbase implements 46 predefined roles with specific privileges on the entire collection[3]. Most of these roles are exclusive to the enterprise version; only three roles can be used in the community version. MongoDB has built-in and user-defined roles that grant privileges to perform the specified actions on a given resource (i.e., database, collection, set of collections, or cluster). Users have no access to the system if they are not assigned to at least one role. The first user created in the database should be a user administrator who has the privileges to manage other users[4]. Although MongoDB is adopted in many solutions due to its dynamic structure, there is no standardization of authorization and access control.

In Colombo and Ferrari [8], the RBAC model in MongoDB is enhanced to support purpose-based policy specification at the document level. However, the proposed approach is limited to MongoDB. Then, the same authors refined the granularity level of access control in MongoDB to support content-based and context-based policies at the field level [10]. They eventually generalized the concept to enforce fine-grained ABAC into document data stores at the document or field level without prior knowledge of the document structure [11]. In Kacimi and Benhlima [14], the work presents an architecture applied to MongoDB for purpose-based access control policies written in XACML.

According to the existing access control features for the document-based database model, we can say that at least one document data store satisfies each of the proposed requirements except *R4*. Although the work in [14] uses XACML in *access control as a service (ACCAAS)* with MongoDB, further implementation is needed to map the defined policy attributes to database values. Hence, the solution is application-specific, but it uses a policy language to express the authorization policy and decide whether the access request is authorized or not.

---

[3] https://docs.couchbase.com/server/current/rest-api/rbac.html.

[4] https://www.mongodb.com/docs/manual/core/authorization.

8   Graph-Structured Data

The data is stored in the form of graphs having object nodes as vertices connected by edges representing the relationships between them. A graph database has no predefined schema and can be seen as a special kind of document-oriented database where some documents act as the relationships connecting other documents [25]. It is scalable and uses shortest path algorithms for improving the efficiency of data queries, but is more complex to manage. There are different graph models, but the *property graph* (see Fig. 5) is the most common model in graph databases.

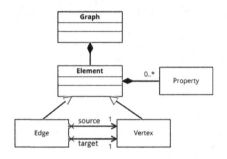

Fig. 5. Property graph database model

Graph databases are mainly used in recommendation systems and social networks, however, there is no standard language for inserting data and traversing graphs yet. Neo4j [21] is the top ranked native graph database[5] with its declarative query language *Cypher*.

Fine-grained access control in the context of graph-structured data is about protecting nodes and edges along with their properties (i.e., attributes). However, one of the key problems is how to describe the object of a permission [15]. This is because usually nodes and edges are not isolated and even contexts in the graph model can be used as an object of a permission, so protecting a single element ignoring the related surroundings results with allowing access to specific subjects although their connecting path could be unauthorized. In some cases, it is also desired to permit/deny specific connections to a particular object. Hence, a way to describe paths or subgraphs to which access rights apply is required. Another problem concerns permission propagation among objects.

Currently, native (e.g., Neo4j) and non-native (e.g., Microsoft Azure CosmosDB [28] and ArangoDB [22]) graph databases provide RBAC. Neo4j supports RBAC with predefined roles (i.e., reader, editor, publisher, architect, and admin) in addition to subgraph and property-level access control [6]. It also has a special database (i.e., system database) for storing the defined privileges.

---

[5] https://db-engines.com/en/ranking/graph+dbms.

A model-based approach is introduced in Morgado et al. [20] using metadata with authorization rules to control access in applications that use graph-oriented databases. It provides a predefined schema for the graph nodes and supports data definition language (DDL) and data manipulation language (DML) operations. This model only allows the specification of positive permissions that have to be defined for each node. The work did not show how the model handles conflicts. In Valzelli et al. [27], the authors proposed an initial solution towards protecting knowledge graphs. A knowledge graph contains all the world's main entities along with their relations. The work introduces a property graph model to specify open and closed policies using authorization edges between subjects (i.e., user and user group) and resources (or resource category). However, they focus only on DAC, MAC, and RBAC which are not sufficient to enforce FGAC. These works provide conceptual approaches that need to be implemented on top of the graph model.

Last but not least, the work in Mohamed et al. [18] tries to couple ABAC with a new declarative language for fine-grained, attribute-based authorization policy, named *XACML for Graph-structured data (XACML4G)* [25]. Even though additional path-specific constraints in terms of graph patterns can be described, the policy rules require specialized processing and the enforcement mechanism needs to be adapted to work in a specific graph data store.

Current access control in graph databases does not meet the requirement *R1*. For instance, the RBAC privileges in Neo4j are limited to reading/updating the database, managing resources (i.e., databases, users, roles, and privileges) as well as editing node labels, relationship types, and property names. Up to the best of our knowledge, content-based FGAC cannot be applied in the existing graph databases (*R2*). The achieved authorization in the enterprise edition of Neo4j is specifying privileges using static commands in terms of actions to be performed (e.g., traverse, read, and match) on particular node labels or relationship types within graphs. These privileges are then granted or denied to custom-defined roles. Requirement *R4* is satisfied since authorization policies can be specified and enforced in the database layer as well as externally (refer to [18]). Finally, existing graph databases and even the recent policy language *XACML4G* did not show rule specification and enforcement taking user context information, e.g., access time and location of the user, into account.

9   Discussion

In the previous sections, we provide the current state of the art of authorization and access control features supported within DBMSs or introduced by research works in relational as well as NoSQL database models. We now relate the requirements defined in Sect. 3 with the previously discussed features taking into consideration that the data model hierarchy in requirement *R1* is structured differently and the term FGAC in requirement *R2* is defined differently for each database model (see *RQ2*).

The relational model has the most sophisticated authorization and access control mechanisms in comparison to all NoSQL models. However, it is not scalable to deal with big interconnected data. The fine-grained content-based model

ABAC can be enforced in the access control systems for relational databases taking environmental conditions into account. Moreover, custom rules can be specified at different levels within the database (e.g., using views) or externally using a policy language such as XACML.

As opposed to relational databases, NoSQL databases trade consistency and security for performance and scalability [13]. The access control approaches available in the literature are specific to certain database models or even data stores. This is due to the lack of a reference model and multiple implementations of the same data model [9]. To address *RQ3*, we summarize the assessment of the requirements for each database model in Table 1.

Table 1. Requirements for each database model

Database model	R1	R2	R3	R4	R5
Relational	✓	✓	✓	✓	✓
Key-Value	✓	×	✓	×	×
Column	✓	✓	✓	×	✓
Document	✓	✓	✓	×	✓
Graph	×	×	✓	✓	×

The key-value model is the simplest with respect to structure and hierarchy, however, it has the least information security support, i.e., basic authorization using labelling, compared to the column, document, and graph models. The column-oriented and document-structured database models received the most attention among the NoSQL ones. The existing access control features together with the research works addressed most of the authorization and access control requirements. It is still challenging to meet the missing requirements and come up with an authorization policy language and enforcement model that fits within one or more non-relational database models. This is because of the lack of a common query language and consistent support that made it hard to switch from one NoSQL data store to another.

Regarding access control for graph databases, Neo4j is more advanced than other graph databases. However, the existing access control features still need to be enhanced to not only provide fine-grained access control for nodes and relationships on the attributes level, but also protecting the graph while traversing it. The proposed research works have two main drawbacks: (1) not generally applicable because graph data stores have different query languages, and (2) extra implementation is required upon changing or adding new policies.

For any application, there is an underlying database within a DBMS either having a specific database model or implementing several ones. For example, ArangoDB is a native multi-model database managing different data models (i.e., key-value, document, or graph) with one declarative query language. There is no access control solution that applies to all database models so far, but it is possible to enforce an access control approach in different DBMSs with a specific model due to similar structure or a specific DBMS with different models because of the common query language. To answer $RQ4$, the defined requirements are generally applicable to typical application scenarios for various DBMSs even with different database models if structural differences are taken into account.

10   Conclusion

Access control ensures information security and protection by enforcing authorizations in terms of which users are permitted (or denied) to perform what operations on which organizational resources. Authorization and access control are open issues in the NoSQL data stores because these database models (i.e., key-value, column, document, and graph) are designed to focus on handling new data sets with less consideration on security. Unlike NoSQL models, the relational model has robust access control mechanisms to protect sensitive information. However, RDBMSs are inefficient in storing and handling big data.

The traditional relational model data is structured into tables with fixed schema where each data entry is equivalent to a row having values for the columns. On the other hand, non-relational models have different forms. Firstly, the key-value model is represented as a hash table with key-value entries. In the column-oriented model, records hold a collection of dynamic columns that are grouped into column families within a key space. The document-based model consists of collections having document entries in the form of key-value pairs or nested documents whereas the graph data structure is solely based on vertices and edges. In this paper, we address authorization and access control, with respect to requirements and features within existing DBMSs or research works, for all database models.

To answer our research questions, we start with defining five requirements to generally apply fine-grained dynamic authorization and access control for different database models regardless of the application scenario (refer to $RQ1$ and $RQ4$). Due to the different hierarchy and fine-grained access control (FGAC) definition for each database model in requirements $R1$ and $R2$ respectively, we discuss them in the context of these database models along with an overview including the meta model structure, authorization and access control features ending with a summary matching the state-of-the-art features with the requirements ($RQ2$). The resource context in requirement $R5$ is also different for some data structures (e.g., graph).

According to our results in Table 1, we indicate whether the requirements are satisfied or not for the relational as well as each of the NoSQL database models ($RQ3$). It can be concluded that the relational database model has advanced authorization and access control features while with the NoSQL models, we can only specify custom authorization policies on different levels, except for the graph model. There it is not yet possible to define policies for individual elements and their properties. However, a policy language for specific NoSQL models is only proposed for graph databases. Last but not least, FGAC based on content and context are currently supported by document and column models only.

As NoSQL data stores are increasingly used today, a lot of research and development have already been focusing on providing more sophisticated authorization and access control features. Still more research is needed for the NoSQL models to achieve a similar maturity level for authorization and access control to that in the relational model.

Acknowledgement. The research reported in this paper has been partly supported by the LIT Secure and Correct Systems Lab funded by the State of Upper Austria. The work was also funded within the FFG BRIDGE project KnoP-2D (grant no. 871299).

References

1. Abadi, D.J., Boncz, P.A., Harizopoulos, S.: Column-oriented database systems. Proc. VLDB Endow. **2**(2), 1664–1665 (2009). https://doi.org/10.14778/1687553. 1687625
2. Agrawal, R., Bird, P., Grandison, T., Kiernan, J., Logan, S., Rjaibi, W.: Extending relational database systems to automatically enforce privacy policies. In: 21st International Conference on Data Engineering (ICDE 2005), pp. 1013–1022 (2005). https://doi.org/10.1109/ICDE.2005.64
3. Alotaibi, A., Alotaibi, R., Hamza, N.: Access control models in NoSQL databases: an overview. JKAU **8**(1), 1–9 (2019)
4. Bertino, E., Samarati, P., Jajodia, S.: An extended authorization model for relational databases. IEEE Trans. Knowl. Data Eng. **9**(1), 85–101 (1997). https://doi.org/10.1109/69.567051
5. Bertino, E., Ghinita, G., Kamra, A.: Access Control for Databases: Concepts and Systems. Now Publishers Inc. (2011)
6. Borojevic, I.: Role-based access control in Neo4j enterprise edition (2017). https://neo4j.com/blog/role-based-access-control-neo4j-enterprise. Accessed Aug 2022
7. Browder, K., Davidson, M.A.: The virtual private database in oracle9ir2. Oracle Technical White Paper, Oracle Corporation 500(280) (2002)
8. Colombo, P., Ferrari, E.: Enhancing MongoDB with purpose-based access control. IEEE Trans. Dependable Secure Comput. **14**(6), 591–604 (2015). https://doi.org/10.1109/TDSC.2015.2497680
9. Colombo, P., Ferrari, E.: Fine-grained access control within NoSQL document-oriented datastores. Data Sci. Eng. **1**(3), 127–138 (2016)
10. Colombo, P., Ferrari, E.: Towards virtual private NoSQL datastores. In: 2016 IEEE 32nd International Conference on Data Engineering (ICDE), pp. 193–204 (2016). https://doi.org/10.1109/ICDE.2016.7498240
11. Colombo, P., Ferrari, E.: Towards a unifying attribute based access control approach for NoSQL datastores. In: 2017 IEEE 33rd International Conference on Data Engineering (ICDE), pp. 709–720 (2017). https://doi.org/10.1109/ICDE.2017.123
12. Dadapeer, N.I., Adarsh, G.: A survey on security of NoSQL databases. Int. J. Innovative Res. Comput. Commun. Eng. **4**(4), 5250–5254 (2016)
13. Dindoliwala, V.J., Morena, R.D.: Survey on security mechanisms in NoSQL databases. Int. J. Adv. Res. CS **8**(5) (2017)
14. Kacimi, Z., Benhlima, L.: XACML policies into MongoDB for privacy access control. In: Proceedings of the Mediterranean Symposium on Smart City Application, SCAMS 2017. Association for Computing Machinery, New York (2017). https://doi.org/10.1145/3175628.3175646

15. Kalajainen, T., et al.: An access control model in a semantic data structure: case process modelling of a bleaching line. Department of CS and Engineering (2007)
16. Kulkarni, D.: A fine-grained access control model for key-value systems. In: Proceedings of the Third ACM Conference on Data and Application Security and Privacy, CODASPY 2013, pp. 161–164. Association for Computing Machinery, New York (2013). https://doi.org/10.1145/2435349.2435370
17. LeFevre, K., Agrawal, R., Ercegovac, V., Ramakrishnan, R., Xu, Y., DeWitt, D.: Limiting disclosure in hippocratic databases. In: 30th International Conference on Very Large Databases, VLDB Endowment, Toronto, Canada, pp. 108–119 (2004)
18. Mohamed, A., Auer, D., Hofer, D., Küng, J.: Extended authorization policy for graph-structured data. SN Comput. Sci. **2**(5), 1–18 (2021)
19. Moreno, J., Fernandez, E.B., Fernandez-Medina, E., Serrano, M.A.: A security pattern for key-value NoSQL database authorization. In: Proceedings of the 23rd European Conference on Pattern Languages of Programs, EuroPLoP 2018. Association for Computing Machinery, New York (2018). https://doi.org/10.1145/3282308.3282321
20. Morgado, C., Busichia Baioco, G., Basso, T., Moraes, R.: A security model for access control in graph-oriented databases. In: 2018 IEEE International Conference on Software Quality, Reliability and Security (QRS), pp. 135–142 (2018). https://doi.org/10.1109/QRS.2018.00027
21. Neo4j: Neo4j documentation (2022). https://neo4j.com/docs/. Accessed Aug 2022
22. Oasis: Access control in ArangoDB (2019). https://www.arangodb.com/docs/stable/oasis/access-control.html. Accessed Aug 2022
23. Sahafizadeh, E., Nematbakhsh, M.A.: A survey on security issues in big data and NoSQL. Adv. Comput. Sci. Int. J. **4**(4), 68–72 (2015)
24. Sandhu, R.: Relational database access controls. Handb. Inf. Secur. Manag. **95**, 145–160 (1994)
25. Sicari, S., Rizzardi, A., Coen-Porisini, A.: Security&privacy issues and challenges in NoSQL databases. Comput. Netw. **206**, 108828 (2022). https://doi.org/10.1016/j.comnet.2022.108828
26. Tankard, C.: Big data security. Netw. Secur. **2012**(7), 5–8 (2012). https://doi.org/10.1016/S1353-4858(12)70063-6
27. Valzelli, M., Maurino, A., Palmonari, M., Spahiu, B.: Towards an access control model for knowledge graphs (2021)
28. Weiss, T., et al.: Azure role-based access control in azure cosmos DB (2022). https://docs.microsoft.com/en-us/azure/cosmos-db/role-based-access-control. Accessed Aug 2022
29. Zahid, A., Masood, R., Shibli, M.A.: Security of sharded NoSQL databases: a comparative analysis. In: 2014 Conference on Information Assurance and Cyber Security (CIACS), pp. 1–8 (2014). https://doi.org/10.1109/CIACS.2014.6861323
30. Zugaj, W., Beichler, A.: Analysis of standard security features for selected NoSQL systems. Am. J. Inf. Sci. Technol. **3**(2), 41–49 (2019)

A Hierarchical Deterministic Wallet Using Ed25519 Digital Signature Scheme

Thang Nguyen-Dinh[1,2], Phuong Nguyen-Nguyen[1,2], Tu Phan[3],
and Khuong Nguyen-An[1,2(✉)]

[1] Faculty of Computer Science and Engineering, Ho Chi Minh City University of
Technology (HCMUT), 268 Ly Thuong Kiet Street, District 10, Ho Chi Minh City,
Vietnam
nakhuong@hcmut.edu.vn
[2] Vietnam National University Ho Chi Minh City, Linh Trung Ward, Thu Duc
District, Ho Chi Minh City, Vietnam
[3] Descartes Network, Ho Chi Minh City, Vietnam
tuphan@descartes.network

Abstract. On the Internet, most financial applications apply public
key cryptography to verify users' identities, manage their digital assets,
authenticate and authorize them, etc. In a blockchain system, this model
is crucial to keep the system working, since there are no intermediaries or
a central database for management. Commonly, users can manage their
key pair using the blockchain wallet, also known as 'crypto wallets.' In
practice, the user has to keep track of many key pairs for each asset,
which is inefficient. We use a hierarchical deterministic wallet (HD wallet) to solve this problem, which can derive hundreds of child wallets
from a single master key-pair. Currently, there are already multiple protocols for an HD wallet for `Secp256k1` while those for `Ed25519` are neither
well-known nor well developed. In this thesis, we will try to analyze and
build an HD wallet for `Ed25519` signature schema.

Keywords: Crypto wallet · Hierarchical deterministic wallet ·
Blockchain wallet · `Ed25519` digital signature scheme · digital signature
algorithm · Edward curve

1 Introduction

Today, blockchain has become a robust trend in financial technology. Blockchain
enables truth-less digital currencies transaction without intermediaries. It helps
to solve the double-spending and censorship problems in traditional finance.
Similar to a transaction in a bank, we need to sign it to provide proof of identity.
In a blockchain system, we use a digital signature scheme (DSS) to perform such
an act. DSS requires a pair of private and public keys, a signing algorithm, and
the corresponding verifying algorithm using those keys. The private key is kept
private and used to sign the transaction, while the public key is accessible by
everyone and used to verify the signature.

© The Author(s), under exclusive license to Springer Nature Singapore Pte Ltd. 2022
T. K. Dang et al. (Eds.): FDSE 2022, CCIS 1688, pp. 240–257, 2022.
https://doi.org/10.1007/978-981-19-8069-5_16

The key pair is preserved and managed using an application called a cryptocurrency wallet (or 'crypto wallet' for short, some people may call it a digital wallet, but that is not entirely correct.) A crypto wallet has access to crypto coins, while a (traditional) digital one does not have access directly to the money. A digital wallet needs to be connected to a bank account or a user's card, and it will spend fiat currency. It also requires registering certain banking services to work. It still costs an extra fee when transferring cross-bank or to another country. With a crypto wallet, the user can transfer cryptocurrency directly to the receiver wallet in an instance (≤ 10 mins) with the fee only proportion to how much he transferred, regardless of the distance. Apart from that, the crypto wallet doesn't require any personal information or third-parties services to work. A crypto wallet doesn't actually "hold" any of your crypto assets; it is just pairs of private and public keys, as mentioned above. It infers the user's balance by tracking his transactions on the blockchain and then calculating how much his balance currently has. From now on, when we mention "wallet", it means crypto wallet or blockchain wallet.

When the user makes a transaction, he uses the wallet to sign his transaction with the private key, which only he has, and sends the transaction to the blockchain network. The blockchain node then validates his transaction using his public key, and when his transaction is approved, his balance will be deduced, and the receiver will get the coins. The public key can also be used as an address of the receiver by hashing or encoding it. For security reasons, the wallet has to create different signatures for different transactions. If not, the attacker can easily impersonate anyone because the signatures are publicly visible on the blockchain. To ensure the security of the signature, the wallet needs to use different key pairs for different transactions. In that case, the user has to keep track of all the used key pairs and make sure he doesn't use one of those the next time he makes a transaction. As the number of transactions grows, the number of key pairs increases tremendously, which makes it a hassle for the users to take care of or back up the wallet.

Apart from that, there is one more problem regarding the advanced users. Commonly, a newcomer uses a single recommended wallet from the market. However, the Internet is never a safe place. There are many disruptions in the world of cybersecurity[1], and so is the blockchain. Most of the current blockchain cryptocurrencies are transparently visible to anyone with access to the Internet. Any user who acknowledges that and is an experienced investor is called an advanced user. With that in mind, advanced users care more about privacy, security, and how to invest in multiple markets. They want to stay anonymous and keep their wallets safe from attackers. Therefore, they found it inconvenient to track how many wallets they owned (how many markets they invested in) and all the key pairs each wallet had used.

That's where the hierarchical deterministic wallet (HD wallet) comes in handy. HD wallet helps advanced users manage multiple wallets and back them up more quickly. The HD wallet helps them back up only the master key pair

---

[1] According to https://www.varonis.com/blog/cybersecurity-statistics.

with a mnemonic code. From a single master key pair, the HD protocol allows the wallet to derive billion of 'child wallets.' Also, in investment, they don't want to put all their eggs in one basket. Holding all your funds in a single wallet is risky, as everything is gone once the user loses his wallet. With HD wallets, he can split his assets into small chunks, each chunk can be put in a different child wallet, and he can easily manage those wallets through the master keys.

There are multiple HD protocols, all of which rely on some DSSs. Currently, most protocols are built for the Secp256k1 elliptic curve which is used in Bitcoin's public-key cryptography and is defined in *Standards for Efficient Cryptography (SEC)*[2], with the standard elliptic curve digital signature algorithm (ECDSA), which has been proven to be "unsafe". Since 2009, a fault attack on ECDSA [1] has already been discussed. After that, there are still certain poor implementations exploited practically in the Console Hacking in 2010 [2] and the Android Bitcoin Wallet Security in 2013 [3].

Given that situation, our work aims to design and implement the very first prototype HD wallet that works for Ed25519 DSS, a fast and high-security signature algorithm proven by Daniel Bierstein and Tanja Lange [10]. The rest of our paper is organized as follows: In Sect. 2 we recall some background on elliptic curve cryptography and related digital signature schemes (DSS), especially the DSS based on the Edwards-curve Ed25519. Next, Sect. 3 presents some related works and technologies relevant to our works. Our main contributions will be presented in Sects. 4, 5, where we propose our solution, design, implement and test the system. And finally, we conclude the paper, discuss some limitations, and propose future works in Sect. 6.

2   Backgrounds

2.1   Blockchain and Digital Signature Algorithm

When the user makes a transaction, he uses the wallet to sign his transaction with the private key, which only he has, and sends the transaction to the blockchain network. The blockchain node then validates his transaction using his public key, and when his transaction is approved, his balance will be deduced, and the receiver will get the coins. The public key can also be used as an address of the receiver by hashing or encoding it. For security reasons, the wallet has to create different signatures for different transactions. If not, the attacker can easily impersonate anyone because the signatures are publicly visible on the blockchain. A simple way to pursue that is to use different key pairs for different transactions. In that case, the user has to keep track of all the used key pairs and make sure he doesn't use one of those the next time he makes a transaction. As the number of transactions grows, the number of key pairs increases tremendously, which makes it a hassle for the users to take care of or back up the wallet.

Let's illustrate the process of making a transaction in a blockchain ecosystem. Blockchain technology includes a peer-to-peer network called a blockchain

---

[2] Certicom Research, http://www.secg.org/sec2-v2.pdf.

network, a ledger of transactions called blockchain, and a consensus protocol. Supposed that Alice wants to send Bob 10 BTC. Alice then uses her wallet to make a transaction and signs it. After that, the wallet broadcasts the transaction to the blockchain network. Every node that receives the transaction will validate the authority to know if Alice made the transaction, the timestamp to prevent the double-spending transaction, and other information, such as if Alice has at least 10 BTC to send to Bob, etc. When a transaction is valid, it will be put into a block until that block is full of transactions (about a hundred transactions per block). Next, the node appends that block to create a new blockchain, then uses the consensus protocol to know which new blockchain will be used in the network. This consensus process takes about 10 min. Finally, when the new blockchain has a block that contains Alice's transaction, the transfer is completed, and Bob now has 10 BTC.

As mentioned earlier, a crypto wallet consists of a key pair called private and public keys. Throughout the transaction process, all the end-user needs to do is to make sure the transaction is signed. Hence, a blockchain is simply a chain of blocks containing digital signatures of transactions. The vital check of the validation process is signature verification. Blockchain is truthless and has no intermediary. The signature is the only thing that the blockchain can authenticate the user. If blockchain technology does not use a proper DSS, a crypt-analytical issue can break down the whole system, where no users can clarify which transactions are their own or who have made a transaction.

2.2 Elliptic Curve Cryptography

Elliptic curve cryptography (ECC) is a branch of public key cryptography known as asymmetric-key cryptography. An elliptic curve E defined over a finite field F_p is given by the following equation

$$y^2 \equiv x^3 + a_1 x + a_2 \pmod{p},$$

where the condition $4a_1^3 + 27a_2^2 \not\equiv 0 \pmod{p}$ must hold to exclude singular curve. The equation above is called a short Weierstrass equation, which can use to represent most of the elliptic form. The set of all pairs $(x, y) \in F_p \times F_p$ together with an imaginary point at infinity Θ satisfying the equation is the set of points on the elliptic curve. Interestingly, the points on an elliptic curve can form a cyclic group. It means that when we perform an operation with a curve point (adding with itself, doubling, tripling, etc.) using the curve's algebraic addition laws, we can get the new point that also belongs to the curve. The resulting point will "jump around" on the curve, and when we keep adding the point to itself, the resulting point will eventually return to the starting point. After that, the point repeatedly cycles through the group of points, and that's why we call it a cyclic group. With that behavior, we can generate a pair of public key with the integer as the private key, and the public key as the scalar multiplication of the base point and the private key. Other rules and necessary parameters are also required to make ECC work, but right now, we only need to focus on how it generates the key pair and its security. ECC security depends on the elliptic curve discrete logarithm problem (ECDLP). Given an elliptic curve E, we consider a primitive element P and another element T. The *discrete logarithm problem* is finding an integer d, where

$$d \in [1, \#E] \text{ satisfies } P + P + \ldots + P \text{ ("+" } d \text{ times)} = dP = T.$$

The ECDLP is infeasible if the elliptic curve parameters are carefully chosen [4]. As mentioned above, we interpret the integer d as the private key, T as the public key, and the exact number of point points E of a curve. The number of points on the curve can be counted by trying all the possible values for x in F_p, but this is inefficient if the p is a large prime. There exists a theorem related to this, called Haskel's theorem. However, Haskel's theorem only gives an upper and lower bound for the number of points on an elliptic curve [4], which is

$$p + 1 - 2\sqrt{p} \leq \#E \leq p + 1 + 2\sqrt{p}.$$

In other words, finding the exact numbers of points on a curve is computationally difficult, which means the brute-force attack is an absurd idea, to begin with. There exists a faster algorithm for computing the order of a curve, Schoof's algorithm, which runs in polynomial time [5]. However, this proves that it's hard to figure out the private key, as the algorithm provides "how many times we need to add the point to itself to go back to the base point", not how to get the exact integer that produces the public key.

Note that in practice, a point $P(x, y)$ can be compressed to an integer (y's LSB in the first byte $\|$ x). The first byte of y can be 0x02 for even y, or 0x03 for odd y (negative y) with the given x. For instance, a point $P(6, 8)$ can be compressed to the integer 0x026 in hexadecimal format. The actual number is almost 256-bit long. This is just a plain example.

2.3   Elliptic Curve Digital Signature Algorithm

A digital signature algorithm is an algorithm to sign and verify the authority of the signature. The elliptic curve digital signature algorithm (ECDSA) is the standard DSS for ECC. It was designed based on the ElGamal DSS and is applicable for most types of elliptic curves. In the Bitcoin blockchain, ECDSA is used with the Secp256k1 curve according to the Bitcoin Wiki, as mentioned in the Introduction section. Until now, the Bitcoin blockchain still uses ECDSA with some adjustments to make it work for them, said that the vulnerability of the Secp256k1 curve. However, as time goes by, the drawbacks of the ECDSA start to show up, along with the security of the Secp256k1 curve. To dive into that, let's go through ECDSA. Denote that n is the prime field of the elliptic curve E, G is the base point of the elliptic curve, H is a hash function, q is the randomly generated private key in the range $[1, n-1]$ and Q is the corresponding public key. Due to the page number limitation of this paper, we only present an abstract version of the signature algorithm in Fig. 1 below.[3]

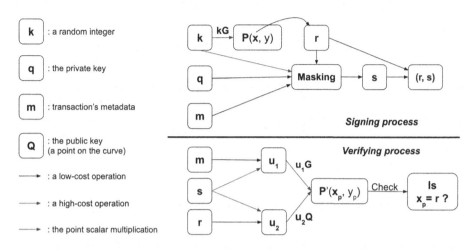

Fig. 1. ECDSA's signing and verifying processes

In short, the math behind the signature is to calculate a random point from a random integer k and the base point G, then takes out the point x-axis to get r, after that combine it with the signature proof $s \equiv k^{-1} * (H(m) + rq)$ mod n. For the verifying, we check whether $x_p = r'$, where x_p is the x-axis of the point $P' = [s^{-1} * H(m)]G + [s^{-1} * r]Q$. The problem with ECDSA is that, we have to calculate modular multiplicative inverse in both the signing and verifying processes. The modular inverse is an expensive modulo computation. In modular arithmetic, to find a multiplicative inverse of an integer a with a prime p, we first compute if $\gcd(a, p) = 1$ to know if a exists a modular inverse. ECC requires one more condition than modular arithmetic: the point needs to be on the curve, which means the coordinates have to satisfy the curve equation and follow the curve's addition laws. That's why signing a message takes a lot of trial and error just to find a suitable nonce, hence causing ECDSA heavily depends on the safety of the pseudo-random number generator (PRNG) for k. Moreover, to ensure the private key won't be leaked, the nonce has to be randomly generated for every signature. Or else, the private key can be retrieved as follow

Step 1: Assume that the signature s_1 and s_2 use the same nonce, which means $r_1 = r_2 = r$. The hash values of the two messages are $H(m_1) = M_1$ and $H(m_2) = M_2$.

Step 2: $s_1 - s_2 \equiv k^{-1} * (M_1 + rq) - k^{-1} * (M_2 + rq) \mod n$

---

[3] The readers interested in the detailed implementation and the maths behind the scene can find those at https://www.rfc-editor.org/rfc/rfc6979.html, which also includes the proof-of-correctness of the signature algorithm.

Step 3: $s_1 - s_2 \equiv k^{-1} * (M_1 + rn - M_2 - rn) \mod n$

Step 4: $s_1 - s_2 \equiv k^{-1}(M_1 - M_2) \mod n$

Step 5: $k \equiv (M_1 - M_2)(s_1 - s_2)^{-1} \mod n$, the attacker now retrieves the nonce k

Step 6: Since $s \equiv k^{-1} * (H(m) + rq) \mod n \Rightarrow q \equiv (sk - H(m)) * r^{-1} \mod n$, simply substitute nonce k into the equation, the attacker can access your private key.

This error has been exploited in the real world, as stated in [2]. Specifically, it's not about the collision of the random number generator but because the implementation uses the static nonce. This is a big flaw, and, as a result, Sony suffered from that mistakes. Another vulnerability caused by a poor implementation is the [3], which caused multiple Android Bitcoin wallets exposed to thieves.

2.4   Edwards-Curve Digital Signature Algorithm with Ed25519 Curve

The Edwards-curve digital signature algorithm (EdDSA) is a DSS based on the Schnorr signature scheme for the Edwards curve type. The Edwards curve was first discovered by Harold M. Edwards [9]. A general Edwards curve has the equation:

$$ax^2 + y^2 \equiv 1 + dx^2y^2 \pmod{n}.$$

For the twisted Edwards-curve Ed25519, it has the prime field $n = 2^{255} - 1$ and the co-factor $h = 8$, which is the same with those of the Curve25519 curve. Actually, the Montgomery curve Curve25519 is the counterpart of the Ed25519 curve, as they are bi-rationally equivalent. A map exists between those two curves to transform from one to the other and vice versa (proved in [10]). Therefore; the Ed25519 curve also supports Montgomery ladders [7], which is an algorithm to calculate the point in constant-time. An extra note is the Ed25519 curve uses a point encoding scheme rather than a standard point compression. A point $P(x, y)$ is presented as a 32-octet string, interpreted as a little-endian integer. To encode a point $P(x, y)$:

Step 1: Encode the $y-$coordinate as a little-endian string of 32 octets. The last octet's most significant bit (MSB) is always zero.

Step 2: Copy the least significant bit (LSB) of the x-coordinate to the MSB of the last octet string. Resulting in an encoded point with 256 bits length, with the 256-bit to be the LSB of x, called x_0. Decoding a point takes more work than encoding.

Step 3: Clearing the x_0, the MSB of the octet string, to obtain y. If $y \geq p$, decoding fails.

Step 4: x can be retrieved by computing $x^2 \equiv (y^2 - 1)/(dy^2 + 1) \mod p$.

Step 5: Denote $u = (y^2 - 1), v = (dy^2 + 1)$, w is the candidate root. Calculate $w \equiv uv^3(uv^7)^{(p-5)/8} \mod p$.

Step 6: There are three cases:

- Case 1: If $vw^2 \equiv u \mod p$, then $x = w$,
- Case 2: If $vw^2 \equiv -u \mod p$, then $x = w \times 2^{(p-1)/4}$,
- Case 3: Otherwise, no square root exists. Decoding fails.

Step 6: If $x = 0, x_0 = 1$, decoding fails. Else, if $x_0 \equiv x \mod 2$ then $x = x$, if not then $x = p - x$.

The main reason for point encoding rather than point compression is to ensure the ability to be distinguished from a string. Standard representations of elliptic-curve points are easily distinguishable from uniform random strings.[4] Thus, this already improves the security of the Ed25519 curve by one level.

The outstanding key difference of the Ed25519 curve to the Secp256k1 curve is the addition laws. For twisted Edwards, the addition laws are "complete," which means there are no exceptional cases, and the laws are the same for all kinds of points. Edward curve, by default, doesn't have an imaginary point-of-infinity. All of its points are 'actual' points on the curve. Therefore, it can have uniform addition laws since there is no irregularity. The key generation for the curve Ed25519 is also different, which will be illustrated in the digital signature algorithm. Edwards-curve digital signature algorithm (EdDSA) is a digital signature scheme using a variant of Schnorr's signature based on twisted Edwards curves. The abstract version in Fig. 2 below presents both the key generation and its use in the EdDSA.[5]

We can see that the private key is split in half. One half is to produce the public key, while the other half is combined with the hashed message to generate the deterministic random r. Hence, there is no random nonce needed in the algorithm, and also makes EdDSA create the deterministic signature, which means we will have the same signature for the same message. This helps EdDSA become strong existential unforgeability, compared to ECDSA, which has multiple valid signatures for a single message.

On the other hand, most of the operations are hash and point scalar multiplication (the bit pruning simply sets some bits to 0 and 1). At the same time, ECDSA involves calculating the modular multiplicative inverse in both signing and verifying processes. This reduces the cost and time consumed in the processes and prevents a specialized attack for ECDSA, a side-channel attack. Since the elliptic curve's multiple parameters are accessible from the internet, the attacker can track the computational time of the algorithm and, from there, infers the private scalar. EdDSA prevents the attacker from knowing the start time of the algorithm and the time consumed. The attacker calculates the algorithm time simply by tracking the sent time of the containing public point message (since the point is only compressed, which is noticeable) and the signed message. As stated above, the point encoding scheme makes the point information

---

[4] "This poses a problem for many cryptographic protocols using elliptic curves: censorship-circumvention protocols, for example, and password-authenticated key-exchange protocols", as stated in According to SafeCurves, https://safecurves.cr.yp.to/ind.html by the author of Ed.

[5] The readers can find the details of the algorithm at https://datatracker.ietf.org/doc/html/rfc8032.

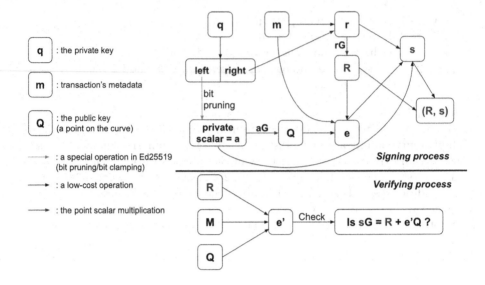

Fig. 2. EdDSA signing and verifying process

masked and indistinguishable from a random message. And the scalar multiplication of EdDSA is constant-time because it inherits the Montgomery ladder. Therefore, EdDSA is practically safe from most side-channel attacks. Another notable breakthrough is that, throughout the process, the private key is not used directly to sign, ensuring that there is no information about the private key can be leaked. Justify from ECDSA and EdDSA. We can see that EdDSA indeed has better security and performance.

3   Related Works and Technology

3.1   Bitcoin Improvement Proposal 32

The crucial part of an HD protocol is the child key derivation (CKD) function. The CKD function helps manage and derive the child key from the master key pair. Bitcoin Improvement Proposal 32 (BIP32)[6] is the pioneer HD protocol, defined for standard ECDSA and Secp256k1 curve. In BIP32, Pieter Wuille introduced the first key derivation scheme. To ensure the child keys do not depend solely on the parent key, BIP32 extends private and public keys with an extra 256 bits of entropy. This extension, called the chain code, is identical to corresponding private and public keys and consists of 32 bytes. The key with the extension is called an extended key. In addition, there are two ways to derive a child key: hardened or normal (non-hardened). The differences between them are the child key's index and the parent key used as an input for the derivation function. The normal derivation will derive a child key with the index in the

---

[6] Available at https://github.com/bitcoin/bips/blob/master/bip-0032.mediawiki.

range of 0 to $2^{31} - 1$ and use the parent public key (the point on the elliptic curve can be calculated from the private key or used by the public key directly) as the necessary input. The index varies from 2^{31} to $2^{32} - 1$, and the private parent key is used for hardened derivation. One note is that the parent key must be extended. BIP32 defined some rules for the CKD function, which are:

1. Private parent key $\rightarrow$ private child key: can be derived using normal derivation and hardened derivation.
2. Public parent key $\rightarrow$ public child key: can be derived using normal derivation.
3. Private parent key $\rightarrow$ public child key: can be derived using hardened derivation.
4. Public parent key $\rightarrow$ private child key: this case is not possible.

BIP32 provides an HD protocol and a tree structure for key management. From a single master key pair, the HD wallet can generate multiple levels of child key, each parent key can derive about $2^{32} - 1$ child keys (level 1), and each child key can derive grandchild key $2^{32} - 1$ child keys (level 2), etc.

However, there is a key leakage problem regarding security issues. By any chance, if an attacker can access the child private key, he can only retrieve one child wallet for a standard case. In the case of HD wallets, if he gets his hand on the wallet's master public key and any child private key, he can calculate the master private key. which means the user lost all of their crypto assets. This dangerous attack is known as the key recovery attack.

Also, the Ed25519 curve can't be directly applied with BIP32. The BIP32's CKD function applies to most of the elliptic curve but not the digital signature algorithm. The Ed25519 DSS didn't use the private key of the Ed25519 curve directly in both the generation of the public key and the signature. Whereas BIP32's CKD version requires the extended key to be the multiplier for the public key. The signing process is also different because the private key used in the Ed25519 DSS is hashed and split into two parts to sign a message. The bit clamping process is crucial to Ed25519 DSS as it has a small co-factor $h = 8$. If the lower bits are not cleared, the attacker can retrieve the private key by simply trying to perform a brute-force point multiplication by 8.

3.2   Satoshi Labs Improvement Proposal 10

Our studies found that the Satoshi Labs Improvement Proposal 10[7] (SLIP10) can "solve" the key leakage problem by applying BIP32's derivation scheme on two curves, the NIST P-256 curve and the Ed25519 curve. We focused on how they made the derivation work for the Ed25519 curve. As presented above, the key generation of the Ed25519 curve is different from other curves by the bit clamping process, and the Ed25519 DSS's signing process is also different. SLIP10 adapted BIP32's derivation scheme by using the produced hashes directly as secret keys (here, we re-word the secret key as the produced hash of the private key to

---

[7] Available at https://github.com/satoshilabs/slips/blob/master/slip-0010.md.

distinguish it from the actual private key used in Ed25519 DSS). This also caused the normal derivation of the Ed25519 curve impossible since the relation between its private key and the public key is not direct point multiplication. Hence, SLIP10 unintentionally solved the key leakage problem for Ed25519. The trade-off is that the public key derivation is not viable.

3.3 Hierarchical Deterministic Keys over a Non-linear Keyspace

In [11], Khovratovich and Law proposed another way to adapt the BIP32 for Ed25519 DSS by discussing the problem of hierarchical deterministic keys over a non-linear keyspace. The method is slightly different from the one in the SLIP23[8]. They skipped the problem of 'bit clamping' by deriving new keys using only 224-bits scalar. This method, however, reduced the security of the signature scheme to enable public key derivation. Thus it brought back the leakage problem. In addition, the author mentioned some other weaknesses of their approach: the child private key is not a valid EdDSA extended private key, the child private key will be vulnerable to timing attacks, and the most important point is that the signature procedure is no longer compatible with EdDSA DSS.

4   Our Approach

4.1   Architecture Analysis and Our General Proposal

We acknowledged that the advantages of public-key derivation significantly impact the financial application of the blockchain system. It removes the need for an intermediary to keep an eye on the buyers' addresses, as the receiver wallet can deduce which child wallet is responsible for storing a crypto asset. The sender only needs to know the receiver's address and transfer usually, similar to the case of sending to a non-HD wallet. In addition, the public key derivation comes along with the HD protocols to help manage the keys efficiently. Rather than constantly generating a private key and then the public one, we can check one's balance with only the master public key.

The key leakage was not a problem to apply an HD protocol with the Secp256k1 curve since the curve key space grows linearly, and Bitcoin does come up with a solution, that is to hash the public key to masking them rather than using the public key directly as the address. Therefore, the only weakness lies in the side-channel attacks. When it comes to application with Ed25519 DSS, the problem is brought up again due to the non-linear key space of the Ed25519 curve, i.e., the point jumps around a smaller bound and won't reach the point of infinity. Within the SLIP23, the bound is more negligible just for the cost of public key derivation. Cardano blockchain used that approach, though. In our studies, we found a write-up (see [6]) about key recovery attacks and even a discussion on Solana [8] that this approach is detrimental to the system. We couldn't agree more, as the main reason we proposed the Ed25519 DSS is for

---

[8] Available at https://github.com/satoshilabs/slips/blob/master/slip-0023.md.

better security and performance, and the Cardano approach tweaked that to bring back the public key derivation.

When choosing which DSS to use, the side channel attack is the most vulnerable attack to ECC, and this problem has been going on for ECDSA for a while. That's why we decide to choose Ed25519 DSS over ECDSA to prioritize the safety of the curve from those attacks. This also comes with faster performance since the Ed25519 DSS has no modular inverse operations and has a constant-time scalar multiplication algorithm.

4.2 Proposed Solution on Hardened Key Derivation with Ed25519

We proposed that, prefering to the [6] and [8] discussions, the wallet should apply the SLIP10's HD protocol implementation for Ed25519 curve for better security against the side-channel and key recovery attacks. The wallet will be a *non-custodial hybrid wallet*, which has zero users' private information, has access to the internet, and stores the seed of the master key pair in a safe place to manage the keys efficiently. Also, we believe anyone should have access to any of the wallets to be bug-free. Hence, we implemented an open-source library for the other developers. They can use it, contribute to it (merge more blockchains, etc.) and audit our works. Furthermore, we will use this library as a core functionality that supports the cryptography mechanism in our web wallet.

Our work does not only share an identical problem with the problem statement. We realize that we could do better with the support of BIP44[9], we can create wallets that hold multiple native tokens of different blockchains. We decided our HD wallet will support the blockchain using Ed25519 curve as well as Secp256k1 curve (two famous curves of the blockchain community). They are Bitcoin, Ethereum, and Solana. As we studied, there are almost no non-custodial hot wallets that support different kinds of coin holders. Even the existing libraries limit their support to a specific blockchain.

The library is supposed to be easy to maintain, read and contribute to the community. We organize as in Fig. 3.

We name our library hdcore[10] meaning the *cores of our HD wallets*. The library is divided into two following parts:

- The /src folder comprises the /wallet folder, which is the implementation of API for each chosen blockchain. There is also a constant file including all general information about the blockchain (index, URL, etc.) And an account file where we generalize the wallet folder. Users can choose their blockchain wallet through this file.
- The /test folder contains test cases for every function.

The library will support the following features of an HD wallet:

- Mnemonic code generation;

---

[9] Available at https://github.com/bitcoin/bips/blob/master/bip-0044.mediawiki.
[10] Available at https://github.com/npsables/hdcore.

– Key pair generation;
– Key tree derivation;
– Address generation (for each blockchain);
– Verification of keys and addresses;
– Balance checker;
– Transaction builder (signing and broadcasting the transaction).

5   Implementation and Testing

5.1   Our Implemented Library

Our library adapts the implementation of the SLIP10 protocols and expands for the Secp256k1 curve and their blockchain transaction problem. For the sake of our work in this paper, we will only present the core function of the Ed25519 blockchain since others will follow the same schema and rules (just different dependencies).

We designed our work for developers who only use it for one specific blockchain or implement multiple of them. We also acknowledge that every blockchain has different features (especially transactions). For example, Bitcoin uses the UTXO model (individual coins) for wallet assets, while Solana uses the Account/Balance model. This led to different implementations in transaction functions. Aiming for upgrade-ability, readability, and ease of use, we organized as follows:

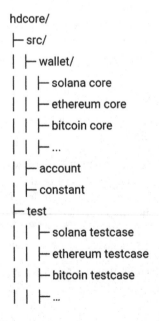

```
hdcore/
├─ src/
│  ├─ wallet/
│  │  ├─ solana core
│  │  ├─ ethereum core
│  │  ├─ bitcoin core
│  │  ├─ ...
│  ├─ account
│  ├─ constant
├─ test
│  ├─ solana testcase
│  ├─ ethereum testcase
│  ├─ bitcoin testcase
│  ├─ ...
```

Fig. 3. General library structure

- We create a *COMPONENTS* JSON object with constant information of every supported blockchain. This *COMPONENTS* belongs to file */src/constant.ts* (.ts is the standard for Typescript file). We made use of the JSON architecture for legibility. Users can immediately see a blockchain's function and how to access them through a few lines of code. Unlike Tomi Jaga's wallet [12], they use an OOP structure which is very hard to read. Also, it would become more redundant when we created more blockchain dictionaries and added more features for every blockchain. Meanwhile, in our JSON object, developers can add more lines with different indexes and add a new function to their blockchain file (solana.ts, etc.). Check out the Fig. 4 below for more details.
- For the users who want to implement the functions generally, we create */src/accounts.ts* for this purpose. It includes the function to access these values and supports every element of the key derivation process (Fig. 5).

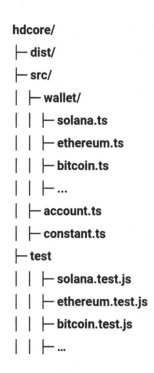

Fig. 4. Typescript library structure

To handle the Ed25519 curve arithmetic, we use the tweetnacl-js library. The library uses Asymmetric Cryptography in NaCl that applied Bernstein's Curve25519 elliptic-curve Diffie-Hellman key exchange and will use the Ed25519 elliptic-curve signature scheme from Subsect. 2.4. One different thing is that, they didn't use the principle we have shown for scalar multiplication with the Ed25519 curve. They decided not to implement the conversion of points on

`Ed25519` to Montgomery form and back. Instead, they perform a new ladder with a completely new addition and double points in one add function (Fig. 6).

5.2   The Proposed System and Implementation

We choose to implement a web wallet[11] so that we don't have to deal with version control and different kinds of operating systems (Android, iOS, etc.) The web wallet is a non-custodial hot wallet where users can sign in, generate accounts in different blockchains, and send and receive native tokens. The users have absolute control over private keys for every blockchain address, and the wallet provider has no access to them (Fig. 7).

We can provide an address service to bring back the use case with a middle merchant. The address service[12] provides API for public wallet management and searching (in the transaction). We apply the Flask framework and MongoDB for our module. The system contains a total of four APIs: **getaddress** to search for a child address of a wallet; **createdefault** to make sure whenever a new wallet is created, there is at least one child wallet available; **pushaddress** to push a specific child wallet's address to the server, and of course, a **deleteaddress** to remove a specific child wallet's address from the server.

```
23    const COMPONENTS: any = {
24      "0": {
25        index: "0",
26        hex: "0x80000000",
27        symbol: "BTC",
28        name: "Bitcoin",
29        link: "https://bitcoin.org/",
30      },
31
32      "1": {
33        index: "1",
34        hex: "0x80000001",
35        symbol: "BTCT",
36        name: "Testnet (all coins)",
37        key_pair_master: create_bitcoin_testnet_pair,
38        get_address: get_bitcoin_testnet_address,
39        transaction: bitcoin_tn_tx,
40
41      },
42
43      "501": {
44        index: "501",
45        hex: "0x800001f5",
46        symbol: "SOL",
47        name: "Solana",
48        link: "https://solana.com",
49        key_pair_master: create_solana_pair,
50        get_address: get_solana_address,
```

Fig. 5. COMPONENTS JSON example

---

[11] Available at https://github.com/thangND026317/hd-wallet-ui.
[12] Available at https://github.com/npsables/address_service.

```
set25519(p[0],gf0);
set25519(p[1],gf1);
set25519(p[2],gf1);
set25519(p[3],gf0);
for (i = 255;i >= 0;--i) {
  u8 b = (s[i/8]>>(i&7))&1;
  cswap(p,q,b);
  add(q,p);
  add(p,p);
  cswap(p,q,b);
}
```

Fig. 6. Different implementation in Montgomery Ladder

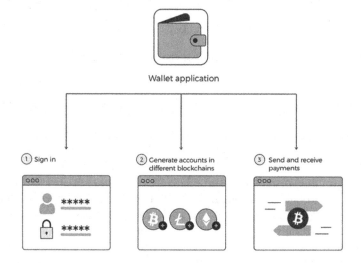

Fig. 7. Example of web wallet flow

Overall, we suggest that the ecosystem should be similar to the figure below (Fig. 8).

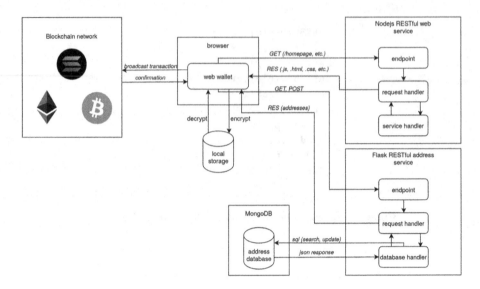

Fig. 8. Overview of the entire system

6   Conclusion, Limitation, Future Work, and Discussion

In this work, we analyzed the HD wallet architecture, including the security of its implementation and the related DSS. We implemented a library and a prototype web wallet to demonstrate our solution. We proposed a workaround to the bit-clamping problem of the `Ed25519` curve and fit it with a properly designed HD protocol. Even though it's still a prototype, we hope it could help researchers and practitioners in the related area know how to apply the same way with better HD protocols, a better curve, or even create an HD wallet that surpasses our work.

The implemented library only supports three out of a thousand existing blockchains. This will require a lot of time and contribution from the community and ourselves. The library is still heavy on dependencies, many of which can be rewritten more efficiently. So we take on recommendations from NIST and the community to develop our project without creating it independently.

The web wallet we created is still simple and doesn't reach the level of industrial production with hundreds of people behind it. Our works didn't provide a way to authorize and limit the user's access. The microservice architect we use can give availability but is very hard to maintain and update. The client-server model is also lost compared to the decentralization of the blockchain network. There is still plenty of room for development in our wallets.

We can put more effort into the web wallet and make it more user-friendly. The centralized client-server for both the web wallet and address service can be replaced with the Inter-Planetary File System (IPFS), a peer-to-peer network protocol for storing and sharing data in a distributed file system. IPFS uses content-addressing to uniquely identify each file in a global namespace connecting all computing devices. It also provides a decentralized database so users can participate in maintaining the software. We can also investigate the new authenticity mechanism for our decentralized network. Since password-based login is an insecure approach to online interactions, multi-factor schemes add friction, reducing user adoption and productivity.

Acknowledgment. We acknowledge Ho Chi Minh City University of Technology (HCMUT), VNU-HCM, for supporting this study.

References

1. Schmidt, J., Medwed, M.: A fault attack on ECDSA. In: Workshop on Fault Diagnosis and Tolerance in Cryptography (FDTC) 2009, pp. 93–99 (2009). https://doi.org/10.1109/FDTC.2009.38
2. Console Hacking 2010 - PS3 Epic Fail, Archived 15 December 2014, at the Wayback Machine, pp. 123–128 (2014)
3. Android Security Vulnerability, Bitcoin, 11 August 2013. https://bitcoin.org/en/alert/2013-08-11-android
4. Bos, J.W., Costello, C., Longa, P., Naehrig, M.: Selecting Elliptic Curves for Cryptography: An Efficiency and Security Analysis. IACR: Cryptology ePrint Archive, p. 130 (2014). http://eprint.iacr.org/2014/130
5. Izu, T., Kogure, J., Noro, M., Yokoyama, K.: Efficient implementation of Schoof's algorithm. In: Ohta, K., Pei, D. (eds.) ASIACRYPT 1998. LNCS, vol. 1514, pp. 66–79. Springer, Heidelberg (1998). https://doi.org/10.1007/3-540-49649-1_7
6. Internet archive: Web 3 Research, Key recovery attack on BIP32-Ed25519, 2 December 2018. https://web.archive.org/web/20210513183118/https://forum.w3f.community/t/key-recovery-attack-on-bip32-ed25519/44
7. Joye, M., Yen, S.-M.: The montgomery powering ladder. In: Kaliski, B.S., Koç, K., Paar, C. (eds.) CHES 2002. LNCS, vol. 2523, pp. 291–302. Springer, Heidelberg (2003). https://doi.org/10.1007/3-540-36400-5_22
8. Solana Labs, Ed25519 BIP32, 10 October 2019. https://github.com/solana-labs/solana/issues/6301
9. Edwards, H.: A normal form for elliptic curves. Bull. Am. Math. Soc. **44**, 393–423 (2007). https://doi.org/10.1090/S0273-0979-07-01153-6
10. Bernstein, D.J., Duif, N., Lange, T., Schwabe, P., Yang, B.Y.: High-speed high-security signatures. J. Cryptogr. Eng. **2**, 124–142 (2011). https://doi.org/10.1007/978-3-642-23951-9_9
11. Khovratovich, D., Law, J.: BIP32-Ed25519: hierarchical deterministic keys over a non-linear keyspace. In: 2017 IEEE European Symposium on Security and Privacy Workshops (EuroS&PW), pp. 27–31 (2017). https://doi.org/10.1109/EuroSPW.2017.47
12. Jaga, T.: Thenewboston HD Wallet, 10 July 2021. https://github.com/tomijaga/tnb-hd-wallet

A Secure Framework for Internet of Medical Things Security Based System Using Lightweight Cryptography Enabled Blockchain

Joseph Bamidele Awotunde[1]([✉]) [ID], Sanjay Misra[2] [ID], and Quoc Trung Pham[3]([✉]) [ID]

[1] Department of Computer Science, Faculty of Information and Communication Sciences,
University of Ilorin, Ilorin 240003, Kwara State, Nigeria
awotunde.jb@unilorin.edu.ng
[2] Department of Computer Science and Communication, Østfold University College, Halden,
Norway
Sanjay.misra@hiof.no
[3] School of Industrial Management, Ho Chi Minh City University of Technology (VNU-HCM),
HCMC, Vietnam
pqtrung@hcmut.edu.vn

Abstract. The Internet of Medical Things (IoMT) is a growing paradigm that offers several efficient and productive solutions for the treatment of various ailments for both patients and medical professionals. The IoMT has many advantages, but security remains a problem that must be overcome. The inexperienced IoMT users' lack of security and privacy consciousness and the possibility of multiple middleman attacks for getting the healthcare information, seriously puts the use of IoMT in jeopardy. Therefore, this paper proposes a lightweight cryptography enabled with blockchain for enhancing IoMT-based security and privacy. The study utilizes lightweight cryptography to securely uploading the data to the cloud database for privacy preservation, and the Blockchain technology is use to securely store the data in the cloud server. The experimental results of the proposed model revealed a better result with compare with prevailing methods. The proposed system achieves an accuracy of 98% of security level.

Keywords: Internet of medical of things · Blockchain technology · Lightweight cryptography · Security and privacy · Cloud computing

1 Introduction

All technological breakthroughs have been centered on data. The use of technologies that enable interconnectedness to establish communications with multiple services has been advocated among various organizations and vendors [1]. Healthcare is one of several industries where blockchain and Internet of Medical Things (IoMT) are being used extensively for applications like secure storage, interactions, and automation technologies [2, 3]. IoMT devices lack security and self-protection capabilities, are resource

T. K. Dang et al. (Eds.): FDSE 2022, CCIS 1688, pp. 258–272, 2022.
https://doi.org/10.1007/978-981-19-8069-5_17

restricted, and is extremely vulnerable to compromise [4]. Blockchain is one of the innovative aspects that has aided this development. Blockchain technology has been used to decentralize communication between many clients while preserving confidentiality and unlinkability in a fully decentralized setting without a central authority. Blockchain has been suggested for a variety of services and solutions by blockchain proponents.

One of the suggested methods for enhancing the IoMT-based environment is the implementation blockchain paradigm [5]. Despite the robustness and tamper-proof nature of blockchain, but due to its transparency, significant privacy and trustworthiness issues have been brought up. When it comes to patient history information, the primary and most important cryptographic method is to encrypt sensitive information [6]. The platform for sending and receiving patient health records is thought to be the digital healthcare system [7]. The majority of the current healthcare systems, however, lack adequate access control and encryption technologies, therefore they lack security measures. The key component of effective healthcare is the dissemination of medical data to authenticate users. Blockchain offers a peer-to-peer and decentralized network system, which is necessary and useful in IoMT-based notwork to decentralized the nodes within the network [8]. It is a blockchain that is consortium- and permission-managed, which indicates that every peer is known to the network. All concerned parties benefit from the confidentiality which is a security requirement that it offers [9].

There are a number of lightweight cryptography techniques available to address the issues raised above, but they are less effective in terms of adaptability and confidentiality [10]. The field of cryptography is developing, and new methods of attack, design, and deployment are being thoroughly researched [11]. The state-of-the-art method known as "Lightweight Cryptography (LWC)" is one of them [12]. A cryptographic technique or protocol designed for deployment in limited settings is known as lightweight cryptography. The LWC can be implemented in various environments like contactless smart cards, RFID tags, sensors, healthcare device among others. Secure is one of the most promising and reliable solutions to these problems. The LWC, which enables users to encrypt data on their own without a third party's assistance. Additionally, LWC offers sufficient security, and not necessarily take advantage of the efficiency-security trade-offs [10].

The LWC was employed for two major reasons namely:

a. End-to-end communication effectiveness end nodes must implement a symmetric key method in order to achieve end-to-end security. The cryptographic operation with a restricted quantity of energy consumption is crucial for resource - constrained devices, such as rechargeable batteries appliances. End devices can use less energy when the lightweight symmetric key method is used.
b. Application to devices with less resources: The LWC primitives have a smaller physical footprint than the traditional cryptographic ones. The use of additional network connections with less resource-intensive devices is made possible by the LWC primitives.

Some end nodes could be able to integrate general-purpose microprocessors, and in such systems, software characteristics are significant. However, because to their restricted cost and energy consumption, the cheapest devices can only integrate application-specific ICs, where hardware characteristics are of utmost importance.

Because it is effective and has a less environmental impact, LWC helps to secure networks of smart items. We think that while designing networks, lightweight primitives should be taken into account. It is now viable to employ lightweight block ciphers in particular [13, 14].

Additionally, blockchain is a new platform with immutability qualities that offer secure administration, authentication, and financial transactions, and secure access management for IoMT devices [15]. IoMT is a cloud-based internet connection in which user data is processed and collected centrally. The institution must also be able to diagnose patients who are located remotely in order to deliver smart healthcare. Significant challenges with the IoMT-based framework include data security, prices, memory, sustainability, trustworthiness, and transparency between many ecosystems. Since the user's legitimacy is in doubt owing to an open internet setting, it is crucial to manage information confidentiality and authenticity. There are a number of strategies that are mostly concerned with addressing security difficulties, include attacks using stolen smartcards, timing, denial of service, and forgeries, among others. To identify the people involved in transactions, blockchain technology adheres to the principles of complete privacy. Immutability, better data sharing, increased security, and the elimination of a centralized third party are the driving forces for the usage of blockchain in IoMT-based systems [16], and for distributed applications with lower overhead expenses [17]. In addition to extra legal standards, IoMT-based platforms have several special security and privacy issues.

Therefore, this study explores the use of lightweight cryptography and blockchain to solve the security and privacy issues in IoMT-based system. Specifically, this paper use LWC to secure the patient data on the IoMT platform [18] to address the concerns about the confidentiality of transactions between blockchain nodes, and serious security risks to critical IoMT environments [1]. The paper provides the following key contributions:

(i)   to guarantee the confidentiality and integrity of user data, a LWC authentication and authorisation architecture was developed for the Blockchain-enabled IoMT environments.

(ii)   Make a suggestion for an enhanced multi-user enhanced secure LWC that assigned roles to safely enquire across specified search queries in the distributed ledger.

(iii) the patient initially encrypts the data before uploading it to the blockchain.

Once the data owner has finished the encryption, the proposed model offers the data owner a facility that will not allow access until they require policy revocation or deletion, through other procedures. Blockchain architecture. Provides rigorous decentralized assurance of patient data sets' privacy and integrity. Each patient will have sovereignty control over their data attributable to blockchain technology. The blockchain enables secure key management between personal servers and implantable medical devices, and between local and remote systems in the cloud. Secure access to the patient information stored on cloud servers is also available to authorized users. The cloud servers' blockchain is where all of the healthcare data is kept.

The rest of the article is summarized as below: Sect. 2 presents the related work, section explain and give the full description of the proposed model. The results and discussion with experimental investigations was presented in Sect. 4. Finally, the conclusion and future scope was presented Sect. 5.

2 Related Work

Blockchain is a tamper-proof, decentralized data warehouse. Consequently, blockchain technology may be utilized to maintain patient medical records, and can be extremely important for maintaining and effectively sharing healthcare data in the domain of healthcare. IoMT consists of a vast number of interconnected items, including sensors, computers, embedded systems, actuators, cellphones, and more [19–21]. Traditional communication protocols including HTTP, TCP, and IP are ineffective at supporting M2M communication, according to studies conducted by authors in [22, 23]. The authors in [24] also put forth a three-layered design with artifacts, linguistic, and internet-oriented layers. In [25, 26], the authors discussed the security issues and solutions of the three-layer architecture are covered in depth, and following is a summary: (a) perception layer: timing attack, man in the middle (MITM) attack, node capture, DoS attack, and malicious node assaults can all happen in this layer; (b) Network layer: The key issues with this layer are identity authentication issues, privacy exposure to prevent various attacks within the layer, such attack are DoS attack, MITM attack, replay attacks, eavesdropping attack, and so on; (c) Application layer: This attack includes pricey protection, identity authentication, and difficulties with data and information exposure.

The majority of IoMT devices used in healthcare settings are susceptible to several cyber threats and assaults. Due to the fact that patient data is housed on the hospital's cloud server, data security is essential [27]. The most difficult challenge in the IoMT framework has been security, and choosing an algorithm that solves all issues with lightweight confidentiality is difficult. The LWC technique has been utilized for IoT in a number of disciplines, including cluster head selection, resource management, supply chain management, and crime prevention. The authors in [28] have provided a brief overview of the function of multi-criteria making decisions assessment in healthcare. For the goal of selection in IoMT, many LWC methodologies have been used. For example, the authors in [29] established a multi-criteria decision support system for dementia patients. Similar to that, multicriteria decision making analysis may be applied to contract decision-making, and tendering procedures in the healthcare industry [30].

One of the most important problems that has to be solved is authentication. The authentication model to secure IoT may be satisfied by a number of authentication mechanisms, including untraceability, perfect forward secrecy, mutual authentication, anonymity, and both cryptosystems and non-cryptosystems are employed by the authentication protocols [31]. These methods are divided into four groups: flat, hierarchical, distributed, and centralized. The following criteria and traits, such as the enrollment phase, two-way identification, offline phase, extra hardware, numerous identities, and several authentication tokens, are used to categorize these approaches. For an IoT context focused on the cloud, certain authentication mechanisms are suggested, and devices with limited resources, which are the two fundamental elements of IoMT and will be described further [25, 32].

Authentication in an IoMT context focused on the cloud, and to use this crypto-graphic techniques, a user's device must be verified on an authorization server. Each user has their own individual secret code. Using a two-tier authentication process and the updated Diffie-Hellman mechanism, SaaS-agent handles unregistered devices. The login and password are validated at the first layer. By inputting a predetermined series of actions on a phony server interface, the user gets validated in the second layer if they are successful. The authors suggested the appropriate authentication procedures in light of the aforementioned facts. Using the three functions of user, destination server, and ID-based authentication using a server provided by an ID is demonstrated. For mutual authentication, two hash values are computed by the ID provider and sent to the user and the destination server. Elliptic Curve Cryptography is presented as a further ID-based strategy (ECC). The suggested inter-cloud authentication mechanism links all cloud servers together, and the user just needs to use one account to access them. You may find a thorough analysis of these methods in [33].

Security and privacy in the IoMT are further challenged by identity management and authentication. Identity management entails identifying the distinctive things, and authentication confirms the parties' identification relationships after that. With the Internet of Things, authentication is essential for maintaining privacy, and accessibility can be hampered without it. If an enemy could establish their legitimacy, they would have access to all data, jeopardizing its integrity, availability, and confidentiality [34]. In the IoMT, user identification and authentication is a major problem. The most popular types of identification are password and username combinations, and parties in electronic systems authentication. The contemporary internet would face more security vulnerabilities as a result of the high rate of heterogeneity and the enormous scale of IoMT systems. Network and protocol intelligence services used for IoMT are significantly impacted by heterogeneity [35]. Security solutions must accommodate varied hardware requirements, and must provide IoT systems with authorisation and authentication. Physical constraints on communications and devices are another security concern. IoMT devices include low-power, small-area CPUs, and even the tiniest devices must adhere to Internet Protocols. IoMT device restrictions prevent information from being processed at faster than light speeds [36]. This indicates that the available memory, CPU, and energy are constrained. To reconcile the conflicting demands of robust performance and modest resource usage, difficult security forms are required. Power and size limitations have an impact on the attempts to uphold honesty, and privacy in IoMT systems [37].

An active daily living (ADL) identification framework that employs sensor data, such as that from mobile phones, and directs time-series sensor fusion processing was given by the authors of [38]. The ADL Recorder Application used patient smartphone with various intelligent sensors to capture real-time data. The location of indoor Wi-Fi, speech processing, and proximity sensor localization are the main technologies in this research, and the merging of time-series sensor data. Using the combined data from various sensors, The ADL Recognition System can accurately characterize a person's ADL and identify recurring trends in their life. Different settings have been used to improve network traffic and battery life in order to satisfy long-term requirements. The authors of [39] have created a cloud exchange and retrieval solution for medical data that is Blockchain-enabled. Each record is given a hash value, which is used to keep it safely.

However, this platform does not check a participant's legitimacy, thus someone might register as a patient or doctor and continually store false information. As the system creates hash values and saves them, it also does not distinguish between diverse data forms, such as images, text, or numbers.

A Blockchain-based repository was created by the authors of [40] to share medical information with increased protection. However, there is always possibility of malfunction, which results in system inefficiency. Data latency may occur, for example, if the patient is referred to a different hospital and sees a new doctor. Individuals who aggregate the data into ledgers are not compensated in any other way. A Blockchain-based reliance on the protection for storing healthcare data has been presented in a research study [41], and mining is done using Proof of Work (PoW) methods. Data security and integrity are achieved through the use of encryption and hashing. This technique, however, does not allow for data exchange and necessitates a lot of computing power and extra time for mining. The authors of [42] described a framework for storing and transmitting healthcare data that consists of two Blockchain systems. The research demonstrates that it is superior in terms of security and record-sharing. However, it is extremely costly and impractical owing to the use of two distinct Blockchain applications. Furthermore, there is no method for data verification in the proposed technique. A thorough analysis of the function of Blockchain in healthcare systems has also been published in [43].

Hence, it is concluded that any approaches should not sacrifice security in order to achieve high performance. Therefore, this study proposes a LWC for authorization and authentication achitectureal system for Blockchain-enabled IoMT platform in accordance with joint likelihood function. When data is distributed, it creates and assigns random numbers in order to provide a secure link for data collecting. In-depth simulations are used to evaluate the proposed architecture. The suggested system supports reciprocal authentication and offers information privacy, according to results analysis.

3 Material and Methods

The suggested authentication system employs a LWC mechanism for the challenge transmission and answer verification phases. The system characteristics and security level determine how many rounds are used. Then a secure connection is established after authentication. Multiple messages are sent across two nodes (that is, a sensor, a server, or an end user). The process is initiated by sending a message along with a set of encrypted identification data from one node to another. If the receiving node possesses the appropriate cipher identity information, subsequently sends the 'end' message attached with the received identity suit, agreeing to mutual authentication or concluding the contact in another manner. Authorization communications are transferred between two nodes to carry out verification in a satisfactory authentication procedure, and create a safe route. Applying the permission guidelines specified in the smart contract, this connection is then utilized to acquire additional data. Some presumptions are taken into account when conducting the trials. The following are the assumption: (i) One or more IoT devices may be owned by a user; (ii) The secret key is secured; (iii) user has an account on Ethereum; (iv) IoMT sensor, device and user are both linked to the blockchain; and (v) The user's own smart contract will be carried out. A decentralized

Blockchain will be used to create a distributed smart contract framework, and to gain full system management, all users activate unique smart contracts. The proposed model framework is depicted in Fig. 1.

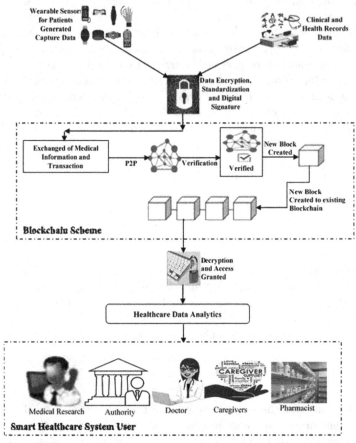

Fig. 1. The proposed Lightweight Cryptography with Blockchain-enabled IoMT-based system architecture.

3.1 Proposed Encryption and Decryption Authentication Architecture

It is anticipated that each user in the IoMT-based infrastructure with Blockchain capabilities will receive their own set of keys. Additionally, it is presumable that the authenticated user has saved data on the devices. Mutual authentication is carried out by two IoMT-based devices, X and Y. A number.

R_{nx} is chosen at random by X from a pool of numbers with the bounds $0 \leq R_{nx,1} \leq \log(id_{max}/2)$ where id_{max} the maximum length of an identification number in bits is. Following the steps outlined below, the message is encrypted with the help of Y's public key and transmitted to Y along with the selected number.

Step 1: $X \rightarrow Y: \vartheta_a = E(PuK_y(X, R_{nx}, 1))$

ϑ_a gets the message at Y and decrypts it to determine what it is intended to say.

Step 2: $\epsilon_{a,1}, R_{nx,1} \leftarrow DE_{prKy}(\vartheta_a)$

The validation was carried out in this instance for consensual authentication. When equality is achieved, Y selects a random number R_{ny} within the range of $0 \leq R_{ny,1} \leq \log(id_{max/2})$ and answers as

Step 3: $\vartheta_b = E(PuK_x(R_{ny,1}, Y \times R_{nx}))$

When X gets Y's reply, it decrypts it as

Step 4: $R_{ny}, \epsilon_y \leftarrow DE_{prKx}(\vartheta_b)$

The acceptance is contingent on ϵ_y and $Y \times R_{nx}$ being equal. X calculates the response and transmits it to Y if it is approved.

Step 5: $\vartheta_c = E(PuK_y(X, R_{ny,1}, R_{nx,2}))$

where $R_{nx,2}$ is constrained to be within the range $0 \leq R_{ny,1} \leq \log(id_{max/2})$. Up to the $(n + 1)^{th}$ message transmission, X and Y interact through challenge and answer exchanges. When X gets the $(n + 1)^{th}$ message, it decrypts the message and gathers the following information.

Step 6: $(R_{ny,z}\epsilon_{y,z}) \leftarrow DE_{prKx}(\vartheta(n - 1))$

In this case, if $\epsilon_{y,z} = Y \times R_{ny,z}$., X calculates the answer ϑ_b. And transmits it to Y as follows:

Step 7: $\vartheta_n = E(PuK_y(X, R_{nx}, z, 0))$

Y decrypts the message and receives the following:

Step 8: $(\epsilon_{y,z+1}) \leftarrow DE_{prKy}(\vartheta_n)$

Next looks for.

Step 9: $(\epsilon_{y,z+1}) = (X, R_{ny,z}) \& \tau = 0$

If the aforementioned requirements are met, the related devices have successfully verified one another or have failed in some other way. The reciprocal authentication mechanism in the suggested framework uses n-passes. The system characteristics and encryption algorithm's security level both affect the value of n. Notably; the suggested framework is preferred to have a 64-bit security level. Tn, X and Y choose two numbers from R_{nx} and R_{ny} at random that are associated by the formula $\log R_{nx}$ and $\log R_{ny} = 64$. Three passes through these steps are required for mutual device authentication.

4 Results and Discussion

The proposed system makes used of Hyperledger Calliper as a tool for the blockchain network. It is compatible with a variety of Hyperledger architectures, including Fabric, Composer, Sawtooth, Iroha, and others. Moreover, the proposed model implemented LWC for encryption and decryption to provide secure, lightweight encryption mechanism. The Calliper tool is crucial tohis presented study's verification and implementation of the framework and numerous parameters. The parameters in Calliper tool includes encryption and decryption times, latency, throughput, and computational cost are some of the parameters. The configuration parameters in the experimental setup are changed in accordance with evaluation, including update, add, delete, and revoke policies, as well as block size, block time, endorsement policy, channel, and keyword search.

The amount of time needed to retrieve outcomes and reflect them on the interactive platform is known as read latency. 100 transactions' initial read latency is recorded for analysis, then, 500 transactions were used for the performance of the proposed system to get results. The read throughput and read latency statistics for 500 transactions are shown in Figs. 2 and 3, accordingly. The graph's trend indicates that there are more transactions per second as time goes on. The time needed to read data from each block increases as the number of transactions rises, and as a result, the linear curve is produced. The volume of transactions affects the throughput of the proposed Blockchain model. When the results were analyzed, it has been found that the system's throughput grows as the number of transactions does.

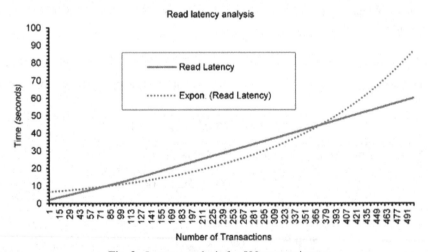

Fig. 2. Latency analysis for 500 transactions.

The duration needed to confirm a transaction is known as transaction latency. It may be estimated by taking the confirmation time out of the submission time. The size of a transaction affects transaction delay. Additionally, a larger transaction requires more resources to process, which adds to the latency. The size of the transaction affects transaction delay. Figure 4 clearly shows that the system's throughput grows with time,

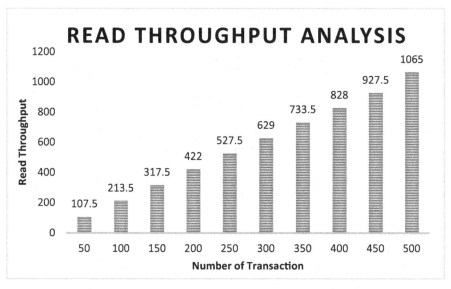

Fig. 3. Throughput for 500 transactions in the Blockchain.

this indicates that the volume and frequency of transactions affect the throughput of the proposed Blockchain technology.

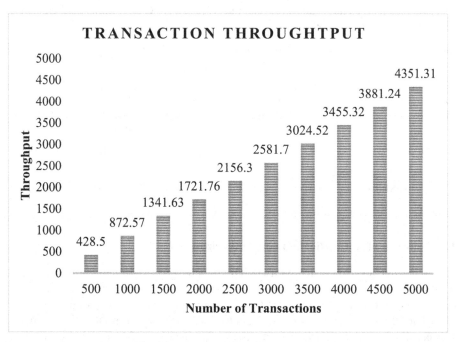

Fig. 4. Throughput for 500 transactions.

4.1 The Comparison of Both Encryption and Decryption Performance

Table 1 show the results of IoMT-based patients data LWC encryption performance, the performance metrics are computing time, computing memory, processor consumption and power consumption respectively. The same size of patient data plaintext was encrypted (500 kb), the patient data plaintext comprises age, blood group, sickness, diseases diagnosed, medical laboratory reports and so on.

Table 1. Cryptography encryption performance

Data size	Cryptography	Computation time (s)	Computing memory (kb)	Processor consumption (%)	Battery consumption (w)	Accuracy (%)
500 kb	AES	0.025	2.37	0	1.56E−05	94%
	RSA	5.487	2.08	0.7	0.004141	73%
	AESRSA	5.502	4.17	0.7	0.005091	70%
	Lightweight	0.261	1.35	0.3	1.29E−07	98%

Table 2 show the results of IoMT-based patients data LWC decryption performance, the performance metrics are computing time, computing memory, processor consumption and power consumption respectively. The same size of patient data plaintext was encrypted (500 kb). The results show that the proposed LWC algorithms perform better across the performance metrics used.

Table 2. Cryptography decryption performance

Data size	Cryptography	Computation time (s)	Computing memory (kb)	Processor consumption (%)	Battery consumption (w)	Accuracy (%)
500 kb	AES	0.022	2.32	0	1.50E−05	93%
	RSA	5.48	2.03	0.6	0.00411	75%
	AESRSA	5.480	4.03	0.6	0.00502	73%

4.2 Esiliency of Authentication and Authorization

The associated keys and matching mote IDs are believed to be reliably pre-configured. Assume that R_n, the chosen random number, has m bits. The level of security is therefore $(R_n - 1)m/2$ bits. The encryption strategy is a foundational component of the proposed mutual authentication framework. Random numbers are used for mutual authentication between devices, as was previously mentioned. So, in order to fake a legitimate device, an eavesdropper needs to produce legitimate messages. The eavesdropper, however, is unable to produce legitimate signals since they lack knowledge of random numbers. The results of the investigation demonstrate how secure the suggested encryption method is in comparison to others. Additionally, it defends against MITM and impersonator threats.

5 Conclusion and Future Scope

Recently, exciting research is being conducted in a number of domains, including healthcare, using LWC and Blockchain technologies. One of the most dynamic areas of Blockchain research is the integration of healthcare with IoT. The health sector manages a vast volume of data that must be analyzed systematically. The digitalization of clinical records is a developing trend. The smart contract has the potential to be used in many Blockchain applications in the future to obtain the best performance. Blockchain-based technologies for maintaining the ledger have been the subject of substantial research, particularly in the field of healthcare systems. Very few of these use cases, however, addressed vital infrastructures that contained delicate data and systems as assets. While blockchains like Ethereum offer their users significant levels of privacy, integrity, and greater transparency, there still significant privacy and security hazards associated with their use in critical areas like IoMT-based systems. Several blockchains do have these privacy problems because one of their key design tenets is the distribution of ledgers. Consequently, with all the extra security and privacy capabilities, thus, any blockchain framework's performance should be thoroughly examined before being used in latency-sensitive settings. Therefore, this paper proposed a hybrid model using LWC enabled Blockchain technology for IoMT-based platforms to protect the patients' medical data. The suggested approach deals with the issue of reciprocal authenticity and permission and offers a creative solution. The findings of the measuring performance and data analysis show that the suggested approach boosts security while processing data more quickly and with less communication overhead. Future work will consider using a better security algorithm like scalable encryption, intrusion detection model with blockchain to further secure the IoMT-based systems. Future work will attempt to assess the proposed system's hardware in a practical environment.

References

1. Tahir, M., Sardaraz, M., Muhammad, S., Saud Khan, M.: A lightweight authentication and authorization framework for blockchain-enabled IoT network in health-informatics. Sustainability 12(17), 6960 (2020)
2. Ali, A., et al.: An Industrial IoT-Based Blockchain-enabled secure searchable encryption approach for healthcare systems using neural network. Sensors 22(2), 572 (2022)
3. Awotunde, J.B., Misra, S., Ayoade, O.B., Ogundokun, R.O., Abiodun, M.K.: Blockchain-based framework for secure medical information in internet of things system. In: Misra, S., Tyagi, A.K. (eds.) Blockchain Applications in the Smart Era, pp. 147–169. Springer International Publishing, Cham (2022). https://doi.org/10.1007/978-3-030-89546-4_8
4. Nguyen, D.C., Pathirana, P.N., Ding, M., Seneviratne, A.: Blockchain for secure EHRs sharing of mobile cloud based e-health systems. IEEE Access 7, 66792–66806 (2019)

5. Vaiyapuri, T., Binbusayyis, A., Varadarajan, V.: Security, privacy and trust in IoMT enabled smart healthcare system: a systematic review of current and future trends. Int. J. Adv. Comput. Sci. Appl. **12**(2), 731–737 (2021)
6. Egala, B.S., Pradhan, A.K., Badarla, V., Mohanty, S.P.: Fortified-chain: a blockchain-based framework for security and privacy-assured internet of medical things with effective access control. IEEE Internet Things J. **8**(14), 11717–11731 (2021)
7. Kim, S.K., Huh, J.H.: Artificial neural network blockchain techniques for healthcare system: focusing on the personal health records. Electronics **9**(5), 763 (2020)
8. Ogundokun, R.O., Arowolo, M.O., Misra, S., Awotunde, J.B.: Machine learning, IoT, and Blockchain integration for improving process management application security. In: Misra, S., Tyagi, A.K. (eds.) Blockchain Applications in the Smart Era, pp. 237–252. Springer International Publishing, Cham (2022). https://doi.org/10.1007/978-3-030-89546-4_12
9. Awotunde, J.B., Chakraborty, C., Folorunso, S.O.: A secured smart healthcare monitoring systems using Blockchain Technology. In: Ghosh, U., Chakraborty, C., Garg, L., Srivastava, G. (eds.) Intelligent Internet of Things for Healthcare and Industry, pp. 127–143. Springer International Publishing, Cham (2022). https://doi.org/10.1007/978-3-030-81473-1_6
10. Katagi, M., Moriai, S.: Lightweight Cryptography for the Internet of Things, vol. 2008, pp. 7–10. Sony Corporation (2008)
11. Hassan, A.: Lightweight cryptography for the Internet of Things. In: Arai, K., Kapoor, S., Bhatia, R. (eds.) Proceedings of the Future Technologies Conference (FTC) 2020, Volume 3, pp. 780–795. Springer International Publishing, Cham (2021). https://doi.org/10.1007/978-3-030-63092-8_52
12. AbdulRaheem, M., et al.: An enhanced lightweight speck system for cloud-based smart healthcare. In: Florez, H., Pollo-Cattaneo, M.F. (eds.) Applied Informatics: Fourth International Conference, ICAI 2021, Buenos Aires, Argentina, October 28–30, 2021, Proceedings, pp. 363–376. Springer International Publishing, Cham (2021). https://doi.org/10.1007/978-3-030-89654-6_26
13. Ning, L., Ali, Y., Ke, H., Nazir, S., Huanli, Z.: A hybrid MCDM approach of selecting lightweight cryptographic cipher based on ISO and NIST lightweight cryptography security requirements for internet of health things. IEEE Access **8**, 220165–220187 (2020)
14. Ogundokun, R.O., Awotunde, J.B., Adeniyi, E.A., Ayo, F.E.: Crypto-Stegno based model for securing medical information on IOMT platform. Multimedia Tools Appl. **80**(21–23), 31705–31727 (2021). https://doi.org/10.1007/s11042-021-11125-2
15. Jan, M.A., et al.: Security and blockchain convergence with Internet of Multimedia Things: current trends, research challenges and future directions. J. Netw. Comput. Appl. **175**, 102918 (2021)
16. Rahmani, M.K.I., et al.: Blockchain-based trust management framework for cloud computing-based internet of medical things (IoMT): a systematic review. Comput. Intell. Neurosci. **2022**, 1–14 (2022). https://doi.org/10.1155/2022/9766844
17. Adeniyi, E.A., Ogundokun, R.O., Misra, S., Awotunde, J.B., Abiodun, K.M.: Enhanced security and privacy issue in multi-tenant environment of green computing using Blockchain technology. In: Misra, S., Tyagi, A.K. (eds.) Blockchain Applications in the Smart Era, pp. 65–83. Springer International Publishing, Cham (2022). https://doi.org/10.1007/978-3-030-895 46-4_4
18. Abdulraheem, M., Awotunde, J.B., Jimoh, R.G., Oladipo, I.D.: An efficient lightweight cryptographic algorithm for IoT security. Commun. Comput. Inform. Sci. **1350**, 444–456 (2020)
19. Mukherjee, A., Ghosh, S., Behere, A., Ghosh, S.K., Buyya, R.: Internet of Health Things (IoHT) for personalized health care using integrated edge-fog-cloud network. J. Ambient. Intell. Humaniz. Comput. **12**(1), 943–959 (2020). https://doi.org/10.1007/s12652-020-021 13-9

20. Ferrag, M.A., Maglaras, L., Derhab, A.: Authentication and authorization for mobile IoT devices using biofeatures: recent advances and future trends. Secur. Commun. Netw. **2019**, 1–20 (2019)
21. Awotunde, J.B., Ayoade, O.B., Ajamu, G.J., AbdulRaheem, M., Oladipo, I.D.: Internet of things and cloud activity monitoring systems for elderly healthcare. In: Scataglini, S., Imbesi, S., Marques, G. (eds.) Internet of Things for Human-Centered Design: Application to Elderly Healthcare, pp. 181–207. Springer Nature Singapore, Singapore (2022). https://doi.org/10. 1007/978-981-16-8488-3_9
22. Li, S., Xu, L.D., Zhao, S.: The internet of things: a survey. Inf. Syst. Front. **17**(2), 243–259 (2014). https://doi.org/10.1007/s10796-014-9492-7
23. Granjal, J., Monteiro, E., Silva, J.S.: Security for the internet of things: a survey of existing protocols and open research issues. IEEE Commun. Surv. Tutorials **17**(3), 1294–1312 (2015)
24. Gou, Q., Yan, L., Liu, Y., Li, Y.: Construction and strategies in IoT security system. In: 2013 IEEE international conference on green computing and communications and IEEE internet of things and IEEE cyber, physical and social computing, pp. 1129–1132. IEEE (2013)
25. Ma, Z., Shang, X., Fu, X., Luo, F.: The architecture and key technologies of Internet of Things in logistics. In: International conference on cyberspace technology (CCT 2013), pp. 464–468. IET (2013)
26. Awotunde, J.B., Jimoh, R.G., Folorunso, S.O., Adeniyi, E.A., Abiodun, K.M., Banjo, O.O.: Privacy and security concerns in IoT-based healthcare systems. In: Patrick Siarry, M.A., Jabbar, R.A., Abraham, A., Madureira, A. (eds.) The Fusion of Internet of Things, Artificial Intelligence, and Cloud Computing in Health Care. IT, pp. 105–134. Springer, Cham (2021). https://doi.org/10.1007/978-3-030-75220-0_6
27. Rani, S.S., Alzubi, J.A., Lakshmanaprabu, S.K., Gupta, D., Manikandan, R.: Optimal users based secure data transmission on the internet of healthcare things (IoHT) with lightweight block ciphers. Multimedia Tools Appl. **79**(47–48), 35405–35424 (2019). https://doi.org/10. 1007/s11042-019-07760-5
28. Frazão, T.D., Camilo, D.G., Cabral, E.L., Souza, R.P.: Multicriteria decision analysis (MCDA) in health care: a systematic review of the main characteristics and methodological steps. BMC Med. Inform. Decis. Mak. **18**(1), 1–16 (2018)
29. Dimitrioglou, N., Kardaras, D., Barbounaki, S.:. Multicriteria evaluation of the Internet of Things potential in health care: the case of dementia care. In: 2017 IEEE 19th Conference on Business Informatics (CBI), vol. 1, pp. 454–462. IEEE (2017)
30. Drake, J.I., de Hart, J.C.T., Monleón, C., Toro, W., Valentim, J.: Utilization of multiple-criteria decision analysis (MCDA) to support healthcare decision-making FIFARMA, 2016. J. Market Access Health Policy **5**(1), 1360545 (2017)
31. Ferrag, M.A., Maglaras, L.A., Janicke, H., Jiang, J., Shu, L.: Authentication protocols for internet of things: a comprehensive survey. Secur. Commun. Netw. **2017**, 1–41 (2017). https:// doi.org/10.1155/2017/6562953
32. Castellani, A.P., Bui, N., Casari, P., Rossi, M., Shelby, Z., Zorzi, M.:. Architecture and protocols for the internet of things: a case study. In: 2010 8th IEEE International Conference on Pervasive Computing and Communications Workshops (PERCOM Workshops), pp. 678–683. IEEE (2010)
33. Saadeh, M., Sleit, A., Qatawneh, M., Almobaideen, W.: Authentication techniques for the internet of things: a survey. In: 2016 Cybersecurity and Cyberforensics Conference (CCC), pp. 28–34. IEEE (2016)
34. Awotunde, J.B., Folorunso, S.O., Bhoi, A.K., Adebayo, P.O., Ijaz, M.F.: Disease diagnosis system for IoT-based wearable body sensors with machine learning algorithm. In: Bhoi, A.K., Mallick, P.K., Mohanty, M.N., de Albuquerque, V.H.C. (eds.) Hybrid Artificial Intelligence and IoT in Healthcare. ISRL, vol. 209, pp. 201–222. Springer, Singapore (2021). https://doi. org/10.1007/978-981-16-2972-3_10

35. Elhoseny, M., Ramírez-González, G., Abu-Elnasr, O.M., Shảwkat, S.A., Arunkumar, N., Farouk, A.: Secure medical data transmission model for IoT-based healthcare systems. IEEE Access **6**, 20596–20608 (2018)
36. Shackelford, S.J., Mattioli, M., Myers, S., Brady, A., Wang, Y., Wong, S.: Securing the Internet of healthcare. Minn. JL Sci. & Tech. **19**, 405 (2018)
37. Abiodun, M.K., Awotunde, J.B., Ogundokun, R.O., Adeniyi, E.A., Arowolo, M.O.: Security and information assurance for IoT-based big data. In: Misra, S., Tyagi, A.K. (eds.) Artificial Intelligence for Cyber Security: Methods, Issues and Possible Horizons or Opportunities. SCI, vol. 972, pp. 189–211. Springer, Cham (2021). https://doi.org/10.1007/978-3-030-722 36-4_8
38. Wu, J., Feng, Y., Sun, P.: Sensor fusion for recognition of activities of daily living. Sensors **18**(11), 4029 (2018)
39. Chen, Y., Ding, S., Xu, Z., Zheng, H., Yang, S.: Blockchain-based medical records secure storage and medical service framework. J. Med. Syst. **43**(1), 1–9 (2019)
40. Fan, K., Wang, S., Ren, Y., Li, H., Yang, Y.: Medblock: efficient and secure medical data sharing via blockchain. J. Med. Syst. **42**(8), 1–11 (2018)
41. Li, H., Zhu, L., Shen, M., Gao, F., Tao, X., Liu, S.: Blockchain-based data preservation system for medical data. J. Med. Syst. **42**(8), 1–13 (2018)
42. Zhang, A., Lin, X.: Towards secure and privacy-preserving data sharing in e-health systems via consortium blockchain. J. Med. Syst. **42**(8), 1–18 (2018)
43. Zubaydi, H.D., Chong, Y.W., Ko, K., Hanshi, S.M., Karuppayah, S.: A review on the role of blockchain technology in the healthcare domain. Electronics **8**(6), 679 (2019)

Signature Algorithms on Non-commutative Algebras Over Finite Fields of Characteristic Two

Duong Thu May[1], Do Thi Bac[1], Nguyen Hieu Minh[1(✉)], A. A. Kurysheva[2], A. A. Kostina[3], and D. N. Moldovyan[3]

[1] TNU - University of Information and Communication Technology, Thai Nguyen, Vietnam
{dtmay,dtbac}@ictu.edu.vn, hieuminhmta@gmail.com
[2] Institute of Cryptographic Science and Technology, Hanoi, Vietnam
[3] St. Petersburg Federal Research Center of the Russian Academy of Sciences, St. Petersburg, Russia

Abstract. The paper considers digital signature algorithms with a hidden group, security of which is based on the computational difficulty of solving a system of many quadratic equations with many unknowns. The attention is paid to an implementation of the said type of algorithms on finite non-commutative associative algebras set over the finite fields of characteristics two. The use of the latter type of algebraic support is aimed to improving the performance and reducing the hardware implementation cost. A new algebraic algorithm with a hidden group is introduced, in which a four-dimensional non-commutative algebra is used as algebraic support. In the used algebra the vector multiplication operation is defined by a sparse basis vector multiplication table. Decomposition of the non-commutative algebra into set of commutative subalgebras is studied. The formulas describing the number of the subalgebras of every type are also presented. It is shown that the factorization of the order of the hidden group is non-critical for the security of the signature algorithm, so one can apply the $GF(2^z)$ fields with a sufficiently large number of different values of the degree z, including those that are equal to a Mersenne exponent.

Keywords: Digital signature · Post-quantum cryptography · Algebraic signature algorithm · Non-commutative Algebra · Finite Associative algebra · Hidden group

1 Introduction

One of the current modern challenges in the field of applied and theoretical cryptography is the development of practical post-quantum algorithms for electronic digital signature (EDS), i.e., algorithms resistant to attacks using conventional and quantum computers (quantum attacks). For the latter, polynomial algorithms for solving the problems of factorization (IF) and discrete logarithm (DL) [1, 2] are known, so post-quantum EDS algorithms should be based on other types of computationally difficult problems.

© The Author(s), under exclusive license to Springer Nature Singapore Pte Ltd. 2022
T. K. Dang et al. (Eds.): FDSE 2022, CCIS 1688, pp. 273–284, 2022.
https://doi.org/10.1007/978-981-19-8069-5_18

To develop practical post-quantum EDS algorithms, an approach based on the computational complexity of the hidden DL [3] and associated with the use of finite noncommutative associative algebras (FNAA) was previously proposed. In algorithms of this type, a secret hidden group is used, in which exponentiation operations are performed when generating a public key and generating an EDS, which lead to setting a hidden DL as a basic cryptographic primitive. Recently, a new approach to constructing EDS algorithms with a hidden group has been proposed, which has led to a new concept for constructing EDS algorithms with a hidden group [4], which retains the techniques for constructing them, however, the basic primitive has been changed, which has become the computational difficulty of solving systems from many quadratic equations with many unknowns. In the new concept, at the initial stage, the problem of substantiating resistance to quantum attacks is eliminated, since a quantum computer is not effective for solving these systems [5, 6]. At the same time, EDS algorithms with a hidden group, built on its basis, are comparable in performance and sufficiently small sizes of the public key and signature with EDS algorithms based on a hidden DL.

To improve the performance of algebraic algorithms with a hidden group, one can use FNAA as an algebraic support, given by sparse multiplication tables of basis vectors (MTBV) [7]. Previously, the variant of using FNAA given over prime fields $GF(p)$ of odd characteristic p was mainly considered [8–10]. An additional increase in the performance of EDS algorithms and a decrease in the hardware implementation cost can be ensured by using FNAA set over finite fields of characteristic two $GF(2^z)$ (due to the lower circuitry complexity of the implementation of the multiplication operation in the fields $GF(2^z)$). The key difference of using the fields $GF(2^z)$ versus $GF(p)$, when designing EDS algorithms with a hidden group is a certain restriction while selecting the bit length of the field elements.

This paper discusses the features of using FNAA defined over finite fields of characteristic two as an algebraic support for EDS algorithms with a hidden group. A sparse MTBV and appropriate values of the extension degree z of the fields $GF(2^z)$ are proposed for setting FNAAs as algebraic supports of the EDS algorithms with a hidden group. Decomposition of the four-dimensional FNAAs into set of commutative subalgebras has been studied. A new EDS algorithm is proposed as candidate for practical post-quantum EDS algorithms.

2   FNAA Problem

Finite m-dimensional algebras are defined as a finite m-dimensional vector space with an additionally defined closed operation of multiplication of all possible pairs of vectors, which is left and right distributive with respect to addition. This paper considers a variant of defining algebras over finite fields $GF(2^z)$, whose elements are all possible binary polynomials of degree at most $z - 1$, and the multiplication operation is the multiplication of binary polynomials modulo an irreducible binary polynomial of degree z. An element of the algebra $\mathbf{A}$ can be represented as an ordered set of its coordinates $a_i \in GF(2^z)$, i.e., $\mathbf{A} = (a_0, a_1, ..., a_{m-1})$, or as a sum of its components $a_i \mathbf{e}_i$, i.e., in the form $\mathbf{A} = \sum_{i=0}^{m-1} a_i \mathbf{e}_i$, where $\mathbf{e}_i$ are basis vectors.

The operation of multiplying vectors $\mathbf{A}$ and $\mathbf{B} = \sum_{j=0}^{m-1} b_j \mathbf{e}_j$ is usually defined by the rule of multiplying each component of the vector $\mathbf{A}$ with each component of the vector $\mathbf{B}$:

$$\mathbf{AB} = \sum_{i,j=0}^{m-1} a_i b_j (\mathbf{e}_i \mathbf{e}_j),$$

where the multiplication of coordinates is performed in the field $GF(2^z)$, and all possible products of pairs of basis vectors $\mathbf{e}_i \mathbf{e}_j$ are replaced by the corresponding one-component vectors of the form $\lambda \mathbf{e}_k$ (λ is a structural constant) indicated in the cells at the intersection of the i-th row and the j-th column in some specially composed MTBV. If a given multiplication operation has the property of non-commutativity and associativity, then we have FNAA.

As a rule, the well-known MTBV for specifying MTBV over finite simple fields $GF(p)$ of odd characteristic p can also be used to specify FNAA over fields $GF(2^z)$. The exception is MTBV, in which the property of non-commutativity is ensured not by the asymmetry (with respect to the main diagonal of the table passing from the upper left corner to the lower right corner) of the distribution of basis vectors, but by the asymmetry of the distribution of the structural constant equal to the value -1. Examples of the latter type are the MTBV, which defines a finite quaternion algebra [11], and the MTBV from the papers [12, 13]. In general, there are various diverse ways of setting FNAA over finite fields of characteristic two, including methods of unified assignment of FNAA [9, 14] of various even dimensions (methods for constructing MTBV, expressed by a single mathematical formula, including the value of the dimension m as a parameter).

For the construction of productive EDS algorithms with a hidden group, four-dimensional sparse MTBV [7] are of interest, for example, MTBV presented as Table 1. Properties of FNAA over a simple finite field $GF(p)$ (for odd p) with the multiplication operation given in Table 1 are studied in [7]. All properties presented in [7] carry over to the case of an algebra over the field $GF(2^z)$. The following provisions are of interest for further consideration:

1. Algebra given in Table 1 contains the global two-sided unit, specified as a vector $\mathbf{E} = (\mu^{-1}, \lambda^{-1}, 0, 0)$.
2. The invertibility condition for the vector $\mathbf{A} = (a_0, a_1, a_2, a_3)$ is the inequality $a_0 a_1 \neq \lambda a_2 a_3$.
3. The order of the multiplicative group of the algebra is equal to the value $\Omega = 2^z (2^z - 1)(2^{2z} - 1)$.
4. Vectors of the form $\mathbf{L} = (1, 1, 0, 0)$ for all possible $\sigma \in GF(2^z)$ are scalar vectors (a scalar vector is called a vector $\mathbf{L}$, such that for any vector $\mathbf{V}$ and for some scalar value σ the relation $\mathbf{LV} = \mathbf{VL} = \sigma \mathbf{V}$ holds true).

Table 1. Specification of the multiplication operation of the four-dimensional FNAA ($\lambda \in GF(2^z)$; $\lambda \neq 0$) [7]

	e_0	e_1	e_2	e_3
e_0	e_0	0	0	e_3
e_1	0	e_1	e_2	0
e_2	e_2	0	0	λe_1
e_3	0	e_3	λe_0	0

3   Main Types of Commutative Groups

When constructing EDS algorithms with a hidden group, the structure of the FNAA used as an algebraic support is important from the point of view of decomposition into commutative subalgebras. The method for studying the structure of FNAA given over the field $GF(p)$ [7] can generally be applied to FNAA given in Table 1 over the field $GF(2^z)$. The performed consideration of the FNAA structure for the last case showed the following:

1. Four-dimensional FNAA given in Table 1 over the field $GF(2^z)$, splits into commutative subalgebras of order 2^{2z}, which intersect pairwise strictly in the set of scalar vectors.
2. Commutative subalgebras are of three different types, distinguished by the structure of their multiplicative group.
3. Three types of commutative subalgebras define the existence of the following three different types of commutative groups in FNAA:
3.1). Commutative groups with two-dimensional cyclicity (groups with two generators of the same order [14, 15]), the order of which is equal to the value $\Omega_1 = (2^z - 1)^2$;
3.2). Cyclic commutative groups, the order of which is equal to the value $\Omega_2 = 2^{2z} - 1$;
3.3). Cyclic commutative groups, the order of which is equal to the value $\Omega_3 = 2^z(2^z - 1)$.

In EDS algorithms with a hidden group, it is of interest to use commutative groups with two-dimensional cyclicity as the latter. The choice of a random group of this type is specified during the formation of a secret key as the generation of two random vectors **G** and **H** of order $2^z - 1$, forming its basis (the minimum system of group generators).

The generation of the basis <**G**, **H**> of a group with two-dimensional cyclicity can be performed according to the following algorithm:

1. Generate a random vector **R** of order $2^z - 1$.
2. If **R** is a scalar vector, then go to step 1.
3. Generate a random binary polynomial $\rho \in GF(2^z)$ of order $2^z - 1$.
4. Generate a random number k ($1 < k < 2^z - 1$) and calculate the vector $\mathbf{H} = \rho \mathbf{R}^k$.

5. Take a pair of vectors $\mathbf{G} = \mathbf{R}$ and $\mathbf{H}$ as the basis of the group.

4 Comparison of Two Types of EDS Algorithms with a Hidden Group

Algorithms of EDS, the security of which is based on the computational difficulty of the hidden DL, will be called algorithms of the first type. Accordingly, the second type will include EDS algorithms, the security of which is based on the computational difficulty of solving a system of many quadratic equations with many unknowns.

Consider the main items of similarity:

1. EDS algorithms of both types refer to algebraic crypto algorithms, i.e., as their algebraic support, finite algebras, or more precisely, FNAA of various dimensions, are used.
2. Each type uses a hidden commutative group (usually two-dimensionally cyclic, but hidden groups with a cyclic structure can be used).
3. The secret key includes numbers and vectors as its elements.
4. The public key includes vectors as its elements.
5. The digital signature includes numbers and vector $\mathbf{S}$ as its elements.
6. The operations of raising vectors to a natural power of large size (from 80 to 256 bits and more) are essentially used.

The difference includes the following significant points:

1. The dimension of the FNAA used as an algebraic support for algorithms of the first type is chosen based on the requirement that there be a sufficiently large number of commutative groups and that the order of such groups be divisible by a prime number of a sufficiently large size. For algorithms of the second type, the presence of a large prime divisor of the order of the hidden group is not a fundamental requirement, and the dimension of FNAA plays a significant role, since it is the coefficient of increase in the number of quadratic equations when reducing systems of vector quadratic equations to systems of scalar quadratic equations (quadratic equations over a field over which FNAA).
2. The structure of the MTBV, according to which the multiplication operation is specified in FNAA, in algorithms of the first type does not have a direct impact on the security value, and in algorithms of the second type it does, since it determines the number of terms in quadratic equations that make up a single system of equations with many unknowns, the computational difficulty of solving which determines security of the EDS algorithm.
3. The use of numbers as elements of a secret key in EDS algorithms of the first type is fundamental, since they constitute the value of the discrete logarithm in the hidden group, and in algorithms of the second type they play an auxiliary role in the framework of the method of increasing the performance of the EDS generation procedure. At the same time, the disclosure of these numerical values does not lead to a critical decrease in security.

4. Using the vector **S** as a signature element in the EDS algorithms of the first type has an auxiliary value, and in the second type algorithms it is of fundamental importance. In the first, an EDS can be a pair or a triple of numbers, and in the second, it can be a single element in the form of a vector **S**. In the algorithms of second type, the vector **S** is required because of its multiple occurrences in the signature verification equation, the latter being a vector equation given in a non-commutative algebra.

In the algorithms of the first type, the exponentiation operations are the operations of setting the basic computationally difficult problem. In algorithms of the second type, exponentiation operations are used as a means of setting parameters and calculating a vector **S** that satisfies a test equation with multiple occurrences of **S**.

5   On the Choice of the $GF(2^z)$ Field for Specifying the FNAA as a Carrier of EDS Algorithms of the Second Type

The elements of the field $GF(2^z)$, binary polynomials of degree at most z, are naturally written as z-bit strings. In this case, the addition operation is a bitwise addition modulo two, and the multiplication is implemented as a multiple execution of arithmetic shifts of bit strings and the indicated addition operations. To eliminate the operation of arithmetic division, the operation of multiplication in $GF(2^z)$, is given modulo an irreducible polynomial of small weight (three-term or five-term polynomials). The mentioned points provide a fairly fast execution of the multiplication operation, and hence the exponential operation, in the fields $GF(2^z)$, with software and hardware implementation on various technical platforms.

In algebraic EDS algorithms with a hidden group based on the computational difficulty of solving systems of quadratic equations, the choice of a hidden group of prime order is not the most preferable case, since factorization of its order into divisors of small size is not critical to ensure stability. However, to improve the performance of the signature generation procedure, techniques are used that include the calculation of inverse values modulo equal to the order of the hidden group. This will determine the occurrence of relatively frequent cases of the need to repeat calculations (associated with the fact that the values from which it is necessary to calculate the inverses may not be coprime with the modulus) if the indicated order contains simple divisors of small size.

For the practical elimination of this point, the most convenient is the use of fields $GF(2^z)$, in which the number z is the Mersenne degree, which sets the simple value of the number $2^z - 1$ [16]. In the range of z values of interest for the application under consideration, there are the following six Mersenne numbers: $61, 89, 107, 127, 521$, and 607. There are no Mersenne powers in the range from 127 to 521. However, it is also acceptable to use values of z such that $2^z - 1$ contains two or three large prime divisors. In this case, a divisor of 30 bits or more can be considered large. Our calculations showed that there are natural values of this type of z (see Table 2) and they occur more often than Mersenne numbers, significantly expanding the possibilities of choosing various combinations of the field expansion degree $GF(2^z)$, and the FNAA dimension.

Table 2. Values of the degree of field expansion $GF(2^z)$, which are of interest in the development of EDS algorithms of the second type

Degree z	Number of prime divisors of the value $2^z - 1$	Divisor size, bits
61	1	61
89	1	89
101	2	43 and 59
103	2	39 and 63
107	1	107
109	2	30 and 80
127	1	127
137	2	65 and 73
139	2	43 and 97
149	2	67 and 83
173	3	41, 56 and 78
199	2	38 and 162

6 An Example of an Algebraic Algorithms of an EDS of the Second Type

Let us use as an algebraic support a four-dimensional FNAA defined over the field $GF(2^z)$ with the degree of extension $z = 149$. In this case, the operation of multiplication of four-dimensional vectors is determined from Table 1. As structural constants λ and μ we take unit binary polynomials, i.e., $\lambda = \mu = 1$.

To generate a secret key, use the following procedure:

1. Generate a basis $<\mathbf{G}, \mathbf{H}>$ of a random commutative group with two-dimensional cyclicity, in which each of the vectors has an order equal to the value $q = 2^{149} - 1$ $= 713623846352979940529142984724747568191373311$.
2. Generate random pairwise non-permutable reversible vectors $\mathbf{A}$, $\mathbf{B}$, and $\mathbf{D}$, each of which is also non-permutable with the vector $\mathbf{G}$.
3. Generate random natural numbers x, w and u $(1 < x, w, u < q)$.
4. Calculate the four-dimensional vectors $\mathbf{G}_x = \mathbf{G}^x$, $\mathbf{G}_u = \mathbf{G}^u$ and $\mathbf{H}_w = \mathbf{H}^w$ (the vectors $\mathbf{G}$, $\mathbf{H}$, $\mathbf{G}_x$, $\mathbf{G}_u$ and $\mathbf{H}_w$ are pairwise permutable as they belong to the commutative group generated by the basis $< \mathbf{G}, \mathbf{H} >$).

At the output of the secret key generation procedure, we obtain its value in the form of a set of vectors $\mathbf{A}$, $\mathbf{B}$, $\mathbf{D}$, $\mathbf{G}$, $\mathbf{H}$, $\mathbf{G}_x$, $\mathbf{G}_u$ and $\mathbf{H}_w$ and numbers x, w and u, with the total size equal to ≈ 652 bytes (in fact, the vectors $\mathbf{G}_x$, $\mathbf{G}_u$ and $\mathbf{H}_w$ may not be included in the secret key, since they can be calculated using the formulas from paragraph 4 of the described procedure, in this case we have a secret key having size ≈ 429 bytes).

The procedure for generating a public key in the form of a set of four-dimensional vectors $\mathbf{Y}_1$, $\mathbf{Z}_1$, $\mathbf{Y}_2$, $\mathbf{Z}_2$ and $\mathbf{P}$, depending on the secret key, consists in performing calculations according to the following formulas:

$$\mathbf{Y}_1 = \mathbf{AGB}, \ \mathbf{Z}_1 = \mathbf{DHA}^{-1}, \tag{1}$$

$$\mathbf{Y}_2 = \mathbf{AH}_w\mathbf{B}, \ \mathbf{Z}_2 = \mathbf{DG}_x\mathbf{A}^{-1} \text{ and } \mathbf{P} = \mathbf{AG}_u\mathbf{HA}^{-1}. \tag{2}$$

Note that instead of (2), formulas with the exponentiation operation can be used:

$$\mathbf{Y}_2 = \mathbf{AH}^w\mathbf{B}, \ \mathbf{Z}_2 = \mathbf{DG}^x\mathbf{A}^{-1} \text{ and } \mathbf{P} = \mathbf{AG}^u\mathbf{HA}^{-1}. \tag{3}$$

The application of formulas (3) refers to the case when the vectors $\mathbf{G}_x$, $\mathbf{G}_u$ and $\mathbf{H}_w$ are removed from the secret key. The length (size) of the public key is ≈ 373 bytes.

EDS Generation Procedure.

1. Using some specified 384-bit hash function f_H, a hash value $h = h_1\|h_2\|h_3 = f_H(M)$ is calculated from the electronic document M to be signed (the sign $\|$ denotes the concatenation operation).
2. Calculate the integer values of n and d using the following two formulas:

$$n = \frac{xh_2 + uh_3 - h_1}{h_1 - h_2} \bmod q \quad and \tag{4}$$

$$d = \frac{wh_2 + h_3 - h_1}{h_1 - h_2} \bmod q. \tag{5}$$

3. Calculate the EDS in the form of a four-dimensional vector $\mathbf{S}$ using the formula

$$\mathbf{S} = \mathbf{B}^{-1}\mathbf{G}^n\mathbf{H}^d\mathbf{D}^{-1}. \tag{6}$$

The computational complexity of the EDS generation procedure can be approximately estimated as two operations of exponentiation of four-dimensional vectors, which are converted into ≈ 3576 multiplication operations in the field $GF(2^{149})$. Signature size is ≈ 75 bytes.

EDS Verification Procedure

1. A 384-bit hash value $h = h_1\|h_2\|h_3 = f_H(M)$ is calculated from the signed document, which is represented as a concatenation of three 128-bit numbers h_1, h_2 and h_3.
2. Check the following test equation holds true

$$(\mathbf{Y}_1\mathbf{SZ}_1)^{h_1} = (\mathbf{Y}_2\mathbf{SZ}_2)^{h_2}\mathbf{P}^{h_3}. \tag{7}$$

3. If equality (7) is satisfied, then the digital signature for the document M is recognized as authentic, otherwise the digital signature is rejected.

The computational complexity of the EDS verification procedure is approximately equal to three operations of exponentiation of four-dimensional vectors, which are converted into ≈ 5364 multiplication operations in $GF(2^{149})$.

It is easy to see that the calculation of the secret key from the public key is associated with the solution of a system of 9 quadratic vector equations with 8 unknowns $\mathbf{A}$, $\mathbf{B}$, $\mathbf{D}$, $\mathbf{G}$, $\mathbf{H}$, $\mathbf{G}_x$, $\mathbf{G}_u$ and $\mathbf{H}_w$, given over the used four-dimensional FNAA. The form of vector equations is given by formulas (1) and (2), supplemented by the conditions for the permutability of the vector $\mathbf{G}$ with the vectors $\mathbf{H}$, $\mathbf{G}_x$, $\mathbf{G}_u$ and $\mathbf{H}_w$. The indicated system of vector equations (consistent by construction) is reduced to a system of 36 equations with 32 unknowns, defined over the field $GF(2^z)$ with 149-bit order.

The correctness of the described EDS algorithm is easily proved by demonstrating that the correctly calculated EDS passes the EDS verification procedure in accordance with the EDS generation procedure. Indeed, let the four-dimensional vector $\mathbf{S}$ be a correctly calculated EDS.

Then we have the following proof of the correctness of the proposed EDS algorithm (we calculate successively the left and right parts of the verification Eq. (7):

$$
\begin{aligned}
\mathbf{K}_L &= (\mathbf{Y}_1\mathbf{S}\mathbf{Z}_1)^{h_1} = \left(\mathbf{AGBB}^{-1}\mathbf{G}^n\mathbf{H}^d\mathbf{D}^{-1}\mathbf{DHA}^{-1}\right)^{h_1} = \\
&= \left(\mathbf{AG}^{n+1}\mathbf{H}^{d+1}\mathbf{A}^{-1}\right)^{h_1} = \mathbf{AG}^{nh_1+h_1}\mathbf{H}^{dh_1+h_1}\mathbf{A}^{-1} = \\
&= \mathbf{AG}^{\frac{xh_2+uh_3-h_1}{h_1-h_2}h_1+h_1}\mathbf{H}^{\frac{wh_2+h_3-h_1}{h_1-h_2}h_1+h_1}\mathbf{A}^{-1} = \\
&= \mathbf{AG}^{\frac{xh_1h_2+uh_1h_3-h_1h_2}{h_1-h_2}}\mathbf{H}^{\frac{wh_1h_2+h_1h_3-h_1h_2}{h_1-h_2}}\mathbf{A}^{-1};
\end{aligned}
$$

$$
\begin{aligned}
\mathbf{K}_R &= (\mathbf{Y}_2\mathbf{S}\mathbf{Z}_2)^{h_2}\mathbf{P}^{h_3} = \left(\mathbf{AH}^w\mathbf{BB}^{-1}\mathbf{G}^n\mathbf{H}^d\mathbf{D}^{-1}\mathbf{DG}^x\mathbf{A}^{-1}\right)^{h_2}\mathbf{P}^{h_3} = \\
&= \left(\mathbf{AG}^{n+x}\mathbf{H}^{w+d}\mathbf{A}^{-1}\right)^{h_2}\left(\mathbf{AG}^u\mathbf{HA}^{-1}\right)^{h_3} = \\
&= \mathbf{AG}^{nh_2+xh_2}\mathbf{H}^{wh_2+dh_2}\mathbf{A}^{-1}\mathbf{AG}^{uh_3}\mathbf{H}^{h_3}\mathbf{A}^{-1} = \\
&= \mathbf{AG}^{nh_2+xh_2+uh_3}\mathbf{H}^{dh_2+wh_2+h_3}\mathbf{A}^{-1} = \\
&= \mathbf{AG}^{\frac{xh_2+uh_3-h_1}{h_1-h_2}h_2+xh_2+uh_3}\mathbf{H}^{\frac{wh_2+h_3-h_1}{h_1-h_2}h_2+wh_2+h_3}\mathbf{A}^{-1} = \\
&= \mathbf{AG}^{\frac{xh_1h_2+uh_1h_3-h_1h_2}{h_1-h_2}}\mathbf{H}^{\frac{wh_1h_2+h_1h_3-h_1h_2}{h_1-h_2}}\mathbf{A}^{-1} = \mathbf{K}_L.
\end{aligned}
$$

Since the verification Eq. (7) is satisfied, the correctly generated EDS passes the verification procedure as a genuine signature, i.e., the proposed EDS algorithm with a hidden group works correctly.

7 Comparison with Well-Known Multidimensional Cryptography Algorithms

Known two-key cryptalgorithms (EDS algorithms, algorithms for public key-distribution and public encryption), based on the computational difficulty of solving systems of many quadratic equations with many unknowns, refer to multidimensional cryptography [5,

6]. With that cryptalgorithms, the proposed algorithm has commonality in the basic computationally difficult problem underlying their security. Otherwise, it is completely different from the algorithms of multidimensional cryptography. The following important differences can be noted:

1. In cryptalgorithms of multidimensional cryptography, the developer of the algorithm develops functions of many variables that determine the form of quadratic equations that form a single system of equations. In the proposed algorithm, the system of quadratic equations follows from the equations defining the relationship between the secret key and the public key, which are compiled as part of the developed procedure for generating a public key depending on the secret key.
2. In two-key cryptalgorithms of multidimensional cryptography, functions of many variables over fields $GF(2^z)$ of a relatively small order, equal to values from 2^4 to 2^{16}, are developed. Accordingly, systems of many quadratic equations arise over such fields. In the proposed algebraic algorithm with a hidden group, the resulting system of quadratic equations is given over fields of a sufficiently large order equal to 2^{149}.
3. In cryptalgorithms of multidimensional cryptography, the number of quadratic equations included in a single system can be greater than, equal to, or less than the number of unknowns. In the proposed EDS algorithm, the number of equations in the system of quadratic equations can be equal to or greater than the number of unknowns.
4. The size of the EDS in both compared EDS algorithms is rather small, and the size of the public key in the EDS algorithms of multidimensional cryptography is hundreds of times larger than the size of the public key in the proposed algebraic algorithm with a hidden group.

Abstracting from the specific type of quadratic equations included in a single system, the difficulty of solving which determines the level of security of the cryptalgorithm, to assess the latter, we can propose a general informal indicator ψ equal to the product of the number of unknowns η by the binary logarithm of the order of the field over which quadratic equations are given. Based on the comparison of the value of the index ψ for various EDS algorithms, it is possible to make some preliminary comparative estimates of the security according to the criterion "higher values of ψ correspond to a higher security level". However, final estimates about the value of stability can only be made on the basis of a detailed consideration of the computational complexity of each particular system of quadratic equations.

A comparison of several well-known EDS algorithms of multidimensional cryptography and the proposed algebraic EDS algorithm is given in Table 3. Comparison shows a number of significant advantages of EDS algorithms with a hidden group.

8   Conclusion

It is shown that in algebraic digital signature algorithms with a hidden group, which are based on computational difficulty of solving many quadratic equations, the factorization of the order of the hidden group is not critical. The latter makes it possible to use the

Table 3. Comparison with known EDS algorithms of multidimensional cryptography

EDS algorithm	EDS size, byte	Public key size, byte	Number of quadratic equations (unknowns)	The order of the field over which the equations are given	Index Ψ
[5]	–	--	27 (27)	2^{16}	432
Rainbow [17]	33	16065	27 (33)	2^8	264
QUARTZ [6]	16	72704	100 (107)	2^4	428
Rainbow [18] (3 different versions)	66... 204	>150000 ... >1900000	64 (96) ... 128 (204)	$2^4, 31,$ 2^8	384 ... 1632
[4]	160	512	28 (28)	$>2^{256}$	>7168
Proposed	75	373	36 (32)	2^{149}	4768

FNAA set over finite fields $GF(2^z)$ as algebraic support of the said type of signature algorithms, providing improving their performance. Additionally, performance can be improved setting the FNAA by sparse MTBV. Using a four-dimensional FNAA (over the $GF(2^{149})$ set by a sparse MTBV field) a new signature algorithm with a hidden group is proposed as candidate for practical post-quantum EDS algorithms. Study of the decomposition of the said four-dimensional FNAA into the set of commutative subalgebras has shown suitability for its application as algebraic support of signature algorithms with a hidden group. Similar implementations using six-dimensional FNAA are also of interest, but this requires studying the structure of the latter or, at least, establishing the structure of the commutative groups contained in them.

Funding. This research is partially supported by RFBR (project # 21–57-54001-Vietnam) and by Vietnam Academy of Science and Technology (project # QTRU01.13/21–22).

References

1. Shor, P.W.: Polynomial-time algorithms for prime factorization and discrete logarithms on quantum computer. SIAM J. Comput. **26**, 1484–1509 (2017)
2. Smolin, J.A., Smith, G., Vargo, A.: Oversimplifying quantum factoring. Nature **499**(7457), 163–165 (2013)
3. Moldovyan, A.A., Moldovyan, N.A.: Post-quantum signature algorithms based on the hidden discrete logarithm problem. Comput. Sci. J. Moldova **26**(3(78)), 301–313 (2018)
4. Moldovyan, D., Moldovyan, A., Moldovyan, N.: A new concept for designing post-quantum digital signature algorithms on non-commutative algebras. Voprosy kiberbezopasnosti **1**(47), 18–25 (2022). https://doi.org/10.21681/2311-3456-2022-1-18-25
5. Shuaiting, Q., Wenbao, H., Yifa, L., Luyao, J.: Construction of extended multivariate public key cryptosystems. Int. J. Netw. Secur. **18**(1), 60–67 (2016)
6. Jintai, D., Dieter, S.: Multivariable Public Key Cryptosystems. https://eprint.iacr.org/2004/350.pdf (2004). Accessed 30 June 2022

7. Moldovyan, D.N.: A practical digital signature scheme based on the hidden logarithm problem. Comput. Sci. J. Moldova **29**(2(86)), 206–226 (2021)

8. Moldovyan, N.A., Moldovyan, A.A.: Digital signature scheme on the 2×2 matrix algebra. Vestnik of Saint Petersburg Univ., Appl. Math. Comput. Sci. Control Processes **17**(3), 254–261 (2021)

9. Moldovyan, N.A., Moldovyan, A.A.: Finite non-commutative associative algebras as carriers of hidden discrete logarithm problem. In: Bulletin of the South Ural State University. Ser. Mathematical Modelling, Programming & Computer Software (Bulletin SUSU MMCS), vol. 12, no. 1, pp. 66–81 (2019)

10. Moldovyan, N.A., Moldovyan, A.A.: Candidate for practical post-quantum signature scheme. Vestnik of Saint Petersburg Univ., Appl. Math. Comput. Sci. Control Processes **16**(4), 455–461 (2020)

11. Moldovyan, N.A., Abrosimov, I.K.: Post-quantum electronic digital signature scheme based on the enhanced form of the hidden discrete logarithm problem. Vestnik of Saint Petersburg University. Applied Mathematics. Computer Science. Control Processes **15**(2), 212–220 (2019). https://doi.org/10.21638/11702/spbu10.2019.205

12. Moldovyan, N.A.: Signature schemes on algebras, satisfying enhanced criterion of post-quantum security. Bull. Acad. Sci. Moldova, Math. **2**(93), 62–67 (2020)

13. Moldovyan, N.A.: Unified method for defining finite associative algebras of arbitrary even dimensions. Quasigroups Relat. Syst. **26**(2), 263–270 (2018)

14. Moldovyan, N.A., Moldovyanu, P.A.: New primitives for digital signature algorithms. Quasigroups Relat. Syst. **17**(2), 271–282 (2009)

15. Moldovyan, N.A.: Fast signatures based on non-cyclic finite groups. Quasigroups Relat. Syst. **18**(1), 83–94 (2010)

16. Crandall, R., Pomerance, C.: Prime Numbers - A Computational Perspective. Springer, New York (2002)

17. Ding, J., Schmidt, D.: Rainbow, a new multivariable polynomial signature scheme. In: Ioannidis, J., Keromytis, A., Yung, M. (eds.) ACNS 2005. LNCS, vol. 3531, pp. 164–175. Springer, Heidelberg (2005). https://doi.org/10.1007/11496137_12

18. Rainbow Signature: One of three NIST post-quantum signature finalists. https://www.pqcrainbow.org/,(2021). Accessed 30 June 2022

Design a Smart Lock System Using Fingerprint and Password for Enhancing Security

Phat Nguyen Huu[1]([✉])[iD], Duy Nguyen Quang[1], Hieu Nguyen Trong[2], Pha Pham Ngoc[2], and Quang Tran Minh[3,4]

[1] Hanoi University of Science and Technology (HUST), Hanoi, Vietnam
phat.nguyenhuu@hust.edu.vn, duy.nq182465@sis.hust.edu.vn
[2] National Institute of Patent and Technology Exploitation (NIPTECH), Hanoi, Vietnam
{nthieu,pnpha}@most.gov.vn
[3] Ho Chi Minh City University of Technology (VNU-HCM), Hochiminh, Vietnam
[4] Vietnam National University Ho Chi Minh City (VNU-HCM), Hochiminh, Vietnam
quangtran@hcmut.edu.vn

Abstract. This paper focuses on designing a security system for a smart door lock using fingerprint sensors and passwords. The security system will consist of two layers, namely, fingerprint identification and password confirmation. A fingerprint sensor module will be integrated into the door for users to confirm fingerprints. The fingerprint sensor will take the fingerprint and forward it to the microcontroller for comparison. If the printout matches the saved fingerprint, the system will go to the password confirmation. The user needs to enter the correct password to unlock. If the user enters the wrong password more than five times, it will have to wait five minutes to continue and only those who are given the ID number can change the password. The system has results with an accuracy of 86.36% that can be applied for practical applicability.

Keywords: Fingerprint · Sensor · Password · Security key · Encryption · Information security

1 Introduction

Today, in regard to security systems, it is one of the primary concerns in this competitive world where a man cannot find a way to provide security for his secrets. Besides, they found an alternative that provides better security and is more reliable. This is the era where everything is connected through a network and anyone can get information from anywhere in the world. Therefore, the ability of information to be hacked is a serious issue. Because of these risks, it is important to have a personal identification system in place to access private information. Today, personal identification is becoming an important issue worldwide. Among the mainstream personal identification methods, we mainly see password and identification card techniques. Nowadays, passwords are very

T. K. Dang et al. (Eds.): FDSE 2022, CCIS 1688, pp. 285–298, 2022.
https://doi.org/10.1007/978-981-19-8069-5_19

easy to hack and identity cards can be lost, and thus making these methods unreliable [1–4].

There are several unpleasant situations when a person locks themselves outside their home or office because of the key inside or sometimes thieves break the lock and steal everything. These situations always make it difficult for the user to lock the door with the key. Although smart cards are used in several places, someone may lose or forget the card. In other situations, several people look after the home or office and keep the keys safe. However, the person in charge of the keys may not be present or have gone for an emergency that can cause unexpected delays. These are the complications that people may encounter when using keys or smart cards. That is the basis for the fingerprint-based door lock system to work. If the fingerprint of someone is saved in the system, they will not experience any delay to enter the room. Fingerprint recognition is one of the most secure systems since they never match those of others. Therefore, unauthorized access can be restricted by designing a key that stores the fingerprints of one or more authorized users and unlocks the system when a match is found.

However, the fingerprint-only locking system becomes unsafe with the rapid development. Therefore, we design a locking system with two security layers including fingerprint identification and password to increase the security of the device.

The rest of the paper includes five parts and is organized as follows. Section 1 presents an overview of the monitoring and detecting system. Section 2 presents several related works. Sections 3 and 4 present and design the proposed system. Section 5 will evaluate the proposed model and analyze the results. In the final section, we give conclusions and future research directions.

2   Related Work

Today, smart locks using fingerprints and other techniques such as RFID and GSM modules have become very popular and there have been many works on this topic [5–11].

The authors [11] have shown that in the traditional locking system, passwords and other security measures have been used in high rating fingerprint sensor module. The paper also goes into detail on fingerprint recognition. These steps are similar to the identification process in fingerprint sensor modules.

The author [6] proposes an advanced method to implement and design fingerprint door locks using GSM technology, alarm system, surveillance camera system, and password. This security system provides various security features such as limiting who is not allowed access and keeping a record of who has ever passed through it. If a thief tries to break through the door, an alarm system is set up to alert those nearby. A GSM module is used to send SMS to the owner and a webcam is used to record videos of people trying to break the lock. The fingerprint scanner R305 is interfaced with the Arduino-ATMEGA328P microcontroller to control the door locking and unlocking process. The LCD control panel displays some basic commands to guide the user. If any user has not saved their fingerprint on the sensor, their automatic access will be denied.

The authors [7] designed an improved smart door lock with a fingerprint interface. They use Atmel Atmega328p, fingerprint sensor, GSM module, motor driver, and some other hardware devices. The fingerprint sensor will be integrated into the door panel and face outside of the door. Therefore, people cannot access the control system from the outside. The latches will be fixed inside the door plate. The thickness of the door can therefore help with the durability of the latch. They use several pins in the control panel to divide the force between the pins if trying to push in. The fingerprint sensor will take the fingerprint of the user and forward it to the microcontroller to match its profile. If the print matches one of the fingerprints in the memory of the microcontroller, it locks or unlocks the latch based on its current state. If the fingerprint is unfamiliar to the microcontroller, the buzzer will ring and the user will have to try again.

In general, the above-mentioned papers all assessed that fingerprint recognition technology has higher security and convenience for users when compared to traditional mechanical keys or cryptographic keys, or RFID cards. However, fingerprint locks also have unsafe risks due to modern counterfeiting technology. The authors also mentioned additional technologies used together with fingerprint recognition technology to enhance security such as GSM module alerting users or simultaneous use of RFID cards and recognition. Therefore, we choose the option of using fingerprint recognition and password simultaneously for smart lock devices in this paper.

3   System Design

3.1   Fingerprint Reader

To be able to use fingerprints for unlocking, they need a fingerprint reader to store and confirm. In the market, the hardware devices with fingerprint and recognition functions are quite diverse and affordable with the rapid development. Therefore, we chose the JM-101 module for the design of the fingerprint lock layer because of its cost and simplicity.

The device parameters are shown in Tables 1 and 2.

3.2   Communication Protocol

The JM-101 module has two protocols for communicating with external devices, UART, and USB. In this paper, we use the UART protocol to transmit and receive packets between the JM-101 module and the microcontroller.

UART [8] is an asynchronous serial receiver. In asynchronous serial communication, the receiver and receiver do not maintain the same clock. Besides, the data will be encapsulated into frames and will need to specify the following parameters since the two parties can transmit and receive the data correctly.

For asynchronous transmission and reception to happen successfully, the participating devices must agree on the amount of time for a bit to transmit. In other words, the baud rate must be set the same and it is called the Baud rate.

Table 1. Operation parameter of JM-101 module.

Parameter	Valuable
Operating voltage	3.6V–6V
Current	40 mA–60 mA
Resolution (pixels)	256 × 288
Pixel density	500dpi
Data transfer protocol	UART, USB
Baud rate (default)	57600 bps
Capacity	150 fingerprints
Recognition time	Less than one second

Table 2. Features of each pin of JM-101 module.

No.	Name	Type	Function
1	+5V	Input	Power for the module
2	TX	Output	Output of the serial signal
3	RX	Input	Input of the serial signal
4	GND	–	Grounding
5	Touch	Output	Output the sensor signal (default high)
6	TouchVin	Input	Sensor power supply (3.3V)
7	D+	–	USB D+
8	D-	–	USB D-

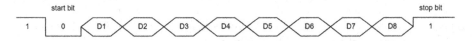

Fig. 1. UART transmission frame example [12, 13].

The baud rate is the number of bits transmitted in one second. In this paper, we use a baud rate of 9600 bps controlled by timer 1 (UART mode 1).

Besides the baud rate, the transmission frame is an important factor in the success of transmission and reception. Figure 1 is the UART transmission frame used in the paper. This transmission frame is preceded by a start bit followed by 8 bits of data (LSM sent first, MSB sent last) as shown in Fig. 1.

The transmit and response packet formats in the JM-101 module [9] include command, data transmission, and response packets.

3.3   Fingerprint Collection of JM-101

The fingerprint collection process of the JM-101 module is shown in Fig. 2.

The steps in the fingerprint collection process are shown in Algorithm 1.

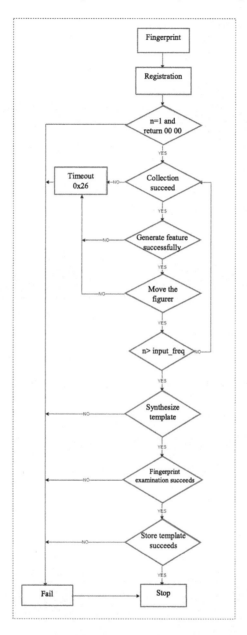

Fig. 2. Fingerprint collection procedure in JM-101 module.

Algorithm 1. Fingerprint collection algorithm.

1: **Step 1:** Get ID from the system
2: **if** The specified ID is invalid **then**
3:     Return 0B 00 00H
4: **end if**
5: **if** Input number configuration error **then**
6:     Return 25 00 00H
7: **end if**
8: **if** The fingerprint database is full **then**
9:     Return 1F 00 00H
10: **end if**
11: **if** The specified ID exists **then**
12:     Return 22 00 00H
13: **end if**
14: Check the validity of the successful command
15: Return 00 00 00H
16: Enter the first time you enter a fingerprint
17: **Step 2:** Wait for successful image collection
18: Returns 00 01 0NH
19: **Step 3:** Wait for successful feature creation, return 00 02 0NH
20: **if** Unsuccessful **then**
21:     Returns 00 20 0NH and waits for successful image acquisition again
22: **end if**
23: **Step 4:**
24: **if** The first import is successful **then**
25:     Return 00 03 0NH and go back to **step 2**
26:     Repeat until the specified n times are successfully entered into a fingerprint
27: **end if**
28: **Step 5:** Combines previously acquired fingerprint characteristics into a sample fingerprint
29: **if** Successful **then**
30:     Return 00 04 F0H
31: **else**
32:     Return 0A 04 F0H
33: **end if**
34: **Step 6:**
35: Check the entered fingerprint matches the stored fingerprint (by setting the bit4 parameter high or low)
36: **if** Password is the same **then**
37:     returns 27 05 F1H
38: **else**
39:     returns 00 05 F1H
40: **end if**
41: **Step 7:** Save the collected fingerprint
42: **if** It is not archived **then**
43:     Return 01 06, F2H and end of the process
44: **end if**
45: **if** Successful **then**
46:     Return 00 06 F2H
47: **end if**
48: **Step 8:**
49: **if** PS Cancel command is received **then**
50:     Terminate the process and return a response packet
51: **end if**

3.4 Password Lock Layer Design

When the user successfully confirms the fingerprint, they will be asked to enter a password to unlock it successfully. At this key layer, we use a 4×4 keyboard for the user to enter the password. To save passwords, we use the AT24C02 memory chip. The password confirmation process is shown in Fig. 3.

The steps in password confirmation are shown on Algorithm 2.

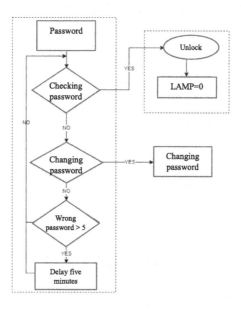

Fig. 3. Password confirmation process.

Algorithm 2. Password confirmation algorithm.

1: **Step 1:** Display requires the user to enter the password
2: **Step 2:**
3: **if** The user enters the correct password stored in the memory chip **then**
4:     The system will notify to enter the correct password and unlock
5:     The indicator light will turn off to notify the lock has been opened.
6: **end if**
7: **Step 3:**
8: **if** the user forgets the password **then**
9:     Press the change password button to switch to the changed password state
10:     After successfully changing the password, you will return to enter the password.
11: **end if**
12: **Step 4:**
13: **if** The user does not remember the ID to change the password and continues to enter the wrong password more than 5 times **then**
14:     The system will send a warning to the user about the number of incorrect entries exceeding the allowed number of times and temporarily stop the user from entering the password for 5 minutes
15:     After 5 minutes, the user can continue to enter the password and the process goes back to **Step 1**
16: **end if**

The process of changing the password is shown in Fig. 4.

The steps in the process of changing the password are shown on Algorithm 3.

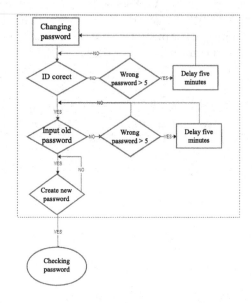

Fig. 4. Password change process.

Algorithm 3. Changing password algorithm.

1: **Step 1:** Display requires the user to enter ID
2: **Step 2:**
3: **if** The user enters the correct ID stored **then**
4:      The system will notify to enter the correct ID
5:      The system will ask the user to enter the old password
6: **end if**
7: **if** The user enters the wrong ID more than five times **then**
8:      The system will notify the user about the number of incorrect entries
9:      The system will have to wait 5 minutes to continue using the system
10: **end if**
11: **Step 3:** The user is asked to enter the current password
12: **if** The current password is entered correctly **then**
13:     The user can proceed to the final step of creating a new password
14: **end if**
15: **if** Enter incorrectly more than 5 times **then**
16:     The system warn
17:     The user found that the number of incorrect entries is more than the allowed limit
18:     The user has to wait 5 minutes to continue changing the password
19: **end if**
20: **if** The user forgets the current password **then**
21:     There is no other way for them to change the password
22: **end if**
23: **Step 4:** The user is asked to enter a new password
24: **Step 5:** It is a sequence of 6 characters.
25: Enter new password
26: The user re-enters the new password
27: The system will check

4   System Diagram

The complete state diagram is shown in Fig. 5. The details of the operation of the system are as follows.

IDLE Status:

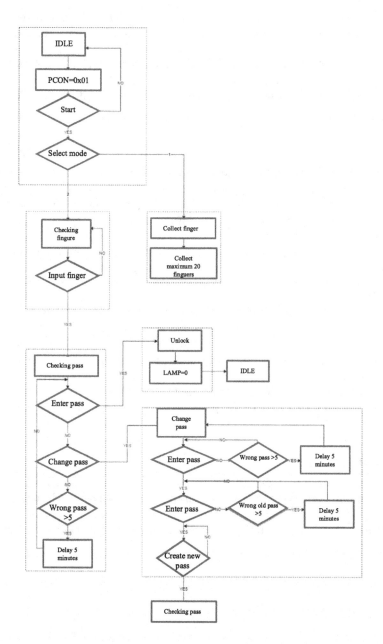

Fig. 5. State diagram of the smart lock system.

We check the start condition. Firstly, the system will be idle and the user needs to press the **START** button to activate it. The user then needs to choose the next feature, that is, fingerprint collection or fingerprint verification, to unlock. Finally, the system will then switch to the state selected by the user.

CHECK FINGER Status:

If the user chooses to confirm a fingerprint, the system will send a request to confirm the fingerprint. The user then needs to place a finger with the fingerprint stored in the system on a device for verification. If the verification fingerprint matches the saved fingerprint, the system will enter the **CHECK PASS** state. If the fingerprints do not match, the user can re-verify and the system does not limit the number of re-verification times. Users can verify fingerprints until successfully.

COLLECT FINGER State:

If the user selects the fingerprint collection feature, the system will go to this state. The system will send a request to collect fingerprints, users need to place the finger that needs to be fingerprinted with the device on the sensor surface. The system will report successful collection if the new fingerprint is valid and stored in the device. If the fingerprint is invalid or an error occurs during collection, the user can collect it again. Up to 20 users can collect fingerprints each time this feature is selected. After 20 times, if the user wants to collect more, they need to reset the system and re-select the fingerprint collection feature.

CHECK PASS State:

In this state, the system will send a password to request to the user. They need to enter the exact string of characters previously saved to unlock. If the correct password is entered, the system will indicate successful unlocking and the indicator light will turn off. If they entered incorrectly, the users have five times to re-enter. If the users still enter the wrong input after five times, they have to wait five minutes for the next input.

If the users want to change the password, they have to press the CHANGE PASS button. The system will switch to the password change state. If the users forget the password, they can neither unlock nor change the password.

CHANGE, PASS State:

In this state, the system will initially send a request to enter the ID, which is the sequence of numbers that the user is given to change the password. If the correct ID is entered, the system will go to the step of entering the current password, if it is wrong 5 times, the system will stop working for 5 min before allowing the user to re-enter it.

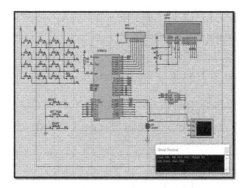

Fig. 6. Diagram of hardware devices in smart-lock.

Fig. 7. Mounting system on the whiteboard.

After successfully changing the password, the user is returned to CHECK PASS state to enter the password.

The schematic diagram and the actual product are shown in Figs. 6 and 7.

5   Experiment and Discussion

The authors [10] proposed a way to check the working accuracy of fingerprint recognition and collection by performing each feature 30 times. In this paper, we therefore perform the examination of 21 cases based on the existing fingerprints. The details of the hardware devices are shown in Figs. 6 and 7.

Tables 3 and 4 illustrate the fingerprint collection and validation features that are tested to ensure proper functioning.

Table 3. Result of fingerprint collection feature.

No.	Result	Notice
1	Not enrolled	Finger existed
2	Enrolled	–
3	Enrolled	–
4	Enrolled	–
5	Not enrolled	Time out
6	Enrolled	–
7	Enrolled	–
8	Enrolled	–
9	Enrolled	–
10	Enrolled	–
11	Enrolled	–
12	Not enrolled	Finger existed
13	Not enrolled	Finger existed
14	Not enrolled	Finger existed
15	Not enrolled	Finger existed
16	Not enrolled	Finger existed
17	Not enrolled	Finger existed
18	Not enrolled	Finger existed
19	Not enrolled	Finger existed
20	Not enrolled	Finger existed
21	Not enrolled	Time out
22	Not enrolled	Time out

In Table 3, we see that the JM-101 module works accurately with the fingerprint collection feature. In case of waiting time to enter fingerprints or invalid fingerprint, images will have time-out errors. The saved fingerprints will receive an error. The unsaved fingerprints were all collected successfully.

In Table 4, the JM-101 module works relatively accurately with the fingerprint recognition feature. Cases of waiting time to enter fingerprints or invalid fingerprint images will have time-out errors. Fingerprints saved when entered are recognized.

Table 4. Result of fingerprint verification feature.

No.	Result	Notice
1	Verified	
2	Verified	–
3	Verified	–
4	Verified	–
5	Verified	–
6	Not verified	Time out
7	Verified	–
8	Verified	–
9	Verified	–
10	Verified	–
11	Verified	–
12	Verified	–
13	Verified	–
14	Verified	–
15	Verified	–
16	Verified	–
17	Verified	–
18	Verified	–
19	Verified	–
20	Verified	–
21	Not verified	Time out
22	Not verified	Time out

6 Conclusion

In the paper, we have presented the steps to build a fingerprint and password security layer for a smart lock system. The features worked relatively accurately with the stated goal. We hope to improve the security of door lock systems and the safety of users with this product.

In the future, we will develop more AI algorithms as well as integrate facial recognition features to increase the security of the system.

Acknowledgment. This research is funded by Vietnam National University Ho Chi Minh City (VNU-HCM) under grant number NCM2021-20-02

References

1. Kassem, A., Murr, S.E., Jamous, G., Saad, E., Geagea, M.: A smart lock system using wi-fi security. In: 2016 3rd International Conference on Advances in Computational Tools for Engineering Applications (ACTEA), pp. 222–225 (2016). https://doi.org/10.1109/ACTEA.2016.7560143
2. Tilala, P., Roy, A.K., Das, M.L.: Home access control through a smart digital locking-unlocking system. In: TENCON 2017–2017 IEEE Region 10 Conference, pp. 1409–1414 (2017). https://doi.org/10.1109/TENCON.2017.8228079
3. Pandit, V., Majgaonkar, P., Meher, P., Sapaliga, S., Bojewar, S.: Intelligent security lock. In: 2017 International Conference on Trends in Electronics and Informatics (ICEI), pp. 713–716 (2017). https://doi.org/10.1109/ICOEI.2017.8300795
4. Shanthini, M., Vidya, G., Arun, R.: IoT enhanced smart door locking system. In: 2020 Third International Conference on Smart Systems and Inventive Technology (ICSSIT), pp. 92–96 (2020). https://doi.org/10.1109/ICSSIT48917.2020.9214288
5. Sarma, M., Gogoi, A., Saikia, R., Bora, D.J.: Fingerprint based door access system using Arduino. Int. J. Sci. Res. Eng. Manage. (IJSREM) 4(8), 1–5 (2020)
6. Alnabhi, H., Al-naamani, Y., Al-madhehagi, M., Alhamzi, M.: Enhanced security methods of door locking based fingerprint. Int. J. Innov. Technol. Explor. Eng. 9(3), 1173–1178 (2020). https://doi.org/10.35940/ijitee.B7855.019320
7. Paul, P., Achib, M.A.A., Hossain, H.S., Hossain, M.K.: Smart door lock system with fingerprint interface. Technical Report pp. 1–13, October 2019. https://doi.org/10.13140/RG.2.2.10806.83523
8. Calcutt, D., Cowan, F., Parchizadeh, H.: 8051 Microcontrollers: an Applications-Based Introduction. Elsevier, Newnes, Amsterdam (2004)
9. Sanirahman: Jm-101 optical fingerprint module user manual, pp. 1–34, January 2017, version 1.8
10. Efunbote, M., Adeleke, M., Fagbemi, O., Orelaja, O., Jokojeje, R.: Development and experimentation of a security door lock system using biometric fingerprint architecture. Int. J. Recent Res. Electr. Electron. Eng. (IJRREEE) 5(3), 6–15 (2018)
11. Anu, Dinesh, B.: A smart door access system using finger print biometric system. Int. J. Med. Eng. Inf. 6(3), 274–280 (2014). https://doi.org/10.1504/IJMEI.2014.063175
12. Dakua, B.R., Hossain, M.I., Ahmed, F.: Design and implementation of UART serial communication module based on FPGA. In: ICMEIE-2015, pp. 1–5, June 2015
13. Saha, S., Rahman, M.A., Thakur, A.: Design and implementation of a BIST embedded high speed RS-422 utilized UART over FPGA. In: 2013 Fourth International Conference on Computing, Communications and Networking Technologies (ICC-CNT), pp. 1–5 (2013). https://doi.org/10.1109/ICCCNT.2013.6726481

Machine Learning and Artificial Intelligence for Security and Privacy

Towards an Attention-Based Threat Detection System for IoT Networks

Thanh-Nhan Nguyen[1,3], Khanh-Mai Dang[1,3], Anh-Duy Tran[1,3],
and Kim-Hung Le[2,3(✉)]

[1] University of Science, Ho Chi Minh City, Vietnam
`{ntnhan18,dkmai18}@apcs.fitus.edu.vn`
`taduy@fit.hcmus.edu.vn`
[2] University of Information Technology, Ho Chi Minh City, Vietnam
`hunglk@uit.edu.vn`
[3] Vietnam National University, Ho Chi Minh City, Vietnam

Abstract. The proliferation of the Internet of Things (IoT) serves demands in our life ranging from smart homes and smart cities to manufacturing and many other industries. As a result of the massive deployment of IoT devices, the risk of cyber-attacks on these devices also increases. The limitation in computing resources of IoT devices stops people from directly operating antivirus software on them. Therefore, these devices are vulnerable to cyber-attacks. In this research, we present our novel approach that could be applied to construct a lightweight Network Intrusion Detection System (NIDS) on IoT gateways. We utilize TabNet-the Google's recently developed model for tabular data-as our detection model. The evaluation results on BOT-IoT and UNSW-NB15 datasets prove the ability of our proposal in intrusion detection tasks with the accuracy of 98,53% and 99,43%. Finally, we experiment with our approach on the Raspberry Pi 4 to prove the lightweight characteristic to deploy on IoT gateways.

Keywords: Intrusion detection system · IoT devices · TabNet

1 Introduction

Ever since the creation of Internet of Things (IoT) devices, they have been transforming our world drastically. Nowadays, IoT devices appear everywhere and serve different industries such as smart homes, smart cities, supermarkets, healthcare, manufacturing, and many others. According to recent research, the number of global IoT devices grew to 12.2 billion active endpoints in 2021 and is predicted to reach 27 billion in 2025 as the consequence of supply constraint ease [11].

However, protecting an IoT network is a challenging problem due to the limitations in its computational power. This limitation makes deploying security software on IoT devices infeasible. Different types of attacks have been constantly

---

T. N. Nguyen and K. M. Dang—These authors equally contributed.

reported throughout the years with the most famous attack being botnet. In 2016, the Mirai botnet was reported as the main culprit that took down the whole Dyn DNS service which caused many frequently used websites to be inaccessible [2]. In today's world, botnet and DDoS attacks are still the most common attacks on IoT networks.

To protect an IoT network, commonly, an Intrusion Detection System (IDS) is installed on IoT gateways to monitor network traffic and alert if there are any suspicious network activities [31]. There are three reasons for this approach. First, IoT devices are energy-constraint and are limited in computational capability, so running the IDS directly on these devices affects their functionality. Second, an IoT gateway connects to all IoT devices in the network and can capture all inbound and outbound traffic of that network. Third, the IDS should lie near the IoT network to avoid interference with traffic from other networks.

Therefore, in this work, we tackle the intrusion detection problem for IoT networks by creating a lightweight Anomaly-based Intrusion Detection System. Recently, Google has introduced TabNet, a new deep learning model that is specially designed to work with tabular data. To the best of our knowledge, there has not existed any scholarly work on applying TabNet in security fields. The number of work carries out on the dataset dedicated to IoT (such as the BOT-IoT dataset) is meager.

Concretely, the authors aim to use TabNet to build a (lightweight) IDS for a network of IoT devices. In contrast to some works that suggest using CNN models for attack classification, the authors want to use a pure deep learning approach. Our method can perform multi-class classification to detect the type of attacks. To assess the capability of our method, we evaluate the performance of the TabNet model on two datasets: BOT-IoT and UNSW-NB15.

Overall, our main contributions are:

- Apply an attention-based model to detect attacks on security fields. TabNet uses an attention mechanism to focus on specific sets of attributes at each step for each instance.
- Evaluate the ability of the TabNet model to detect unknown attacks. Besides detecting correctly the types of attacks, the authors also test if the model can detect unknown attacks that it has not seen before. The experiment shows very promising results for this part.
- Prove the deployment of TabNet on lightweight devices. To show that the model can actually work on a constrained device so that it can be deployed in the real world, the authors use a Raspberry Pi 4 to assess TabNet's performance. Such an experiment consolidates the practicality of our proposed solution.

The rest of this paper is structured as follows: Sect. 2 provides some popular approaches relating to the intrusion detection problem. Section 3 present the architecture overview of our proposed IDS and the detail of TabNet-our detection model. In Sect. 4, we provide further information on the dataset we used, the evaluation environment, and metrics. Section 4.4 contains experimental results and discussion. Finally, we conclude our work in Sect. 5.

2   Related Works

2.1   Device Classification

Because of the heterogeneity of IoT devices, knowing what type of devices are making communications give us more advantages in monitoring the network. This section discusses some recent approaches for the device classification task.

In 2018, L. Bai et al. proposed a deep learning approach using the LSTM-CNN architecture for classifying device's type [4]. The author claimed that this method was the first to leverage time-series information of network traffic. The approach works by capturing packets and separating them into different flows, each one belongs to a specific device in the network using the MAC address contained in packets' headers. The main classification model is based on the LSTM-CNN architecture and it shows very good performance.

In 2019, S. Marchal et al. proposed AuDI, an autonomous system that can learn and effectively identify the type of IoT devices [21]. To handle the difficulty of dealing with devices that have sparse communications periods, the authors suggest modeling the network's periodic communications. This technique uses a hybrid architecture that utilizes both an IoT Gateway and a cloud service. The IoT Gateway is used to generate devices' fingerprints and send them to a kNN model hosted on the Cloud. Another takeaway from this work is that the fingerprint generated from the IoT Gateway can be used to create some policies to manage the network.

2.2   Machine Learning IDS

Recently, in 2020, M. Eskandari et al. proposed Passban IDS, a deployable IDS that can run on a Raspberry Pi [8]. Passban IDS is constructed to be a one-class classifier, meaning it can only distinguish between normal and abnormal network traffic. The core algorithm in Passban IDS is iForest, a tree-based machine learning algorithm designed based on normal Random Forest. The system also provides a web-based user interface for convenient use. From experiments, Passban IDS shows very good performance on a Raspberry Pi when tested with 4 different attacks.

I. Hafeez et al. proposed IoT-KEEPER, an IDS that uses unsupervised learning to detect malicious traffic [10]. IoT-KEEPER uses Software Defined Network to create a virtual network to monitor and filter traffic. After the detection phase, the system creates network policies to block malicious traffic flow. The authors also improved the model so that it can detect the exact type of attack. Their experiment shows very good results for this approach. Furthermore, the authors prove that IoT-KEEPER can operate on a resource-constrained IoT device.

2.3   Deep Learning IDS

In 2019, X. Zhang et al. proposed an approach that make use of a Convolutional Neural Network (CNN) model and decision tree algorithms [32]. The authors suggest converting directly the tabular data into images using a method called P-Zigzag. After the conversion, the images are fed into a CNN model called GoogLeNetNP, an improved model from GoogLeNet. GoogLeNetNP's purpose is to classify different categories of attacks. Next, for each category of attacks, a gcForest model is used for classifying sub-category attacks.

Also in 2019, E. Anthi et al. proposed an approach that uses 3 layers to perform classification [1]. The first layer is to classify the type of IoT devices and build a normal profile of those devices. The second layer is to distinguish between malicious packets and normal packets. The third layer is to classify the type of an attack based on 4 categories. The authors suggested using Weka to make the datasets balanced. The authors also tested 9 classifiers to compare their detection performance.

To tackle the detection problem with a different approach, T.-D. Nguyen et al. proposed DÏoT, a federated self-learning anomaly detection system for IoT [27]. The core algorithm in DÏoT is designed using Gated Recurrent Units (GRUs), a component that is widely used for series data. Another prominent feature of DÏoT is that it creates a specific model for each type of device. Using federated learning helps the whole system to reduce bias and enhance privacy without losing performance. Furthermore, the system works well with unknown attacks and reports no false alarms when evaluated in a real-world smart home deployment setting.

Another approach that tackles the anomaly detection problem using a CNN model is IMIDS proposed by K.-H. Le et al. in 2022 [19]. The authors demonstrated CNN's performance using a simple self-designed CNN model in the IDS. To improve the accuracy, the authors apply a Generative Adversarial Network (GAN) model to synthesize more samples for minor classes in the dataset. This helps increase the performance of the IDS since the dataset is highly imbalanced [26].

Also in 2022, X.-H. Nguyen et al. proposed Realguard, a lightweight network intrusion detection system for IoT Gateways [28]. Realguard's core detection model is a simple self-designed neural network that contains only 5 hidden layers and 34315 parameters. To reduce the memory footprint and increase the speed in the feature extraction phase, the authors proposed a feature extractor based on the Damped Incremental Statistics algorithm. The whole model is tested on a Raspberry Pi 4 to show its potential to be deployed on real IoT Gateways.

D.-T. Nguyen et al. proposed MidSiot, a Multistage Intrusion Detection System for Internet of Things [6]. The overall system contains 3 main stages: classifying the type of IoT devices, distinguishing between malicious network traffic and benign network traffic, and detecting the type of attacks. The authors remove redundant features using Pearson's correlation coefficient to increase the system's robustness. Furthermore, to deal with the problem of imbalanced datasets, the authors use SMOTE to synthesize new data points for minor classes. The proposed IDS is expected to deploy to IoT gateways using edge deployment frameworks presented in [7,18,20].

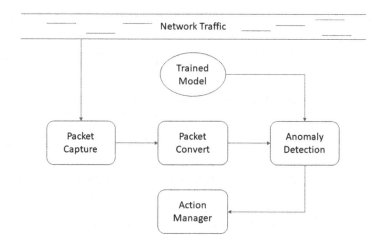

Fig. 1. Proposed IDS

3 Proposed IDS

3.1 Architecture Overview

In this section, we discuss our proposed IDS in general. Overall, our proposed IDS contains three main components:

- **Packet Capture block:** This block is responsible for capturing raw packets and storing them in PCAP files. This block uses the TCPDump program to perform the capturing process.
- **Packet Convert block:** This block converts the PCAP files received from the previous block into CSV files. During the conversion, it also extracts network flows from the packets and generates analysis features for those flows. This block uses CICFlowMeter [9], a network traffic flow analyzer, to perform the extraction and features generation.
- **Anomaly Detection block:** This block is the main component of our IDS. It is responsible for reading the CSV files, loading up the model, and performing classification. Since our model is trained offline, this block does not handle any training process. Our approach does not need to perform any data preprocessing before the classification takes place. Finally, TabNet is chosen as our core model for this detection block.

For the Packet Capture block and the Packet Convert block, we use a bash script [30] to execute the TCPDump program to capture packets and call CICFlowMeter to make conversions accordingly. For that reason, we only explain in detail the Anomaly Detection block. Figure 1 illustrates our overall system.

3.2 Attack Detection Model

As mentioned in Sect. 3.1, we use TabNet [3], a deep learning model designed specifically for tabular data, as our core model to perform attack classification.

TabNet is created to be an end-to-end deep learning model, which means we can train the model using pairs of input-output samples. The training process of TabNet uses gradient descent-based methods to update the model's weights. The authors also designed TabNet to work without needing any preprocessing steps for input data.

The structure of TabNet includes one or multiple similar blocks called decision steps. Each decision step may choose a different set of features to make a prediction, and at the end, all the predictions of each step are combined in a voting manner. Such an idea is called sequential attention. Before the samples are fed into decision steps, the model merely applies batch normalization on raw features without the need for global normalization. Each decision step then receives the same features f from the batch normalization block. The ith decision step receives the processed information from the $(i-1)^{th}$ step to decide which features to use and outputs the processed feature representation which is then aggregated into the overall decision.

Furthermore, the feature selection process is instance-wise, meaning for each sample the model may focus on a different set of features. Interestingly, TabNet's authors claimed that multiple decision steps behave as if it mimics an ensemble classifier. Figure 2 illustrates the architecture of TabNet's decision steps.

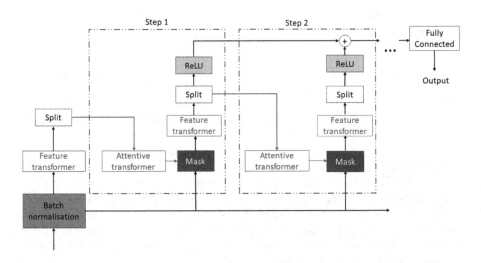

Fig. 2. TabNet's architecture [3]

A decision step contains two smaller networks: an attentive transformer and a feature transformer. Those two transformers are also the core components in a decision step.

A feature transformer is a neural network in which there are multiple layers organized into two types of smaller networks. One type is shared across different decision steps, and the other type is decision step-dependent. Figure 3 shows the architecture of a feature transformer. The authors stated in the original

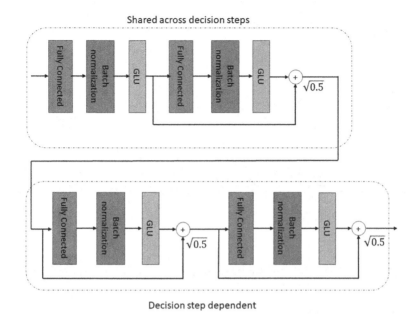

Fig. 3. Feature transformer's architecture

work that sharing some layers between decision steps helps the model to become "parameter-efficient and robust learning with high capacity". The authors also reasoned that using "normalization with $\sqrt{0.5}$ stabilizes the learning process by ensuring that the variance throughout the network does not change dramatically." The output of a feature transformer is transferred to the attentive transformer of the next decision step and the overall output in a voting manner.

An attentive transformer is responsible for selecting features to make reasoning in a step. The structure of an attentive transformer comprises a fully connected layer, batch normalization, and a Sparsemax normalization. Figure 4 illustrates the architecture of the attentive transformer. The prior scales block gives the attentive transformer how much each feature has been used in previous steps. The attentive transformer creates a mask to indicate what features should be used in this step. The mask also functions as a way to explain the model, looking at the mask, we will know what features are being used.

4   Evaluation Results

4.1   Evaluation Environment

Regarding machine learning models, we use a dedicated server to conduct our experiments. Specifically, we use this server to train the TabNet model with different configurations and evaluate those models. The specification of the server is as follows:

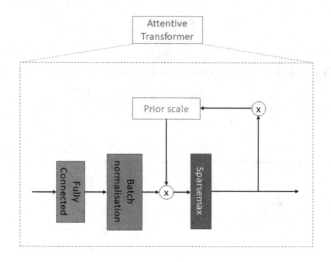

Fig. 4. Attentive transformer's architecture

- Processor: CPU Intel Xeon Gold 5220R
- Memory: RAM 256 GB
- Graphic card: GPU Nvidia A100 40 GB
- Operating System: Ubuntu 20.04 LTS

Besides training the models, we also use this server to preprocess the datasets. Since TabNet is a not very large neural network and there is no pretrained model for TabNet, we train the whole model from the beginning. After the training process, the models can be loaded and evaluated directly on this server or they can be transferred to a Raspberry Pi.

For the evaluation of constrained devices, we use a Raspberry Pi 4 with the following specifications:

- Processor: CPU Broadcom BCM2711
- Memory: RAM 4 GB
- Operating system: Ubuntu 22.04 LTS

Even though the Raspberry Pi is very resource-limited, it can still perform classification at a blazing fast speed.

4.2 Evaluation Metrics

To evaluate our approach, we use the following metrics: Accuracy, Precision, Recall, and F1-score.

Accuracy. Accuracy measures correctly classified records over the total number of samples. Accuracy is good for showing the overall performance of the model.

$$Accuracy = \frac{TN + TP}{TN + FP + TP + TN}$$

Precision. In the context of our experiments, the precision score is the fraction of the correctly attacking records over the total number of attacking records detected by the model.

$$Precision = \frac{TP}{TP + FP}$$

Recall. The recall score is the fraction of the number of attacks the model could detect over the total number of attacks in the ground truth labels. The recall score has the ideal value of 1 when the model can detect all the attacks in the dataset.

$$Recall = \frac{TP}{TP + FN}$$

F1-Score. F1-score is the harmonic mean of precision and recall, namely, it is easier to judge a model performance based on F1-score. F1-score has the maximum score of 1 when both Precision and Recall return 1, which means the model could correctly detect and classify all attack records in the dataset.

$$F1\_score = 2 \times \frac{Precision \times Recall}{Precision + Recall}$$

4.3   Datasets

To evaluate our work, we use the BOT-IoT dataset and the UNSW-NB15 dataset. Both datasets are popular and were created by the Cyber Range Lab of UNSW Canberra. In the following subsections, we provide detailed information about these two datasets.

BOT-IoT. The BOT-IoT dataset [12–17] is created by designing a realistic network environment combining of normal network traffic and botnet traffic behaviors. In our experiment, we use the small version of the BOT-IoT dataset, which contains 3 million records. As in the original dataset, this small one contains all attack categories and subcategories. The dataset contains 5 classes: DDoS, DoS, OS and Service Scan, Keylogging, Data exfiltration, and Normal. From the 5 main categories mentioned, BOT-IoT divides them into 11 smaller sub-categories. This dataset is highly imbalanced, while the DDoS class contains 1926167 records, the Theft class only contains 75 records.

UNSW-NB15. UNSW-NB15 dataset [22–25, 29] is a popular dataset in the field of Intrusion Detection System. The Cyber Range Lab of UNSW Canberra uses the IXIA PerfectStorm tool to simulate normal and contemporary synthetic attack behaviors. The dataset contains 9 kinds of attacks: Fuzzers, Analysis, Backdoors, DoS, Exploits, Generic, Reconnaissance, Shellcode, and Worms. UNSW-NB15 dataset is also highly imbalanced. The Normal class contains about 2 million records, while the Worms class only has 174 rows.

4.4 Results and Discussion

In this section, we show and analyze the experimental results of our proposed approach. As mentioned in Sect. 4.3, the BOT-IoT contains 5 main categories and 11 more detailed sub-categories inside the 5 main ones. Table 1 presents the performance when testing on 11 subcategories of the BOT-IoT dataset, 5 main categories of the BOT-IoT dataset, and 10 classes of the UNSW-NB15 dataset. Both datasets are augmented using the SMOTE [5] technique.

Table 1. The highest results in different metrics. A high F1-score means high Precision and Recall, which indicates the ability to correctly classify attacks and a low attack missing rate.

Dataset	Accuracy	Precision	Recall	F1-score
BOT-IoT	0,9853	0,9865	0,9853	0,9857
BOT-IoT (main categories only)	0,9943	0,9943	0,9943	0,9943
UNSW-NB15	0,9795	0,9784	0,9795	0,9767

Table 2 and Table 3 presents the scores in different metrics when testing on 11 subcategories and 5 main categories of the BOT-IoT dataset. Our approach achieves a high F1-score for most of the classes.

Table 2. The precision, recall, and F1-score per class when experimenting on 11 subclasses of the BOT-IoT dataset

Category	Precision	Recall	F1-score
DDoS, HTTP	0,3088	0,9747	0,4690
DDoS, TCP	0,9833	0,9747	0,9809
DDoS, UDP	**1,0000**	0,9991	0,9995
DoS, HTTP	0,5540	0,9527	0,7006
DoS, TCP	0,9646	0,9812	0,9729
DoS, UDP	0,9992	**1,0000**	0,9996
Normal	**1,0000**	0,9759	0,9878
Reconnaissance, OS_Fingerprint	0,5601	0,7616	0,6455
Reconnaissance, Service_Scan	0,9177	0,8457	0,8802
Theft, Data_Exfiltration	**1,0000**	**1,0000**	**1,0000**
Theft, Keylogging	0,5185	**1,0000**	0,6829

Table 3. The precision, recall, and F1-score per class when experimenting on 5 main classes of the BOT-IoT dataset. Our approach has a good performance on detecting *DDoS* attacks. The model also classifies correctly benign traffic, hence, the model does not raise any false alarms.

Category	Precision	Recall	F1-score
DDoS	0,9977	0,9915	0,9946
DoS	0,9908	0,9973	0,9940
Normal	1,0000	0,9873	0,9936
Reconnaissance	0,9857	0,9989	0,9923
Theft	0,8125	0,9286	0,8667

We also compare our results with results from MidSIoT [6] in terms of F1-score in Table 4. Our approach performs better compared to MidSIoT in the class Normal and Theft, results in other classes are competitive. However, MidsIoT did not evaluate the Theft class due to the problem of too few samples.

Table 4. F1-score per class comparision between TabNet and MidsIoT on BOT-IoT dataset. Our approach performs better comparing to MidSIoT on the class Normal and Theft, results on other classes are competitive.

Category	TabNet	MidsIoT
DDoS	0,9946	0,9995
DoS	0,9940	0,9989
Normal	**0,9936**	0,3636
Reconnaissance	0,9923	0,9999
Theft	**0,8667**	–

For the UNSW-NB15 dataset, we perform experiments to evaluate our approach and also compare it with IMIDS [19]. Table 5 shows the precision, recall, and F1-score of every class in the UNSW-NB15 dataset. Table 6 presents the comparison between our work with IMIDS. When compared to IMIDS, our approach has a better performance in terms of F1-score for most of the classes. For the class DoS and Worms, our approach has lower scores. Nevertheless, in the remaining classes, our method and IMIDS are competitive.

We also conduct performance assessments using a Raspberry Pi 4 as mentioned in Sect. 4.1. Regarding this experiment, we transfer the model into the Raspberry Pi along with the testing set from the BOT-IoT dataset. This model is trained on the preprocessed and augmented training set from the BOT-IoT dataset. The result is very promising with the average time to perform prediction being approximately 302 μs per network flow. Total RAM usage is measured to be about 667MB including the memory used for loading the whole testing set and the TabNet model. The testing set consists of 442630 network flows.

Table 5. The precision, recall, and F1-score per class when experimenting on 10 classes of the UNSW-NB15 dataset.

Category	Precision	Recall	F1-score
Normal	1,0000	0,9856	0,9927
Generic	0,9164	0,8436	0,8785
Fuzzers	0,4268	0,8795	0,5747
DoS	0,2739	0,2655	0,2696
Reconnaissance	0,7941	0,7237	0,7573
Exploits	0,8067	0,7015	0,7504
Analysis	0,0960	0,3710	0,1525
Backdoors	0,1163	0,3590	0,1757
Shellcode	0,3671	0,7835	0,5000
Worms	0,1226	0,3824	0,1857

Table 6. F1-score per class comparison between TabNet and IMIDS on UNSW-NB15 dataset. Our approach has a better performance in terms of F1-score for most of the classes.

Category	TabNet	IMIDS	IMIDS with ctGAN
Normal	**0,9956**	0,9918	0,9906
Generic	**0,9899**	0,9861	0,9865
Fuzzers	**0,5451**	0,5151	0,5173
DoS	0,0695	**0,4465**	0,4376
Reconnaissance	**0,8152**	0,7582	0,7011
Exploits	**0,7101**	0,5555	0,5522
Analysis	0,0290	**0,1514**	0,1206
Backdoors	0,0839	**0,1069**	0,0930
Shellcode	**0,5587**	0,2642	0,2432
Worms	0,0000	**0,2014**	0,1244

Detecting Unknown Attacks. Our proposed IDS has a good performance in detecting unknown attacks. To prove the ability to detect unknown-attack, we conduct experiments on 2 categories: DoS and DDoS of the BOT-IoT dataset. With the DoS category, the testing set comprises records from DoS, UDP subcategories. With the experiment on the DDoS category, the testing set composes of DDos, UDP records. Both of the testing sets contain 20% of normal data. The training sets of two experiments contain records from the remaining subcategories in the Dos and DDoS categories respectively. Table 7 shows the accuracy for this experiment.

Table 7. Results when testing with unknown attacks

Subcategory	Accuracy
DoS, UDP	99,93%
DDoS, UDP	99,99%

5 Conclusions

We have proposed a new approach for building an IDS system for IoT Gateways that uses an attention-based model as the core classification model. From our literature review, TabNet has not been used in the intrusion detection field before. Therefore, applying such an advanced model to the intrusion detection field is an innovative decision. The approach achieves the accuracy of **98,53%** and **99,43%** when classifying 11 subcategories and 5 main categories in the BOT-IoT dataset, respectively. Regarding the UNSW-NB15 dataset, the model's accuracy is **97,47%**. Besides, we also compare our approach with existing works using the F1-score metric. When comparing TabNet with existing approaches such as MidSIoT [6] and IMIDS [19], the results are highly competitive. For some attack categories, our results are even better. Moreover, **our approach achieves 99,93% accuracy when testing with unknown attacks**. Finally, we **test our approach on a Raspberry Pi 4 to prove the lightweight characteristic** to deploy on IoT gateways. In conclusion, our method achieves good performance in the task of intrusion detection and is suitable for resource-constrained devices.

Acknowledgements. This research is supported by research funding from Faculty of Information Technology, University of Science, Vietnam National University - Ho Chi Minh City.

References

1. Anthi, E., Williams, L., Słowińska, M., Theodorakopoulos, G., Burnap, P.: A supervised intrusion detection system for smart home IoT devices. IEEE Internet Things J. **6**(5), 9042–9053 (2019)
2. Antonakakis, M., et al.: Understanding the mirai botnet. In: 26th USENIX Security Symposium (USENIX Security 17), pp. 1093–1110. USENIX Association, Vancouver, BC, August 2017. https://www.usenix.org/conference/usenixsecurity17/technical-sessions/presentation/antonakakis
3. Arik, S., Pfister, T.: Tabnet: attentive interpretable tabular learning (2021)
4. Bai, L., Yao, L., Kanhere, S.S., Wang, X., Yang, Z.: Automatic device classification from network traffic streams of internet of things. In: 2018 IEEE 43rd Conference on Local Computer Networks (LCN), pp. 1–9. IEEE (2018)
5. Bowyer, K.W., Chawla, N.V., Hall, L.O., Kegelmeyer, W.P.: SMOTE: synthetic minority over-sampling technique. CoRR abs/1106.1813 (2011). http://arxiv.org/abs/1106.1813
6. Dat-Thinh, N., Xuan-Ninh, H., Kim-Hung, L., Nassar, H.: Midsiot: a multistage intrusion detection system for internet of things. Wirel. Commun. Mob. Comput. **2022** (2022). https://doi.org/10.1155/2022/9173291

7. Do, X.T., Le, K.H.: Towards remote deployment for intrusion detection system to IoT Edge Devices. In: Balas, V.E., Solanki, V.K., Kumar, R. (eds.) Recent Advances in Internet of Things and Machine Learning. Intelligent Systems Reference Library, vol. 215, pp. 301–316. Springer, Cham (2022). https://doi.org/10.1007/978-3-030-90119-6_24

8. Eskandari, M., Janjua, Z.H., Vecchio, M., Antonelli, F.: Passban IDS: an intelligent anomaly-based intrusion detection system for IoT edge devices. IEEE Internet Things J. **7**(8), 6882–6897 (2020). https://doi.org/10.1109/JIOT.2020.2970501

9. Habibi Lashkari., A., Draper Gil., G., Mamun., M.S.I., Ghorbani., A.A.: Cicflowmeter https://www.unb.ca/cic/research/applications.html

10. Hafeez, I., Antikainen, M., Ding, A.Y., Tarkoma, S.: IoT-keeper: detecting malicious IoT network activity using online traffic analysis at the edge. IEEE Trans. Network Serv. Manage. **17**(1), 45–59 (2020)

11. Hasan, M.: State of IoT 2022: number of connected IoT devices growing 18% to 14.4 billion globally (2022). https://iot-analytics.com/number-connected-iot-devices

12. Koroniotis, N.: Designing an effective network forensic framework for the investigation of botnets in the internet of things (2020)

13. Koroniotis, N., Moustafa, N.: Enhancing network forensics with particle swarm and deep learning: the particle deep framework. CoRR abs/2005.00722 (2020). https://arxiv.org/abs/2005.00722

14. Koroniotis, N., Moustafa, N., Schiliro, F., Gauravaram, P., Janicke, H.: A holistic review of cybersecurity and reliability perspectives in smart airports. IEEE Access **8**, 209802–209834 (2020). https://doi.org/10.1109/ACCESS.2020.3036728

15. Koroniotis, N., Moustafa, N., Sitnikova, E.: A new network forensic framework based on deep learning for internet of things networks: a particle deep framework. Future Gener. Comput. Syst. **110**, 91–106 (2020). https://doi.org/10.1016/j.future.2020.03.042, https://www.sciencedirect.com/science/article/pii/S0167739X19325105

16. Koroniotis, N., Moustafa, N., Sitnikova, E., Slay, J.: Towards developing network forensic mechanism for botnet activities in the IoT based on machine learning techniques. In: Hu, J., Khalil, I., Tari, Z., Wen, S. (eds.) MONAMI 2017. LNICST, vol. 235, pp. 30–44. Springer, Cham (2018). https://doi.org/10.1007/978-3-319-90775-8_3

17. Koroniotis, N., Moustafa, N., Sitnikova, E., Turnbull, B.: Towards the development of realistic botnet dataset in the internet of things for network forensic analytics: Bot-IoT dataset (2018). https://doi.org/10.48550/ARXIV.1811.00701, https://arxiv.org/abs/1811.00701

18. Le, K.H., Le-Minh, K.H., Thai, H.T.: Brainyedge: an AI-enabled framework for IoT edge computing. ICT Express (2021). https://doi.org/10.1016/j.icte.2021.12.007, https://www.sciencedirect.com/science/article/pii/S2405959521001727

19. Le, K.H., Nguyen, M.H., Tran, T.D., Tran, N.D.: Imids: an intelligent intrusion detection system against cyber threats in IoT. Electron. **11**(4) (2022). https://doi.org/10.3390/electronics11040524, https://www.mdpi.com/2079-9292/11/4/524

20. Le Minh, K.H., Le, K.H., Le-Trung, Q.: Dlase: a light-weight framework supporting deep learning for edge devices. In: 2020 4th International Conference on Recent Advances in Signal Processing, Telecommunications & Computing (SigTelCom), pp. 103–108 (2020). https://doi.org/10.1109/SigTelCom49868.2020.9199058

21. Marchal, S., Miettinen, M., Nguyen, T.D., Sadeghi, A.R., Asokan, N.: Audi: toward autonomous IoT device-type identification using periodic communication. IEEE J. Sel. Areas Commun. **37**(6), 1402–1412 (2019). https://doi.org/10.1109/JSAC.2019.2904364

22. Moustafa, N., Creech, G., Slay, J.: Big data analytics for intrusion detection system: statistical decision-making using finite dirichlet mixture models. In: Palomares Carrascosa, I., Kalutarage, H.K., Huang, Y. (eds.) Data Analytics and Decision Support for Cybersecurity. DA, pp. 127–156. Springer, Cham (2017). https://doi.org/10.1007/978-3-319-59439-2_5

23. Moustafa, N., Slay, J.: UNSW-NB15: a comprehensive data set for network intrusion detection systems (UNSW-NB15 network data set). In: 2015 Military Communications and Information Systems Conference (MilCIS), pp. 1–6 (2015). https://doi.org/10.1109/MilCIS.2015.7348942

24. Moustafa, N., Slay, J.: The evaluation of network anomaly detection systems: statistical analysis of the UNSW-NB15 data set and the comparison with the KDD99 data set. Inf. Secur. J. Global Perspect. **25**(1–3), 18–31 (2016)

25. Moustafa, N., Slay, J., Creech, G.: Novel geometric area analysis technique for anomaly detection using trapezoidal area estimation on large-scale networks. IEEE Trans. Big Data **5**(4), 481–494 (2019). https://doi.org/10.1109/TBDATA.2017.2715166

26. Nguyen, P.C., Nguyen, Q.T., Le, K.H.: An ensemble feature selection algorithm for machine learning based intrusion detection system. In: 2021 8th NAFOSTED Conference on Information and Computer Science (NICS), pp. 50–54 (2021). https://doi.org/10.1109/NICS54270.2021.9701577

27. Nguyen, T.D., Marchal, S., Miettinen, M., Fereidooni, H., Asokan, N., Sadeghi, A.R.: Dïot: a federated self-learning anomaly detection system for IoT (2018). https://doi.org/10.48550/ARXIV.1804.07474, https://arxiv.org/abs/1804.07474

28. Nguyen, X.H., Nguyen, X.D., Huynh, H.H., Le, K.H.: Realguard: a lightweight network intrusion detection system for IoT gateways. Sensors **22**(2) (2022). https://doi.org/10.3390/s22020432, https://www.mdpi.com/1424-8220/22/2/432

29. Sarhan, M., Layeghy, S., Moustafa, N., Portmann, M.: NetFlow datasets for machine learning-based network intrusion detection systems. In: Deze, Z., Huang, H., Hou, R., Rho, S., Chilamkurti, N. (eds.) BDTA/WiCON -2020. LNICST, vol. 371, pp. 117–135. Springer, Cham (2021). https://doi.org/10.1007/978-3-030-72802-1_9

30. Tiwatthanont, P.: Tcpdump and cicflowmeter. https://github.com/iPAS/TCPDUMP_and_CICFlowMeter

31. Tran, B.S., Ho, T.H., Do, T.X., Le, K.H.: Empirical performance evaluation of machine learning based DDoS attack detections. In: Balas, V.E., Solanki, V.K., Kumar, R. (eds.) Recent Advances in Internet of Things and Machine Learning. Intelligent Systems Reference Library, vol. 215, pp. 283–299. Springer, Cham (2022). https://doi.org/10.1007/978-3-030-90119-6_23

32. Zhang, X., Chen, J., Zhou, Y., Han, L., Lin, J.: A multiple-layer representation learning model for network-based attack detection. IEEE Access **7**, 91992–92008 (2019). https://doi.org/10.1109/ACCESS.2019.2927465

Security and Privacy Issues and Solutions in Federated Learning for Digital Healthcare

Hyejun Jeong[✉] and Tai-Myoung Chung[✉]

College of Computing, Sungkyunkwan University, Suwon, Republic of South Korea
june.jeong@g.skku.edu, tmchung@skku.edu

Abstract. The advent of Federated Learning has enabled the creation of a high-performing model as if it had been trained on a considerable amount of data. A multitude of participants and a server cooperatively train a model without the need for data disclosure or collection. The healthcare industry, where security and privacy are paramount, can substantially benefit from this new learning paradigm, as data collection is no longer feasible due to stringent data policies. Nonetheless, unaddressed challenges and insufficient attack mitigation are hampering its adoption. Attack surfaces differ from traditional centralized learning in that the server and clients communicate between each round of training. In this paper, we thus present vulnerabilities, attacks, and defenses based on the widened attack surfaces, as well as suggest promising new research directions toward a more robust FL.

Keywords: Federated learning · Security · Privacy · Vulnerabilities · Attacks · Threats · Defenses

1 Introduction

Digital health has rapidly grown, and the COVID-19 outbreak accelerated its evolution. However, HIPAA reported that there were 712 healthcare data breaches in 2021, exceeding 2020 by 11% [25], and Verizon confirmed that data breaches in the healthcare industry increased by 58% during the pandemic. An Electronic Health Record (EHR) contains a wealth of sensitive private information about each patient, such as name, social security number, financial information, current and previous addresses, and medical history. However, traditional digital healthcare relies on centralized AI techniques that operate on a single location such as a server or data center for analytics; thus, it requires data collection. It is often not only time and resource-consuming but likely to violate stringent privacy protection policies, such as GDPR, CCPA, and HIPAA, that mandate securing patient health-related data management.

Federated Learning (FL) decouples the use of AI techniques from gathering data by training a global model in a distributed manner under the orchestration of a central server (often referred to as an aggregator) and multiple local

T. K. Dang et al. (Eds.): FDSE 2022, CCIS 1688, pp. 316–331, 2022.
https://doi.org/10.1007/978-981-19-8069-5_21

clients. The server updates the global model by aggregating the local models' parameters, trained using each end-device data. In other words, data does not leave the data-owning devices, so it reduces the risk of raw training data being exposed in the middle of communication. FL thus came to light for its data privacy improvement, allowing learning without data leakage in situations where personal information must be protected. The advantages hold great promise to leverage AI techniques in the healthcare sector while complying with privacy policies.

Despite the benefits, FL opens new attack surfaces and vulnerabilities that adversaries can exploit to harm the global model or leak the data. The expanded attack surfaces necessitate an updated vulnerability analysis to minimize the threat probabilities considering the rapidly growing needs of digital healthcare. This paper aims to introduce various vulnerabilities, attacks, and defenses, as well as open challenges and future directions toward more robust federated learning in the healthcare industry.

The rest of the paper is structured as follows: Sect. 2 identifies vulnerabilities, Sect. 3 categorizes attack methods by exploiting them, and Sect. 4 introduces defense methods. Section 5 suggests future research directions, and finally, we conclude the paper in Sect. 6.

2   Sources of Vulnerabilities

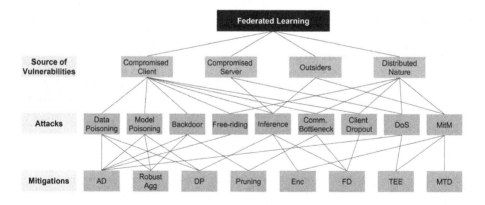

Fig. 1. A taxonomy of federated learning: vulnerabilities, attacks, and defenses.

Identifying vulnerabilities in a system helps to mitigate and prevent potential attacks. FL creates a shared model by aggregating locally computed updates using client-specific data. FL involves three entities in **a distributed nature**: **clients** in which each of them computes a local model based on its own dataset, **a server** that aggregates the local model updates to recompute the latest global model, and **communication channels** that the clients and the server communicate. Figure 1 visualizes the relationship between the vulnerabilities, attacks, and defense strategies in a vanilla FL framework.

Compromisable Clients. The FL workflow involves multiple clients computing local models based on each site-specific dataset inaccessible to other clients or the server. Thus, each client is a source of vulnerability. *Compromised clients* entail the following:

– clients unable to keep a stable connection to the server
– clients equipped with insufficient computing resources for a model training
– clients having insufficient quality or quantity of data for a fair contribution
– clients with malicious intents to disturb the process or to plant backdoors

A Compromisable Server or an honest-but-curious server may attempt to infer the training data from the updates, alter the model parameters, and manipulate the aggregation algorithm [9]. The server is also vulnerable to flooding endangering its availability.

Outsiders or Eavesdroppers intercept communications between the participating parties and steal the model parameters. They also can launch consecutive attacks, such as inference or MitM attacks, using the stolen information. The outsiders also might theft the final model parameters at the deployment phase to launch inference-time attacks.

A Distributed Nature opens attack surfaces related to communication, such as free-riding, DoS, MitM attacks, or communication bottlenecks. The participating clients' not uniform data distribution and resources have additionally introduced non-malicious failure, resulting in detrimentally impacted model performance and extended training time.

3   Attacks and Threats

By exploiting the vulnerabilities mentioned in Sect. 2, attackers aim to achieve two objectives: performance degradation and data leakage at training or testing

Table 1. The severity and short description of threats

Threats	Severity	Description
Poisoning (Subsect. 3.1)	High to Medium	Alter the training data or model parameters to modify the model's behavior in a malicious direction
Inference (Subsect. 3.2)	High to Medium	Analyze the global or local model parameters to infer the information in the training dataset
Backdoor (Subsect. 3.3)	High	Insert hidden backdoor to train the global model on malicious tasks while the main tasks are not affected
Comm Bottleneck (Subsect. 3.4)	High	Congested communication due to the large size of the payload of the trained model parameters
Free-riding (Subsect. 3.5)	Medium	Fake contribution to effortlessly gain the global model
MitM (Subsect. 3.6)	Medium to low	Steal the model parameters in-between the endpoints to breach data or launch consequent attacks
DoS (Subsect. 3.7)	Low	Flood the server to harm its availability
Client Dropout (Subsect. 3.8)	Low	Forceful or accidental dropping out of participating clients due to resource instability

time. Various actors attempt to harm a global model performance by disrupting its convergence, modifying the training data or the model updates, contribution-less participation, and incurring latency. The severity and short descriptions of each threat are summarized in Table 1.

3.1 Poisoning Attacks

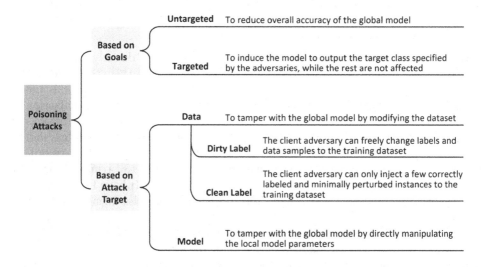

Fig. 2. A taxonomy of poisoning attacks.

FL framework is known as especially vulnerable to poisoning attacks due to its distributed and data-isolated nature. In poisoning attacks, the adversaries impact either the training dataset or local models in order to modify the behavior of the target model in some undesirable ways [9]. Poisoning attacks can be categorized based on the adversarial goal: untargeted and targeted attacks. Untargeted attacks, also known as random attacks, aim to reduce the overall accuracy of a global model. On the other hand, targeted attacks aim to induce the model to output the target class specified by the adversaries, while the other classes are predicted ordinarily. Targeted attacks are generally more complicated than random ones because it has a specific goal to achieve [33] while minimizing their influences on non-targeted classes. Figure 2 summarizes the categories of poisoning attacks. Based on what the adversaries attempt to manipulate, poisoning attacks are categorized into *data poisoning* and *model poisoning*.

Data Poisoning attacks allow adversaries on the client side to alter the training dataset to compromise data integrity and modify the model's behavior in an attacker-chosen direction. These attacks begin in the training phase, during local data collection [40]. Data poisoning attacks fall into clean-label and dirty-label poisoning attacks. For the clean-label attacks, the adversary injects a few correctly labeled and minimally perturbed instances into the training data as if the adversarial or evasion attacks. In the FL environment, however, because the raw data instances are only observable to the data owner, dirty-label attacks prevail in which adversaries can freely change labels and data samples as they wish to misclassify [6]. A representative dirty-label poisoning attack is a label-flipping attack, flipping the labels of two different classes to induce the global model to misclassify one class to another.

Model Poisoning attacks allow client-side adversaries to directly modify the local model parameters at the training phase before sending them to the server. The adversarial clients also manipulate the model hyperparameter, such as the learning rate, number of the local epoch, the batch size, and the optimization objective, to manipulate the training rules before the local training. The attacks improved stealthiness by optimizing the local model for both training loss and an adversarial objective to avoid deviation from the global model [9,13]. Accordingly, robust aggregation rules, such as Krum [8], Bulyan [18], trimmed-mean, coomed [55] were proposed; however, recent works [13,46,51] have broken them by tailoring model updates in a malicious direction. It has also been shown that only one non-colluding malicious client achieves targeted misclassification with 100% confidence while ensuring the convergence of the global model [6]. Model poisoning attacks are far more effective than data poisoning attacks because the malicious client's updates are tuned to maximize the damage to the overall model performance while remaining stealthy [6,9].

3.2 Inference Attacks

Inference attacks target participant privacy during both the training and testing phases. A compromised client, an honest-but-curious server, or outsiders may want to infer participating clients' training data. This type of attack is not explicit to FL but has been rampant in ML or DL. A DL model contains data properties that appear unrelated to the main tasks, mainly because the gradients of a given layer are computed using this layer's features and errors backpropagated from the layer above [33]. Hence, trained model gradients contain extra information about the unintentional features of participants' training data [33,36]. The attackers thus infer a substantial amount of private information such as *membership*, *properties*, and *class representatives*.

Membership Inference attacks are arguably the most basic privacy attack that infers the presence of a particular sample in the sensitive training dataset [36]. The attackers, for example, may learn whether a particular patient profile was used to train the model linked with a disease, exposing that the particular patient went to the hospital for the associated disease [33]. Shokri et al. [47] constructed shadow models that imitate the target model's behavior to distinguish the target model's output on membership versus non-members of its training dataset. Nasr et al. [41] exploit the vulnerability of the SGD algorithm, gradually influencing some parameters to adapt themselves towards reducing the loss.

Property Inference attacks allow an adversarial party to infer whether the training dataset has specific general properties seemingly unrelated to the model's primary task. For instance, a model is originally trained on facial images to predict if someone's mouth is open (primary task); the attacker's goal is to infer whether the training dataset is gender-balanced (inferred property) [45]. Adversarial clients can identify when a property appears and disappears in the data during the training phase by inferring from the history of global models [36].

Class Representatives Inference attacks allow adversarial parties to reconstruct sensitive training data features by taking advantage of their correlation with the model output [58]. It had been demonstrated that attackers could correctly characterize features of the class from simple models, such as logistic regression and decision trees, with no false positives [15]. Recent efforts utilize Generative Adversarial Networks (GANs) to produce synthetic class representations from training data [21,27,58] or even recover the exact training images or texts from the gradients [17,36,44]. Nevertheless, it is less feasible in FL scenarios since GAN-generated representatives are only similar to the training data when the training datasets of participants are similar (i.e., IID) [36].

3.3   Backdoor Attacks

Backdoor attacks include adversarial clients inserting triggers into the training data or model updates in order to train a global model on both backdoor and main tasks. On test data with the same trigger embedded, the model produces false-positive predictions with high confidence. Adversaries have also reinforced the detection evasion strategy by tuning the backdoored models to not diverge from other models [50]. For example, Bagdasaryan et al. [3] rewards the model for backdoor task accuracy and penalizes it for deviating from what the aggregator considers benign. Xie et al. [54] proposed a Distributed Backdoor Attack that decomposes a global trigger pattern into separate small local patterns and embeds them into the training sets of multiple adversarial parties. Their efforts reached a higher attack success rate than inserting one global pattern. Because the malevolent behavior only appears when the triggers are present at test time, it is difficult and time-consuming to identify the existence of backdoor attacks.

3.4   Communication Bottleneck

Although FL has reduced communication costs by transmitting training models rather than much larger quantities of data, the communication overhead is still of the utmost importance, especially with larger deep learning models [40]. Participating clients are typically large in number and have slow or unstable internet connections [28]. System heterogeneity—an inequality of computation and communication capabilities across the clients—causes asymmetric arrival timing at the server. Considering that 1 to 1000 clients participate in typical federated learning [22], accumulated delayed uplink time will ultimately result in a substantial delay in training time.

3.5   Free-Riding Attacks

Free-riding attacks refer to an effortless extraction of a trained model; attackers benefit from the global model while not contributing to the training process. Exploiting the distributed nature and the server's blindness, they obtain the trained global model without affording their computing resources and data [30]. Free-riders generate fake updates without training with their local datasets because they have to send something to the server on each round, even if they do not update the local model parameter during the iterative federated optimization [14]. As such, the attackers steal intellectual property and breach privacy.

3.6   Man-in-the-Middle Attacks

In a Man-in-the-Middle (MitM) attack, the attackers position themselves in a conversation between the endpoints either to eavesdrop or to impersonate one of the participants, making it appear as if a normal exchange is taking place [35]. They aim to jeopardize confidentiality by eavesdropping, integrity by manipulation, and availability by interrupting the communication [7]. The attackers intercept the client-server connection and replace the model parameters with malicious updates or make a shadow model to enable consecutive attacks such as model poisoning, backdoor, or inference attacks.

3.7   DoS Attacks

Denial-of-Service (DoS) attacks include an insider (compromised client) or outsider flooding a server with traffic to compromise resource availability. DoS attacks thus disrupt the server with receiving, computing, and sending model parameters. It has been a known threat in the computer network domain for a long time. For instance, Fung et al. [16] simulated three types of DoS attacks by increasing training time, bandwidth, and CPU usage at the server and clients. As the model could not be adequately trained, making a final model will be much more expensive in computation and communication.

3.8   Client Dropout

Clients could be accidentally or forcefully dropped out of the procedure, which may yield ineffective results and raise concerns about fairness. Mobile devices on the client-side might frequently be offline or on slow and costly connections at any time owing to user behaviors or the unpredictable network environment in which they are located [22]. However, because a server cannot tell whether the clients are malicious or heavily non-IID, it may exclude the clients from future rounds, thus producing a less generalized global model [5].

4 Mitigation Techniques

Fig. 3. A Category of mitigation techniques

A server has to secure the system by only examining the local model parameters. As illustrated in Fig. 1, a single technique can mitigate multiple issues or attacks simultaneously. A Fig. 3 categorize the mitigation techniques. In this section, we introduce various mitigation strategies.

4.1 Anomaly Detection

Anomaly or outlier detection is a proactive strategy that employs analytical and statistical methods to filter out malicious occurrences that do not conform to an expected pattern or activity [40]. This technique primarily addresses poisoning, backdoor, free-riding, and DoS attacks [16]. Fang et al. [13] proposed LFR (Loss Function-based Rejection) and ERR (Error Rate-based Rejection) that reject client participation which negatively impacts the global model. Baruch et al. [4] and Sun et al. [48] employed norm thresholding of client model update to remove models with boosted model parameters exceeding a specified threshold. ZeKoC [11] and FLAME [42] leverage various clustering algorithms, DBSCAN and HDBSCAN, to detect deviating clients. FoolsGold [16] prevents Sybil-based attacks, inspired by the fact that Sybil clients' gradients have unexpectedly high cosine similarities because they are trained for the same malicious objectives.

However, anomaly detection techniques could easily fail when clients with highly non-IID datasets join. The detection algorithm may misclassify the benign clients as abnormal because of the unique distribution of model parameters owing to learning from the non-IID dataset.

4.2 Robust Aggregation

Robust aggregation is a widely studied proactive strategy to reduce the impact of malicious model updates, used as a defense technique against poisoning and backdoor attacks. According to Shejwalkar et al. [46], robust aggregation algorithms (AGRs) remove the suspicious client based on the following criteria:

1. Distances from the benign gradients [6,8,10,18,55]

2. Distributional differences with benign gradients [6,31,48]
3. Differences in L_p-norms of benign and malicious gradients [48]

The first criteria-based methods measure the pair-wise cosine distance between all clients [2,10] or Euclidean distances between all clients and the global model [8,18,55] to identify malicious clients. Lu et al. [31] followed the second criteria to address free-riding attacks; they measured the clients' potential contributions using Gaussian Distribution. Sun et al. [48] followed the second and third criteria to address label-flipping attacks. Inspired by the distinct weight distribution of malicious and benign clients, they calculated the L2 norm of local weights and compared it with a specified threshold. The server omits suspicious clients whose value is below the threshold from further aggregation. Wang et al. [51] did not directly analyze the model parameter in the parameter space. Found that Penultimate Layer Representations (PLRs) in latent space are highly differentiating features for the poisonous models, they measured the Euclidean distance of the PLRs to estimate the trust score of local models' updates to determine the amount of weight on each local model when it comes to aggregation.

The degree of non-IID is directly proportional to the impact of attacks because when the data distributions are highly non-IID, it is difficult for an aggregation algorithm to detect and remove the malicious clients reliably [46]. Regarding that IID data assumption often does not hold in practice, implementing a robust AGR without any assumptions comes as a challenge.

4.3   Pruning

Pruning refers to reducing the model size by dropping neurons, thus relaxing computational complexity and communication bottleneck [19,24], as well as addressing backdoor attacks [52]. Inspired by that backdoors exploit the spare capacity in the neural network, Wu et al. [52] dropped the backdoor attack success rate by removing spare neurons that might have been trained for backdoor tasks and fine-tuning the parameters after the training phase.

4.4   Differential Privacy

Differential Privacy (DP) introduces additional noise to the client's sensitive data so that the attacker cannot meaningfully distinguish a single data record from the rest [9]. DP is initially believed to withstand privacy attacks, such as inference attacks, but it can also inherently defend against poisoning and backdoor attacks [34]. Miao et al. [37] bounded the norm of malicious updates by adaptively setting a proper clipping threshold throughout the training process to eliminate backdoors and enhance the main task accuracy.

Although DP is one of the preferred techniques due to its low computational overhead and privacy quantification properties, inserted perturbation often suggests a trade-off between performance and privacy. To this extent, Nguyen et al. [42] estimate a minimal amount of noise to ensure the elimination of backdoors while maintaining the benign performance of the global model.

4.5   Moving Target Defense

Moving Target Defense (MTD) is a proactive defense strategy against MitM attacks. Continually randomizing FL system modules obscures the vulnerability source from attackers, thereby increasing the cost and complexity of locating the exact target [40]. As such, the added dynamics consequently reduce the likelihood of successful attacks and increase the system resiliency while limiting the disclosure of system vulnerabilities and opportunities for attacks [40]. Zhou et al. [59] introduced ADS-MTD, a double-shuffle system comprising model and client-shuffling components. Specifically, MTD takes place in the second phase as a hierarchical multi-shuffler structure to dynamically and efficiently assess and eliminate malicious FL participants to enhance the aggregated model's integrity and availability.

4.6   Trusted Execution Environment

A Trusted Execution Environment (TEE) protects the FL system during a training phase by allocating a separate region for code execution and data handling. TEE guarantees integrity and confidentiality of computations while incurring lower overhead but higher privacy compared to encryption-based methods [38]. TEEs, however, have limited memory for computation in order to keep the Trusting Computing Base as small as possible [39] to minimize the attack surface [29]. Thus, Mo et al. [39] proposed PPFL that enlarges its memory capability by greedy layer-wise training and aggregation. They demonstrated that PPFL achieved comparable accuracy while dealing with data heterogeneity and accelerating local training processes.

4.7   Encryption-Based Methods

Encryption-based methods apply *Homomorphic Encryption (HE)* and/or *Secure Multi-party Computation (SMC)* to the model updates to combat privacy-related attacks, inference, and MitM attacks. Further, they can be combined with a perturbation-based method (i.e., DP) for more robustness.

Homomorphic Encryption enables data to be processed without decryption, and the outcome of a homomorphic operation after decryption is equivalent to the operation on plain data. Since only encrypted parameters are communicated, and the server only views and computes over the encrypted parameters, it thus can protect the data from inference attacks by a compromised server or eavesdroppers [12].

However, its effectiveness comes at a substantial amount of computational, communicational, and memory overhead hampering its applicability [32]. Zhang et al. [56] thus proposed BatchCrypt that sped up training time while reducing communication overhead by encoding the gradients into long integers in a batch followed by gradient-wise aggregation.

Secure Multi-party Computation is a cryptographic protocol that distributes a computation process across multiple parties, with no single party having access to the data of the others. For instance, an encryption key may be divided into shares so that no individual possesses all the components needed to reassemble the key completely. SMC is a preferred approach because it is 1000 times faster than HE [26]. Hao et al. [20] and Truex et al. [49] integrate SMC and Gaussian-based DP to mitigate privacy threats launched by multiple colluding clients, balancing performance and privacy guarantee trade-offs by injecting a reduced amount of perturbation with the aid of SMC.

Applying SMC to FL, on the other hand, generally demands all parties to produce and exchange secret shares with all other parties. This procedure inevitably introduces a substantial communication overhead, exponentially growing with the number of participants [26].

4.8 Federated Distillation

Federated Distillation (FD) [23] is a variant of the model compression techniques [40] to effectively handle communication bottlenecks and heterogeneity and to combat inference attacks. FD refers to transferring knowledge from a large and fully trained teacher model to another small student model without losing validity. Sharing knowledge instead of model weights saves communication and computational costs in resource-restricted local devices as well as protects the model information from being interpreted for inference attacks [40,53]. Zhang et al. [57] built an auxiliary generator in a server to fine-tune the model aggregation procedure. Exploiting its powerful processing capability, the server safely explores knowledge in local models and adapts them to global models.

5   Future Research Direction

Despite the intensive studies on FL, there still exists room for improvement. In this section, we suggest future research direction that needs more attention.

Standardization. Multiple institutions across the globe use different languages, and each institution has its own convention to format data instances. It means that local models are trained on differently formatted data instances, thus might incurring unnecessary deviation. Hence, the local models should go through a proper preprocessing step to standardize different types and contents of data.

Various Type of Data. Data are often not limited to a single type; for example, EHR contains texts, images, or tables. Numerous papers are, however, limited in that they have tested their methods on simple image datasets, such as the variety of MNISTs or CIFAR-10. Thus, their superiority might not stand out on text or a combination of multi-types of datasets. Moreover, most papers on backdoor attacks had been only simulated on image classification tasks. More experiments with various types of datasets are needed for more practicality.

Incentive Mechanism. A sufficient incentive mechanism is needed as well. Large institutions are highly likely to have enough data (in terms of quality and quantity) to build a model that makes predictions with reasonable confidence. If the coordination deteriorates performance, security, or privacy, they have no reason to participate and contribute, consuming their resources or risking privacy. A robust data quality verification could be a possible solution for encouragement. By ensuring that variable data produces a more generalizable and performance-enhanced global model, they may be willing to join.

Balancing Trade-off. Although multiple efforts have tried to prevent sudden client dropout, privacy is not well-preserved at the moment. For example, a server inquires about clients' geolocation to form a homogeneous group for client selection to deal with system heterogeneity [1]. Nishio et al. [43] limit their global model to a simple DNN structure at the cost of accuracy. More research should be conducted to find a harmonious balance between privacy and performance in applying FL to real-world practice.

United and Non-orthogonal Defense Techniques. All defensive methods are not mutually exclusive; a single defense technique can thwart multiple attacks. Nevertheless, existing countermeasures are mostly studied separately and orthogonal [59]. For example, some encryption-based methods come at a high communication cost, causing communication bottlenecks, and perturbation-based methods sacrifice performance. Defense objectives should be congratulated for more practicality.

6 Conclusion

Federated Learning has been suggested as a new paradigm for utilizing AI techniques in data-sensitive industries. To train a comparable AI model thus far, data have been collected centrally, putting privacy at risk and incurring substantial communication costs. Such data collection, however, is no longer possible due to stringent regulations. FL comes with the benefit of creating well-performing ML/DL models without data disclosure or collection as if being trained on extensive data. It did, however, enlarge attack surfaces and introduce new vulnerabilities. Immense research works have been conducted to mitigate the vulnerabilities, yet open challenges still exist prohibiting its practical application. We expect that with this survey on vulnerabilities, attacks, and defense, researchers would pay greater attention to the unmet needs.

Acknowledgement. This research was supported by Healthcare AI Convergence Research & Development Program through the National IT Industry Promotion Agency of Korea (NIPA) funded by Ministry of Science and ICT (No. S1601-20-1041).

References

1. AbdulRahman, S., Tout, H., Mourad, A., Talhi, C.: FedMCCS: multicriteria client selection model for optimal IoT federated learning. IEEE Internet Things J. **8**(6), 4723–4735 (2020)
2. Awan, S., Luo, B., Li, F.: CONTRA: defending against poisoning attacks in federated learning. In: Bertino, E., Shulman, H., Waidner, M. (eds.) ESORICS 2021. LNCS, vol. 12972, pp. 455–475. Springer, Cham (2021). https://doi.org/10.1007/978-3-030-88418-5_22
3. Bagdasaryan, E., Veit, A., Hua, Y., Estrin, D., Shmatikov, V.: How to backdoor federated learning. In: International Conference on Artificial Intelligence and Statistics, pp. 2938–2948. PMLR (2020)
4. Baruch, G., Baruch, M., Goldberg, Y.: A little is enough: circumventing defenses for distributed learning. In: Advances in Neural Information Processing Systems, vol. 32 (2019)
5. Benmalek, M., Benrekia, M.A., Challal, Y.: Security of federated learning: attacks, defensive mechanisms, and challenges. Revue des Sciences et Technologies de l'Information-Série RIA: Revue d'Intelligence Artificielle **36**(1), 49–59 (2022)
6. Bhagoji, A.N., Chakraborty, S., Mittal, P., Calo, S.: Analyzing federated learning through an adversarial lens. In: International Conference on Machine Learning, pp. 634–643. PMLR (2019)
7. Bhushan, B., Sahoo, G., Rai, A.K.: Man-in-the-middle attack in wireless and computer networking-a review. In: 2017 3rd International Conference on Advances in Computing, Communication & Automation (ICACCA)(Fall), pp. 1–6. IEEE (2017)
8. Blanchard, P., El Mhamdi, E.M., Guerraoui, R., Stainer, J.: Machine learning with adversaries: byzantine tolerant gradient descent. Adv. Neural Inf. Process. Syst. **30** (2017)
9. Bouacida, N., Mohapatra, P.: Vulnerabilities in federated learning. IEEE Access **9**, 63229–63249 (2021)
10. Cao, X., Fang, M., Liu, J., Gong, N.Z.: Fltrust: byzantine-robust federated learning via trust bootstrapping. arXiv preprint arXiv:2012.13995 (2020)
11. Chen, Z., Tian, P., Liao, W., Yu, W.: Zero knowledge clustering based adversarial mitigation in heterogeneous federated learning. IEEE Trans. Netw. Sci. Eng. **8**(2), 1070–1083 (2020)
12. Fang, H., Qian, Q.: Privacy preserving machine learning with homomorphic encryption and federated learning. Future Internet **13**(4), 94 (2021)
13. Fang, M., Cao, X., Jia, J., Gong, N.: Local model poisoning attacks to {Byzantine-Robust} federated learning. In: 29th USENIX Security Symposium (USENIX Security 20), pp. 1605–1622 (2020)
14. Fraboni, Y., Vidal, R., Lorenzi, M.: Free-rider attacks on model aggregation in federated learning. In: International Conference on Artificial Intelligence and Statistics, pp. 1846–1854. PMLR (2021)
15. Fredrikson, M., Jha, S., Ristenpart, T.: Model inversion attacks that exploit confidence information and basic countermeasures. In: Proceedings of the 22nd ACM SIGSAC Conference on Computer and Communications security, pp. 1322–1333 (2015)
16. Fung, C., Yoon, C.J., Beschastnikh, I.: The limitations of federated learning in sybil settings. In: 23rd International Symposium on Research in Attacks, Intrusions and Defenses (RAID 2020), pp. 301–316 (2020)

17. Geiping, J., Bauermeister, H., Dröge, H., Moeller, M.: Inverting gradients-how easy is it to break privacy in federated learning? Adv. Neural Inf. Process. Syst. **33**, 16937–16947 (2020)
18. Guerraoui, R., Rouault, S., et al.: The hidden vulnerability of distributed learning in byzantium. In: International Conference on Machine Learning, pp. 3521–3530. PMLR (2018)
19. Haddadpour, F., Kamani, M.M., Mokhtari, A., Mahdavi, M.: Federated learning with compression: unified analysis and sharp guarantees. In: International Conference on Artificial Intelligence and Statistics, pp. 2350–2358. PMLR (2021)
20. Hao, M., Li, H., Luo, X., Xu, G., Yang, H., Liu, S.: Efficient and privacy-enhanced federated learning for industrial artificial intelligence. IEEE Trans. Ind. Inf. **16**(10), 6532–6542 (2019)
21. Ho, S., Qu, Y., Gu, B., Gao, L., Li, J., Xiang, Y.: DP-GAN: differentially private consecutive data publishing using generative adversarial nets. J. Netw. Comput. Appl. **185**, 103066 (2021)
22. Huang, W., Li, T., Wang, D., Du, S., Zhang, J.: Fairness and accuracy in federated learning. arXiv preprint arXiv:2012.10069 (2020)
23. Jeong, E., Oh, S., Kim, H., Park, J., Bennis, M., Kim, S.L.: Communication-efficient on-device machine learning: Federated distillation and augmentation under non-iid private data. arXiv preprint arXiv:1811.11479 (2018)
24. Jiang, Y., et al.: Model pruning enables efficient federated learning on edge devices. IEEE Trans. Neural Netw. Learn. Syst. (2022)
25. Journal, H.: December 2021 healthcare data breach report, June 2022. https://www.hipaajournal.com/december-2021-healthcare-data-breach-report/
26. Kanagavelu, R., et al.: Two-phase multi-party computation enabled privacy-preserving federated learning. In: 2020 20th IEEE/ACM International Symposium on Cluster, Cloud and Internet Computing (CCGRID), pp. 410–419. IEEE (2020)
27. Khosravy, M., Nakamura, K., Hirose, Y., Nitta, N., Babaguchi, N.: Model inversion attack by integration of deep generative models: Privacy-sensitive face generation from a face recognition system. IEEE Trans. Inf. Forensics Secur. **17**, 357–372 (2022). https://doi.org/10.1109/TIFS.2022.3140687
28. Konečnỳ, J., McMahan, H.B., Yu, F.X., Richtárik, P., Suresh, A.T., Bacon, D.: Federated learning: Strategies for improving communication efficiency. arXiv preprint arXiv:1610.05492 (2016)
29. Li, W., Xia, Y., Lu, L., Chen, H., Zang, B.: Teev: virtualizing trusted execution environments on mobile platforms. In: Proceedings of the 15th ACM SIGPLAN/SIGOPS International Conference on Virtual Execution Environments, pp. 2–16 (2019)
30. Lin, J., Du, M., Liu, J.: Free-riders in federated learning: attacks and defenses. arXiv preprint arXiv:1911.12560 (2019)
31. Lu, Y., Fan, L.: An efficient and robust aggregation algorithm for learning federated CNN. In: Proceedings of the 2020 3rd International Conference on Signal Processing and Machine Learning, pp. 1–7 (2020)
32. Lyu, L., et al.: Privacy and robustness in federated learning: attacks and defenses. arXiv preprint arXiv:2012.06337 (2020)
33. Lyu, L., Yu, H., Yang, Q.: Threats to federated learning: a survey. arXiv preprint arXiv:2003.02133 (2020)
34. Ma, Y., Zhu, X., Hsu, J.: Data poisoning against differentially-private learners: attacks and defenses. arXiv preprint arXiv:1903.09860 (2019)
35. Mallik, A.: Man-in-the-middle-attack: understanding in simple words. Cyberspace: Jurnal Pendidikan Teknologi Informasi **2**(2), 109–134 (2019)

36. Melis, L., Song, C., De Cristofaro, E., Shmatikov, V.: Exploiting unintended feature leakage in collaborative learning. In: 2019 IEEE Symposium on Security and Privacy (SP), pp. 691–706. IEEE (2019)
37. Miao, L., Yang, W., Hu, R., Li, L., Huang, L.: Against backdoor attacks in federated learning with differential privacy. In: ICASSP 2022–2022 IEEE International Conference on Acoustics, Speech and Signal Processing (ICASSP), pp. 2999–3003. IEEE (2022)
38. Mo, F., Haddadi, H.: Efficient and private federated learning using tee. In: Proceedings of EuroSys Conference on, Dresden, Germany (2019)
39. Mo, F., Haddadi, H., Katevas, K., Marin, E., Perino, D., Kourtellis, N.: PPFL: privacy-preserving federated learning with trusted execution environments. In: Proceedings of the 19th Annual International Conference on Mobile Systems, Applications, and Services, pp. 94–108 (2021)
40. Mothukuri, V., Parizi, R.M., Pouriyeh, S., Huang, Y., Dehghantanha, A., Srivastava, G.: A survey on security and privacy of federated learning. Future Gener. Comput. Syst. **115**, 619–640 (2021)
41. Nasr, M., Shokri, R., Houmansadr, A.: Comprehensive privacy analysis of deep learning: passive and active white-box inference attacks against centralized and federated learning. In: 2019 IEEE Symposium on Security and Privacy (SP), pp. 739–753. IEEE (2019)
42. Nguyen, T.D., et al.: Flame: taming backdoors in federated learning. Cryptology ePrint Archive (2021)
43. Nishio, T., Yonetani, R.: Client selection for federated learning with heterogeneous resources in mobile edge. In: ICC 2019–2019 IEEE International Conference on Communications (ICC), pp. 1–7. IEEE (2019)
44. Pan, X., Zhang, M., Ji, S., Yang, M.: Privacy risks of general-purpose language models. In: 2020 IEEE Symposium on Security and Privacy (SP), pp. 1314–1331. IEEE (2020)
45. Parisot, M.P.M., Pejo, B., Spagnuelo, D.: Property inference attacks on convolutional neural networks: influence and implications of target model's complexity. CoRR abs/2104.13061 (2021). https://arxiv.org/abs/2104.13061
46. Shejwalkar, V., Houmansadr, A.: Manipulating the byzantine: optimizing model poisoning attacks and defenses for federated learning. In: NDSS (2021)
47. Shokri, R., Stronati, M., Song, C., Shmatikov, V.: Membership inference attacks against machine learning models. In: 2017 IEEE Symposium on Security and Privacy (SP), pp. 3–18 (2017). https://doi.org/10.1109/SP.2017.41
48. Sun, Z., Kairouz, P., Suresh, A.T., McMahan, H.B.: Can you really backdoor federated learning? arXiv preprint arXiv:1911.07963 (2019)
49. Truex, S., et al.: A hybrid approach to privacy-preserving federated learning. In: Proceedings of the 12th ACM Workshop on Artificial Intelligence and Security, pp. 1–11 (2019)
50. Wang, H., et al.: Attack of the tails: yes, you really can backdoor federated learning. Adv. Neural Inf. Process. Syst. **33**, 16070–16084 (2020)
51. Wang, N., Xiao, Y., Chen, Y., Hu, Y., Lou, W., Hou, Y.T.: Flare: defending federated learning against model poisoning attacks via latent space representations. In: Proceedings of the 2022 ACM on Asia Conference on Computer and Communications Security, pp. 946–958 (2022)
52. Wu, C., Yang, X., Zhu, S., Mitra, P.: Mitigating backdoor attacks in federated learning. arXiv preprint arXiv:2011.01767 (2020)
53. Wu, C., Wu, F., Lyu, L., Huang, Y., Xie, X.: Communication-efficient federated learning via knowledge distillation. Nature Commun. **13**(1), 1–8 (2022)

54. Xie, C., Huang, K., Chen, P.Y., Li, B.: Dba: Distributed backdoor attacks against federated learning. In: International Conference on Learning Representations (2019)
55. Yin, D., Chen, Y., Kannan, R., Bartlett, P.: Byzantine-robust distributed learning: towards optimal statistical rates. In: International Conference on Machine Learning, pp. 5650–5659. PMLR (2018)
56. Zhang, C., Li, S., Xia, J., Wang, W., Yan, F., Liu, Y.: {BatchCrypt}: Efficient homomorphic encryption for {Cross-Silo} federated learning. In: 2020 USENIX Annual Technical Conference (USENIX ATC 20), pp. 493–506 (2020)
57. Zhang, L., Shen, L., Ding, L., Tao, D., Duan, L.Y.: Fine-tuning global model via data-free knowledge distillation for non-iid federated learning. In: Proceedings of the IEEE/CVF Conference on Computer Vision and Pattern Recognition, pp. 10174–10183 (2022)
58. Zhang, Y., Jia, R., Pei, H., Wang, W., Li, B., Song, D.: The secret revealer: generative model-inversion attacks against deep neural networks. In: Proceedings of the IEEE/CVF Conference on Computer Vision and Pattern Recognition, pp. 253–261 (2020)
59. Zhou, Z., Xu, C., Wang, M., Ma, T., Yu, S.: Augmented dual-shuffle-based moving target defense to ensure CIA-triad in federated learning. In: 2021 IEEE Global Communications Conference (GLOBECOM), pp. 01–06. IEEE (2021)

pPATE: A Pragmatic Private Aggregation of Teacher Ensembles Framework by Sparse Vector Technique Based Differential Privacy, Paillier Cryptosystem and Human-in-the-loop

Phat T. Tran-Truong[1,2] and Tran Khanh Dang[1(✉)]

[1] Ho Chi Minh City University of Food Industry, Ho Chi Minh City, Vietnam
{phatttt,khanh}@hufi.edu.vn
[2] HCMC University of Technology, VNU-HCM, Ho Chi Minh City, Vietnam

Abstract. With advances of deep learning models, Artificial Intelligence (AI) has been applied into various fields to aid human. Some domains where sensitive data with privacy concerns are pivotal, for example medical care, are no exception. Dealing with that, a private learning framework satisfying differential privacy - a gold standard to protect privacy, namely Private Aggregation of Teacher Ensembles (PATE) has gained popularity. However, this framework needs to train a large number of models in disjoint private training datasets, thereby in plethora of cases, it can not be leveraged. In this paper, we propose pPATE - a pragmatical framework that is based on PATE but it uses a sparse vector technique to achieve differential privacy and demonstrate that with small manual efforts of human (expert) in the development loop, our solution can train privacy-preserving models that have approximate accuracy as ground-truth models. Moreover, we extend PATE framework pragmatically in a distributed setting so that it not only aggregates privately but also secures confidentiality and privacy when multi-parties collaborate.

Keywords: PATE · Data privacy · Trustworthy AI · Privacy in deep learning · Sparse vector technique

1 Introduction

Thanks to the development of hardware and big data technologies, deep learning models that are based on neural networks in turn surpass previous machine learning methods in various fields. AI applications are now ubiquitous. Some fields dealing with personal data like medical treatment, finance, face recognition, have also integrated AI into processes. However, models are trained to learn sensitive data without "privacy by design", can be the sources of data breaches [1,2]. In addition, with the General Data Protection Regulation (GDPR) [3]

© The Author(s), under exclusive license to Springer Nature Singapore Pte Ltd. 2022
T. K. Dang et al. (Eds.): FDSE 2022, CCIS 1688, pp. 332–346, 2022.
https://doi.org/10.1007/978-981-19-8069-5_22

coming into force, it is crucial to develop privacy-preserving learning methods by which AI technologies can overcome privacy-related concerns for mass adoption.

Since the invention of differential privacy, there have plenty of directions which attempt to make learning algorithms differentially private in both theory and practice. However, in the context of deep learning, many former works fail due to non-convexity optimization, stochasticity of learning and huge number of steps of iterations that jeopardize privacy parameters. Recently, there are two popular approaches that are widely utilized for training privacy-preserving deep learning models based on differential privacy [2]: differential private stochastic gradient descent (DP-SGD) [5] and PATE framework [6]. While DP-SGD is tailored for deep learning models in which stochastic gradient descent is mainly utilized, PATE uses teacher-student architecture [7] to distill knowledge from ensembles of sensitive teacher models to a privacy-preserving student model. Comparing to DP-SGD, PATE framework has some advantages:

- Model-agnostic: because of training each teacher model on disjoint training datasets, so theoretically we can train each shard of training dataset with different learning models, both deep learning models and traditional machine learning models;
- Model-extension capability: using model ensembles that make this framework to be trained distributed easily, for examples, an idea extending PATE that multi-organizations can collaborate to train was proposed in [8];
- Model-training method: using semi-supervised learning based approaches, for detail, needs a small set of labelled private data to train each teachers and a large amount of unlabelled data to query teacher ensembles for making privacy-preserving pseudo-labels for training student (also called Query-By-Committee (QBC)). This not only protects privacy but also saves human labor cost for label annotation and helps to learn with not enough data;

However, the original PATE [6] degrades accuracy because it incurs epistemic uncertainty by taking advantages of a large numbers of teachers' votes (set of {50, 100, 250} independent models in the authors' experiments) agreeing on a label. As the result, each teacher model usually has a low quality due to limited or unrepresented datasets. This is also not suitable for personal resources or even small and medium sized companies/organizations. Moreover, PATE framework uses a large number of unlabelled data but each piece of data consumes an amount of privacy cost. As soon, privacy budget is exhausted. This makes original PATE unables to adapt to more scalable deep learning tasks with massive datasets. We realize that by applying another differentially private mechanism such as sparse vector technique combining with small efforts of human (also called human-in-the-loop) can outcome student models that achieve approximate accuracy as ground-truth model with a fixed privacy cost.

In distributed setting, PATE framework seems to be a promising solution, beside federated learning [9] - a learning framework designed for distributed and collaborated learning. Although, firstly federated learning is not designed with privacy preservation in mind, there are accelerating works for characterizing the private learning federated setting [9]. On the other hand, PATE framework is designed for learning with privacy concerns and is simpler than federated learning due to collaborate with only data's labels instead of numerous weight or gradient round communications.

In fact, when extending PATE framework for distributed applications, there have not only the privacy-related problems in aggregated results but also privacy and security concerns in communication and computation since multi-parities join hand distrustly. First and foremost, each party who train their own model on their private dataset do not releases their plain predictions for other parties in collaboration. Besides, they also do not want to leak privacy via their predictions. Finally, the aggregating party who is responsible for aggregating results from multi-forces could inspect the results for inferring more information. This is a honest-but-curious (semi-honest) party. By leveraging Paillier crytosystem scheme, we provide a pragmatic solution in this attack model.

The main contributions of this paper are summarized as follows:

- Firstly, we propose a pragmatic learning framework by which it can outcome privacy-preserving deep learning models that have approximate accuracy as ground-truth models by attendance of experts for directing models' prediction expectations.
- Secondly, by leveraging the another techniques, namely sparse vector technique, our proposed learning framework has an acceptable and fixed privacy budget that can answer super larger numbers of prediction requests.
- Thirdly, we explore PATE framework in distributed learning applications. Our solution that is based on Paillier crytosystem scheme can be applied pragmatically for multi-party learning and is error-prone with a honest-but-curious parties.

The rest of the paper is organized as follows: in Sect. 2, we will explain some backgrounds used in our proposed solutions including: differential privacy, PATE framework, techniques for incorporating human-machine (human-in-the-loop) and Paillier cryptosystem scheme. After that, we will display our proposed solution in Sect. 3. Then, we will review some related works that pinned research directions in Sect. 4 and draw conclusions in Sect. 5.

2   Preliminary

2.1   Differential Privacy

Differential Privacy [10] is a standard for data privacy guarantee built on a solid mathematical foundation that ensures that the presence or absence of a data point will not affect "too much" the outcome of an algorithm, a model, or a data mining process.

Formally, a randomized mechanism M satisfies ϵ-differential privacy if for two adjacent datasets D, D' (differ by a single data point) with any output set $S \subseteq R$ (result domain). We have

$$ln(\frac{P[M(D) \in S]}{P[M(D') \in S]}) \leq \epsilon \tag{1}$$

The quantity ϵ in the above formula is also known as the privacy budget. The smaller the privacy budget (meaningfully $\epsilon < 1$), the safer the mechanism M in term of privacy protection.

Technically, process can satisfy differential privacy by randomizing. More broadly, to achieve this criterion we often use noise-adding techniques based on a statistical distribution, although we can use other ways to generate randomness, such as sampling. One of the noise distributions that is commonly used in differential privacy is Laplace distribution. We can add noise using the Laplace mechanism as follows:

$$M(D) = f(D) + Lap(\frac{\Delta f}{\epsilon}). \tag{2}$$

In [10], it was proved that this noise-adding mechanism satisfies the criterion of ϵ-differential privacy where $f(D)$ is the output of a computation, Δf is the sensitivity function - the largest distance between two results of a computation on two adjacent datasets:

$$\Delta f = max_{D,D'}||f(D) - f(D')||_1. \tag{3}$$

Differential privacy has become a "de facto" privacy protection standard due to be able to protect privacy a variety of problems such as: privacy of a model, a process, collected data, the results of a model, etc. In addition, an another reason for which makes differential privacy extremely effective in both analysis and application is its composability shown by composition theorem:

Theorem 1 (Sequential composition theorem). *Suppose a set of privacy mechanisms $M = \{M_1, M_2, ..., M_n\}$ are executed sequentially on a dataset, each M_i guarantees ϵ_i-differential privacy then M will satisfy $(\sum_{i=1}^{n} \epsilon_i)$-differential privacy.*

Thanks to the sequential composition theorem, the implementation of privacy protection that satisfies ϵ-differential privacy in both practice and analysis as follows: decomposing an algorithm or a process into smaller steps. Then, adding adaptive noises for bounding each step to satisfy ϵ_i-differential privacy. The whole process will be differentially private with a privacy budget equal to the sum of ϵ_i. And:

Another property that is mathematically guaranteed by differential privacy is that it remains private despite post-processing: if mechanism M satisfies ϵ-differential privacy, then after series of operations $F = F_n(F_{n-1}(...(F_2(F_1)))$ (random or deterministic), $F(M(D))$ still ensures ϵ-differential privacy.

While ϵ-differential privacy is a good criterion, it is so tight to apply other mechanism than Laplace mechanism. One of the ways to relax ϵ-differential privacy is to allow this standard to fail with a small probability. That is (ϵ, δ)-differential privacy: a randomized mechanism M satisfying (ϵ, δ)-differential privacy if for two adjacent datasets D, D' with any output set $S \subseteq R$ (result domain). We have:

$$P[M(D) \in S] \leq e^{\epsilon} * P[M(D') \in S] + \delta \tag{4}$$

Therefore it can be considered that this criterion guarantees ϵ-differential privacy with probability $1 - \delta$ with δ very small, namely $\delta << \frac{1}{N}$, where N is the number of points in the training set because otherwise it is possible to expose $\delta * N \geq 1$ data points.

When using the (ϵ, δ)-differential privacy criterion, we can use the Gaussian noise addition mechanism:

$$M(D) = f(D) + \mathcal{N}(0, \Delta f^2 \delta^2). \tag{5}$$

In [10], it was proven that if $\epsilon < 1$ and $\sigma > f_2 \sqrt{2ln(1.25/\delta)}/\epsilon$ then $M(D)$ satisfies (ϵ, δ)-differential privacy. Unlike the Laplace mechanism, which can only use the sensitivity function L_1, the Gaussian mechanism can use both L_1 and L_2 - Euclidean distance. Beside the composition theorem $((\epsilon, \delta)$-differential privacy satisfies $(\sum_{i=1}^{n} \epsilon_i, \sum_{i=1}^{n} \delta_i)$-differential privacy), the another reason for the popularity of (ϵ, δ)-differential privacy and the Gaussian mechanism is the advanced composition theorem:

Theorem 2 (Advanced composition theorem). *Suppose k-fold mechanism which each satisfies (ϵ, δ)-differentially private mechanism then for any $\epsilon, \delta, \delta' > 0$, it satisfies $(2\epsilon\sqrt{2kln(1/\delta')}, k\delta + \delta')$-differential privacy.*

By using advanced composition theorem for an iterative process with k-times, privacy budget ϵ degrades with $\tilde{O}(\sqrt{k})$ instead of $O(k)$ by standard composition theorem. In [5], the authors devise a method called moment accountant, that is even tighter than advanced composition theorem that eliminate factor $ln(1/\delta)$ on ϵ (ϵ degrades by $O(\sqrt{k})$) and remain the same on δ by using numerical analysis at each step of bounding. For detail, the authors use the moment generator function (MGF) to limit privacy loss. The privacy loss at an $o \in R$ output is defined:

$$c(o; M, aux, D, D') = ln \frac{P[M(aux, D) = o]}{P[M(aux, D') = o]}. \tag{6}$$

In which, D, D' are two adjacent data sets; aux is the input's extra information, M is the privacy protection mechanism. Then the function of generating moment at order λ:

$$\alpha_M(\lambda; aux, D, D') = log E_{o \sim M(aux, D)}[e^{\lambda c(o; M, aux, D, D')}]. \tag{7}$$

We need to limit this moment

$$\alpha_M(\lambda) = max_{aux, D, D'} \alpha_M(\lambda; aux, D, D'). \tag{8}$$

In [5], The author proved two theorems of this moment expression:

Theorem 3 (Composability). *Suppose that a mechanism M consists of a sequence of adaptive mechanisms $M_1, ..., M_k$ where $M_i : \prod_{j=1}^{i-1} R_j \times D \to R_i$. Then, for any output sequence $o_1, ..., o_{k-1}$ and any λ*

$$\alpha_M(\lambda; d, d') = \sum_{i=1}^{k} \alpha_{M_i}(\lambda; o_1, ...o_{i-1}, d, d') \tag{9}$$

where α_M is conditioned on M_i's output being o_i for $i < k$.

Theorem 4 (Tail bound). *For any $\epsilon > 0$, the mechanism M is (ϵ, δ)-differentially private for*

$$\delta = min_\lambda e^{\alpha_M(\lambda) - \lambda\epsilon}. \tag{10}$$

Moment accountant method keeps track of cumulative MGF after each step by Theorem 3 and uses Theorem 4 to search optimal each privacy budget for the next step.

2.2 Private Aggregation of Teacher Ensembles (PATE)

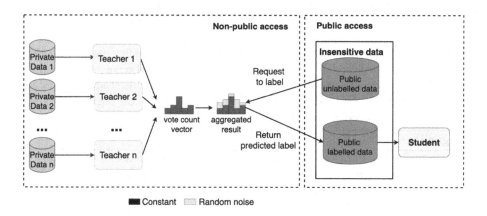

Fig. 1. PATE framework

PATE (Fig. 1) achieves differential privacy by following subsample-and-aggregate fashion [12]. The private dataset is divided by k-fold for some disjoint private computations on each fold then all results are aggregated via an differential private mechanism. Intuitively, by limiting affect of a single sensitive data in the results of only one teacher rather than the whole dataset (assuming that there are no duplication or not too much duplications in the datasets), this makes each sensitive data likely to blend in the crowd of each teacher's dataset, thereby it is more private. In more technical aspect, by some aggregation mechanisms like Report Noisy Arg-Max to find max value of noisy label count aggregation of teacher's ensemble and dataset have not got too much sensitive data, we can usually get "privacy for free" with no additional privacy cost.

In vanila PATE [6], aggregating results from k results from k teacher models will count and add noise according to Laplace mechanism to satisfy ϵ-differential privacy, then get the maximum value, this mechanism is called LNMax Aggregator (Algorithm 1). In improved version [11] instead of using Laplace mechanism, the authors use Gaussian mechanism. This mechanism is called GNMax Aggregator: $argmax_i(\sum_{n=1}^{k} \hat{h}_n(x_j) + \mathcal{N}(0, \sigma^2))$. Moreover, the authors also observe that the aggregated results of teachers' ensemble seem more accurate when they strongly agree on a label with its vote result is higher than a threshold. So they add a condition that maximum value of all label counts should be higher than a large threshold comparing to k teachers (e.g. $> 0.6k$) before aggregation by reporting Noisy Arg-Max mechanism. The authors name this mechanism confident-GNMax Aggregator. This observation bears resemblance to a special technique, namely sparse vector technique in differential privacy theory.

Finally, the aggregation mechanism of k teacher models can not used in practice since the noise-addition mechanism allows only a limited number of queries and the model parameters are not protected, e.g. such as DP-SGD, the model parameters are sanitized. Therefore, the authors have proposed to train the student model from distilling knowledge of these teacher models. To train the student model, a large amount of unlabeled (non-sensitive) public data is needed. These data are fed into k teacher models to create pseudo-labels. And the privacy loss will be accounted according to moment accountant method. After being labeled, this data will be used to train the student model. So the ensemble of teacher models are only used for limited number of m unlabelled public data despite of a large number of them. Note that this student model is not trained with sensitive data. The end user or attacker can only access this student model for prediction (Fig. 1).

Algorithm 1: Vanila PATE (2017) [6]

Input: Private dataset D_T with n data point, public dataset D_S with m data point $\{x_1, x_2, ..., x_m\}$, set of k teacher models $\{\hat{h}_1, \hat{h}_2, ..., \hat{h}_k\}$ are trained on disjoint private dataset
$$D_T = D_{T_1} \cup D_{T_2} \cup, ..., \cup D_{T_k}, \text{ privacy parameter } \lambda > 0$$
$\tilde{D}_S \leftarrow \emptyset.$
for $x_j \in D_s$ **do**
  Output $\tilde{y}_j \leftarrow argmax_i(\sum_{n=1}^{k} \hat{h}_n(x_j) + Lap(\frac{1}{\lambda}))$.
  $\tilde{D}_S \leftarrow \tilde{D}_S \cup (x_j, \tilde{y}_j)$.
end
Train $\hat{h}_s$ on $\tilde{D}_S$.

2.3   Human-in-the-Loop

Traditionally, machine learning application is assumed that it is developed to automatically aid human with some specific tasks and eliminate fully human intervention. Recently, many researches have been showed that machine learning needs attendance of human, specially experts, to become much better [13]. Firstly, human can help model to maximize accuracy by adding their knowledge bases that need years to gain. Secondly, model could converge faster with assistants of human to select represented data to direct model approach to result expectations. Finally, with human relevant tasks in the development and production loop, training machine learning model becomes more efficient thanks to human perception for leaving useless steps out.

In general, human can help machine learning model by some techniques such as: human annotation, active learning and transfer learning. Human annotation is an combination of both auto and manual labelling in the annotation process to assure precision and accuracy. Active learning are techniques that help to select represented data making learning process faster and more accurate. And transfer learning is a well-known technique to adapt knowledge from pre-trained models of related tasks to make learning process faster and avoid from cold start.

2.4 Paillier Cryptosystem

Paillier cryptosystem [19] is a well-known partial homomorphic encryption scheme based on public key cryptography which preserves operations of addition of two ciphertexts that is $D_{priv}(ADD_{pub}(E_{pub}(m_1), E_{pub}(m_2))) = m_1 + m_2$. The scheme works as following:

Key Generation

1. Choose randomly and independently two large prime numbers p and q such that $\gcd(pq, (p-1)(q-1)) = 1$, where $gcd()$ is a greatest common divisor function.
2. Compute $n = pq$ and $\lambda = lcm(p-1, q-1)$, where $lcm()$ is a least common multiple function.
3. Select random integer g where $g \in \mathbb{Z}^*_{n^2}$ ($g \in [1, n^2]$).
4. Calculate the modular multiplicative inverse: $\mu = (L(g^\lambda \bmod n^2))^{-1} \bmod n$, where function L is defined as $L(x) = \frac{x-1}{n}$. If μ does not exist start step 1 again.

– The public key is (n, g).
– The private key is (λ, μ).

Encrytion
  Let m ($0 \le m < n$) be the plaintext to be encrypted:

1. Select random r where $0 < r < n$.
2. Compute ciphertext as: $c = g^m \cdot r^n \bmod n^2$.

Decryption
  Let c ($c \in \mathbb{Z}^*_{n^2}$) be the ciphertext to decrypt:

1. Compute the plaintext message as: $m = L(c^\lambda \bmod n^2) \cdot \mu \bmod n$.

3 The Proposed Approach

3.1 Sparse Vector Technique Based Aggregation

Intuitively, in PATE, student model's quality is depend on aggregation results of ensemble of teacher models. However, vanilla PATE seems so hard to control teacher models' quality for the reasons that need a large number of teacher models to bargain cumulative privacy loss. In [6], the authors bound MGF at each request for predicting for Algorithm 1 setup:

Theorem 5. *Suppose that on neighboring databases D, D', the label counts n_j differ by at most 1 in each coordinate. Let M be the mechanism that reports $argmax_j\{n_j + lap(\frac{1}{\gamma})\}$. Then M satisfies $(2\gamma, 0)$-differential privacy. Moreover, for any λ, aux, D and D':*

$$\alpha(\lambda; aux, D, D') \leq 2\gamma^2\lambda(\lambda + 1). \tag{11}$$

Proof (Proof (from [6, Theorem 2])).

By Theorem 5, with each prediction consumes 2γ privacy loss, we can account the cumulative privacy loss according to advanced composition theorem. When the cumulative privacy loss exceeds a threshold (theoretically 1, however in practise, it is accepted < 10 now) deep learning models become meaningless about privacy preservation. If we want to minimize MGF of privacy loss, we should calibrate noise with γ as small as possible (corresponding $lap(\frac{1}{\gamma})$ is large). However, this requires k - number of teachers is large so that it does not make noisy argmax - $argmax_j\{n_j + lap(\frac{1}{\gamma})\}$ change label after calibrating noise.

Sparse vector technique [10] is a special differential private technique that instead of achieving differential privacy by calibrating noise according to (advanced) composition theorem, it adds noise to results and report only noisy values exceeds the public given threshold. Sparse vector technique is suitable for differential private process that answers a large number of queries and privacy degrades only when small number of sensitive queries occur, specified by parameter cutoff T. Sparse vector technique based differential private process will answer as many as possible numbers of "above threshold" queries, and output $\perp$ when is asked "below threshold" queries. When number of sensitive queries that are below threshold exceed T, differential private process will halt.

Algorithm 2: Sparse Vector Technique [10]

Input : Dataset D, query set $Q = \{q_1, ..., q_m\}$, privacy parameters $\epsilon, \delta > 0$, unstable query cutoff T, threshold ω

$c \leftarrow 0, \lambda \leftarrow \sqrt{32Tlog(\frac{1}{\delta})}/\epsilon, \hat{\omega} \leftarrow \omega + Lap(\lambda)$.

for $q \in Q$ *and* $c \leq T$ **do**

    $\hat{q} \leftarrow q + Lap(2\lambda)$.

    if $\hat{q} > \hat{\omega}$ **then**

        | Output $\top$.

    else

        | $c \leftarrow c + 1$.

        | Output $\perp$.

    end

end

So by leveraging sparse vector technique (Algorithm 2), it is suitable for deep learning models to predict large a number of public unlabelled data. Besides, we only needs to train a small number of teacher models to according to sparse vector technique as long as the noisy vote $\hat{q}$ is above the threshold. We usually pay no privacy cost for stable queries and only pay for small number of abnormally unstable queries Fig. 2. In [14], the authors have proposed a model-agnostic differentially private learning mechanism based on sparse vector technique Algorithm 3. So we leverage that work for initializing PATE.

Algorithm 3: Sparse Vector Technique based initialization for ensembles of teacher models in PATE [14]

Input: Private dataset D_T, public dataset $D_S = \{x_1, x_2, ..., x_m\}$, query
set $Q = \{q_1, ..., q_m\}$, cutoff T, privacy parameters $\epsilon, \delta > 0$, failure probability β

$c \leftarrow 0, \lambda \leftarrow \sqrt{32T log(\frac{1}{\delta})/\epsilon}$
$k \leftarrow 34\sqrt{2}\lambda ln(4mT/min(\delta, \beta/2))$
$\omega \leftarrow 2\lambda ln(2m/\delta), \hat{\omega} \leftarrow \omega + Lap(\lambda)$.
Arbitrarily split D_T into k non-overlapping chunks of size n/k,
$D_T = \{D_{T_1}, D_{T_2}, ..., D_{T_k}\}$.
for $j \in [k]$ **do**
| Train teacher model $\hat{h}_j$ on disjoint private dataset D_{T_j}
end
for $j \in [m]$ and $c \leq T$ **do**
| $\hat{q}(D) \leftarrow argmax_i(\sum_{n=1}^{k} \hat{h}_n(x_j))$.
| $\hat{d} \leftarrow max\{0, \hat{q}(D) - argmax_{i \neq \hat{q}(D)}(\sum_{n=1}^{k} \hat{h}_n(x_j)) - 1\} + Lap(2/\lambda)$.
| **if** $\hat{d} > \hat{\omega}$ **then**
| | Output ⊤.
| **else**
| | $c \leftarrow c + 1$.
| | $\hat{\omega} \leftarrow \omega + Lap(\lambda)$
| | Output ⊥.
| **end**
end

Theorem 6 (Privacy guarantee of Algorithm 3). *Algorithm 3 is (ϵ, δ)-differential private.*

Proof. Overall, Algorithm 3 satisfies sparse vector technique based $(\epsilon, \delta/2)$-differential privacy that outputs sequence m of $\{⊤, ⊥\}$, ⊤ means that our ensembles of teacher models have strongly agreed on either label 1 or 0. If it only outputs ⊥, then we have all same outputs despite of input data, thereby formally it is 0-differential privacy or nothings to leak. When sparse vector technique based private mechanism outputs ⊤, it will check a final output based on distance to instability framework. There are two cases: firstly, distance to instability framework also outputs ⊤, we will pay no privacy cost. In second case, it outputs some ⊥ then each will occur with probability $1 - \frac{\delta}{2m}$. So after at most m queries, the subroutine of releasing based on distance to instability framework will satisfy $(0, \delta/2)$-differential privacy. Thereby by all, Algorithm 3 is a sequential composition of sparse vector technique with $(\epsilon, \delta/2)$-differential privacy and $(0, \delta/2)$-differential privacy. That satisfies (ϵ, δ)-differential privacy.

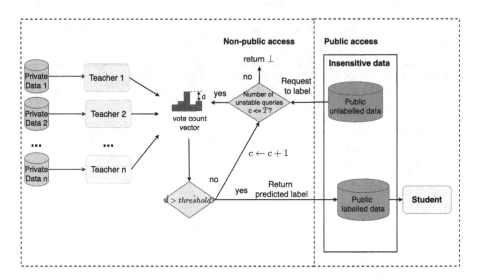

Fig. 2. Sparse vector technique based aggregation of PATE framework

3.2   Improving PATE Framework with Human-in-the-Loop

1) All models (teachers-student) should start with a pre-trained model.

In [14], the authors analyze a model agnostic private learning framework which could be considered as a theoretical aspect of PATE. According to their works, in realizable case, PATE framework can probably approximately correct-learn (PAC-learn) with finite Vapnik-Chervonenkis dimension (VC-dimension). However if we allow PATE learn agnostically, accuracy could not be as same as expectation. Besides, the authors also analyze connection between each teacher ensembles' accuracy and their aggregated results:

Theorem 7. *If* k *binary classifiers* $\{h_1, h_2, ..., h_k\}$ *are guaranteed to make at most* B *mistakes in predicting the* m $\{\tilde{y}_1, \tilde{y}_2, ..., \tilde{y}_m\}$ *labels then*

$$|\{i \in [m] : \sum_{n=1}^{k} \mathbb{1}(h_n(x_i) \neq \tilde{y}_i) > \frac{k}{3}\}| < 3B. \qquad (12)$$

So if we want aggregated results of teacher ensembles would have high probability to be the true label, we should control each teacher's accuracy and their votes so that at least $\frac{2}{3}$ of them agree on a label. Thereby, we propose that all teachers and student should share a pre-trained model which is trained by small number of labelled public data.

2) Human annotation with unstable queries for more accurate teacher ensembles' aggregated results.

Under a sparse vector technique based differential private aggregation mechanism, if the number of unstable queries do not exceed of cutoff value T then it is safe to protect private dataset when publishing model. On the other hand, data which is used for querying teacher ensembles is from the public dataset having no privacy concerns. The auxiliary of public dataset in the problem of learning on private dataset in fact is a relaxation.

Our observation is that unstable queries could be a valuable data that can help model to be more accurate. Unstable queries are queries that teacher ensembles do not strongly agree on a label. In Algorithm 3, when dealing with them, the algorithm chooses to pass (output $\perp$). So with the help of human or expert to decide to what is the true label, as long as the number of unstable queries do not exceed of cutoff value T, we can help the final model to be more accurate and converge toward the actual tasks.

For a realistic case, let imagine there are k hospitals to collaborate to diagnosis patients' disease by building their own models. Independently, there are half of models diagnosis with result A, and the other half is with result B. So there are actually valuable cases that need to record for improving overall model in general and each hospital's model in particular. Human annotation presents in our proposed solution is like the hospital will delegate doctor council (experts) to diagnosis and decide what is the true result.

Algorithm 4: Sparse vector technique based initialization for ensembles of teacher models in PATE with expert annotation

---

Input: Private dataset D_T, public dataset $D_S = \{x_1, x_2, ..., x_m\}$, query
set $Q = \{q_1, ..., q_m\}$, cutoff T, privacy parameters $\epsilon, \delta > 0$, failure
probability β

Initiate Algorithm 3 with D_T, D_S, T, ϵ, δ.

if $j \in [m]$: output x_j of Algorithm 3 is $\perp$ and $c \leq T$ **then**
  $\quad Result \leftarrow askExpert(x_j)$
  $\quad$ Output $Result$.
else
  $\quad$ Output $\top$.
end

3.3 Distributed Deployment with Paillier Cryptosystem

PATE framework shows potentials for applications in distributed setting although it is more challenging. Specially, security and privacy problems relate when there are mutual communications between computing parties. Our proposed solution with attendance of experts to guide the framework can be leveraged for coordination among party separation including: the parties in roles of building each local teacher model, aggregation service and building student for secure communication and computation.

For detail, following Paillier cryptosystem scheme, the expert council will generate pair of (public, private) key. The teacher ensembles take that public key to encrypt their predictions and send encrypted message to aggregation service. The aggregation service will take sum of them. Then the expert council will decrypt the aggregated results by their private key. If the results show a strong consensus of teacher ensembles then they are passed to party who is responsible for building student model, else the expert council will decide which is the true value of this data before passing it to the next stage (Fig. 3).

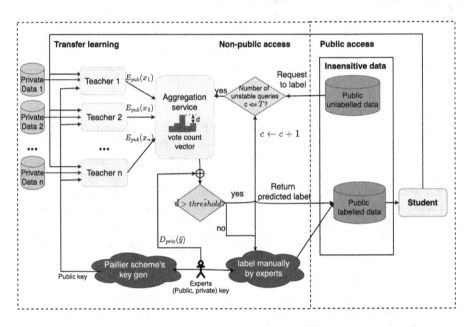

Fig. 3. Our proposal PATE-based framework

4   Related Work

Differential Privacy and Deep Learning. Many works have attempted to integrate differential privacy into deep learning. Notably, in [15] which shows the potentials of combination by achieving acceptable trade-off between accuracy and privacy. However, for the reason that privacy accountant is kept per parameter, this method is not applicable in both theory and practise. DP-SGD [5] reduces significantly limitations of former works, however since it achives differential privacy by noise-adding mechanism to gradient vectors in SGD process, thereby its sensitivity is proportional to model parameters which raises larger privacy loss when model is deeper. Moreover, by gradient clipping technique, DP-SGD also causes information loss and can not achieve high as acurate as non-private model. On the other hands, the proposed moment accountant method in [5] for keeping track of privacy loss random variable has ameliorated drastically the privacy loss tracking method.

Private Aggregation of Teacher Ensembles (PATE). Another promising approach for deep learning models to achieve differential privacy is PATE [6,11]. In [14], the authors have proposed sparse vector technique based differential private aggregation and characterized accuracy guarantee of the model agnostic private learning framework. Besides, the authors also provide theorems in term of sample complexity in both realized and agnostic cases.

In [16], the authors demonstrate how the number of teacher models on disjoint private datasets degrades significantly accuracy and propose transfer learning by training all models (teachers and student) with sharing common layer with public data before fine-tuning with private datasets for each of the teachers. In [17], by using another relaxation of differential privacy, namely, label differential privacy for a definition that instead two datasets are different by one data, this notion is based on that two datasets are different by one label, this method can help to achieve more accurate than vanilla PATE. On an another side, in [8], the authors show the potential of PATE in distributed manner by combining Yao's garbled circuit [18] and PATE for collaborative training.

5 Discussion and Conclusion

In conclusion, we have proposed a solution that could be applicable for learning with privacy preservation by design which is initialized with an acceptable fixed privacy budget and could answer large number of prediction queries. Furthermore, our proposed solution based on PATE framework could be extended to adapt for security and privacy requirements of distributed and collaborated learning framework.

In the next step, we will demonstrate our solution in empirical experiments. Moreover, our up-and-coming works can direct to develop both practical and theoretical aspects of our solution. Firstly, our solution could be analyzed in privacy guarantee for averaging the privacy loss random variables, specially by Rényi differential privacy standard instead of (ϵ, δ)-differential privacy. Secondly, we could implement more complex learning methods to preserve accuracy relationship between teachers-student such as in recent semi-supervised learning and self-supervised learning methods. Thirdly, our proposed solutions could be pragmatically integrated with active learning methods to be more scalable in more complex tasks with massive dataset. Finally, in distributed setting, active attack models with dishonest parties or Byzantine attacks are taken into our considerations.

References

1. Ha, T., Dang, T.K., Le, H., Truong, T.A.: Security and privacy issues in deep learning: a brief review. SN Comput. Sci. **1**(5), 1–15 (2020). https://doi.org/10.1007/s42979-020-00254-4
2. Dang, T.K., Truong, P.T.T., Tran, P.T.: Data poisoning attack on deep neural network and some defense methods. In: International Conference on Advanced Computing and Applications (ACOMP), vol. 2020, pp. 15–22 (2020). https://doi.org/10.1109/ACOMP50827.2020.00010
3. Council of European Union, Council regulation (EU) no 269/2014 (2014). http://eur-lex.europa.eu/legal-content/EN/TXT/?qid=1416170084502&uri=CELEX:32014R026
4. Ha, T., Dang, T.K., Dang, T.T., Truong, T.A., Nguyen, M.T.: Differential privacy in deep learning: an overview. In: International Conference on Advanced Computing and Applications (ACOMP), vol. 2019, pp. 97–102 (2019). https://doi.org/10.1109/ACOMP.2019.00022
5. Abadi, M., et al.: "Deep learning with differential privacy. In: Proceedings of the ACM SIGSAC Conference on Computer and Communications Security (ACM CCS), pp. 308–318 (2016)
6. Papernot, N., Abadi, M., Erlingsson, Ú., Goodfellow, I., Talwar, K.: Semi- supervised knowledge transfer for deep learning from private training data, Oct 2016
7. Hinton, G., Vinyals, O., Dean, J.: Distilling the knowledge in a neural network (2015)
8. Choquette-Choo, C.A.: Capc learning: Confidential and private collaborative learning (2021)
9. Kairouz, P., et al.: Advances and open problems in federated learning. Foundations and Trends®. Mach. Learn. **14**(1-2), 1–210 (2021)
10. Dwork, C., Roth, A.: The algorithmic foundations of differential privacy. Foundations and Trends in Theoretical Computer Science (2014)
11. Papernot, N., Song, S., Mironov, I., Raghunathan, A., Talwar, K., Erlingsson, Ú.:Scalable private learning with pate (2018)
12. Nissim, K., Raskhodnikova, S., Smith, A.: Smooth sensitivity and sampling in private data analysis. In: Proceedings of the Thirty-Ninth Annual ACM Symposium on Theory of Computing, STOC 2007, 75–84. Association for Computing Machinery, New York (2007)
13. Monarch, R.: Munro. Active learning and annotation for human-centered AI. Simon and Schuster, Human-in-the-Loop Machine Learning (2021)
14. Bassily, R., Thakkar, O., Thakurta, A.G.: Model-agnostic private learning. In: Neural Information Processing Systems (NeurIPS 2018), pp. 7102–7112 (2018b)
15. Shokri, R., Shmatikov, V.: Privacy-preserving deep learning. In: Proceedings of the 22nd ACM SIGSAC Conference on Computer and Communications Security (2015)
16. Wang, L., et al.: Enhance pate on complex tasks with knowledge transferred from non-private data. IEEE Access **7**, 50081–50094 (2019)
17. Malek, M., et al.: Antipodes of label differential privacy: PATE and ALIBI. arXiv preprint arXiv:2106.03408 (2021)
18. Yao, A.C.-C.: How to generate and exchange secrets. In: 27th Annual Symposium on Foundations of Computer Science (sfcs 1986). IEEE (1986)
19. Paillier, P.: Public-key cryptosystems based on composite degree residuosity classes. In: Stern, J. (ed.) EUROCRYPT 1999. LNCS, vol. 1592, pp. 223–238. Springer, Heidelberg (1999). https://doi.org/10.1007/3-540-48910-X_16

Vietnamese Text's Writing Styles Based Authorship Identification Model

Khoa Dang Dong[1] and Dang Tuan Nguyen[2(✉)]

[1] University of Information Technology, VNU-HCM, Ho Chi Minh City, Vietnam
khoadd.14@grad.uit.edu.vn
[2] Saigon University, Ho Chi Minh City, Vietnam
dangnt@sgu.edu.vn

Abstract. Identification of authorship is a research topic in natural language processing that has been interesting in recent years. Previously, texts were studied through a large variety of feature extraction methods to identify the author of the content. Advanced approaches based on deep learning have recently been applied to authorship attribution. This paper introduces a new model called ViBert4Author (V4A), a fine-tuning version of the pre-trained PhoBERT language model with the addition of dense layer and soft-max through combining the same algorithms. The feature extraction method is used for author classification in Vietnamese literature. In addition, our article also introduces a dataset that has been collected based on self-developed tools, the dataset on building over 800 works from 8 authors named VN-Literature. We also performed many tests on English datasets to evaluate the model: blogs, emails published on Kaggle, and pre-trained multi-languages for testing. We give a comprehensive analysis of the advantages and disadvantages of the proposed method. In addition, we evaluate the extraction of additional features (stylometric and hybrid features) in our assessment of approaches using the F1-score measure. The results show that our proposed model has improved performance over previous methods, in which the model that combines stylistic features and modern methods achieves outstanding performance.

Keywords: Authorship attribution · Stylometric · Pre-trained language model · Hybrid feature

1 Introduction

In the scope of this paper, we study the verification of authorship in the field of Vietnamese literature. Authorship Attribution (AA) is the task of allocating text to the correct author among a closed group of potential authors. Then, the attribution of authorship is considered as the task of identifying the author of a text.

The most significant difference between AA and other text classification tasks is the need to capture the specific style of each author. This area has attracted attention because of its relevance to many applications, including identifying the author of anonymous documents or phishing emails (Chask 2005; Lambers and Veenman 2009; Iqbal et al. 2010), and plagiarism detection (Kimler 2003; Gollub et al. 2013).

Existing AA methods focus on capturing each author's writing style through models such as SVM (Schwartz et al. 2013), CNN (Shrestha et al. 2017) and RNN (Bagnall 2015). The stylistic features recorded through n-grams of words and characters and syntactic and semantic information (Ding et al., 2016) were used in this task. In addition to learning features directly from the original text (such as n-gram words and characters), specific models use stylometric features, such as text length and output frequency-side of the first characters (Stamatatos, 2013). Huang et al. 2020 introduce latent-style features such as each user's emotional orientation of tweets and gets good results.

In machine learning approaches, author attribution can be thought of as a form of text classification. Let $D = \{d_1, d_2, ..., d_n\}$ be a set of documents and $A = \{a_1, a_2, ..., a_n\}$ is a fixed set of authors. The main task of copyright allocation is assigning an author A for each document in D. Most deep learning models have given significant results in various text classification tasks. Pre-trained language models can be fine-tuned for a target task with a few labeled training samples. (Wang et al., 2021) integrates RoBERTa fine-tuning and user writing styles for AA tweets, achieving the most modern results to date.

In this research, we proposed an approach based on the transfer learning technique through fine-tuning a pre-trained language model for Vietnamese named PhoBERT. We add a dense layer and soft-max activation to classify the author; the model is trained over several epochs. Our testing was performed with the VN-Literature dataset we collected through a crawler tool developed to collect and extract data from the Internet. Collected data are Vietnamese literary works with specifically identified authors and made public on the Internet. Unlike most deep learning methods for AA, V4A requires neither preprocessing nor feature engineering. Our method provides a state-of-the-art (SOTA) approach through transfer learning, with significantly improved relative accuracy. In addition, we also conduct an evaluation and comparison with other methods to show the architecture's strengths and weaknesses. We also build an overall architecture, combining style with hybrid features, to improve the macro averaged F1-score. Our evaluation was based on the published standard English corpus: Blog Attribution corpus (introduced by Schler et al., 2004) and Enron Email (by the Federal Energy Regulatory Commission). We performed the test by using pre-trained multilingual models (BERT, XLM-R and DitilBERT) with transfer learning techniques.

The following section presents the research related to the problem of author classification. Section 3 presents the self-built corpus and an overview of the compared corpus. Section 4 details our existing and proposed architectures. Section 5 describes the results obtained. Section 6 discusses our method, as well as future works. Finally, Sect. 7 describes our conclusions.

2   Related Work

Traditionally, previous studies have been based on feature extraction such as Fig. 1 from the content (such as the Bag-of-Words (BoW), Term-Frequency Inverse-Document-Frequency (TF-IDF) method) word or N-gram level, etc.) or writing style (such as the use of punctuation, capital letters, numbers, the author's POS tag (in the study of E. Stamatatos 2009). However, some proposed approaches using Convolutional Neural

Network (CNN) for AA tasks are more widely available, especially transfer learning methods. In addition, the authors use ensemble methods as described in Fig. 2 to propose their models. The following section presents recent studies of these methods.

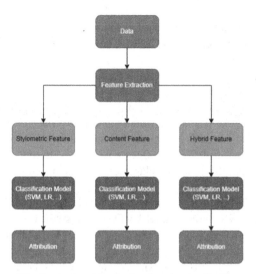

Fig. 1. Authorship Attribution classic pipeline

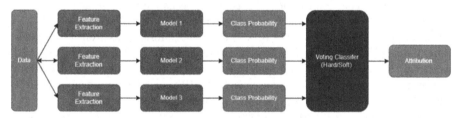

Fig. 2. Authorship Attribution Ensemble model

Usually, the set of features analyzed in a text is divided into five categories (according to E. Stamatatos 2009): vocabulary, structure, specific content, syntax, and features. Lexical features are defined as a set of characters and words of an individual. Such features include the distribution of uppercase letters, special characters, the average length of words used per sentence, and other characteristics. This set of features describes an author's lexical richness. Structural features tell us about how writers organize elements in a text, such as the number of paragraphs and sentences or their average length. Iyer et al. (2019) dealt with identifying the author of a manuscript of any literary work based on a pre-trained model with 50 authors. The model completes the task as a text classification problem with multi-class labels and proposes a supervised machine learning model with stylometric feature extraction. The accuracy has increased significantly after being cross-validated, with the optimization reaching nearly 93%.

The issue of authorship of short texts collected from Twitter was examined in the scientific work of Huang et al. (2022). The authors proposed a method of learning text representation using the joint development declaration of n-gram words and characters as input to NN. In addition, authors used an additional set of features with 10 elements: text length, number of usernames, subject, emoji, URL, numeric expression, time expression, date expression, month, degree of polarization and degree of subjectivity. Models provided for verification are CNN and LSTM. The method has an accuracy of 83.6% on a corpus containing 50 authors.

An approach based on a common implementation of words, n-grams, and latent Dirichlet allocation (LDA) has been proposed by Anwar et al. (2018). The LDA-based approach allows for processing sparse data and volumetric texts, providing a more accurate representation. The described approach is an unsupervised computational method that can account for the dataset's heterogeneity, multiple text styles, and the Urdu language's specificity. It was tested on 6000 texts written by 15 authors in Urdu. Use the improved sqrt-cosine similarity as the classifier. As a result, the accuracy achieved is 92.89%.

Dmitrin et al. (2018) present the analysis and application of different NN architectures (RNN, LSTM, CNN, bidirectional LSTM). The study was conducted based on three datasets in Russian (Habrahabr blog - 30 authors, average text length 2000 words; vk.com - 50 and 100 authors, average text length 100 words; Echo.msk.ru - 50 and 100 authors, average text length 2000 words). CNN achieved the best results (87% for the Habrahabr blog, 59% and 53% for 50 and 100 authors with vk.com, respectively). In addition, the author found that character tri-grams are not very good for short texts from social networks. In contrast, for longer texts, tri-grams and tetra-grams achieve almost the same accuracy (84% for social media) tri-grams, 87% for tetra-grams).

Convolutional Neural Networks (CNN) can extract formations from raw signals during the user's speech or vision processing. Ruder et al. 2016 explored word- and character-level CNNs for AA and found that character-level CNNs tend to perform better than other simple approaches based on SVM. (Rhodes) An n-gram model with 3, 4 and 5 g as input to a multi-layer CNN was applied max-over-time pooling.

Adaku Uchendu et al. (2020) used human-written and machine-written texts (CTRL, GPT, GPT2, GROVER, XLM, XL-NET, PPLM, FAIR) to perform authorship verification between texts written by writers and text generators. Most machine-written texts are significantly different from human texts, which makes it easier to identify the author. However, the generated documents with GPT2, GROVER and FAIR models give better quality than other methods used, which leads to confusion in the classification process. For this study, the author used a convolutional neural network (CNN) because the CNN architecture is suitable for representing each author's characteristics. In addition, the author has improved the CNN implementation by using n-gram word and part-of-speech (PoS) tags. The classification result of "human-machine" ranges from 81–97%, depending on the generation methods.

3 The Corpora

This paper presents a self-collected corpus through the tool we developed. Collected data are Vietnamese prose works based on eight authors with 839 different works. Raw data is collected and stored as files and not preprocessed. The data stored in the structured form is a CSV format document, including the data fields: work, title, content, and author (Table 2). The work is represented by an author that does not include co-authors, which does the work of identifying authorship based on style clearer, optimizing classification for better results. Specific content is literary works; each work will be a collection of many sentences and will have different lengths. In our testing, we looked at the length profile of each homologous text to reduce the standard deviation between sentences. The following Table 1 presents the statistics of the data we collected.

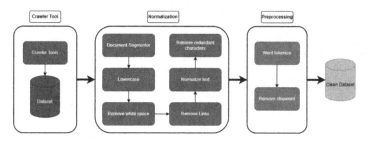

Fig. 3. Overview of our data collection and processing tools

Next, we evaluate the model through two publicly available datasets from the Internet, Blog Authorship Corpus and Enron Email. Many different authors have studied these two datasets in recent years to perform the task of identifying the author of a text in a list of N potential authors on each dataset. Details of the datasets are presented below.

The Authorship Corpus blog (publicly available on Kaggle[1]) consists of 19,320 bloggers who collected posts from blogger.com in August 2004. It was introduced by Schler et al. as part of a study on the effects of age and gender on blogging. The archive combines 681,288 posts and over 140 million words - or about 35 posts and 7250 words per person. Each blog is stored in a separate file, the name of which indicates the blogger's id# and the gender, age, industry and astrological sign provided by the blogger herself.

Table 1. Statistics of collected datasets

# No	# Author	# Works	# Sentence	# Percentage
1	Hồ Biểu Chánh	325	63547	43.61
2	Khái Hưng	144	19178	13.16
3	Vũ Trọng Phụng	125	18331	12.58
4	Nam Cao	80	12182	8.36
5	Ngô Tất Tố	73	11648	7.99
6	Nhất Linh	41	11478	7.87

(continued)

Table 1. (*continued*)

# No	# Author	# Works	# Sentence	# Percentage
7	Nguyễn Huy Tưởng	30	6970	4.78
8	Đào Trinh Nhất	21	2375	1.62
	Total	839	145709	100

Table 2. Collected data storage details

# Works	# Title	# Content	# Author
Tắt đèn	Chương I	Bắt đầu từ gà gáy một tiếng, trâu bò lục tục kéo thợ cầy đến đoạn đường phía trong điểm tuần. Mọi ngày, giờ ấy, những con vật này cũng như những người cổ cầy, vai bừa kia, …	Ngô Tất Tố
.	…	…	…

Enron Email is a document repository containing more than 0.5 million emails. This data was initially made public and posted to the web by the Federal Energy Regulatory Commission during the investigation. It includes the data of 150 users, most of whom are senior Enron managers. This dataset was used in the study of Klimt and Yang 2004 on the email classification problem. The data is publicly available here[2]. The Enron Email Archive has been researched for several tasks, including authorship analysis in Halvani et al., 2020.

For our tests, we consider the eight authors with the most significant number of documents in each dataset to provide the most objective assessment of the proposed model and the VN-Literature dataset. Table 3 presents summary statistics on the length and number of documents per author for each dataset tested. Thereby showing the similarity of the Enron Email and VN-Literature datasets, the similarity in text size here is the length of each text and the number of documents of each author. Finally, we selected the top 8 authors with the most text for the Blog dataset.

Table 3. Summary statistics on each author's average length and the number of documents on the dataset

# Dataset	# Avg. Num. Tokens	# Avg. Num. Texts
VN-literature	208	18212
Enron email	201	8745
Blog authorship	538	1709

---

[1] https://www.kaggle.com/datasets/rtatman/blog-authorship-corpus.

[2] https://www.cs.cmu.edu/~enron.

4   The Methodologies

4.1   A Brief Introduction to Authorship Attribution Task

Authorship Attribution (AA) is the process of assigning an author to an anonymous document based on the characteristics of the script. Several attribution methods have been developed for natural languages, such as English, Russian, Chinese, and Dutch. However, the number of works related to Vietnamese is still limited. Many machine learning models have been tested, including communication machine learning and deep learning models. However, it is not often mentioned that combined stylometric and deep learning models or the transfer learning techniques used can significantly impact classifier performance. Therefore, we propose to study their use in this regard by building a model of possible author identification for a particular Vietnamese text rather than in prose works through the combination of writing style and PhoBERT model (a pre-trained language model for Vietnamese). We evaluated these models on a large dataset in Vietnamese collected through self-developed tools by eight different authors. We also compared them with other existing methods. The test results show that our model provides the best results and can attribute the text's author with an accuracy of 84.7%. Furthermore, compared with related methods, the results indicate that our proposed method is suitable for allocating copyright.

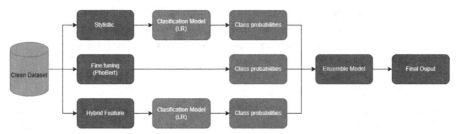

Fig. 4. Overview of our proposed method model (V4A) combining writing style, feature synthesis, and the BERT language model

First, we introduce a baseline model. Accordingly, the problem AA can be reduced to the text classification problem, in which this problem is defined according to Aggarwal and Zhai (2012) when given a set of training documents as training data $D = \{X_1, X_2, \ldots, X_i\}$, where each $X_i \in D$ has a label in the set of labels $\{1..k\}$. First, the training data is used to build the classification model. Then, for the incoming unlabeled data, the classification model predicts the label for it. We will discuss each approach in the next section and present our proposed method.

4.2   Traditional Method

Traditionally, AA has relied on the extraction of content-related features (e.g., Bag-Of-Words) (BoW), Term frequency-inverse document frequency (TF-IDF) at the word or n-gram level, etc.) or author's stylistic features, according to research by Stamatatos (2009) (e.g., the use of punctuation, capital letters, numbers, POS tag) of an author.

Then construct a classifier that trains on these features, such as the popular Logistic Regression (LR) used by Madigan et al. (2005), Anwar et al. (2018). In addition, we also use other machine learning models such as Multinomial Naive Bayes, Decision Tree, Random Forest.

1. **Multinomial Naive Bayes**: This algorithm is to predict and classify databases based on observational data and statistics, based on the Bayes theorem of probability. Multinomial Naive Bayes is a popular supervised learning algorithm in machine learning because it is relatively easy to train and achieves high performance (I. Rish et al., 2001).
2. **Logistic Regression:** A binary classification algorithm, a simple, well-known and most important method in machine learning. By analyzing the relationship between all available independent variables, the Logistic regression model predicts a dependent data variable (Genkin et al., 2007; Hosmer Jr et al., 2013). However, in natural language processing, this method requires manual features extracted from the data to classify text in the test we used for TF-IDF, Stylometric and Char n-gram.
3. **Decision Tree:** The decision tree is the most powerful and popular method for classification (Pranckeviciu, 2017). The decision tree algorithm is also considered as a structure tree, where each node represents a test attribute, each branch is a test result, and each leaf node is a class label target variable.
4. **Random Forest:** Random forest is a supervised machine learning method to solve classification and regression tasks (Davidson, 2017). The Random Forest model is very effective for classification problems because it mobilizes hundreds of smaller internal models with different rules simultaneously to make the final decision.

4.3 Deep Learning

Convolutional Neural Network (Text-CNN): Convolutional Neural Network (CNN) is a multi-layer neural network architecture developed for classification (Kim et al., 2014). By using convolutional layers, it is possible to detect the combined features. In our test, we used together a pre-trained word embedding of 157 different languages (fastText[3]) suggested by Grave et al., 2018. This embedding turns a word into a 300-dimensional vector. Finally, we use a soft-max function that uses the results to predict labels for the text.

Bidirectional Long Short-Term Memory (Bi-LSTM): Bi-LSTM (Schuster et al., 1997) is a well-known variant of Recurrent Neural Networks (RNN) (Medsker et al., 1999). Bi-LSTM can be trained using all available input information in the past and continuously over a selected time frame. This method is considered very powerful in classification problems, and most of its classification results achieve high performance. Therefore, we intend to use it to compare with other classification models in this task.

4.4 Transformers Model

The transfer learning model has recently attracted the attention of researchers in the field of NLP because of its outstanding effectiveness. Above all, transformers models are an

---

[3] https://fasttext.cc/docs/en/crawl-vectors.html.

advanced architecture that relies on attention mechanisms and deep neural networks, replacing recurrent layers inside the auto encoder-decoder with particular layers called multi-head self-attention (Yang et al. 2019). The most prominent is the language model BERT stands for Bidirectional Encoder representations from transformers, proposed by Devlin et al., 2019. BERT and its variants, such as DistilBERT (Sanh et al., 2020), XLM-R (Conneau et al. 2020), and especially PhoBERT (Nguyen et al., 2020), have affirmed its strength in natural language processing tasks in recent years.

4.5 Proposed Model

While researching and examining previous studies on the issue of authorship attribution, we found that there is no proposed model for combining pre-trained language models with stylometric features. That led us to introduce a new model, ViBert4Author (V4A), a simple fine-tuning of PhoBERT with a dense layer and softmax enabled, trained in several epochs for authorship. The output size of the dense layer corresponds to the number of authors in the corpus.

For Vietnamese, the state-of-the-art (SOTA) method was first developed and called PhoBERT (by Nguyen et al., 2020) to solve Vietnam's NLP problems. PhoBERT is a pre-trained model that shares the same idea as RoBERTa, a BERT replication study proposed by Liu et al., 2019 and has been modified for Vietnamese. BERT, widely used in research in recent years, is a contextual word representation model built using bidirectional transformers and based on a masked language model. As described by Sun et al. (2020), to use BERT as a classifier, a simple dense layer with a softmax activation function is combined with the final hidden state h header of the first token [CLS] through a weight matrix W and prediction probability of label c in the following way:

$$p(c|h) = softmax(Wh)$$

Then, all weights, including the weight of BERT and the weight of W, are adjusted to maximize the log probability of correct labels. Finally, the training is done using the Cross-Entropy loss function. In this study, we implement PhoBERT, a pre-trained language mode from the Transformer library (Wolf et al., 2020), trained on a large Vietnamese corpus. Fine-tune BERT for AA task was done on Google Colab Tesla T4-PCIE-16GB.

Inspired by previous studies, we have incorporated writing style features into V4A. Through 2 models called V4A + Style and V4A + Style + Hybrid Feature combined with the Logistic Regression model. For hybrid features, we extract based on n-grams with character-level bi-grams and tri-grams through an LR classifier. Finally, we collect the BERT model's output probabilities by stylometric and hybrid features, which are reassembled and classified using an additional LR classifier. Such a model will examine the content, writing style and synthesis of features. The architecture of V4A + Style + Hybrid Feature is shown in Fig. 4.

5 Results

The parameters we choose for the tested architectures in the study are shown in Table 4. We ran tests on eight authors for all three datasets presented above. Our model was trained on 5 epochs for each test. The results are shown in Tables 5 and 6. We retained 20% of the data for the test set using stratified approach sampling, i.e., stratified approach sampling, the ratio of the proportions of each class is kept equal in the train and test sets. We compare the proposed approach with traditional and deep learning models using the feature extraction methods presented earlier. In addition, we compare our approach with the word-level TF-IDF - LR model with root word removal and word breaks. We also add a benchmark for the performance of an LR trained only on stylistic features and an additional LR trained on Char N-gram hybrid features.

Table 4. Parameters of the experiments

Approach	Model	Parameter	Value
Traditional	Logistic Regression	Penalty	12
		max_iter	100
		C	1
		random_state	0
	Decision Tree	min_samples_split	2
		min_samples_leaf	1
	Random Forest	n_estimators	1000
		random_state	0
Deep Neural Network	TextCNN/BiLSTM	filter_size	32
		dropout	0.5
		batch_size	256
		epoch	40
State-of-the-art	BERT	Config	bert-base-cased
		Epochs	5
		train_batch_size	16
	XLM-Roberta	Config	xlm-roberta-base
		Epochs	5
		train_batch_size	16
	DistilBERT	Config	distilbert-base-multilingual-cased
		Epochs	5
		train_batch_size	16
	PhoBERT	Config	vinai/phobert-base
		Epochs	5
		train_batch_size	16

In this study, we focus on evaluating based on the VN-Literature dataset we built ourselves. Thereby, it is evident that the proposed model V4A (fine-tuning from pre-trained language model PhoBERT) works well with the author identification problem in Vietnamese literature. For our dataset, V4A outperforms traditional machine learning models using TF-IDF. We see the highest Random Forest model in conventional machine learning models with a measured accuracy of 70.8%. The most superior deep neural network model is BiLSTM combined with pre-trained word embedding fastText with improved accuracy of 71%. However, with the proposed model, the results are more impressive, with outstanding accuracy reaching over 80% with multilingual models such as BERT, XLM-RoBERTa and DistilBERT, especially with the PhoBERT language model due to its advantages. Moreover, it is built in Vietnamese, giving better accuracy, up to 84.6%; combining writing style and hybrid features helps increase accuracy.

Two other datasets also included in our experiment gave awe-inspiring results. Data preparation will take a long time with the Enron Email dataset containing much unimportant information. We decided to delete short emails or emails containing special characters and signatures. Experimental results show improvement of State-of-the-art models (ignoring experience with monolingual PhoBERT) with traditional models based on TF-IDF and deep learning models with word embedding, average accuracy increase of more than 13.3%.

The more significant challenge is with the Blog Authorship dataset, which is a large dataset, so we only selected the top 8 authors in our test, providing an average word count of about 1700 for each author, and providing enough data for model training and evaluation. Our testing shows that traditional machine learning and deep learning models still do not perform as well as the proposed model combining pre-trained multilingual models and feature techniques. Nevertheless, the results show a significant improvement in accuracy at 9.8%.

Table 5. A detailed description of the results of our tests based on two English datasets

Approach	Model	Enron Email		Blog Authorship	
		F1-score	Accuracy	F1-score	Accuracy
Traditional	Multinomial Naive Bayes + TF-IDF	0.66977	0.70135	0.76848	0.7723
	Logistic Regression + TF-IDF	0.77525	0.78213	0.81147	0.80994
	Decision Tree + TF-IDF	0.61214	0.61934	0.57477	0.57054
	Random Forest + TF-IDF	0.71755	0.72705	0.75432	0.75439
	Style-based + LR	0.26352	0.29123	0.25001	0.28801

(continued)

Table 5. (*continued*)

Approach	Model	Enron Email		Blog Authorship	
		F1-score	Accuracy	F1-score	Accuracy
	Char n-gram + LR	0.37402	0.42573	0.48668	0.50183
Deep Neural Network	TextCNN + fastText	0.68931	0.68043	0.67924	0.67893
	BiLSTM + fastText	0.69238	0.6911	0.69787	0.69696
State-of-the-art	BERT	0.83691	0.83977	0.85235	0.85088
	BERT + Style + LR	0.83031	0.83509	0.85306	0.85161
	BERT + Style + Char N-gram + LR	0.83031	0.83509	0.85371	0.85234
	DistilBERT	0.83793	0.84211	0.84892	0.84795
	DistilBERT + Style + LR	0.83262	0.83743	0.84658	0.84576
	DistilBERT + Style + Char N-gram + LR	0.83147	0.83626	0.84649	0.84576
	XLM-RoBERTa	0.81929	0.82456	0.87018	0.86879
	XLM-RoBERTa + Style + LR	0.81835	0.82339	0.87248	0.87098
	XLM-RoBERTa + Style + Char N-gram + LR	**0.81935**	**0.82456**	**0.8721**	**0.87061**

Table 6. A detailed description of the results of our tests based on the Vietnamese dataset (VN-Literature)

Approach	Model	VN-Literature	
		F1-score	Accuracy
Traditional	Multinomial Naive Bayes + TF-IDF	0.58882	0.57809
	Logistic Regression + TF-IDF	0.61171	0.59391
	Decision Tree + TF-IDF	0.70874	0.69257
	Random Forest + TF-IDF	0.72491	0.70858
	Style-based + LR	0.27518	0.3151
	Char n-gram + LR	0.25494	0.315
Deep neural network	TextCNN + fastText	0.58061	0.57679
	BiLSTM + fastText	0.72297	0.71057
State-of-the-art	BERT	0.82161	0.81315

(*continued*)

Table 6. (*continued*)

Approach	Model	VN-Literature	
		F1-score	Accuracy
	BERT + Style + LR	0.82569	0.81616
	BERT + Style + Char N-gram + LR	0.82485	0.81539
	DistilBERT	0.8251	0.81665
	DistilBERT + Style + LR	0.82608	0.81645
	DistilBERT + Style + Char N-gram + LR	0.82582	0.81626
	XLM-RoBERTa	0.79102	0.78143
	XLM-RoBERTa + Style + LR	0.79775	0.7858
	XLM-RoBERTa + Style + Char N-gram + LR	0.79743	0.78522
	PhoBERT	0.85108	0.84624
	PhoBERT + Style + LR	0.85398	0.84769
	PhoBERT + Style + Char N-gram + LR	**0.85422**	**0.84789**

6 Discussion

Our research combined a Vietnamese language model with the writing style and feature extraction methods to achieve outstanding scores for task AA. We can improve the results by using dense layers, and the activation function used is softmax based on the pre-trained language model PhoBERT. The approach of BERT and PhoBERT focuses mainly on the inherent element of word representation, syntax and context without requiring any preprocessing. Previous studies (Sari et al. 2018) have shown that using type and matching features improves the accuracy of AA tasks. We also offer that adding such features and pre-trained language models can improve the macro-averaged F1-score. Our proposed model V4A fine-tuning from the pre-trained language model PhoBERT shows similar effects. That indicates that our model will work well when each author has enough training data. However, having the data available to all authors is not easy in practice. In addition, the representation of short paragraphs by the authors also causes some asymmetry in the data.

There are many possible methods to extend this study. Our experiments on three datasets: VN-Literature, Enron Email, and Blog Authorship, have successfully utilized transformers-based language and representation models. In addition, we have done it with other pre-trained multilingual models that are variations of BERT and have had a positive effect. In further works, we will focus on building a more extensive experimental dataset with a more significant number of authors; Next, we will attempt to extract additional typographic, association, profiling, or content-related features.

7 Conclusion

The development of science and technology led to the birth of more modern advanced research. Deep learning and transformers techniques are gradually becoming more popular in natural language processing; Feature engineering and text preprocessing are becoming less and less necessary. In this work, we presented V4A, a fine-tuning-based approach based on pre-trained PhoBERT for author classification. In addition, we also introduce a self-developed dataset for the task of author classification in Vietnamese literature. Our model works best when the author has enough training data, no significant label imbalance, and the text is too short. In addition, in this task, we also applied more style features (like previous authors) and hybrid features to V4A, which improved, significantly the increase in F1-Score compared to the model overall figure. Future work will explore more features for V4A, build more datasets with a larger number of authors, and review and suggest ways to deal with large data imbalances. Finally, explore other pre-trained language models and expand our approach to Authorship Attribution.

References

Chaski, C.E.: Who's at the keyboard? authorship attribution in digital evidence investigations. International Journal of Digital Evidence **4**, 1–13 (2005)

Lambers, M., Veenman, C.J.: Forensic authorship attribution using compression distances to prototypes. In: Proceeding of the 3rd International Workshop on Computational Forensics, 13–24 (2009)

Iqbal, F., Binsalleeh, H., Fung, B.C.M., Debbabi, M.: Mining write prints from anonymous e-mails for forensic investigation. Digit. Investig. **7**(1–2), 56–64 (2010)

Kimler: Using style markers for detecting plagiarism in natural language (2003)

Huang and Mizuho IWAIHARA: Authorship Attribution Based on Pre-Trained Language Model and Capsule Network (2022)

Gollub, T., et al.: Recent trends in digital text forensics and its evaluation – plagiarism detection, author identification, and author profiling (2013)

Schwartz, R., Tsur, O., Rappoport, A., Koppel, M.: Authorship attribution of micro messages. In: Conf. Empirical Methods in Natural Language Processing, pp. 1880–1891 (2013)

Shrestha, P., et al.: Convolutional neural networks for authorship attribution of short texts (2017)

Bagnall, D.: Author identification using multi–headed recurrent neural network. In: Working Notes Papers of the CLEF 2015 Evaluation Labs, vol. 1391 (2015)

Ding, S.H.H., Fung, B.C.M., Iqbal, F., Cheung, W.K.: Learning stylometric representations for authorship analysis. In: IEEE Transactions on Cybernetics, pp. 107–121 (2016)

Stamatatos, E.: A survey of modern authorship attribution methods. J. Am. Soc. Inform. Sci. Technol. **60**(3), 538–556 (2009)

Huang, W., Su, R., Iwaihara, M.: Contribution of improved character embedding and latent posting styles to authorship attribution of short texts, pp. 261–269. Springer (2020)

Wang, X., Iwaihara, M.: Integrating RoBERTa fine-tuning and user writing styles for authorship attribution of short texts (2021)

Iyer, R.R., Rose, C.P.: A machine learning framework for authorship identification from texts. arXiv Prepr. arXiv: 1912.10204 (2019)

Anwar, W., Bajwa, I.S., Choudhary, M.A., Ramzan, S.: An empirical study on forensic analysis of urdu text using LDA-based authorship attribution (2018)

Dmitrin, Y.V, Botov, D.S, Klenin, J.D, Nikolaev, I.E.: Comparison of deep neural network architectures for authorship attribution of Russian social media texts (2018)

Uchendu, A., Le, T., Shu, K., Lee, D.: Authorship attribution for neural text generation (2020)

Ruder, S., Ghaffari, P., Breslin, J.G.: Character-level and multi-channel convolutional neural networks for large-scale authorship attribution. arXiv Prepr. arXiv:1609.06686 (2016)

Klimt, B., Yang, Y.: A new dataset for email classification research. In: Boulicaut, J.F., Esposito, F., Giannotti, F., Pedreschi, D. (ed.), Machine Learning: ECML (2004)

Aggarwal, C., Zhai, C.: A survey of text clustering algorithms. In: Aggarwal, C.C., Zhai, C. (eds.) Mining Text Data, pp. 77–128. Springer, US (2012)

Kim, Y.: Convolutional neural networks for sentence classification. In: Proceedings of the 2014 Conference on EMNLP, pp. 1746–1751 (2014)

Schuster, M., Paliwal, K.K.: Bidirectional recurrent neural networks. IEEE Trans. Signal Process. **45**(11), 2673–2681 (1997)

Medsker, L., Jain, L.C.: Recurrent Neural Networks: Design and Applications. CRC Press (1999)

Yang, X., Yang, L., Bi, R., Lin, H.: A comprehensive verification of transformer in text classification. In: China National Conference on Chinese Computational Linguistics, pp. 207–218. Springer (2019)

Conneau, A., et al.: Unsupervised cross-lingual representation learning at scale (2020)

Nguyen, D.Q., Nguyen, T.A.: PhoBERT: Pre-trained language modelsfor vietnamese. In: Findings of the Association for Computational Lin-guistics: EMNLP 2020, pp. 1037–1042. Association for ComputationalLinguistics, Online (2020)

Liu, Y., et al.: RoBERTa: a robustly optimized BERT pretraining approach. arXiv:1907.11692 (2019)

Grave, E., Bojanowski, P., Gupta, P., Joulin, A., Mikolov, T.: Learning word vectors for 157 languages. In: Proceedings of the Eleventh International Conference on Language Resources and Evaluation (LREC 2018). European Language Resources Association (ELRA), Miyazaki, Japan (2018)

Sari, Y., Stevenson, M., Vlachos, A.: Topic or style? exploring the most useful features for authorship attribution. In Proceedings of the 27th International Conference on Computational Linguistics, pp. 343–353. Association for Computational Linguistics, Santa Fe, New Mexico, USA (2018)

Application of Machine Learning in Malware Detection

Trinh Van Quynh[1]([✉]), Vu Thanh Hien[1], Vu Thanh Nguyen[2], and Huynh Quoc Bao[1]

[1] HUTECH University, Ho Chi Minh City, Vietnam
{vt.hien,hq.bao}@hutech.edu.vn
[2] Ho Chi Minh City University of Food Industry, Ho Chi Minh City, Vietnam
nguyenvt@hufi.edu.vn

Abstract. In this paper, we propose applying machine learning techniques to solve the problem of static malware analysis based on features extracted from executable files to minimize errors when detecting new malicious code or its variants. Our improved model is based on two datasets EMBER 2018 and SOREL-20M, for training and testing. The results of the study have achieved an accuracy of 99.94% (AUC). The malware detection rate is 98.78% with 1% false-positive rate (FPR) and 97.49% with 0.1% false-positive rate on the test dataset after reducing 36.54% features from the original dataset.

Keywords: PE features · Machine learning · Malware detection

1 Introduction

Most businesses and individuals depend on computer networks and information systems to process and store data in today's digital economy. Organizations and enterprises transform their paper-based content into digital forms and create new business models based on these digital assets. Facebook, Netflix, Baidu, etc., are typical examples of businesses that have been very successful in exploiting such digital resources. In parallel with the intense explosion of information technology, data, and the development of the global Internet, the risks of information insecurity are becoming more serious and dangerous, in which malicious code is the greatest threat because of its ability to spread on computer systems and perform illegal attacks. Moreover, malicious code is increasingly evolving with diverse variations, with increasingly sophisticated concealment and concealment techniques. According to AV-TEST [1], as of February 2022, the total number of newly discovered malware worldwide reached 920.66 million and 218.81 million potentially dangerous software. And every second, there will be an average of 4.9 new malicious codes. With rapid growth, complexity, and limited human resources, new malware detection is a big challenge for businesses, governments, and end-users [2]. Reliance on signature-based malware detection has proven ineffective against new malware or new variants. Experts and researchers have been trying to use machine learning techniques, and deep learning to accurately detect new malicious code. This study improves and evaluates a machine learning model that does static analysis of executable

© The Author(s), under exclusive license to Springer Nature Singapore Pte Ltd. 2022
T. K. Dang et al. (Eds.): FDSE 2022, CCIS 1688, pp. 362–374, 2022.
https://doi.org/10.1007/978-981-19-8069-5_24

files to classify them as malicious or benign. The study uses two datasets, EMBER 2018 [3–5] and SOREL-20M [6, 7], containing data extracted from known executable files of malicious and benign files.

This research will focus on researching, comparing, and proposing techniques to improve the machine learning model trained on the original dataset with the model proposed by the dataset's authors. Besides improving the accuracy of the model, we have also proposed an architecture that reduces the memory consumption as well as the computational cost when analyzing data and finding the optimal value.

2 Related Works

The selection of input features is a significant task in any machine learning research. In the case of malware detection by static analysis, these features can be all or part of raw information extracted from files. Using all the raw data from the file will slow down the detection speed and not meet the actual needs because new malicious code appears every second. For this reason, researchers often extract a piece of information from executable files to build machine learning models. The methods used mainly recently are [8–21]: Signature extraction, extracting information of functions called from the dynamically linked library, extracting binary string, extracting the assembly code, extract header information.

Several studies on applying machine learning to malware analysis have been published, clearly showing its superiority. Various methods such as dynamic analysis of system function calls, monitoring access to the registry, and analysis based on the hidden Markov model have also been proposed for dynamic malware analysis.

Kolter and Maloof [8] proposed using n-grams by combining a 4-byte sequence to produce about 255 million distinct n-grams. This paper proposes to use a probabilistic approach to determine the good feature and use the best 500 n-grams for analysis. The paper proposed to use the Naive Bayes algorithm, Support Vector Machine (SVM), and J48 decision tree to analyze their data. The data used for analysis was mainly obtained from Sourceforge and VX Heavens (actual data not disclosed) with 1971 benign executables and 1651 malicious executables. This study uses a small sample set, and the author does not publish the dataset, so it is difficult to determine the research accuracy, especially when dealing with a more extensive data set. A similar study was performed by Bagga [22] using this approach with Microsoft's malware classification, which is a supposedly large data set. However, this research focuses on malware classification rather than malware detection.

Raman et al. [9], from the product incident response team of Adobe Systems Inc., proposed a method for malware classification by extracting the seven least correlated features from the executable files. The extracted features are DebugSize, ImageVersion, IatRVA, ExportSize, ResourceSize, VirtualSize, NumberOfSections. A dataset containing 100,000 malicious executables and 16,000 benign executables was used for testing.

Various models were tested on this dataset. The J48 decision tree obtained the best results among the tested models: true-positive rate of 98.6% and false-positive rate of 5.7%. The model after training has been released as a free tool for malware classification, but the dataset has not been published to perform any form of comparative study.

H. Pham et al. [11] proposed a method to reduce the feature size of the EMBER 2017 Feature Version 1 dataset by 30% in 2018, which achieved a detection rate of up to 99.394% with a false positive rate of 1% and 97.572% with a false positive rate of 0.1%. However, the malicious and benign samples in this dataset were extracted entirely from unencrypted or unpackaged files.

Phil Roth et al. [3–5], provided the EMBER 2018 dataset with one million samples, including 2381 features in 2018 in which the training set contains 800,000 samples and the test set contains 200,000 samples. Malicious samples were collected from samples that appeared in 2017 and 2018, including those with or without encryption or encapsulation techniques, and benign samples were collected from files that occurred before 2018. The author's proposed model achieves an accuracy of 96.498% with 1% false-positive rate and 3.502% false-negative rate.

Richard Harang and Ethan M. Rudd [6, 7] from security companies Sophos and FireEye report that commercial malware detection models are trained on tens to hundreds of millions of data samples. Thus, EMBER is too small a dataset compared to real datasets, and they provided the SOREL-20M dataset with the same number of features as the EMBER dataset with nearly 20 million samples. It contains 12,699,013 training samples, 2,495,822 validation samples, and 4,195,042 tests to help researchers approach closer to the natural environment. In addition, Richard and his colleagues also provide nearly 10 million malicious files that have been disabled to help researchers create data sets for different research purposes. The author's proposed machine learning model has an accuracy of 97.979% with 1% false-positive rate and 2.021% false-negative rate.

3   The Proposed Approach

When using machine learning to detect malware, PE files are not used to be put directly into the training or testing model, but these files must be analyzed in some way to extract useful characteristics. In order for the study to be more favorable and closer to the real environment, the criteria of the study are to choose the available datasets and contain new malware samples.

With the goal of minimizing computation time and cost, we perform feature analysis and search for optimal values on a data set 20 times smaller, the study used two data sets with similar characteristics, EMBER 2018 created by Endgame [23] security company and SOREL-20M provided by Sophos [23, 24] security company. These are two balanced datasets between classes with new malware samples from 2018 and contain features extracted from millions of Windows executable files (PE) detailed in Table 1.

Table 1. Data statistics

Dataset	Train set	Validation set	Test set	No. features
EMBER 2018	1,000,000	0	200,000	2381
SOREL-20M	12,699,013	2,495,822	4,195,042	2381

In this study, we use LightGBM – a framework developed in 2017 by Microsoft. LightGBM is a gradient boosting framework that uses tree-based learning algorithms. LightGBM, XGBoost, or CatBoost are state-of-the-art algorithms, and they all support parallel computation, but LightGBM is more powerful than the previous XGBoost algorithm. LightGBM is developed from decision tree algorithm based on gradient-based one-side sampling (GOSS), exclusive feature bundling (EFB), and splitting technique using use histogram. Therefore, it is faster and less memory usage, and possible to reduce the communication cost when training in parallel. To speed up the training as well as reduce the size of the model, we perform dataset analysis and feature selection before training the machine learning model. Moreover, this feature selection and analysis is only performed on the 20 times smaller dataset EMBER 2018 and uses the features from this analysis to apply to the SOREL-20M dataset 20 times larger to save memory consumption, and computation cost.

The first method is to remove all features with no or low variance. This means that all features with the same value or values with minor deviation (0.000003) for all samples will be deleted. After performing this technique, set A has 1761 features. In the second method, we select set B with 1749 features, in which the selected features are the features that have the most correlation with the label. Finally, performing the intersection ($\cap$) between two sets A and B, we get a set C with 1511 features. The formula determines the set of features of C:

$$C = A \cap B, \text{ with } \forall x \in C \text{ then } x \in A \text{ and } x \in B.$$

The dataset, including all features in C, selected from the original dataset will be chosen as the training set for the model.

The specific steps are as follows:

(1) Divide the dataset into training and test sets, analyze the variance on the features and the correlation between features and labels on the EMBER, then create a dataset named s-EMBER by selecting 1511 best features from EMBER;

(2) Using Bayesian hyperparameter optimization algorithm to optimize parameters of LightGBM model to build P_E-LightGBM model and train on s-EMBER;

(3) Use the P_E-LightGBM model to predict and export prediction results.

(4) Create a dataset named s-SOREL-20M by selecting 1511 best features from SOREL-20M.

(5) Using the optimal hyperparameter achieved in step (2) to build the P_S-LightGBM model and train on the s-SOREL-20M;

(6) Use P_S-LightGBM model to predict and export prediction results.

The specific experimental procedure is shown in Fig. 1.

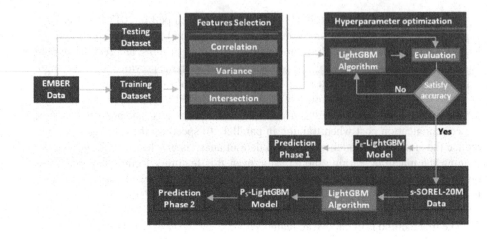

Fig. 1. Proposed machine learning workflow

4 Experiment

We use the EMBER2018 dataset with 1 million samples split into two datasets for training and testing. The training dataset consists of 800,000 samples, of which 300,000 are labeled as malicious, 300,000 are labeled as benign, and the remaining 200,000 are unlabeled. In this study, we only used 600 thousand labeled samples to train and optimize the P_E-LightGBM model. Then the optimal hyperparameter set of the P_E-LightGBM model is used to train the P_S-LightGBM model on the s-SOREL-20M dataset to save training costs and the process of performing analysis of the features.

4.1 Experiment Environment

The hyperparameter optimization of the P_E-LightGBM model was trained asynchronously using GPUs on four Dell Precision T7820 computers with Xeon Bronze 3104 processor, nVIDIA GPU Quadro P6000 24GB, and 128GB of RAM. The P_S-LightGBM model was trained parallel on an HP Intel(R) Xeon(R) Gold 6230 server CPU @ 2.10GHz, 40 Cores, and 512GB of RAM.

We use the below software and libraries based on Anaconda 2020 distribution.

- Python 3.7.7
- Scikit-Learn
- NumPy
- LIEF
- Pandas
- MatPlotLib
- LightGBM
- Optuna
- and some other libraries support the above libraries.

4.2 Experiment Results

In this study, we use the feature selection technique by statistical method. The method used is the analysis of variance on all 2381 features and the correlation between 2381 features and labels.

We first normalize the data using the max-min strategy to rescale all the values according to the formula (1) and (2):

$$X_{std} = \frac{(X - min(X))}{max(X) - min(X)} \tag{1}$$

$$X_{scaled} = X_{std} * [max(X) - min(X)] \tag{2}$$

where X is the value of the feature, max(X) is the largest value of X, min(X) is the smallest value of X, X_{scaled} is the feature normalization value. And then, we calculate the variance of the feature by the formula (3):

$$S^2 = \frac{1}{n-1} \sum_{i=1}^{i=n} (X_i - \overline{X})^2, n = 800,000 \tag{3}$$

We use only 800,000 labeled samples in the EMBER dataset with 1,000,000 samples. Where S^2 is variance, X_i is the value of the one observation, $\overline{X}$ is the mean value of all observations.

From Fig. 2a. and Fig. 2b., observe that it is possible to keep about 1700 without losing too much model performance too much. By using the function VarianceThreshold from Scikit-learn framework with threshold = 0.000003, we get a set named A with 1761 features.

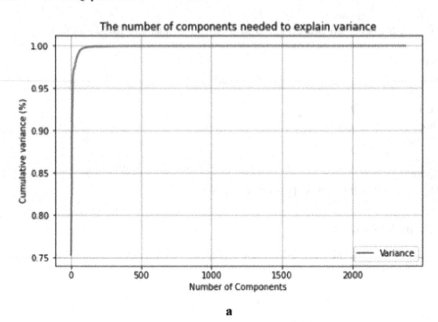

a

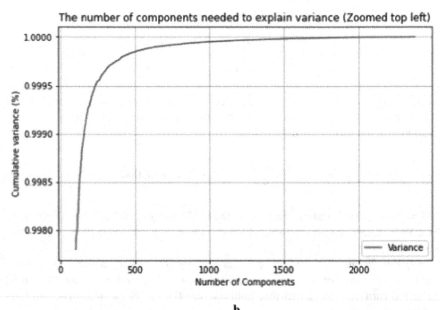

b

Fig. 2. a. Feature variance. b. Feature variance (zoomed top left corner)

Next step, We calculate the correlation between each feature with the label and then plot it out to do the observation as Fig. 3a.

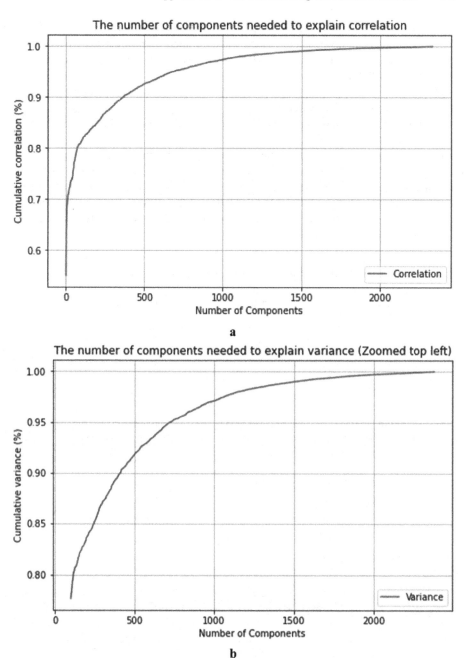

Fig. 3. a. Correlation between features and labels. b. Correlation between features and labels (zoomed top left corner)

From Fig. 3a. and Fig. 3b., we observe that keeping about 1700 features that will not change the model's performance too much when training. Performing feature selection with a correlation value greater than 0.005, we obtain set B with 1749 features that correlate most with the label.

In the last step, completing the intersection of two feature sets, A and B above, we receive a collection of 1511 features.

We train and optimize the P_E-LightGBM model on the s-EMBER dataset with 1511 features obtained in stage (2).

Performing asynchronous distributed training with the Optuna library with the input parameter space as shown in Table 2. we obtain an optimal parameter set in Table 3.

In the last step, this is an important phase, we use the optimal set of hyperparameters obtained from training the model on 1511 features on the s-EMBER dataset to train the model on a dataset 20 times larger, by this approach we can reduce analysis as well as the computational cost to find the best model. Fortunately, we got the expected results.

Table 2. Hyperparameter-turning space for optimizing model

Parameters	Search space	Datatypes
Objective	Binary	String
Metric	Metric	String
Boosting_type	gbdt	String
Lambda_l1	1.4e-08 → 1.6	Float
Lambda_l2	3.4e-06 → 4.0	Float
Num_leaves	2 → 256	Integer
max_depth	7 → 16	Integer
Num_boost_round	500 → 2500	Integer
Feature_fraction	0.4 → 0.52	Float
Bagging_fraction	0.8 → 1.0	Float
Bagging_freq	3 → 7	Integer
Learning_rate	0.07 → 0.9	Float
Min_child_samples	20 → 200	Integer

Table 3. The optimal hyperparameter set.

Parameters	Value	Datatypes
Objective	Binary	String
Metric	Metric	String
Boosting_type	gbdt	String

(continued)

Table 3. (*continued*)

Parameters	Value	Datatypes
lambda_l1	2.50523e-06	Float
Lambda_l2	0.0177153	Float
Num_leaves	245	Integer
Max_depth	16	Integer
Num_boost_round	1058	Integer
Feature_fraction	0.433775	Float
Bagging_fraction	0.961283	Float
Bagging_freq	3	Integer
Learning_rate	0.0798828	Float
Min_child_samples	191	Integer

Training P_E-LightGBM and P_S-LightGBM models with the obtained hyperparameters set s-EMBER and s-SOREL-20M and then test on the test set respectively, we get the results as shown in Table 4.

Table 4. Test results on P_E-LightGBM and P_S-LightGBM model

Model	Detection rate with 1% FPR	Detection rate with 0.1% FPR	No. of features
P_E-LightGBM	96.558%	88.266%	1511
P_S-LightGBM	98.776%	97.492	1511

4.3 Model Performance Comparison

For convenience, this paper temporarily names the machine learning model of the two authors of the EMBER 2018 and SOREL-20M datasets as E-LightGBM and S-LightGBM, respectively.

As shown in Fig. 4, the optimal results of the P_E-LightGBM model have better performance than the E-LightGBM model. Fortunately, the P_S-LightGBM model results are also better than the S-LightGBM model as expected in Fig. 5. Thus, with the proposed analysis and optimization techniques in this problem, we have achieved the desired results on both models, saving more than 20 times the computational cost if analyzed and optimized directly on the SOREL-20M dataset.

Below is a detailed comparison table of the model's performance (Table 5)

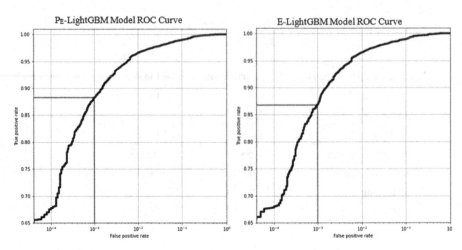

Fig. 4. P_E-LightGBM and E-LightGBM Area under the ROC Curve

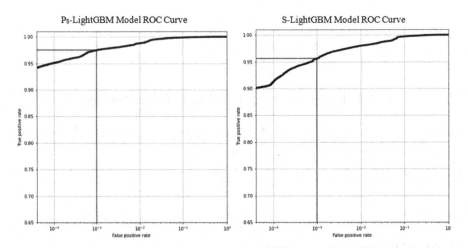

Fig. 5. P_S-LightGBM and S-LightGBM Area under the ROC Curve

Table 5. Performance comparison between machine learning models

Model	Detection rate with 1% FPR(%)	Detection rate with 0.1% FPR(%)	AUC (%)	No. of features
P_E-LightGBM	96.5580	88.2660	99.6531	1511
EMBER-LightGBM	96.4980	86.8080	99.6429	2381
P_S-LightGBM	98.7760	97.4920	99.9375	1511
S-LightGBM	97.9789	95.6151	99.8462	2381

5   Conclusion

This study proposes to improve LightGBM predictive model performance based on the Bayes hyper-parameter optimization algorithm. In particular, Bayes hyper-parameter optimization is used to find an optimal set of parameter combinations for the model, which improves the performance of the LightGBM model when making predictions. The pager has also presented an effective approach in the application of machine learning techniques to the problem of malware identification to the identification and detection of malicious code in order to minimize the computing time at the characteristic selection step as well as optimize the model performance phase.

Although the improved model has achieved the expected results, there is still the possibility of improvement in the feature selection techniques using important specialties identified from previously trained machine learning models. However, it should also be noted that this method is quite expensive when training models on the combination of features.

References

1. AVTest: AV-ATLAS analyzes for you. AV-TEST. Available: https://portal.av-atlas.org. Accessed 12 May 2021
2. The (ISC): Cybersecurity workforce study. The (ISC), 2020. Available: https://www.isc2.org/Research/Workforce-Study. Accessed 12 May 2021
3. Hyrum, S.: Anderson and Phil Roth. EMBER: An Open Dataset for Training Static PE Malware Machine Learning Models (2018)
4. Roth Phil: EMBER Improvements. The Conference on Applied Machine Learning in Information Security, 2019. Available: https://www.camlis.org/2019/talks/roth. Accessed 10 Nov 2020
5. Phil, R.: Elastic malware benchmark for empowering researchers. The Conference on Applied Machine Learning in Information Security, Available: https://github.com/elastic/ember. Accessed 10 Sep 2020
6. Harang, R., Rudd, E.M.: Sorel-20 m: a large scale benchmark dataset for malicious PE detection. Sophos-ReversingLabs, 2020. Available: https://ai.sophos.com/2020/12/14/sophos-reversinglabs-sorel-20-million-sample-malware-dataset/. Accessed 10 Apr 2021
7. Harang, R., Rudd, E.M.: Sorel-20 m: a large scale benchmark dataset for malicious PE detection. Sophos-ReversingLabs, 2020. Available: https://github.com/sophos-ai/SOREL-20M. Accessed Mar 2021
8. Kolter, J.Z., Maloof, M.A." Learning to detect malicious executables in the wild. In: Proceedings of the Tenth ACM SIGKDD International Conference on Knowledge Discovery and Data Mining (2006)
9. Raman, K., et al.: Selecting features to classify malware. InfoSec Southwest (2012)
10. Huang, W., Stokes, J.W.: MtNet: a multi-task neural network for dynamic malware classification. In: Caballero, J., Zurutuza, U., Rodríguez, R.J. (eds.) Detection of Intrusions and Malware, and Vulnerability Assessment, pp. 399–418. Springer International Publishing, Cham (2016). https://doi.org/10.1007/978-3-319-40667-1_20
11. Pham, H.D., Le, T.D., Vu, T.N.: Static PE malware detection using gradient boosting decision trees algorithm. In: Dang, T., Küng, J., Wagner, R., Thoai, N., Takizawa, M. (eds) Future Data and Security Engineering. FDSE 2018. Lecture Notes in Computer Science

12. Oyama, Y., Miyashita, T., Kokubo, H.: Identifying useful features for malware detection in the ember dataset. In: Seventh International Symposium on Computing and Networking Workshops (CANDARW) (2019)
13. Galen, C., Steele, R.: Evaluating performance maintenance and deterioration over time of machine learning-based malware detection models on the EMBER PE dataset. In: Seventh International Conference on Social Networks Analysis, Management and Security (SNAMS) (2020)
14. El Merabet, H.: A first approach to malware detection using residual networks. In: International Journal of Computer Science, Communication & Information Technology (CSCIT) (2019)
15. Abdessadki, I., Lazaar, S.: A new classification based model for malicious PE files detection. Int. J. Comput. Netw. Inf. Secur. 11(6), 1–9 (2019). https://doi.org/10.5815/ijcnis.2019.06.01
16. Kolosnjaji, B., Zarras, A., Webster, G., Eckert, C.: Deep learning for classication of malware system call sequences. In: Australasian Joint Conference on Articial Intelligence (2019)
17. Heller, K., Svore, K., Keromytis, A.D., Stolfo, S.: Oneclass support vector machines for detecting anomalous windows registry accesses. In: ICDM Workshop on Data Mining for Computer Security (2003)
18. Attaluri, S., McGhee, S., Stamp, M.: Profile hidden markov models and metamorphic virus detection. J. Comput. Virol. 5(2), 151–169 (2009). https://doi.org/10.1007/s11416-008-0105-1
19. Ronen, R., Radu, M., Feuerstein, C., Yom-Tov, E., Ahmadi, M.: Microsoft malware classification challenge (2018)
20. Norouzi, M., Souri, A., Zamini, M.S.: A data mining classification approach for behavioral malware detection. J. Comput. Netw. Commun. (2016)
21. Souri, A., Hosseini, R.: A state-of-the-art survey of malware detection approaches using data mining techniques. Hum. Cent. Comput. Inf. Sci. 8 (2018)
22. Bagga, N.: Measuring the Effectiveness of Generic Malware Models. San Jose State University (2017)
23. Roth, P.: Introducing ember: an open source classifier and dataset. Elastic . Available: https://www.elastic.co/blog/introducing-ember-open-source-classifier-and-dataset. Accessed 20 Sep 2020
24. Sophos, A.I.: Sophos-ReversingLabs (SOREL) 20 Million sample malware dataset. Sophos. Available: https://ai.sophos.com/2020/12/14/sophos-reversinglabs-sorel-20-million-sample-malware-dataset/. Accessed 12 May 2021

Smart City and Industry 4.0 Applications

Text Classification Models and Topic Models: An Overall Picture and a Case Study in Vietnamese

Khang Nhut Lam[1(✉)], Vu-Luan Le Tran[1], and Jugal Kalita[2]

[1] Can Tho University, Can Tho, Vietnam
lnkhang@ctu.edu.vn
[2] University of Colorado, Colorado, USA
jkalita@uccs.edu

Abstract. Document classifiers are supervised learning models in which documents are assigned labels based on models that are trained on labeled datasets. The accuracy of a classifier depends on the size and quality of training datasets, which are costly and time-consuming to construct. Besides, a suitable word representation method may improve the quality of the text classifier. In this paper, we study the effect of different word representation methods on 16 classification models trained on a labeled dataset. Then, we experiment with the ability to discover latent topics using 6 topic models. Based on experimental results using combination of classification models and topic models, we propose a method to label datasets for training classification models using topic models and classification models. Although we perform experiments on a Vietnamese document dataset, our approach may apply to any datasets and does not require any labeled datasets for bootstrapping.

Keywords: Annotating documents · Word representation methods · Text classification models · Topic models · Labeling datasets

1 Introduction

Text classification helps save time in searching, sorting, organizing and managing a collection of textual documents effectively. Classification models are supervised-learning approaches based on annotated training datasets. The size and quality of the training datasets significantly affect the accuracy of classifiers. Constructing training datasets for classification models costs effort and is time-consuming. In addition, a classifier trained on a dataset in a particular domain may not classify documents in other domains. Some published efforts have developed methods to enlarge the labeled datasets for training the classification models by bootstrapping from small labeled datasets. Pavlinek and Podgorelec [51] proposed a semi-supervised classification method based on self-training. A small labeled dataset and a much larger unlabeled dataset were passed through the self-training algorithm to enlarge the labeled dataset, to a

© The Author(s), under exclusive license to Springer Nature Singapore Pte Ltd. 2022
T. K. Dang et al. (Eds.): FDSE 2022, CCIS 1688, pp. 377–392, 2022.
https://doi.org/10.1007/978-981-19-8069-5_25

size suitable for training two supervised classification models, Naïve Bayes (NB) and Support Vector Machine (SVM). All labeled and unlabeled data were fed to a topic model in the self-training algorithm to obtain the topic distribution. Then, the unlabeled data were moved iteratively into a labeled set until the pre-defined semantic similarity threshold based on topic distribution and cosine similarity was reached. The authors performed experiments using their proposed approach with the Latent Dirichlet Allocation (LDA) topic model, the so-called ST LDA, to label data for training the SVM and NB classification models. The highest accuracies of the ST LDA with NB and the ST LDA with SVM on the 20 Newsgroups were 73.39±0.54, and 65.73±1.03, respectively. Chen et al. [11] presented a descriptive LDA (DescLDA) scheme for dataless text classification. LDA was combined with a describing device to infer Dirichlet prior, which was later used by the LDA to discover latent topics from unlabeled documents. Multiclass text classification experiments on the 20Newsgroups with 20 topics showed that the accuracy of the DescLDA using category descriptions (–0.72) is better than the DescLDA model using just category labels (~ 0.44) and the supervised LDA model (–0.56), but lower than the SVM model (~ 0.75). Fu et al. [20] extracted topic terms using several LDA models, then clustered topics by computing the divergence similarity between word distributions of two topics and applying the K-means algorithm. Finally, they manually checked and merge similar clusters to generate the final categories. Multi-LDA models were used to classify new documents. Their experiments showed that the LDA model helped extract meaningful topic terms. The highest F-score of their model to construct the categorization system was about 0.8.

In this paper, we take advantage of the ability of topic models to discover latent topics in documents and the power of the classification models to study an effective method for annotating datasets from unlabeled documents. Besides, generating word embeddings is an important step in text classification models. We use several word representation methods to convert words in documents to vectors that can be fed into models. Our study compares the performance of word embedding methods for text classification models in Vietnamese. The contributions of this paper are enumerated below.

- We summarize several word represention methods.
- We discuss classification models and draw an overall picture of classifiers.
- We brief several topic models and perform comparison among topic models.
- A method to annotate datasets from unlabeled documents is proposed using a topic model and two text classification models.

The rest of our paper is organized as follows. Section 2 describes several word representation methods. Summaries of classification models and topic models are presented in Sect. 3 and Sect. 4, respectively. A method to assign categories to documents is proposed in Sect. 5. Section 6 shows experimental results and Sect. 7 concludes the paper.

2 Word Representation Methods

Word representation methods are used to create embeddings of words by mapping words to vectors of real numbers. Word embeddings can represent the semantics of words and express the contextual relationship among words. A fundamental embedding technique is the TF-IDF (Term Frequency - Inverse Document Frequency) [55]. The TF-IDF weight is used to evaluate the importance of words or terms in the text. The higher the TF-IDF value the greater is the importance of a word or term in a document.

One of the most popular and efficient methods to represent words based on neural networks is Word2Vec [43], including a Continuous Bag-of-Words (CBOW) model and a Skipgram model. These models obtain representation of words by capturing the contextual relations among words. Given a sequence of training words $w_1, w_2, ..., w_T$, the CBOW method predicts a target word w_t or a missing word using the context of words; whereas, the Skipgram model predicts a target context of a given word w_t. FastText [6] is a library for learning word representations. Each word is represented as a bag of character N-grams. A vector representing a word is the sum of vectors of character N-grams which that word comprises.

Wordpiece [56] is a method for representing words using subword segmentation approach. A language model is built on a training subword dataset. Byte Pair Encoding (BPE) [57] is very similar to Wordpiece. The major difference is that Wordpiece creates new subwords by maximizing the likelihood of the training data, whereas BPE generates subwords by the most frequent byte pair.

3 Text Classifiers

Text classification models are supervised machine learning and usually consist of 4 steps: feature extraction, dimension reduction, classifier selection, and evaluation [32]. A training dataset D consists of M documents $\{d_1, d_2, ..., d_i, ..., d_M\}$ such that each document d_i is assigned a class value c drawn from a set of k discrete classes. This training dataset is used to train a classification model. Given a new document whose class is unknown, the trained model or the classifier predicts the class for this document.

3.1 Overview of Text Classifiers

The Naïve Bayes classifier (NBC) and Logistic Regression classifier (LRC) are linear classifiers. NBC is a probabilistic classifier based on the Bayesian theorem [4] with an assumption of conditionally independent features, which turns out to be the limitation of this classifier [54]. A basic and simple classification methods is the k-Nearest Neighbor (kNN) classifier which uses the kNN algorithm [17] to classify documents. The kNN classifier can yield an error rate less than that of NBC [58]. However, kNN works less efficiently on documents with many unusable or out-of-vocabulary words [64], costs high amount of time searching neighbors, and depends on the metric distance algorithm used.

The decision tree classifier (DTC) has a tree-like structure generated from the training dataset using a recursive divide-and-conquer approach. The decision tree starts from the root node, splits the data into subsets based on a "best" feature. This splitting process is repeated on each derived subset until leaf nodes are created. The drawbacks of the decision tree are over-fitting, and noise caused by large trees [9]. Some decision tree classifiers are ID3 [52], C4.5 [53], and CART [7].

The Support Vector Machine (SVM) [65] is a linear classification algorithm that finds an optimal hyperplane separating data points of different classes in a high dimensional space. SVM outperforms other text classification models [16, 28] such as the NBC, Rocchio, C4.5, and kNN classifiers on the Reuters-21578 dataset. However, Yu's [70] experiments show that NBC outperforms SVM in erotic poem classification. The drawbacks of SVM classifiers are the high algorithm complexity and memory requirement [54], and the lack of transparency in results [30].

Bagging [8] and Boosting [1] are ensemble learning methods for classification which can improve the performance of a prediction model by combining several simple base models or weak learners [10]. Random Forest is a bagging algorithm that generates a forest with multiple decision trees and classifies a new given document by taking a majority vote of all predictions [62]. Random Forest is better than bagging and as good as boosting [18].

Linear Discriminant Analysis (LDAc) and Quadratic Discriminant Analysis (QDA) [19] are two types of Discriminant Analysis (DA) classifiers [41]. An unknown sample is classified into the class which maximizes the discriminant function. When each class has an individual covariance matrix, it leads to the QDA whose the decision boundaries are quadratic curves; if the variance of all classes is equal, it leads to the LDA whose discriminant function is simplified from quadratic to linear [63].

Deep learning approaches have significantly contributed to solve complex tasks over large datasets, help avoid problems of high dimensionality and spareness of data [71]. Several deep learning classification models are Convolutional Neural Network (CNN) [35], Long Short-Term Memory Network (LSTM) model [25], and Gated Recurrent Unit (GRU) [12].

3.2 Overall Picture of Classifiers

It is not easy to compare all classification models because the classification task for which it has been designed, and thus training and testing datasets may be different. However, for drawing an overall picture of classifiers, we attempt to compare classifiers with the same tasks and datasets.

The experiments in eroticism classification on the Dickinson Erotic Poem dataset [37] showed that NBC with self-feature selection (81.0% accuracy) outperformed SVM with self-feature selection (76.2% accuracy) [70]. Yu suggested that the processes of stemming and removing stopwords were necessary to improve the accuracy of NBC and SVM classifiers.

Irani et al. [27] performed experiments with NBC and C4.5 on the Tweet text and web-page content associated with tweets to predict a tweet belongs to a trend or not. C4.5 achieved the highest F1-measure of 79% on the tweet text and 90% on web-page content and took the longest time to build the model.

NBC achieved F1-measures of 0.77% and 0.74% on the two tasks, respectively. After several experiments, interestingly the authors suggested the use of NBC even though NBC did not perform as well as the C4.5 classifier.

Several classification models [49] have been used to classify short text and sentiment on several datasets taken from the UCI machine learning repository [15]. The experiments showed that GRU worked well on a simple dataset, but was not good on datasets with very short phrases such as book titles [49]. Random Forest and AdaBoost did not work well, in addition to the neural network based approaches on the Farm Advertisement Dataset. The BiLSTM classifier is better than the LSTM classifier and is the best classifier in 3 dataset experiments [49].

Kim [48] experimented with CNN to determine discriminative phrases in a text with a max-pooling layer, and compared CNN classifiers with other classifiers. Experimenting on several benchmark datasets annotated as negative and positive classes, the CNN model outperformed other existing models such as dynamic CNN with k-max pooling [29] and conditional random fields with posterior regularization [69]. On the Subjectivity dataset [50] involving sentences labeled objective or subjective classes, the CNN model was not as good as Naïve Bayes SVM, and multinomial Naïve Bayes [68], and Gaussian dropout and fast dropout [67]. Experiments on classifying a question into 6 types of questions using the TREC question dataset [36] showed that SVMs were the best classifiers [59] compared to CNN models and the dynamic CNN with k-max pooling [29].

Kim claimed that Kim's CNN model was better than other existing CNNs because it had more capacity due to the use of multiple filters and feature maps [48]. In addition, Kim found that word2vec significantly improves the performance of classification. However, Kim was unable to conclude whether it was because of the architecture or the enormous size of the Google dataset. In this paper, we will experiment with several classification models on a Vietnamese dataset to establish which model is the best for classifying Vietnamese documents. Besides, several embedding approaches will also be trained on the same Vietnamese dataset to establish the best technique.

4   Topic Models

Given a document collection $D = \{d_1, d_2..., d_m, ...d_M\}$ with a total of N words in a dictionary $W = \{w_1, w_2, ..., w_n, ..., w_N\}$, a topic model explores latent semantic structures or topics of documents based on word distribution. A topic associated with a document contains a list of weighted words that convey the most information about the document, the so-called *topic terms* or *terms*. A topic model is also known as a generative model for documents [61]. Most topic models, except the Top2Vec and BERTopic models, need to know the k underlying latent topics $Z = \{z_1, z_2, ..., z_k\}$ in the corpus. The rest of this section briefly presents topic models and the overall pictures of them.

4.1   Overview of Topic Models

TF-IDF [55] can be used to reveal the topic terms in documents. The result of the TF-IDF model is a term-by-document matrix. This method is based on the bag-of-word approach and word frequency count, which do not take the position and context of words into account. In addition, words with the highest TF-IDF weight might not make sense as the topic terms of documents. To address the drawbacks of TF-IDF, Latent Semantic Indexing or Latent Semantic Analysis (LSA) [13] was introduced using SVD for dimensionality reduction. LSA tries to map documents with high dimensional vectors to lower dimensional vectors, the so-called *latent semantic space*, using the SVD method. LSA is based on dimension reduction of the corpus, using ad-hoc heuristics. To overcome this drawback, the probabilistic Latent Semantic Analysis (pLSA) [26] model was introduced. LSA and pLSA have some drawbacks, such as the model can not assign probabilities to new documents outside the training dataset and the number of parameters increases linearly with the number of documents. These problems are overcome by the Latent Dirichlet Allocation (LDA) [5] which uses the Dirichlet multinomial distribution. The common ideas among the LSA, pLSA, and LDA are that they use the bag-of-words technique to represent documents, and they model topics as a distribution of words. As a result, topic terms extracted using these models may not express the main topic of the documents. To overcome issues of the existing topic model, LDA2Vec [45] is a model that combined the LDA and Word2vec Skipgram.

The weakness of LSA, pLSA, LDA, and LDA2Vec is that the number of topics needs to be known. Top2Vec [2] unearths, by itself, the number of latent topics among documents by finding the number of dense areas of documents found in the semantic space, which is created jointly by document and word embeddings using Doc2vec Distributed Bag of Words [34]. An outstanding advantage of Top2Vec is that there is no need to preprocess datasets such as removing stopwords, stemming, and lemmatizing words in text.

BERTopic [22] takes advantage of pre-trained models. This topic model generates BERT embeddings for a document using the *sentence-transformers* package. BERTopic also performs the UMAP algorithm [40] for dimension reduction on document vectors and the HDBSCAN [39] for clustering documents. Then, a class-based TF-IDF (c-TF-IDF) is used to compute the importance value of each word in a cluster. The most important words, which are words with the highest c-TF-IDF scores, in each cluster are considered as topic terms.

4.2   Overall Picture of Topic Models

Several studies perform comparison among topic models. The authors have found that LDA is better than LSA. In particular, the best coherence values achieved with LDA on scientific unstructured text documents with 10 topics and 20 topics are 0.504 and 0.548; while these values with LSA are 0.4801 and 0.405 [44]. On the IMDB movie reviews and National Institutes of Health corpus with 10 topics, the average coherence values of topics generated by LDA are 0.07 and 0.06, and the values generated by LSA are 0.11 and 0.32 [31]. Besides, LDA is also better than Non-Negative Matrix Factorization when performing on a large corpus of Covid'19[1] with 10 topics [42].

---

[1]   https://www.sketchengine.eu/covid19/.

Moody performs experiments with the LDA2Vec model on the Twenty Newsgroups dataset with 20 topics and finds that the best average topic coherence is 0.57 [45]. Comparing the performance of the LDA and LDA2Vec on the Aviation Safety Reports comprising 59,876 reports in 20 topics shows the LDA2Vec outperforms the LDA and is more reliable [38]. The average coherence of LDA2Vec is about 0.49. Hasan et al. [23] also find that LDA2Vec achieves higher accuracy (85.66%) than LDA (62.45%) on 22,675 Bangla news documents with 9 types. Both Luo and Shi [38] and Hasan et al. [23] claim that LDA2vec is more reliable and more flexible than LDA.

Angelove [2] compares pLSA, LDA, and Top2Vec by calculating the probability weighted amount of information. The results show that Top2Vec consistently provides more information than pLSA and LDA. Based on our best knowledge, we could not find any papers that evaluate the coherence although there are many studies used Top2Vec to discover topic terms [3, 21].

5   Label Documents for Training Classification Models

Given documents and k number of classes or topics, we follow guidelines of Lam et al. [33] by using a topic model to extract terms for each topic, and document-topic matrix. Topics in the numeric form are converted to natural language form manually by experts. After using a topic model to assign topics to documents, we compute coherence scores of topic terms in each topic label. We notice that the topic with the lowest coherence score comprises ambiguous documents which need to be considered again, and denote this topic by $Topic_{bias}$. We use 2 additional classification models to re-assign topics or labels to documents. The process of assigning labels to documents has 5 steps, as presented in Fig. 1.

- Step 1 - Train classification model A: We initially assume that documents labeled with topics by the topic model are acceptable, except documents labeled with $Topic_{bias}$. To make it easy for discussion, we make an assumption that $Topic_1$ is the $Topic_{bias}$. A Dataset$_D$ comprises the documents labeled by the topic model, not including documents labeled with $Topic_{bias}$. We feed all documents and their labels in Dataset$_D$ to train the classification model A. After the training step, classifier A can classify documents into $(k-1)$ topics.
- Step 2 - Remove inappropriately labeled documents in Dataset$_D$: Documents in Dataset$_D$ have their labels removed to create a Dataset$_{D'}$, and are fed into classifier A to classify documents into $(k-1)$ topics. Next, for each document, we compare its label assigned by classifier A with its label assigned by the topic model; if it does not match, we label this document with $Topic_{bias}$ and remove it from Dataset$_{D'}$. This step is repeated until there are no changes in Dataset$_{D'}$. Finally, the documents in Dataset$_{D'}$ are labeled by classifier A and are accepted correctly.
- Step 3 - Train classification model B: We use the documents labeled by classifier A as a dataset to train classification model B.
- Step 4 - Classify the remaining documents: All documents labeled as $Topic_{bias}$ by the topic model and by the process in Step 2 have their labels removed

and fed to the two classifiers A and B. For each document, if its labels by classifier A and classifier B are similar, we accept this label as the final label of the document, otherwise, this document is labeled as $Topic_{bias}$.

– Step 5 - Combine results: Finally, we simply combine documents labeled and change the $Topic_{bias}$ to the original topic assigned by the topic model.

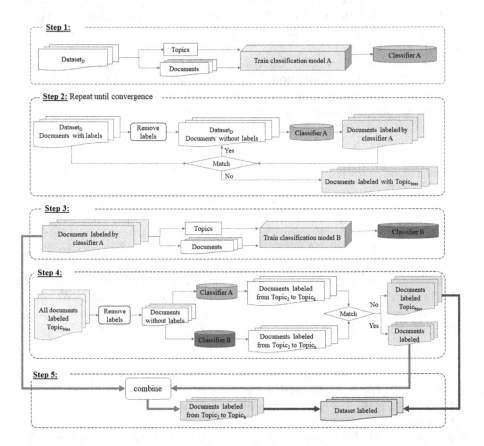

Fig. 1. Process for labeling a training classification dataset using a topic model and topic classification models

6   Experiments

First, we present the dataset used and steps to pre-process the dataset. Then, we discuss the methods used to evaluate models. Next, we analyze the effect of classifiers and word embedding methods for classifying Vietnamese documents using an annotated training classification dataset. We experiment with the ability to discover latent topics of topic models. Finally, we perform experiments with the model for annotating a training datatset for classification models

6.1   Data Pre-processing

In this study, we use the VNTC dataset[2] [24] comprising about 84,000 articles on 10 topics extracted from popular online magazines in the Vietnamese language, such as vnexpress.net, tuoitre.vn, thanhnien.vn, and nld.com.vn. The Beautiful-Soup[3] library is used to clean the data. Then, we normalize text in the documents into the Unicode character set and normalize diacritics written above or below the vowel. Next, the Underthesea[4] toolkit is used to segment Vietnamese words. In addition, we remove 1,942 stopwords using the Vietnamese stopword list provided by Le Van Duyet[5]. After the pre-processing step, we collect about 6,5 million words in total with about 94,258 unique words.

6.2   Classification Models and Word Embeddings

We want to compare the performance of classifiers. In addition, one of our goals is to compare the effect of different word represention methods on classifiers so that we use several methods for representing words for each classifier. We experiment with 16 classifiers with several word embedding methods using the original VNTC dataset. As discussed in Sect. 2, there are several word embedding methods available, we experiment to find which method is more effective in text classification.

- TF-IDF: We use the *TfidfVectorizer* and *TruncatedSVD* functions in the Scikit-learn[6] library to obtain representations of words.
- Word2Vec: Both Word2Vec CBOW (denoted as CBOW) and Word2Vec Skipgram (denoted as Skipgram) are used to generate word embeddings on the VNTC dataset using parameters of 300-dimensional vectors and a context window size of 10. We additionally use pre-trained CBOW word vectors provided by Vu et al. [66], and pre-trained Skipgram word vectors provided from PhoW2V [46].
- FastText: We generate word embeddings using FastText on the VNTC dataset, and use pre-trained word embeddings of FastText[7].
- WordPiece: We only use pre-trained WordPiece embeddings provided by BERT-base, multilingual cased[8] [14].
- BPE: We use pre-trained BPE embeddings provided by PhoBERT[9] [47].

Figure 2 presents the accuracies of classifiers using CBOW, Skipgram and FastText embedding approaches, each of which comprises pre-trained models and trained models on the VNTC dataset. Although the number of word embeddings

---

[2]   https://github.com/duyvuleo/VNTC.
[3]   https://www.crummy.com/software/BeautifulSoup/bs4/doc/.
[4]   https://pypi.org/project/underthesea/.
[5]   https://github.com/stopwords/vietnamese-stopwords.
[6]   https://scikit-learn.org/.
[7]   https://fasttext.cc/.
[8]   https://github.com/google-research/bert.
[9]   https://huggingface.co/vinai/phobert-base.

constructed by ourselves is significantly smaller than the number of pre-trained word embeddings, the classifiers using our trained word embeddings help achieve higher accuracies than the ones using pre-trained word embeddings. Therefore, we use our trained word embeddings including CBOW, Skipgram, and FastText for further experiments. In addition, we use pre-trained WordPiece and BPE word embeddings. The accuracies of classifiers are presented in Fig. 3.

We additionally experiment with BERT and PhoBERT classifiers. The BERT classifier using WordPiece embedding method and the PhoBERT classifier using BPE embedding method achieve accuracies of 86.13% and 86.53%, respectively. The SVM classifiers using TF-IDF for feature extracting outperforms other classifiers with the highest accuracy of 92.14%. TF-IDF is the best feature extraction method for all classifiers. WordPiece and BPE are worse than TF-IDF, but much better than CBOW and other embedding approaches.

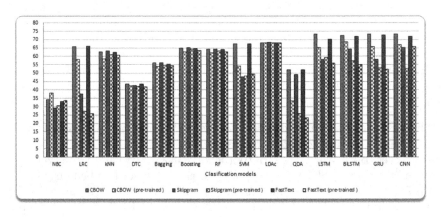

Fig. 2. Accuracies of classifiers using trained word embeddings and pre-trained word embeddings

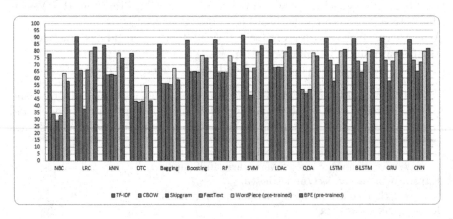

Fig. 3. Accuracies of 14 classifiers on the original VNTC dataset

6.3 Comparing Performance of Topic Models

Topic coherence measure is used to evaluate topic models [60]. To perform experiments on topic models, we do not take into account the labels of documents. In particular, we create a dataset for topic models, the so-called VNdocs, by removing all labels of documents in the VNTC dataset and mixing them. The outputs of the topic models are term-topic matrices, where the topic values are discrete numbers.

For the Top2Vec model, we follow the guide of Ghasiya et al. [21] and Arora et al. [3] to extract 50 terms for each topic. Based on the suggestion of the BERTopic's authors[10], if the number of set terms is high, it can "negatively impact topic embeddings". We extract 30 terms for each topic by the BERTopic model. For the LSA, pLSA, LDA, and LDA2Vec topic models, we extract 100 terms for each topic. Table 1 shows the topic coherence values of topic models.

Table 1. The topic coherence values of terms on each corresponding topic discovered using the topic models in the VNdocs dataset

Topic model	LSA	pLSA	LDA	LDA2Vec	Top2Vec	BERTopic
Topic 1	0.684	0.486	0.664	0.394	0.474	0.392
Topic 2	0.390	0.406	0.555	0.510	0.869	0.843
Topic 3	0.356	0.575	0.475	0.207	0.551	0.898
Topic 4	0.655	0.376	0.673	0.522	0.563	0.629
Topic 5	0.391	0.377	0.652	0.413	0.552	0.882
Topic 6	0.344	0.464	0.727	0.398	0.300	0.798
Topic 7	0.361	0.434	0.582	0.422	0.317	0.819
Topic 8	0.730	0.490	0.873	0.419	0.325	0.899
Topic 9	0.447	0.460	0.565	0.435	0.413	0.900
Topic 10	0.435	0.469	0.765	0.361	0.466	0.859
Average	**0.479**	**0.454**	**0.653**	**0.408**	**0.483**	**0.792**

The results show that BERTopic has the highest average coherence value of 0.792, but there is a wide range between the lowest coherence value (0.392 of Topic 1) and the greatest coherence value (0.900 of Topic 9). The LDA achieves the average coherence value of 0.653, and the LDA2Vec has the lowest average coherence value of 0.408.

6.4 Labeling Documents for a Training Classification Dataset

Topic models are used to extract terms belonging to each topic in numeric form and manually label them with a topic in natural language form. Three people

---

[10] https://maartengr.github.io/BERTopic/index.html.

were requested to label topics for given terms. The agreement values between them are 36.67% for LSA, 60.67% for pLSA, 70% for LDA, 10% for LDA2Vec, 50% for Top2Vec, and 73,33% for BERTopic. The agreement between volunteers and the coherence values of words on corresponding topics is confirmed. Once again LDA and BERTopic discover topics better than LDA2Vec and Top2Vec. In addition, the BERTopic and LDA topic models extract topic terms with the highest average coherence values, shown in Table 1. Therefore, we use the LDA and BERTopic models to assign labels to documents for training classification models. For comparison purpose, we also compute the coherence scores for each topic in the original VNTC dataset, presented in Table 2. The results show that the topic terms extracted on each topic in the original VNTC dataset have lower average coherence scores than the terms extracted on each topic in the VNdocs dataset, as shown in Table 1.

Next, we evaluate the accuracy of the labels assigned to documents using the topic models only. The LDA and BERTopic models to assign the labels to documents have accuracies of 66.02% and 31.7%. Then, we continually use our proposed method to label documents on outputs of topic models using SVM as the classification model A and NBC as the classification model B, the so-called SVM-NBC. The accuracies of the approach for labeling documents using the LDA-SVM-NBC and BERTopic-SVM-NBC are 66.12% and 53.78%, respectively.

Table 2. The topic coherence values of terms on each corresponding topic discovered using the topic models in the original VNTC dataset

LDA topic model- average coherence score: 0.582									
Topic 1	Topic 2	Topic 3	Topic 4	Topic 5	Topic 6	Topic 7	Topic 8	Topic 9	Topic 10
0.385	0.535	0.413	0.624	0.521	0.668	0.548	0.787	0.583	0.755
BERTopic topic model- average coherence score: 0.583									
Topic 1	Topic 2	Topic 3	Topic 4	Topic 5	Topic 6	Topic 7	Topic 8	Topic 9	Topic 10
0.390	0.535	0.413	0.624	0.521	0.668	0.548	0.787	0.587	0.755

7   Conclusion

We have briefly presented, analyzed, and compared several word embedding approaches, text classification models, and topic models. We have proposed a method to automatically assign labels to documents for text classification using a topic model and two text classification models. Although we have not performed experiments on datasets in other languages, our approach may apply to any datasets and does not require any labeled datasets for bootstrapping. For future work, we will discover combinations between other topic models and classification models to improve the results.

References

1. Amit, Y., Geman, D.: Shape quantization and recognition with randomized trees. Neural Comput. **9**(7), 1545–1588 (1997)
2. Angelov, D.: Top2vec: Distributed representations of topics. arXiv preprint arXiv:2008.09470 (2020)
3. Aroraa, J., Patankara, T., Shaha, A., Joshia, S.: Artificial intelligence as legal research assistant. In: CEUR Workshop Proceedings (CEUR-WS.org) (2020)
4. Bayes, F.: An essay towards solving a problem in the doctrine of chances. Biometrika **45**(3–4), 296–315 (1958)
5. Blei, D.M., Ng, A.Y., Jordan, M.I.: Latent dirichlet allocation. J. Mach. Learn. Res. **3**, 993–1022 (2003)
6. Bojanowski, P., Grave, E., Joulin, A., Mikolov, T.: Enriching word vectors with subword information. Trans. Assoc. Comput. Linguist. **5**, 135–146 (2017)
7. Breiman, L., Friedman, J., Olshen, R., Stone, C.: Classification and regression trees (CART).: Belmont. Wadsworth International Group, CA, USA (1984)
8. Breiman, L.: Bagging predictors. Mach. Learn. **24**(2), 123–140 (1996)
9. Breslow, L.A., Aha, D.W.: Simplifying decision trees: A survey. Knowl. Eng. Rev. **12**(01), 1–40 (1997)
10. Bühlmann, P.: Bagging, boosting and ensemble methods. In: Handbook of Computational Statistics, pp. 985–1022. Springer (2012). https://doi.org/10.1007/978-3-642-21551-3_33
11. Chen, X., Xia, Y., Jin, P., Carroll, J.: Dataless text classification with descriptive LDA. In: Proceedings of the AAAI Conference on Artificial Intelligence, vol. 29 (2015)
12. Cho, K., Van Merriënboer, B., Bahdanau, D., Bengio, Y.: On the properties of neural machine translation: Encoder-decoder approaches. arXiv preprint arXiv:1409.1259 (2014)
13. Dennis, S., Landauer, T., Kintsch, W., Quesada, J.: Introduction to latent semantic analysis. In: 25th Annual Meeting of the Cognitive Science Society, Boston, Mass, p. 25 (2003)
14. Devlin, J., Chang, M.W., Lee, K., Toutanova, K.: BERT: Pre-training of deep bidirectional Transformers for language understanding. arXiv preprint arXiv:1810.04805 (2018)
15. Dua, D., Graff, C.: UCI machine learning repository. irvine, ca: University of california, school of information and computer science (1997). http://archive.ics.uci.edu/ml
16. Dumais, S., Platt, J., Heckerman, D., Sahami, M.: Inductive learning algorithms and representations for text categorization. In: Proceedings of the Seventh International Conference on Information and Knowledge Management, pp. 148–155 (1998)
17. Fix, E., Hodges, J.L.: Discriminatory analysis. Nonparametric discrimination: Consistency properties. Int. Stat. Review/Revue Internationale de Statistique **57**(3), 238–247 (1989)
18. Franklin, J.: The elements of statistical learning: data mining, inference and prediction. Math. Intell. **27**(2), 83–85 (2005). https://doi.org/10.1007/BF02985802
19. Friedman, J., Hastie, T., Tibshirani, R., et al.: The elements of statistical learning, vol. 1. Springer series in statistics, New York (2001)
20. Fu, R., Qin, B., Liu, T.: Open-categorical text classification based on multi-LDA models. Soft. Comput. **19**(1), 29–38 (2015)

21. Ghasiya, P., Okamura, K.: Investigating COVID-19 news across four nations: A topic modeling and sentiment analysis approach. IEEE Access **9**, 36645–36656 (2021)
22. Grootendorst, M.: BERTopic: Leveraging BERT and c-TF-IDF to create easily interpretable topics. Zenodo, Version v0 4 (2020)
23. Hasan, M., Hossain, M.M., Ahmed, A., Rahman, M.S.: Topic modelling: A comparison of the performance of Latent Dirichlet Allocation and LDA2vec model on Bangla newspaper. In: 2019 International Conference on Bangla Speech and Language Processing (ICBSLP), pp. 1–5. IEEE (2019)
24. Hoang, V.C.D., Dinh, D., Le Nguyen, N., Ngo, H.Q.: A comparative study on Vietnamese text classification methods. In: 2007 IEEE International Conference on Research, Innovation and Vision for the Future. pp. 267–273. IEEE (2007)
25. Hochreiter, S., Schmidhuber, J.: Long short-term memory. Neural Comput. **9**(8), 1735–1780 (1997)
26. Hofmann, T.: Unsupervised learning by probabilistic latent semantic analysis. Mach. Learn. **42**(1), 177–196 (2001)
27. Irani, D., Webb, S., Pu, C., Li, K.: Study of trend-stuffing on Twitter through text classification. In: Collaboration, Electronic messaging, Anti-Abuse and Spam Conference (CEAS) (2010)
28. Joachims, T.: Text categorization with support vector machines: learning with many relevant features. In: Nédellec, C., Rouveirol, C. (eds.) ECML 1998. LNCS, vol. 1398, pp. 137–142. Springer, Heidelberg (1998). https://doi.org/10.1007/BFb0026683
29. Kalchbrenner, N., Grefenstette, E., Blunsom, P.: A convolutional neural network for modelling sentences. arXiv preprint arXiv:1404.2188 (2014)
30. Karamizadeh, S., Abdullah, S.M., Halimi, M., Shayan, J., javad Rajabi, M.: Advantage and drawback of Support Vector Machine functionality. In: 2014 international conference on computer, communications, and control technology (I4CT), pp. 63–65. IEEE (2014)
31. Kherwa, P., Bansal, P.: Topic modeling: a comprehensive review. EAI Endorsed Trans. Scalable Inform. Syst. 7(24) (2020)
32. Kowsari, K., Jafari Meimandi, K., Heidarysafa, M., Mendu, S., Barnes, L., Brown, D.: Text classification algorithms: a survey. Information **10**(4), 150 (2019)
33. Lam, K.N., Truong, L.T., Kalita, J.: Using topic models to label documents for classification. In: Dang, T.K., Küng, J., Takizawa, M., Chung, T.M. (eds.) FDSE 2020. CCIS, vol. 1306, pp. 443–451. Springer, Singapore (2020). https://doi.org/10.1007/978-981-33-4370-2_32
34. Le, Q., Mikolov, T.: Distributed representations of sentences and documents. In: International Conference on Machine Learning, pp. 1188–1196. PMLR (2014)
35. LeCun, Y., Bottou, L., Bengio, Y., Haffner, P.: Gradient-based learning applied to document recognition. Proc. IEEE **86**(11), 2278–2324 (1998)
36. Li, X., Roth, D.: Learning question classifiers. In: COLING 2002: The 19th International Conference on Computational Linguistics (2002)
37. Lord, G., et al.: Exploring erotics in Emily Dickinson's correspondence with text mining and visual interfaces. In: Proceedings of the 6th ACM/IEEE-CS joint conference on Digital libraries (JCDL 2006), pp. 141–150. IEEE (2006)
38. Luo, Y., Shi, H.: Using LDA2vec topic modeling to identify latent topics in aviation safety reports. In: 2019 IEEE/ACIS 18th International Conference on Computer and Information Science (ICIS), pp. 518–523. IEEE (2019)
39. McInnes, L., Healy, J., Astels, S.: HDBSCAN: Hierarchical density based clustering. J. Open Source Softw. **2**(11), 205 (2017)

40. McInnes, L., Healy, J., Melville, J.: Umap: Uniform manifold approximation and projection for dimension reduction. arXiv preprint arXiv:1802.03426 (2018)

41. McLachlan, G.J.: Discriminant analysis and statistical pattern recognition, vol. 544. John Wiley & Sons (2004)

42. Mifrah, S., Benlahmar, E.: Topic modeling coherence: A comparative study between LDA and NMF models using COVID'19 corpus. Int. J. Adv. Trends Comput. Sci. Eng. 5756–5761 (2020)

43. Mikolov, T., Chen, K., Corrado, G., Dean, J.: Efficient estimation of word representations in vector space. arXiv preprint arXiv:1301.3781 (2013)

44. Mohammed, S.H., Al-augby, S.: LSA & LDA topic modeling classification: Comparison study on e-books. Indonesian J. Elect. Eng. Comput. Sci. **19**(1), 353–362 (2020)

45. Moody, C.E.: Mixing Dirichlet topic models and word embeddings to make LDA2vec. arXiv preprint arXiv:1605.02019 (2016)

46. Nguyen, A.T., Dao, M.H., Nguyen, D.Q.: A pilot study of text-to-SQL semantic parsing for Vietnamese. arXiv preprint arXiv:2010.01891 (2020)

47. Nguyen, D.Q., Nguyen, A.T.: PhoBERT: Pre-trained language models for Vietnamese. arXiv preprint arXiv:2003.00744 (2020)

48. Nowak, J., Taspinar, A., Scherer, R.: Convolutional neural networks for sentence classification. In: The 2014 Conference on Empirical Methods in Natural Language Processing (EMNLP), p. 1746–1751 (2014)

49. Nowak, J., Taspinar, A., Scherer, R.: LSTM recurrent neural networks for short text and sentiment classification. In: Rutkowski, L., Korytkowski, M., Scherer, R., Tadeusiewicz, R., Zadeh, L.A., Zurada, J.M. (eds.) ICAISC 2017. LNCS (LNAI), vol. 10246, pp. 553–562. Springer, Cham (2017). https://doi.org/10.1007/978-3-319-59060-8_50

50. Pang, B., Lee, L.: A sentimental education: Sentiment analysis using subjectivity summarization based on minimum cuts. arXiv preprint cs/0409058 (2004)

51. Pavlinek, M., Podgorelec, V.: Text classification method based on self-training and LDA topic models. Expert Syst. Appl. **80**, 83–93 (2017)

52. Quinlan, J.R.: Induction of decision trees. Mach. Learn. **1**(1), 81–106 (1986)

53. Quinlan, J.R.: C4.5: programs for machine learning. Elsevier (2014)

54. Ranjan, M.N.M., Ghorpade, Y., Kanthale, G., Ghorpade, A., Dubey, A.: Document classification using LSTM neural network. J. Data Mining Manag. **2**(2), 1–9 (2017)

55. Salton, G., Buckley, C.: Term-weighting approaches in automatic text retrieval. Inf. Process. Manag. **24**(5), 513–523 (1988)

56. Schuster, M., Nakajima, K.: Japanese and Korean voice search. In: 2012 IEEE International Conference on Acoustics, Speech and Signal Processing (ICASSP), pp. 5149–5152. IEEE (2012)

57. Sennrich, R., Haddow, B., Birch, A.: Neural machine translation of rare words with subword units. arXiv preprint arXiv:1508.07909 (2015)

58. Sharma, S., Agrawal, J., Sharma, S.: Classification through machine learning technique: C4.5 algorithm based on various entropies. Int. J. Comput. Appli. **82**(16) (2013)

59. Silva, J., Coheur, L., Mendes, A.C., Wichert, A.: From symbolic to sub-symbolic information in question classification. Artif. Intell. Rev. **35**(2), 137–154 (2011)

60. Stevens, K., Kegelmeyer, P., Andrzejewski, D., Buttler, D.: Exploring topic coherence over many models and many topics. In: Proceedings of the 2012 Joint Conference on Empirical Methods in Natural Language Processing and Computational Natural Language Learning, pp. 952–961 (2012)

61. Steyvers, M., Griffiths, T.: Probabilistic topic models. Handbook of Latent Semantic Analysis. Edited by Landauer, T.K., McNamara, D.S., Dennis, S., kintsch, W., Erlbaum, N.J: Information Science in Korea using Topic Modeling. J. Korean Soc. Inf. Manag. **30**(1), 7–32 (2007)

62. Taser, P.Y.: Application of bagging and boosting approaches using decision tree-based algorithms in diabetes risk prediction. In: Multidisciplinary Digital Publishing Institute Proceedings, vol. 74, p. 6 (2021)

63. Tharwat, A.: Linear vs. quadratic discriminant analysis classifier: a tutorial. Int. J. Appli. Pattern Recogn. **3**(2), 145–180 (2016)

64. Trstenjak, B., Mikac, S., Donko, D.: KNN with TF-IDF based framework for text categorization. Proc. Eng. **69**, 1356–1364 (2014)

65. Vapnik, V.: The nature of statistical learning theory. Springer Science & Business Media (2013). https://doi.org/10.1007/978-1-4757-3264-1

66. Vu, X.S., Vu, T., Tran, S.N., Jiang, L.: ETNLP: A visual-aided systematic approach to select pre-trained embeddings for a downstream task. arXiv preprint arXiv:1903.04433 (2019)

67. Wang, S., Manning, C.: Fast dropout training. In: International Conference on Machine Learning, pp. 118–126. PMLR (2013)

68. Wang, S.I., Manning, C.D.: Baselines and bigrams: Simple, good sentiment and topic classification. In: Proceedings of the 50th Annual Meeting of the Association for Computational Linguistics (Volume 2: Short Papers), pp. 90–94 (2012)

69. Yang, B., Cardie, C.: Context-aware learning for sentence-level sentiment analysis with posterior regularization. In: Proceedings of the 52nd Annual Meeting of the Association for Computational Linguistics (Volume 1: Long Papers), pp. 325–335 (2014)

70. Yu, B.: An evaluation of text classification methods for literary study. Liter. Lingu. Comput. **23**(3), 327–343 (2008)

71. Zhang, J., Li, Y., Tian, J., Li, T.: LSTM-CNN hybrid model for text classification. In: 2018 IEEE 3rd Advanced Information Technology, Electronic and Automation Control Conference (IAEAC), pp. 1675–1680. IEEE (2018)

Deep Hybrid Models for Forecasting Stock Midprices from the High-Frequency Limit Order Book

Duc-Phu Nguyen[1,2], Nhat-Tan Le[3], Tien-Thinh Nguyen[1,2],
Thanh-Phuong Nguyen[4], Tien-Duc Van[5], Son-Tu Phan[6],
and Khuong Nguyen-An[1,2(✉)]

[1] Faculty of Computer Science and Engineering,
Ho Chi Minh City University of Technology (HCMUT),
268 Ly Thuong Kiet Street, District 10, Ho Chi Minh City, Vietnam
{phu.nguyen.cse,ntthinh,nakhuong}@hcmut.edu.vn
[2] Vietnam National University Ho Chi Minh City, Linh Trung Ward, Thu Duc
District, Ho Chi Minh City, Vietnam
[3] Fulbright University, Ho Chi Minh City, Vietnam
tan.le@fulbright.edu.vn
[4] New Mexico State University, Las Cruces, USA
ntphuong@nmsu.edu
[5] Orient Commercial Joint Stock Bank (OCB), Hochiminh City, Vietnam
[6] Descartes Network, Ontario, Canada
tuphan@descartes.network

Abstract. This paper aims to develop deep learning models for forecasting stock's mid-price movements based on the high-frequency limit order book (LOB) data. We acquire a relatively large (∼15GB) dataset from the well-known Wharton Research Data Services (WRDS), which contains Millisecond Trade and Quote, consolidated from "Daily Product" in WRDS. Stock prices in millisecond are carefully aggregated to stock prices in seconds so that stock price trends remains relatively the same after the aggregation. To predict the stock price, we apply popular machine learning models: ResNet50, LSTM, and two of their hybrid forms. Our tested results are comparable with other recent studies regarding accuracy and F1-score.

Keywords: Stock · Order book · Market prediction · Automatic trading · Machine learning · Convolutional neurons network · Long-short term memory

1 Introduction

In recent years, deep learning methods have greatly contributed to many practical applications in different areas of finance, such as *Fraud detection, portfolio management, credit scoring, stock market prediction,* or *algorithmic trading* [16].

T. K. Dang et al. (Eds.): FDSE 2022, CCIS 1688, pp. 393–406, 2022.
https://doi.org/10.1007/978-981-19-8069-5_26

Among them, the stock market prediction has always been one of the most attractive areas.

More specifically, due to an increasing number of daily traders, there is a demand for more accurate and efficient tools that can support daily traders to make better decisions and profits on stock markets. In the literature, several deep learning models are used to predict price movements in a short interval. The results of these works can form a foundation to construct a helpful tool for "intraday" traders, an automatic trading bot. Gandhmal et al. [5], and [12] provided a detailed analysis and review of stock market prediction techniques.

Given in Fig. 1, we observe the dominance of Recurrent Neural Network (RNN), Deep Multi-Layer Perceptron (DMLP), and Convolutional Neural Network (CNN) over the remaining models, which might be expected, since these models are the most commonly preferred and supported ones in deep learning techniques.

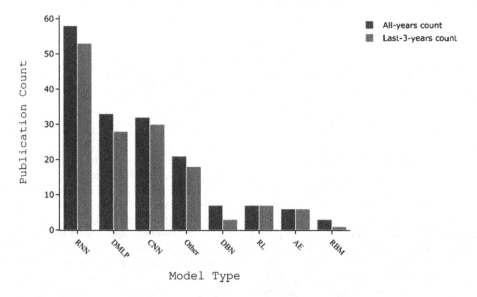

Fig. 1. Histogram of publication count in model types (2020). (source [12]).

In this paper, we use the order book data in the last 5 min to predict the stock price for the next 5 min (explained in Sect. 4.4). Our data set includes 200 million records about the best bid price, the best ask price, and their corresponding volumes of seven popular NASDAQ stocks, from April 1, 2018, to April 30, 2018. The data is carefully manipulated and labeled to set up the research problem rightly. Our obtained results by using popular machine learning models: ResNet50, LSTM, and two of their hybrid forms are promising in terms of accuracy and F1-score. All four models have accuracy and F1-score above 70%.

The paper is organized into seven sections. Section 1 introduces the research problem . Section 2 presents some "order book" and machine learning-related knowledge. Section 3 discuss the methodologies proposed by previous researchers in solving the research problem. We introduce our data and present clearly the way we process it in Sect. 4. Our proposed models are explained and evaluated in Sects. 5 and 6, respectively. Section 7 summarizes the paper, evaluates what we have achieved and what we have not, as well as some plans for the future of the research problem.

2 Backgrounds

2.1 Local Spatial Structure

This section highlights a potential feature, known as the local spatial structure, of our LOB data. One example of that feature is that the larger the ask size at the current level, the less likely the future best ask price might reach a greater level. Some statistical evidence for local spatial structure in limit order books is given in the research [13]. In particular, a detailed analysis across 489 stocks primarily drawn from S&P500 and NASDAQ-100 is conducted in [13] to show that the conditional movement of the future price depends locally on the current limit order book state. In this paper, we select neural networks as our main models due to their great capacity to explore the spatial structure of our data.

2.2 Deep Residual Learning

Since AlexNet [11] was introduced, the state-of-the-art CNN architecture is going more sophisticated. The descendants of it, VGGNet and GoogleNet, had 19 and 22 layers respectively [4], compared to 5 of AlexNet. However, vanishing gradient causes challenging problems regarding training deep neural networks - as the gradient is back-propagated to earlier layers, repeated multiplication may make the gradient infinitely small. As a result, when the network goes deeper, its performance halts or even starts degrading rapidly, which is called a *degradation* problem [8]. Deep Residual Learning (ResNet) was first introduced by He et al. [8] in order to address the degradation problem. The core idea of ResNet is introducing a so-called "identity shortcut connection" that skips one or more layers, as shown in Fig. 2.

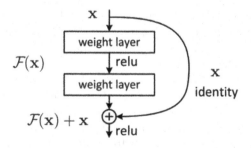

Fig. 2. A residual block in ResNet. ((source [8]).

ResNet50 is a well-known variant of ResNet in which there are 50 convolutional layers, introduced by He et al. [8].

2.3 Long-Short Term Memory

Long-Short Term Memory (LSTM) was first introduced by Hochreiter and Schmidhuber in 1997 [9]. LSTM is a variant of RNN in which a gating mechanism is provided. According to Goodfellow et al. [6], the original idea of the LSTM model is to **create self-loops** to **remain the gradient** for a longer duration. These self-loops are weighted by a gating mechanism, controlled by other hidden units, rather than fixed. This innovation gives LSTM a huge advantage in many applications, such as unconstrained handwriting recognition, speech recognition, image captioning, etc. In the finance industry, LSTM has also gained its popularity thanks to its unique property in processing time-series data, which contributes to our decision to go along with LSTM models in the paper[1].

LSTM block, also called the "LSTM cell", has the same input and output as the RNN but possesses an internal self-loop and gating units in addition. The self-loop is controlled by a **forget gate** unit $f_i^{(t)}$ for time step t and cell i.

3 Related Works

Thanks to recent advances, it is impossible not to notice the rising of deep learning techniques. Therefore, we were encouraged to apply deep learning techniques to discover knowledge from the limit order book. In the survey conducted by Ozbayoglu [12], many works have been done using high-frequency data from the limit order book as input for deep learning models.

In 2017, in Tsantekidis et al. [15], CNN models are used to predict the midprice changes based on the order book data in the first 14 d of June 2010 provided by Nasdaq Nordic. The data contains ten levels of orders on each side (bid and ask). Each level holds the size and the price of the order. After normalizing and labeling data, Tsantekidis et al. [15] divided the data set into samples, each sample containing a 100-length sequence of orders. Therefore, the model's input data has the shape of (100, 40). The performance of the proposed CNN architecture beats other techniques such as Support Vector Machine (SVM), and Multi-Layer Perception (MLP) [15]. The best performance of the CNN model is 59.44% in the F1-score, compared with 49.42% of SVM and 55.95% of MLP. Also in 2017, Tsantekidis et al. [14] published another paper that used LSTM instead of CNN. With the same preprocessing process, the LSTM achieved better performance with 66.33% in F1-score.

Doering et al. [3] published a paper about using CNN to forecast high-frequency market microstructure in 2017. Doering et al. used CNN architecture with high complexity in order to exploit hidden patterns autonomously. Using data including every bid and ask order placed, as well as order cancellation and trade matched from June 2007 to June 2008, provided by London

---

[1] Discussed in Sect. 5.

Stock Exchange, Doering et al. implemented a CNN model based on CaffeNet, and GoogleNet [3]. The best result when using both order book and information about order flow is 48.3% for price trend prediction, and 68.2% for price volatility prediction [3].

Sirignano [13] in 2018, published a paper about using deep learning, "spatial neural network", to predict price movements based on the limit order book. The detailed limit order book, including 50 levels on each side (bid and ask), was reconstructed from NASDAQ Level 3 data by LOBSTER. Events such as order placements, cancellations, and matched trades were recorded. At each level, the price and size of the order were kept as well as the timestamp. The paper used data from 489 stocks, mainly drawn from S&P500 and NASDAQ-100 [13]. After experiments with the model proposed in the paper, Sirignano concludes that neural networks performed significantly better in modeling the distribution of best ask and best bid prices compared to linear regression [13]. Also discussed in the paper, the "spatial neural network" proposed by Sirignano has a lower error, lower computational cost, and greater interpretability than the original neural network.

Another research from Zhang et al. [17] used a mixture of convolutional filters and LSTM, called DeepLOB, to produce a deep learning model with better performance. The paper used two datasets: the dataset from Nasdaq Nordic, which was used by Tsantekidis et al. [14,15], and the dataset provided by London Stock Exchanges. The dataset from London Stock Exchange had the same format as the one from Nasdaq Nordic, in which each entry has 40 columns, including ten levels of price and size of the bid and ask orders. After normalizing and labeling with the similar concept found in [15] and [14], the data was used as input to a model whose architecture consists of convolutional layers to capture the spatial structure of the limit order book and LSTM modules to capture long time dependencies. The performance of the experiments is better than the ones of other papers studied by Zhang et al. [17] for the first dataset. The model also performed well for the second dataset and even for the stocks that were not part of the training data set.

4   Data Preparation

4.1   Data Overview

Dataset used in the paper belongs to Wharton Research Data Services (WRDS). The Consolidated Quotes we employ in the paper are the "Daily Product" from WRDS, which contain Millisecond Trade and Quote, updated daily. The quotes information of seven different stocks, i.e., Apple Inc. (AAPL), Advanced Micro Devices (AMD), Amazon.com Inc (AMZN), Facebook Inc. (FB), Microsoft (MSFT), nVIDIA (NVDA), Tesla Inc. (TSLA). The reason behind these choices is that they are among the most popular stocks in the market in 2020, according to NASDAQ[2]. All these stocks combined around 200 million records about the

---

[2] https://www.nasdaq.com/articles/10-most-popular-stocks-on-nasdaq.com-in-2020-2021-01-04.

best level of the order book, from April 1, 2018, to April 30, 2018. This results in about 15GB of data which we believe to be enough for training our models.

4.2 Data Aggregation

We first aggregate the original data measured in milliseconds into the data measured in seconds. We take the average of the bid prices and ask prices, with their sizes as weights. Meanwhile, the size of bid and request orders is calculated by the mean of all orders in each second. In particular, the bid price at t (second), denoted by Bid price$_t$, is computed as:

$$\text{Bid Price}_t = \frac{\sum_i \text{Bid Price}_{t,i} \times \text{Bid Size}_{t,i}}{\sum_i \text{Bid Size}_{t,i}}.$$

where Bid Price$_{t,i}$ and Bid Size$_{t,i}$ are the bid price and bid volume size at milliseconds between $t-1$ (second) and t (second).

The bid volume at time t (second), denoted by Bid size$_t$, is computed as:

$$\text{Bid Size}_t = \frac{\sum_i \text{Bid Size}_{t,i}}{\sum_i 1},$$

The ask price and ask volume size at each second are also computed similarly as above. The mid-price at each second is the average of bid and ask prices at each second.

4.3 Normalization

Since different stocks have different scales, it is important to normalize the data to archive a more general model. Our purpose is to create models that can predict buying or selling signals for many stocks from various industries. We use standardization ($z-$score) $x_{\text{norm}} = \dfrac{x - \bar{x}}{\sigma_{\bar{x}}}$, which is also used in [14,15, 17], to normalize each data point with the mean and standard deviation of the corresponding stock.

4.4 Time Intervals

This paper uses the data available in the last 5 min to predict the stock price in the next 5 min. In real-life intraday trading, real-life investors also tend to use various time intervals, such as a period of 1, 5, 15, 30 min, or even longer. The main reason for us to choose 5-min intervals is that longer intervals may lead to memory problems in the training phase, while shorter intervals may be difficult for investors to oversee the trading actions and stabilize the model efficiency.

To this aim, we slide a window with a length of 300 (seconds) along with the length of the averaged data, resulting in a dataset in which each record is a $(300, 4)$ matrix. Since we aim to predict the movement of stock mid-price, we need to ensure that the mid-price after aggregation and the original mid-price are relatively the same. Figure 3 illustrates the original mid-price computed from the averaged data of AMZN stock and the corresponding mid-price calculated after aggregation. As we can see, the shape of the two lines is relatively the same. Also, we remove the records whose either bid price or ask price equals zero to reduce the noise when calculating the mid-price.

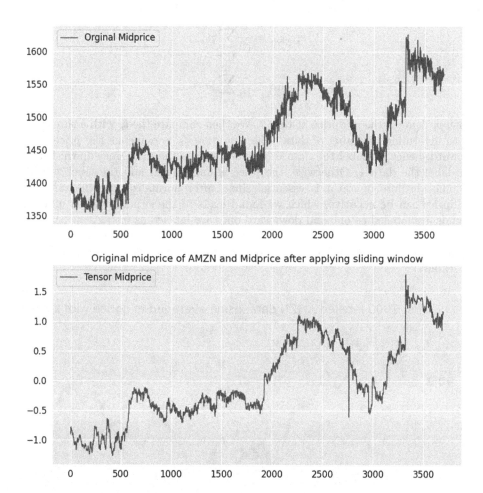

Fig. 3. The original mid-price and mid-price after aggregation for AMZN data.

4.5   Labeling

Labeling is an important part to set up correctly our research problem. Unsuitable labeling can lead to meaningless models. In this paper, we follow the labeling method proposed by Tsantekidis et al. [14,15] and Zhang et al. [17]. In particular, the percentage of change in price is calculated by

$$\ell_t = \frac{m_{after} - m_{before}}{|m_{before}|}, \tag{1}$$

where m_{after} denotes the mean of the next 10 mid-prices and m_{before} is the mean of the previous 10 midprices:

$$m_{before} = \frac{1}{10} \sum_{i=1}^{10} p_{t-i}, \tag{2}$$

$$m_{after} = \frac{1}{10} \sum_{i=1}^{10} p_{t+i}, \tag{3}$$

with p_t denotes the midprice at time t. We then compare the ℓ_t with a threshold α to determine the label of data. The condition $\ell_t > \alpha$ means the price goes upward; hence we label the data 0, $\ell_t < -\alpha$ means the price goes down; hence we label the data 1. Otherwise, the price is unchanged, and the label will be 2. The absolute operator is essential since, after normalization, the value of midprice can be negative, which we found leads to the situation when upward trends are labeled as one and downward ones are labeled as 0.

Figure 4 shows that the produced label is relatively correct. Labels seem to demonstrate suitably the trend of data. The frequency of the label set is shown in Table 1.

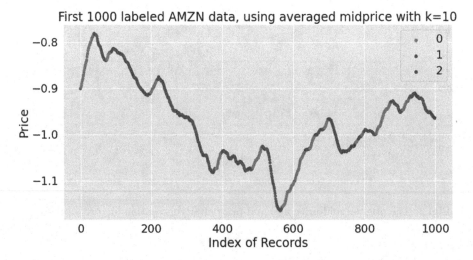

Fig. 4. The first 1000 labeled AMZN data point, using averaged mid-price.

Table 1. Percentage of labels using averaged mid-price.

Stock	% Upward	% Downward	% Unchange
AMZN	38.23	37.42	24.35
AMD	33.22	33.56	33.22
AAPL	26.48	26.57	46.95
FB	32.48	32.33	35.19
TSLA	39.61	38.09	22.3
NVDA	40.44	40.16	19.4
MSFT	36.21	34.72	29.07

Note that in all the above experiments and also in our final model, $\alpha = 0.01$ is applied. The parameter α determines how much change in the price makes us willing to trade. The bigger the value of α is, the more data is labeled as unchanged. Since 1% of the price can be considered as an acceptable profit, we decide to use $\alpha = 0.01$ for our models.

5   Models

In this section, we apply popular machine learning models: LSTM, ResNet50, and two of their hybrid forms to solve our research problem.

5.1   LSTM

We use Keras [2], a python open-source library, to implement the LSTM model , pictured in Fig. 5. The activation and recurrent activation of the LSTM layer are both set as default, which is tanh and *sigmoid* function. The reason we decide to choose 600 units is to increase the complexity of the model, which will be trained with around 20 million records.

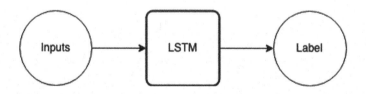

Fig. 5. LSTM model, built with Keras.

5.2   ResNet

ResNet is one of the state-of-the-art architectures in CNN areas. Therefore, in the thesis, ResNet50, as discussed in Subsect. 2.2, is the CNN representation.

The model we used is already designed by TensorFlow [1] through the Tensor-Flow Hub library[3]. The ResNet model summary is illustrated in Fig. 6. The KerasLayer version of ResNet50, developed by TensorFlow Hub, is used as a feature extractor. A 3-unit Dense layer follows the ResNet50 to classify data into three classes.

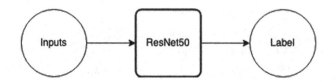

Fig. 6. ResNet model, built with Keras and TensorFlow Hub.

5.3   Two Proposed Combinations of LSTM and ResNet

As we discussed above, Ozbayoglu et al. [12] suggested that the hybrid form of CNN and LSTM may have better outcomes. This prediction encourages us to propose two new models, i.e. two different hybrid forms of LSTM and CNN, in our case, ResNet50. Our purpose is to determine whether these combos produce better performances. The hybrid models, namely Hybrid and ResLSTM, will be discussed in the following part.

Hybrid Model 1. One hybrid model is to use ResNet50 as a feature extractor we used in Subsect. 5.2. But we replace the fully connected layer at the top with an LSTM layer.
    The model is shown in Fig. 7.

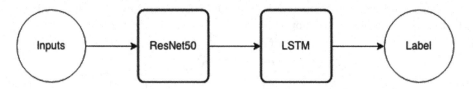

Fig. 7. The first proposed model, built with Keras and TensorFlow Hub.

Hybrid Model 2. In the second combination, we consider both ResNet50 and LSTM as feature extractors, which means we combine the result from the ResNet50 and LSTM layers into one single vector. The final feature vector, then, go through a full-connected layer and classify the input data. The model is shown in Fig. 8.

---

[3] https://www.tensorflow.org/hub.

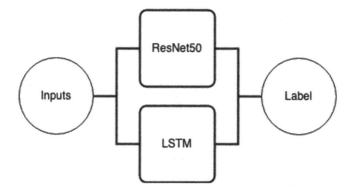

Fig. 8. The second proposed model, built with Keras and TensorFlow Hub.

5.4 Training Method

We divided the dataset into seven separate parts. Each part contains data from other symbols, ordered as (AMZN, AMD, AAPL, FB, TSLA, NVDA, MSFT). We trained our model with each smaller dataset and tested it with the following set, which means there are a total of seven times of training and six times of evaluations. The result will be shown in Sect. 6. The loss function used is "categorical cross-entropy", which is also used in [14, 15, 17].

$$\mathfrak{L}(W) = -\sum_{i=1}^{L} y_i \times \log \hat{y}_i,$$

where $L = 3$ is the number of labels, W represents the parameters of models. The true label and the predicted label are denoted as y_i and $\hat{y}_i$, respectively. Also used in [15], [14],[17], the Adaptive Moment Estimation algorithm "ADAM" [10] is used as optimization algorithm. Both categorical cross-entropy and ADAM algorithms are implemented by Keras [2].

6 Evaluation

In this section, we present the evaluation method for the performance of all four models proposed in Sect. 5.

6.1 Evaluation Methods

The metrics discussed above will be demonstrated in detail as follows. TP, TN, FP, and FN denote the number of true positive, true negative, false positive, and false negative cases.

$$\text{Accuracy} = \frac{\text{TP} + \text{TN}}{\text{TP} + \text{FP} + \text{TN} + \text{FN}}$$

$$\text{Precision} = \frac{\text{TP}}{\text{TP} + \text{FP}}$$

$$\text{Recall} = \frac{\text{TP}}{\text{TP} + \text{FN}}$$

$$\text{F1-Score} = 2 \times \frac{\text{Precision} \times \text{Recall}}{\text{Precision} + \text{Recall}}$$

$$\kappa = \frac{2 \times (\text{TP} \times \text{TN} - \text{FP} \times \text{FN})}{(\text{TP} + \text{FP}) \times (\text{FP} + \text{TN}) - (\text{TP} + \text{FN}) \times (\text{FN} + \text{TN})}.$$

Since we have three classes, namely upward, downward and stable, we should consider the Kappa coefficient for multi-classes, discussed by Grandini et al. [7]

$$\kappa = \frac{c \times s - \sum_k^K p_k \times t_k}{s^2 - \sum_k^K p_k \times t_k},$$

where

- $c = \sum_k^K \text{TP}_k$ the total number of TP of each class.
- s the total number of elements.
- $p_k = \text{TP}_k + \sum \text{FP}_k$ the total number of times that class k was predicted.
- $t_k = \text{TP}_k + \sum \text{FN}_k$ the total number of times that class k truly occurred.

6.2   Models Performance

This section discusses the performance of models measured with our training data. The dataset is divided into seven parts, each containing one kind of stock. We trained the model with the first set and evaluated it with the following ones. The process was repeated six times. For the ResNet50 and two hybrid forms of LSTM and ResNet50, we run the training with 20 epochs. Meanwhile the LSTM is trained 10 times (epochs = 10).

As we can see, although being the simplest, LSTM performs better than any model, followed by ResLSTM and Hybrid. The worst performance belongs to ResNet50 when the accuracy is only 82.5%, shown in Table 2. In the evaluation phase, we find out the result is not that good compared to training performance. The detailed results of the evaluation on the final dataset of models are shown in Table 3. The result we achieved is reasonably competent, compared with other research. Our LSTM model performs better than the LSTM model of Tsantekidis et al. [14], which achieved 0.5, 75.92%, 60.77%, 66.33% for Cohen's κ, Mean Precision, Mean Recall, and Mean F1-Score, respectively. The CNN model, proposed by Tsantekidis et al. [15], had the performance of 0.35, 65.54%, 50.98%, 55.21% for the same metrics above. Compared with the result from Zhang et al. [17], who proposed the hybrid form of CNN and LSTM, our models achieve worse performance. Notes that the dataset, the models, the training methods, and other hyper-parameters in this paper are different from these papers.

Table 2. Performance of models after trained with seven datasets.

Models	Accuracy	Cohen's κ	Mean precision	Mean recall	Mean F1-Score
LSTM	87.42	0.8108	88.54	86.17	87.17
ResNet	82.5	0.7367	84.53	80.21	82.1
Hybrid	84.21	0.7623	85.92	82.29	83.84
ResLSTM	84.9	0.7727	86.74	82.87	84.52

Table 3. Performance of models in the final evaluation.

Models	Accuracy	Cohen's κ	Mean precision	Mean recall	Mean F1-score
LSTM	79.58	0.6917	81.69	76.97	78.86
ResNet	76.32	0.6464	80.04	70.58	76.35
Hybrid	75.91	0.6351	79.3	69.96	74.95
ResLSTM	71.94	0.5737	74.76	75.43	70.95

7   Conclusion and Future Work

7.1   Limitation, Future Work and Discussion

The order book information proves helpful when it comes to predicting the mid-price changes; however, it is not the only factor that affects the stock price. Other aspects such as financial indicators, politics, the state of the world economy, and news also contribute to the price of stocks. Further research needs to address these factors, along with the information from the order book.

Regarding machine learning models, since the technology develops at a very high speed, future research shall keep pace with the newest techniques to achieve better performance. Models should also be able to rank the magnitude of the price changes to suggest better trading decisions.

7.2   Conclusion

This paper aims to apply popular machine learning models: ResNet50, LSTM, and two of their hybrid forms to predict the stock mid-price in the next 5 min based on the book data available in the last 5 min. The relatively large ($\sim$15GB) dataset from the well-known Wharton Research Data Service is well processed to get the most insight into our research problem. Our proposed models work relatively well on our dataset, with the tested results comparable with other recent studies regarding accuracy and F1-score.

Acknowledgment. We acknowledge Ho Chi Minh City University of Technology (HCMUT), VNU-HCM, for supporting this study.

References

1. Abadi, M., et al.: Tensorflow: Large-scale machine learning on heterogeneous systems (2015)
2. Chollet, F., et al.: Keras (2015). https://keras.io
3. Doering, J., Fairbank, M., Markose, S.: Convolutional neural networks applied to high-frequency market microstructure forecasting. 2017 9th Computer Science and Electronic Engineering (CEEC), pp. 31–36. IEEE (2017) market microstructure forecasting. 2017 9th computer science and electronic engineering (ceec), IEEE, 2017 **2017**, 31–36 (2017)
4. Fend, V.: An overview of resnet and its variant
5. Gandhmal, D.P., Kumar, K.: Systematic analysis and review of stock market prediction techniques. Comput. Sci. Rev. **34**, 100190 (2019)
6. Goodfellow, I., Bengio, Y., Courville, A., Bengio, Y.: Deep learning, vol. 1. MIT Press Cambridge (2016)
7. Grandini, M., Bagli, E., Visani, G.: Metrics for multi-class classification: an overview, arXiv preprint arXiv:2008.05756 (2020)
8. He, K., Zhang, X., Ren, S., Sun, J.: Deep residual learning for image recognition. In: Proceedings of the IEEE Computer Society Conference on Computer Vision and Pattern Recognition, pp. 770–778, 2016-December (2016)
9. Hochreiter, S., Schmidhuber, J.: Long short-term memory. Neural Comput. **9**, 1735–1780 (1997)
10. Kingma, D.P., Ba, J.: Adam: A method for stochastic optimization, arXiv preprint arXiv:1412.6980 (2014)
11. Krizhevsky, A., Sutskever, I., Hinton, G.E.: ImageNet classification with deep convolutional neural networks. ACM International Conference Proceeding Series, pp. 145–151 (2012)
12. Ozbayoglu, A.M., Gudelek, M.U., Sezer, O.B.: Deep learning for financial applications: A survey. Appli. Soft Comput. J. **93**, 106384 (2020)
13. Sirignano, J.A.: Deep learning for limit order books. Quant. Finance **19**, 549–570 (2019)
14. Tsantekidis, A., et al.: Using deep learning to detect price change indications in financial markets. In: 25th European Signal Processing Conference (EUSIPCO), pp. 2511–251 (2017)
15. Tsantekidis, A., Passalis, N., Tefas, A., Kanniainen, J., Gabbouj, M., Iosifidis, A.:Forecasting stock prices from the limit order book using convolutional neural networks. In: Proceedings - 2017 IEEE 19th Conference on Business Informatics, CBI 2017, vol. 1, pp. 7–12 (2017)
16. Zavadskaya, A., et al.: Artificial intelligence in finance: Forecasting stock market returns using artificial neural networks (2017)
17. Zhang, Z., Zohren, S., Roberts, S.: DeepLOB: Deep convolutional neural networks for limit order books. IEEE Trans. Signal Process. **67**, 3001–3012 (2019)

An Image Denoising Model Based on Nonlinear Partial Diferential Equation Using Deep Learning

Quan Dac Ho[1,2,3] (iD) and Hieu Trung Huynh[3(✉)] (iD)

[1] Faculty of Mathematics and Computer Science, University of Science, Ho Chi Minh City, Vietnam
hodacquan@iuh.edu.vn
[2] Vietnam National University, Ho Chi Minh City, Vietnam
[3] Faculty of Information Technology, Industrial University of Ho Chi Minh City, Ho Chi Minh City, Vietnam
hthieu@ieee.org

Abstract. In this paper, we present a deep neural network-based framework for solving nonlinear partial differential equations (PDEs) and applying in denoising image. A loss function that relies on form PDEs, initial and boundary condition (I/BC) residual was proposed. The proposed loss function is discretization-free and highly parallelizable. The network parameters are determined by using stochastic gradient descent algorithm. We demonstrated the performance of proposed method in solving nonlinear partial diferential equation and applying image denoising. The experimental results from this method were compared to the efficient PDE's numerical method. We showed that the method attains significant improvements in term image denoising.

Keywords: Nonlinear diffusion equation · Neural network · Deep learning · Image denoising

1 Introduction

Image processing is an important task in the field of computer vision. It can reduce the effect of noise on video processing, image analysis, and tracking. In fact, the image denoising is one of classical problems and has been investigated by several research groups. The classical denoising methods based on the correlation among pixels or image patches in the original images includes spatial domain filtering [1–3] and variational methods [4–12]. Normally, these methods can eliminate noise reasonably but may have the cost of blurring image or computation [13]. The transform techniques are developed for transforming image from the initial spatial domain to other domains [14]. The popular methods based on this technique includes Fourier transform, cosine transform, wavelet transform, etc. These methods aim to differentiate the characteristics of information and noise in the transform domain. They have the limitations of selecting the cut-off frequency, filter function behavior, bases (wavelet bases), etc.

Recently, the convolutional neural network (CNN) based methods have been developed and applied sufficiently in many computer vision tasks including image denoising. F. Ashouri et al. [15] proposed a new PDE learning model for image denoising. Vincent et al. [16] and Xie et al. [17] proposed an approach based on multi-layer perception models including autoencoders. A trainable nonlinear reaction diffusion model based on a feed-forward deep network was proposed by Chen et al. [18]. The early approach based on deep learning for denoising image was proposed by Zhang et al. [19]. They also introduced a fast and flexible denoising convolutional neural network [20]. Although these methods are effective and have a short running time, their learning process often requires the time complexity.

Based on the superiority of partial differential equation (PDE) and its application in the field of physics, biology, image processing, etc., the PDE-based models have advantages over many traditional models in processing complex images while considerable computation is often required. Especially nonlinear diffusion equation (NDE) has a very important role in image processing. For the past decades, the use of PDEs in image processing has become an effective technique. In this study, we investigate in an approach for image denoising based on PDEs. The main idea is to represent an image as a function $u(t, \mathbf{x})$ in $\mathbb{R}^2$. The function satisfies a time dependent PDE that characterizes the given problem. The PDE's solution produces the processed image at the scale t. The diffusion equation is usually represented by

$$\frac{\partial u(t, \mathbf{x})}{\partial t} - \text{div}(c(u, t, \mathbf{x}) \nabla u(t, \mathbf{x})) = 0 \text{ in } I \times \Omega, \tag{1}$$

where $I = [0, T]$ is the scaling (time) interval for some $T > 0$, $\Omega \in \mathbb{R}^2$ is a simply bounded rectangular domain, $c(\cdot)$ is named as *diffusivity* and depends on the model. It can be a scalar, a scalar function of coordinates (inhomogeneity) or a tensor (anisotropy). Furthermore, if the diffusivity depends on $u(t, \mathbf{x})$, the Eq. (1) becomes NDE. In case of $c = 1$, we attain a simple linear model of the heat equation that leads to the following Cauchy problem

$$\frac{\partial u(t, \mathbf{x})}{\partial t} = \Delta u(t, \mathbf{x}) \text{ in } I \times \Omega, \tag{2}$$

$$u(0, \mathbf{x}) = u_0(\mathbf{x}) \text{ on } \Omega. \tag{3}$$

Solutions of this Eq. (2) can be expressed as a Gaussian function with $G_\sigma(\mathbf{x})$ convolution, namely:

$$u(t, \mathbf{x}) = G_\sigma * u_0(x). \tag{4}$$

The Gauss function [21, 22] $G_\sigma(\mathbf{x})$ is a fundamental solution of the linear heat equation, it has been possible to replace the classical convolution of an initial image with G_σ by solving the linear heat equation for a corresponding time $t = \sigma$ with initial condition given by the original image. It is well known that Gaussian smoothing (linear diffusion) is a convolution operation that is used to 'blur' images and remove image noising which led to the fact that edges of image are blurred. In order to eliminate this weakness, nonlinear diffusions are chosen. Many nonlinear second order diffusion equations have been employed in image denoising. The idea is to modify the heat equation by adding the diffusivity coefficient depending on space activity in a given part of an image, measured by the norm of the image gradient $|\nabla u|$. For small values of $|\nabla u|$, the large values of the diffusivity are expected to perform stronger smoothing. In regions with large value of $|\nabla u|$, smaller diffusivity is expected to slow down the diffusion process and protect delicate image features. Perona and Malik introduced their anisotropic diffusion scheme [12]. The model can be written as

$$\frac{\partial u(t, \mathbf{x})}{\partial t} - \operatorname{div}\left(c\left(|\nabla u|^2\right)\nabla u(t, \mathbf{x})\right) = 0, \tag{5}$$

where $c(\cdot)$ is the diffusivity function and $|\nabla u|$ is the edge detector. The function c is chosen such that $c(s^2) \to 0$ when $s \to \infty$, and $c(s^2) \to 1$ when $s \to 0$. The idea of (5) is that the diffusion coefficient is small around the image edge as the gradient of image intensity is large, as a result, the smoothing will be less on the edge of the image. The diffusion is high as the gradient is small, which results in more smoothing in the flat area of the image. Hence the nonlinear diffusion preserves the edges of images and protects the brightness of image simultaneously. In [4], authors selected the function c as convolution of a Gaussian kernel G_σ and the image gradient of $u(t, \mathbf{x})$. The model is based on the equation

$$\frac{\partial u(t, \mathbf{x})}{\partial t} - \operatorname{div}\left(c\left(|G_\sigma * \nabla u|^2\right)\nabla u(t, \mathbf{x})\right) = 0. \tag{6}$$

In [23], authors offered two adaptive versions of PM model, the first model is α-PM equation, which has the following form

$$\frac{\partial u(t, \mathbf{x})}{\partial t} = \operatorname{div}\left(\frac{\nabla u(t, \mathbf{x})}{1 + (|\nabla u|/K)^\alpha}\right), \tag{7}$$

where α is a fixed constant. The second one is $\alpha(x)$-PM defined by

$$\frac{\partial u(t, \mathbf{x})}{\partial t} = \operatorname{div}\left(\frac{\nabla u(t, \mathbf{x})}{1 + (|\nabla u|/K)^{\alpha(x)}}\right). \tag{8}$$

where $\alpha(x)$ is chosen as

$$\alpha(\nabla G_\sigma * u_0) = 2 - \frac{2}{1 + k|\nabla G_\sigma * u_0|^2}. \tag{9}$$

or

$$\alpha(\nabla G_\sigma * u) = 2 - \frac{2}{1 + k|\nabla G_\sigma * u|^2}. \tag{10}$$

Traditionally, the solutions for these PDEs have been attained based on the analytical approaches. However, they are quite complicated and impossible in many applications. These issues could be addressed by numerical approaches. They include popular methods such as finite difference methods (FDMs) [24], finite element methods (FEMs) [25]. These methods determine an approximate solution at a number of discrete points and interpolate the solution elsewhere in domain. However, these methods have disadvantages including the local treatment of solution, the models obtained from these methods are not only tremendously expressive but also very costly to evaluate and store [26]. In order to overcome these limitations, in this paper, we propose a new approach based on the unsupervised learning method, called DNDE (deep nonlinear diffusion equation), for solving PDEs by using deep neural network (DNN) model.

2   A Deep Learning Algorithm for Solving Nonlinear Diffusion Equation

Let the noisy image be a given gray scaled intensity map $u_0(x) : \Omega \to [0, 255]$ for the image domain $\Omega \in \mathbb{R}^2$. . The nonlinear diffusion equation (NDE) was first proposed in [12] in filtering the noise. The sequence of continuous images $u(t, \mathbf{x})$ was built on the abstract scale t and through the nonlinear diffusion equation to remove the noise during the scaling time. It can be described by:

$$\frac{\partial u(t, \mathbf{x})}{\partial t} = \operatorname{div}(c(t, \mathbf{x}) \nabla u(t, \mathbf{x})) \text{in } I \times \Omega, \tag{11}$$

$$\frac{\partial u(t, \mathbf{x})}{\partial n} = 0 \text{ on } I \times \partial\Omega, \tag{12}$$

$$u(0, x) = u_0(\mathbf{x}) \text{ on } \Omega, \tag{13}$$

where $\partial\Omega$ is boundary Ω, and n is the outward unit normal vector to $\partial\Omega$; c is a given non-increasing function. There are several choices for $c(s)$ [6, 7]. If $c(t, \mathbf{x})$ is constant, (11) is called the isotropic heat diffusion equation. If $c(t, \mathbf{x}) = c(|\nabla u|^2)$, (11) is called the Perona and Malik (PM) [12].

The discretization-based numerical methods such as FDMs and FEMs can be used to approximate the solution of PDEs (11) (12) (13) in [25]. As discussed, these methods are very expensive and requires a large resource for storing and calculating. Moreover, they are not straightforward to obtain solutions. Utilizing neural networks to solve PDEs allows us to attain PDE's solution directly that can alleviate the requirement of evaluation and memory.

Let $\theta \in \mathbb{R}^m$ be the parameters of the artificial neural network (ANN). The solution of the NDE can be approximated by the nonlinear output function $f(t, \mathbf{x}; \theta)$ of ANN, where $f : [0, T] \times \Omega \to \mathbb{R}$ maps the spatiotemporal coordinates t and $\mathbf{x}$ to the scalar output field of the NDE. For a given ANN model, one of important steps is to find the network parameters that optimize the predefined criteria. Traditionally, these criteria are based on the mean square error defined by

$$\theta^* = argmin \int_T \int_\Omega |u(t, \mathbf{x}) - f(t, \mathbf{x}; \theta)| dx dt, \tag{14}$$

where $u(\cdot)$ denotes the true solution of NDE.

In this work, we develop a deep learning method for solving of (11) (12) (13) called DNDE (deep nonlinear diffusion equation). In which boundary conditions (BCs) of (12) are the pixel values of image edges. Let a PDE residual field $r : \Omega \times [0, T] \to \mathbb{R}$ be defined to reflect how well the function $f(\cdot)$ approximates the solution of (11)

$$r(t, \mathbf{x}) = \frac{\partial f(t, \mathbf{x})}{\partial t} - \text{div}(c(t, \mathbf{x}) \nabla f(t, \mathbf{x})). \tag{15}$$

Given a PDE residual field form (15), we can define the desired loss functions. Consider a set of n_{rs} points $\left\{ \left(t_j^{rs}, \mathbf{x}_j^{rs} \right) \right\}_{j=1}^{n_{rs}}$ which are sampled from the space-time $(0, T] \times \Omega$, a set of n_{ic} points $\left\{ \left(0, \mathbf{x}_j^{ic} \right) \right\}_{j=1}^{n_{ic}}$ correcsponding to the initial condition, and sets of n_{bc} points $\left\{ \left(t_j^{bc}, \mathbf{x}_j^{bc} \right) \right\}_{j=1}^{n_{bc}} \in [0, T] \times \Gamma^i$ for the enforcement of the BCs. The parameters of neural network can be determined by minimizing the mean square error

$$err = e^{rs} + e^{ic} + e^{bc}, \tag{16}$$

where

$$e^{rs} = \frac{1}{n_{rs}} \sum_{j=1}^{n_{rs}} |r(t_j^{rs}, \mathbf{x}_j^{rs})|^2 = \frac{1}{n_{rs}} \sum_{j=1}^{n_{rs}} |e_j^{rs}|^2, \tag{17}$$

$$e^{rs} = \frac{1}{n_{rs}} \sum_{j=1}^{n_{rs}} |r(t_j^{rs}, \mathbf{x}_j^{rs})|^2 = \frac{1}{n_{rs}} \sum_{j=1}^{n_{rs}} |e_j^{rs}|^2, \tag{18}$$

$$e^{bc} = \frac{1}{n_{bc}} \sum_{i=1}^{n_{bc}} \left| f\left(t_j^{bc}, \mathbf{x}_j^{bc} \right) - g_i\left(t_j^{bc}, \mathbf{x}_j^{bc} \right) \right|^2 = \frac{1}{n_{bc}} \sum_{j=1}^{n_{bc}} |e_j^{bc}|^2, \tag{19}$$

and $n_{bc} = \sum_{i=1}^{n_b} n_{b,i}$.

The process, called PDE sampling, generates a set of training points on Ω, $\left\{ \left(t_j^{rs}, \mathbf{x}_j^{rs} \right) \right\}_{j=1}^{n_{rs}}$. The set $\left\{ \left(0, \mathbf{x}_j^{ic} \right) \right\}_{j=1}^{n_{ic}}$ is generated by the initial sampling process and the set $\left\{ \left(t_j^{bc}, \mathbf{x}_j^{bc} \right) \right\}_{j=1}^{n_{bc}}$ is generated by the boundary sampling process. The parameters are chosen to be minimizing (16) using stochastic gradient descent (SGD) and its modern variants [27, 28]. In summary, the algorithm for image denoising is described as follows.

DNDE Algorithm

Require: Space-time domain;

Require: DNN (deep neural network);

Require: Image I_0;

Require: n_{rs}, n_{ic}, n_{bc} are the initial numbers of training points for NDE, initial, and boundary conditions, respectively;

Require: Space-time domain Ω, $[0, T]$, time step τ ;

Require: η is maximum number of epochs;

Require: ϵ is an error threshold;

Set:

$$u(0, \mathbf{x}) = u_0(\mathbf{x}) = \mathbf{I}_0;$$

$$\xi = 0;$$

$$A, B = size(\mathbf{I}_0);$$

$$P = \frac{T}{\tau};$$

$$n_{ic} = A \times B;$$

$$n_{bc} = A \times B \times 4$$

$$n_{rs} = A \times B \times P;$$

Repeat

1.   Compute $f(t, \mathbf{x})$ from DNN;
2.   Compute *err* using (16);
3.   **if** $err < \epsilon$ **then** break;
4.   Update DNN's parameters with parameters n_{ic}, n_{bc}, and n_{rs};
5. $\xi = \xi + 1;$

Until ($\xi \geq \eta$).

3 Experimental Results

In this section, we present the results of three experiments to show the performance of DNDE. The experiments were implemented in Python on a PC with Intel Core i5 (3470). The algorithm was run on a single NVIDIA GEFORCE GTX 1060 6GB. Denoising image performance was measured in terms of the peak-signal-to noise ratio (PSNR) and mean absolute error (MAE), which are defined by Durand et al. [29]:

$$PSNR(u, u_0) = 10log_{10} \frac{AB \times 255^2}{||u - u_0||_{L^2}^2}, \tag{20}$$

$$MAE(u, u_0) = \frac{||u - u_0||_{L^2}}{AB},\qquad(21)$$

where the image size is $A \times B$ and u_0, u denote the original image and result image, respectively.

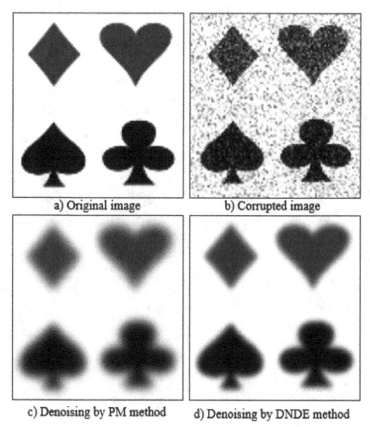

a) Original image   b) Corrupted image

c) Denoising by PM method   d) Denoising by DNDE method

Fig. 1. Denoising results from spade-heart-diamond-club image (100×100). (a) Original image. (b) Noisy image corrupted by Gaussian white noise with SD of 0.1. (c) Result from the PM model. (d) Result from the DNDE model

Table 1. Quantitative comparison between PM model and DNDE model for denoising spade-heart-diamond-club

Model	PSNR	MAE
PM	15.768	0.108
DNDE	17.932	0.079

The first experiment is on the spade-heart-diamond-club image with resolution of 100 x 100 pixels. It is corrupted by Gaussian white noise with standard deviation (SD) of 0.2. The original and corrupted images are shown in Fig. 1(a) and (b), respectively. The denoising results by using PM model and our DNDE for the scale $t_{10}(\tau = 10e^{-1})$ are shown in Fig. 1(c) and (d). Visually, we can see that the proposed DNDE can give a sharper image, while the PM method give a blurred image. Table 1 presents the quantitative comparison on PSNR, MAE. The DNDE attain the PSNR of 17.93, while the PM method has the PSNR of 15.77. For MAE criterion, the proposed method has the values of 0.079, which is smaller than the MAE from the PM method.

a) Original image   b) Corrupted image

c) Denoising by PM method   d) Denoising by DNDE method

Fig. 2. Denoising results from Lena image (100 × 100). (a) Original image. (b) Noisy image corrupted by Gaussian white noise with SD of 0.1. (c) Result from the PM model. (d) Result from the DNDE model

In the second experiment, we evaluated the image denoising results on the Lena image with the resolution of 100 x 100 pixels. The Gaussian white noise with the standard deviation (SD) of 0.1 was added. The original and corrupted images are shown in Fig. 2(a) and (b), respectively. The image denoising results by using PM model and our DNDE for the scale $t_{10}(\tau = 10e^{-1})$ are shown in Fig. 2(c) and (d). Visually, we can see that the PM method give a blurred image while the DNDE can offer a clearer image. The quantitative comparison on PSNR, MAE are presented in Table 2. The DNDE attains the PSNR of 19.13 that is larger than PSNR from the PM method with the value of 18.02. For MAE criterion, the proposed method has the values of 0.076, which is smaller than the MAE from the PM method.

Table 2. Quantitative comparison between PM model and DNDE model for denoising Lena

Model	PSNR	MAE
PM	18.021	0.091
DNDE	19.129	0.076

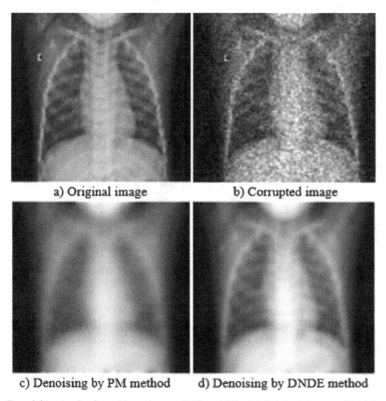

a) Original image   b) Corrupted image

c) Denoising by PM method   d) Denoising by DNDE method

Fig. 3. Denoising results from X-ray image (100 × 100). (a) Original image. (b) Noisy image corrupted by Gaussian white noise with SD of 0.1. (c) Result from the PM model. (d) Result from the DNDE model

Our third experiment is on a chest X-ray image. The original image and the corrupted image with Gaussian white noise are shown in Fig. 3(a) and (b), respectively. Figure 3(c) and (d) illustrate the denoising results by using PM model and our DNDE for the scale

$t_{10}(\tau = 10e^{-1})$. We can see that the result image from the DNDE is clearer than that from the PM method. The PSNR and MAE from the DNDE are 23.87 and 0.049, respectively, while those from the PM method are 22.40 and 0.054, respectively. We can improve these results for clinical use in the future (Table 3).

Table 3. Quantitative comparison between PM model and DNDE model for X-ray

Model	PSNR	MAE
PM	22.404	0.054
DNDE	23.874	0.049

From the Fig. 1, Fig. 2, and Fig. 3, it is evident that the DNDE exhibited better results as compared to PM in image denoising while preserving edges. It is obvious that the DNDE not only shows no speckles but also preserver the image edges.

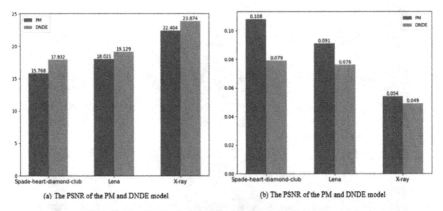

(a) The PSNR of the PM and DNDE model   (b) The PSNR of the PM and DNDE model

Fig. 4. The PSNR and MAE of the PM and DNDE model

Figure 4 shows quantitative comparison PSNR in DNDE model has higher value than PM model in all experiments and MAE of DNDE have lower value than PM model in all experiments. It is proved that proposed DNDE denoise better than PM model.

4   Conclusion

Partial differential equations play an important role in many fields. Many problems in practical applications such as physics, engineering, biology, economy, and image processing are modeled by PDEs. Many image denoising models based on NDE are developed and applied. However, NDE's solution is determined based on traditional numerical method. In this paper, we introduce the DNDE model applying in image denoising. The experimental results show that the proposed DNDE can give better results than PM model in image denoising.

References

1. Bouboulis, P., Slavakis, K., Theodoridis, S.: Adaptive kernel-based image denoising employing semi-parametric regularization. IEEE Trans. Image Process. **19**(6), 1465–1479 (2010)
2. Takeda, H., Farsiu, S., Milanfar, P.: Kernel regression for image processing and reconstruction. IEEE Trans. Image Process. **16**(2), 349–366 (2007)
3. Yang, R., Yin, L., Gabbouj, M., Astola, J., Neuvo, Y.: Optimal weighted median filtering under structural constraints. IEEE Trans. Signal Process. **43**(3), 591–604 (1995)
4. Catté, F., Lions, P.-L., Morel, J.-M., Coll, T.: Image selective smoothing and edge detection by nonlinear diffusion. SIAM J. Numer. Anal. **29**(1), 182–193 (1992)
5. Fan, L., Li, X., Guo, Q., Zhang, C.: Nonlocal image denoising using edge-based similarity metric and adaptive parameter selection. Science China Inf. Sci. **61**(4), 1–3 (2018). https://doi.org/10.1007/s11432-017-9207-9
6. Grewenig, S., Zimmer, S., Weickert, J.: Rotationally invariant similarity measures for nonlocal image denoising. J. Vis. Commun. Image Represent. **22**(2), 117–130 (2011)
7. Gu, S., Xie, Q., Meng, D., Zuo, W., Feng, X., Zhang, L.: Weighted nuclear norm minimization and its applications to low level vision. Int. J. Comput. Vis. **121**(2), 183–208 (2017)
8. Hu, Y., Jacob, M.: Higher degree total variation (HDTV) regularization for image recovery. IEEE Trans. Image Process. **21**(5), 2559–2571 (2012)
9. Fan, L., Li, X., Fan, H., Feng, Y., Zhang, C.: Adaptive texture-preserving denoising method using gradient histogram and nonlocal self-similarity priors. IEEE Trans. Circuits Syst. Video Technol. **29**(11), 3222–3235 (2018)
10. Zhang, L., Zuo, W.: Image restoration: From sparse and low-rank priors to deep priors [lecture notes]. IEEE Signal Process. Mag. **34**(5), 172–179 (2017)
11. Lou, Y., Zeng, T., Osher, S., Xin, J.: A weighted difference of anisotropic and isotropic total variation model for image processing. SIAM J. Imaging Sci. **8**(3), 1798–1823 (2015)
12. Perona, P., Malik, J.: Scale-space and edge detection using anisotropic diffusion. IEEE Trans. Pattern Anal. Mach. Intell. **12**(7), 629–639 (1990)
13. Fan, L., Zhang, F., Fan, H., Zhang, C.: Brief review of image denoising techniques. Visual Computing for Industry, Biomedicine, and Art **2**(1), 1–12 (2019). https://doi.org/10.1186/s42492-019-0016-7
14. Jain, P., Tyagi, V.: Spatial and frequency domain filters for restoration of noisy images. IETE J. Educ. **54**(2), 108–116 (2013)
15. Ashouri, F., Eslahchi, M.R.: A new PDE learning model for image denoising. Neural Comput. Appl. **34**(11), 8551–8574 (2022)
16. P. Vincent, H. Larochelle, Y. Bengio, and P.-A. Manzagol, "Extracting and composing robust features with denoising autoencoders," in *Proceedings of the 25th international conference on Machine learning*, 2008, pp. 1096–1103
17. J. Xie, L. Xu, and E. Chen, "Image denoising and inpainting with deep neural networks," *Adv. Neural Inf. Process. Syst.*, vol. 25, 2012
18. Chen, Y., Pock, T.: Trainable nonlinear reaction diffusion: A flexible framework for fast and effective image restoration. IEEE Trans. Pattern Anal. Mach. Intell. **39**(6), 1256–1272 (2016)
19. Zhang, K., Zuo, W., Chen, Y., Meng, D., Zhang, L.: Beyond a gaussian denoiser: Residual learning of deep cnn for image denoising. IEEE Trans. Image Process. **26**(7), 3142–3155 (2017)
20. Zhang, K., Zuo, W., Zhang, L.: FFDNet: Toward a fast and flexible solution for CNN-based image denoising. IEEE Trans. Image Process. **27**(9), 4608–4622 (2018)
21. Koenderink, J.J.: The structure of images. Biol. Cybern. **50**(5), 363–370 (1984)
22. A. P. Witkin, "Scale-space filtering," in *Readings in Computer Vision*, Elsevier, 1987, pp. 329–332

23. Guo, Z., Sun, J., Zhang, D., Wu, B.: Adaptive Perona-Malik model based on the variable exponent for image denoising. IEEE Trans. Image Process. **21**(3), 958–967 (2011)
24. Yahya, A.A., Tan, J., Hu, M.: A blending method based on partial differential equations for image denoising. Multimedia Tools and Applications **73**(3), 1843–1862 (2013). https://doi.org/10.1007/s11042-013-1586-6
25. Shih, Y., Rei, C., Wang, H.: A novel PDE based image restoration: convection–diffusion equation for image denoising. J. Comput. Appl. Math. **231**(2), 771–779 (2009)
26. Saloma, C.: Computational complexity and the observation of physical signals. J. Appl. Phys. **74**(9), 5314–5319 (1993)
27. Black, M.J., Sapiro, G., Marimont, D.H., Heeger, D.: Robust anisotropic diffusion. IEEE Trans. Image Process. **7**(3), 421–432 (1998)
28. Monteil, J., Beghdadi, A.: A new interpretation and improvement of the nonlinear anisotropic diffusion for image enhancement. IEEE Trans. Pattern Anal. Mach. Intell. **21**(9), 940–946 (1999)
29. Durand, S., Fadili, J., Nikolova, M.: Multiplicative noise removal using L1 fidelity on frame coefficients. J. Math. Imaging Vis. **36**(3), 201–226 (2010)

Recommendations in E-Commerce Systems Based on Deep Matrix Factorization

Nguyen Thai-Nghe, Nguyen Thanh-Hai, and Tran Thanh Dien[✉]

Can Tho University, Can Tho city, Vietnam
{ntnghe,nthai.cit,thanhdien}@ctu.edu.vn

Abstract. E-commerce systems (including online shopping, entertainment, etc.) play an increasingly important role and have become popular in digital life. These systems have also become one of the cores, and vital issues for many businesses, especially from the recent COVID-19 pandemic, the importance of online e-commerce systems are very necessary. Techniques in recommendation systems are widely used to support users in finding suitable products/items in online systems. This work proposes using deep matrix factorization for recommendation in online e-commerce systems. We provide a detailed architecture of a deep matrix factorization as well as make a comparison with the standard matrix factorization model. Experimental results on ten published data sets show that the deep matrix factorization model can work well for recommendations in online e-commerce systems.

Keywords: Deep matrix factorization · Matrix factorization · Recommender systems · E-commerce systems

1 Introduction

E-commerce systems play an increasingly important role and have become popular with the strong development of mobile devices. E-commerce has also become one of the cores and vital issues for many businesses if they do not keep up with the trends. As observed from the recent COVID-19 pandemic, the importance of e-commerce has been seen. After the quarantine period, people are gradually getting used to e-commerce and using it regularly. The positive points that e-commerce brings bring attraction to buyers and sellers. It can greatly affect marketing and advertising while we only spend the low cost. The internet connects computers and mobile devices in a world of things, and the transmission of information through advertising takes place extremely easily and quickly to millions worldwide through a few simple steps.

However, we also realize that besides the benefits that e-commerce can bring, there are also some disadvantages. This includes much information irrelevant to the user's interests or interests. Since then, users have spent much time filtering

T. K. Dang et al. (Eds.): FDSE 2022, CCIS 1688, pp. 419–431, 2022.
https://doi.org/10.1007/978-981-19-8069-5_28

out unnecessary information, leading to negative emotions when users have to receive too many advertisements for some stores and e-commerce brands.

The recommender system that has emerged in recent years uses artificial intelligence algorithms to provide automatic recommendations to users based on data about past behavior/actions from the data collected by a vast of analytics actions to guide customers and suggest products they may like or are interested in them. This helps customers make shopping decisions that match their needs and preferences. With the nature of e-commerce systems, buyers and sellers may not need to meet face-to-face, and purchase and sale transactions will mainly be done on websites or mobile applications, so the need for automated assistants to suggest sales is essential. Of course, having a smart, friendly, knowledgeable customer "expert" is a big challenge. So researchers will often integrate recommendation techniques into e-commerce systems that make intelligent predictions about customer preferences, identifying customer groups by interest similarity to provide notifications or suggestions that they may care about or are interested in.

This study proposes using the deep matrix factorization method [1,2] to provide suggestions/recommendations to customers in online e-commerce systems. The advantage of this approach is that it replaces the DOT product in the standard matrix factorization with a deep neuron network for a better non-linear combination, thus, getting better prediction results. Experiments are evaluated on vast data sets that include more than 30 million reviews on the Amazon site and several other data sources.

This paper is organized as follows: A short introduction on recommendation approaches for e-commerce systems is given in Sect. 2. In Sect. 3, we present our architecture, including factorization matrix methods to develop workflow processes. In Sect. 4, we propose a set of changed operations to customize the workflow. Experimental results are introduced in Sect. 5. Finally, Sect. 6 concludes the paper with an outlook on future research.

2   Related Work

According to [1], the learners and the lecturers can meet face-to-face in traditional learning. Therefore, they can use the printed book tutorials as their lectures. However, in distance education, learners cannot interact with their lecturers. Therefore, online learning materials would be helpful resources for learners to obtain knowledge. In the research, the authors proposed a deep matrix factorization model that extended from the standard matrix factorization model to recommend learning resources based on learners' capacities. The experimental results that used data from students' learning outcomes at a university provided valuable course recommendations for learners.

Another study of [3] reviewed the research trends linking recommendation systems' advanced technical aspects. Based on more than 135 top-ranking articles and top-tier conferences published in Google Scholar period 2010 to 2021, the authors systematized the trend in recommendation system models, the technologies used in recommendation systems, and the business fields of the recommendation systems. The study showed that the content-based filtering recommendation model was one of the earliest models to have been used, along with collaborative filtering-based recommendation models. However, hybrid systems that can complement the strengths and weaknesses of the content-based and collaborative filtering recommendation models are more appropriately used. It also showed that the filtering models of the recommendation systems using techniques such as text mining, KNN, clustering, matrix factorization, and neural network were used for a long period. However, applying neural network technology to a recommendation system has recently increased. In addition, several studies that aim to improve the performance of recommendation systems are actively conducted and expanded.

The authors in [4] have studied the implicit regularization of gradient descent over deep linear neural networks for matrix completion and sensing. A model referred to as deep matrix factorization. They presented theoretical and empirical arguments questioning a nascent view by which implicit regularization in matrix factorization can be captured using simple mathematical norms. [5] proposed a novel matrix factorization model with neural network architecture. Firstly, they construct a user-item matrix with detailed ratings and non-preference implicit feedback. Then, with this matrix as the input, the authors present a deep structure learning architecture to learn a common low-dimensional space for the representations of users and items. After that, they designed a new loss function based on binary cross-entropy, in which we consider both explicit ratings and implicit feedback for better optimization. The experimental results show the proposed model's effectiveness and the loss function.

For recommendation in online/e-commerce systems, the authors in [6] have explained how recommender systems help E-commerce sites increase sales and analyzed six sites that use recommender systems, including several sites that use more than one recommender system. Based on the examples, they created a taxonomy of recommender systems, including the interfaces they present to customers, the technologies used to create the recommendations, and the inputs they need from customers. Finally, they concluded with ideas for new applications of recommender systems to E-commerce. [7] developed a recommendation system to achieve realistic prediction results, which is done by building the system based on the customers' behavior and cooperating with the statistical analysis to support decision-making, to be employed on an e-commerce site, and to increase its performance. The experimental results showed that using statistical methods improves decision-making to increase the accuracy of recommendation lists suggested to customers. The authors in [8] have proposed a hierarchical recommendation system to increase the performance of the e-commerce recommendation system. Their approach has a two-level hierarchical structure: The first level uses bidirectional encoder representations to represent textual information of an item (title, description, and a subset of item reviews), efficiently and accurately; The second level is an attention-based sequential recommendation model that uses item embeddings derived from the first level of the hierarchical structure. Results in the real-world dataset show that the proposed approach provides at least 10% better HR@10 and NCCG@10 performance than other review-based models. Other works can be found in [3,9,10].

In this work, we propose using deep matrix factorization to provide customer recommendations in online e-commerce systems. The advantage of this approach is that it replaces the DOT product in the standard matrix factorization with a deep neuron network for a better non-linear combination, thus, getting better prediction results.

3   Matrix Factorization for Recommendation

In recommender systems, we usually collect the user-item-rating matrix data. Let denote X as that matrix, u as a user, i as an item, and r as a rating. The main purpose of recommender systems is to predict the empty rating in the matrix X, which means that the users have not seen the items. After prediction, the items with the highest prediction score are recommended to the users.

One state-of-the-art method in this area is Matrix Factorization. This is a well-known method in recommender systems [3,11,13]. It decomposes a matrix X (each row of X is a user, each column is an item, and each element is a rating of the user on that item, respectively) to two small matrices P and Q such that we can reconstruct X from these two P and Q matrices (as presented in Fig. 1 and Eq. (1)).

$$X \approx PQ^T \tag{1}$$

where $P \in \mathbb{R}^{|U| \times K}$; $Q \in \mathbb{R}^{|I| \times K}$; K is number of latent factors, $K << |U|, K << |I|$. The latent factors P and Q can be obtained from optimizing the objective function as the following (Equation (2)):

$$\mathcal{O}^{MF} = \sum_{(u,i) \in \mathcal{D}^{train}} \left(r_{ui} - \sum_{k=1}^{K} p_{uk} q_{ik} \right)^2 + \lambda(||P||_F^2 + ||Q||_F^2) \tag{2}$$

$\lambda \in (0..1)$ is a regularization and $|| \cdot ||_F$ is the Frobenius norm. One benefit of the Matrix Factorization approach is its flexibility in dealing with various data aspects. This is one of the techniques in feature/dimensionality reduction. Thus, it works well for large data sets. Details of these methods are described in [11–13].

4   Proposed Approach

The main idea of the Matrix factorization model is that it decomposes the big matrix into two smaller ones. Then, each element of the big matrix is approximated from the two smaller matrices using a DOT product, as presented on the left side of Fig. 2. The DOT product is running very fast. Thus it can work

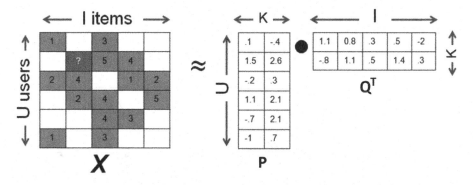

Fig. 1. Matrix factorization method for recommendation systems

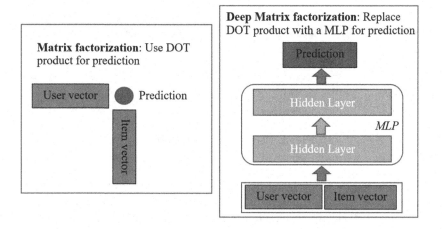

Fig. 2. Matrix factorization vs Deep matrix factorization

well for larger data sets. However, it is a linear combination between two latent factors of the user and the item.

To tackle this linear combination, the Deep matrix factorization replaces the DOT product by deep neuron networks for a better non-linear combination, as presented on the right side of Fig. 2. Therefore, this study proposes using Deep Matrix Factorization (DMF), which is extended from the matrix factorization [1, 2,14], for recommendation in online e-commerce systems. The model is described in detail in Fig. 3. The proposed model has four layers. First, an input layer represents the current user/item; second, an embedding layer for reducing the user and item features' dimensions (the latent factors); Third, the DOT product is replaced by a deep neuron network for a better non-linear combination. Fourth, two embedding features are concatenated as the Multilayer Perceptron (MLP) layer input. Finally, an output layer for the prediction score. In this model, the MLP and the latent factors are trained simultaneously.

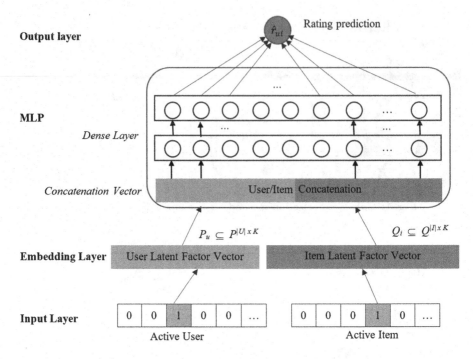

Fig. 3. Deep matrix factorization

The MLP can be set up by adding more hidden layers or changing the number of neurons depending on different datasets/domains. In this study, the number of nodes/neurons is selected using a hyper-parameter search, which will be carefully presented in the experimental results section.

5   Evaluation

Ten published data sets in e-commerce/online systems are used for evaluation. In addition, the standard measures in recommender systems are used for comparison.

5.1   Data Sets

Datasets 1, 2, and 3: These datasets are extracted from the Amazon product reviews on Office Products, Fashion, and Cell Phones and Accessories[1] These datasets include reviews (ratings, text, helpfulness votes), product metadata (descriptions, category information, price, brand, and image features), and links (also viewed/also bought graphs). However, we use three attributes in this work: user ID, item ID, and ratings.

---

[1] https://nijianmo.github.io/amazon/index.html..

Table 1. Data sets used for experiments

No	Dataset name	Number of Users	Number of Items	Number of Ratings
1	Amazon – Office Products	306,800	3,404,914	5,581,313
2	Amazon – Fashion	186,189	749,233	883,636
3	Amazon – Cell Phones	589,534	6,211,701	10,063,255
4	Anime Recommendation	4,714	7,157	419,943
5	Book Recommendation	105,283	340,556	1,149,780
6	Food.com Recipes and Interactions	226,570	231,637	1,132,367
7	Movielens 100k	610	9,724	100,836
8	Restaurant Data with Consumer Ratings	138	130	1,161
9	Retailrocket recommender system	1,407,580	235,061	2,756,101
10	R1 - Yahoo! Music User Ratings of Musical Artists	167,184	28,757	10,000,000

Dataset 4: Anime Recommendations Database[2] This data set contains information on user preference data on anime. Each user can add anime to their completed list and give it a rating.

Dataset 5: Book Recommendation Dataset[3] This dataset contains the book rating information. Ratings (Book-Rating) are either explicit, expressed on a scale from 1–10 (higher values denoting higher appreciation), or implicit, expressed by 0.

Dataset 6: Food.com Recipes and Interactions[4] This dataset consists of recipes and reviews by the users on Food.com (formerly GeniusKitchen).

Dataset 7: Movilens 100k[5] This dataset was collected from the MovieLens website. The data set is about ratings of the users for movies.

---

[2] https://www.kaggle.com/datasets/CooperUnion/anime-recommendations-database..

[3] https://www.kaggle.com/datasets/arashnic/book-recommendation-dataset..

[4] https://www.kaggle.com/datasets/shuyangli94/food-com-recipes-and-user-interactions..

[5] https://grouplens.org/datasets/movielens/.

Dataset 8: Restaurant Data with Consumer Ratings[6] This dataset was used for a study where the task was to generate a top-n list of restaurants according to consumer preferences and find the significant features.

Dataset 9: Retailrocket recommender system dataset[7] The dataset consists of three files: a file with behavior data), a file with item properties, and a file that describes a category tree. The data has been collected from a real-world e-commerce website. It is raw data, i.e., without any content transformations. However, all values are hashed due to personal issues. The events are encoded by: "view" is set to 1, "add to cart" is set to 2, and "transaction" is set to 3.

Dataset 10: R1 - Yahoo! Music User Ratings of Musical Artists[8] This dataset represents a snapshot of the Yahoo! Music community's preferences for various musical artists. The rating values are from 1 to 100. However, this data is too big, so we just used the first ten million ratings for the experiment.

5.2   Evaluation Metrics

The root means squared error (RMSE) and absolute error (MAE) are used to evaluate the models. They are calculated by Eqs. (3) and (4), respectively.

$$\sqrt{\frac{1}{n}\sum_{i=1}^{n}(r_{ui}-\hat{r}_{ui})^2} \tag{3}$$

$$\frac{1}{n}\sum_{i=1}^{n}|r_{ui}-\hat{r}_{ui}| \tag{4}$$

where r_{ui} is the true value, $\hat{r}_{ui}$ is the predicted value, and n is the number of samples in the test set.

5.3   Train/test Split and Dealing with Cold-Start Problem

In the experiments, the data sets were randomly shuffled and split into 67% for training and 33% for testing. This may cause the cold-start problem (new user/item problem), which is the users/items that exist in the test sets but have not appeared in the training set. The simple way to treat these new users/items is to return the global average rating for all new users/items.

5.4   Experimental Results

In the first experiment, we performed the hyper-parameter search to look for the best number of neurons and the best number of hidden layers of the MLP in the Deep matrix factorization model. The relationship between the RMSE

---

[6] https://www.kaggle.com/datasets/uciml/restaurant-data-with-consumer-ratings..

[7] https://www.kaggle.com/datasets/retailrocket/ecommerce-dataset..

[8] https://webscope.sandbox.yahoo.com/catalog.php?datatype=r.

and the number of neurons is presented in Fig. 4. These results show that the RMSE did not change much when we added more neurons (other data sets also gave the same results). Thus, we used 128 neurons for all the data sets in this work. Similarly, when adding more hidden layers to the model, the RMSE is not improved so much. Thus, we only used one hidden layer for all data sets. This helps reduce the training time.

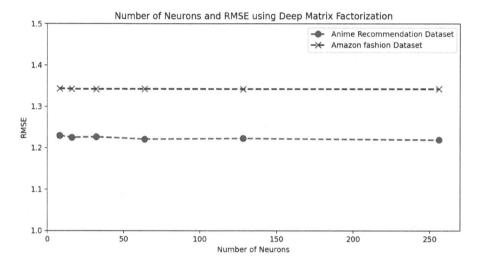

Fig. 4. Relationship between the RMSE and the number of neurons

In the second experiment, we look for the best number of latent factors in both the matrix factorization and deep matrix factorization as presented in Fig. 5 (other data sets are similar). In the matrix factorization model, the number of latent factors is from 40 to 60 for getting good RMSE results. On the other hand, in the deep matrix factorization model, the RMSE results are nearly stable when we change the number of latent factors. Thus, we have used 10 latent factors for all the data sets.

In the third experiment, we look for the best number of epochs in both the matrix factorization and deep matrix factorization as presented in Fig. 6 (other data sets are similar). In the matrix factorization model, the number of epochs is from 10 to 30 for good RMSE results. On the other hand, in the deep matrix factorization model, the RMSE results are nearly stable when we change the number of epochs. Thus, we have used 2 epochs for all data sets to get better training times.

After finding good parameters, the matrix factorization (using DOT product) and deep matrix factorization (using MLP) are performed on ten e-commerce data sets. Detailed comparison results of the RMSE and MAE are presented in Tables 2 and 3.

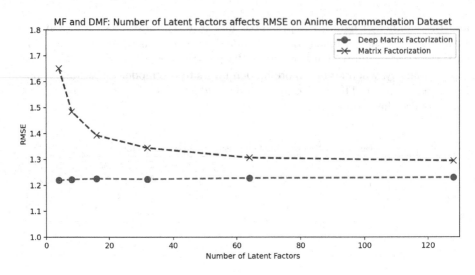

Fig. 5. Number of latent factors

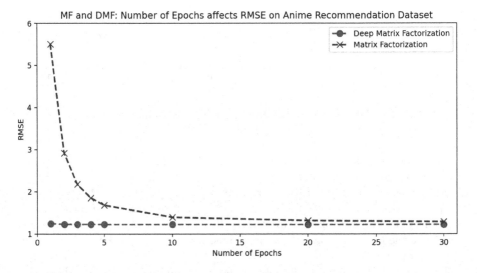

Fig. 6. Number of epochs

From the experimental results, deep matrix factorization can reduce the error in both RMSE and MAE. This means replacing a linear combination with a non-linear one in the matrix factorization can get better results. Please note that in data set 10 (R1 Yahoo! Music), the rating values are from 0 to 100. Thus, the RMSE and MAE are higher than other data sets with ratings from 1 to 5.

Moreover, the advantage of these factorization models is their dimensionality reduction feature. For example, the user/item collaborative filtering methods (using K-nearest neighbors) can not run on large data sets (e.g., data sets 1, 3,

Table 2. RMSE comparison of the matrix and deep matrix factorization

No	Dataset	Matrix Factorization	Deep Matrix Factorization
1	Amazon – Office Products	3.321	**1.295**
2	Amazon – Fashion	3.191	**1.409**
3	Amazon – Cell Phones	3.364	**1.433**
4	Anime Recommendation	1.395	**1.223**
5	Book Recommendation	4.492	**3.368**
6	Food.com Recipes and Interactions	2.818	**1.280**
7	Movielens 100k	1.172	**0.885**
8	Restaurant Data with Consumer Ratings	1.002	**0.691**
9	Retailrocket recommender system	0.857	**0.231**
10	R1 - Yahoo! Music	31.866	**29.127**

Table 3. MAE comparison of the matrix and deep matrix factorization

No	Dataset	Matrix Factorization	Deep Matrix Factorization
1	Amazon – Office Products	2.869	**1.013**
2	Amazon – Fashion	2.813	**1.177**
3	Amazon – Cell Phones	2.935	**1.160**
4	Anime Recommendation	1.012	**0.930**
5	Book Recommendation	3.015	**2.759**
6	Food.com Recipes and Interactions	2.107	**0.865**
7	Movielens 100k	0.830	**0.683**
8	Restaurant Data with Consumer Ratings	0.792	**0.603**
9	Retailrocket recommender system	0.740	**0.097**
10	R1 - Yahoo! Music	22.373	**21.082**

9, 10) due to an out of memory on 16 Gb RAM. In contrast, the deep matrix factorization method can work well.

We also investigate the loss during training and validation phases as presented in Fig. 7 (on data set 4 - Anime, other data sets have similar results). For the matrix factorization, the loss becomes stable after 8–10 epochs, while the deep matrix factorization needs 1–2 epochs.

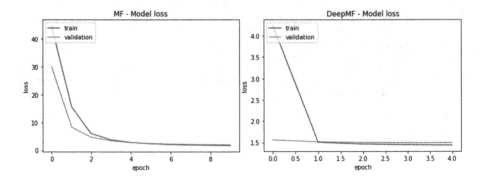

Fig. 7. Loss comparison on matrix factorization and deep matrix factorization

6 Conclusion

This work proposes using deep matrix factorization for recommendation in online e-commerce systems. We provide a detailed architecture of a deep matrix factorization as well as make a comparison with the standard matrix factorization model. Experimental results on ten published data sets show that the deep matrix factorization model can work well for recommendations in online e-commerce systems.

References

1. Dien, T.T., Thanh-Hai, N., Thai-Nghe, N.: An approach for learning resource recommendation using deep matrix factorization. J. Inf. Telecommun. (2022). https://doi.org/10.1080/24751839.2022.2058250
2. Zhang, F., Song, J., Peng, S.: Deep matrix factorization for recommender systems with missing data not at random. Conference Series, J. Phys. **1060**, pp. 012001 (2018). https://doi.org/10.1088/1742-6596/1060/1/012001
3. Ko, H., Lee, S., Park, Y., Choi, A.: A survey of recommendation systems: recommendation models. Tech. Appl. Fields Electro. **11**, 141 (2022). https://doi.org/10.3390/electronics11010141
4. Arora, S., Cohen, N., Hu, W., Luo, Y.: Implicit regularization in deep matrix factorization. In: Proceedings of the 33rd International Conference on Neural Information Processing Systems. Curran Associates Inc., Red Hook, NY, USA, Article 666, 7413–7424 (2019)

5. Xue, H.-J., Dai, Xinyu., Zhang, J., Huang, S., Chen, J.: Deep matrix factorization models for recommender systems. In: Proceedings of the Twenty-Sixth International Joint Conference on Artificial Intelligence (IJCAI-17), pp. 3203–3209 (2017).https://doi.org/10.24963/ijcai.2017/447

6. Ben Schafer, J., Konstan, J., Riedl, J.: Recommender systems in e-commerce. In: Proceedings of the 1st ACM conference on Electronic commerce (EC '99). Association for Computing Machinery, New York, NY, USA, pp. 158–166 (1999). https://doi.org/10.1145/336992.337035

7. Abdul Hussien, F.T., Rahma, A.M.S., Abdulwahab, H.B.: An E-Commerce recommendation system based on dynamic analysis of customer behavior. Sustain. **13**(19) 10786 (2021). https://doi.org/10.3390/su131910786

8. Islek, I., Gunduz Oguducu, S.: A hierarchical recommendation system for E-commerce using online user reviews. Electron. Commer. Res. Appl. **52**, 101131, ISSN 1567–4223, (2022). https://doi.org/10.1016/j.elerap.2022.101131

9. Handschutter De, P., Gillis, N., Siebert, X.: A survey on deep matrix factorizations. Comput. Sci. Rev. **42**, 100423, ISSN 1574–0137 (2021). https://doi.org/10.1016/j.cosrev.2021.100423

10. Yuanzhe, P.: A Survey on Modern Recommendation System based on Big Data. arXiv, (2022). https://doi.org/10.48550/ARXIV.2206.02631

11. Koren, Y., Bell, R., Volinsky, C.: Matrix factorization techniques for recommender systems. Comput. **42**, 30–37 (2009)

12. Thai-Nghe, N., Drumond, L., Krohn-Grimberghe, A., Schmidt-Thieme, L.: Recommender system for predicting student performance. Procedia Comput. Sci. **1**, 2811–2819 (2010)

13. Thai-Nghe, N., Schmidt-Thieme, L.: Factorization forecasting approach for user modeling. J. Comput. Sci. Cybern. **31**(2), 133–148 (2015)

14. Guo, H., Tang, R., Ye, Y., Li, Z., He, X.: DeepFM: A factorization-machine based neural network for CTR prediction. In: Proceedings of the 26th International Joint Conference on Artificial Intelligence, IJCAI'17, AAAI Press, pp. 1725–1731 (2017)

AttendanceKit: A set of Role-Based Mobile Applications for Automatic Attendance Checking with UHF RFID Using Realtime Firebase and Face Recognition

Trung-Dung Tran[1,2], Kha-Tu Huynh[1,2], Phu-Quang Nguyen[1,2], and Tu-Nga Ly[1,2(✉)]

[1] International University, Ho Chi Minh City, Vietnam
`vernytran@icloud.com`, {`hktu,nqphu,ltnga`}`@hcmiu.edu.vn`
[2] Vietnam National University, Ho Chi Minh City, Vietnam

Abstract. Traditional attendance monitoring has disadvantaged wasting time and resources. While an automatic attendance monitoring system enables students to check their attendance in offline classes. This paper we propose an AttendanceKit tool to check the automatic their attendance using real-time Ultra-High Frequency (UHF) RFID technology combined with face recognition in a suite of mobile applications for institution, lecturers, parents, and students. This can assist us overcome the disadvantages of manual inspection and get a very precise outcome. The back-end system's real-time updates will trigger automatic push notifications to the students' mobile devices, prompting them to access the app and verify their attendance. They will also include the attendance monitoring features that allow the instructor to evaluate or determine the attendance status of each student. After receiving a request from a student, the application enables lecturers to manually monitor attendance in the event of unforeseen student concerns. In addition, our technique can automatically compile reports and analysis on each student's learning status in each class and the class overall to provide the lecturers, parents, and the institution with the aggregate percentage of students who are committed to attending class. Our experiments show that some initial simulations of the system provide a more complete picture of how the new system operates and interacts, followed by an evaluation based on the learning outcomes of the class. Our system takes time and accuracy into account. In addition, our results present a complete performance study of the system with RFID and genuine mobile devices, as well as a novel machine learning platform that can be deployed on actual devices in reality for commercial.

Keywords: AttendanceKit · UHF RFID · Role-based mobile applications · Face recognition · Realtime firebase · Automatic attendance system

1 Introduction

According to [1], class attendance can be indicative of class quality and student performance. Participating in class enables students to interact with one another and with

© The Author(s), under exclusive license to Springer Nature Singapore Pte Ltd. 2022
T. K. Dang et al. (Eds.): FDSE 2022, CCIS 1688, pp. 432–446, 2022.
https://doi.org/10.1007/978-981-19-8069-5_29

lecturers, which can have a positive impact on their ability to study and apply course material in their future careers. This is the reason why many colleges mandate class attendance as a criterion for assessing and evaluating student performance. Traditional attendance tracking conducted manually by inspecting pupils face-to-face or through the use of forms in class has several residual flaws that can be addressed by an automated information system. This proposed attendance method decreases class management resource and time expenditures [2].

Recently, our research proposed the development of long-range UHF RFID technology with the high-definition camera to automate attendance monitoring system from 1 m to 3 m range in real-time database based on MongoDB (see Figs. 2b and 5 [3]) and showed the performance with and without using RFID based on analysis the attendance of student's and evaluated class' learning outcome of AI and CA, see Figs. 12 and 13 [4] respectively.

Unlike the system suggested [3], our biometric authentication system combines face recognition technology. This can result in a more advanced and usable system with more precision and provide more data for monitoring and analysis. In addition, the system encourages students to take a more active role in checking attendance by sending immediate notifications to the application on their mobile devices and utilizing the camera and microphone for security authentication.

Our principal contributions include the following:

Firstly, a set of macOS and iOS role-based usable and deployable applications, which is very new because few researchers such as firebase realtime database, mobile app or institutions can develop or try to implement anything on Apple platforms previously due to the difficulty of hardware dependency and its exclusivity, because iOS is the second major mobile operating system, this means a great deal, and the Android version will be much easier to develop. The algorithm is then fed a series of 5-second-long videos containing the faces of students. A collection of student faces is compared with the image captured by the camera on the mobile device, and attendance is recorded if the two IDs matched, stored ID via vectors in the database after trained and current ID via mobile app.

Secondly, utilizing the information system described [3, 4], we continue to assess the performance of the learning outcomes to illustrate the utility of automatic RFID in improving the quality of learning. RFID tags and mobile device's camera are combined to reach our current target of teaching or security-based facial. We leverage Apple's native ARKit framework [5] to identify and match a 3D grid mask on the student's face, as well as a Convolution Neural Network (CNN) FaceNet [5] TensorFlow [6] implementation model, converted to Core ML [7]. The timing and precision of our system are then determined.

In Section 2, where they will analyze existing research and create the framework for this approach, all relevant publications are provided. In Section 3, procedures ranging from hardware attribute measuring through software creation are illustrated. Section 4 presents the results of tests using the established system. The authors conclude with a summary of completed work and suggestions for future improvements.

2 Literature Review

2.1 Attendance System-based RFID

Referring to [1, 3, 4], there are a number of prevalent roll call methods that utilize the RFID component of the management system. For the purpose of employee identification, the research team developed a real-time RFID system comprising an 6C tag, a web-based interface stored on a server, and a database behind. In this instance, the distance between the card reader was fixed at approximately 5 centimeters. In a similar manner, the authors [1] provide a method for predicting average reading time and automatically calculating student attendance percentage based on collected and stored data. These technologies have been realized as web development programming languages and frameworks, but they perform badly in terms of real-time and optimized data traffic. The system presented [3, 4] prefers to use more complex technologies and frameworks, such as Node.js and MongoDB [8], to enhance the system's performance.

Our previous study [3, 4] established an automated attendance system based on radio frequencies with long-distance ranges (1 m to 3 m) and a power range of 18 dBm to 24 dBm (see Fig. 3b [3] and Fig. 2 [4]). This leads us to examine the student's status by displaying the student's name in real-time in case of card fraud and to remind students of the number of lessons via email, see Figure 10 [3], so that they are more aware of the situation and more inclined to attend class, as well as automatically digitizing and visualizing the sessions in terms of statistics for the teacher (see Figs. 8 and 9 [3]). Our latest research [4] introduced an automatically generate a weekly report about student's learning status in each class and provide the overall proportion of students' commitment to attending classes for the lecturer. It brings some initial simulations of the system to give a more detailed picture of how the new system works and interacts. Besides, this manuscript provides a detailed performance analysis about the system with RFID and camera, then has an evaluation based on class' learning outcome. The time, precision, and accuracy of system are considered.

2.2 Integrated RFID and Face Recognition

The use of RFID for roll call does not guarantee that the person using the card is the one calling. To address these concerns, researchers [9–11] included facial recognition into RFID roll call technology. The paper [10] describes a face-recognition-based method for automating the checking of attendance. The paper offers a method for acquiring training sets and testing sets utilizing a camera and the PCA (Principal Component Analysis) algorithm for learning. In addition, the system includes log file maintenance that keeps records of each student over the duration of the system. With a detection rate of 98.7 percent and a recognition rate of 95 percent, the archival performance is quite good at the time of writing. The required distance for face inspection is incredibly small (50 cm), yet its use in practice is challenging. In the work [9], the author proposes a technique for the office checkup task in a surveillance monitoring system based on the combination of facial recognition and RFID tags. The system is specially linked to a SQL Server database, allowing for greater synchronization than conventional surveillance management solutions. Using a close-range RC522 card reader, this system scanned tags and confirmed 200 to 300 photographs with an accuracy of 93.5–95.3%. Another author [19] proposed integrating deep learning face recognition and RFID technology, followed by an analysis of standard face recognition technology using deep learning neural network recognition technology.

2.3 Firebase Real-time Database and RFID

The author [12] proposed an attendance system for doctors has also been designed using RFID cards and Node MCU based on real-time database made in Google Firebase. This real-time database is also connected to the back end of the web application. Local cache on the device is used by the Realtime database SDKs to serve and store the changes when the users are suddenly switched from online to offline. Meanwhile, the author [13] used centralized Firebase as one of Google's mobile platforms to develop high-quality apps. It is a real-time and cloud-hosted NoSQL database which is used to store and synchronize between the existing users. The author [14], moreover, proposed mobile application is integrated with hardware scanner which scans the fingerprints of the student and uses Google Cloud firebase to store the fingerprint records. The attendance of respective subjects will be automatically marked, and the respective changes will be reflected in student android app. The author [15] introduced a tool for recording student attendance history in a time efficient and digitalized manner using biometric sensor and firebase. This is the IOT based autonomous class attendance. By applied Google assistant, the attendance was logged using RFID card to access the database and trained to calculate the average attendance [16] for iOS.

3 Proposed System

In this study, our group proposes a fully built system that links to a middleware macOS application called "RFID Dashboard" that was developed with Java JDK version 16 (Developed with IntelliJ) and the Gradle Build Tools [17] structure. Hopeland CL7206B7A [18] UHF RFID reader would be used by the system. In addition, we have a quadrupole of iOS mobile applications referred to as "Institution", "Students", "Teachers," and "Parents" that employ a role-based architecture. All these applications are known as "AttendanceKit (with RFID)" and employ Google Firebase [19] as their backend and database. Programming in Swift 5 [20] for iOS applications utilizing the SwiftUI, UIKit, ARKit, AVKit, SceneKit, Core Data, Core ML [7], and Vision frameworks (Developed in Xcode). To enable an end user (Institution) to create accounts for other end users: Students, Lecturers, and Parents. We also have a simple Node.js backend (Express.js).

Supporting RFID and utilizing Face Recognition on mobile devices, the newly integrated capability in our system enables us to track student attendance in class by utilizing Face Recognition. The FaceNet recognizer described in the paper [5], TensorFlow implementation [6] are used and exported into Apple's Core ML [7] format using Cocoa Pods [21] and coremltools [22] for use on real iOS devices. Since this ML model is embedded within the application, the 5-second-long face sample videos of the students will be converted into 50 vectors per individual (10 vectors per second) and kept in the real-time database for further comparison. Apple's Create ML [23] software is used to create the model for the voice recognition component and has a 5-second voice sample for each student. Currently the Android version of our system is not developed yet but will be available soon and will deploy into academic scenarios. Our team also reused the hardware placement mentioned in Sect. 3.2 of [3, 4].

3.1 System Architecture

Figure 1 shows our architecture of the attendance system, which employs long-range RFID, macOS middleware, and iOS applications. The system's architecture employs an admin-user structure. RFID Dashboard is a Java application for macOS that must be installed on a computer in order to read data from a reader and receive tag data. The reader should be positioned so that it can read the tags worn by pupils as they enter and leave the classroom (the optimal location for the reader can be found in the section titled "Tag reading range"). Either a TCP LAN connection or a USB serial port is necessary for the two devices to communicate. It is also possible to utilize the middleware application for macOS as a client of the system, allowing it to communicate information about tags to the Firebase database.

This piece of middleware is only capable of displaying one thing on the screen, and that is the most recent tag it read. If this tag was not being read, it would display "Currently not reading." It has two responsibilities while you are using it: First, the data from the read tag is entered into the realtime Database. The second step is to collect the token for the connected mobile device and the most recent information about the student's classroom course. Finally, a message is composed and sent to the student as a reminder to check attendance.

The mobile applications are developed in Swift 5 with SwiftUI (iOS 14 or later), and the targeted functionality is role-based access. When we ultimately release it, each of the roles that occur in an academic setting the institution, the students, the lecturers, and the parents will have their own mobile app, complete with features suited to that

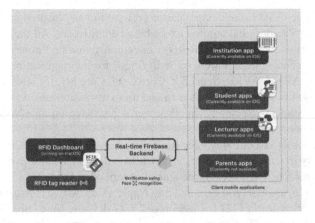

Fig. 1. System architecture diagram

position in order to deliver the optimal user experience for that role. They all utilize the same server and database for the Firebase platform.

3.2 Software Analysis

This project, named AttendanceKit, consists of five distinct applications with distinct functions shown in Fig. 2. The first is the middleware application namely "RFID Dashboard" for connecting to the reader and sending messages to the cloud center on macOS. Gradle settings were chosen primarily because they are compatible with the Firebase Admin SDK. Originally, Firebase did not provide a solution for a desktop application to use it; only mobile, web, and games were supported. However, with the Admin SDK, which also includes options for Node.js and Python, we have a small opening to implement it with Java, luckily the SDK provided from the manufacturer also works in Java. This is used as a connector to the reader as well as a message builder for FCM to send notifications to student devices in real-time.

The student application is the second application in the set. This is the most crucial iOS application since it implements the face recognize method and monitors student attendance in real time with a wonderful user experience by providing instant notifications and opening the camera quickly for verification. In addition, it logs arrival and departure times and provides further reports and analyses. Students cannot create accounts for themselves since the institution must collect face samples for the training database and security purposes. They can only reset or update their password with the aid of Firebase Authentication and their registered email address (OAuth 2.0).

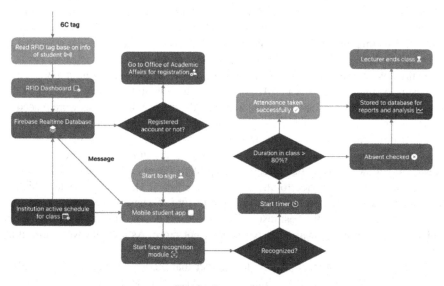

Fig. 2. System flow

The third application in the package is the app for the institution; its primary function is to take a sample of the student's face and create an account for them, their professors, and their parents. Due to security concerns, only a few copies of this program will be put on a limited number of mobile phones, and only a few departments, such as Student Affairs or Academic Affairs, will have access to this application. In addition to its primary function of generating accounts and collecting samples, the system may coordinate class schedules, exam schedules, information, summary reports and analyses, reader configuration, etc. All these features are currently being created.

The fourth app, the lecturer app (which is still in development), provides the lecturer with the ability to monitor their students, view reports and analysis, and reschedule classes created by the institution. This app also allows lecturers to manually check attendance for students who forgot to bring their RFID tag to campus. Lastly, the parent app to remotely watch the child and check the report will be built after an inquiry to the institution. We are still debating whether we should develop this app owing to student privacy concerns.

The minimum target for deployment is iOS 14 because the user interface was written using the SwiftUI framework. In addition, we implemented numerous frameworks, libraries, and extensions required for the iOS development process, including CocoaPods, Firebase, RxSwift, Alamofire, and many others.

3.3 Face Recognition

In this attendance monitoring system, face recognition is the major security measure. By doing a literature analysis on this topic, we discover that most of the prevalent AI platforms and tools, such as TensorFlow, PyTorch, Keras, etc., utilized in our previous research [3, 4] cannot be deployed on actual mobile devices due to hardware requirements. The cameras of these mobile devices on iOS and Android have their own configuration and SDK to implement it, not only a web-based notebook such as Google Colab or Kaggle. To implement the pretrained model FaceNet [5], therefore, we will need to export it into Apple's Core ML format [7], namely .mlmodel.

At first, we attempted to develop an image classification model without any lines of code using Apple's native Create ML tool [23], which is quite cool. We separated the face samples of three persons into three files, and the remaining samples were placed in an "unknown" category. It first works great, but when we try to detect up to four people, it produces inaccurate results, so we ignore it (this method works, but we will need to manually train each of the students faces on campus every time there is a new student if we want to get the model to be correct, so we pass this method in the end).

The second time, we tried to utilize TuriCreate tool [24], also by Apple, which is superior because we can specify the model architecture. We have three models who have already been trained. For the best results, ResNet-50 is chosen. This manner, our model produces accurate results with only ten people, not more. As a result, we ignore it as well.

We investigated constructing a Python server that recognizes faces using FaceNet [5] or ArcFace [21]. Then, our iOS application will send the image to the server and receive the response. It will yield the most accurate findings, but there is a catch: "We must wait for the network; this application cannot recognize in real time." Therefore, we attempted to convert a TensorFlow model to Core ML [7] format utilizing coremltools [22] to utilize it in our iOS application. After converting the facenet.pb model to the facenet.mlmodel format, we embedded it into our project and used numerous frameworks to make it compatible with the device, such as Alamofire [25], RxSwift [26], TensorFlow-experimental [6], etc.

In brief, this is an embedding paradigm in which all valuable image information is incorporated into vector. FaceNet compresses an individual's face into a vector of 128 values. Ideally, the embeddings of related faces would be identical. We gather the student's face sample as a 5-second-long video (like how the iPhone collects the native FaceID sample) and export it as a collection of 512 Double components. In addition to resizing the input to 160×160 pixels prior to putting it into a CVPixelBuffer for analysis, our model has turned the face sample video to Double 512 vectors. Remember that the vector we just constructed is a database of faces. Once we have additional face samples, we will employ the FaceNet model, convert it to a new vector, and then calculate the distance between the two vectors as shown in Fig. 3. The closest vector in the database is the outcome of the prediction process. Assume if we have 100 students, for instance, we will have $50 \times 100 = 5000$ vectors. How to quickly locate the nearest vector? For loop is not the optimal approach, so we study k-Means Clustering, k-d Tree, or kNN instead.

Fig. 3. Firebase real-time database of FaceNet recognition

3.4 Firebase

Firebase [19] is a Google-developed platform that facilitates the development, administration, and expansion of mobile applications. It makes it easier for programmers to create programs that are both faster and more secure. On the Firebase side, programming is not required, which makes it easier to optimize the usefulness of its features. Android, iOS, the web, and Unity may all profit from its services. Cloud storage is provided. NoSQL is used as the database for storing the information that is being maintained. Firebase was once known as Envolve and acted as an API-based provider of online chat services to several websites. It gained popularity because to developers' use of it to ease the real-time transfer of application data, such as the state of a game, among its players. In direct response to this, Envolve's architecture and chat system were finally separated.

In 2012, business founders James Tamplin and Andrew Lee moved the Envolve architecture in a new direction, resulting in what is currently known as the current Firebase. We opted to add Firebase and a lot of it's services into our project since it can provide feature support for a wide range of mobile devices and provide us with user-friendly backend tools in order for us to create this system.

4 Simulation Results

4.1 RFID Dashboard

This middleware reader connector and message builder just displays the tag ID of the current tag it reads using the manufacturer Java SDK see Fig. 4a. In the background, it uses the Firebase Admin SDK to build a message based on the tag ID it just read. The message sends notifications to mobile phones using a device token, see Fig. 4b. When the student logs in for the first time, this token is saved in the real-time database and is replaced if the student reinstalls the application. To register our app with FCM, we will also need a .json key issued by Google and a.p8 key provided by the Apple Push Notification Service Center (APNS Center).

(a)   (b)

Fig. 4. (a) RFID Dashboard (b) IntelliJ Gradle environment with FCM message builder

4.2 Mobile Applications

4.2.1 Students' Application

This mobile application is intended for use by all the students who are enrolled at the Institution see Fig. 5a. Its primary purpose is to enable the students to receive the notification that is transmitted instantly from the RFID Dashboard (delay at 5 seconds each time, do not spamming continuously) and to make it possible for them to face check with the recognition module shown in Fig. 5d. After the user has interacted with the notification, the application will proceed directly to the login session shown in Fig. 5b; however, if the student has already logged in, they will not be required to do so again. Then, a sheet view will modally be pop-up on the screen from the bottom of the screen and start to face checking. The algorithm and the process behind this module is the method of KNN and a pretrained FaceNet model [27], both of which will be detailed in further detail below. Following the completion of the check, the student will be notified by alert as to whether it was successful shown in Fig. 5e. If the answer is affirmative, the application will continue to the class timer session, the data from which will be gathered later for the purpose of class performance analysis as well as many other objectives.

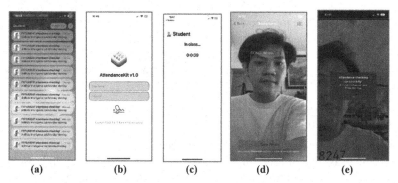

Fig. 5. (a) Notification to attendance checking (b) Login (c) Processing (d) Face checked (e) Attendance checking successfully

4.2.2 Institution's Application

This application will only be manually installed in a few department's devices within the organization, so that only a few departments will have access to the system. It will not be made available for extensive distribution to the general population. This application's major purpose is to allow admin users to create accounts for all the possible roles within the system. This includes students, instructors, and parents. In addition, it possesses a considerable number of other features that are still being developed. These capabilities allow it to remotely manage all tag readers, configure the amount of electricity being used, create class schedules, or administer an examination, etc.

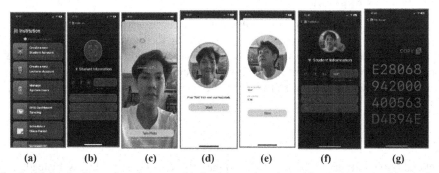

Fig. 6. (a) Institution app main menu (b) Student registration view (c) Face checking before register (d) 5 seconds face video recording (e) Face recorded and sample naming (f) Back to registration view with face recorded and button for checkout (g) RFID real-time tag ID syncing from reader

When we pick "Create a new Student Account" from the main menu see Fig. 6a, a new screen will appear where we can enter the student's information shown in Fig. 8b. This data consists of the student's ID, full name, and password, and it will be connected to the current RFID tag, which can be obtained remotely through the "Dashboard Syncing" section of the app shown in Fig. 6c. You can also capture a video of the student's sample face by touching the large face icon in the middle of the software's interface shown in Fig. 6d. This will take you to a unique perspective from which you can record the video shown in Fig. 8e. After completing all steps, a check mark will appear on top of the circle shown in Fig. 8f to indicate that you can now proceed to the checkout shown in Fig. 6g.

4.2.3 Lecturer's Application

This application, on the other hand, allows the lecturers of the institution to see the analysis of the class and of each student shown in Fig. 7. Because currently we do not have actual data to build out the graphs and charts, we will put a sample of it on the main screen, it also had a login session like the student app.

Fig. 7. Lecturer app interface with sample student's attendance report

4.2.4 Parent's Application

This software, like the Lecturer app, allows users to access student class performance reports and analyses, but it restricts users to only seeing their own children. The Lecturer app, on the other hand, allows users to view the reports and analyses of all students. Because this application is still in the process of being developed and because it raises certain concerns regarding the students' right to privacy, we will decide regarding this matter later.

4.3 Backend

Backend is the portion of an application that the user cannot directly access. Instead, it is the responsibility of the backend to supply the frontend with the functionality required for optimal operation. To fulfill the aim, a solid backend must be constructed. To determine what type of backend is required, the following questions must be answered. What type of backend might be implemented? Would the backend be server-based or serverless?

What types of databases are the most effective? How will authentication be performed? And based on the requirements, a serverless backend built on the Firebase platform was selected. Firebase is a Backend-as-a-service (BaaS) from Google that employs a software development kit (SDK) that supports JavaScript, Angular, JavaScript/Node.js, C++, Swift, Objective-C, and Java programming. Backbone, Ember, and React are also supported via database bindings. It has some of the most useful packages for mobile applications development processes such as Realtime database, Firestore, Storage, Cloud Messaging, Cloud Functions, Authentication, and some more. The SDK was integrated into the front-end mobile projects using the following snippets:

Realtime Database: Firebase also supplied the project with an appropriate database. The project utilized a NoSQL database type to hold all attendance, student, and course information in separate collections (i.e., table). The database was meticulously developed to give fully customizable data requests. This allows mobile applications to retrieve exactly the data they need, decreasing the number of calls between the frontend and backend, hence making the application more efficient. Even though NoSQL databases lack a schema, a structure was required to organize data within the database. We use this database to store information of the users (Students, Lecturers and Parents), their real device token ID as well as the RFID tags information. In the meantime, we will also use two other databases from Firebase SDK to store the data which will be mentioned below are Firestore and Storage. Hosting As the application must be accessible at any time and from any location, it was placed in the cloud. Firebase delivers hosting for mobile applications, static and dynamic content, and microservices that are seamless, quick, and safe. When the project is deployed to Firebase, numerous features will be available. When the project is initially launched, it is given a domain name that can be modified later to the appropriate domain name. Administrators could deploy many versions of a project and easily switch between them without losing any data. When the attendance system was deployed, it was provided with this domain (https://attendancekit-492b3-def ault-rtdb.asia-southeast1.firebasedatabase.app) and 10GB of storage space. We chose to host this database in Singapore, which is the closest choice to Vietnam shown in Fig. 8 (a).

(a)   (b)

Fig. 8. (a) Firebase realtime database of FaceID and RFID tag; (b) Firestore

Firestore: This project's second database was Firestore, a newer version of Realtime Database that supports many more functions. However, we only utilize this database for storing user authentication information, as it is the only way to allow an end user (Institution) to create accounts for other client users (Students, Lecturers and Parents). By separating the data into several databases inside the same SDK, we can utilize it more efficiently because it is a NoSQL, hence limiting our querying possibilities. In addition, this is the only way to grant permission for the Institution end user to create accounts for other users. (Firebase was designed for mobile developers to easily give users the option to sign up using an authenticator such as "Sign in with Google" or "Sign in with Facebook" or "Sign in with Apple," but not to manually grant an end user permission to create accounts for other users). The technique we utilized to accomplish this is referred to as an "Admin Module" shown in Fig. 8 (b).

Authentication: After integration, it was time to construct the project's authentication component. Firebase simplifies authentication for developers and end users. A user's identity must be known for an application to provide a personalized experience and maintain data security. Firebase offers a variety of user authentication methods. The administrator can enable or disable any of the various authentication methods, including email address, Facebook, Twitter, GitHub, and Google. The user information contains a unique identifier that is guaranteed to be unique across all service providers and unchanging for a particular authorized user. This UID is used to identify users and the portions of the backend system to which they have access to read, write, or delete. Firebase will also maintain the user session, ensuring that users remain signed in even if the browser or application is restarted. As noted previously in the section on the admin module, our system does not permit client users to establish their own accounts, so the Institution admin must manually create these accounts in their application. Firebase Authentication will then allow users to reset their passwords through the institution's email domain if they forget them.

4.4 The Performance of Face Recognition

Fig. 9. Face recognition process and evaluating

Because we implemented the pretrained model FaceNet, the performance of the face recognition module is the same as the performance of the FaceNet module. This is because of how the FaceNet module was trained (which is a notably immensely powerful one). Most of the time, it will return to a match of 90–100% (see Fig. 9 and respectively), but there are certain instances in which, if we tried to recognize it in the dark, it would dip down to 70%. Before integrating it into the app for students, we first tested the module on its own, which required us to isolate it into a distinct app. The quality of the sample video that lasts only five seconds will determine how successfully the data will be uploaded to the backend and converted into vectors (an ideal video recorded is in bright light condition with the face always in the center and turn the head around continuously, like the method of Apple's FaceID). For now, we have not implemented the flow or rules for the user to follow to get the best sample yet, but we will in the future.

5   Conclusion

This paper proposes an AttendanceKit tool to check the automatic attendance of institution, lecturers, parents, and students using real-time UHF RFID technology with four circularly polarized antennas, combined with an automated tag reading range of 1 m to 3 m and face recognition via mobile applications. This technology enables instructors and students in evaluating or determining each student's attendance status. Real-time updates to the backend system will send automatic push alerts to the students' mobile devices, urging them to open the app and confirm their attendance. Our trials demonstrate that our approach delivers a more comprehensive depiction of how the new system operates and interacts, followed by an evaluation based on the class's learning outcomes. In addition, our finding provides a comprehensive evaluation of the system's performance with RFID and authentic mobile devices. However, more parental involvement-enhancing elements can be added in the future. To increase security, speech recognition and fingerprinting are being examined.

Compliance with Ethical Standards

Funding. This research is funded by Vietnam National University Ho Chi Minh City (VNU-HCM) under grant number C2022-28-10.

References

1. Adeniran, T., et al.: Design and implementation of an automated attendance monitoring system for a Nigerian university using RFID. Afr. J. Comput. ICT 72–89 (2019)
2. Anitha, G., Devi, P.S., Sri, J.V., Priyanka, D.: Face recognition based attendance system using MTCNN and Facenet. Zeichen Journal **6**(8), 189–195 (2020)
3. Chiem, Q.-, Huynh, K.-T., Nguyen, M.-T., Tran, M.-D., Nguyen, X.-P.P., Ly, T.-N.: Attendance monitoring using adjustable power UHF RFID and web-based real-time automated information system. In: Dang, T.K., Küng, J., Chung, T.M., Takizawa, M. (eds.) FDSE 2021. LNCS, vol. 13076, pp. 392–407. Springer, Cham (2021). https://doi.org/10.1007/978-3-030-91387-8_25
4. Tran, M.D., et al.: performance analysis of automatic integrated long-range RFID and webcam system. SN Comput. Sci. **3**(6), 1–14 (2022)

5. Schroff, F., Kalenichenko, D., Philbin, J.: Facenet: a unified embedding for face recognition and clustering. In": Proceedings of the IEEE Conference on Computer Vision and Pattern Recognition, pp. 815–823. GitHub repository FaceNet: https://github.com/davidsandberg/facenet (2015)
6. TensorFlow Document. Available: https://www.tensorflow.org/
7. Core ML Document. Available: https://developer.apple.com/documentation/coreml
8. MongoDB Document. Available from: https://docs.mongodb.com/guides/
9. Hoang, V.-D., et al.: A solution based on combination of RFID tags and facial recognition for monitoring systems. In: 5th NAFOSTED Conference on Information and Computer Science (NICS), pp. 384–387. IEEE (2018)
10. Kar, N., et al.: Study of implementing automated attendance system using face recognition technique. Int. J. Comput. Commun. Eng. 1(2), 100 (2012)
11. Tsai, M.L., Jian, J.X., Wang, C.M.: Access control management system integrating deep learning face recognition and RFID technology. Int. J. Comput. Consumer Control (IJ3C) 10(2) (2021)
12. Choudhury, A., Choudhury, A., Subramanium, U., Balamurugan, S.: HealthSaver: a neural network-based hospital recommendation system framework on flask webapplication with realtime database and RFID based attendance system. J. Ambient Intell. Humaniz. Comput. 1–14 (2021)
13. Vijayalakshmi, V.J.: Centralized attendance monitoring system. In: 2020 6th International Conference on Advanced Computing and Communication Systems (ICACCS), pp. 1288–1291. IEEE (Mar 2020)
14. Ahirao, P., Michael, A.V.: MYP: digital attendance system using google cloud firebase and Gradle. In: 2nd International Conference on Advances in Science & Technology (ICAST) (Apr 2019).
15. Hossain, I.A., Hossain, I., Banik, M., Alam, A.: IOT based autonomous class attendance system using non-biometric identification. In: 2018 Joint 7th International Conference on Informatics, Electronics & Vision (ICIEV) and 2018 2nd International Conference on Imaging, Vision & Pattern Recognition (icIVPR), pp. 268–271. IEEE (Jun 2018)
16. Niharika, M., Karuna Sree, B.: IoT based attendance management system using google assistant. In: Pandian, A.P., Palanisamy, R., Ntalianis, K. (eds.) ICCBI 2019. LNDECT, vol. 49, pp. 21–31. Springer, Cham (2020). https://doi.org/10.1007/978-3-030-43192-1_3
17. Gradle Document. Available: https://gradle.org/guides/
18. Hopeland CL7206B Document. Available: https://www.hopelandrfid.com/
19. Firebase Document. Available: https://firebase.google.com/
20. Swift 6 & SwiftUI Document. Available: https://www.swift.org/
21. CocoaPods Document. Available: https://cocoapods.org
22. Coremltools Document. Available: https://pypi.org/project/coremltools/
23. Create ML Document. Available: https://developer.apple.com/machine-learning/create-ml/
24. Apple's TuriCreate Document. Available: https://github.com/apple/turicreate
25. Alamofire Tutorial with Swift (Quickstart) (codewithchris.com) Document. Available: https://codewithchris.com/alamofire/
26. RxSwift: Reactive Programming in Swift Document. Available: https://github.com/ReactiveX/RxSwift.
27. Adhinata, F.D., Tanjung, N.A.F., Widayat, W., Pasfica, G.R., Satura, F.R.: Real-time masked face recognition using FaceNet and supervised machine learning. In: Triwiyanto, T., Rizal, A., Caesarendra, W. (eds.) Proceedings of the 2nd International Conference on Electronics, Biomedical Engineering, and Health Informatics: ICEBEHI 2021, 3–4 November, Surabaya, Indonesia, pp. 189–202. Springer Nature Singapore, Singapore (2022). https://doi.org/10.1007/978-981-19-1804-9_15

Poses Classification in a Taekwondo Lesson Using Skeleton Data Extracted from Videos with Shallow and Deep Learning Architectures

Ha Thanh Thi Hoang, Chau Ngoc Ha, Dat Tien Nguyen,
Truong Nhat Nguyen, Tuyet Ngoc Huynh, Tai Tan Phan,
and Hai Thanh Nguyen[✉]

College of Information & Communication Technology, Can Tho University,
Can Tho, Vietnam
pttai@cit.ctu.edu.vn, nthai.cit@ctu.edu.vn

Abstract. Sports is an important activity to help maintain and improve human health, help fight diseases, create flexibility for the body, and contribute to training the spirit of competition, spirit teammates, and increase soft human skills. The current sports practice has great support from technical technology, contributing to sports to achieve many high achievements. Currently, many technological techniques are applied to support sports for practicing and monitoring matches. For example, Video Assistant Referee re-examines videos to support the referee's accurate decisions on a specific situation in football matches and applications in poses recognition of aerobics and martial arts sports. This study uses Fast Forward Moving Picture Experts Group (FFMPEG) technique to extract images from the video of Taekwondo and generate skeleton data from extracted frames with MoveNet. Then, we perform the poses classification tasks for TAEGEUK IN JANG lesson with deep learning architectures such as shallow convolutional neural networks, VGGNet, Inception, and Long Short-Term Memory networks. These architectures are modified to receive 1-Dimensional data as input, including key points of the skeleton. Poses recognition tasks in sports lessons use skeleton data to eliminate noise in the images, such as background behind practitioners and unrelated objects, and only focus on the movement/direction of the poses. Our proposed method has achieved good accuracy in the data, including 35 videos (more than 25,000 frames) distinguishing 20 poses in a basic Taekwondo lesson.

Keywords: Taekwondo lesson · Poses classification · Action recognition · Skeleton

1 Introduction

In recent years, human action recognition (HAR) has become a research area in which many people are interested. The purpose of HAR is to analyze activ-

© The Author(s), under exclusive license to Springer Nature Singapore Pte Ltd. 2022
T. K. Dang et al. (Eds.): FDSE 2022, CCIS 1688, pp. 447–461, 2022.
https://doi.org/10.1007/978-981-19-8069-5_30

ities from videos or images. From there, HAR systems aim to correctly classify the input data into its basic activity category. For example, as stated in [1], depending on their complexity, human activities are classified into: gestures, atomic actions, human-to-object or human-to-human interactions, group actions, behaviors, and events. Gestures are considered primitive movements of a person's body parts that can correspond to specific movements of that person. Atomic actions are human actions that describe a specific action that can be part of a more complex activity. Human-object or human-human interaction is a human activity involving two or more people or objects. Group action is an activity performed by a group or individual. Human behavior refers to the physical behavior related to the individual's mood, character, and mental state. Finally, events are high-level activities that describe social behavior among individuals and indicate one's intentions or social roles. HAR has applications in various domains, including surveillance, human-computer interaction (HCI), video reclamation, understanding of visual information, etc. However, the most important application of action recognition is video surveillance [2].

Taekwondo is one of Korea's most systematic and scientific traditional martial arts, teaching more than just physical fighting skills. First, Taekwondo is the correct way to use a Taekwondo "kick" or any part of the body represented by a kick[1]. Second, it is a way to control or quell the fighting and keep the peace. So Taekwondo means "use all body parts in the right way to stop fighting and contribute to a better and more peaceful world". Today, it has become a global sport, gaining international fame and becoming one of the official sports of the Olympic Games. In [3], the popularity of Taekwondo has grown significantly as it has expanded into a modern Olympic sport, with competitions currently held in 210 countries on five continents. In South Korea, the birthplace of the sport, there are currently 10,774 Taekwondo athletes, of whom approximately 9,800 (90.96%) are classified as student-athletes (¡13 years, 1587; 13–15 years, 2690; 16–18 years, 3021; 19–22 years, 2502). Besides, it is a fairly popular subject taught in universities.

Following are the main contributions of the research:

– We extracted a skeleton from 2-Dimensional (2D) images into 1D data using MoveNet. The pose classification tasks in Taekwondo were performed on 1D data faster than image classification on 2D images. However, the performance still obtains a rather good average accuracy with more than 0.9904 on the test set. In addition, skeleton data focus on movements and directions of poses. At the same time, images can contain gender, background, skin color, brightness, etc., which cause noise in image classification tasks.
– We compared the architectures of deep learning, including shallow convolutional neural networks and deep convolutional neural networks such as Inception, VGGNet, and Long Short-Term Memory.

The rest of the paper is organized as follows. First, we will discuss several related studies in Sect. 2. After that, we will elaborate on our architecture

---

[1] https://www.teamusa.org/usa-taekwondo/v2-getting-started-in-taekwondo/what-is-taekwondo, accessed on 01 August 2022.

and algorithms in Sect. 3. Subsequently, our experiments for the system will be explained (Sect. 4). In conclusion, we will summarize our studies' key features and development directions (Sect. 5).

2 Related Work

Artificial Intelligence (AI) is growing rapidly and is used in image/video processing and recognition with almost complete accuracy. Application of deep learning in HAR is widely applied in monitoring, fitness, sports, etc., to increase objectivity and accuracy, make recommendations or train distance sports.

2.1 Deep Learning in Human Action Recognition

The problem of HAR is not too new, many articles in [4–9] have been presented along with many proposed solutions and architecture of deep learning networks. A study in [4] gave a novel, useful taxonomy and a review of deep learning HAR methods based on color videos, skeleton sequences, and depth maps. Besides, some datasets and effective tricks in action recognition deep learning methods have also been introduced. In [7], the authors thought that extracting motion history images from RGB videos and sending them online for training would be ineffective, so they proposed a human motion recognition method based on the improved motion history image, mainly from the following aspects, such as removing redundant motion sequences, applying rainbow coding. The authors in [9] proposed a novel approach for HAR based on a hybrid deep learning model. They used the proposed approach evaluated on the UCF Sports, UCF101, and KTH datasets, giving an average of 96.3 percent (on the KTH dataset). In [10], a novel method for HAR using a deep learning network was proposed with features optimized using particle swarm optimization [11]. The features extracted from the video sequence's spatiotemporal volume were the binary histogram, Harris corner points, and wavelet coefficients. The particle swarm optimization technique with a multi-objective fitness function was used to reduce the computational complexity of the system. The proposed framework has achieved an average recognition rate of 91% on UT interaction set 1, 88% on UT interaction set 2, 91% on SBU interaction dataset and 94% on Weizmann dataset. The work [12] presented the simultaneous utilization of video images and inertial signals that are captured in a video camera and a wearable inertial sensor within a fusion framework in order to achieve a more robust HAR compared to the situations where each sensing modality is used individually. Experiments were conducted using the publicly available dataset UTD-MHAD in which simultaneous video images and inertial signals are captured for 27 actions. The results have indicated that both the decision-level and feature-level fusion (two types of fusion are considered) approaches generate higher recognition accuracies than when each sensing modality is used individually. The highest accuracy of 95.6% was obtained for the decision-level fusion approach.

2.2 Deep Learning Techniques in Sports Action Recognition Tasks

Spatio-temporal and high-level data availability have driven recent progress in sports analytics. Video-based action recognition in sports has contributed significantly to these advances.Studies [13–16] are an example of diversity in sports action recognition. In the model of [13], videos were represented as sequences of features, extracted using the well-known Inception neural network, and trained on an independent dataset. Then a 3-layered LSTM network is trained for the classification. The proposed neural network architecture achieved competitive results on THETIS dataset, including low-resolution monocular videos of tennis action. The authors in [14] provided a review study on the video-based technique to recognize sports action toward establishing the automated notational analysis system. The authors believed that deep learning approaches such as CNN and RNN have been tremendously used in many works. They provide better accuracy and can eliminate the complex pre-processing phase. However, it has become an issue since each proposed method can only classify certain sports' actions because they have different contexts and features. In [15], the background subtraction method was used to process sports video images to obtain sports action contour and realize sports action segment and feature extraction. This research mainly used the three-stream CNN artificial intelligence deep learning framework based on the convolutional neural network to train the feature vector to establish the sports action recognition classifier and use the representation algorithm soft Vlad based on data decoding to learn action features.

3 Methods

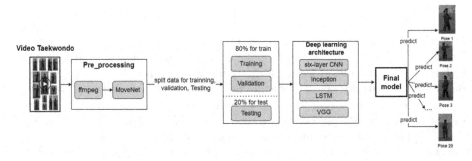

Fig. 1. The proposed architecture of Taekwondo pose detection.

The overall architecture for Taekwondo poses classification tasks based on practical videos of different practitioners exhibited in Fig. 1. As detailed in the figure, proceed to extract the skeleton and divide the data for classification. In addition, we have taken full advantage of convolutional architectures such as CNN-6, VGG, LSTM, and Inception for classifying and identifying similar poses in Taekwondo.

3.1   Data Description

Skeleton-based action recognition is a specific research area of HAR, whose skeleton-based action recognition uses data obtained on the localization of human joints in the three-dimensional environment to perform motion recognition. Depending on the system, 17 joints are generally considered to define the human body, as shown in Fig. 2.

Fig. 2. A skeleton illustration of the human body.

The data includes videos and images about Taekwondo 1 (TAEGEUK IN JANG). We use videos and photos of practitioners of different ages for greater accuracy. First, the videos are cut into multiple frames (50 frames per second), then the images are pre-processed to extract the skeleton. About the data set is the movements of Taekwondo 1, which consists of 20 positions because there are 2 similar poses in position 2 - 15 and position 4 - 18, so we do not describe these poses again. With the dataset of Taekwondo poses, we will divide it into 18 different classes. Next, we will describe the postures and positions of Taekwondo athletes performing TAEGEUK IN JANG lesson (see[2] for more information about the poses in Taekwondo lessons).

- Pose 1: turn left 90°, bring the left leg out into the left walking position towards D (as detailed in Fig. 3), and do a low left-hand block.
- Pose 2: step your right foot forward into a right walking position and punch with your right fist into the middle.
- Pose 3: turn right 180°, step with right foot into right walking position facing C (as detailed in Fig. 3), and do right arm lowering.
- Pose 4: step forward with left foot into left walking position and punch with left fist into the midsection.
- Pose 5: step left 90° with the left foot to forward left pose B (as detailed in Fig. 3) and do a low left-hand block.
- The rest of the poses will be covered in Fig. 3 and[3] obvious way.

---

[2] http://www.trosatkd.se/docs/107/2000/Poomsae.pdf.
[3] http://www.trosatkd.se/docs/107/2000/Poomsae.pdf.

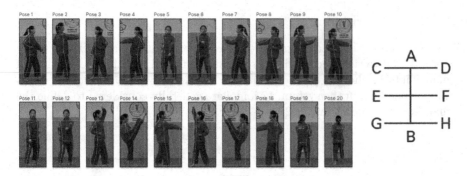

Fig. 3. An illustration of poses and standing positions in TAEGEUK IN JANG lesson.

The data is 1D Taekwondo poses transferred from the images we collect. With the above dataset, we have 25,474 Samples divided into 80% for train, which means 20,377 Samples for training data and 20% for testing, which means 5,097 Samples. As illustrated in Table 1, we divide the data so that the validation is 15% on the Training Set's Sample. The pose_14 and pose_17 have the lowest number of Samples because, in these movements, the execution time is fast, so the number of frames obtained is small.

We build the validation set for evaluating the model's accuracy and setting a checkpoint to save the best weight. The Validation set also helps us to end the data training process when the model has passed and gotten a certain accuracy. We use test sets to make model evaluation easy. The testing set supports us in getting Matthews Correlation Coefficient (MCC), accuracy, and f1-score measures, and we can evaluate the model more objectively from those measures.

3.2   Data Pre-processing

Data is an important part of deep learning techniques. It plays a major role and influences the accuracy of the layered network architecture. In addition, data pre-processing plays a key role in the composition of the problem.

As shown in Fig. 4, firstly, we collect images of postures in Taekwondo. From the original video, we used Fast Forward Moving Picture Experts Group (**FFMPEG**) [17] to cut into frames (50 frames per second). We obtained a set of RGB color images of the movements of post 1. From the above data set, we proceed to layer each posture. Besides, we also proceed to group the same poses.

Table 1. The sample numbers of Training, Validation, and Test Sets.

Class name	Training Set	Validation Set	Test set
pose_1	922	162	283
pose_10	1012	178	303
pose_11	718	126	218
pose_12	991	174	303
Pose_13	887	156	249
Pose_14	132	23	39
Pose_16	826	145	245
Pose_17	123	21	37
Pose_19	831	146	239
Pose_20	1210	213	348
Pose_2_15	2125	375	593
Pose_3	918	162	285
Pose_4_18	2120	373	617
Pose_5	419	73	122
Pose_6	839	148	277
Pose_7	1050	185	300
Pose_8	1020	179	307
Pose_9	956	168	287

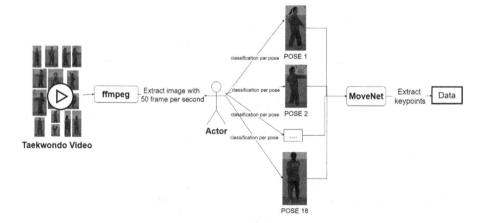

Fig. 4. Data pre-processing steps.

From the layered images, we extract the skeleton features of the movements with **MoveNet** [4], then save it as a file (.csv) from which we proceed to divide

---

[4] https://blog.tensorflow.org/2021/05/next-generation-pose-detection-with-movenet-and-tensorflowjs.html, accessed on 6 August 2022.

and combine the data. With deep learning methods, machine learning can learn those features.

FFMPEG tool is a powerful multimedia processing framework. It allows users to handle media such as decoding, encoding and extracting information, and split video. Most of today's platforms like Windows, macOS, and Linux can use, so we use FFMPEG as a powerful tool for the project. Besides, we also use a skeleton extraction tool called MoveNet. MoveNet extracts the skeleton based on 17 points of the body according to COCO standards. This bottom-up approach uses heat maps to extract points on the human body. The tool for MoveNet to extract is MobileNetV2 with a pyramid network that allows the output of a high-resolution feature map with 4 prediction heads attached to the extractor responsible for the prediction, Person center heatmap, Keypoint regression field, Person keypoint heatmap, 2D per-keypoint offset field. With skeleton data, we focus on the movements and direction of poses. Each sample in Skeleton data includes coordinates of 17 points with 17 pairs of (x, y). Such pairs are then flattened to 34 features before fetching into learning models as 1D data.

3.3   Deep Learning Architectures for Poses Classification Tasks

As the methods are shown in the diagram 1, it is necessary to choose the appropriate deep learning method for the data set to identify the movements correctly. Several methods are presented below to find the most suitable method.

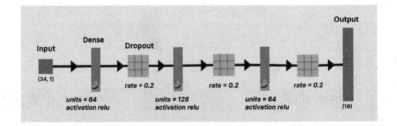

Fig. 5. The proposed six-layer convolutional neural network architecture (CNN-6) for pose detection.

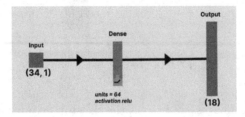

Fig. 6. The proposed one-layer convolutional neural network architecture (CNN-1) for pose detection.

A CNN network is a collection of overlapping Convolution layers using activation functions such as ReLU and Tanh. As shown in Fig. 5, we use a CNN architecture with 6 layers overlapping each. In addition, we will add a dropout layer by this technique. As a result, we can reduce overfitting, so your model will not learn too much dependency between the weights. To be able to evaluate the 6-layer architecture more objectively, we also built a Shallow Learning architecture that is 1 layer CNN (CNN-1) with one Dense layer (the architecture is described in Figure 6).

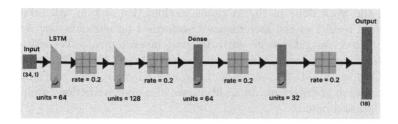

Fig. 7. LSTM architecture for pose detection.

LSTM networks, also known as Long Short Term Memory networks, LSTM network is an improved form of RNN. It can learn remote dependencies. LSTM was introduced by Hochreiter and Schmidhuber (1997) and has since been refined and popularized by many people in the industry. They work extremely well on many different problems, so they have gradually become popular today LSTM is designed to avoid the problem of long-term dependency. Remembering information for a long time is their default property. Therefore, we do not need to train it to be able to remember it. That is, its internals can already be memorized without any intervention. Here we build an LSTM network architecture with 4 layers, with the first 2 layers being the overlapping LSTM layers followed by 2 Dense layers, each layer we intermingle with a Dropout of 0.2 to avoid overfitting when training the model. For more details on the architecture, please refer to Figure 7.

VGG-16 [18] is also a famous convolutional neural network that retains the features of AlexNet but with improvements. In addition, VGG-16 is deeper, consisting of 13 2-way tick layers (instead of 5 compared to AlexNet) and 3 fully connected layers. VGG-16 also inherits ReLU-enabled functionality in AlexNet. In this study, we build a VGG network to fit the 1D form data, which is the key point that we have refined input and 4 VGG blocks. Our architecture has 18 layers, with the first 4 blocks being 4 blocks (Conv1D and MaxPool1D), followed by a flattened layer and 2 dense layers.

Inception-V1 network won the ImageNet competition in 2015[5]. Previous neural network architectures used filters ranging in size from 11×11, 5×5, and 3×3 to as small as 1×1. The Inception block architecture is one discovery made by the paper that combining these filters into the same block can be effective. In our architecture, there are 2 inception blocks, dense layers and flattened layers, to better understand the architecture.

4   Experimental Results

Based on the work done in the Methods section, this section will present the experimental results of the architectures performed on our data set. After the model is tested, we get results with different measurements. We will present the results of measurements like Area under the Curve (AUC), Matthew's Correlation Coefficient (MCC), accuracy, Loss, and F1-score, etc., to evaluate the efficiency of each architecture. In addition, we also give prediction results based on the Confusion matrix.

4.1   Environment Settings

In this section, the experimental process of the proposed method will be presented. The testing process used a dataset of 35 videos containing 20 movements (more than 3000 frames) of different practitioners. During testing, 80% of the video sequence is used for training purposes, while the remaining 20% is used for testing purposes. The validation set aims to select the best model during the training phase. All models are configured with a batch size of 64 and an Adam optimizer with a default learning rate of 0.001, running to 200 epochs. All runtime is performed on Colab, equipped with NVIDIA Geforce MX150 2 GB, connected to a personal Core-i5 with 8GB of RAM.

4.2   Performance Comparison of Various Architectures

The overall average results of deep and shallow architectures illustrated are presented in Table 2. The results of the two shallow architectures achieve 98.5%, but CNN-6 is somewhat superior. During the first 10 epochs, the accuracy of both architectures increased dramatically. CNN-1 architecture peaks in about 90 epochs. CNN-6 architecture is superior to CNN-1 when it only takes about 70 epochs to reach the maximum. These architectures' AUC score, MCC, and accuracy are almost equal.

The classification results on each pose with various architectures are summarized in Table 3. Besides Recall and Precision, the F1 score will balance both values for cases where these two measures are too different. F1-score is called the harmonic mean of precision and recall, so it is a representative index in correctly

---

[5] https://phamdinhkhanh.github.io/2020/05/31/CNNHistory.html, accessed on 06 August 2022.

Table 2. Performance comparison among considered architectures with various metrics.

	CNN-1	CNN-6	LSTM	Inception	VGG
Accuracy on training set	0.99903	0.99933	0.99774	0.99954	0.99773
Loss on training set	0.00461	0.00249	0.00736	0.00130	0.00304
Accuracy on test set	0.98518	0.98588	0.98524	0.98865	0.97764
Loss on test set	0.07413	0.08379	0.14521	0.09259	0.01771
AUC on test set	0.99959	0.99979	0.99947	0.99981	0.99867
MCC on test set	0.98409	0.98485	0.97740	0.98781	0.97612

Table 3. F1-score measurement of CNN-1, CNN-6, LSTM, Inception, and VGG architecture for pose classification task on the test set.

Class name	CNN-1	CNN-6	LSTM	Inception	VGG
Pose_1	0.99	0.99	0.99	0.99	0.99
Pose_10	1.00	0.97	0.99	0.98	0.98
Pose_11	1.00	0.95	1.00	0.99	0.99
Pose_12	0.97	1.00	1.00	1.00	0.98
Pose_13	0.92	0.98	0.98	0.98	0.99
Pose_14	0.92	0.86	0.97	0.99	0.92
Pose_16	1.00	1.00	0.98	0.99	0.99
Pose_17	0.90	1.00	1.00	1.00	0.93
Pose_19	0.91	0.99	1.00	1.00	0.88
Pose_20	1.00	0.99	1.00	1.00	0.99
Pose_2_15	1.00	1.00	0.99	0.99	1.00
Pose_3	1.00	0.97	0.98	0.99	1.00
Pose_4_18	1.00	1.00	1.00	1.00	1.00
Pose_5	0.97	0.97	1.00	0.97	0.97
Pose_6	0.99	0.99	1.00	0.99	0.98
Pose_7	1.00	1.00	1.00	1.00	0.91
Pose_8	1.00	1.00	1.00	1.00	1.00
Pose_9	0.99	1.00	0.99	1.00	1.00
Accuracy	0.99	0.99	0.99	0.99	0.98
Macro avg	0.97	0.98	0.99	0.99	0.97
Weighted avg	0.98	0.99	0.99	0.99	0.98

predicting positive samples. Therefore, we will evaluate the F1-score index in the following to give a more objective assessment. The CNN-1 architecture has an F1-score in all poses above 0.9, but most reach 1.00. The CNN-6 architecture has the lowest results at pose_14 with a value of 0.86. The rest of the poses all

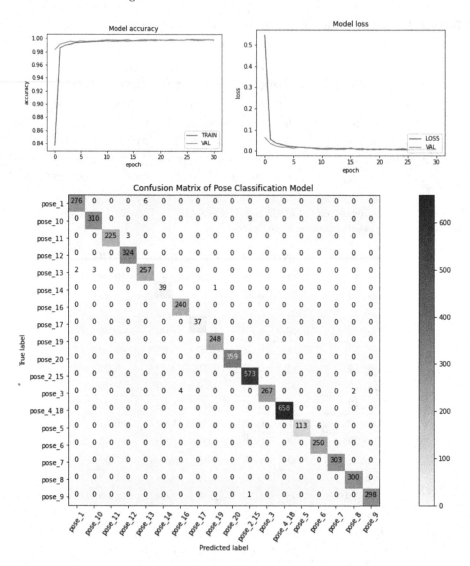

Fig. 8. Accuracy and Loss of Inception architecture during the training and the confusion matrix on the test set.

have results above 0.9. In the LSTM architecture, most poses result in 1.00 or approximately 1.00, the lowest F1-score value is in pose_14 with 0.97, Inception architecture is similar with the lowest result is in pose_5 with 0.97. Finally, the VGG architecture also has the lowest F1-score result in pose_19 with a value of 0.88; the rest all have an F1-score value above 0.9. We will evaluate the performance of each considered architecture in the following paragraphs.

Figure 8 reveals validation results are over 90% on the accuracy train and accuracy test metrics. The model's accuracy increases sharply in the first 5 epochs and reaches the highest value at the 30th epoch. Like Accuracy, Loss of the architecture also reduced the network in the first 5 epochs and reached the lowest value from epoch 30. MCC, AUC score, accuracy scores were 98.7%, 99.94%, 98.8%, respectively. In this architecture, we see a confusion matrix for prediction results achieved in very good postures. The majority of results fall into the diagonal of the matrix means that the classification is correct. The matrix also pointed out a few erroneous results, such as Pose 14, Pose 17, and the best one at Pose 4_18.

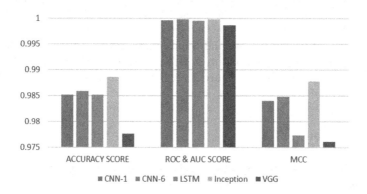

Fig. 9. Column chart shows the results of parameters ACC, ROC AUC, MCC obtained from 5 architectures: CNN-1, CNN-6, LSTM, Inception, and VGG.

The model's accuracy with VGG increases sharply in the first 10 epochs and peaks at the 40th epoch. Like accuracy, the Loss of the architecture also reduces the network in the first 10 epochs and reaches the lowest value from epoch 40. MCC, AUC score, accuracy scores are 97.61%, 99.86%, 97.64%, respectively. The Confusion matrix shows that the model is pretty much wrong at Pose 16.

For LSTM architecture, we obtain all metrics over 97%, most notably AUC scores with 99%. The model's accuracy increases sharply during the first 20 epochs and peaks at the 100th epoch onwards. Like accuracy, the Loss of the architecture also reduces the network in the first 20 epochs and reaches the lowest value from epoch 100-the confusion matrix of the LSTM architecture results in highly accurate posture predictions.

Figure 9 shows that the VGG architecture has the lowest average measurement results among the five mentioned architectures. Going into the analysis of each measurement, the first is about the Accuracy score. It can be seen that all five architectures give very high scores (all over 97%), the highest is the Inception architecture with 98.8%, followed by the CNN-6 architecture (98.6%), then LSTM and CNN-1 architecture (98.5%), and finally VGG architecture with 97.8%. Second, we consider the ROC and AUC score in all five architectures. The classification efficiency is over 99%. The classification efficiency of the Inception architecture is the highest, followed by CNN-1, CNN-6, LSTM, and VGG. Finally, the MCC measurement, according to the Fig. 9, all architectures have high classification results, Inception architecture is approximately 98.8%, next CNN-6 is 98.5%, followed by CNN-1 with 98.4%, then LSTM with 97.7% and the lowest is VGG with 97.6%. Overall, the train and test results of the five architectures in Table 2 show that the VGG architecture performs worst in training and test accuracy. Table 2 shows that Inception architecture is the highest with a score of approximately 100%, followed by CNN-6, CNN-1, LSTM, and VGG architecture. With loss train, we can see that the LSTM architecture has the highest loss train measurement with 0.07%, while the Inception architecture has the lowest Loss train measurement of 0.01%. Regarding the testing accuracy, the Inception architecture achieved the highest of 98.9%, then the CNN-6, CNN-1, LSTM, and VGG architectures. The last is the loss test score, whereby the LSTM architecture has the highest score and is quite different from the rest with 14.5%, followed by the Inception architecture with 9.3%. Next, CNN-6 with 8.4%, CNN-1 with 7.4%, and finally, the VGG architecture has the lowest measure with only 1.8%.

5   Conclusion

In this study, we collected 35 videos related to practical Taekwondo lessons. Then, we presented an approach using skeleton data extracted from these videos to perform poses classification tasks in a Taekwondo lesson with vast deep learning algorithms, including shallow and deep architectures. The skeleton data extracted from video frames can reduce processing time and computational resources compared to performing 2D image classification tasks. In addition, pose classification tasks use skeleton data to eliminate and skip image noise, such as background behind practitioners, brightness, and unrelated objects appearing in images/videos. As observed from the results, Inception obtains the best performance while VGG exhibits the lowest. In addition, we noticed that LSTM reveals worse results than shallow architectures. Further research can work on positioning segmentation and embedding skeleton in videos to support martial arts practitioners visually. The work is expected to enhance the effectiveness of student learning and teachers' assessment in Taekwondo lessons. In addition, the system supports students' self-learning and assessment in their homes easily. It also contributes to AI application in education in the fourth industrial revolution.

Acknowledgements. This study is funded in part by the Can Tho University, Code: TSV2022-33.

References

1. Vrigkas, M., Nikou, C., Kakadiaris, I.A.: A review of human activity recognition methods. Frontiers Robot. Artif. Intell. **2**, (2015). https://doi.org/10.3389 %2Ffrobt.2015.00028

2. Khan, S., et al.: Human action recognition: a paradigm of best deep learning features selection and serial based extended fusion. Sensors **21**(23), 7941 (2021). https://doi.org/10.3390%2Fs21237941
3. Park, S.U., Jeon, J.W., Ahn, H., Yang, Y.K., So, W.Y.: Big data analysis of the key attributes related to stress and mental health in korean taekwondo student athletes. Sustainability **14**(1), 477 (2022). https://doi.org/10.3390%2Fsu14010477
4. Zhang, Z., Ma, X., Song, R., Rong, X., Tian, X., Tian, G., Li, Y.: Deep learning based human action recognition: a survey. In: 2017 Chinese Automation Congress (CAC). IEEE pp. 3780-3785 (2017). https://doi.org/10.1109%2Fcac.2017.8243438
5. Baccouche, M., Mamalet, F., Wolf, C., Garcia, C., Baskurt, A.: Sequential deep learning for human action recognition. In: Salah, A.A., Lepri, B. (eds.) HBU 2011. LNCS, vol. 7065, pp. 29–39. Springer, Heidelberg (2011). https://doi.org/10.1007/978-3-642-25446-8_4
6. Sargano, A.B., Wang, X., Angelov, P., Habib, Z.: Human action recognition using transfer learning with deep representations. In: 2017 International Joint Conference on Neural Networks (IJCNN). IEEE (2017).https://doi.org/10.1109%2Fijcnn.2017.7965890
7. Wang, P.: Research on sports training action recognition based on deep learning. Sci. Programm. **2021**, 1–8 (2021). https://doi.org/10.1155%2F2021%2F3396878
8. Sun, Z., Ke, Q., Rahmani, H., Bennamoun, M., Wang, G., Liu, J.: Human action recognition from various data modalities: a review. IEEE Trans. Pattern Anal. Mach. Intell. pp. 1–20 (2022). https://doi.org/10.1109%2Ftpami.2022.3183112
9. Jaouedi, N., Boujnah, N., Bouhlel, M.S.: A new hybrid deep learning model for human action recognition. J. King Saud Univ. Comput. Inf. Sci. **32**(4), 447–453 (2020). https://doi.org/10.1016%2Fj.jksuci.2019.09.004
10. Berlin, S. Jeba., John, Mala: Particle swarm optimization with deep learning for human action recognition. Multimedia Tools Appl. **79**(25), 17349–17371 (2020). https://doi.org/10.1007/s11042-020-08704-0
11. Kennedy, J., Eberhart, R.: Particle swarm optimization. In: Proceedings of ICNN'95 - International Conference on Neural Networks. IEEE (1995). https://doi.org/10.1109%2Ficnn.1995.488968
12. Wei, H., Jafari, R., Kehtarnavaz, N.: Fusion of video and inertial sensing for deep learning–based human action recognition. Sensors **19**(17), 3680 (2019). https://doi.org/10.3390%2Fs19173680
13. Vinyes Mora, S., Knottenbelt, W.J.: Deep learning for domain-specific action recognition in tennis. In: Proceedings of the IEEE Conference on Computer Vision and Pattern Recognition (CVPR) Workshops, (2017)
14. Rahmad, N.A., As'ari, M.A., Ghazali, N.F., Shahar, N., Sufri, N.A.J.: A survey of video based action recognition in sports. Indonesian J. Electr. Eng. Comput. Sci. **11**(3), 987 (2018). https://doi.org/10.11591%2Fijeecs.v11.i3.pp987-993
15. Jiang, H., Tsai, S.B.: An empirical study on sports combination training action recognition based on SMO algorithm optimization model and artificial intelligence. Math. Prob. Eng. **2021**, 1–11 (2021). https://doi.org/10.1155%2F2021%2F7217383
16. Liu, N., Liu, L., Sun, Z.: Football game video analysis method with deep learning. Comput. Intell. Neurosci. **2022**, 1–12 (2022). https://doi.org/10.1155%2F2022%2F3284156
17. Tomar, S.: Converting video formats with FFmpeg. Linux J. **2006**(146), 10 (2006)
18. Tammina, S.: Transfer learning using VGG-16 with deep convolutional neural network for classifying images. Int. J. Sci. Res. Publ. (IJSRP) **9**(10), p9420 (2019). https://doi.org/10.29322%2Fijsrp.9.10.2019.p9420

Social Distancing Violation Detection in Video Using ChessBoard and Bird's-eye Perspective

An Cong Tran, Trong Huu Ngo, and Hai Thanh Nguyen[✉]

Can Tho University, Can Tho, Vietnam
tcan@cit.ctu.edu.vn, nthai.cit@ctu.edu.vn

Abstract. Thousands of infections, hundreds of deaths every day - these are numbers that speak the current serious status, numbers that each of us is no longer unfamiliar with in the current context, the context of the raging epidemic - Coronavirus disease epidemic. Therefore, we need solutions and technologies to fight the epidemic promptly and quickly to prevent or reduce the effect of the epidemic. Numerous studies have warned that if we contact an infected person within a distance of fewer than two meters, it can be considered a high risk of infecting Coronavirus. To detect a contact distance shorter than two meters and provides warnings to violations in monitoring systems based on a camera, we present an approach to solving two problems, including detecting objects - here are humans and calculating the distance between objects using Chessboard and bird's eye perspective. We have leveraged the pre-trained InceptionV2 model, a famous convolutional neural network for object detection, to detect people in the video. Also, we propose to use a perspective transformation algorithm for the distance calculation converting pixels from the camera perspective to a bird's eye view. Then, we choose the minimum distance from the distance in the determined field to the distance in pixels and calculate the distance violation based on the bird's eye view, with camera calibration and minimum distance selection process based on field distance. The proposed method is tested in some scenarios to provide warnings of social distancing violations. The work is expected to generate a safe area providing warnings to protect employees in administrative environments with a high risk of contacting numerous people.

Keywords: Minimum distance · Bird's eye view · Human recognition · Epidemic · Distancing violation

1 Introduction

Artificial intelligence is present in all areas of human life, from economics, education, and medicine to housework, entertainment, and even the military. But the breakthroughs mostly come from Deep Learning - a small array gradually expanding to each type of work, from simple to complex, like in the field of positioning with tasks that need high accuracy, including drones and uncrewed

T. K. Dang et al. (Eds.): FDSE 2022, CCIS 1688, pp. 462–476, 2022.
https://doi.org/10.1007/978-981-19-8069-5_31

vehicles. In the context that the world is facing COVID-19, with thousands of people infected every day, preventing the spread is the issue that needs the most attention, so distance violation detection approaches through using the camera have become useful. As a result, we can detect and timely prevent the spread of the disease or create favorable conditions. In addition, the technologies tracing the origin of the spread have been proposed and developed so that disease prevention and control take place effectively, promptly, and quickly.

Public places and crowded places such as schools, administrative offices, and hospitals are clear places to spread Covid pathogens. In such places, keeping a distance is one of the important rules in the 5K rule [1][1] of Ministry of Vietnamese Public Health released, including wearing a mask, disinfection, not gathering, declaring health and keeping the minimum distance. Keeping a distance is extremely necessary during the pandemic to prevent the spread of disease. Health experts say that keeping a distance is one of the most important and recommended solutions to prevent the pandemic. However, not everyone understands the role and meaning of distance and considers it a serious rule. Coronavirus disease, as we know, is transmitted mainly through close contact within about two meters. Therefore, there is a very high infection risk, as the Vietnamese Ministry of Health recommended in 2020. Moreover, numerous evidences from research was restated that the 2-meter social distancing rule to reduce COVID-19 transmission [2,3]. Although we know that the advice on 2-meter distancing is a risk assessment of some research, such distance should be longer to ensure safety. Also, the authors in an article [4] in the Lancet journal stated that physical distancing of at least one meter lowers the risk of COVID-19 transmission, but that two meters can be more effective. Exposure occurs when droplets from the nose or mouth of an infected person cough, sneeze, or talk shoot out and into the air, and these elements come into contact with an uninfected person that can cause illness. Many studies have shown that asymptomatic infected people also contribute to the spread of COVID-19 because they can spread the virus before they reveal symptoms.

This study proposes an approach to detect minimum distance violations by the camera to support the implementation of regulations on keeping a distance of two meters when in contact with others. The rest of the work is organized as follows. First, we discuss some related applications and studies in Sect. 4. After that, in Sect. 3, we will elaborate on our workflow and algorithms. Subsequently, our experiments with test cases will be described and explained (Sect. 4). Finally, in conclusion, we will summarize our studies' key features and development plan (Sect. 5).

2   Related Work

With the serious effects of Corona disease, numerous scientists have focused on some solutions to prevent the epidemic in a vast of applications and studies.

[1] https://covid19.gov.vn/bo-y-te-khuyen-cao-5k-chung-song-an-toan-voi-dich-benh-1717130215.htm.

Some studies have attempted to present computer-based methods to monitor social distancing violations. The work in [5] used the YOLOv3 object recognition algorithm to indicate humans in video sequences with a pre-trained algorithm to gather to an extra-trained layer using an overhead human data set. In [6], the authors designed a computer vision-based smart to monitor and automatically detect people who violated safe distancing rules. In another study in [7], the authors evaluated the American people's perceptions of social distancing violations during the COVID-19 pandemic. In work in [8], scientists introduced SocialNet, a method aimed to indicate violations of social distancing in a public crowd scene. The method included two main parts, including a detector backbone and an Autoencoder. The research in [9] deployed the YOLO algorithm to detect social distancing violations in real time. In addition, the authors in [10] presented a drone using a surveillance method implemented in Deep Learning algorithms to indicate whether two people were violating social distancing rules. The authors in [11] used a small neural network architecture to indicate social distancing using a bird's eye perspective. In more studies on deep learning-based method, the study in [12] implemented bounding boxes to indicate group violated the social distancing rules using Euclidean distance and deep learning trained on COCO dataset [13] using YOLO. In [14], the authors introduced a method to detect people in a frame and check whether people violated social distancing by calculating the Euclidean distance between the centroids of the detected boxes. The authors in [15] deployed the "Nvidia Jetson Nano" development kit and Raspberry Pi camera to compute and determine social distance violation cases. The scientists in [16] counted the violations using some analysis techniques on video streams.

Bluezone application[2] provided warnings and contacted people infected with Covid-19. Some outstanding features of the Bluezone application include a scan for nearby Bluezone community, warning when contact with Covid-19 infected person, secure operation, transparency, lightweight, and low battery consumption. In addition, it could support people to make medical declarations right on their phone easily at any time, provide a quick electronic medical declaration using a QR code, and easily track contact history with Bluezone users. In addition, it can submit a report of COVID-19 disease summarized information, suspected infected subjects around the area where you live, provide an Electronic health book, and allows Covid-19 vaccination registration. Health Book application[3] was also an interesting application with some features such as allowing people to register for the Covid-19 vaccine on the app. In addition, it can report any unusual symptoms quickly after getting the COVID-19 vaccine, providing a certificate of vaccination against COVID-19. Moreover, it can support declaring health information and family anytime, anywhere. It can easily track health tracking after connecting the COVID-19 vaccine directly with the personal health record system of the Ministry of Health, easily book an appointment with a medical facility or doctor before visiting, or maybe, talk to your doctor

---

[2] https://bluezone.gov.vn/.

[3] https://play.google.com/store/apps/details?id=com.mohviettel.sskdt.

online for advice and take care of your health. The most obvious common difficulty is that it is hard to monitor accurately. However, now that the policy of loosening the distance is applied, more and more people gather in public places, so using a Camera to monitor is essential and popular.

3   Methods

The camera's approach to detecting distance violations is proposed in Fig. 1.

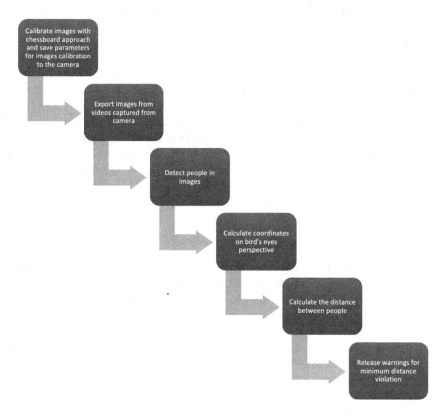

Fig. 1. Steps of the process of building a model to detect distance violations through the camera.

First, we calibrate the Camera with OpenCV to increase the model's accuracy. After this calibration, we can conduct object recognition with the pre-train model to create bounding boxes indicating people's positions. After having these bounding boxes, we can calculate the coordinates of the midpoint of the bottom edge of the bounding box, taking that as a basis to calculate the distance between the objects. Finally, we have deployed the chessboard method to calibrate images from videos captured from the camera's output before converting the image into perspective from camera view to birds'-eye view.

3.1   Object Recognition with Pre-trained Inceptionv2 Model

This study has deployed Inceptionv2 [17] to recognize the object recognition process. Inceptionv1 [18] was originally proposed with about 7 million parameters. It was much smaller than the famous prevailing architectures, like VGG [19] and AlexNet [20]. However, it can achieve a lower error rate, which is also why it is a breakthrough architecture. The modules in Inception perform convolutions with different filter sizes on the input, operate max pooling and concatenate the results for the next inception modules. The introduction of a 1×1 convolution operation greatly reduces the parameters. Although the number of layers in Inceptionv1 is 22, the dramatic parameter reduction has made it a very difficult model to overfit. The Inceptionv2 [17] is a major improvement on the Inceptionv1 that increases accuracy and further makes the model less complex. The significant improvements in the Inceptionv2 model include Multiplying the 5×5 convolution into two 3×3 convolution operations to improve the computation speed. Although this may seem counter-intuitive, a 5×5 convolution is 2.78 times more expensive than a 3×3 convolution. So stacking two 3×3 convolutions leads to a performance increase. Furthermore, Inception factorizes filter convolutions of size $n \times n$ into a combination of $1 \times n$ and $n \times 1$ convolutions. For example, a 3×3 convolution is equivalent to first performing a 1×3 convolution and then performing a 3×1 convolution on its output. They found that this method was 33% in time execution reduction than 3×3 single convolution.

3.2   Calibrate the Camera with Chessboard Corner Detection

Cameras these days have become relatively cheap to manufacture. We have deployed camera calibration from captured images to indicate the geometric parameters of the image formation process. As mentioned in [21], the camera calibration process is an important step in computer vision tasks, especially when metric information about the scene is required. We calibrate the camera to enhance the efficiency of computing the distance between two objects with some changes for the internal parameters of the camera (camera calibration change due to movement of the internal lens) even if it falls to the ground and causes production problems) and external parameters are calculated. There are two types of uncorrected in-camera noise. The first is called barrel distortion and causes a quick view from the sides, while the second type is called pin buffer noise (pincushion distortion) and is flattened from the sides.

We call the matrix known as the denoising camera matrix. OpenCV [22] provides calibration support with various methods. The most famous of these is the Chessboard corner detection [23]. With the chessboard corner detection, we first detect corners in the chess board. Then, we draw detected angles using drawChessboardCorners to generate a new image with circles at the corners found in python. Next, we calculate the camera's internal and external parameters from multiple perspectives of a calibrator. Our final step is to store the parameters returned by feeding the feature points in all images and the equivalent pixels in the two-dimensional image into the calibrated camera function.

The total error represents the accuracy of the camera calibration process. Total error calculation is done by projecting 3D checkerboard points into the image plane using the final correction parameters. A Root Mean Square Error of 1.0 means that, on average, each of these projected points is 1.0 pixels from its actual location. The error is not bound in [0, 1]. It can be considered a distance as an illustration in Fig. 2.

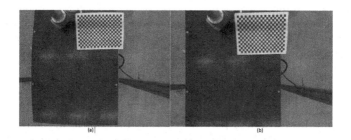

Fig. 2. An original image and its image after calibrating camera.

3.3 Calculate Coordinates on a Detected Object

We used the pre-train model, Inceptionv2, to recognize and track people in the video to indicate whether they violated social distancing or not. After that process, we can get the bounding boxes corresponding to each object (person) in the region of interest (ROI). Then, to calculate the distance between 2 objects, we first have to determine the coordinates of each detected object. The coordinate calculation process consists of 2 steps. At first, we calculate the coordinates of the centroid of the bounding box with formulas Equations of 1 and 2. Then, After having the coordinates of the center of gravity of the bounding box, we go to find the coordinates of the midpoint of the bottom edge of the bounding box and use this point to calculate the distance between 2 objects on the birds'eye view as illustrated in Fig. 3 and calculated by Formulas of 3 and 4.

$$x3 = \frac{x1 + x2}{2} \tag{1}$$

$$y3 = \frac{y1 + y2}{2} \tag{2}$$

$$x4 = x3 \tag{3}$$

$$y4 = y3 + \frac{y2 + y1}{2} = y2 \tag{4}$$

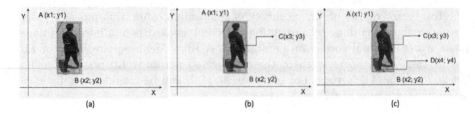

Fig. 3. Calculate coordinates on a detected object: a) Present the original object in the coordinate axis, b) Calculate the coordinates of the center of gravity C(x3; y3) of the bounding box, c) Calculate the Midpoint coordinate D(x4; y4) of bottom edge bounding box

3.4 Calculate Distance Between 2 People

We build a matrix of 3×3 to perform coordinates transformation on 4 points with height and the width of the image[4]. To get the "birds'eyes view" from the top, we employ operations in OpenCV to calculate a perspective transform from four pairs of the corresponding points and generate a matrix of transformations of entities, including two parameters of rect, dst, where rect denotes the list of 4 points in the original image, and dst is the list of converted points. After getting the transformation matrix, we perform a perspective transformation to transform the image's perspective using the transformation matrix, along with the width and height of the image as input. Then, the operation returns the transformed matrix and image. Then there is a transformed matrix taken from the perspective transformation and a list of points to convert. Next, we take the output of the above calculation and start the process of passing the transformation calculation based on the entity transformation matrix: cv2.perspectiveTransform(list_points_to_detect, matrix) where *list_points_to_detect* is the result of the above calculation and *matrix* is the entity transformation matrix.

4   Experiments

4.1   Environmental Settings

We place the camera at 4.9m high from the ground at B as exhibited in Fig. 4. The camera was adjusted so that the length of the frame center to point A is 10.15 m (Fig. 5). In addition, the length from the center of the frame to point A can not affect the results of calculating the distance between objects (Fig. 7).

---

[4] https://pyimagesearch.com/2014/08/25/4-point-opencv-getperspective-transform-example/.

Fig. 4. camera's height

Fig. 5. Distance from camera to the center of bird's eye view.

We set up some procedures to calculate the minimum distance (two meters) between 2 people. First, we use a ruler with a length of two meters which is the minimum distance to prevent the risk of spreading COVID-19 as recommended by the Vietnamese Ministry of Health and numerous studies on Coronavirus disease. Then, we choose this as the minimum distance between the 2 received objects to start calculating the minimum distance. As illustrated in Fig. 6, the distance of 216 pixels is the distance calculated between 2 points from the bird's eye perspective.

Fig. 6. We use a ruler to measure the distance in the pre-determined field

Fig. 7. Calculate the number of pixels of the minimum distance on the bird's eye view

Fig. 8. Four points for transformation and to indicate the pre-determined field.

In addition, we have deployed the process of converting pixels from the camera to birds'eye perspective and marked four points on the ground as four input points for perspective transition with perspective transition (Fig. 8). Here, choosing the order of each image angle is essential. If it is not selected correctly, it can reverse the image angle after conversion. The chessboard method can calibrate the camera to increase the model's accuracy. The method can be highly

Fig. 9. The minimum distance to detect the violations on the birds'eye view.

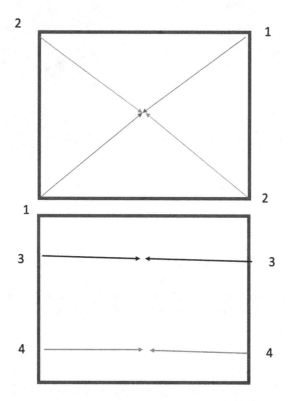

Fig. 10. Experimental participants' movement directions in Scenarios 1, 2, 3, and 4.

affected by the camera calibration and choosing the minimum distance directly from the birds'eye view. Here is an image when taking pixel parameters for a distance of two meters, as exhibited in Fig. 9. We obtain 240 pixels for a distance of two meters in the pre-determined field. Because the process of choosing the minimum distance is based on the distance of 2 points of the 2 rulers displayed on the video, the model's accuracy can depend on the accuracy of the camera calibration process during test cases. The accuracy of the calibration process reaches 0.23 (a smaller value can lead to a higher accuracy). We repeated the experiment more than 20 times for each scenario in the experiments. All of them were sent warnings to the users using the system. We illustrate some results in the following sections with experimental participants' movement directions as illustrated in Fig. 10.

4.2   Scenario 1

Fig. 11. A test case for Scenario 1.

One student moved from the top left corner and the other from the bottom right corner (Fig. 11). The two intersect at the center of the rectangle. We perform the experiments in full light conditions, with the participation of two people, one male, and one female, both wearing yellow shirts. The first object moves from the right side 1m from the bottom right corner. The second opponent moves 1m from the bottom right corner from the left side, and 2 objects move parallel to the bottom edge.

4.3   Scenario 2

One student moved from the top right corner while the other moved from the bottom left corner (Fig. 12). The two intersect at the center of the rectangle. When we test in full light conditions, with the participation of 2 subjects, 1 male and 1 female, wearing yellow shirts. The first enemy moves from the right

Fig. 12. A test case for Scenario 2.

side 1m from the top right corner, the second opponent moves from the left side 1m away from the top right corner, and 2 objects move parallel to the top edge.

4.4   Scenario 3

Fig. 13. A test case for Scenario 3.

One student moved from the midpoint of the upper edge, while the other moved from the midpoint of the lower edge (Fig. 13). Finally, the two intersect at the center of the rectangle. We perform the experiments in full light conditions, with the participation of two female and two male students. One pair wore yellow and black shirts (Fig. 14). The students moved from the 4 corners of the specified area, met, and stopped at the center of the specified area for about three seconds, and then the objects continued to move to the starting corner.

Fig. 14. Another test case for Scenario 3 with many people.

4.5   Scenario 4

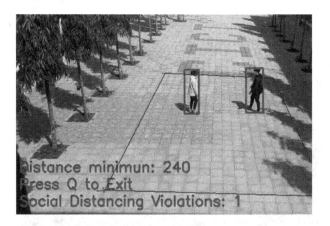

Fig. 15. A test case for Scenario 4.

One student moved from the midpoint of the right side, and the other moved from the midpoint of the bottom left edge (Fig. 15). The two intersect at the center of the rectangle.

5   Conclusion

With the current epidemic situation being complicated with many outbreaks, even though we have a vaccine, keeping our distance still needs to be followed. The risk of transmission is rather low at two meters, so we should maintain a 2 m distance. In this study, we applied the pre-trained InceptionV2 model to recognize human objects in surveillance video, and then from the recognized human objects in each scene, we fine-tuned the camera. With methods of converting coordinates with a chessboard and bird's eye view, calculate distances and provide warnings if violated. The method has been evaluated and tested with scenarios. However, the method's accuracy is based on the transition from the camera view to the birds'eye perspective. In addition, we convert measure units from meter to pixel to calculate distance. This can lead to dependency on the camera calibration process.

References

1. The Ministry of Health, Viatnamese: The ministry of health recommends "5k" to live safely with the epidemic (2020). https://covid19.gov.vn/bo-y-te-khuyen-cao-5k-chung-song-an-toan-voi-dich-benh-1717130215.htm

2. Bunn, S.: COVID-19 and social distancing: the 2 m advice (2020). https://post.parliament.uk/covid-19-and-social-distancing-the-2-metre-advice/

3. Payne, M.: What is the evidence to support the 2-m social distancing rule to reduce COVID-19 transmission? - a lay summary. https://www.healthsense-uk.org/publications/covid-19/204-covid-19-15.html

4. Chu, D.K., et al.: Physical distancing, face masks, and eye protection to prevent person-to-person transmission of SARS-CoV-2 and COVID-19: a systematic review and meta-analysis. The Lancet. **395** (10242), 1973–1987 (2020). https://doi.org/10.1016/s0140-6736(20)31142--9

5. Ahmed, I., Ahmad, M., Rodrigues, J.J.P.C., Jeon, G., Din, S.: A deep learning-based social distance monitoring framework for COVID-19. Sustain. Cities Soc. **65**(102571), 102571 (2021)

6. Goh, Y.M., Tian, J., Chian, E.Y.T.: Management of safe distancing on construction sites during COVID-19: a smart real-time monitoring system. Comput. Ind. Eng. **163**(107847), 107847 (2022)

7. Rosenfeld, D.L., Tomiyama, A.J.: Moral judgments of COVID-19 social distancing violations: the roles of perceived harm and impurity. Personal. Soc. Psychol. Bull. **48**(5), 766–781 (2021). https://doi.org/10.1177%2F01461672211025433

8. Elbishlawi, S., Abdelpakey, M.H., Shehata, M.S.: SocialNet: detecting social distancing violations in crowd scene on IoT devices. In: 2021 IEEE 7th World Forum on Internet of Things (WF-IoT). IEEE (2021). https://doi.org/10.1109

9. Acharjee, C., Deb, S.: YOLOv3 based real time social distance violation detection in public places. In: 2021 International Conference on Computational Performance Evaluation (ComPE). IEEE, December 2021. https://doi.org/10.1109

10. Bharti, V., Singh, S.: Social distancing violation detection using pre-trained object detection models. In: 2021 19th OITS International Conference on Information Technology (OCIT). IEEE, December 2021. https://doi.org/10.1109

11. Saponara, S., Elhanashi, A., Zheng, Q.: Developing a real-time social distancing detection system based on YOLOv4-tiny and bird-eye view for COVID-19. J. Real-Time Image Process. **19**(3), 551–563 (2022). https://doi.org/10.1007

12. Sriharsha, M., Jindam, S., Gandla, A., Allani, L.S.: Social distancing detector using deep learning. Int. J. Recent Technol. Eng. (IJRTE). **10**(5), 146–149 (2022). https://doi.org/10.35940

13. Lin, T.-Y., et al.: Microsoft COCO: common objects in context. In: Fleet, D., Pajdla, T., Schiele, B., Tuytelaars, T. (eds.) ECCV 2014. LNCS, vol. 8693, pp. 740–755. Springer, Cham (2014). https://doi.org/10.1007/978-3-319-10602-1_48 T.-Y., et al.: Microsoft COCO: common objects in context. In: Fleet, D., Pajdla, T., Schiele, B., Tuytelaars, T. (eds.) ECCV 2014. LNCS, vol. 8693, pp. 740–755. Springer, Cham (2014). https://doi.org/10.1007/978-3-319-10602-1_48

14. Kumar, G., Shetty, S.: Application development for mask detection and social distancing violation detection using convolutional neural networks. In: Proceedings of the 23rd International Conference on Enterprise Information Systems. SCITEPRESS - Science and Technology Publications (2021). https://doi.org/10.5220/0010483107600767

15. Karaman, O., Alhudhaif, A., Polat, K.: Development of smart camera systems based on artificial intelligence network for social distance detection to fight against COVID-19. Appl. Soft Comput. **110**, 107610 (2021). https://doi.org/10.1016/j.asoc.2021.107610

16. Mercaldo, F., Martinelli, F., Santone, A.: A proposal to ensure social distancing with deep learning-based object detection. In: 2021 International Joint Conference on Neural Networks (IJCNN). IEEE (2021). https://doi.org/10.1109/ijcnn52387.2021.9534231

17. Szegedy, C., Ioffe, S., Vanhoucke, V., Alemi, A.: Inception-v4, inception-resnet and the impact of residual connections on learning (2016)

18. Szegedy, C., et al.: Going deeper with convolutions (2014). https://arxiv.org/abs/1409.4842

19. Simonyan, K., Zisserman, A.: Very deep convolutional networks for large-scale image recognition (2014). https://arxiv.org/abs/1409.1556

20. Krizhevsky, A., Sutskever, I., Hinton, G.E.: ImageNet classification with deep convolutional neural networks. In: Proceedings of the 25th International Conference on Neural Information Processing Systems - Volume 1, pp. 1097–1105. NIPS 2012, Curran Associates Inc., Red Hook, NY, USA (2012)

21. Laureano, G.T., de Paiva, M.S.V., da Silva Soares, A., Coelho, C.J.: A topological approach for detection of chessboard patterns for camera calibration. In: Emerging Trends in Image Processing, Computer Vision and Pattern Recognition, pp. 517–531. Elsevier (2015). https://doi.org/10.1016

22. Bradski, G.: The OpenCV library. Dr. Dobb's J. Softw. Tools. **25**, 120–123 (2000)

23. Liu, Y., Liu, S., Cao, Y., Wang, Z.: Automatic chessboard corner detection method. IET Image Proc. **10**(1), 16–23 (2016). https://doi.org/10.1049/iet-ipr.2015.0126

3D-FaultSeg-UNet: 3D Fault Segmentation in Seismic Data Using Bi-stream U-Net

Thi DINH Van-Ha[1(✉)] and Nguyen Thanh-An[2]

[1] NguyenDu Secondary School, Ho Chi Minh City, Vietnam
dtvha@thcsnguyenduq1.edu.vn
[2] University of Science, VNU-HCM, Ho Chi Minh City, Vietnam
ntan@hcmus.edu.vn

Abstract. Structural interpretation tasks require the step of fault segmentation, which is mostly performed manually, in seismic samples. Recent approaches represent seismic samples as 3D images and utilize a variety of methods, including Deep Learning. In this research, the authors propose a 3D bi-stream convolutional neural network, derived from U-Net, as an end-to-end model to segment seismic faults. Empirical results prove the power of the 3D bi-stream U-Net whose accuracy reaches 96.30% which outperforms recent works. The proposed network is potential for practical applications in seismic data analysis.

Keywords: Seismic image · 3D Bi-stream U-Net · Fault segmentation

1 Introduction

Seismic data analysis is an essential task in the field of geophysics, in which experts interpret samples to detect faults and abnormality manually. Therefore, automatic fault detection in 3D seismic samples is crucial to reduce the work quantity of experts and provide a stable base for practical applications.

In this research, the authors propose a methodology, based on advancements of convolutional neural networks in the field of deep learning.

- Input: a 3D matrix representing a seismic image,
- Output: a 3D mask representing fault locations.
- Model: an end-to-end 3D convolutional neural network transforming a seismic image to a mask.

The research is strongly inspired by the approaches of seismic image representation and end-to-end neural networks in [5–8]. Deep learning models, especially 3D convolutional neural networks, recently play an important role in the task of learning representation and data transformation. That is a stable and promised background to conduct the research.

To obtain the research targets, the authors propose a 3D convolutional neural network, named 3D Bi-stream U-Net, derived from the original architecture of U-Net [9]. The proposed model has two separated streams which transform and extract visual features of the input seismic image in different ways and hence

T. K. Dang et al. (Eds.): FDSE 2022, CCIS 1688, pp. 477–488, 2022.
https://doi.org/10.1007/978-981-19-8069-5_32

3D Bi-stream U-net gains more useful information in layer-wised feature maps. Additionally, "skip-connection" idea, inspired from U-Net [9] and ResNet [10], is also applied and customized to control the flow and the ration of data transformation. Figure 1 illustrates the general architecture of 3D Bi-stream U-Net.

The proposed method is evaluated in the 3D seismic image data set provided in [1]. The empirical results show that 3D Bi-stream U-Net outperforms recent models with a remarkably higher accuracy in both training and test sets, **0.9731** and **0.9679** respectively.

In conclusion, the research brings two contributions, including

- Continuing the approach of 3D seismic image representation and automatic fault segment detection,
- Proposing an end-to-end 3D convolutional neural network, 3D Bi-stream U-Net, outperforming recent works and promisingly for practical applications.

The article is organized as five sections. Section 1 Introduction brings a general point of view of the research and relevant approaches are mention in Sect. 2 Related Works. Details of the proposed method, 3D Bi-stream U-Net, are discussed in Sect. 3 Method and Sect. 4 Experimental Results brings proofs to show up the power of the method. Finally, Sect. 5 Conclusion summarizes contents of the research and provides new targets for later coming studies.

2   Related Works

In a seismic volume, faults are frequently obvious as reflector discontinuities. By detecting reflection discontinuities, numerous types of fault properties have been proposed to highlight fault sites from a seismic volume. Nonetheless, these attribute volumes can be vulnerable to noise and stratigraphic features that appear as discontinuities in seismic volumes.

In [5], the authors present an approach to improve a pre-computed fault attribute volume and estimate synchronously fault strikes and dips. In order to improve the fault attribute volume, the attribute features are smoothed along fault orientations such that non-fault-related features are muted and fault-related features become more continuous and conspicuous. Then, on the ridges of an increased fault attribute volume, the authors calculate fault samples. Each fault sample parallels to a single seismic sample and is positioned according to the fault's estimated strike and dip. By directly joining oriented fault samples with consistent fault strikes and dips, fault surfaces can be built. The authors further suggest using a perceptual grouping method to infer fault surfaces that reasonably match the positions and orientations of the fault samples in complex scenarios with missing and noisy fault samples. The authors skillfully extract numerous intersecting flaw surfaces and finished fault surfaces with no holes by implementing these techniques to 3D synthetic and real instances.

To detect flaws by measuring reflection continuities or discontinuities, a variety of fault qualities have been proposed. Other seismic discontinuities, such as noise and stratigraphic features, can, nevertheless, affect these properties.

Furthermore, malfunction characteristics inside a fault attribute image are frequently impossible to track continuously.

In [6], the authors present an excellent surface voting approach for improving a fault attribute image so that noisy (non-fault) features are eliminated and fault features become cleaner and more consistent. In this technique, the authors select seed points from the input attribute illustration automatically and utilize them as control points to calculate optimal surface patches that go through the control points and pursue the global maximum fault attribute values. Then, the authors treat all of the computed surfaces as supporters, establishing voting scores for each voter based on defect attribute values smoothed along the surface voter. the authors then take all of the voters' voting scores and create a voting score map as a new fault attribute image, with fault features (with high scores) that are significantly cleaner, sharper, and more constant than those in the input attribute photo. By computing the authors weighted averages of the surface voter orientations, the authors may reliably estimate fault orientations (strikes and dips) using the optimal surface voters. Fault surfaces can be recovered from a voting score map with clean and persistent fault features by simply tacking the fault features along the projected fault directions. The method's computing cost is determined by the number of seed points rather than the size of the seismic volume, making it extremely effective. Our parallel approach can handle more than 1000 seeds in 1 s on an eight-core machine, resulting in ideal voting surfaces and a final voting score map.

The ability to appropriately detect faults in continental sandstone reservoirs in eastern China is critical for better understanding the distribution of residual structural reservoirs and more effective development procedures. The majority of the faults, nevertheless, have minor displacements and ambiguous elements, making it difficult to detect them in seismic data using conventional methods.

In [7], the authors view fault diagnosis to be a problem of labeling a 3D seismic image with ones as faults and zeros elsewhere as an end-to-end binary image segmentation drawback. As a result, The authors created a flaw segmentation method based on a fully convolutional network (FCN) and employed synthetic seismic data to obtain an accurate and sufficient training data set. FCN uses a modified version of the VGGNet architecture (A convolutional neural network was named by the Visual Geometry Group). A classification net can build a heatmap by converting fully linked layers into convolution layers. The addition of the deconvolution layers results in a network that is productive for end-to-end intensive learning. The authors used the fact that a fault binary image is highly skewed, with large zeros and only a few ones on the faults to our advantage. To rectify the imbalance and optimize the parameters of our FCN model, The authors created a balanced cross-entropy loss function. Finally, the FCN model was tested on real-world data, leading to the conclusion that our FCN model can more accurately and efficiently forecast faults from seismic pictures than conventional techniques.

In [8], the authors suggest a technique for identifying and isolating fault surfaces in 3D seismic volumes that is both accurate and reliable. The seismic data is converted into a volume of local-fault-extraction (LFE) estimations, which quantify the probability that a given point is located on a failure surface. By evaluating tilted and inverted sub-volumes over the area of interest, the authors segment the fault surfaces into comparatively tiny linear parts. The use of directional filtering and thresholding improves the seismic discontinuities caused by fault surfaces. Single fault surfaces are separated and named in order of decreasing size after the volume of LFE calculations is skeletonized. The suggested technique yields a visual and semantic illustration of a set of well-defined, cleanly separated, one-pixel-thick, named fault surfaces that may be easily used for seismic interpretation.

3   Method

3.1   General Architecture

The input image is fed to the two branches separately to be down-sampled throughout stacked layers consisting of convolution layers, max-pooling layers, and several additional dropout ones. After that, the outputs of the two branches are concatenated before being fed to an up-sampling flow. Figure 1 shows the general architecture of 3D Bi-stream U-Net.

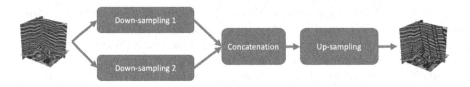

Fig. 1. General architecture of 3D Bi-stream U-Net.

3.2   Branch Architecture

There are two individual branches in 3D Bi-stream U-Net which take the responsibility to transform the input seismic image into feature maps in latent space. Three kinds of layers are utilized in these branches include convolution 3D, max-pooling 3D, and dropout layers.

Table 1 summarizes the branch architecture in details. There are five groups of layers that consist a couple of 3D convolution layers followed a 3D max-pooling with a stride of 2 for each dimension. All convolution layers use the same kernel size of (3×3) and the activation function is ReLU. There two layers of dropout, with a ratio of 0.5, added to the last two groups.

Table 1. Branch architecture in details.

Branch 1	Branch 2	Layer	Size	Activation
conv11	conv12	Conv3D	8, 3×3	ReLU
conv11	conv12	Conv3D	8, 3×3	ReLU
pool11	pool12	MaxPooling3D	$2 \times 2 \times 2$	-
conv21	conv22	Conv3D	16, 3×3	ReLU
conv21	conv22	Conv3D	16, 3×3	ReLU
pool21	pool22	MaxPooling3D	$2 \times 2 \times 2$	-
conv31	conv32	Conv3D	32, 3×3	ReLU
conv31	conv32	Conv3D	32, 3×3	ReLU
pool31	pool32	MaxPooling3D	$2 \times 2 \times 2$	-
conv41	conv42	Conv3D	64, 3×3	ReLU
conv41	conv42	Conv3D	64, 3×3	ReLU
drop41	drop42	Dropout(0.5)	-	-
pool41	pool42	MaxPooling3D	$2 \times 2 \times 2$	-
conv51	conv52	Conv3D	128, 3×3	ReLU
conv51	conv52	Conv3D	128, 3×3	ReLU
drop51	drop52	Dropout 0.5	-	-

Table 2. Details of up-sampling flow architecture.

Name	Action	Parameters	Up-sampling
merge5	concatenate	[drop51, drop52]	
up6	Conv3D	$(64, 2 \times 2)$, ReLU	$\leftarrow$ UpSampling3D $(2 \times 2 \times 2)$
merge6	concatenate	[drop41, drop42, up6]	
conv6	Conv3D	$(64, 3 \times 3)$, ReLU	
conv6	Conv3D	$(64, 3 \times 3)$, ReLU	
up7	Conv3D	$(32, 2 \times 2)$, ReLU	$\leftarrow$ UpSampling3D $(2 \times 2 \times 2)$
merge7	concatenate	[conv31, conv32, up7]	
conv7	Conv3D	$(32, 3 \times 3)$, ReLU	
conv7	Conv3D	$(32, 3 \times 3)$, ReLU	
up8	Conv3D	$(16, 2 \times 2)$, ReLU	$\leftarrow$ UpSampling3D $(2 \times 2 \times 2)$
merge8	concatenate	[conv21, conv22, up8]	
conv8	Conv3D	$(16, 3 \times 3)$, ReLU	
conv8	Conv3D	$(16, 3 \times 3)$, ReLU	
up9	Conv3D	$(8, 2 \times 2)$, ReLU	$\leftarrow$ UpSampling3D $(2 \times 2 \times 2)$
merge9	concatenate	[conv11, conv12, up9]	
conv9	Conv3D	$(8, 3 \times 3)$, ReLU	
conv9	Conv3D	$(8, 3 \times 3)$, ReLU	
conv10	Conv3D	$(1, 1 \times 1)$, Sigmoid	

3.3 Up-Sampling Flow

The details of up-sampling flow architecture is illustrated in Table 2. The outputs of the two branches are concatenated before being fed to a UpSampling3D module with a stride of 2 for each dimension. A 3D convolution layer is utilized to handle the output of each UpSampling3D module.

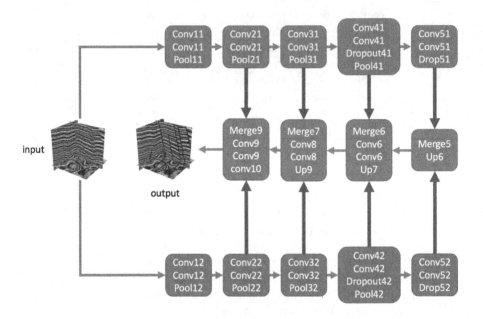

Fig. 2. General architecture of 3D Bi-stream U-Net.

"Merge" layers, including $merge6, merge7, merge8, and merge9$, take responsibility to concatenate the output of the previous layer and feature maps from the two branches, i.e. $[drop41, drop42, up6]$. These "skip connection" steps help to produce feature maps with a variety of transformation levels and thus they are effective to avoid information loss. Figure 2 summarizes the general architecture of the 3D bi-stream U-Net with details of skip connections.

4 Experimental Result

4.1 Data Set

Experiments are conducted to verify the performance of the 3D bi-stream U-Net. For comparison with ease, the authors use the 3D seismic image data set, proposed in [1]. There are respectively 200 and 20 images in the training and test set.

Before being fed to the network, each seismic image with a size of $(128, 128, 128)$ is normalized using the mean, and standard deviation. Formula 1 represents the normalization action.

$$X_i = \frac{X_i - mean(X_i)}{\sigma(X_i)} \tag{1}$$

where,

$$mean(X) = \frac{1}{D_1 \times D_2 \times D_3} \sum_i^{D_i} \sum_j^{D_2} \sum_k^{D_3} X_{i,j,k} \tag{2}$$

$$\sigma(X) = \sqrt{\sum_i^{D_1} \sum_j^{D_2} \sum_k^{D_3} \frac{(X_{i,j,k} - mean(X))^2}{D_1 \times D_2 \times D_3}} \tag{3}$$

in which X_i is a sample image, D_1, D_2, and D_3 are the dimensions of images. $mean(X)$ and $\sigma(X)$ are respectively the mean and standard deviation.

Figure 3 illustrates a sample seismic image from the data set [1]. The sample is represented as 3 slices corresponding to 3 axes. Figure 4 shows a sample image with fault highlighted by red color. These annotations are currently detected manually by geophysics experts.

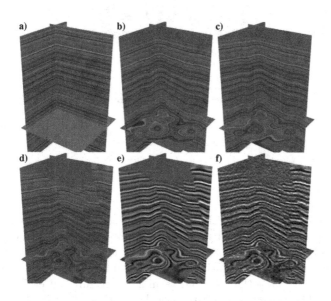

Fig. 3. Sample seismic images in the data set [1].

4.2 Configurations

The 3D bi-stream U-Net is trained using Adam optimizer with a learning rate of $1e - 4$. Model parameters are optimized with a Binary Cross Entropy function

a)

b)

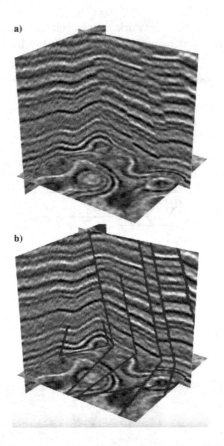

Fig. 4. A sample seismic image with fault highlighted by red color [1] (Color figure online).

(formula 4).

$$H(p,q) = - \sum_{x \in X} p(x) \log q(x) \qquad (4)$$

in which p and q are respectively a prediction and the corresponding ground truth. Accuracy is the selected metric to measure the performance of 3D bi-stream U-Net.

Validation loss is tracked during the training phase to save the model state whenever it reaches a better one and terminates training after 5 epochs with improvement. The learning rate is reduced by 10 times to start a new training step after each time of being terminated.

Training configurations are summarized in Table 3.

The proposed convolutional neural network, 3D bi-stream U-Net, is implemented using TensorFlow library [2] and experiments are conducted using Google Colab virtual machines with GPUs [4].

Table 3. Training configurations for 3D bi-stream U-Net

Configuration	Selection
Optimizer	Adam ($lr = 10^{-4}$)
Loss function	Binary cross entropy
Metrics	Accuracy
Early stopping	5 epochs ($delta = 10^{-5}$)
NumPy random seed	12345
TensorFlow random seed	1234

4.3 Results

The 3D Bi-stream U-Net is trained during total 51 epochs, including 4 stages: 29, 11, 5, and 6 epochs. Stages are separated based on Early Stopping technique [3] with a patience of 5. Table 4 shows experimental results of each stage in details.

Table 4. Training process with 4 stages

Stage	lr	Train. accuracy	Train. loss	Val. accuracy	Val. loss	#Epochs
1	10^{-4}	0.9655	0.0825	0.9630	0.0927	29
2	10^{-5}	0.9695	0.0713	0.9656	0.0855	11
3	10^{-6}	0.9713	0.0668	0.9671	0.0827	5
4	10^{-7}	**0.9731**	**0.0625**	**0.9679**	**0.0821**	6

Figures 5 and 6 respectively illustrate the accuracy and loss in the training and validation sets during the training phase. The accuracy in the two sets gradually increases throughout the 4 stages and reaches peaks of **0.9731** and **0.9676** respectively. On the other hand, losses reduces during the training process and reach **0.0625** and **0.0821** in the two sets.

Comparing to the U-Net derived network, proposed in [1], our 3D Bi-stream U-Net achieves remarkably higher accuracy, which is figured out in Table 5.

Table 5. Accuracy comparison to U-Net derived network proposed in [1]

-	3D Bi-stream U-Net (ours)	U-Net liked [1]
Training accuracy	**0.9731**	0.9500
Validation accuracy	**0.9679**	0.9500
Number of epochs	51	25

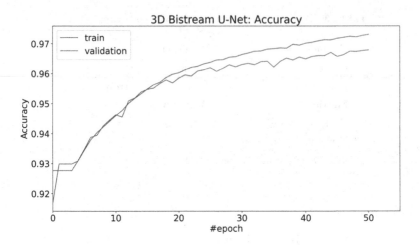

Fig. 5. Training and validation accuracy during the training process.

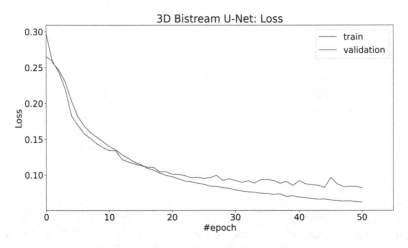

Fig. 6. Training and validation losses during the training process.

As discusses in Sect. 3, the proposed 3D Bi-stream U-Net has two different streams to transform the input seismic image into a latent space. Because network parameters, including weights, biases, etc., are isolated between the two streams, different and various visual features are extracted, which is much more efficient than the ones from a single stream.

The more streams are integrated, the more powerful visual features are extracted. However, computational performance of hardware is limited and hence convolutional neural networks with high complexity of parameters face at more obstacles to be published in practise. Our model, 3D Bi-stream U-Net, has **2,507,905** trainable parameters, which is essential to be optimized.

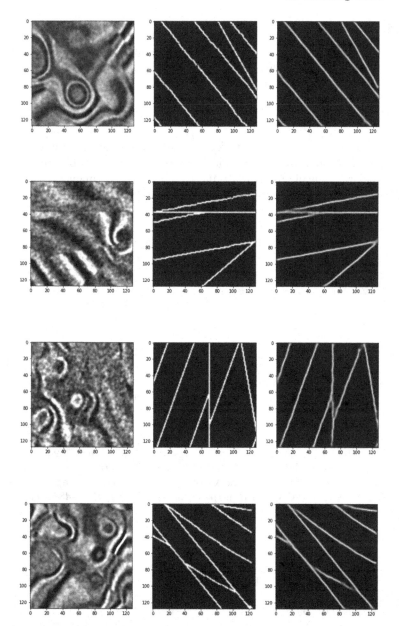

Fig. 7. Central slices of predictions generated by the best model of 3D Bi-stream U-Net: images (left), ground truths (center), predictions (right).

4.4   Sample Predictions

Figure 7 illustrates central slices of predictions generated by the best model of 3D Bi-stream U-Net. The left, center, and right columns consist of central slices of seismic images, ground truths, and predictions respectively.

5   Conclusion

Fault segmentation is an essential task in the field of seismic data analysis. In this research, the authors propose a deep learning-based model, 3D bi-stream U-Net, which transforms seismic images into masks of fault. Experimental results show that 3D bi-stream U-Net out-performs recent models and thus it is potential for practical applications in the field of Geophysics where most of the tasks are manually conducted by experts.

Additionally, the computational cost is the major obstacle to applying convolutional neural networks in practice. Although the 3D bi-stream U-net brings remarkable results, it needs improving to reduce the complexity, which is a challenging target for later-coming research.

References

1. Xinming, W., Liang, L., Shi, Y., Fomel, S.: FaultSeg3D: using synthetic datasets to train an end-to-end convolutional neural network for 3D seismic fault segmentation. Geophysics **84**(3), 35–45 (2019)
2. TensorFlow: Large-Scale Machine Learning on Heterogeneous Systems. http://www.tensorflow.org/
3. Prechelt, L.: Early stopping — but when? In: Montavon, G., Orr, G.B., Müller, K.-R. (eds.) Neural Networks: Tricks of the Trade. LNCS, vol. 7700, pp. 53–67. Springer, Heidelberg (2012). https://doi.org/10.1007/978-3-642-35289-8_5
4. Bisong, E.: Google colaboratory. In: Building Machine Learning and Deep Learning Models on Google Cloud Platform: A Comprehensive Guide for Beginners, pp. 59–64, Apress, Berkeley, CA (2019). https://doi.org/10.1007/978-1-4842-4470-8_7
5. Xinming, W., Zhu, Z.: Methods to enhance seismic faults and construct fault surfaces. Comput. Geosci. **107**, 37–38 (2017). https://doi.org/10.1016/j.cageo.2017.06.015
6. Xinming, W., Fomel, S.: Automatic fault interpretation with optimal surface voting. Geophysics **83**, 067–082 (2018). https://doi.org/10.1190/geo2018-0115.1
7. Wu, J., Liu, B., Zhang, H., He, S., Yang, Q.: Fault detection based on fully convolutional networks (FCN). J. Marine Sci. Eng. **9**(3), 259 (2021). https://doi.org/10.3390/jmse9030259
8. Cohen, I., Coult, N., Vassiliou, A.A.: Detection and extraction of fault surfaces in 3D seismic data. Geophysics **71**, 021–027 (2006). https://doi.org/10.1190/1.2215357
9. Ronneberger, O., Fischer, P., Brox, T.: U-Net: convolutional networks for biomedical image segmentation. In: Navab, N., Hornegger, J., Wells, W.M., Frangi, A.F. (eds.) MICCAI 2015. LNCS, vol. 9351, pp. 234–241. Springer, Cham (2015). https://doi.org/10.1007/978-3-319-24574-4_28
10. He, K., Zhang, X., Ren, S., Sun, J.: Deep residual learning for image recognition. In: CVPR (2015). http://arxiv.org/abs/1512.03385

Applying Artificial Intelligence to Plan Flight Paths for Aircraft at Subsonic Speeds

Nguyen Dang Minh[1], Nguyen Khac Diep[2(✉)], and Pham Tuan Anh[2]

[1] Viettel Aerospace Institute, Hanoi, Vietnam
[2] Institute of Information Technology, AMST, Ho Chi Minh City, Vietnam
diep62@mail.ru

Abstract. The content of the article is in the field of research and manufacture of command and control automation systems, based on reference analysis of actual systems being used at home and abroad. The research results bring benefits and practical effects in the process of supporting the commander in planning and making combat decisions in a timely and accurate manner. Accordingly, the article presents a method to automatically plan flight paths in a complex combat environment for aircraft at subsonic speeds based on nonlinear programming combined with an improved genetic algorithm.

Keywords: Automatic flight path planning · Aircraft · Artificial intelligence · Improved genetic algorithm

1 Problem

Flight path planning for aircraft at subsonic speed is one of the core issues in the planning system to ensure the ability to complete the mission, from a tactical point of view it effectively increases the ability to the survivability of the aircraft until it reaches the target by avoiding obstacles, reducing the possibility of detection and early warning and destruction when flying over the enemy's combat zone, and at the same time ensuring the safety of civilian and allied targets.

The basic content of flight path planning is to select consecutive points that satisfy the binding criteria at the waypoints, combined with geographical, meteorological, and battlefield information in a specific situation to optimize them, to plan valid flight paths.

In the process of setting up the flight route, it is necessary to understand the technical characteristics of the equipment and ground control system, and at the same time master the geographical and meteorological information of the combat area, the position, and movement of the sides, the types, strength, and information of the enemy's defensive firepower, reconnaissance, and electronic warfare equipment. The above information together with its constraints make the flight path planning process a computationally complex multi-criteria non-linear optimization process.

To solve the problem of flight route planning for aircraft flying at subsonic speeds, the methods used can include: meshing method, Voronoi diagram, dynamic programming, and planning in the potential field [1–5]. The above methods all have the common characteristic that they spend too much time performing large-scale iterations, easily get stuck in local minima, and converge early because they do not use heuristics.

To improve the efficiency of classical methods, modern probability algorithms have been developed. Intelligent mining search method to get a good quality quasi-global optimal solution. Although mining algorithms do not guarantee a solution, if they do, they are likely to perform much faster than classical methods. In recent years, many flight path planning methods have been proposed, and most of them are based on high-speed heuristics and execution methods, such as genetic algorithms, mining algorithm A*, D*, and herd intelligence [6–9].

This article will focus on studying the method of flight path planning in a complex combat environment based on the application of an improved genetic algorithm.

2   Constraints of the Flight Path

The two most important goals in planning a flight path for an aircraft to fly at subsonic speeds are to be safe and enforceable (flyable). The safety of the missile is achieved by avoiding obstacles, the flight path is executed when the kinematic constraints and maneuverability of the device are satisfied. To achieve that, the route needs to satisfy the following.

2.1   The Condition of the Bank Angle

This condition constrains the slope α_i, $i = \overline{1 \ldots n}$ to be less than a predefined maximum angle: $\alpha_i \leq \alpha_{max}$.

2.2   Condition of Bank Radius

The radius of banking turn R must be large enough to ensure maneuverability of the device, and not cause the aircraft to be horizontally overloaded during banking turn: $R \geq R_{min}$.

2.3   Condition of the Geodesic Length

A geodesic is a straight line connecting two consecutive turn points, there are three types of short lines with separate constraints.

Conditions on the First Geodesic. The first geodesic from the launch point to the turning point W_1 needs to satisfy the condition that it is large enough for the aircraft to reach the required altitude after leaving the launch pad and fly stably before entering the transition point. Let d_1- be the distance from launch point O to the first turn (see Fig. 1).

$$d_1 = l_1 + R*tan\left(\left|\frac{\alpha_1}{2}\right|\right) \tag{1}$$

d_1 must satisfy the condition:

$$d_1 \leq l_1 + R*tan\left(\left|\frac{\alpha_{max}}{2}\right|\right); \tag{2}$$

with l_1 – the minimum distance for the device to reach the required altitude after launch; R – radius of banking turn at point W_1; α_{max} – maximum bank angle; α_1 – bank angle, missile redirects from OW_1 to W_1W_2;

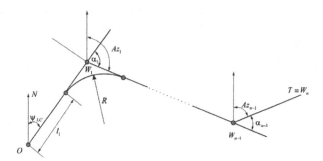

Fig. 1. Conditions on the first geodesic

Conditions on the Intermediate Geodesics. The geodesics other than the first and last (see Fig. 2) have the length d_{i+1}.

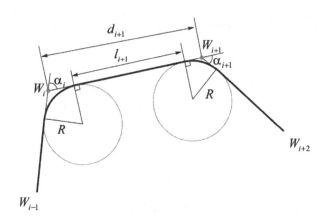

Fig. 2. Geodesics and intermediate waypoints

$$d_{i+1} = R*\left(tan\left(\left|\frac{\alpha_i}{2}\right|\right) + tan\left(\left|\frac{\alpha_{i+1}}{2}\right|\right)\right) + l_{i+1} \tag{3}$$

with α_i, α_{i+1} – bank angles at points W_i, W_{i+1}; l_{i+1} – distance between the end of the bank at W_i and starting point of banking turn at W_{i+1}, $l_{i+1} \geq 0$.

Bank angel α_i must satisfy $|\alpha_i| \leq \alpha_{max}$ is calculated by the formula: $\alpha_i = Az_{i+1} - Az_i$. With Az_i – azimuth of the geodesic $W_{i-1}W_i$;

Conditions on the Last Geodesic. The final path from the last waypoint to the destination coordinates must be of the length d_n, with:

$$d_n = R * tan\left(\left|\frac{\alpha_{n-1}}{2}\right|\right) + l_n + d_{ss}; \tag{4}$$

where: d_{ss} – distance to turn on the reconnaissance sensor; l_n – the distance for the missile to fly stably after finishing the banking turn process, before reaching the position where the reconnaissance sensor is turned on, $l_n \geq 0$ (Fig. 3).

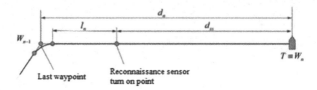

Fig. 3. Conditions on the last geodesic

2.4 Conditions of Avoiding Obstacles, Enemy Combat Zones

The geodesics need to satisfy that they do not intersect with obstacles such as islands, coastal strip, extreme weather area, and enemy combat zone.

2.5 Conditions of Flight Distance Restriction

The total flight distance of an aircraft is finite depending on the amount of fuel, altitude, ambient temperature, and its design. Therefore, the established flight distance is not allowed to exceed the maximum operating capacity in specific environmental and temperature conditions.

3 Methods of Designing Flight Path

This section presents the principle of applying the nonlinear programming method to establish a set of valid paths and also presents an improved genetic algorithm designed based on the unique characteristics of the flight path to find optimal flight paths through cover and mutation processes.

3.1 Characteristics of Objects in the Flight Path Planning Problem

Obstacles, no-fly zones, and areas with extreme weather conditions are represented as a polygon in the coordinate plane used to establish the flight path.

The enemy's area of strong fire defense is represented as a circle centered at the center of the fire zone, the radius is equal to the defense range of the strongest fire can reach.

The flight path is represented as a list of turn points (waypoints), starting with the launch point and ending with the target point the aircraft needs. Waypoints other than the launch point and target point are called intermediate waypoints.

Each intermediate waypoint is encoded in the form of a data field containing information including waypoint coordinates, distance, and azimuth from its immediate predecessor to it, the curve at the waypoint.

The launch point is represented as a data field containing information including: launch point coordinates and launch direction.

The destination point is represented as a data field containing the following information: the coordinates of the target, the distance, and the azimuth from the previous turn to it.

3.2 Objective Function

The criterion for evaluating the flight path is based on the objective function value, in this article, the objective function value is called fitness.

The fitness value evaluates the quality of the flight path based on two factors: total flight distance and total maneuverability (total angle the aircraft must make). The two routes have the same total flight distance, and the route with the lower total maneuverability is evaluated better. However, the factor of total flight distance is still the main factor in determining flight quality. Therefore the parameters Q_f – the parameter that determines the importance of the total flight distance in the fitness value, and Q_S – the parameter that determines the importance of the total maneuver in the fitness value is included to specify the contribution level of each factor. Q_f and Q_S based on the following principles:

$$\begin{cases} Q_f + Q_S = 1; \\ Q_f > 0; \\ Q_S > 0; \\ Q_f > Q_S \end{cases}$$

Experimental results show that with the pairs of values Q_f and Q_S selected according to the above principle, the dispersion of the total flight distance and total mobility depends only on the complexity of the flight situation. The fitness value is calculated according to the formula:

$$fitness = 1 - \frac{Q_f*(f_{max} - f)}{(f_{max} - D)} - \frac{Q_S*(n*\alpha_{max} - S)}{(n*\alpha_{max})}; \tag{5}$$

where: f – total flight distance; f_{max} – the maximum flight distance of the aircraft with the corresponding amount of fuel; D – distance from launcher to target; n – the number of intermediate waypoints; S – total maneuverability in the flight path is calculated by the formula: $S = \sum_{i=1}^{n} |\alpha_i|$, with α_i bank angle at waypoint i.

Accordingly, the smaller the *fitness* value, the better the flight path is evaluated.

3.3 Optimal Flight Path Planning

Optimal flight path planning is performed based on nonlinear programming methods and improved genetic algorithms (IGA). The nonlinear programming method allows to set and check the constraints of the flight path. IGA allows finding the optimal flight path quickly and accurately. The flight path planning process is as follows:

– Step 1: Initialize the valid flight path population.
– Step 2: Select the flight paths participating in the optimal search process.
– Step 3: Create a new flight path by crossover and mutation methods.
– Step 4: Synthesize and evaluate new flight paths.
– Step 5: Check the search stop condition.

To optimize the flight path, it is necessary to repeat steps 2 to 5 until the search stop condition is reached. Figure 4 shows the optimal flight path planning cycle based on a genetic algorithm.

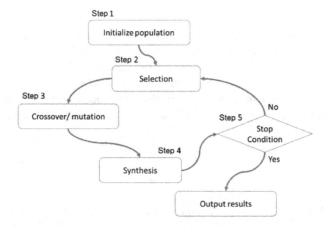

Fig. 4. The cycle of steps to perform optimal flight planning

Below is a description of how to do it step by step.

Initialize the Valid Flight Path Population. To initialize the flight path, it is necessary to first determine the first waypoint according to the conditions set out in the item 2.3 (Conditions on the intermediate geodesics).

The ith waypoints ($i > 1$), are determined by the RRT-smart (Rapidly-exploring Random Tree) method satisfying the conditions set for an intermediate waypoint on the route.

Accordingly, at each $(i-1)^{th}$ waypoint, set up random tree branches such that the angle created by the previous branch and the short path is in the range $[-\alpha_{max}, \alpha_{max}]$, and the length of each branch satisfies the degree condition. The length of the tangent line taking into account the slope at the ith waypoint is equal to the bounding angle. Figure 6 shows the branches at the 2nd waypoint.

Inspect and remove tree branches that violate the conditions of crossing obstacles and dangerous areas. Then randomly select a tree branch from among those that satisfy, or according to the criterion that the distance from the top of the branch to the target is the shortest. Then the selected tree branch is the next geodesic and the top of the tree branch is the ith waypoint.

The process of creating a valid path ends when the path from the ith waypoint to the target satisfies all of the conditions in (2.1) to (2.4) and at the same time the route satisfies the condition in (2.5). Figure 5 shows a valid flight path being initialized.

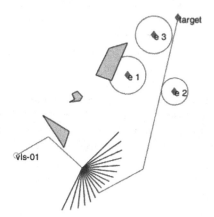

Fig. 5. Initiate a valid flight path.

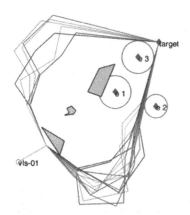

Fig. 6. A set of 20 valid flight paths.

In case the number of intermediate waypoints is greater than a given number or the route does not satisfy the condition (2.5), the route initialization process will start again from the first waypoint.

The route initialization step is repeated until the required number of valid routes is reached.

Select the Flight Paths Participating in the Optimal Search Process. Based on the set of routes initialized in step 1, select a list of n pairs of routes prepared for hybridization and m routes prepared for mutation for optimal search. The roulette selection method [10] was used to make a list based on the fitness value at each flight path in the set. Accordingly, routes with small fitness values will have a higher probability of being selected, which directly affects the convergence speed and quality of newly formed routes.

Generate a New Flight Path by Crossover and Mutation Methods. *Generate   a New Flight Path by Crossover Method.* In this step, a random cross is performed between pairs of routes selected in step 2 to generate an expected number of n new valid routes, the implementation method is similar to concatenating two chromosome segments from two individuals can form a complete new chromosome that has the characteristics of both parents. Accordingly, each route will be randomly split into two segments, a new route will be formed by taking the first segment of the first route and combining it with the second segment of the second route, and vice versa, the first segment of the second route is combined with the second segment of the first route. This crossover does not always produce new valid routes, so it is necessary to try multiple crossovers on the chosen pair of routes. After a finite number of trial crosses, if no new valid routes have been created, the pair in question should be abandoned and proceed with the next pairs.

Figure 7 shows the new flight path (in blue) that combines the segment from the launch point to the 2nd waypoint of the first track with the segment from the 5th waypoint to the target of the 2nd track.

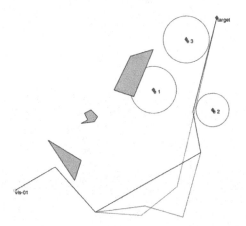

Fig. 7. Valid flight path generated by process of crossover (Color figure online).

Generate a New Flight Path by Mutation Method. In nature, there can be two cases of mutations, that is, a mutation that loses a gene or a mutation that changes the properties of a gene on a chromosome segment. Similarly, if we consider the flight path as a chromosome, the waypoints act as genes. This step will perform the creation of mutations on the flight path and check the satisfaction of the conditions of the newly formed flight path. This process will take place in an oriented random manner.

Method 1: Gene Loss Mutation. Loss mutation will not be performed with the flight path with a number of waypoints less than three, because waypoint 1 and the endpoint are mandatory and cannot be changed.

Gene loss mutation is done as follows: randomly select on the original route waypoint i^{th} (other than required points), delete the selected point from the waypoint list of the original route, check the conditions again valid route, if the conditions are satisfied, the newly created route will be added to the list of new routes and stop the mutation process in the selected original route. For example, in Fig. 8 a new route is created by deleting the 2nd waypoint in the original route.

If the new route is not valid, continue to try to select and delete another point on the original route, after a finite number of attempts fails to create a new route from the original route, the mutation will stop without a new valid flight path is created.

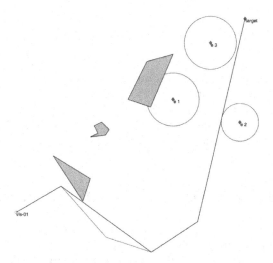

Fig. 8. The mutant lost waypoint number 2 on the original flight path.

Method 2: Mutation of Gene Characteristics. In this method, randomly select a waypoint among the waypoints that can participate in the mutation of the original flight path, create a new point near the selected point and replace the selected point with a newly created point, and check the satisfaction of the newly created flight path. This neighborhood point is designed so that it tends to decrease the roll angle or reduce the stroke length, thereby reducing the total flight distance and smoothing the flight path. Figure 9 shows the new flight path created by genetic modification.

The advantage of this method is a very high success rate, which has the effect of smoothing and refining the flight path.

Synthesize and Evaluate a Set of New Flight Paths. In this step, the old and new routes are synthesized due to the process of hybridization/mutation, based on the fitness quality of each route, eliminate low-quality routes and keep the number of routes in the set at a fixed level to ensure the performance and convergence speed of the algorithm.

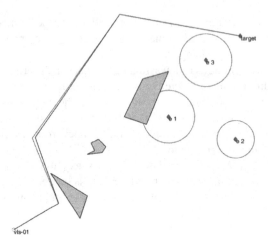

Fig. 9. Example of mutation of gene characteristics

Check the Search Stop Condition. The process of finding the optimal flight path stops when a finite number of times the search cycle from step 2 to step 5 is reached or the fitness value of the objective function for the best flight path remains unchanged after a finite number of loops depending on which condition comes first. After stopping the search, the route with the smallest fitness value will be selected as the optimal route.

4   Results of the Evaluation of the Flight Path Planning Method

The flight path planning software program is implemented in MATLAB environment. To evaluate the planning time in this article, use a personal computer with a central processor CPU with a speed of 3.7 GHz, and a RAM memory of 8 GB.

The flight path is planned in a simulated environment, polygons represent islands, fixed obstacles, or extreme weather areas, and red circles are combat zones with strong enemy fire.

The input condition parameters of the problem are given in Table 1, equivalent to the technical parameters of the flying device, launcher, and target parameter in reality.

Table 1. Conditions parameter to set up the flight path

№	Parameter	Value
1	Distance to destination	120000 m
2	Azimuth destination	60°
3	Take-off direction	10°
4	Stable altitude distance after take-off	4000 m
5	Distance to turn on the reconnaissance sensor	23000 m
6	Bank radius	8000 m
7	Maximum bank angle	90°

Table 2 shows the coordinates (x,y) of the waypoints on the optimal flight route (excluding launch points), the bank angles α_i at the corresponding waypoint, the azimuth az_i and the distance d_i from the point before it (Table 3).

Table 2. Parameters at waypoints

	x	y	α_i	az_i	d_i
W_1	1980.11	11229.79	54.8	10.0	11403.03
W_2	12085.45	15981.07	12.4	64.8	11166.58
W_3	44917.30	23418.34	−19	77.2	33663.67
W_4	103923.05	60000.00	0	58.2	69425.48

Table 3. Route evaluation parameter

№	Parameter	Value	Unit
1	Total flight distance	124984.45	m
2	Total bank angle	1.5057	radian
3	*Fitness*	0.8650	–
4	Search time	3.17	sec

Figures 10 and 11 show the optimal flight path with the condition parameters given in Table 1.

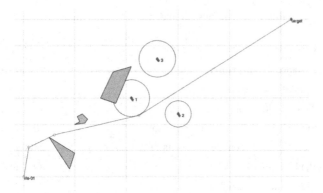

Fig. 10. The best flight route with the parameter given in Table 1.

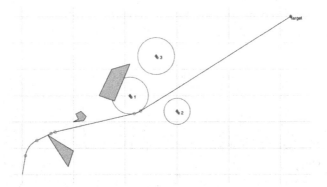

Fig. 11. The trajectory of the aircraft with a radius of 8 km.

5 Conclusion

The article presents the conditions of a valid flight path and the method in principle to plan the optimal flight path for aircraft flying at subsonic speed in complex combat environment conditions by combining modern math tools. In which, it is proposed to use smart random trees in the step of initialization valid flight paths and directional crossover and mutation methods to accelerate the optimal search speed to ensure real-time.

In fact, in an operational combat environment, a task that seems feasible becomes impossible if it is not planned and executed in a timely and accurate manner. Some systems are currently equipped in the Army or do not have the feature to set up a flight path with many waypoints (reducing combat ability) or the feature of setting up flight routes completely manually based on manual operation and experience of the operator, this leads to inaccuracies as well as prolonged operation time, which leads to loss of combat time. Using research results in an automated command and control system brings practical benefits and efficiency in the process of assisting commanders in planning and making combat decisions in a timely and accurate manner.

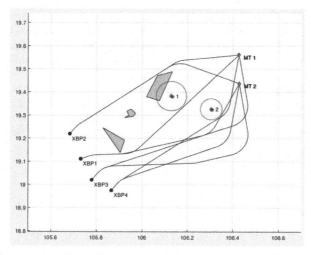

Fig. 12. Simulate simultaneous attacks from multiple directions on the target.

The application of the method also allows the command and control system to plan simultaneous attacks from multiple directions at the same time, increasing weapon efficiency, achieving higher mission completion probability with less weapon usage. Figure 12 simulates simultaneous attacks (XBP1, XBP2, XBP3, XBP4) on two targets MT1, and MT2 from different directions.

References

1. Helgason, R.V., Kennington, J.L., Lewis, K.R.: Cruise missile mission planning: a heuristic algorithm for automatic path generation. J. Heuristics **7**, 473–494 (2001)
2. Andreev, M.A., Miller, A.B., Miller, B.M., Stepanyan, K.V.: Path planning for unmanned aerial vehicle under complicated conditions and hazards. J. Comput. Syst. Sci. Int. **51**(2), 328–338 (2012). https://doi.org/10.1134/S1064230712010030
3. Yakovlev, K., Andreychuk, A.: Any Angle Pathfinding for Multiple Agents Based on SIPP Algorithm. In Proceedings of the 27th International Conference on Automated Planning and Scheduling (ICAPS 2017), pp. 586-593. Pittsburgh, PA, USA (2017)
4. Ghosh, S., Mount, D.: An Output sensitive algorithm for computing visibility graphs. In: Proceedings of the 28th Annual Symposium on Foundations of Computer Science, pp. 11–19. IEEE, Los Angeles, California (1987)
5. Bhattacharya, P., Gavrilova, M.L.: Voronoi diagram in optimal path planning. In: 4th International Symposium on Voronoi Diagrams in Science and Engineering (ISVD 2007), pp. 38–47. Glamorgan (2007). https://doi.org/10.1109/ISVD.2007.43
6. Guoshi, W., Qiang, L., Lejiang, G.: Multiple UAVs routes planning based on particle swarm optimization algorithm. In: Proceedings of the IEEE Conference on Information Engineering and Electronic Commerce, pp. 1–5 (2010)
7. Yang, X., Ding, M., Zhou, C.: Fast marine route planning for UAV Using improved sparse A* ALGORITHM. In :Proc. of the IEEE Conference on Genetic and Evolutionary Computing, pp. 190–193 (2010)

8. Tanil, C.: Improved heuristic and evolutionary methods for tactical missile mission planning. In: Proceedings of the IEEE Aerospace Conference, pp. 1–8 (2012). 978-1-4577-0556-4

9. Zhao, X., Fan, X.: A method based on genetic algorithm for anti-ship missile path planning. In: Proceedings of the IEEE Conference on Computational Sciences and Optimization, pp. 156–159 (2009)

10. Słowik, A., Białko, M.: Modified version of roulette selection for evolution algorithms – the fan selection. In: Rutkowski, L., Siekmann, J.H., Tadeusiewicz, R., Zadeh, L.A. (eds.) Artificial Intelligence and Soft Computing - ICAISC 2004. Lecture Notes in Computer Science (Lecture Notes in Artificial Intelligence), vol. 3070, pp. 474–479. Springer, Heidelberg (2004). https://doi.org/10.1007/978-3-540-24844-6_70

Capacity Building in Government: Towards Developing a Standard for a Functional Specialist in AI for Public Services

Alena Labanava[1][(✉)] ⓘ, Richard Michael Dreyling III[1] ⓘ, Marzia Mortati[2] ⓘ,
Innar Liiv[1] ⓘ, and Ingrid Pappel[1] ⓘ

[1] Tallinn University of Technology, Ehitajate Tee 5, 19086 Tallinn, Estonia
`alena.labanava@taltech.ee`
[2] Politecnico di Milano, Piazza Leonardo da Vinci 32, 20133 Milan, Italy

Abstract. One key aspect related to the spread of data and artificial intelligence (hereinafter AI) related technologies in the public sector is the capability for supervision and implementation of these projects. With AI gaining popularity and spreading in all sectors including the government, the public sector should have enough professionals who are equipped with modern knowledge and practical skills on how to employ AI for public services while taking into account ethical and moral needs. One way to ensure that governments are able to employ these individuals is to build capacities and train these professionals. The paper presents the results of the preliminary research on the competences of a functional specialist in AI for public services. The data was collected through a questionnaire that was sent out to AI professionals with a high level of expertise who represent both public and private sector as well as international organisations. The research shows that there is no unanimous opinion of the role of such specialist. The majority of respondents lean towards seeing him/her/them as an intermediary between the technical side and public policy side, while some respondents consider him/her/them as a technical professional or a data scientist. In any case, a functional specialist in AI for public services is expected to have interdisciplinary knowledge and skills that include technical, business and management and design thinking skills. A detailed list of the required competences has to be defined later when more data is collected. In the preliminary research phase, the list of technical skill has caused the biggest debate.

Keywords: AI in public sector · Functional specialist in AI for public services

1 Introduction

Capacity building in the public sector has a chance to resolve a key issue in adopting next generation data related technologies in government. Currently, although there are many ethical, legal, and social challenges that are associated with Artificial Intelligence implementation in the public sphere [1, 2] that threaten values like transparency, accountability, and inclusion as defined by the UN Sustainable Development Goals (SDGs) [3,

T. K. Dang et al. (Eds.): FDSE 2022, CCIS 1688, pp. 503–516, 2022.
https://doi.org/10.1007/978-981-19-8069-5_34

4] many governments are still attempting to implement these systems with no agreed upon ethical responsibility to the public interest [5, 6].

The use of AI can lead to unintended consequences that often result in marginalized populations becoming even more marginalized, the problem is highlighted when the public sector uses this technology because it can be interpreted as the government legitimizing the effects of these issues [7, 8]. According to Mensah [9] governments and stakeholders should adhere to a strict legal and regulatory regime furthering sustainable development to ensure SDG attainment.

One way which governments could understand and help to mitigate problems and even capitalize on opportunities [10, 11] is to use an AI specialist as the guardian of the moral fabric of society when AI or other data related technologies are used [12]. However, no agreed upon standard for a public sector functional AI specialist exists [13, 14]. Because of this, the AI4GOV EU project seeks to research and create an agreed upon standard for the public sector functional AI specialist in order to reach higher level e-governance for public entities. Additionally, in the light of digital transformation in the public sector, education related to e-governance field is essential and should be done according to the market needs [15].

This exploratory case study will seek to answer the following research questions:

1. How would the role of a functional specialist in AI for the public sector be utilized?
2. What competences should a functional specialist in AI for public services have?

The hypothesis is that the functional AI specialists for public services will fill a supervisory role and be expected to have multidisciplinary competences.

The main contributions of this Paper are: Identify the expert agreement on position/role of a functional specialist in AI for the public sector; and identification of key skills and competences of a functional AI specialist for the public sector.

The paper is organised as follows. The background section contains an overview of the market need of AI specialists and sheds the light on what competencies modern civil servants are expected to have. It also provides information on the AI4GOV master's programme that is meant to train specialists for public sector with a good understanding of how AI can be employed to achieve public goals and are able to successfully manage AI-related projects in the public sector. Coming to a standard on the role of a functional AI specialist would be a step toward being able to build the capacities necessary to have personnel who are able to manage data and AI related project implementation in a manner that is congruent with the values required in the public sector.

2 Background

In 2021 the master's programme AI4GOV was launched as a joint initiative of Universidad Politécnica de Madrid (UPM) in Spain, Politecnico di Milano (PoliMi) in Italy, Friedrich-Alexander-Universität Erlangen-Nürnberg (FAU) in Germany, and Tallinn University of Technology (TalTech) in Estonia. The core objectives of this program are providing education on: (i) the management of AI to help participants gain understanding about adequate management of AI-related services and products, (ii) the adoption of a human-centric approach to AI to increase knowledge and awareness of possibilities and opportunities related to exploiting AI in the public sector, and (iii) the application of AI in real projects, supporting learning through a hands-on approach and developing projects for turning theory into practice.

Building on these objectives, the AI4GOV programme tries to provide added value compared to the many programs, initiatives, and research projects flourishing around the world to push the technology of AI to improve public service provision. AI4GOV differentiates its offer by building on a multi-disciplinary approach that does not see in the technology an answer to the more complex transformations needed in Government. Rather, technological tools are contextualized in the wider need to transform the processes through which Governments formulate and implement new policies. The new public challenges to which Governments are called to respond are requiring from them more inclusion towards societal stakeholders, more responsiveness to their needs, and more transparency to account for their decisions [16, 17].

The main aim of the programme is to prepare a functional specialist in AI for public services who is ready to lead and/or participate in developing user-centred AI-based solutions to ensure societal benefits and taking into account ethical matters. A functional specialist in our consortia means a person who will use the knowledge, skills, and competences they have in the technical, design-centered, and business/management category areas to apply to real life projects in the organisations in which they are employed.

In a real world setting, the technology is just one component that drives the incorporation of new sets of Pragmatic tools and approaches [18]. Building on this vision, AI4GOV is piloting a teaching strategy developed around several pillars listed below:

Design thinking approach, to stimulate creative problem solving, teamwork and action research, and guide participants to develop human-centred solutions;

Project-based learning and team-working on practical projects and real challenges across different types of public institutions, increasing the confidence of students in adopting/procuring the right technology for the relevant societal needs;

Active learning, encouraging peer exchange, dialogue and debate, to create an extensive ecosystem around the adoption of AI in Government beyond the duration of the Master, thus aiming in the long run to contribute to a shift in the mindset of public officials and policy makers;

Focus on governance of AI and ethics to tackle notions of beneficence, human dignity, privacy, accountability, explainability, human autonomy, fairness, equity, and bias.

While the AI4GOV programme serves as an enabler of providing knowledge and skills at the intersection of technology, business and management, design thinking and policy sides, the reason for such an interdisciplinary approach lies in the needs of the labour market. The following sections emphasize that the labour market is in demand of AI-related specialists, while civil service competence frameworks require innovation and technology skills from public servants.

2.1 Overview of the Demand for AI Skills in the Labour Market

As using AI for public services is a relatively new area, there is almost no research on what kind of specialists are in need, what knowledge and skills they should have, what tasks can be given to them, what kind of differences will there be in the knowledge, skills and tasks for civil servants and for private sector employees, which are engaged in public sector projects. Despite this knowledge gap, however, the demand for AI-related skills both in public and private sector is growing tremendously. Further, the gap is more evident in Europe, as most of the research of the AI skills demand is limited geographically and mostly focuses on the US, the UK and a few other developed countries.

According to the KPMG 2021 report in the US AI adoption skyrocketed in the pandemic era. 61% of government decision-makers say AI is at least moderately to fully functional in their organizations [19]. 79% Government decision-makers are confident in AI's ability to improve bureaucratic efficiency. 75% respondents from the Government, which is bigger than in any other industry, agree that they are struggling with selecting the best AI technology [20].

According to the Snaplogic 2019 survey among 300 IT leaders in the US and UK the biggest barrier when executing AI initiatives is lack of skilled talent. Among the top skills in need are 1) coding, programming, and software development skills; 2) an understanding of data governance, security, and ethics as relates to AI/ML; 3) data visualization and analytics skills [21].

As reported by Deloitte survey in 7 countries (Australia, Germany, France, China, UK, US, Canada) one of the major challenges for AI early adopters is moderate-to-extreme AI skill gap [22]. A systematic literature review of AI in Public Governance [23] also highlights skills challenges among the challenges for the use of AI in public governance.

The top three roles needed to fill the gaps include AI researchers, software developers, and data scientists. A lot of companies see the need for business leaders who can make informed decisions and take corresponding actions relying on the interpretations of the results of AI [22].

As noted by the report conducted by EY and commissioned by Microsoft "Artificial Intelligence in the Public Sector: European Outlook for 2020 and Beyond", the public sector is struggling to move from AI pilots and silos to full-scale AI solutions. However, 65% of surveyed European public organizations view AI as a digital priority; 67% of European public organizations have adopted one or more AI use cases; 4% of European public organizations have been able to scale AI and achieve a high outcome, resulting in organizational transformation; and only 11% of European public organizations view themselves as highly competent in terms of AI skills [24].

According to OECD Working Paper that examines AI-related jobs in 2012–2018 in Canada, Singapore, the UK and the US, software engineering and development and operating systems skills that were in the highest demand in 2012 have lost their importance, while natural language processing and deep learning skills, on the contrary, have acquired higher demand. Skills related to big data have been listed among the major skills for AI professionals throughout the examined period [25]. OECD paper "The Human Capital Behind AI" that compares the data of 2013–2015 and 2017–2019 for the US and the UK indicates python and machine learning skills as the most demanded. These are followed by data mining, cluster analysis, natural language processing and robotics. The demand for communication related skills is significantly bigger in the US compared to the UK possibly due to a bigger demand for AI managers. A remarkable observation is the geographical concentration for the need of AI talent in California and London [26].

OECD working paper "Demand for AI Skills in Jobs: Evidence from Online Jobs Posting" provides analysis of AI-related job postings based on the information collected by Burning Glass Technologies from online job platforms for Canada, Singapore, the UK and the US for the period 2012–2018 [25]. The research reveals that the number of AI-related jobs has increased and reached almost 150 000 postings in the US in 2018. The LinkedIn Jobs on the Rise in the US report also includes artificial intelligence practitioners [27].

In the LinkedIn 2019 report "AI Talent in the European Labour Market" it is claimed that Europe is lagging behind the United States. The U.S. employs twice as many AI-skilled individuals than the EU, despite its total labour force being just half the size. One more noticeable figure is related to the concentration of young AI talent, which shows the leadership of Estonia [28].

In the UK the year of 2020 was the highest year to date for the number of online job vacancies related to AI and Data Science, with an increase of 16% from 2019 levels. The annual number of job postings had more than doubled since 2014 [29]. In the LinkedIn Jobs on the Rise UK report, which examined the roles experiencing growth from April to October 2020 comparing to the previous year, jobs in artificial intelligence hold the 15th position with a growth of 40% hired in 2020. Online retailers and social media companies made up a majority of hires within this category [30]. According to LinkedIn Jobs on the Rise Report, in Spain jobs in AI and data science have increased by 64% during 2020 [31]. In France the LinkedIn Jobs on the Rise Report also place Artificial Intelligence on the 15th place with a 40% increase in recruitment in 2020 [32].

Thus, a huge demand for AI-related skills exists in private and public sector across different geographies. With the growth of AI initiatives in the public sector the demand for professionals with AI related skills is going to grow both in public institutions and private companies that deal with public sector projects.

2.2 Overview of the Necessary Civil Service Skills

The work on defining the skills that are required from modern-day civil servants is going on in governments, academia and international organizations. Some countries have developed competency frameworks for civil servants, while some governments and regions are conducting research to identify the missing skills.

Data from the OECD's 2016 survey of Strategic Human Resource Management practices in government (the SHRM Survey) indicates that innovation is among the highest priorities for HR reform across OECD countries. The report defines six core skills for public sector innovation, namely, iteration, data literacy, user centricity, curiosity, storytelling and insurgency [33].

Italy assembled list of skills that an e-leader should have in the e-leadership skills document, including but not limited to: digital knowledge, soft skills, organizational leadership, public administration context, digital public administration, protecting digital citizenship, e-government project management, and open government process activation [34].

In the UK civil service competency framework outlines 10 competencies, which are grouped into 3 clusters: Set Direction; Engage People and Deliver Results. For each competency there is a description of what it means in practice and some examples of effective and ineffective behaviours at all levels [35].

Estonian Competency framework for top executives in the civil service consists of six competencies and is used in the recruitment, selection, evaluation and development of top managers. These competences include: future designer, innovation booster, self-leader, achiever, empowered, value builder [36].

The Public Administration School of Catalonia (EAPC) has published the Competency framework for innovative professionals in public administrations. It describes the eight key skills that are necessary to tackle innovation in the public sector: self-organisation, independent learning, creativity, communication, teamwork, networking, capturing trends and risk management. The publication reflects three primary vectors, the individual, the team, and the organisation. To achieve innovation, the individual needs to be action-oriented; the team needs to be cooperative; and the organisation must be sustainable [37].

Thus, there have been multiple attempts to identify the profile of an innovation leader in the public sector. Competency frameworks use different approaches to describing such a leader. Although these frameworks tend to not specifically include AI-related skills, having IT skills and being innovative and user-centred is something that is expected from a present-day civil servant.

3 Methodology

The methodology selected for this research is an exploratory case study. This method was selected because the research investigates a contemporary phenomenon where new knowledge constructs need to be developed. Moreover, the main research question concerns the "how" of the topic outlined [38].

The goal of the data collection is to examine the opinions of experts on the skillset and the profile of a functional AI specialist for the public sector. The data collection method is questionnaire.

First, respondents were asked to specify the economy sector they are associated with, rank their technical, business/management and design thinking related expertise, describe how AI is used in their organisations if applicable and what experience they have in this area. Second, respondents were offered to evaluate the relevance of skills that had been identified by consortium members expert into the three areas of knowledge offered in the master, namely technical skills on AI, business/management skills, design thinking skills. This initial set was identified also by means of a review of relevant literature, further validated by direct comparison with the ESCO skill and competence concepts, and refined by consortium members (i.e., some of the design thinking related skills taken from ESCO were rephrased).

Through the questionnaire, experts were asked to identify any missing skills from the suggested list, identify the most important skills, and provide an opinion on the selected skills. Then they were required to summarize the adequate level of knowledge needed for a functional specialist in AI for public services. Finally, the respondents were requested to describe the role of a functional specialist in AI for public services. The answers were analysed qualitatively with junior and senior researchers coding the results, creating categories and themes using a combination of MS Word and MS Excel.

The requests were initially sent to the members of the advisory board and the scientific committee of the AI4GOV Master's programme, representing relevant categories of stakeholders for the profile exiting the Master (experts working for public institutions, private companies and international organisations with varying degrees of expertise in the adoption of AI).

4 Results

This section explains the lists of skills that were originally presented for experts' evaluation and presents the analysis of the experts' responses.

The experts were given a list of skills which was derived from early expert interviews to evaluate the most important skills for a functional specialist in AI for public services. The skills which were shown to the experts came in three different categories, technical skills, business and management skills, as well as design-thinking skills.

The technical skills list is as follows: emergent technologies, principles of AI, Data mining, Python, Statistics, Machine learning, Data extraction, transformation and loading tools, Data protection, Prototyping development, Create prototype of user experience solutions, Natural language processing, Deep learning, Knowledge representation and reasoning. The technical skills that experts considered most important for the functional AI specialist are machine learning (71,4%), principles of AI (50%), deep learning (42,86%), data extraction, transformation and loading tools (42,86%), data protection (35,7%), prototype development (35,7%), data representation and reasoning (28,6%), python (28,6%) (Fig. 1).

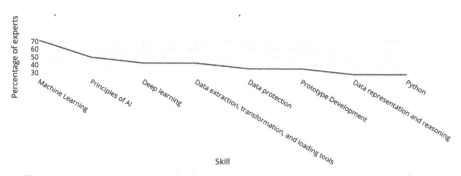

Fig. 1. Most important technical skills for a functional specialist in AI for public services

In addition to picking the most important skills, the experts were asked to provide a list of those skills they thought should be added to the list. Although the majority of the respondents agreed that the list of skills adequately describes the necessary skillset of a functional AI specialist for the public sector, they did describe skills that had not been explicitly added to the list by researchers.

The new skills suggested were divided into several groups during the thematic analysis. The new resulting categories are programming languages, advanced technology skills, prerequisite knowledge and data lifecycle and data use related skills. The identified missing skills that would be ideal for a functional AI specialist to have are:

- Programming languages recommended to be used alongside Python: Java, R;
- Advanced Technology Skills: Cybersecurity, Complex Network Analysis, Advanced Signal Processing Techniques, AI for Image recognition, Artificial Neural Networks, Distributed computing efficiency, Robotics and more;
- Prerequisite knowledge: Specifically, maths and statistics for optimization, Algebra;
- Data Lifecycle and Data use related: Data Engineering, SQL (Query Language), Deployment, Data integration, Machine translation, Visualisation, Interpretation of data, forms of decision making, Data Science, Hadoop, Use of libraries, Designing AI Models.

Some of the skills that were suggested by the respondents in the area of technical skills belong to a different category of skills according to the classifications, although some have a technical element to them. These skills were moved to the relevant group of skills and counted toward the number of times these themes were mentioned, including: ethics of AI, change management, collaborative competences, evidence-based policy making, juridical skills. These results indicated the necessity of the AI specialist, even a technical one, to be engaged in understanding the social aspects of AI and how the technology affects society.

In addition to technical knowledge, competency, and skills requirements another group of skills that was deemed to be relevant to the potential specialist role were business and management skills, which are required for the understanding and implementation of the technical portion of any AI project. The business skills that were given to experts to select included: identify needs and technological responses, ICT project management methodologies, agile project management, business process modelling, define technical requirements, manage contracts, analyze ICT systems, identify user ICT needs, define technology strategy, identify undetected organizational needs, analyze software specifications, apply change management, develop technological improvement strategies, combine business technology with user experience, risk management, monitor social impact, conduct impact evaluation of ICT processes on business, service-oriented modelling, information governance compliance, participate in governmental tenders, manage government funding, prepare government funding dossiers, maintain relationships with stakeholders, problem-solving with digital tools, assess project resource needs, collect customer feedback on applications.

The experts identified the following business and management related skills as the most important: Identify needs and technological responses (42,86%), monitor social impact (35,7%), risk management (28,6%), define technical requirements (28,6%), agile project management (28,6%), maintain relationships with stakeholders (28,6%). Among the missing skills respondents named ethical aspects of AI, juridical skills, domain-specific business knowledge, listening, policy advising, expertise in public and private partnerships (Fig. 2).

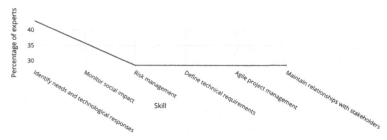

Fig. 2. Most important business and management skills for a functional specialist in AI for public services

Design thinking is an area of concern for the experts initially interviewed. When a design approach is not applied correctly, the adoption of the technology can suffer by diminishing trust in technologies while also reducing effectiveness and efficacy, especially in the e-Governance sphere [39, 40]. Furthermore, an appropriate design approach also supports the adoption of technologies in a human-centric way, thus appearing as central in the correct uptake of AI in Government. Because of this, the AI4GOV program puts a large emphasis on design thinking. The list of skills given to experts to evaluate in this category included: create a work atmosphere of continuous improvement, cope with uncertainty, adapt to changing situations, process qualitative information, monitor sociological trends, provide innovative ideas, thinking creatively and innovatively, applying co-creation techniques and methodologies, communicate requirements through appropriate visualisations, brainstorm ideas, solving problems, identify problems, research and analyse human behaviour, think analytically, use storytelling for meaningful communication, use creative suit software, stimulate creative processes, demonstrate curiosity.

The list of design related skills that the experts consider the most important: applying co-creation techniques and methodologies (42,86%), identify problems (35,7%), create a work atmosphere of continuous improvement (35,7%), stimulate creative processes (35,7%), research and analyse human behaviour (28,6%), cope with uncertainty (28,6%), solving problems (28,6%) (Fig. 3).

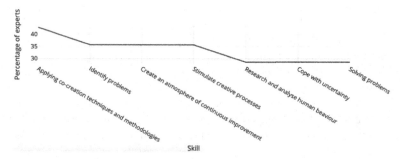

Fig. 3. Most important design related skills for a functional specialist in AI for public services

As for the overall opinion on the role of a functional AI specialist for public services, respondents' opinions are divided. The majority sees this professional as an intermediary between the technical side and public policy side. At the same time, some respondents view this specialist more as a technical professional or data scientist. The experts who advocate for the latter point of view evaluate their technical skills higher than those who see the AI specialist for public services as an intermediary.

The majority of the respondents agreed with the list of skills originally presented by researchers. The necessity for a functional specialist in AI for public services to have interdisciplinary knowledge and skills has not been criticised. The area of technical skills has caused the biggest debate in terms of adding more relevant skills. Although the list of relevant technical skills depends on the context and can hardly be imagined to be vested in one person, the list of compulsory skills for a functional specialist in AI for public services so far seems to be a disputable matter and will be further researched after collecting more data. It is worth noting that among the missing skills in the business and management area the most frequently suggested skill to add was ethics (although respondents phrased it differently, for example, transparency and fairness, ethics by design, responsibility for ethics abuses, ethical aspects of AI, ethical/regulatory AI audits, etc.). Despite being often mentioned as a necessary skill to be added to the list, ethics related matters were not included in the list of the most important skills. The area of design-thinking skills was the least debatable. Among the possible suggestions for improvement was reducing the number of skills and grouping them.

This confirms the hypothesis that the functional AI specialist will have to have multi-disciplinary skills. However, the unexpected finding is that the experts themselves have different conceptions of how a functional AI specialist will be used in the public sector. The discussion will address this topic further.

5   Discussion

The holistic nature of the profile outlined by this research and the potential skills included also helped the experts to implicitly define the role of the functional AI specialist. The answers they gave concerning this role although varying, helped researchers identify problems with creating a standard.

Baskarada and Koronios [13] identified the challenge of hiring data scientists, a role that can be considered to be similar, although different in essence and breadth of skillset, to the conception of the functional AI specialist for the public sector that AI4GOV is developing. In mature data using organizations in the Australian government, those asked could not reach an agreement on how to hire data science personnel. Instead, they recommended conceiving of trying to hire for this role as a team effort with many people focused on different competences and skill areas rather than looking for a "unicorn." This research confirms this concept in principle. The number of technical skills identified by experts would indeed be difficult for a single person to have while also possessing the other skill groups.

The most important technical skills identified are the most common competencies in AI. But the selection of skills to be added to the list indicates that the more technical person in an organization should not be simply well-versed in the use of code for machine learning but should have in-depth knowledge about the foundations of the statistics and mathematics that comprise many of the algorithms that different AI methods use. It would be reasonable to assume that this type of person would be highly technical and with a computer science or engineering background.

The business and management skills would indicate someone closer to a product or project manager who understands the technical side enough to be able to safeguard the moral side of society. The design thinking related skills and competencies concern a professional who would ensure that the working environment and synergies between the product created and the users are maximized. It's noteworthy that the business and design categories are not opposed and could feasibly be embodied in the same person. Again, this is not to say that it is impossible for the functional AI specialist to have the relevant skills in all of the categories. However, due to the division of labour, it is unlikely that this person would do all of the tasks related to development, planning development, training and testing models, and designing everything. Even the hypothetical unicorn data scientist would be unlikely to do the design and business management parts [13].

Although the research focuses on developing a standard for a single professional, organisations should take into account collective competencies and hire teams in that fashion. The standard for the functional AI specialist should take into account a combination of skills that will be required for the role that the organization needs. This is due to the lack of agreement on a role definition for the public sector. The organization should look at how they will use the team and what the team will be required to achieve, and then decide what skills should be added, grouped in which way, and how to take into account the context.

5.1 Limitations

The research takes into account the opinions of fourteen experts, but the data is still being collected and more insights are expected from further research. Most of the experts represent the public sector with very few of them working for the private sector, while the standard is supposed to be applicable to a specialist in any kind of organisation that deals with projects related to public services. A broader set of AI specialists would represent a better data set.

5.2 Future Work

The results of the present research are expected to lay the foundation for developing a standard of a functional specialist in AI for public services, which will describe the required knowledge and skills, tasks and deliverables of such a specialist.

With more data available the occupational profile will become more precise and defined.

The developed standard is expected to be iterative and will be reviewed based on the developments in technology, policy, etc.

6 Conclusion

The original task was to define a role of a functional specialist in AI for public services to help the implementation of data and AI related projects in governments. This research underlines the importance of this position as a way understanding and judging the social impacts of AI initiatives to safeguard the values of societies as they strive to attain the UN SDGs. Currently the research suggests hiring a team of specialists that have all three categories of skills as they apply to the specific context in which the organization will engage the team.

Defining the role and competencies of a functional specialist in AI for public services is important in view of more governments aiming to employ AI in the public sector. Few public organisations consider themselves equipped with enough relevant talents to successfully run AI projects. This situation can and should potentially be fixed with the help of corresponding education programmes like, for example, AI4GOV master's programme.

The need for interdisciplinary knowledge and skills is not disputable. However, what skills exactly should be included into the profile is under debate, especially in the area of technical skills. It is desirable that list of skills does not look like a list of high-level concepts, but is concrete and applicable. At the same time, different AI related projects may require different sets of skills depending on the context. Oftentimes, making an AI-enabled project requires spreading the skills among team-members. The idea of the importance of collective competencies is also illustrated by some of the civil service competency frameworks.

Regarding the role of a functional specialist in AI for public services, there is no unanimous opinion among the AI experts. Some experts view it as a bridge that would connect the public policy and technical side, some think of it as some sort of a technical professional or data scientist. This is probably going to be a matter of a continuous discussion. The role of a functional specialist in AI for public services in each particular case may depend on a lot of factors, like the nature the AI project in a specific domain, competencies and tasks of the other team members, etc. At the same time, it is considered necessary to have a common understanding and a standard profile of a functional specialist in AI for public services to ensure that projects can be deployed with a level of success.

References

1. Aizenberg, E., Van Den Hoven, J.: Designing for human rights in AI. Big Data Soc. **7**(2), 2053951720949566 (2020)
2. Dreyling, R., Jackson, E., Tammet, T., Labanava, A., Pappel, I.: Social, legal, and technical considerations for machine learning and artificial intelligence systems in government. In: Filipe, J., Smialek, M., Brodsky, A., (eds.) Proceedings of the 23rd International Conference on Enterprise Information Systems (ICEIS 2021): Prague, 26 - 28 April 2021, Volume 1, pp. 701–708. SciTePress, Hammoudi, Slimane (2021). https://doi.org/10.5220/001045290 7010708
3. Sachs, J.D., Schmidt-Traub, G., Mazzucato, M., Messner, D., Nakicenovic, N., Rockström, J.: Six transformations to achieve the sustainable development goals. Nature sustainability **2**(9), 805–814 (2019)
4. Gupta, J., Vegelin, C.: Sustainable development goals and inclusive development. Int. Envir. Agre. Polit. Law and Econ. **16**(3), 433–448 (2016). https://doi.org/10.1007/s10784-016-9323-z

5. Shah, H.: Algorithmic accountability. Philosophical Transactions of the Royal Society A: Mathematical, Physical and Engineering Sciences **376**(2128), 20170362 (2018)
6. Cath, C., Wachter, S., Mittelstadt, B., Taddeo, M., Floridi, L.: Artificial Intelligence and the 'Good Society': the US, EU, and UK approach. Sci. Eng. Ethics **24**(2), 505–528 (2017). https://doi.org/10.1007/s11948-017-9901-7
7. Kuziemski, M., Misuraca. M.: AI governance in the public sector: three tales from the frontiers of automated decision-making in democratic settings. Telecommunications policy **44**(6), 101976 (2020)
8. Yigitcanlar, T., Corchado, J.M., Mehmood, R., Yi Man Li, R., Mossberger, K., Desouza, K.: Responsible urban innovation with local government artificial intelligence (AI): a conceptual framework and research agenda. J. Open Innov. Technol. Mark. Compl. **7**(1), 71 (2021)
9. Mensah, J.: Sustainable development: meaning, history, principles, pillars, and implications for human action: literature review. Cogent Social Sciences **5**(1), 1653531 (2019)
10. Allam, Z., Dhunny, Z.A.: On big data, artificial intelligence and smart cities. Cities **89**, 80–91 (2019)
11. Secundo, G., Ndou, V., Del Vecchio, P., De Pascale, G.: Sustainable development, intellectual capital and technology policies: a structured literature review and future research agenda. Technological Forecasting and Social Change 153 (2020). https://doi.org/10.1016/j.techfore. 2020.119917
12. Bennett, S.J.: Investigating the role of moral decision-making in emerging artificial intelligence technologies. In: Conference Companion Publication of the 2019 on Computer Supported Cooperative Work and Social Computing, pp. 28–32 (2019)
13. Baškarada, S., Koronios. A.: Unicorn data scientist: the rarest of breeds. Program (2017)
14. Alekseeva, L., Azar, J., Giné, M., Samila, S., Taska B.: The demand for AI skills in the labor market. Labour Economics, 71, issue C, number S0927537121000373 (2021)
15. Pappel, I., Oolu, K., Pappel, I., Draheim, D.: Driving Forces and Design of the TTÜ e-Governance Technologies and Services Master's Program. In: Kő, A., Francesconi, E. (eds.) EGOVIS 2017. LNCS, vol. 10441, pp. 278–293. Springer, Cham (2017). https://doi.org/10. 1007/978-3-319-64248-2_20
16. Mortati, M., Christiansen, J., Maffei, S.: Design craft in Government, Positioning Paper – Track 4, Conference Proceedings, ServDes 2018, 18-20 June, Milan, Italy. ISBN: 978-91-7685-237-8 (2018)
17. Mortati, M.: The nexus between design and policy: strong, weak, and non-design spaces in policy formulation. Des. J. **22**(6), 1–18 (2019). https://doi.org/10.1080/14606925.2019.165 1599
18. Latour, B.: Waiting for gaia: composing the common world through arts and politics. What is cosmopolitical design? Design, nature and the built environment. Routledge 2017. 41–52 (2017)
19. Batley. M.M.: AI adoption accelerated during the pandemic but many say it's moving too fast: KPMG survey. Retrieved from https://info.kpmg.us/news-perspectives/technology-inn ovation/thriving-in-an-ai-world/ai-adoption-accelerated-during-pandemic.html (2020)
20. Krishna, S., Campana, E., Chandrasekaran, S.: Thriving in AI World. KPMG. (April 2021). Retrieved from https://info.kpmg.us/content/dam/info/en/news-perspectives/pdf/2021/Upd ated%204.15.21%20-%20Thriving%20in%20an%20AI%20world.pdf (2021)
21. Snaplogic: The AI Skills Gap, https://www.snaplogic.com/resources/infographics/ai-skills-gap-research. Last accessed 14 August 2022
22. Deloitte: Future in the balance. How countries are pursuing an AI advantage? Deloitte Center for Technology, Media and Telecommunications report, https://www2.deloitte.com/content/ dam/Deloitte/lu/Documents/public-sector/lu-global-ai-survey.pdf. Last accessed 14 August 2022

23. Zuiderwijk, A., Chen, Y.-C., Salem, F.: Implications of the use of artificial intelligence in public governance: A systematic literature review and a research agenda. Government Information Quarterly **38**(3), 101577 (2021). https://doi.org/10.1016/j.giq.2021.101577, ISSN 0740-624X

24. Microsoft: Artificial Intelligence in the Public Sector. European Outlook for 2020 and Beyond. How 213 Public Organizations Benefit from AI. Report commissioned by Microsoft and conducted by EY, https://info.microsoft.com/rs/157-GQE-382/images/EN-CNTNT-eBook-artificial-SRGCM3835.pdf. Last accessed 14 August 2022

25. Squicciarini, M., Nachtigall, H.: OECD Working Paper. Demand for AI Skills in Jobs: Evidence from Online Job Posting. 25 Mar 2021 No. 2021/03 (2021). https://doi.org/10.1787/3ed32d94-en

26. Samek, L., Squicciarini, M., Cammeraat. E.: OECD Science, Technology and Industry Policy Papers No. 120. 22 Sep 2021. The Human Capital Behind AI. Jobs and Skills Demand from Online Jobs Postings (2021). https://doi.org/10.1787/2e278150-en

27. LinkedIn: Jobs on the Rise in 2021. United States Report, https://business.linkedin.com/talent-solutions/resources/talent-acquisition/jobs-on-the-rise-us. Last accessed 14 August 2022

28. Roca, T.: AI Talent in the European Labour Market. LinkedIn Economic Graph. (November 2019), https://economicgraph.linkedin.com/content/dam/me/economicgraph/en-us/PDF/AI-TAlent-in-the-European-Labour-Market.pdf. Last accessed 14 August 2022

29. UK Government: 9 Key Findings from Understanding the UK AI Labour Market: 2020 Report, 9 key findings from Understanding the UK AI labour market: 2020 Report - GOV.UK (www.gov.uk), last accessed 14 August 2022

30. LinkedIn: Jobs on the Rise. United Kingdom Report, Jobs on the Rise | United Kingdom (linkedin.com), last accessed 14 August 2022

31. LinkedIn: Jobs on the Rise. Spain Report, https://business.linkedin.com/es-es/talent-solutions/resources/talent-acquisition/jobs-on-the-rise-cont-fact, Last accessed 14 August 2022

32. LinkedIn: Jobs on the Rise. France Report, https://business.linkedin.com/fr-fr/talent-solutions/resources/talent-acquisition/jobs-on-the-rise-cont-fact, last accessed 14 August 2022

33. OECD: Core Skills for Public Sector Innovation. (April 2017). https://www.oecd.org/media/oecdorg/satellitesites/opsi/contents/files/OECD_OPSI-core_skills_for_public_sector_innovation-201704.pdf, last accessed 14 August 2022

34. Agenzia per l'Italia Digitale: Competenze di e-leadership, 2. Principi e strategie per la mappatura e la valorizzazione (lg-competenzedigitali.readthedocs.io), last accessed 14 August 2022

35. UK Government: Civil Service Competency Framework 2012–2017. Civil Service Human Resources, cscf_fulla4potrait_2013–2017_v2d.pdf (publishing.service.gov.uk), last accessed 14 August 2022

36. Riigikantselei: Competency Framework, https://riigikantselei.ee/en/supporting-government-and-prime-minister/top-civil-service/competency-framework#innovation-booster, last accessed 14 August 2022

37. Public Administration School of Catalonia: Competency framework for innovative professionals in public administrations. Public Administration School of Catalonia. (July 1, 2020), Comptetency framework for innovative professionals in public administrations (gencat.cat), last accessed 14 August 2022

38. Yin, R.K.: Case Study Research Design and Methods. Thousand Oaks, CA: Sage, p. 282

39. Carter, L., Bélanger. F.: The utilization of e-government services: citizen trust, innovation and acceptance factors. Information Systems Journal **15**(1), 5–25 (2005)

40. Colesca, S.E.: Understanding trust in e-government. Engineering Economics **63**(3) (2009)

On the Feasibility of Machine Learning Models for Customer Spending Prediction Problem

Khang Nguyen Hoang, Long Bui Thanh, Tien Nguyen Thi Thuy,
Cuong Nguyen Quoc, and Tran Tri Dang[✉]

School of Science, Engineering and Technology (SSET), RMIT University,
Ho Chi Minh City, Vietnam
{s3802040,s3748575,s3757934,s3748840,tri.dangtran}@rmit.edu.vn

Abstract. Over the last few years, FinTech (Financial Technology) companies have played a significant role in supporting e-commerce processes and transactions. For individual users, more convenient payment methods were invented to help them purchase more easily. For businesses, it's now a lot easier to understand customers than ever, especially in knowing how they spend their money. In fact, the capability of predicting customer spending power over a period of time is a crucial task for marketers in making strategic decisions about advertising. However, it is not trivial to build such an automatic prediction system due to the numerous models and metrics available combined with the ad-hoc nature of personal purchases. In this paper, as the first step in tackling the above-mentioned problem, we explored the feasibility of applying different machine learning models and metrics to predict customer spending under different contexts. In particular, we applied Beta Geometric/Negative Binomial distribution (BG/NBD), Gamma-gamma, Linear Regression, Random Forest, and Light Gradient Boosting Machine (LightGBM) models to train and predict customer spending. Experimenting with anonymized real-world data supplied by one of the biggest payment providers in Vietnam provided us with valuable insights into the suitability of each model. The result of this research can serve as a foundation for more in-depth work on the same problem in the future.

Keywords: Customer spending prediction, machine learning model ·
Tree-based model · Statistical model

1 Introduction

Customer Lifetime Value (CLV)[1] is a prognostication of the net profit contributed to the whole future relationship with a customer. Customer spending refers to the total money amount individuals and families spend on goods and services for personal use and enjoyment. There were many attempts to forecast customer spending using traditional macroeconomic predictor factors, namely: customer satisfaction [1], sentiment

---

[1] https://en.wikipedia.org/wiki/Customer_lifetime_value.

T. K. Dang et al. (Eds.): FDSE 2022, CCIS 1688, pp. 517–531, 2022.
https://doi.org/10.1007/978-981-19-8069-5_35

[2], or their financial condition [3]. Altogether, these models produce few insights and frequently conclude that customer spending follows a random-walk process [4].

Accurate customer spending prediction brings significant benefits to businesses. Companies can incentivize customers' spending by learning and understanding each person's habits. For example, by knowing the average amount a customer is willing to spend for goods, businesses could encourage her to buy more for prizes such as a coupon [5]. The information is specifically beneficial to marketing and branding campaigns in which marketers can group customers based on their portfolio and choose the target group more effectively. Technology advancements in areas such as machine learning and big data make building such prediction models feasible. In this paper, we describe our work on developing and analyzing machine learning models to predict customer spending under different contexts. Our main goal is to understand the suitability of each model for specific types of customers, spending behaviors, prediction periods, etc. Unlike the CLV problem, our research focuses on near future forecasting only.

The structure of the paper is as follows. In Sect. 2, we present related work. The proposed solutions and its architecture are presented in Sect. 3. In Sect. 4, we describe the details of data collection for each model. Section 5 presents and compares the performances between models. Finally, in Sect. 6, we draw a conclusion and suggest potential future improvements.

2 Related Work

There are many studies around building a machine learning model to learn about the customers. Traditional marketing, like brand loyalty and sale events, is not enough for the expected return on investment [6]. To know how the customer is valuable to the business, CLV is a reliable metric to estimate [18]. Although our research problem focuses on forecasting customer spending in a near future with a flexible time frame, it can be seen as a variant of the CLV problem. In the CLV area, Cui and Curry conducted extensive Monte Carlo simulations to compare predictions based on the multinomial logit model and Support-Vector Machine (SVM) [7]. In all cases, SVM out predicted the logit model. In their simulation, the overall mean prediction rate of the logit was 72.7%, whereas the hit rate for SVM was 85.9%. The results prove the effectiveness of machine learning models in this field. In the video game industry, Chen et al. suggested that convolutional neural network structures are the most efficient in predicting the economic value of individual players [8]. According to Chen et al.'s research, they perform better in terms of accuracy, scale to big data, and significantly reduce computational time. Furthermore, they can work directly with raw sequential data and thus do not require any feature engineering process.

Feature engineering and data cleaning techniques for predicting the next purchase are employed in our research. Martínez et al. [9] focused on the future customer behavior prediction for managing resources in marketing and sales departments. The predicted behaviors support making strategic decisions during production, and inventory planning at the warehouse. Logistic Lasso Regression, Extreme Learning Machine, and Gradient tree boosting were evaluated. The data was given by a large manufacturer located in central Europe, from January 2009 until May 2015, with around 190,000 orders for all customers [9]. The author also applies 10-fold cross-validation to prevent overfitting problems on the training data set. Therefore, the models were more generalizable to predict the unknown outcome where the prediction was for the next-month purchase. The limitation of this work compared to ours is that it can predict customer spending in the next month only, while our system can predict any period.

In another paper [10], the researchers proposed a solution for predicting what items will be bought later, after the customers make their purchases. The authors proposed Customer Purchase Prediction model, which is a two-stage method. Firstly, they study product correlations to predict client preferences. Secondly, they learn customers' product preferences to determine which prospective products are most likely to be bought.

Martínez et al. research [9] proposed a solution to determine whether the user will purchase anything shortly. Meanwhile, Qiu et al.'s paper [1] predicted what associate goods based on the previous one be bought in the next purchase. Together, the two papers can predict what products would be purchased in a different period and forecast the sales at a specific time.

3   Proposed Method

This section introduces two statistical models and three machine learning models that we implemented. The two selected statistical models are the BG/NBD model and the Gamma-gamma sub-model. Meanwhile, the three machine learning models include Linear Regression, Random Forest and LightGBM.

3.1   Statistical Models

BG/NBD
BG/NBD [11] is a statistical model that is used to estimate the number of transactions that an individual is going to make in the future. The model makes various assumptions:

- At any point in time, a customer can decide to make a transaction.
- Probability of buying is unique for each user and follows Poisson distribution.
- Each customer can churn after a transaction.
- Probability of churn is unique for each user and follows beta distribution.

The model carries out two processes: transaction process and dropout process. Transaction process follows Poisson distribution with λ varies among customers following gamma distribution with shape r and scale α. The dropout process with probability p varies among customers following beta distribution with shape parameters a and b. The equation of this model can be expressed as following:

$$E(Y(t)|X = x, t_x, T, r, \alpha, a, b) =$$

$$\frac{a+b+x-1}{a-1} * \frac{\left[1 - \left(\frac{\alpha+T}{\alpha+T+t}\right)^{r+x} {}_2F_1\left(r+x, b+x; a+b+x-1; \frac{t}{\alpha+T+t}\right)\right]}{1 + \delta_{x>0}\frac{a}{b+x-1}\left(\frac{\alpha+T}{\alpha+t_x}\right)^{r+x}} \quad (1)$$

where Y(t) is the expected number of transactions for each customer, x is the frequency of each customer, t_x points to the recency and T represents the range between today and the last purchasing date.

Gamma-Gamma Sub-model

Gamma-Gamma sub-model [16] is another statistical model for making forecasts on average profit for each customer. The model assumes the average transaction values vary across customers but do not vary over time for any given individual. Average transaction values vary among customers following gamma distribution with parameters y, p and q. Refer to the Gamma-Gamma model formula below:

$$E(M|p,q,m_x,x) = \frac{\gamma + m_x x}{p_x + q - 1} = \left(\frac{q-1}{px+q-1}\right) * \frac{\gamma p}{q-1} + \left(\frac{px}{px+q-1}\right) m_x \quad (2)$$

where m_x represents the monetary value of each customer and M is the expected value of transactions.

To make forecasts on customers' spending, these two statistical models are implemented and their results are multiplied with each other. The BG/NBD estimates the number of transactions. Meanwhile, the Gamma-Gamma sub-model forecasts the average profit of each transaction. Multiplying the two gives us the forecast on the total spending.

3.2 Machine Learning Models

Linear Regression

Linear Regression is a ubiquitous approach for financial forecasting modeling [12, 13]. The approach is used extensively in practical applications due to its simplicity to implement and explainability to non-technical parties. Multiple linear regression (MLR) is one of the linear regression models where there are one dependent variable and multiple independent variables of which parameters are linear [14]. The point of implementing MLR is to discover the relationships between the known independent variables and the dependent variable. These relationships are expressed mathematically in the form coefficients. The mathematical representation of a MLR model can be written as:

$$y_t = \beta_0 + \beta_1 x_{1t} + \beta_2 x_{2t} + \ldots + \beta_k x_{kt} + \varepsilon_t (t = 1, 2, \ldots, n) \quad (3)$$

where y is the dependent variable and x are the independent variables. β represents the population slope coefficients of each variable. In the context of this paper, y is a customer spending prediction; x are the lag features and customer-related data.

Random Forest

Random Forest is a Supervised Machine Learning algorithm that is frequently employed in Classification and Regression issues [15]. It is an ensemble algorithm known as Bagging or Bootstrap Aggregation. In this algorithm, Bootstrap is a statistical technique for estimating data sample statistics. Usually, the estimated result contains large errors with small sample size. To enhance the result, the means of several random subsamples are computed together. The architecture of Random Forest is depicted in Fig. 1.

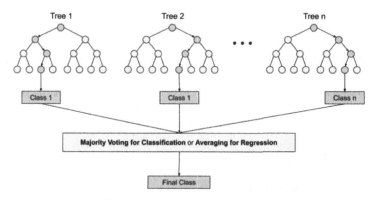

Fig. 1. Random forest architecture.

With Random Forest, the algorithm trains several Decision Tree models from bootstrapped samples with replacement in parallel [15]. The output is produced in the final aggregation stage, combining all sub-model outputs based on majority voting [15] as shown in Fig. 1. This step is most effective when the sub-models are minimally correlated [15]. Therefore, random forest limits random features set for individual trees. As a result, each tree is unique with less feature space. We determine the feature importance by calculating and averaging the drop in error [15] (sum squared error and Gini score for regression and classification respectively) at each feature split point. The feature importance score increases with the drop level.

LightGBM

Since Microsoft announced LightGBM, it is widely used due to its efficiency, accuracy and high-speed. This algorithm is based on the Gradient Boosting Decision Tree algorithm (GBDT). LightGBM can tackle the problem of GBDT because GBDT must make a tradeoff between accuracy and efficiency. For each feature, to calculate the information gain of possible split points, the algorithm must go through all data instances. Therefore, as the number of features and instances increases, the computational complexity increases. Hence, dealing with big data is time consuming [14].

The LightGBM can successfully prevent extra computation for zero feature values by bundling numerous exclusive features to fewer dense features. By constructing a table for each feature to store the data with nonzero values, it may improve the fundamental histogram-based approach towards disregarding the zero feature values. In short, Light-GBM safely identifies such features and bundles them into a single feature to reduce the complexity to O(#data * #bundle) instead of O(#data * #features) where #bundle is smaller than #feature [14].

4 Experiment

In this section, we perform experiments with the aforementioned models. The section covers the data preparation method, experiment setups, and chosen performance metrics.

4.1 Data for Statistical Models

The data are available from 01/07/2020 to 31/12/2021 and will be used to build and test the statistical model approach. The data will be divided into two parts: one from 01/07/2020 to 31/11/2021 is used as calibration data to fit the statistical model; the leftover from 01/12/2021 to 31/12/2021 is used to benchmark the performance of the fitted model.

The statistical models are built around four predictors:

- Recency: number of days since a customer's last purchase;
- Monetary: The average or total sales value of the customer;
- Frequency: Number of transactions;
- Age: number of days since the date of a customer's first purchase.

For all of these predictors, they can be derived from the historical transaction data. This set of predictors is fitted into the BG/NBD model and the model will predict the number of purchases each customer would make in the next one month. Meanwhile, the Gamm-Gamma model then accepts frequency and monetary then predicts the average spending amount for each customer. Combining the two results gives us the predicted customer spending in the next one month.

4.2 Data for Machine Learning Models

The crucial log we are interested in is the Transaction Log. Besides, we collect some data from user profiles. We would further engineer these features before fitting them into the Machine Learning models.

Feature Generation

To convert the time-series transaction log to tabular data, we aggregate the transaction amount (statistical data revolve around the amount of money spent by customers), transaction count (the number of transactions), and other transaction-related information for each customer from the past up to a specific time. We call this time "standing point". We compute min, max, sum, and average transaction amount over the last 1, 2, 3, 7, 30, 60, 90, and 180 days. The intuition is that we want to capture what happened in previous days and months together with a farer past events.

On the other hand, we use the future data after this point together with lead_time and duration to compute our target values, spending amount in the future. For example, if the lead time value is seven and the duration period is three, we calculate the future spending amount for three days starting at seven days from now. Both lead time and duration have randomized values from 0 to 30.

We have 24-month data (2020 to 2022) to specify the standing points as the first date of each month starting from 1/7/2020 to 1/11/2021. The duration to generate sample features is six months before the standing point. Whereas, the duration to generate the target value is two months after the standing point.

Dataset Preparation Procedure

We have a daily transaction log. However, one customer can have multiple transactions per day. Firstly, we aggregate the daily transaction log for each customer. In the second step, we aggregate the transaction-related features for customers at each standing point. After this step, we have 18 datasets for each standing point. Next, we join the aggregated transaction-related-feature-only datasets with customer data from the user profile log and save them. We save the 2021–11-01 dataset as our test set. Meanwhile, we merge the datasets for other months for the train set. The train and test set has 4,549,835 and 894,825 samples respectively with five categorical features and 78 numerical features.

Experiment Setup

Train models on the whole dataset.

In this experiment setup, we train one model for each algorithm with the whole dataset. However, 75% of the dataset has a target value of zero due to the churn users or small duration values. Meanwhile, the max target value could reach 100M. Therefore, the dataset is very imbalanced. We will try to target this problem by building different models for different groups in the following experiment setup.

Because there are many experiment setups, we will only choose the best performing algorithm on the whole dataset for the follow-up experiment setup.

Train models based on user quality.

In this experiment setup, we build three models for three different groups of user quality. There are three user quality levels: active (high, low) and churn.

- Churn users: Users don't have any transactions within three months.
- High-quality users: Active (not churn) users who make transactions monthly for the last three months.
- Low-quality users: Active users but not high-quality users.

75% of churn users don't spend in our prediction period compared to only 25% of high-quality users. Moreover, lag features would make a higher impact with high-quality users because the values for each month are different. Whereas, for churn users, lag features for 30 days, 60 days, and 90 days are the same.

Train models based on duration and lead.

Duration and lead values are uniformly distributed between 0 and 30. The longer the duration, the higher the amount the customers spend. Meanwhile, the farther the lead time (prediction to be in the far future), the less accurate the forecast is. In this experiment setup, we split the dataset into three segments of duration and three segments of lead time and train nine models for all combinations of duration period and lead time segments. Table 1 displays our segmentation details.

Table 1. Duration and lead segments.

Lead	Duration
Close lead (lead $< = 7$ days)	Short duration (duration $< = 7$ days)
	Medium duration ($7 <$ duration $< = 14$ days)

(continued)

Table 1. (*continued*)

Lead	Duration
	Long duration (duration > 14 days)
Medium lead (7 < lead < = 14 days)	Short duration (duration < = 7 days)
	Medium duration (7 < duration < = 14 days)
	Long duration (duration > 14 days)
Far lead (lead > 14 days)	Short duration (duration < = 7 days)
	Medium duration (7 < duration < = 14 days)
	Long duration (duration > 14 days)

Evaluation Metrics.

Table 2. Evaluation metrics.

	Pros	Cons	Justification & Consideration
RMSE	Can penalize outliers. Provide a more complete picture on error distribution. Easy to interpret. Keeps the original units. [17]	Can't compare different units. Sensitive to outliers	It is the most common metric for the time-series problem. We are forecasting customer spending, with wealthy customers usually being the minority. Large errors are undesirable because we would target the wrong groups of customers
MAE	Simple, interpretable. Better for uniform error distribution. Keeps the original units. [17]	Can't compare different units and penalize outliers	It is simple and interpretable that tells us the average of actual errors. We might have unusually large values due to seasonal campaigns. We don't want our model to be too sensitive to these outliers. Hence, we want to use MAE with RMSE to have different views

(*continued*)

Table 2. (*continued*)

	Pros	Cons	Justification & Consideration
MAPE	Scale independence and ease of interpretation. Compare between different units	Doesn't work well with zero or near-zero values. Percentage error can make no sense	A percentage gives a better idea of how accurate the model is. However, we need to filter out customers with zero spending. Moreover, the error might be misleading because while the percentages are equal, the absolute errors are way higher for the higher values

Looking at one metric alone is not enough. We need to look at our model in different angles to have a more accurate estimation of our model performance. We evaluate our model by calculating Root Mean Squared Error (RMSE), Mean Absolute Error (MAE), and Mean Absolute Percentage Error (MAPE) (Table 2).

5   Result and Discussion

5.1   Statistical Model

Table 3. Performance of statistical model.

	RMSE (VND)	MAE (VND)	MAPE (%)
30 days	765,629	15,646	8,206
14 days	729,752	7,555	2,429
7 days	731,364	3,716	1,066

The results are benchmarked forecasts results made by the statistical model on the test dataset in three timespan variances: 7 days, 14 days, and 30 days. Overall, for MAE and MAPE, as the value of timespan increases, the model forecasts resulted in worse performance (Table 3). However, the RMSE metric did not follow the pattern of the other two metrics and remained relatively the same with the best value at VND 731,364 on the seven days forecast. The best MAE result is at the seven days timespan with VND 3,716 and appears to have doubled as the timespan doubled. Lastly, for the MAPE value, the model performed worst at 82.06 on the 30 days forecast. Even with the best one at 10.66 in seven days, it is still considered as bad, subjectively, compared to the corresponding value of other models.

5.2   Machine Learning Models

Build Models on the Whole Dataset

Table 4. Model performance for Linear Regression, Random Forest, and LightGBM.

	RMSE	MAE	MAPE
Train set			
Linear Regression	1,151,463	278,539	8.19
Random Forest	2,156,706	284,502	9.85
LightGBM	1,151,513	305,382	13.06
Test set			
Linear Regression	878,323	270,435	7.40
Random Forest	1,092,498	270,060	6.80
LightGBM	863,647	287,599	7.50

When looking at Table 4, the performance of the Linear Regression and LightGBM models are similar and better than that of Random Forest. Since the Random Forest model has significantly higher RMSE in both train and test set, we can conclude that it is more affected by high spenders compared to the other two algorithms. Meanwhile, the three models have quite similar MAPE values which are around 7. All metrics errors on the train set are higher than the test set, indicating that the models generalize well on the unseen data. For the follow-up experiment setup, we will choose LightGBM to build the models.

Train Models Based on User Quality.
Based on their spending patterns, we categorize users into three groups: Churn User, Low User, and High User. The training and testing performance for all groups are presented in Table 5.

Table 5. Model performance of all sub-models by user quality.

	RMSE Train	MAE Train	MAPE Train
Train set			
Churn User	675,863	137,321	10.48
Low User	1,244,619	353,179	11.81
High User	1,905,922	719,539	10.60
Aggregation Result	1,131,753	295,672	13.41
Original Result (Whole dataset)	1,151,513	305,382	13.06

(*continued*)

Table 5. (*continued*)

	RMSE Train	MAE Train	MAPE Train
Test set			
Churn User	473,243	133,036	5
Low User	989,396	350,797	7.80
High User	1,586,081	664,269	11.00
Aggregation Result	859,330	274,024	7.50
Original Result (Whole dataset)	**863,647**	**287,599**	**7.50**

In general, the aggregation result after training three sub-models by user quality is slightly better in all metrics in both train and test set compared to the original result. However, the improvement between the aggregation results and the original dataset is quite small (4,000 VND and 10,000 VND for RMSE and MAE respectively). When looking at each sub-model's performance, the churn users' errors are lower than the low-quality users' errors which is lower than the high-quality users' errors. Intuitively, churn users tend not to spend anymore. From exploring the dataset, we observe that the percentages of target values equal zero are 68%, 36% and 0.7% for churn, low-, and high-quality users respectively.

Train Models Based on Lead and Duration.

Table 6. Model performance of all sub-models by lead & duration.

	RMSE Train	MAE Train	MAPE Train
Train set			
Close Lead			
Small Duration	1,000,968	271,184	12.37
Medium Duration	1,165,965	304,141	13.65
Long Duration	1,116,193	319,955	13.57
Medium Lead			
Small Duration	991,497	273,422	12.25
Medium Duration	1,086,570	294,880	12.66
Long Duration	1,167,025	319,746	13.63
Far Lead			
Small Duration	1,090,937	280,388	12.19
Medium Duration	1,091,708	289,560	7.33
Long Duration	1,159,745	318,801	13.56

(*continued*)

Table 6. (*continued*)

	RMSE Train	MAE Train	MAPE Train
Aggregation Result	1,125,461	304,343	13.16
Original Result (Whole dataset)	1,151,513	305,382	13.06
Test set			
Close Lead			
Small Duration	827,762	259,003	7.40
Medium Duration	715,580	280,768	7.40
Long Duration	856,991	302,284	7.90
Medium Lead			
Small Duration	805,547	264,695	6.70
Medium Duration	888,146	276,806	7.00
Long Duration	928,619	305,233	7.60
Far Lead			
Small Duration	929,573	266,595	7.20
Medium Duration	850,753	274,671	7.30
Long Duration	859,750	300,605	7.70
Aggregation Result	**863,680**	**287,024**	**7.50**
Original Result (Whole dataset)	**863,647**	**287,599**	**7.50**

In general, the aggregated results after training nine sub-models by lead and duration segments show no improvement compared to the original model (Table 6). When comparing individual models, we also see that the errors of all models for all metrics are not significantly different.

By averaging the results group by lead segment, we can observe in Fig. 2 that farer lead segment not resulting in less accurate results. There are two possible reasons for this. Firstly, the original assumption is not valid. Secondly, our models perform badly in all cases. From this, we could either revalidate our assumptions or try to tune the models for better results. Because we use the same feature sets for all nine models, this can also become the reason for not improving the performance.

In Fig. 3, by averaging the results group by duration segment, we can observe that longer duration segments tend to result in higher errors which hold true to our original assumptions.

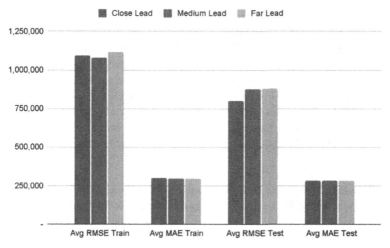

Fig. 2. Average results group by lead for all sub models by lead & duration.

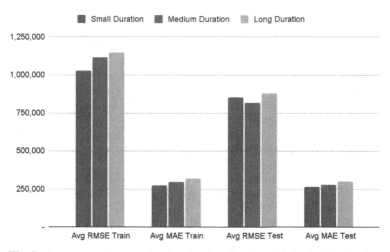

Fig. 3. Average results group by duration for all sub models by lead & duration

6   Conclusion and Future Work

To sum up, in this paper, there are some proposed methods including statistical models and traditional machine learning models to predict customer spending in the future based on their historical behavior.

The extracted findings during this work are summarized as follows. The statistical model is not flexible enough to make predictions based on different lead and duration input. Its input must be a constant and stick to one lead and one duration. For the machine learning model, the input can be flexible to any lead and duration which is a huge advantage compared to the others. To increase the performance, we have experimented with different setup, splitting on the input (lead, duration) or by user's quality. By splitting them into different models, we can capture the trend of the duration as larger it is, the error is larger when building the segmented models related to lead and duration. However, there is no significant improvement based on different types of splits.

As future work, the plan is to focus on building a machine learning model to optimize the result and its speed. The proposed solution is to conduct a different feature set for each type of segment model. For example, the model with close lead and small duration should not include lag features larger than 30 days and so on. Besides, if the customers are identified as a churn user, they will be predicted by the churn user model. Otherwise, their input goes into lead and duration segment models based on their lead and duration input.

Acknowledgement. This project would not have been possible without the guidance from the ZaloPay's technical mentor. He had given us plenty of dedicated feedbacks in the project. Besides, we would like to thank ZaloPay for allowing us to access the anonymized payment data. Without it, our work would not be further processed.

References

1. Fornell, C., Rust. R.T., Dekimpe, M.G., The effect of customer satisfaction on consumer spending growth. Journal of Marketing Research **47**(1), 28–35 (2010). https://doi.org/10.1509/jmkr.47.1.28 Accessed 12 April 2022
2. Mehra, Y.P., Martin, E.: Why Does Consumer Sentiment Predict Household Spending?. FRB Richmond Economic Quarterly **89**(4), pp. 51–67 (Fall 2003). Available at SSRN: https://ssrn.com/abstract=2184918 Accessed 12 April 2022
3. Shea, J.: Myopia, Liquidity Constraints, and Aggregate Consumption: A Simple Test. Journal of Money, Credit and Banking **27**(3), 798–805 (1995). https://doi.org/10.2307/2077751. Accessed 12 April 2022
4. Hall, R.: Stochastic Implications of the Life Cycle-Permanent Income Hypothesis: Theory and Evidence. Journal of Political Economy **86**(6), 971–987 (1978). https://doi.org/10.1086/260724 Accessed 12 April 2022
5. Fay, J.: In Search of Spending — Part 1. Medium (2022). [Online]. Available: https://medium.com/swlh/in-search-of-spending-part-1-b50487c0f55a. Accessed: 12 Apr 2022
6. Yoo, S., Hanssens, D.: Modeling the Sales and Customer Equity Effects of the Marketing Mix. UCLA Anderson School of Management (2022)
7. Cui, D., Curry, D.: Prediction in Marketing Using the Support Vector Machine. Marketing Science **24**(4), 595–615 (2005). Accessed: 12 Apr 2022
8. Chen, P., Guitart, A., del Rio, A., Perianez, A.: Customer lifetime value in video games using deep learning and parametric models. In: 2018 IEEE International Conference on Big Data (Big Data) (2018). Accessed: 12 Apr 2022
9. Martínez, A., Schmuck, C., Pereverzyev, S., Pirker, C., Haltmeier, M.: A machine learning framework for customer purchase prediction in the non-contractual setting. European Journal of Operational Research **281**(3), 588–596 (2020). Accessed: 12 Apr 2022
10. Qiu, J., Lin, Z., Li, Y.: Predicting customer purchase behavior in the e-commerce context. Electronic Commerce Research **15**(4), 427–452 (2015). Accessed: 12 Apr 2022
11. Fader, P.S., Hardie, B.G.S., Lee, K.L.: Counting your customers the easy way: an alternative to the Pareto/NBD Model. Mark. Sci. **24**(2), 275–284 (2005)

12. Yuan, M., Ekici, A., Lu, Z., Monteiro, R.: Dimension reduction and coefficient estimation in multivariate linear regression. Journal of the Royal Statistical Society: Series B (Statistical Methodology) **69**(3), 329–346 (2007)
13. Marill, K.: Advanced statistics: linear regression, part i: simple linear regression. Acad. Emerg. Med. **11**(1), 87–93 (2004)
14. Chen, X., Jun, H.U., Deng, J.: Weight correction model of condition assessment for substation equipment based on multiple linear regression method. High Voltage Apparatus **53**(1), 14–19 (2017)
15. Brownlee, J.: Bagging and Random Forest Ensemble Algorithms for Machine Learning. Machine Learning Mastery (2022). [Online]. Available: https://machinelearningmastery.com/bagging-and-random-forest-ensemble-algorithms-for-machine-learning/. Accessed: 06 Aug 2022
16. Fader, S.P., Hardie, G.S.B.: The Gamma-Gamma Model of Monetary Value (2022). [online] Brucehardie.com. Available at: <http://www.brucehardie.com/notes/025/gamma_gamma.pdf> Accessed 14 September 2022
17. Chai, T., Draxler, R.: Root mean square error (RMSE) or mean absolute error (MAE)? – Arguments against avoiding RMSE in the literature. Geoscientific Model Development **7**(3), 1247–1250 (2014). https://doi.org/10.5194/gmd-7-1247-2014 Accessed 14 September 2022
18. Castéran, H., Waarden, L.M., Reinartz, W.: Modeling Customer Lifetime Value, Retention, and Churn. Springer. [Online]. Available: https://doi.org/10.1007/978-3-319-57413-4_21.pdf

Forecasting the Opening and Closing Price Trends of Stock Using Hybrid Models and Artificial Intelligence Algorithm

Nguyen Dinh Thuan[✉], Nguyen Minh Nhut, Nguyen Thi Viet Huong, and Dang Vu Phuong Uyen

University of Information Technology, VNU-HCM, Ho Chi Minh, Vietnam
thuannd@uit.edu.vn, {17520867,19521595,19520345}@gm.uit.edu.vn

Abstract. The stock has been a long-standing and potential investment field until now, attracting much investment in this field every year. In particular, favorite stocks such as Dow Jones Industrial Average (DJIA), Tesla Inc (TSLA), and Meta Platforms Inc (META) have attracted many investments in recent years. The volatility of stock prices is very unpredictable, causing many difficulties for investors in this field. Furthermore, this study uses artificial intelligence models such as Autoregressive Integrated Moving Average (ARIMA), Support Vector Regression (SVR), Linear Regression (LR), and Gated Recurrent Unit (GRU) to predict closing prices and opening prices of three stock DJIA, TSLA, and META. Furthermore, proposing hybrid methods of the above models to improve and improve the accuracy of stock price prediction. The comparison results will be based on three evaluation parameters: RMSE, MAE, and MAPE.

Keywords: DJIA prediction · TSLA prediction · META prediction · Artificial intelligence · Deep learning · Machine learning · ARIMA · SVR · LR · GRU · Hybrid model

1 Introduction

Stock price prediction is an area of investment and research with a lot of potential and challenges in recent years. Investing in securities is no longer a new topic, yet it still attracts many investors to this field every year and is expected to remain a hot topic in the coming years. Besides, famous stocks such as Dow Jones Industrial Average (DJIA) [1], Tesla Inc (TSLA) [2], and Meta Platforms Inc (META) [3] are attracting investors' attention today. However, the movements of these securities are very unpredictable and make it difficult for investors to decide about buying and selling securities.

Many studies on stock price prediction have yielded quite positive results. However, the results of these methods are still limited and need more research and proposals to help predict more accurately about stock prices. In this study, we use models in artificial intelligence and regression to solve the following problems:

© The Author(s), under exclusive license to Springer Nature Singapore Pte Ltd. 2022
T. K. Dang et al. (Eds.): FDSE 2022, CCIS 1688, pp. 532–546, 2022.
https://doi.org/10.1007/978-981-19-8069-5_36

- First, use existing stock prediction single models to predict the prices of three stocks DJIA, TSLA, and META.
- Second, propose a new method (using the hybrid model) to improve accuracy.
- Finally, compare the hybrid and single models to find the model with the best accuracy in this study to predict future stock prices.

2 Related Works

Khaled A. Althelaya et al. [4] conducted S&P500 price predictions from 2010 to 2017 through two variants of Deep Recurrent Neural Network, stacked LSTM, bidirectional LSTM, and bidirectional GRU. This study adjusted the units and epochs and used the MAE, RMSE, and R-Squared indexes to rate the models. The results show that the SLSTM model achieves optimal results than the remaining models.

Mohammad Almasarweh et al. [5] study forecasting ASE bank stock market data using the ARIMA model. Through RMSE, they predicted the closing price of ASE and selected parameters suitable for the above data set with ARIMA (1,1,2) having an optimal RMSE evaluation index more than other models with the same value is 1.4.

Searching for kernels in the SVR model gives better prediction results between kernels when predicting daily and minute prices of various stock prices such as BBAS3, PETR4, and many others. Bruno Miranda Henrique et al. [6] used RMSE and MAPE indexes to evaluate the fit between Linear kernel, Radial kernel, and Polynomial kernel.

Gourav Bathla's research [7] on predicting stock price using LSTM and SVR. In it, LSTM is compared with SVR to predict S&P 500, NYSE, NSE, BSE, NASDAQ, and Dow Jones Industrial Average for testing and analysis. The results show that LSTM shows more accuracy than SVR.

Mehar Vijh et al. [8] researched stock closing price prediction using machine learning techniques. In this work, Artificial Neural Network and Random Forest techniques are used for predicting the next day's closing price for five companies operating in different fields based on evaluation through 2 parameters, RMSE and MAPE. The results show that ANN is better than RF because it gives better RMSE and MAPE values.

The authors [9], to deal with the nonlinearity in the data, proposed a hybrid model between the prediction rule ensembles (PRE) technique and deep neural network (DNN). The dataset used in this study uses The Indian stock price data. Prediction results are based on the mean absolute error (MAE) and the RMSE. Results show that the performance of the hybrid prediction model is better than that of the single prediction model. DNN and ANN with RMSE parameters improved from 5% to 7%.

3 Research Method

3.1 Linear Regression Model

Regression is a supervised learning algorithm. A regression model is a model that describes the relationship between a set of independent variables and one or more dependencies [10]. Linear regression is both a statistical algorithm and a machine learning algorithm. Regression has the following general expression:

$$f(x) = a + bX$$

In there, $f(x)$ is the output, X is the input, a is constant, and b is the coefficient of the linear equation. The Linear Regression (LR) model is illustrated with the following formula:

$$f(x) = w_0 + w_1x_1 + \ldots + w_nx_n$$

In there, w_0, w_1, w_n are the regression coefficients. An illustrative case for this algorithm is shown in Fig. 1 below.

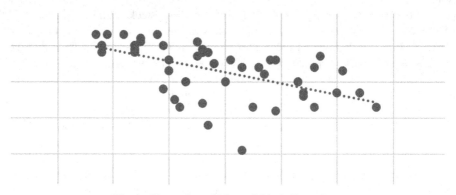

Fig. 1. Illustration of LR model in 2-dimensions

3.2 ARIMA Model

Autoregressive Integrated Moving Average (ARIMA), one of the classic models in time series forecasting research, combines the autoregression model - AR (a linear model that predicts current value based on past values) and moving average model - MA (which is a linear model of the current value based on past errors) and adjust the order d of difference I to ensure a stationary series [11] Adjusting the ARIMA series to a stationary series result in time-constant mean and variance.

Like the ARIMA model, ARMA is created from a combination of two linear models AR and MA. However, the value of order d of the difference I is now 0. So, the equation of the ARMA model [5]:

$$ARMA(p, q) = AR - MA(q)$$

Nevertheless, there is an additional difference I for ARIMA (p, d, q) [5]:

$$ARIMA(p, d, q) = AR(p) + I(d) - MA(q)$$

The two parameters p and q are the numbers of lagged observations used as predictors in the AR model and the number of past error values used as predictors in the AR model, respectively. MA model.

Besides, we have the entire equation of the autoregression model [11]:

$$AR(p) = Y_t = c_1 + \alpha_1 Y_{t-1} + \alpha_2 Y_{t-2} + \ldots + \alpha_p Y_{t-p} + \varepsilon_t$$
$$= c_1 + \sum_{i=1}^{p} \alpha_i Y_{t-i} + \varepsilon_t$$

And the moving average model [12]:

$$MA(q) = Y_t = c_2 + \beta_1 \varepsilon_{t-1} + \beta_2 \varepsilon_{t-2} + \ldots + \beta_q \varepsilon_{t-q}$$
$$= c_2 + \sum_{i=1}^{q} \beta_i \varepsilon_{t-i}$$

So, the full ARIMA mode has the form:

$$ARIMA(p, d, q) = Y_t = AR(p) + I(d) - MA(q)$$
$$= (c_1 + \alpha_1 Y_{t-1} + \alpha_2 Y_{t-2} + \ldots + \alpha_p Y_{t-p} + \varepsilon_t)$$
$$- (c_2 + \beta_1 \varepsilon_{t-1} + \beta_2 \varepsilon_{t-2} + \ldots + \beta_q \varepsilon_{t-q})$$
$$= \left(c_1 + \sum_{i=1}^{p} \alpha_i Y_{t-i} + \varepsilon_t \right) - \left(c_2 + \sum_{i=1}^{q} \beta_i \varepsilon_{t-i} \right)$$

Finally, to build the ARIMA model, we use the British the Box - Jenkins method with the following flows (Fig. 2):

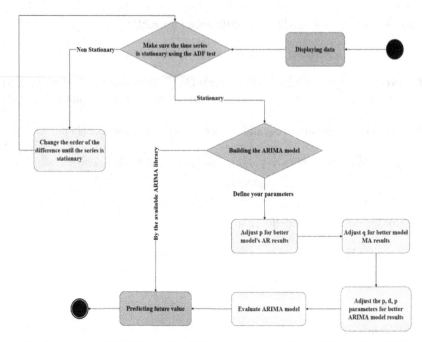

Fig. 2. Complete ARIMA model building process using Box Jenkins method. [13].

3.3 Support Vector Regression Model

Support Vector Regression, a popular model regression, is built on top of a Support Vector Machine to predict the value of a continuous variable, just like Linear Regression (Fig. 3).

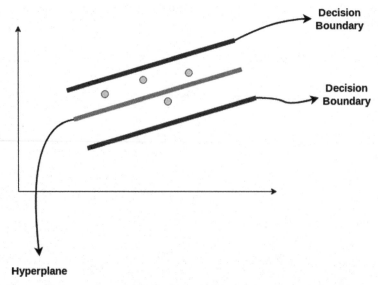

Fig. 3. Illustration of SVR model [15].

In this model, the SVR has two boundary lines (red line) and a hyperplane (green line) which is defined by selecting the path with the maximum number of points.

Kernel Function is a function used to take data as input and convert it into a suitable data form. The kernel uses the math functions provided in the Support Vector Machine [14] (Table 1).

Table 1. Some kernels used in this article[1,2].

Kernel Function	Formulas	Function Representation
Sigmoid	$K(x_i, x) = \tanh(\gamma x_i^T x + r)$	Fig. 4. Sigmoid Kernel Graph.
Polynomial	$K(x_i, x)$ $= (x_i^T x + 1)^d \ with \ d$ $= 1, 2, ...$	Fig. 5. Polynomial Kernel Graph.
Gaussian Kernel Radial Basis Function.	$K(x_i, x) = e^{-(\frac{\|x-y\|^2}{2\sigma^2})}$	Fig. 6. Gaussian Kernel Radial Basis Function.

---

[1] https://www.analyticsvidhya.com/blog/2020/03/support-vector-regression-tutorial-for-machine-learning/.

[2] https://www.geeksforgeeks.org/major-kernel-functions-in-support-vector-machine-svm/.

3.4 GRU Model

The Gated Recurrent Unit algorithm, GRU, is a variant of LSTM to increase the calculation speed but still ensure the quality of the model [15]. GRUs have been shown to perform better when building on small and less frequent data sets. A GRU model consists of two gates: a reset gate (which controls the previous state utilizing a sigmoid activation function) and an update gate (which is intended to figure out how to update the GRU by combining the old state and the potential state). Therefore, it can be said that the reset gate manages short-term dependencies, and the update gate manages long-term dependencies.

3.5 Hybrid Model

The authors [16] in their study proposed a hybrid method between ARIMA and ANN models in time series prediction. Based on that idea, we propose more hybrid models based on this idea in this study.

Time series data has two components: linear and non-linear. The hybrid idea combines these two components to give the final predicted result. The following equation represents these two components:

$$y_t = L_t + N_t$$

In there, y_t is the time series value, L_t is the linear component, and N_t is the non-linear component.

First, use a linear model to predict the linear component and time series values. Then, use the non-linear model to predict the non-linear component from the error value obtained from the linear model. The equation illustrates how to calculate the error value from the linear model:

$$e_t = y_t - \widehat{L_t}$$

The non-linear model will predict the error values obtained from the prediction of the non-linear model, illustrated by the following equation:

$$e_t = f(e_{t-1}, e_{t-2}, \ldots, e_{t-n}) + \varepsilon_t$$

In there, e_t is the error value after using the predictive linear model at time t, y_t is the value of the time series at time t, and $\widehat{L_t}$ is the predicted value of the linear model at time t. The non-linear model will be used to predict the value of e_t– the error value obtained from the prediction by the linear model. f is the non-linear function defined by the non-linear model, ε_t is a random value obtained at t.

From the above two equations, we get that $\widehat{N_t}$ is the predictive value for the non-linear component, and $\widehat{L_t}$ is the predictive value for the linear component. The result of the forecast value at time t to be found is $\widehat{y_t}$ illustrated in the following equation:

$$\widehat{y_t} = \widehat{L_t} + \widehat{N_t}$$

In this study, a new hybrid model is proposed. Linear models are ARIMA and LR, and non-linear models are SVR and GRU. Then, the hybrid and single models will be compared to find the model that gives the best stock forecasting accuracy and performance in this study.

The input is a dataset of predicted time series values. The processing steps include selecting the necessary attributes, choosing the appropriate models, and preprocessing the data. The data is then fed to the models for training. Here, two models are used, linear and non-linear, to predict two components, respectively, the linear component and the non-linear component. After using the linear model (LR, ARIMA) to predict, we obtain the output as a linear component of the time series. The error value is the difference between the linear model's predicted value and the actual value. Next, use non-linear models (SVR, GRU) to predict the error value obtained from the linear model; this is called the non-linear component of the time series. The two results obtained from the non-linear and linear model will be hybrid to make the final prediction, and then performance and accuracy evaluation will be carried out. [Fig. 7].

The process of the hybrid model goes through the following steps:

Step 1: Prepare and preprocess the data and find the appropriate model for the forecast time series.

Step 2: Train the linear model with the training dataset and then make predictions on the test dataset. Calculate the error value of the predicted result and practice with the actual result.

Step 3: Use the nonlinear model to predict the errors of the results in Step 2.

Step 4: Crossing the prediction result (linear component) in Step 2 and predicting the error value (nonlinear component) in Step 3 gives the prediction result of the hybrid model.

Step 5: Evaluate the model based on three parameters, RMSE, MAPE, and MAE, to find the model with the best predictive results in this study.

3.6 Evaluation Methodology

In this research, predictive models are evaluated according to three criteria: MAE, MAPE, and RMSE.

– Mean Absolute Error – MAE

$$MAE = \frac{1}{n} \sum_{i=1}^{n} |y_i - \widehat{y_i}|$$

– Mean Absolute Percentage Error – MAPE

$$MAPE = \frac{1}{n} \sum_{i=1}^{n} \left| \frac{y_i - \widehat{y_i}}{y_i} \right|$$

– Root Mean Squared Error

$$RMSE = \sqrt{\frac{1}{n} \sum_{i=1}^{n} (y_i - \hat{y_i})^2}$$

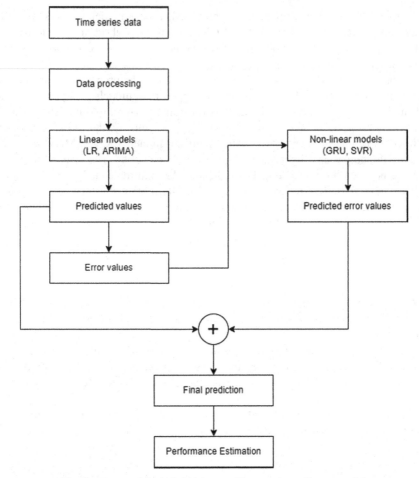

Fig. 7. Figure of the hybrid between linear and non-linear models

With n is sample size of dataset, y_i is the actual value at time t, $\overline{y_i}$ the mean value at time t and $\widehat{y_i}$ is the predicted value of time t.

4 Analysis

4.1 Visualization

In this study, we use three stocks, DJIA, TSLA, and META, obtained from Yahoo! Finance[3] from July 1, 2020, to July 1, 2022. In addition, we also preprocess the data, including setting the DJIA price at $10 units and TSLA and META at $100 units to make the prediction process easier.

Figure 8 and Fig. 9 illustrate the movements of DJIA securities' opening and closing prices.

---

[3] https://finance.yahoo.com/.

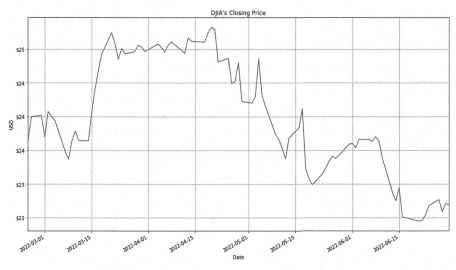

Fig. 8. The figure of the closing price of DJIA's chart.

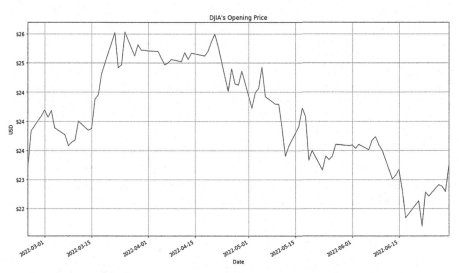

Fig. 9. The figure of the opening price of DJIA's chart.

4.2 Splitting Data

At the same time, we split the data sets into 70% training data - 30% testing data and 80% training data - 20% testing data.

5 Result

With the ARIMA model, we use the function in the pmdarima library with three default parameters, p = 0, d = 1, and q = 0, which are selected based on the lowest Criteria

(AIC) index to choose the optimal model than the rest of the models. Regarding the SVR, we build the GridSearch function to search for parameters suitable for each data set and found that DJIA and META are suitable for the Sigmoid kernel and TSLA with two 'RBF' with opening price and sigmoid with a price close the door. The LR model is similar to SVR but with two parameters, fit_intercept being True and copy_X being True. The last single model, GRU, has been built by us based on the columns "High - Low", "Open - Close", SMA 7, SMA 14, and standard deviation. For each set, the tree will be structurally similar: six layers (1 input layer, four hidden layers, and one output layer), 60 units in each layer, 60 epochs, and 40 steps per epoch (Table 2).

Table 2. Evaluation of single models with the opening and closing of the DJIA's price.

Model		RMSE		MAPE		MAE	
		Opening	Closing	Opening	Closing	Opening	Closing
ARIMA	7 – 3	0.013836	**0.004603**	**1.71%**	**1.83%**	**0.003908**	**0.004234**
	8 – 2	0.236857	0.355452	2.60%	3.31%	0.005922	0.007487
SVR	7 – 3	1.196857	1.451735	5.20%	4.67%	0.011973	0.010698
	8 – 2	**0.009572**	0.02619	5.75%	5.46%	0.013146	0.012427
LR	7 – 3	0.013746	0.022762	102.25%	153.96%	0.236819	0.355426
	8 – 2	0.013836	0.01321	3.85%	10.36%	1.19685	1.45173
GRU	7 – 3	0.236857	0.355452	**1.71%**	3.31%	0.009114	0.026149
	8 – 2	1.196857	1.451735	2.60%	3.31%	0.013569	0.022762

Given DJIA stock's opening and closing prices, the ARIMA model is more suitable than the rest in terms of most indicators such as MAE, MAPE, and RMSE. While the DJIA's closing price prediction is not as good as the SVR model (expressed through RMSE), the other values of the ARIMA model are much better (Table 3).

Table 3. Evaluation of single models with the opening and closing of the META's price.

Model		RMSE		MAPE		MAE	
		Opening	Closing	Opening	Closing	Opening	Closing
ARIMA	7 – 3	0.06132	0.04275	50.14%	51.81%	0.100232	0.103549
	8 – 2	0.08822	0.089388	**30.28%**	**20.20%**	0.058071	0.037876
SVR	7 – 3	0.10655	0.108099	38.21%	38.74%	0.077607	0.078226
	8 – 2	4.58268	4.586287	53.82%	54.77%	0.104779	0.106266

(*continued*)

Table 3. (*continued*)

Model		RMSE		MAPE		MAE	
		Opening	Closing	Opening	Closing	Opening	Closing
LR	7 – 3	3.65451	3.646051	2017.0%	2023.7%	4.582058	4.585659
	8 – 2	**0.00957**	0.023162	1843.8%	1844.6%	3.654422	3.645958
GRU	7 – 3	**0.01375**	**0.022762**	**3.85%**	**6.98%**	**0.009114**	**0.016706**
	8 – 2	0.06132	0.04275	50.14%	51.81%	**0.013569**	**0.022762**

Unlike DJIA, META stock is more suitable when using the GRU model with the ratio of 70% of training sets and 30% of test sets through RMSE, MAE, and MAPE indexes (Table 4).

Table 4. Evaluation of single models with the opening and closing of the TSLA's price.

Model		RMSE		MAPE		MAE	
		Opening	Closing	Opening	Closing	Opening	Closing
ARIMA	7 – 3	0.4484	0.4913	47.45%	52.87%	0.3834	0.4293
	8 – 2	0.1354	0.1376	14.16%	14.65%	0.1136	0.1165
SVR	7 – 3	0.3264	0.2899	30.24%	30.15%	0.2924	0.2603
	8 – 2	0.2145	0.3199	20.51%	29.73%	0.1784	0.2862
LR	7 – 3	20.3505	20.4770	2298.5%	2321.4%	20.3495	20.4760
	8 – 2	22.1215	22.0442	2662.5%	2660.8%	22.1208	22.0436
GRU	7 – 3	**0.0668**	**0.0650**	**6.17%**	**6.00%**	**0.0526**	**0.0519**
	8 – 2	**0.0542**	**0.0748**	**4.95%**	**7.14%**	**0.0419**	**0.0623**

The GRU model with the ratio of 80% training set and 20% test set of the GRU model gave more consistent results with the TSLA stock price.

Table 5 for DJIA in the case of 7–3, the hybrid algorithm that most accurately predicts the opening and closing prices is ARIMA + GRU. In the 8–2 case, the hybrid algorithm that predicts the best opening and closing prices is LR + GRU.

Table 6 shows the META in the case of 7–3. The hybrid algorithm that predicts the most accurate opening price is LR + GRU, and the hybrid algorithm that predicts the most accurate closing price is ARIMA + GRU. In the case of 8–3, the hybrid algorithm that predicts the most accurate closing price is ARIMA + GRU, and the hybrid algorithm that predicts the most accurate closing price is LR + GRU.

Table 5. Evaluation of hybrid models with DJIA Opening & Closing Price.

Model		RMSE		MAPE		MAE	
		Opening	Closing	Opening	Closing	Opening	Closing
ARIMA – GRU	7 – 3	**0.0018**	**0.0015**	**0.57%**	**0.42%**	**0.0013**	**0.0010**
	8 – 2	0.0030	0.0032	1.05%	1.01%	0.0024	0.0024
ARIMA – SVR	7 – 3 (rbf)	0.0106	0.0053	4.23%	1.92%	0.0097	0.0044
	8 – 2 (rbf)	0.0135	0.0142	5.57%	5.93%	0.0128	0.0135
LR – GRU	7 – 3	0.0035	0.0031	1.31%	1.19%	0.0030	0.0027
	8 – 2	**0.0025**	**0.0025**	**0.89%**	**0.79%**	**0.0020**	**0.0018**

Table 6. Evaluation of hybrid models with META Opening & Closing Price.

Model		RMSE		MAPE		MAE	
		Opening	Closing	Opening	Closing	Opening	Closing
ARIMA – GRU	7 – 3	0.0094	**0.0103**	2.47%	**2.87%**	0.0059	**0.0069**
	8 – 2	**0.0069**	0.0081	**2.59%**	3.18%	**0.0052**	0.0064
ARIMA – SVR	7 – 3 (rbf)	0.2030	0.2081	91.01%	93.64%	0.1934	0.1987
	8 – 2 (rbf)	0.1150	0.0816	58.12%	41.07%	0.1133	0.0792
LR – GRU	7 – 3	**0.0083**	0.0156	**2.42%**	6.26%	**0.0057**	0.0135
	8 – 2	0.0104	**0.0052**	4.72%	**2.08%**	0.0093	**0.0041**

Table 7. Evaluation of hybrid models with TSLA Opening & Closing Price

Model		RMSE		MAPE		MAE	
		Opening	Closing	Opening	Closing	Opening	Closing
ARIMA – GRU	7 – 3	0.0572	0.0543	5.24%	5.12%	0.0476	0.0460
	8 – 2	0.0557	0.0540	5.36%	5.11%	0.0443	0.0439
ARIMA – SVR	7 – 3 (rbf)	0.8104	0.8995	89.94%	100.96%	0.7479	0.8425
	8 – 2 (rbf)	0.2017	0.2093	22.31%	23.30%	0.1692	0.1766
LR – GRU	7 – 3	**0.0432**	**0.0351**	**3.94%**	**3.22%**	**0.0356**	**0.0283**
	8 – 2	**0.0295**	**0.0360**	**2.86%**	**3.39%**	**0.0240**	**0.0289**

Table 7 about TSLA shows that the hybrid algorithm with the best accuracy is the LR + GRU algorithm with the lowest error with all three evaluation parameters RMSE, MAPE, MAE, and in both cases, 7–3 and 8 -2 when predicting the opening and closing prices.

The above six tables show that the hybrid model gives a much lower error than the conventional single model. Because LR is a regression algorithm that performs exceptionally well in a single regular model, GRU is a deep learning algorithm that works well in small error prediction. Therefore, the LR + GRU result is the algorithm for the best accuracy in the study and has great potential for use to predict future cryptocurrency prices.

6 Conclusion

In this study, we divided the training and testing data sets by 70% - 30% and 80% - 20% and used single and combined algorithms to predict the prices of various types. DJIA, META, and TSLA stocks with the best possible accuracy. It is possible to show the error in the model through standard measures, and most models have less error, the better; the variant model of RNN (GRU) - black box model, although challenging to explain how the internal structure will affect the output, but this model has many approaches to achieve the expectation, and the ARIMA model learned more from the training data than the machine models, conventional linear learning such as LR and SVR has high errors. Although ARIMA learns relatively well, like the two regression models LR and SVR, the predicted values only show neutrality along a straight line, giving little meaning to the model. Thanks to the excellent performance in the LR's conventional model, the good learning in the time series of the ARIMA, and the excellent learning in the small error prediction of the GRU model, the combination of ARIMA-GRU and LR-GRU have high accuracy. It is pretty accurate in research and has excellent potential to be used to predict future stock prices. Through the process of survey, experiment, and analysis, we determined that the accuracy of the LR - LSTM and ARIMA - LSTM models are over 90%. In the subsequent research, we hope to be able to supplement stock price prediction through investors' emotions.

Acknowledgement. This research is funded by Vietnam National University HoChiMinh City (VNU-HCM) under grant number DS2022–26-03.

References

1. Chun, S.-H., Jang, J.-W.: A new trend pattern-matching method of interactive case-based reasoning for stock price predictions. Sustainability **14**(3), 1366 (2022). Last accessed 14 August 2022
2. Pawar, K., Jalem, R.S., Tiwari, V.: Stock market price prediction using LSTM RNN. Emerging trends in expert applications and security, pp. 493–503. Springer, Singapore (2019). Last accessed 14 August 2022
3. Srivastava, T., et al.: A Deep Learning (LSTM) Approach for Future Stock Price Prediction. Available at SSRN 4160606 (2022). Last accessed 14 August 2022
4. Althelaya, K.A., El-Alfy, E.M., Mohammed, S.: Stock market forecast using multivariate analysis with bidirectional and stacked (LSTM, GRU). In: 2018 21st Saudi Computer Society National Computer Conference (NCC), pp. 1–7. IEEE (2018). Last accessed 14 August 2022

5. Almasarweh, M., Alwadi, S.: ARIMA model in predicting banking stock market data. Modern Applied Science **12**(11), 309 (2018). Last accessed 14 August 2022
6. Henrique, B.M., Sobreiro, V.A., Kimura, H.: Stock price prediction using support vector regression on daily and up to the minute prices. The Journal of Finance and Data Science **4**(3), 183–201 (2018). Last accessed 14 August 2022
7. Bathla, G.: Stock price prediction using lstm and svr. In: 2020 Sixth International Conference on Parallel, Distributed and Grid Computing (PDGC), p. 211–214. IEEE (2020)
8. Vijh, M., Chandola, D., Tikkiwal, V.A., Kumar, A.: Stock closing price prediction using machine learning techniques. Procedia Computer Science **167**, 599–606 (2020)
9. Manujakshi, B.C., Kabadi, M.G., Naik, N.: A hybrid stock price prediction model based on pre and deep neural network. Data **7**(5), 51 (2022)
10. Ashfaq, N., Nawaz, Z., Ilyas, M.: A comparative study of different machine learning regressors for stock market prediction. arXiv preprint arXiv:2104.07469 (2021). Last accessed 15 August 2022
11. Stoean, R., Stoean, C., Sandita, A.: Evolutionary regressor selection in ARIMA model for stock price time series forecasting. In: International Conference on Intelligent Decision Technologies, pp. 117–126. Springer, Cham (2017). Last accessed 15 August 2022
12. Nguyen, D.-T., Le, H.-V.: Predicting the price of bitcoin using hybrid ARIMA and machine learning. In: International Conference on Future Data and Security Engineering, pp. 696–704. Springer, Cham (2019). Last accessed 15 August 2022
13. Hyndman, R.J., Khandakar, Y.: Automatic time series forecasting: the forecast package for R. Journal of Statistical Software **27**, 1–22 (2008). Last accessed 15 August 2022
14. Rohmah, M.F., Putra, I.K.G.D., Hartati, R.S., Ardiantoro, L.: Comparison Four Kernels of SVR to Predict Consumer Price Index. In: Journal of Physics: Conference Series **1737**(1), 012018. IOP Publishing (2021). Last accessed 15 August 2022
15. Gupta, U., Bhattacharjee, V., Bishnu, P.S.: Stock- net—gru based stock index prediction. Expert Systems with Applications **207**, 117986 (2022). Last accessed 15 August 2022
16. Zhang, G.P.: Time series forecasting using a hybrid ARIMA and neural network model. Neurocomputing **50**, 159–175 (2003). Last accessed 15 August 2022

Artificial Intelligence Use in e-Government Services: A Systematic Interdisciplinary Literature Review

Richard Michael Dreyling III$^{(\boxtimes)}$ [ID], Tanel Tammet [ID], and Ingrid Pappel [ID]

Tallinn University of Technology, Ehitajate Tee 5, 19086 Tallinn, Estonia
`richard.iii@taltech.ee`

Abstract. The objective of this paper is to conduct an interdisciplinary systematic literature review of the current state of the art related to the use of Artificial Intelligence in the field of e-Government services that includes technical applications. The study uses the systematic literature review methodology prescribed for software science. Of over 500 resulting articles, the final relevant number of articles is 29. The results include a large cross-section of disciplinary approaches. One surprise result is that even technical articles considered the ramifications of the use of AI in government services on underserved populations. The field of use of AI in government services for service provision is still a new area of investigation and more literature is being published constantly. Because of this, a recommendation for potential areas of future research include readiness assessment frameworks and security.

Keywords: Artificial intelligence · Government services · Literature review

1 Introduction

Governments have begun to use AI in various ways to increase effectiveness and efficiency [1] Different governments and organizations have found AI useful in the provision of government services, or in providing governance.

Artificial intelligence has the potential to be a transformative technology but it also comes with potential drawbacks. As governments insist on learning how to use AI, the potential for it to have a negative effect on citizens' lives must be considered. Issues like bias that can be the result of historical data or hard coded into the algorithms can have a larger impact on those sections of societies least able to defend themselves. This can include bias in policing, or even credit decisions [2].

The systematic literature reviews previously conducted research to answer some of the important questions about AI and its uses in government, public governance, sustainable development and business models [1, 3, 4]. However, the unique situation in which the social effects of AI can depend on less obvious technological aspects it is necessary to conduct a holistic literature review that combines all of the interdisciplinary parts of the research to understand how the use of AI in government services can be

© The Author(s), under exclusive license to Springer Nature Singapore Pte Ltd. 2022
T. K. Dang et al. (Eds.): FDSE 2022, CCIS 1688, pp. 547–559, 2022.
https://doi.org/10.1007/978-981-19-8069-5_37

achieved without causing harm to the populace through bias, legal issues, or breaches of privacy [2].

An understanding of technical topics as they apply to the problem of the application of AI to the provision of government services is largely absent in the literature. The literature review of AI use in public governance conducted by Zuiderwijk et al. [2019] gives a thorough format to approach the research questions [1]. However, this literature review disqualified all technical literature and the inclusion of the technological element has the potential to provide interesting insights in the area of using AI for government services.

The objective of this literature review is to conduct an interdisciplinary systematic literature review to understand the field as it concerns technologies involved as well as the uses of AI in public governance as it applies to e-government services. As presented in Burgers et al. [2019] an interdisciplinary approach will be followed to bring together disparate perspectives on the same problem to help better understand the application at hand [5].

The methodology of this research modeled Kitchenham's [2009] systematic literature methodology [6]. The primary purpose of this research is to answer the research questions to understand the literature as it stands currently in the field across many disciplines.

Research questions:

1. How has the use of AI in public services been researched?
What disciplines and approaches are prevalent in the literature?

Main contribution:
This paper gives results as to research items specifically relevant to the topic of the use of AI in public services.

2   Methodology

The methodology of this research modeled Kitchenham's [2009] systematic literature methodology [6]. The primary purpose of this research is to answer the research questions to understand the literature as it stands currently in the field across many disciplines. As such, quite broad research questions were selected to give an indication of the existing literature.

2.1   Keywords and Search Process

The search process included the databases Web of Science and Scopus. These were chosen because they have a large number of disciplines and are known as general research databases that give an accurate picture of the literature that is currently available. The general databases were in this case chosen to limit the amount of bias and conduct the review in as systematic a manner as possible. Initially, a search which included all of the potential keywords separated by "OR" returned results of over 10,000 between the two databases. After this initial search adjustments were made using the top results as feedback to try to hone the results to be more relevant to the research questions. The final selection of keywords was placed for the Scopus query as follows: "(TITLE-ABS-KEY ("Artificial Intelligence" OR "AI") AND TITLE-ABS-KEY ("Public Sector" OR "Government") AND TITLE-ABS-KEY ("Public Service" OR "Government Service" OR "EGovernance" OR "E-Governance" OR "E-Government" OR "Egovernment"))." A search for a similar keyword string and Boolean values was placed in Web of Science. However, the search criteria in Web of Science were "All Fields" as the "TITLE-ABS-KEY" which search titles, abstracts and keywords were not available. These keywords were chosen because they would accurately narrow the specific items that would apply to the research questions through the boolean requirements. The "ORs" selected in the keyword search were designed to cover all potential analogous terms. With the terms, "AI" and "Artificial Intelligence" the idea was that the keywords would cue on the general terminology even if the article discussed a more specific component technology of AI, such as machine learning (ML) or natural language processing (NLP). The Scopus search yielded 566 results. The Web of Science search returned 321 records.

2.2 Inclusion and Exclusion Criteria

The inclusion and exclusion criteria were chosen to be able to get an idea of multiple disciplines as they apply to the research questions. Because of the interdisciplinary nature of the topic, the discipline of the article was not used as a refining technique, to avoid unintentionally disqualifying articles pertinent to the topic. All languages were considered, as well as unpublished materials to attempt to ameliorate English language and publication bias. However, the majority of the articles returned were in the English language.

Inclusion Criteria

- All disciplines.
- Topic relevant to research questions.
- AI used for e-government or public services.
- AI use or application in Public Services as a part of the purpose of the research.
- Consideration of the application of AI in public services discussed.

Exclusion Criteria

- Editorials, letters, book chapters, presentations are not included.
- AI is only part of research methodology not the subject being researched.
- Pure technical article without explicit application to a government or e-service.
- AI is not directly part of providing an e-service or government service.
- AI mention is incidental.
- Early non-AI chatbots.

Duplicates were removed. 384 records were present after duplicate removal. Then the researcher conducted an initial review of titles and abstracts to determine which of these were relevant to the topic. All of the search results were given values of yes, no, and maybe.

2.3 Quality Evaluation

After the initial review of abstracts and titles, all relevant and possibly relevant articles were read to determine a final judgment of relevance and quality. For each of the articles, a quality evaluation was conducted based on the table format given in [7]. Table two gives metrics for rating empirical studies based on the type of data collection. And Table one takes into account table two's score as well as the relevant categories for the quality assessment. These tables give an indication of how complete a piece of research could be based upon metrics like the amount of data collected depending upon the method of collection. For example, different numbers are required when doing face to face qualitative interviews than when considering questionnaires. From these table based metrics, the author derived a percentage quality score by evaluating each point. Due to not all studies having scores in all of the categories, only relevant ones, the quality scores varied to a large degree. The table used for statistical collation and analysis of the quality numbers primarily used the percentage to try to judge articles on as level a basis as possible. This percentage was derived by the following equation: (Score / Potential Relevant Score * 100). The number of articles for consideration in the data extraction portion of the review-was 29, specific numbers at each stage will be discussed in section three. The author read the literature that was accepted for the study. Coding took place within the documents looking for connections and congruities from the broad research.

The search conducted yielded 29 articles which were found from a total of 386 records after the initial application of the deduplication. After the title and abstract review n = 66. Upon further review and quality check, the number of articles selected for study was 29.

2.4 Data Collection and Analysis

The author read the literature that was accepted for the study and coded the documents looking for connections and congruities from the research. Once coding was complete, the author analyzed the codes and data for similarities and through lines in the research while paying special attention to the methodology and discipline of the research.

3 Results

The preliminary answers are stated in this chapter.

3.1 Search Results

As stated above, the search conducted yielded 29 articles which were found from a total of 386 records after the initial application of the timeliness criteria and removal of duplication. After the title and abstract review n = 66. Upon further review and quality check, the number was 29.

These items can be seen in alphabetical order in Table 1. The Systematic Identifier "S" with a number is used for clarity so the reader knows which items were selected for the study and which were referenced in other areas. Where applicable, the overall ACM citation number will be used at the end of the sentences as prescribed by citation rules.

3.2 Answers to Research Questions

As previously stated, the research questions are as follows:

1. How has the use of AI in public services been researched?
2. What disciplines and approaches are prevalent in the literature?

Contrary to expectation, the contributions made by the items included in the study were primarily dealing with practical applications of AI in public services. Because the research area is so new, the hypothesized trend was to see a variety of theories which would explain how the use of AI in public services would work. However, even the overviews of the state of the art had the goal primarily of stating the ways in which AI was used in public services currently and could be in the future. This could be because of the particular angle through which the author is finding the gap in research. Several articles [13, 14, 23, 31] analyzed the phenomenon from theoretical perspectives like the Technology adoption model [23], public value theory, problematization, and digital inclusion. One also suggested a maturity model for e-invoicing to build toward. AI capabilities in automated public services [29].

Due to the nature of the inquiry as well as the field itself, it is expected that the relevant items would be multidisciplinary in many ways. The fields which investigate the use of AI in public services are varied. Below, the discipline through which the items were approached are shown. Information research and public administration comprised the largest portion of the accepted papers. Research focusing on the data science and computational intelligence of AI in public services were the other approach that was apparent. The other disciplines had a single item each, including one article that was pure data science (Fig. 1).

This literature review resulted in an interesting categorical distribution of the types of contributions that were made in the field. Because of the interdisciplinary basis of the inquiry many different types of contributions were made, but many of them may be organized into categories based on the ending contribution. For example, there are multiple overviews of how AI can be implemented in government services including [8–10, 17, 20, 36]. In addition, there are multiple different overviews of AI implementations that have specific geographical regions as a component of the research. These are [22, 23, 25, 28]. These two categories, comprise the majority of the articles in related categories in the study. Not all of these articles are from the same discipline. In addition, some other articles gave an overview of an implementation of a technology or technologies that use AI in public services in the context of a specific region or geography [11, 22, 30, 31, 33]. Only one article [16] specifically measured citizen opinion about using AI systems in public services, which means that only one directly related to user experience or user

Table 1. Texts selected for study

Identifier	Authors	Title
[8]	Ahn M.J., Chen Y.-C	Artificial intelligence in government: Potentials, challenges, and the future
[9]	Akkaya, C; Krcmar, H	Potential Use of Digital Assistants by Governments for Citizen Services: The Case of Germany
[10]	Al-Mushayt O.S	Automating E-Government Services with Artificial Intelligence
[11]	Anwer, MA; Shareef, SA; Ali, AM	Smart Traffic Incident Reporting System in e-Government
[12]	Balta D., Kuhn P., Sellami M., Kulus D., Lieven C., Krcmar H	How to Streamline AI Application in Government? A Case Study on Citizen Participation in Germany
[13]	Chatterjee S., Khorana S., Kizgin H	Harnessing the Potential of Artificial Intelligence to Foster Citizens' Satisfaction: An empirical study on India
[14]	Chen, T; Ran, LY; Gao, X	AI innovation for advancing public service: The case of China's first Administrative Approval Bureau
[15]	Dreyling R., Iii, Jackson E., Pappel I	Cyber security risk analysis for a virtual assistant G2C digital service using FAIR model
[16]	Drobotowicz K., Kauppinen M., Kujala S	Trustworthy AI Services in the Public Sector: What Are Citizens Saying About It?
[17]	Engin Z., Treleaven P	Algorithmic Government: Automating Public Services and Supporting Civil Servants in using Data Science Technologies
[18]	Fatima S., Desouza K.C., Buck C., Fielt E	Business model canvas to create and capture AI-enabled public value
[19]	Gunaratne H., Pappel I	Enhancement of the e-Invoicing Systems by Increasing the Efficiency of Workflows via Disruptive Technologies
[20]	Henman P	Improving public services using artificial intelligence: possibilities, pitfalls, governance
[21]	Hong, S; Kim, Y; Park, J	Big data and smat (sic.) city planning: The case of Owl Bus in Seoul

(*continued*)

Table 1. (*continued*)

Identifier	Authors	Title
[22]	Kuziemski M., Misuraca G	AI governance in the public sector: Three tales from the frontiers of automated decision-making in democratic settings
[23]	Marri A.A., Albloosh F., Moussa S., Elmessiry H	Study on the Impact of Artificial Intelligence on Government E-service in Dubai
[24]	Medhane D.V., Sangaiah A.K	PCCA: Position Confidentiality Conserving Algorithm for Content-Protection in e-Governance Services and Applications
[25]	Misuraca G., Van Noordt C., Boukli A	The use of AI in public services: Results from a preliminary mapping across the EU
[26]	Mittal P	A multi-criterion decision analysis based on PCA for analyzing the digital technology skills in the effectiveness of government services
[27]	Montoya L., Rivas P	Government AI Readiness Meta-Analysis for Latin America and the Caribbean
[28]	Nam T	How did Korea use technologies to manage the COVID-19 crisis? A country report
[29]	Pappel I., Gelashvili T., Pappel I	Maturity Model for Automatization of Service Provision and Decision-Making Processes in Municipalities
[30]	Park S., Humphry J	Exclusion by design: intersections of social, digital and data exclusion
[31]	Petersen A.C.M., Cohn M.L., Hildebrandt T.T., Møller N.H	'Thinking problematically' as a resource for AI design in politicised contexts
[32]	Rafail P., Efthimios T	Knowledge Graphs for Public Service Description: The Case of Getting a Passport in Greece
[33]	Snowdon J.L., Robinson B., Staats C., Wolsey K., Sands-Lincoln M., Strasheim T., Brotman D., Keating K., Schnitter E., Jackson G., Kassler W	Empowering Caseworkers to Better Serve the Most Vulnerable with a Cloud-Based Care Management Solution

(*continued*)

Table 1. (*continued*)

Identifier	Authors	Title
[34]	van Noordt C., Misuraca G	New Wine in Old Bottles: Chatbots in Government: Exploring the Transformative Impact of Chatbots in Public Service Delivery
[35]	Van Noordt C., Misuraca G.,	Evaluating the impact of artificial intelligence technologies in public services: Towards an assessment framework
[36]	Wirtz, BW; Weyerer, JC; Geyer, C	Artificial Intelligence and the Public Sector-Applications and Challenges

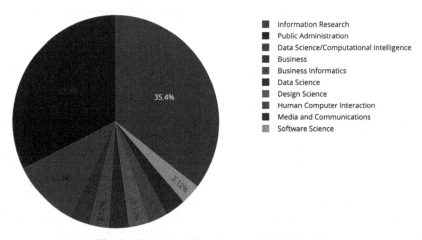

- Information Research
- Public Administration
- Data Science/Computational Intelligence
- Business
- Business Informatics
- Data Science
- Design Science
- Human Computer Interaction
- Media and Communications
- Software Science

Fig. 1. Discipline of items accepted for the study

interactions and how the public felt. Design of AI techniques and Systems which would implement AI in public services were another large category, with four articles [11, 19, 24, 32]. Theoretical analyses comprised a smaller number of articles in this study, only three articles analyzed AI in public services specifically from a theoretical perspective, or proposed a new theoretical way to look at the phenomenon. One article [18] designed an approach which was essentially a method of completing a business model canvas as a way to aid in the creation of AI enabled government services. [26, 27, 29] proposed discussed readiness levels. [27] specifically explained readiness in a geography. And [29] proposed a maturity model in the context of readiness as a specific geography builds toward the ability to implement a higher level of AI enabled government services (Fig. 2).

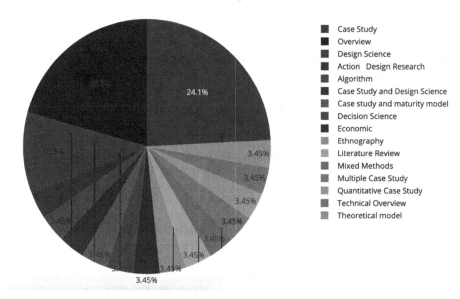

Fig. 2. Methodologies of items accepted for study

The methodologies used in the articles were disparate. The largest percentage of them came in the form of case studies and overviews of the topic. These categories together represented 44.8% of the articles. Only one paper [15] specifically focused on security at all in the area of the use of AI in public services.

4   Discussion and Limitations

This study takes into account the best of the researcher's knowledge at the time of this writing but the process is iterative. The keywords are indicative of the current state of the art as it pertains to the use of artificial intelligence in the provisioning of government services, but with such a new area of study new research will constantly be published. The focus of this paper is a novel area of research even though it is well known that researchers have been publishing research in artificial intelligence for a very long time. This can be considered a limitation of this study. Because it is such a new area of research, the total number of studies that meet the criteria of this piece of research is likely drastically lower because the focus on the use of AI in public services is low. Even though many governments have vision documents referring to how they would like to deploy AI in their governments, in reality very few have gone to the production phase of operation [37]. This logically means that of the case studies that are included in this research many of them, even if not explicitly stated, primarily derived from cases which have not had real implementation and citizen interaction to gain user feedback or understanding how the technical solution can affect the social environment.. As of the writing of this paper, few projects have been implemented in a production environment that has run long enough to see differences in the before and after state or what the projects have achieved [38].

One theme that came through in the analysis of all the documents is the concept of "can" versus "should." Many of the overviews [2, 35] and previous literature reviews [1] approach the topic from a primarily non-technical disciplinary perspective. In these subjects, one would expect discussions of ethereal topics such as the conceptual, "Given the ability to use a technology to increase efficiency and effectiveness of a public service, should society do this?" This is especially considering the potential and documented exponential downsides for those populations in societies who have historically been underserved. This makes sense to question the ethical ramifications and was in accordance with the hypotheses of the author prior to beginning the study. However, what was not expected was that some of the more technical articles also considered these issues. For example, in the article discussing optimizing the bus lines in South Korea for the late night hours, the authors state:

"The most profitable late night bus routes generally connect downtown and high income neighborhoods. From an equity point of view, however, the government could not implement the service only in those areas. If the government did implement such a service, low income neighborhoods would be further marginalized and the already unequal regional distribution of public infrastructure would have been exacerbated. This is why governments sometimes make decisions that conflict with evidence guided by the analysis of big data" [21]

This quotation shows that the researchers involved believed that they could optimize the use of the public service of late-night buses. However, they also had the understanding of how this technological improvement would affect the social environment in this area.

In addition, the author did not expect that particular case studies would compare the programs of multiple parts of a specific country, similar at least in the national law, if not the state, and give both the benefits and drawbacks of these programs considering the intent of the programs when they were implemented [30]. These case studies gave insight into the lives of citizens affected by these programs. This understanding is important if politicians and policy makers are going to implement these programs, they should understand in depth the way these programs will affect citizens.

Several areas that lacked a strong breadth of work became apparent during this study. Given that data protection and privacy is an often-mentioned topic in the introduction section of many papers on AI use in public services, it is unexpected that only one of the papers in the study dealt with security [15]. This paper discussed cybersecurity risk. However, there would seem to be a large gap for researchers wanting to research security in this area because an evaluation of risk is only an introductory amount of work that could be done.

Some studied proposed maturity models related to the topic [14, 29]. Only one study [29] suggested the necessity for preambular requirements to build to a successful implementation of AI, in the form of a maturity model for EDRMS systems that would be, at the highest level, able to integrate into an AI system in a public service. Because of the lack of production implementations of AI in public services from which researchers can derive insights, and the pilot-first approach to the use of AI in the public sector, the next step for research would be to establish a framework for AI readiness assessments in the public sector including feasibility studies for pilots. This is common practice in the private sector and could have the effect of more successful AI related public service projects and less waste and loss from projects that currently go to the pilot phase but do not have prerequisite elements for a successful pilot. It would be useful to have more projects that have been completed which use AI in order to discuss with the departments and creators of the projects the outcomes of them and the effect on public services.

5 Conclusion

The many overviews even in the past five years suggest that the science in the area of artificial intelligence implementation in the specific area of public services is not yet established. The future direction of research in this area should do a better job of melding the technical with the social in an interdisciplinary manner and also include the way these technologies will affect the lives of citizens. It is one thing to give specific economic indicators of time saved in measures of efficiency and effectiveness, but the impact on citizens should also be measured. Only one of the studies accepted into this systematic literature review looked at the ramifications of an example of an AI enabled public service and that study [15] did this from an almost theoretically vanilla IT implementation. Perhaps another person can write a maturity model of the literature research into the use of AI in public services. Ideally, public policy makers and politicians should have academically cogent research that goes as far as quantitatively discussing the impact of the issues that arise when AI is implemented in the public sector. This could be accomplished through analyzing the ramifications of things like black box decision-making in AI determination of credit worthiness and other items that should be but are not often regulated. If it can be shown that an AI system will cause a percentage of the population to lose a certain amount of economic potential in currency, then politicians will have a better understanding of how regulation or implementation will impact the citizenry. If systems currently do not have the ability to explain the methods through which they decide who should and should not have access to benefits or services, the considerations of accountability of decision makers and systematic decision making are very important.

Acknowledgements. This work in the project "ICT programme" was supported by the European Union through European Social Fund.

References

1. Zuiderwijk, A., Chen, Y., Salem, F.: Implications of the use of artificial intelligence in public governance: a systematic literature review and a research agenda. Government Information Quarterly **38**(3), 101577 (2021)
2. Wirtz, B., Weyerer, J.C., Sturm, B.J.: The dark sides of artificial intelligence: An integrated AI governance framework for public administration. Int. J. Public Adm. **43**(9), 818–829 (2020)
3. Di Vaio, A., Palladino, R., Hassan, R., Escobar, O.: Artificial intelligence and business models in the sustainable development goals perspective: a systematic literature review. J. Bus. Res. **121**, 283–314 (2020)

4. de Sousa, W.G., de Melo, E.R.P., Bermejo, P.H.D.S., Farias, R.A.S., Gomes, A.O.: How and where is artificial intelligence in the public sector going? A literature review and research agenda. Government Information Quarterly 36(4), 101392 (2019)
5. Burgers, C., Brugman, B.C., Boeynaems, A.: Systematic literature reviews: four applications for interdisciplinary research. J. Pragmat. 145, 102–109 (2019)
6. Kitchenham, B.O., Brereton, P., Budgen, D., Turner, M., Bailey, J., Linkman, S.: Systematic literature reviews in software engineering–a systematic literature review. Inf. Softw. Technol. 51(1), 7–15 (2009)
7. Beecham, S., Baddoo, N., Hall, T., Robinson, H., Sharp, H.: Motivation in software engineering: a systematic literature review. Inf. Softw. Technol. 50(9–10), 860–878 (2008)
8. Ahn, M.J., Chen, Y.C.: Artificial intelligence in government: potentials, challenges, and the future. In: The 21st Annual International Conference on Digital Government Research, pp. 243–252 (2020)
9. Akkaya, C., Krcmar, H.: Potential use of digital assistants by governments for citizen services: The case of Germany. In: Proceedings of the 20th Annual International Conference on Digital Government Research pp. 81–90 (2019)
10. Al-Mushayt, O.S.: Automating E-government services with artificial intelligence. IEEE Access 7, 146821–146829 (2019)
11. Anwer, M.A., Shareef, S.A., Ali, A.M.: October. Smart traffic incident reporting system in e-government. In: Proceedings of the ECIAIR 2019 European Conference on the Impact of Artificial Intelligence and Robotic (2019)
12. Balta, D., Kuhn, P., Sellami, M., Kulus, D., Lieven, C., Krcmar, H.: How to streamline AI application in government? A case study on citizen participation in Germany. In: International Conference on Electronic Government, pp. 233–247. Springer, Cham (2019)
13. Chatterjee, S., Khorana, S., Kizgin, H.: Harnessing the Potential of Artificial Intelligence to Foster Citizens' Satisfaction: An empirical study on India. Government information quarterly 101621 (2021)
14. Chen, T., Ran, L., Gao, X.: AI innovation for advancing public service: The case of China's first Administrative Approval Bureau. In: Proceedings of the 20th Annual International Conference on Digital Government Research, pp. 100–108 (2019)
15. Dreyling, R., Jackson, E., Pappel, I.: Cyber Security Risk Analysis for a Virtual Assistant G2C Digital Service Using FAIR Model. In: 2021 Eighth International Conference on eDemocracy & eGovernment (ICEDEG), pp. 33–40. IEEE (2021)
16. Drobotowicz, K., Kauppinen, M., Kujala, S.: Trustworthy AI Services in the Public Sector: What Are Citizens Saying About It?. In: International Working Conference on Requirements Engineering: Foundation for Software Quality, pp. 99–115. Springer, Cham (2021)
17. Engin, Z., Philip Treleaven, P.: Algorithmic government: automating public services and supporting civil servants in using data science technologies. The Computer Journal 62(3), 448–460 (2019)
18. Fatima, S., Desouza, K., Buck, C., Fielt, E.: Business model canvas to create and capture AI-enabled public value. In: Proceedings of the 54th Hawaii International Conference on System Sciences, p. 2317 (2021)
19. Gunaratne, H., Pappel, I.: Enhancement of the e-invoicing systems by increasing the efficiency of workflows via disruptive technologies. In: International Conference on Electronic Governance and Open Society: Challenges in Eurasia, pp. 60–74. Springer, Cham (2020)
20. Henman, P.: Improving public services using artificial intelligence: possibilities, pitfalls, governance. Asia Pacific Journal of Public Administration 42(4), 209–221 (2020)
21. Hong, S., Kim, Y., Park, J.: Big data and smat city planning: The case of Owl Bus in Seoul. In: 2018 IEEE International Conference on Big Data (Big Data), pp. 4492–4500. IEEE (2018)

22. Kuziemski, M., Misuraca, G.: AI governance in the public sector: Three tales from the frontiers of automated decision-making in democratic settings. Telecommunications policy **44**(6), 101976 (2020)
23. Al Marri, A., Albloosh, F., Moussa, S., Elmessiry, H.: Study on the impact of artificial intelligence on government E-service in Dubai. In: 2019 International Conference on Digitization (ICD), pp. 153–159. IEEE (2019)
24. Medhane, D.V., Sangaiah, A.K.: PCCA: Position confidentiality conserving algorithm for content-protection in e-governance services and applications. IEEE Transactions on Emerging Topics in Computational Intelligence **2**(3), 194–203 (2018)
25. Misuraca, G., van Noordt, C., Boukli, A.: The use of AI in public services: results from a preliminary mapping across the EU. In: Proceedings of the 13th International Conference on Theory and Practice of Electronic Governance, pp. 90–99 (2020)
26. Mittal, P.: A multi-criterion decision analysis based on PCA for analyzing the digital technology skills in the effectiveness of government services. In: 2020 International Conference on Decision Aid Sciences and Application (DASA), pp. 490–494. IEEE (2020)
27. Montoya, L., Rivas, P.: Government AI readiness meta-analysis for Latin America and The Caribbean. In: 2019 IEEE International Symposium on Technology and Society (ISTAS), pp. 1–8. IEEE (2019)
28. Nam, T.: How did Korea use technologies to manage the COVID-19 crisis? A country report.". International Review of Public Administration **25**(4), 225–242 (2020)
29. Pappel, I., Gelashvili, T., and Pappel, I.: Maturity Model for Automatization of Service Provision and Decision-making Processes in Municipalities. In: Proceedings of Sixth International Congress on Information and Communication Technology, pp. 399–409. Springer, Singapore (2022)
30. Park, S., Humphry, J.: Exclusion by design: intersections of social, digital and data exclusion. Inf. Commun. Soc. **22**(7), 934–953 (2019)
31. Petersen, A.C., Cohn, M.L., Hildebrandt, T., Møller, N.H.: 'Thinking Problematically' as a Resource for AI Design in Politicised Contexts. In: CHItaly 2021: 14th Biannual Conference of the Italian SIGCHI Chapter, pp. 1–8 (2021)
32. Petersen, A.C., Cohn, M.L., Hildebrandt, T., Møller, N.H.: 'Thinking Problematically' as a Resource for AI Design in Politicised Contexts. In: CHItaly 2021: 14th Biannual Conference of the Italian SIGCHI Chapter, pp. 1–8 (2021)
33. Snowdon, J.L., Robinson, B., Staats, C., Wolsey, K., Sands-Lincoln, M., Strasheim, T., Kassler, W.: Empowering caseworkers to better serve the most vulnerable with a cloud-based care management solution. Applied Clinical Informatics **11**(04), 617–621 (2020)
34. Noordt, C.V., Misuraca, G.: New wine in old bottles: Chatbots in government. In: International Conference on Electronic Participation, pp. 49–59. Springer, Cham (2019)
35. van Noordt, C., Misuraca, G.: Evaluating the impact of artificial intelligence technologies in public services: towards an assessment framework. In: Proceedings of the 13th International Conference on Theory and Practice of Electronic Governance, pp. 8–16 (2020)
36. Wirtz, B.W., Weyerer, J.C., Geyer, C.: Artificial intelligence and the public sector—applications and challenges. Int. J. Public Adm. **42**(7), 596–615 (2019)
37. Misuraca, G., Van Noordt, C.: AI Watch-Artificial Intelligence in public services: Overview of the use and impact of AI in public services in the EU. JRC Working Papers, (JRC120399) (2020)
38. van Noordt, C., Misuraca, G.: Artificial intelligence for the public sector: results of landscaping the use of AI in government across the European Union. Government Information Quarterly, 101714 (2022)

Face Recognition Based on Deep Learning and Data Augmentation

Lam Duc Vu Nguyen[1,2], Van Van Chau[1,2], and Sinh Van Nguyen[1,2(✉)]

[1] School of Computer Science and Engineering, International University, Ho Chi Minh City, Vietnam

[2] Vietnam National University, Ho Chi Minh City, Vietnam
nvsinh@hcmiu.edu.vn

Abstract. Face recognition is one of the most popular applications in video surveillance systems and computer vision. The researches of face recognition in recent years have been shown that their applications are widely used in practice. Particularly, during the pandemic of Covid-19, there were a lot of researches relating to face recognition with and without mask. The accuracy of the face recognition algorithms is depended on technical issues, implemented solutions and models of data processing. In this paper, we propose an improved method for face recognition based on deep learning techniques and data augmentation. Our contribution of the proposed method is focused on the following steps: (1) obtaining and pre-processing data for training dataset based on image processing techniques (i.e. noise removal, mask wearing). (2) Creating a trained model of new dataset based on the Inception Resnet-v1. (3) Building an application for face recognition in timekeeping of a company. We use the two popular face datasets which are open source and publicity available: Casia-WebFace [1] for training and LFW [2] for validation. Comparing the several methods, the accuracy of our method is higher in case with mask and the processing time is very fast in the real time.

Keywords: Face detection · Face recognition · Deep learning · CNN models · Inception-resnet data augmentation

1 Introduction

The research and application of computer vision, computer graphics, image processing and machine learning in recent years brings us a lot of advantages [3–6]. They are applied in many fields like 3D simulation, game industry, medical diagnostics or digital heritages. These knowledge and solutions are also popular and widely used in the systems of security, access control, check-in and check-out, objects tracking and monitoring, identify verification services, etc., and proved usefully and efficiently. The researches in face recognition system have been becoming popular along with development of artificial intelligence and deep learning techniques [7,8]. A facial recognition system is an application capable of matching a human face from a digital image or a video frame of a

© The Author(s), under exclusive license to Springer Nature Singapore Pte Ltd. 2022
T. K. Dang et al. (Eds.): FDSE 2022, CCIS 1688, pp. 560–573, 2022.
https://doi.org/10.1007/978-981-19-8069-5_38

camera with a given image in the database system. Using the machine learning methods and deep learning techniques are best solutions to obtain the high accuracy and adapt real time processing. Transfer learning and image augmentation are additional techniques in image processing and machine learning that can help improving precision of the face recognition systems.

The existing identify systems like fingerprints, palm recognition, ID and passwords, etc., are developed and widely used in practice. However, these methods existed limitations such as fake images of fingers and palms, or missing the user name and password to check-in. Therefore, the needs for using face recognition system is increasing recent years because of its accuracy and necessary in both security system and objects monitoring system.

In order to build a facial recognition system, the training dataset plays an important role in implementation of the system. Numerous facial datasets have been published online so that anyone can download them for free testing. These datasets are very huge, containing millions of images of various peoples. Therefore, researchers can skip the data collection phase and concentrate on training the model. The computer hardware is also getting more and more powerful to be able to train models. Wearing a face mask is now commonly used as part of standard to prevent infection during the pandemic of COVID-19. This is requirements for us in public spaces or on the means of transportation. Therefore, a system that recognizes people with face mask is necessary in any organizations or companies.

The system ought to be real-time and robotized. One suitable solution for these requirements is deep learning. This technology can help us recognize people with face mask automatically. Although the numerous facial datasets are available and free for accessing in the several researches. However, the facial dataset with mask is not available at present. In this research, we apply the image processing techniques to wear a mask on each face of the existing facial data. The dataset is then used for training data of our model. After reviewing the state-of-the-art methods, we propose a method for face recognition in both mask and without mask. Our contribution focus on data creation and data augmentation. The improved points have been shown the accuracy in face recognition with mask.

The remainder of the paper is structured as follows. Section 2 presents the state-of-the-art methods, several applications, tools and techniques for building application in practice. Section 3 describes in detail our proposed method including system design of the application. We present the implementation and obtained results in Sect. 6. Section 5 includes discussion and evaluation. The last section is our conclusion and future work.

2   Related Works

In this section, we explore the several methods for face recognition and its application in practice. The two important points that researchers want to obtain are accuracy and time processing. In order to improve accuracy of image classification, Alex Krizhevsky et al. [9] (called AlexNet) presented a new CNN architecture model based on increasing layers with the support of computational power.

The advantage of this CNN architecture is that the model can extract more features from each layer. After that, they are combined to enrich information of the object for prediction step. Moreover, the activation function ReLU is used as an additional computation step to speed-up the training process of the model compared to sigmoid function. However, the limitation come from size selection (11×11) of the first convolutional layer that can be difficult to deal with smaller size of pictures in practice. Karen et al. [10] proposed an idea to build templates using blocks. The VGG Block includes three parts: a convolutional layer, an activation function, and a pooling layer. The order and number of the block are optional. At the end, a fully connected layer and SoftMax is inserted to make prediction. Unlike AlexNet [9], that model use 3×3 filters to help reduce computation, which reduces time and parameters. In contrast, they increase the depth of CNN that lead to increase accuracy of the network model.

In the traditional approach, the neural nework layers are stacked together as thickly as possible to create a model that can learn complex rules. However, a very deep neural network can cause the problem of overfitting. Another problem is vanishing gradient: the gradient is too small, that make it impossible for layers to learn in backpropagation. Furthermore, since the picture's information area changes with each image, choosing the optimal kernel size is crucial. Szegedy et al. [11] suggested a new solution for building neural networks. Instead of being "deeper," the network would become "wider." Different kernels operate on the same input. Then, to form block output, all kernel's output are concatenated along the channel dimension. For example, a block includes four parallel paths. To extract information from different spatial sizes, the first three paths used different convolutional layers from 1×1, 3×3, and 55. The max pooling layer (3×3) is used in the last path. All output must be the same size across the fourth paths, which is a requirement for the concatenation step. Each layer must have appropriate padding. The neural network (as previously indicated) is consuming cost. Therefore, the authors include an extra layer 1×1 convolution before 3×3 and 5×5 convolutions to reduce the number of input channels.

Kaiming et al. [12] presented another solution (namely residual block) to defeat the vanishing/exploding gradient. Instead of making the network wider, this approach introduces a technique called skip connection. It let data skip several layers and connect directly to the output. The implementation of this block is simple. Input x and f(x) are directly added together to create an output of block. This kind of architecture requires x and f(x) to have the same shape. If the result x + f(x) approximates x (can be assumed as x + f (x) = x), the residual block is easy to learn (it means all weights and bias of the layer will be pushed to 0).

Christian et al. [11] presented a method for improving inception deep learning model for image classification. With numerous variants of the inception network were established, each of later versions is better compared to the previous one. In the next research project [13], authors suggested a solution to improve the accuracy and reduction of the computational complexity. Instead of using large filters (e.g. 5×5 or 7×7), it can be expensive in computation, authors suggested to decompose them into smaller filters.

Considering the spatial factorization, the researchers can continue to factorize n × n kernel into a combination of 1 × n and n × 1 kernels. When the number of filters is the same, 1 x n and n × 1 kernels are $(1 \times n + n \times 1)/n^2 = 2/n$ cost of n × n kernel. Therefore, this combination is $1 - 2/n$ cheaper than the original kernel. For instance, a 3×3 convolution is divided into 1×3 convolution followed by a 3×1 convolution. They found this method is $1 - 2/n = 0.3$ cheaper than the single 3×3 convolution. In practice, they figured out that this factorization does not work on early layer, but it produces incredibly good results on the grid of medium size. In order to reduce the grid size, Christian [13] use a pooling layer and a convolutional layer to process and combine them to produce the output of block. From these improvements, many architectural models had been introduced: Inceptionv1, Inceptionv2, Inceptionv3, Inceptionv4. The model in this research is based on Inception Resnet v1. The inception-resnet v1 is introduced in [14]. It is a hybrid network insprired by the inception model and residual model. This combination increases the number of layers while keeping the accuracy and performance.

Another research namely FaceNet is introduced by Florian et al. [15]. The purpose is to represent faces in Euclidean space, where the distance can used to compare similarity. The architecture of FaceNet is described as follows. A batch of images fed into a deep architecture (this architecture is designed to turn images into vectors). These vectors are then normalized to unit vectors using the L2 method. The pictures (as vector form) is then processed through triplet loss to distributed embedding the notation of similarity and dissimilarity. To the face-mask recognition, Warot Moungsouy et al. [16,17] proposed a method based on residual inception networks. Authors introduced a masked-face dataset based on the Casia-WebFace dataset [1]. It consists of 2236161 masked-face images. Then, both Casia-WebFace dataset and new dataset are combined to train the model. The proposed method was based on FaceNet using Inception-Resnet-v1 architecture. They test with several model and the best model was the fine-tuned FaceNet with the retrain Inception Block A on the new dataset. This model achieved 99.2% accuracy on masked-face test dataset. They also figure out that adding masked-face image into training data, it improve the accuracy of the model 0.6%

Besides, the transfer learning is known as a machine learning form where a model is built for a specific task and then reused on a second task as the starting point to be modified. It is used in deep learning as a pre-trained model in computer vision and natural language processing tasks to develop neural network models on these problems. The transfer learning is very useful in deep learning problems because most real-world problems usually have billions of labeled data, and this requires complex models. It is an effective technique for optimization, time saving and achieving better performance. Developers can use transfer learning to merge different applications into one. They can quickly train new models for complex applications. Moreover, transfer learning is a good tool to improve the accuracy of computer vision models. At the end of this research work, we present a facial recognition application for attendance system based on a deep learning model. We utilize transfer learning by using three pre-trained convolution neural networks and train them on our data which contains 10 different classes where each class includes 20 facial images. The three networks showed very high performance in terms of high prediction accuracy and reasonable training time. Therefore, face recognition based on deep learning can greatly improve the recognition speed and accuracy. The last and not lead, many existing API, Libraries, tools and techniques can help us to implement our application like OpenCV, TensorFlow, PyTorch.

3   Our Proposed Method

3.1   Overview

This section present our proposed method. We create an effective model for both recognizing masked faces and without masked faces. As mentioned in the Introduction, the method consist of three steps. In the first step, we obtain the datasets from the publish sources Casia-WebFace [1] and LFW [2]. They are the face images without face masks. Therefore, after pre-processing these data (i.e. noise removal) we use the image processing techniques to wear a mask on each face. In the second step, we use the new datasets for building our training data model based on inception resnet-v1. The last step is creating an application for testing our face recognition system. The detail of each step is described in the following sections.

3.2   Pre-processing Data

Cleaning Data: The dataset Casia-WebFace [1] is used for face verification and face identification tasks including 494414 face images of 10575 peoples. Each image has a size of $250 \times 250 \times 3$ (width $\times$ height $\times$ channel) and saved as a jpg file. To avoid any noise in the image, an algorithm iterates through all images and detects face coordinates. Thus, the face in the image will be extracted from the background. In this section, the MTCNN model is used for face detection. This model includes three nets: P-Net, R-Net and O-Net to process and obtain the coordinates of the bounding box as a rectangle. Finally, we apply an image processing method to format, resize image to have a uniform of width and height, change the color to RGB and save image into a new folder (see Fig. 1). The algorithm (Algorithm 1) below is proposed to clear data.

Creating Mask: After cleaning process, a new dataset of faces is created, however these faces do not have masks. Thus, we now create a mask on each face image. Firstly, a list of mask images will be retrieved from the internet that contain ten different mask images. All of them are processed by using an edited photo application to filter out the background. The purpose is to randomly select masks, thereby creating diverse images when feeding them into the model. The functions of application allows process the picture. Using a certain threshold to

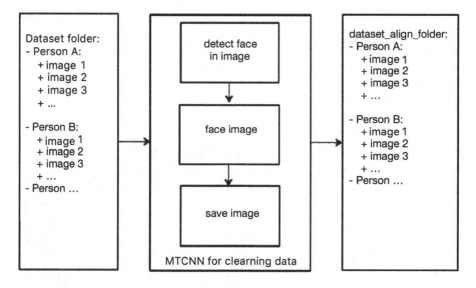

Fig. 1. Using MTCNN to clean data

Algorithm 1. Algorithm for clearing dataset

Input: the dataset from Casia-WebFace [1]
Output: Our new dataset

1: **for** each image in the dataset **do**
2:       image = openImage(each_file)
3:       list_face_coordinates = MTCNN.detect_faces(image)
4:       **if** length(list_face_coordinates) == 1 **then**
5:           [xmin, ymin, xmax, ymax] = list_face_coordinates[0]
6:           face_image = image[ymin:ymax, xmin:xmax]
7:           face_image = resize(image)
8:           save(face_image)
9:       **else**
10:           print(the number of faces is incorrect)
11:           continue
12:       **end if**
13: **end for**

---

enable the mask separated from the background and obtain a mask image. In order to determine the coordinates points on the face for processing, a technique called facial landmark [18,19] is used. This technique will mark important points of the face according to sixty-eight coordinates. We based on this information to wear mask on the face. Many solutions can be applied to cover a mask on the face like determining points around mouth, nose or chin, etc.

In this case, we map the mask to corresponding points on the face using the homography algorithm. Each face has different features and situation, applying this algorithm gives us a better result because the mask is rotated and resized based on the shape of face. We want to overlay both cheeks and nose with a mask, so the corresponding points in this case from 1 to 15 and 29. Figure 2 illustrates how the points on the face and the mask are connected. If the coordinates of the face change, the coordinates of the mask also change, so the mask will fit more close to the face (see Fig. 2). The next algorithm (Algorithm 2) show the way to wear a mask on the face:

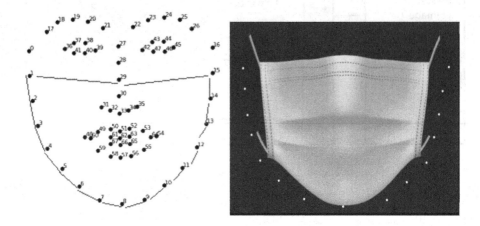

Fig. 2. Creating a mask for the face

3.3   Creating Trained Model

In this section, we apply the FaceNet concept to create our model. As mentioned in [15], the picture is converted into 128-D embedding using triplet loss function. In the very first model, triplet loss function is used to train the model, but the result is bad. The loss value decreases gradually and the model eventually corrupts. The problems come from batch size and the label of each batch. The Casia-WebFace dataset has 10575 labels with a batch size of 512. Therefore, there is a small chance for images of the same person to exist in one batch, while triplet loss function requires triplets (anchor, positive, and negative). For this reason, we apply the FaceNet concept to convert image into embedding; but other factors like loss function and model architecture will be changed. After training, we will remove the last layer (dense net 10575) and add an l2 normalizer to the model. The final model for embedding is described as in Fig. 3. We use the Inception-resnet-v1 [14] to train our model. The model is added more Batch Normalization Layers to normalize input data and modify the last layer to get the 128-element embedding. This model is a stack of Stem, Inception-Resnet-A, Reduction A, Inception-Resnet-B, Reduction-B, Inception-Resnet-C. The cross-entropy is chosen to train the model, so the last layer must encode the image into an n-number vector, where n is equal to the number of people in the dataset.

Algorithm 2. Algorithm for wearing a mask on the face

Input: The data without mask
Output: The data with mask

1: **for** each face image in the dataset **do**
2:     image = openImage(each_file)
3:     xminM, xmaxM, yminM, ymaxM //M: mouth
4:     landmarks = detect_68_landmarks_and_mouth(image)
5:     **if** (landmarks is not null) and (len(landmarks) = 68) **then**
6:         coord_points_face = ([point[0], point[1]] for points in landmarks[1:16])
7:         coord_points_face.append(landmarks[29][0], landmarks[29][1])
8:         mask_image = choose_a_random_mask()
9:         coord_points_mask = get_coord_points_mask()
10:         matrix_HG = findHG(coord_points_mask, coord_points_face)
11:         mask_image_HG = cv2.warpPerspective(mask_image,matrix_HG,imageSize)
12:         image_with_mask = wear_mask_HG(image, mask_image_HG)
13:         save(image_with_mask)
14:     **else**
15:         mask_image = choose_a_random_mask()
16:         mask_image = resize(xmaxM - xminM, ymaxM - yminM)
17:         image&mask = wear_mask_default(image, mask_image, xminM, yminM)
18:         save(image&mask)
19:     **end if**
20: **end for**

Due to the requirement of cross entropy, dense net has 10575 units before going to loss function because there are 10575 different persons in the dataset and one image belongs to only one person. But we do not want to classify 10575 people in a dataset or train again each time we add a new person. Therefore, we keep a dense net with 128 units to learn the features of the face before going to a dense net of 10575 (see Fig. 4).

Training Process: Although the dataset has 10575 people, but the image number of each person are not the same that lead to generate noise. To solve this problem, for each epoch, a training dataset must be created in which each person has the same number of images. After that, each person includes fifteen images are chosen from the "no mask" dataset and fifteen images are chosen from the "mask" dataset. We apply processing techniques to augment the data. This will help the model predict better in different conditions (e.g. angle, light, size). Because the data is processed at random, we make a double of data to increase the amount of data in one epoch. Currently, we have 634500 ($30 \times 10575 \times 2$) images in the training dataset. We use several functions like change contrast, change brightness, flip, and crop an image, then combine them together to generate new images.

Prediction Process: This model was inspired by the FaceNet model. It means the model learns to distinguish between different people and group the images

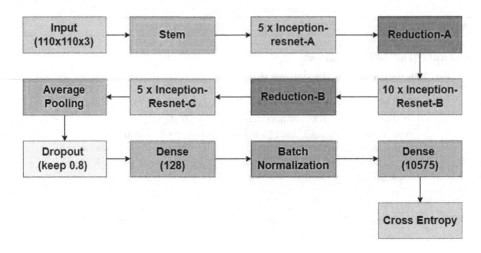

Fig. 3. Stem block

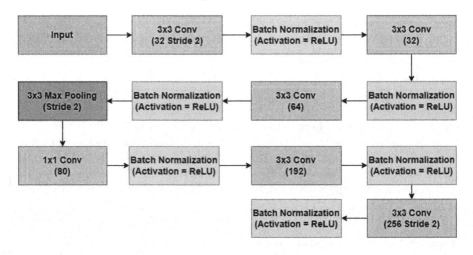

Fig. 4. Our proposed architectural model

of the same people into the same cluster. This approach is more efficient and we do not need to train our model again each time a new image is added. In detail, we generate an embedding of a new person and save it. To recognize an image, the model converts the image to embedding and uses a function to measure the similarity of this embedding with database embedding. The obtained result is a pair with the most similarities.

3.4   Building an Application

In this section, we build an application for testing our model. It is served as a real application to test and evaluate our model. Our application is performed

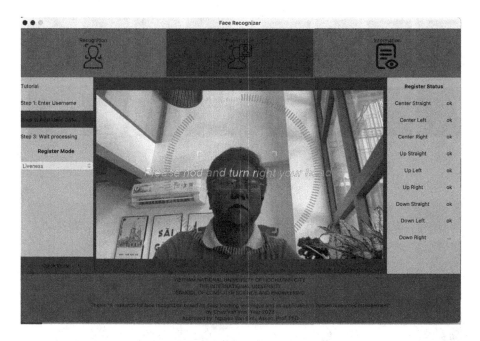

Fig. 5. Our application for testing and evaluating

on a single Laptop (MacBook Pro 8-Core CPU, 14-Core GPU) and its camera. The user interface of the application is created as follows (see Fig. 5).

4   Implementation and Results

In this section, we implement our proposed method and application for face recognition system. We perform our method by using Python, TensorFlow. The model and data are trained on Google Collab Pro. The application is then built based on our model to describe how it is used in the face recognition system. We implement all functions based on Python API to process data, to augment images, to train the training data. The Inception-Resnet v1 is implemented using Keras. To wear a mask on each face image, we use the API "FacialMask-DataSet.py". The output of this step is presented as follows: The face detection is performed by using existing source code in [20]. The obtained result is matched with data in the database (see Fig. 6 and Fig. 7)

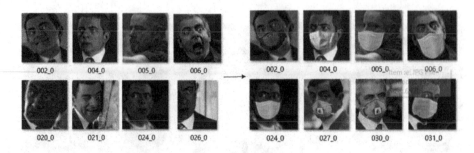

Fig. 6. Wearing a mask on each face image [1]

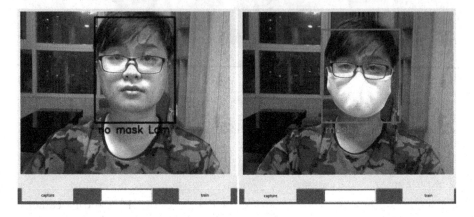

Fig. 7. Face recognition is worked well with both masked face and non-masked face

5   Discussion and Evaluation

In order to evaluate our model, we test and run with many times of epochs. After running 49 epochs (see Fig. 8a), The loss value decrease dramatically in the first ten epochs; after that, this value decreases slowly and is stable from 35 to 49.   The goal is to evaluate how our model can process both the face with and without mask. We combine the "no mask LFW" and "mask LFW" into one dataset. The obtained result is plotted in Fig. 8b. The accuracy increases after each epoch. Starting from the epoch twenty, accuracy increase insignificantly, staying around 90%.

To compare with the existing method, the FaceNet-PyTorch [21] in python library includes several versions of the FaceNet model. In this research work, we use the Casia-Webface version. This model is trained with the same dataset that we used. The dataset LFW and its variants will be reused in this experiment.

Our model will be the model at epoch 49, which is the latest model. At first, two models will convert images from the "no mask LFW" dataset into database embedding. Each label will have only one embedding. Then two models will predict data in two cases: LFW (with mask) and LFW (without mask). In this

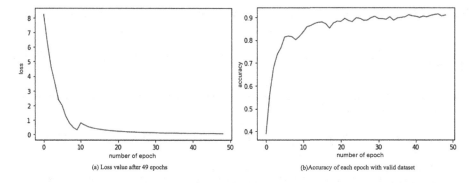

(a) Loss value after 49 epochs   (b)Accuracy of each epoch with valid dataset

Fig. 8. Evaluation of the stable and accuracy of our model

test we do not use a threshold to maximize the accuracy of two models, so the unknown answer will be zero (see Table 1).

Table 1. Comparison of the precision, recall, accuracy and F1 between our model and the existing methods

Model (training dataset)	Data type	Precision	Recall	Accuracy	F1
Facenet pytorch (Casia-Webface)	Without mask	0.9875	0.9961	0.9758	0.9918
	With mask	0.5860	0.1697	0.1632	0.2632
Facenet pytorch (VGGFace2)	Without mask	**0.9969**	**0.9993**	**0.9957**	**0.9981**
	With mask	0.7024	0.4844	0.4772	0.5734
Our model	Without mask	0.9740	0.9896	0.9268	0.9817
	With mask	**0.9644**	**0.9817**	**0.8992**	**0.9730**

Comparing to other models, the accuracy of our model is better in case with mask and a little lower in case without mask. In order to improve for both cases (with and without mask), we can increase the number of epochs to run until meet the accuracy of our expectation.

6   Conclusion and Future Work

In this research work, we explore the several methods for face recognition and their application in practice. The methods are based on machine learning techniques are very popular and suitable for almost cases in practical applications nowadays. We proposed a method that is based on the Inception Resnet-v1 to implement our model. The obtained results have been shown the accuracy of our model (see Table 1). It is higher than the existing methods in case with mask. It can be adapted with real context of pandemic of Covid-19 at present. Besides, we built successful an application that will be applied in the company for timekeeping. This application can help the company to check-in, check-out and control their staffs every days. The work in the future can be extended an applied in other security systems as mentioned in the Introduction.

References

1. Yi, D., Lei, Z., Liao, S., Li, S.Z.: Learning face representation from scratch (2014). https://arxiv.org/abs/1411.7923
2. Huang, G.B., Mattar, M., Berg, T., Learned-Miller, E.: Labeled faces in the wild: a database for studying face recognition in unconstrained environments. In: Workshop on Faces in Real Life Images: Detection, Alignment, and Recognition (2008)
3. Nguyen, S.V., Tran, H.M., Maleszka, M.: Geometric modeling: background for processing the 3D objects. Appl. Intell. **51**(8), 6182–6201 (2021). ISSN: 1573–7497
4. Van Nguyen, S., Le, S.T., Tran, M.K., Tran, H.M.: Reconstruction of 3D digital heritage objects for VR and AR applications. J. Inf. Telecommun. **6**(3), 254–269 (2021). https://doi.org/10.1080/24751839.2021.2008133. ISSN: 2475–1839
5. Van Nguyen, S., Nguyen, D.A., Pham, L.Q.S.: Digitalization of administrative documents - a digital transformation step in practice. In: 8th NAFOSTED Conference on Information and Computer Science (NICS), pp. 519–524. IEEE (2021). 978-1-6654-1001-4/21/$31.00
6. Van Nguyen, S., Tran, H.M., Le, T.S.: Application of geometric modeling in visualizing the medical image dataset. SN Comput. Sci. **1**(5), 1–15 (2020). https://doi.org/10.1007/s42979-020-00266-0
7. Suganthi, S.T., Ayoobkhan, M.U.A., Venkatachalam, K.V., Bacanin, N., Stepan, H., Pavel, T.: Deep learning model for deep fake face recognition and detection. PeerJ Comput. Sci. **8**, e881 (2022). https://doi.org/10.7717/peerj-cs.881
8. Teoh, K.H., Ismail, R.C., Naziri, S.Z.M., Hussin, R., Isa, M.N.M., Basir, M.S.S.M.: Face recognition and identification using deep learning approach. J. Phys. Conf. Ser. **1755**, 012006 (2021)
9. Krizhevsky, A., Sutskever, I., Hinton, G.E.: ImageNet classification with deep convolutional. J. Commun. ACM **60**(6), 84–90 (2017). https://doi.org/10.1145/3065386
10. Simonyan, K., Zisserman, A.: Very deep convolutional networks for large-scale image recognition. In: International Conference on Learning Representations (2015). http://arxiv.org/abs/1409.1556
11. Szegedy, C., et al.: Going deeper with convolutions (2014). https://doi.org/10.48550/arXiv.1409.4842
12. He, K., Zhang, X., Ren, S., Sun, J.: Deep residual learning for image recognition. In: IEEE Conference on Computer Vision and Pattern Recognition (CVPR 2016), pp. 770–778 (2016)
13. Szegedy, C., Vanhoucke, V., Ioffe, S., Shlens, J., Wojna, Z.: Rethinking the inception architecture for computer vision. In: IEEE Conference on Computer Vision and Pattern Recognition (CVPR), pp. 2818–2826 (2016). https://doi.org/10.1109/CVPR.2016.308
14. Szegedy, C., Ioffe, S., Vanhouke, V., Alemi, A.A.: Inception-v4, inception-ResNet and the impact of residual connections on learning. In: AAAI 2017 Proceedings of the Thirty-First AAAI Conference on Artificial Intelligence, pp. 4278–4284 (2017)
15. Schroff, F., Kalenichenko, D., Philbin, J.: FaceNet: a unified embedding for face recognition and clustering. In: IEEE Conference on Computer Vision and Pattern Recognition (CVPR) 2015, pp. 815–823 (2015). https://doi.org/10.1109/CVPR.2015.7298682

16. Moungsouy, W., Tawanbunjerd, T., Liamsomboon, N., Kusakunniran, W.: Face recognition under mask-wearing based on residual inception networks. Appl. Comput. Inf. (2022). https://doi.org/10.1108/ACI-09-2021-0256
17. Masood, S., Ahsan, U., Munawwar, F., Rizvi, D.R., Ahmed, M.: Scene recognition from image using convolutional neural network. J. Procedia Comput. Sci. **167**, 1005–1012. https://doi.org/10.1016/j.procs.2020.03.400. ISSN 1877–0509
18. Sun, K., et al.: High-resolution representations for labeling pixels and regions (2019). arXiv:1904.04514v1 [cs.CV]
19. Liang, S., Zhou, Z., Guo, Y., Gao, X., Zhang, J., Bao, H.: Facial landmark disentangled network with variational autoencoder. J. Appl. Math. **37**(2), 290–305 (2022)
20. AIZOOTECH. Github FaceMaskDetection. Accessed July 2022. https://github.com/AIZOOTech/FaceMaskDetection
21. Timesler, Facenet-pytorch. https://github.com/timesler/facenet-pytorch

An Approach for Similarity Vietnamese Documents Detection from English Documents

Hai Thanh Nguyen, Anh Duy Le, Nguyen Thai-Nghe,
and Tran Thanh Dien[(✉)]

Can Tho University, Can Tho, Vietnam
{nthai.cit,ldanh,thanhdien}@ctu.edu.vn, ntnghe@cit.ctu.edu.vn

Abstract. Currently, many studies are measuring the similarity between documents in a specific language, such as Vietnamese - Vietnamese and English - English. However, situations have recently appeared in the problem of copying articles. For example, English sources have been translated into Vietnamese and edited into their manuscripts. As a result, it is considered cross-language plagiarism. Therefore, this study has applied a new approach: translate from English to Vietnamese documents, then calculate and compare the translated document with documents modified or copied from a translated document. In the study, the main focus is on stages such as Translating English documents into Vietnamese, preprocessing documents, and determining the similarity between documents. The determination of similarity between documents mentioned in this topic is Cosine similarity based on Term Frequency (TF), Inverse Document Frequency (IDF), and word order similarity in the text. Combine these two metrics to give a similar result that is more accurate and convincing. The data is collected in 7 topics with related topics with the number of 15 documents with lengths from 2000 to more than 8000 words, successfully built a document translation integration system based on Google Translate Application Programming Interface (API) and similarity checking, Precision and Recall measures show very positive results over 80%.

Keywords: Similar document detection · Similarity · Cross plagiarism · Translation · Cosine similarity · Documents similarity

1 Introduction

Recently, with the development of information technology, which serves many demands of society. The data about the texts is also growing in diversity and contains much necessary information. The internet is an environment containing huge information and knowledge for people in the world searching for some information. Therefore, some people are copying the content of others, such as documents, articles, reviews, etc., and making them become their own.

Copying ideas and content from documents or articles online is a problem in the university environment and scientific article submission systems. Violators have many ways to proceed with copying and turning them into their ideas

T. K. Dang et al. (Eds.): FDSE 2022, CCIS 1688, pp. 574–587, 2022.
https://doi.org/10.1007/978-981-19-8069-5_39

by copying from English documents and converting them into the Vietnamese language, then submitting their articles to scientific journals.

Anti-copying by measuring the similarity between documents is a very important and necessary task. This work aims to improve the quality of articles by filtering and rejecting manuscripts with higher similarity. In addition, copyright protection and the quality of the journal and publisher systems are expected to improve.

The main objective of this study focuses on an approach to detecting similar Vietnamese documents from a given English document. First, given the original English document in advance, we translate it to a Vietnamese document. Then, the translated document is compared and calculated the similarity with a repository that includes Vietnamese documents for the similarity comparison to detect documents that have similar content to the original document.

The remaining sections are organized as follows. First, related work is presented in Sect. 2. Next is Sect. 3 (Method), our proposed method to apply translation and find similarities between documents. Next, the results of the experiments are shown in Sect. 4 (Experimental results). Finally, Sect. 5 (Conclusion) summarizes the results we have achieved.

2   Related Work

Calculating documents' similarities has always been an interesting topic for researchers. There are many studies on finding similarities between documents. Semantic similarity is also applied in such fields as Suggesting learning resources [1] through semantic-based search to develop suitable learning materials. Furthermore, question classification based on approximate semantics in retrieving more than 35 million question-answer pairs [2] has also been applied.

The application of cosine similarity, TF-IDF is also used much in some outstanding studies, such as the recommended system [3–5]; Plagiarism detection [6–8]. Application of cosine similarity TF-IDF to detect plagiarism is a popular method and gives positive results. It is considered a good and optimal method to find similarities between documents. Survey on approaches to measuring similarity between documents [9] has also been mentioned through evaluation methods such as: Based on strings, based on characters, and based on the corpus is prebuilt and Term-based. By comparing the similarity between texts, the authors in [10] also proposed a method to evaluate the similarity between sentences and sentences, based on semantics and combined with similarity word order to calculate the similarity between documents. The authors at [11] focused on the candidate retrieval task and aimed to extract the minimal set of highly potential source documents accurately. The paper proposed a fusion of concept-based and keyword-based retrieval models.

Because of internet development, multilingual plagiarism is increasing, and the source of documents in different languages is shared everywhere. As a result, access to multilingual document content has become easy. The authors at [12] also mentioned using translation tools and applications to copy the content. The authors proposed an approach focusing on keywords in the text. The text content used a segmentation architecture to analyze and find similarities, then applied the model to trace the origin of documents with related paragraphs. The results were very positive.

Multilingual plagiarism is a form that has emerged recently. This is also an aspect that many researchers are interested in, some researchers at [13–23] have mentioned this issue. Detecting multilingual plagiarism is still difficult, a big challenge for researchers. Violators can use translation tools to translate into other languages, edit some parts, and make them become their documents or articles.

3   Method

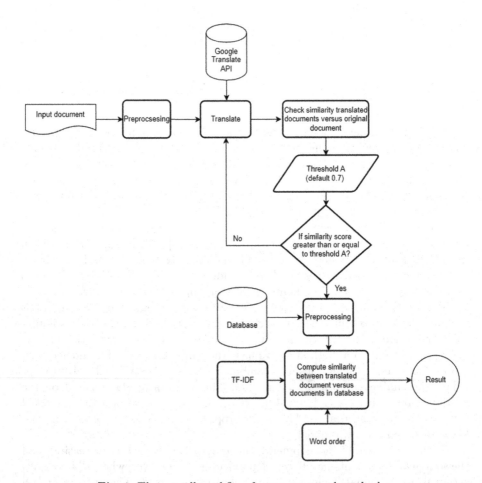

Fig. 1. The overall workflow for our proposed method.

Figure 1 illustrates the proposed overall architecture with the main stages, including translating and evaluating the translated text into Vietnamese and preprocessing the translated text and documents in the repository. Then, we compare the similarity between the input documents and the documents in the repository by applying Cosine to combine TF-IDF and word order. Finally, we use machine-based translation with Google Translate API to translate English documents into Vietnamese. It can be among the best-supported machine translation tools at the moment, with the translated sentences still meaningful and easy to understand.

3.1   Translation Phase and Translation Evaluation

Translating that document into Vietnamese is necessary to check whether an English document is similar to the Vietnamese documents in the repository. The input document can have a .docx or .doc extension, so it is necessary to perform the preprocessing task; preprocessing here means converting the word or pdf format into .txt format for translation and processing. After translation, we need to check the document translated from English is valid for use by evaluating the meaning of the original English document with translated document. We need to check to ensure the translated document has not changed too much and makes enough sense to use. We recommend 4 steps to check as in Algorithm 1.

Algorithm 1. Compare reverse translation in English and original English document

Input: File: reverse translation and original file English.
1: Call (A) is the English original.
2: (B) is the Vietnamese version translated from (A).
3: Then brings (B) translated back to English and called it as (C). (C) denotes the English reverse translation version.
4: Finally, calculate the difference between (C) and (A) to determine that the difference between the original content and translated content is trivial.
Output: Result of calculating TF-IDF in similarity scores.

To evaluate content between reverse translation English and original English documents, we use TF-IDF to calculate the similarity scores. We suggest default threshold A is 0.7 for an overall assessment of the translation content.

3.2   Similarity Calculation Phase of Documents

The final stage is to evaluate the similarity of Vietnamese documents translated from English with Vietnamese documents in the repository. At this stage, we recommend evaluating the similarity with the following steps:

Preprocessing: Some documents are in the repository with the standard scientific paper format, with some sections needing to be removed. The preprocessing process can go through several main steps, as follows:

- We extract and retrieve document content information. Then, we only keep content from the Introduction section to the Conclusion section. Because in many articles, the content mainly covers from Introduction to Conclusion, the rest can be removed as acknowledgments and references.
- We perform sentence segmentation and word separation tasks through supported libraries such as nltk[1] if the document is in English and underthesea[2] if the document is Vietnamese.
- We convert texts back to lowercase and remove extra characters like (!#%$&@, etc.). We need to remove extra characters from the content because it will affect the result, such as Agriculture, Animals. Medicine, Biotechnology and Food Technology. These characters often have no useful meaning and influence the comparison results. Therefore, removing these extra characters is an important step.
- Stop words are also removed in Vietnamese documents, including "is, so, but, and so on". With Vietnamese documents, we can delete stop words using tools such as StopWords dictionary[3].

Calculate Cosine Similarity Based on TF-IDF: It is a very popular technique for calculating similarities between documents. This method is a combination of TF and IDF methods. The weight w_{ij} is calculated by the frequency of occurrence of the keyword ti in the text d_j and the rarity of the keyword ti in the corpus, called similarity SimS as revealed in Eq. 1.

$$SimS = weigh(i,j) = \begin{cases} (1 + log_{(f_{ij})})log(\frac{N}{df_i}) & f_{ij} \geq 1 \\ 0 & f_{ij} = 0 \end{cases} \tag{1}$$

Calculate Similarity Based on Word Order: Word order similarity[4] is an important factor affecting text similarity. For example, texts containing the same vocabulary but with different locations can have different meanings. It is called similarity SimR. The formula calculates word order similarity [24]:

$$SimR = 1 - \frac{|R_1 - R_2|}{|R_1 + R_2|} = 1 - \frac{\sqrt{\sum_{i=1}^{m}(r_{1i} - r_{2i})^2}}{\sqrt{\sum_{i=1}^{m}(r_{1i} + r_{2i})^2}} \tag{2}$$

For example, with T1 = {dog, bite, cat} and T2 = { cat, bite, dog }, the top two sentences contain a set of similar and nearly identical words, only the order

---

[1] https://www.nltk.org/.
[2] https://github.com/undertheseanlp/underthesea.
[3] https://github.com/stopwords/vietnamese-stopwords.
[4] http://fit.vimaru.edu.vn/vi/content/nghien-cuu-ki-thuat-danh-gia-do-tuong-dong-van-ban-ung-dung-trong-so-sanh-van-ban-tieng-viet.

of the pair of words "cat" and "dog" is different. If only based on the similar semantic self of the text, if two documents contain the same set of words, they can give the same result, which means sim(T1, T2)=1. However, the above two sentences have different orders, so the meaning is not the same. The difference between the two sentences is word order.

The author in [24] gives a method to evaluate word order similarity .For each pair of documents T_1 and T_2, determine the set of distinct vocabularies of both texts T $= T_1 \cup T_2$.

The word order feature vector of two documents, denoted $R_1 = (r_{11}, r_{12}, ..., r_{1m})$ and $R_2 = (r_{21}, r_{22}, ..., r_{2m})$, calculated based on the set T

- The word order vector represents where each word in T is located in the corresponding text
- For each word $w_i \in$ T, find the correct or closest word in T_1 to determine the weight for the element r_{1i} in R_1 in one of the following three cases:
  + If the word w_i is in T_1 then r_{1i} is the ordinal number of that word in T_1
  + Find the word in T_1 that is closest in meaning to w_i, using the method of semantic similarity between two words. If this measure exceeds the threshold θ given, r_{1i} is the ordinal number of that word in T_1.
  + If not found or similarity between the words in T_1 and w_i If the threshold is not exceeded, set r_{1i} to 0.

Combine SimS and SimR: TF-IDF-based similarity and word order similarity are equally important. Therefore, we combine both calculation Eq. 1 and Eq. 2 to have the following general Eq. 3 to ensure the accuracy of the method of calculating text similarity.

$$Sim = a * SimS + b * SimR \ (a = b = 0.5) \tag{3}$$

4 Experimental Results

4.1 Experimental System Specifications

We evaluate the proposed method in Fig. 1 by deploying the experiments on a computer equipped with an Intel®Core™i5-8600k, 16 GB RAM, VGA AMD Radeon™RX 580 8 GB, Ubuntu 18.04.1. Translation time, precision, and recall are measured and evaluated when we calculate similarities between documents and search documents in the repository. In addition, we also built a system that integrated the proposed method for similar Vietnamese document detection tasks from a given English document.

4.2 Data description

Table 1 reveals the information on English papers for translation to Vietnamese collected at Can Tho University Journal of Science (CTUJS), including 15 documents (.docx) related to 7 topics. The collected data is in the full format of

Table 1. Collected data

No.	Abbreviation	Topic	The number of documents
1	AG	Agriculture	3
2	AV	Animal & Veterinary	2
3	BT	Biotechnology	2
4	SE	Social Economic	2
5	SH	Social science & Humanities	2
6	FT	Food Technology	2
7	LA	Law	2
Total			**15**

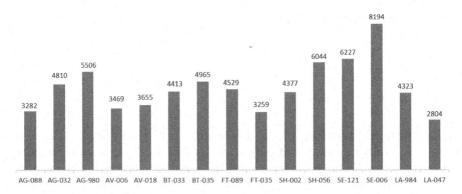

Word count in each document

Fig. 2. Words count of 15 samples

a scientific paper so that the file can include numerous sections such as Digital Object Identifier (DOI), Title, Authors, Abstract, Introduction, Method, Results, Conclusion, Acknowledgment, and References.

Figure 2 shows the word count of all 15 sample documents, the highest proportion is in the topic of social economics with more than 8194 words, and the lowest is in the topic of law with more than 2804 words. This statistic is meant to measure how long it takes to translate a document from English to Vietnamese to evaluate the performance of the translation module.

4.3 Evaluation

Table 2 shows that we recommend 3 levels of time to send requests to the API: 15s-45s, 5s-15s, and 5s-10s. The purpose of frequency requests is to limit the number of requests sent to the API in a short time, preventing the API mark this as spam. Generally, the frequency results with 5s-10s are very good and fast document translation, but the API will often mark this as spam and block

Table 2. Time translation of 15 samples

No.	Samples	Total words	Frequency request	Time processing
1	AG-088	3282	15 s–45 s	22:41
2	AG-032	4810		35:33
3	AG-980	5506		48:19
4	AV-006	3469		29:26
5	AV-018	3655		24:06
6	BT-033	4413	5 s–15 s	19:57
7	BT-035	4965		24:02
8	FT-089	4529		22:21
9	FT-035	3259		23:01
10	SH-002	4377		15:58
11	SH-056	6044	5 s–10 s	14:46
12	SE-121	6227		16:47
13	SE-006	8194		18:22
14	LA-984	4323		11:37
15	LA-047	2804		8:27

requests for a short time. With the remaining frequency, the translation time has increased greatly but will not be considered spam by the API.

Table 3. The similarity scores using Cosine TF-IDF to compare between original English and reverse translate English

No.	Samples	Cosine TF-IDF
1	AG-088	0.74
2	AG-032	0.70
3	AG-980	0.67
4	AV-006	0.76
5	AV-018	0.75
6	BT-033	0.73
7	BT-035	0.69
8	FT-089	0.73
9	FT-035	0.76
10	SH-002	0.81
11	SH-056	0.80
12	SE-121	0.75
13	SE-006	0.80
14	LA-984	0.84
15	LA-047	0.86

Table 3 illustrates the results of the Cosine measure between the original English document and the reverse translation as described in 3.1 shows that after the reverse translation, the meaning of the reverse translation does not change much. The search results on the Law topic (Code: LA) give very positive results. We noticed that the Law topic only contains texts, not many statistic numbers, and rarely does not contain math formulas or data tables like some other topics such as Biotechnology, Food Technology, Agriculture, etc.

These results showed only a partial reverse translation content compared with the original English version. We can see that most sentences from the reverse translation also have some sentences that are kept unchanged. Most sentences can be replaced with synonyms or can be rephrased. Generally, the meaning remains the same as the original and does not change much.

Through the process of studying the Pangasius belly hydrolysate by neutrase enzyme, the belly Pangasius was defated; it showed a kinetic index Vmax = 1.283 µmol tyrosine per minute, Km = 0.377 g protein with reliability R2 = 0.997, enzyme/substrate ratio (E/S) (0.652 mg enzyme/0.975 g protein). Hydrolysis efficiency of tyrosine according to enzyme/substrate 42.69%, ortho-phthaldialdehyde efficiency of the enzyme/substrate was 52.51% at 240 minutes. Subsequently, the belly Pangasius protein hydrolysate was dry-sprayed at 180°C. After drying, the moisture and water activity of dried fish protein hydrolysates were 6.05% and 0.55, respectively. Both commercial peptone and protein hydrolysate from Pangasius belly were used as nitrogen components for Bacillus subtilis growth media at the time from 0 to 72 hours at 37oC and pH = 7, then the powder medium hydrolysed by enzyme neutrase was higher than the commercial peptone medium. In addition, the result from the activity of enzyme protease in the two media for at time of 4, 8, 12, 16, 20, 24 hours, at 37oC and pH = 7 showed that the activity of protease in hydrolysed protein medium from the belly Pangasius was similar to commercial peptone.	Qua quá trình nghiên cứu quá trình thủy phân bụng cá tra bằng enzym neutrase, bụng cá tra đã được khử trùng; nó cho thấy chỉ số động học Vmax = 1,283 µmol tyrosine mỗi phút, Km = 0,377 g protein với độ tin cậy R2 = 0,997, tỷ lệ enzyme / cơ chất (E / S) (0,652 mg enzyme / 0,975 g protein). Hiệu suất thủy phân tyrosine theo enzyme / cơ chất là 42,69%, hiệu suất ortho-phthaldialdehyde của enzyme / cơ chất là 52,51% ở 240 phút. Sau đó, dịch thủy phân protein trong bụng cá tra được phun khô ở 180 ° C. Sau khi làm khô, độ ẩm và hoạt độ nước của sản phẩm thủy phân protein cá khô lần lượt là 6,05% và 0,55. Cá peptone thương mại và dịch thủy phân protein từ bụng cá tra đều được sử dụng làm thành phần nitơ cho môi trường sinh trưởng Bacillus subtilis tại thời điểm từ 0 đến 72 giờ ở 37oC và pH = 7, sau đó môi trường bột thủy phân bằng enzyme neutrase cao hơn môi trường peptone thương mại. Ngoài ra, kết quả từ hoạt động của enzyme protease trong hai môi trường tại thời điểm 4, 8, 12, 16, 20, 24 giờ, ở 37oC và pH = 7 cho thấy hoạt tính của protease trong môi trường protein thủy phân từ cá tra trong bụng tương tự như peptone thương mại.

Fig. 3. English text (left) and text translated to Vietnamese (right)

Fig. 3 exhibited on the right side is the Vietnamese translation from the English original (left side). With the improvement of the Google Translate Tool, integrating machine learning and deep learning techniques to improve the meaning of the translation has made the content of the translations easier to understand. However, the content and sentences after the translation are still full of meaning.

To evaluate the proposed method's efficiency, we have created some document samples from the source documents after they were translated. The first column in Table 4 shows how to create samples with original documents, and the second column is the ratio of copies. The first row is to copy 10%–30% of the original post and make corrections, replacing some sentences or vocabulary. And the second row, to copy and paste documents with significant changes, we copy at a rate of 40%–60% by making corrections to the original document, paraphrasing some sentences, and sorting word order. Then, finally, we copy 70%–100% from the original translated document to create new documents without changes.

The result is shown in Table 4; we measure the performance by two metrics, precision and recall [25] calculated in two cases. Given a threshold of x, in Case 1, we search documents that own similarity within the given threshold (the similarity score < x), while in Case 2, we consider documents that have the similarity score be equal to or higher than the threshold (the similarity score ≥ x). Case

2 is a sample document copied from the previous Vietnamese translation. The precision and recall measurement results have shown very positive results. We use precision and recall [26], Precision in Formula 4 is conducted from the documents retrieved, and the Recall in Formula 5 is based on the relevant documents in the collection. In the equation, *RelRetrieved* is relevant documents returned from the considered repository, *RelinCollection* is relevant documents in such collection, and *Retrieved* is the number of retrieved documents.

$$Precision = \left| \frac{RelRetrieved}{Retrieved} \right| \qquad (4)$$

$$Recall = \left| \frac{RelRetrieved}{Rel\,in\,Collection} \right| \qquad (5)$$

An English document can create a new Vietnamese document after being translated into Vietnamese with minor changes or keep it the same as the original one. Detecting which Vietnamese documents are translated from the original one is still possible. The thresholds that we apply to find similar documents are 0.3 (30%), 0.5(50%), and 0.7(70%).

Our proposed method combines the translation tool and calculates the similarity between documents to detect a document copied or edited from another language to determine the documents suspected of plagiarism. To evaluate the efficiency, we created the test data by copying and editing the translations to produce a new document to verify that the translation can be used by keeping or changing some parts.

For most documents, after being translated into the language to be copied, the violator can use 10%–30% or 40%–60% edited copy to make it harder to detect. It is impossible to copy 90%–100% because the translation needs to be reviewed and edited a few more parts to make the document's content coherent and easy to understand. The machine-based translation is just one of the approaches we recommend for multilingual plagiarism detection.

Table 4. Similar documents Search Results in Precision and Recall scores with 10 considered suspicious documents.

Datasets	Copy ratio	Case 1		Case 2	
		Precision	Recall	Precision	Recall
Copy and paste with minor similarity - 10	10%–30%	0.9125	0.9250	0.9129	0.9489
Copy and paste with moderate similarity - 10	40%–60%	0.9233	0.8912	0.9412	0.9144
Copy and paste with significant similarity - 10	70%–100%	1.0000	0.9012	1.0000	0.9012
Average		0.9362	0.9058	0.9423	0.9215

Figure 4 shows that case 2 gives more positive results than case 1. Precision and recall have improved compared to case 1. Both cases are equal when tested at a copy threshold of 70% above. It shows that it is possible to copy from another language. A violator can use translation tools, and the violator can translate

Precision, Recall in 2 cases

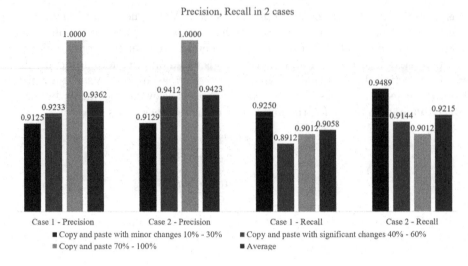

Fig. 4. Performance comparison in Precision, Recall of 2 cases.

any document from language A to language B, edit more or less, or keep all the translation content. Applying the proposed method as in Sect. 3 shows that it is possible to find similarities between documents translated into a specified language.

4.4 Implementation

We also built an integrated system that supports translation from English to Vietnamese with Google Translate API and similarity detection.

Fig. 5 shows that with the similarity check application, users can upload documents with .docx, .pdf extensions. Next, the system automatically converts to .txt, and they can select the test thresholds to be checked like 10%, 20%, 30%, 40%, and 50%. For document preprocessing and similarity checking, we use Flask[5], a Python framework for building the backend.

After the user uploads the document, the returned documents (as illustrated in Fig. 6) can have similar contents compared to the considered document. After processing, the system will return the results in the following order in the table, including No., file name, TF-IDF similarity, and word order similarity, synthesizing 2 measures to produce a common measure.

---

[5] https://flask.palletsprojects.com/.

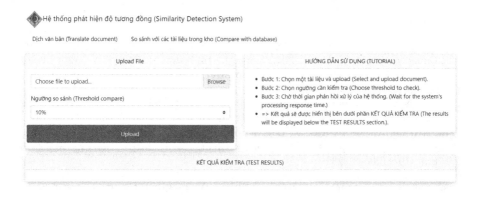

Fig. 5. Similarity Check

STT (No.)	File	SimS (TF-IDF)	SimR (Word order)	Sim = SimS + SimR
1	01-Sample-LA Click to view	0.485	0.372	0.429
2	17-Sample-LA Click to view	0.782	0.664	0.723

KẾT QUẢ KIỂM TRA (TEST RESULTS)

Ngưỡng kiểm tra (Threshold): 30%

Thời gian xử lý (Time processing): 00h:01m:28s

Tổng số file (Total file): 2

Fig. 6. Check results presented in the web interface.

5   Conclusion

With the proposed system model, this study solved the problem of building a translation module from English to Vietnamese using the API service from Google Translate and calculating similarity scores with documents copied, edited, or changed few contents when translated from English to Vietnamese.

The initial results are very positive, providing new research directions in the future to further improve the quality of the system so that it can better and more thoroughly evaluate the problem of multilingual plagiarism. In addition, the system can work relatively well with documents with many similarities.

With the current system, we need to research different similarity checking techniques such as semantic similarity, synonyms, and antonyms. Furthermore, we will apply some techniques to highlight similar sentences compared to sentences in the considered repository. In addition, further work can improve the preprocessing techniques to increase the speed of checking and collect more data to supplement the database.

Acknowledgement. This study is funded in part by the Can Tho University, Code: TDH2022-04.

References

1. Dien, T.T., Han, H.N., Thai-Nghe, N.: An approach for plagiarism detection in learning resources. In: Dang, T.K., Küng, J., Takizawa, M., Bui, S.H. (eds.) FDSE 2019. LNCS, vol. 11814, pp. 722–730. Springer, Cham (2019). https://doi.org/10.1007/978-3-030-35653-8_52
2. Chan, N.N., Roussanaly, A., Boyer, A.: Learning resource recommendation: an orchestration of content-based filtering, word semantic similarity and page ranking. In: Rensing, C., de Freitas, S., Ley, T., Muñoz-Merino, P.J. (eds.) EC-TEL 2014. LNCS, vol. 8719, pp. 302–316. Springer, Cham (2014). https://doi.org/10.1007/978-3-319-11200-8_23
3. Yunanda, G., Nurjanah, D., Meliana, S.: Recommendation system from microsoft news data using tf-idf and cosine similarity methods. Build. Inf. Technol. Sci. 4(1), 277–284 (2022). http://ejurnal.seminar-id.com/index.php/bits/article/view/1670
4. Renuka, S., Raj Kiran, G.S.S., Rohit, P.: An unsupervised content-based article recommendation system using natural language processing. In: Jeena Jacob, I., Kolandapalayam Shanmugam, S., Piramuthu, S., Falkowski-Gilski, P. (eds.) Data Intelligence and Cognitive Informatics. AIS, pp. 165–180. Springer, Singapore (2021). https://doi.org/10.1007/978-981-15-8530-2_13
5. Bagul, D.V., Barve, S.: A novel content-based recommendation approach based on lda topic modeling for literature recommendation. In: 2021 6th International Conference on Inventive Computation Technologies (ICICT), pp. 954–961 (2021)
6. Resta, O.A., Aditya, A., Purwiantono, F.E.: Plagiarism detection in students' theses using the cosine similarity method. Sinkron : jurnal dan penelitian teknik informatika 5(2), 305–313 (2021). https://polgan.ac.id/jurnal/index.php/sinkron/article/view/10909
7. Chavan, H., Taufik, M., Kadave, R., Chandra, N.: Plagiarism detector using machine learning. Int. J. Res. Eng. Sci. Manag. 4(4), 152–154 (2021). http://journals.resaim.com/ijresm/article/view/677
8. Fauzi, R., Iqbal, M., Haryanti, T.: Design and implementation of a final project plagiarism detection system using cosine similarity method. IJAIT (Int. J. Appl. Inf. Technol.), 1–16 (2022). https://journals.telkomuniversity.ac.id/ijait/article/view/4146
9. Ehsan, N., Shakery, A.: Candidate document retrieval for cross-lingual plagiarism detection using two-level proximity information. Inf. Process. Manag. 52(6), 1004–1017 (2016). https://www.sciencedirect.com/science/article/abs/pii/S0306457316300784
10. Gomaa, W., Fahmy, A.: A survey of text similarity approaches. Int. J. Comput. Appl. 68 (2013)
11. Roostaee, M., Sadreddini, M.H., Fakhrahmad, S.M.: An effective approach to candidate retrieval for cross-language plagiarism detection: a fusion of conceptual and keyword-based schemes. Inf. Process. Manag. 57(2), 102150 (2020). https://www.sciencedirect.com/science/article/abs/pii/S0306457318310148
12. Feng, G., et al.: Question classification by approximating semantics. In: Proceedings of the 24th International Conference on World Wide Web, pp. 407–417 (2015)
13. Ceska, Z., Toman, M., Jezek, K.: Multilingual plagiarism detection. In: Dochev, D., Pistore, M., Traverso, P. (eds.) AIMSA 2008. LNCS (LNAI), vol. 5253, pp. 83–92. Springer, Heidelberg (2008). https://doi.org/10.1007/978-3-540-85776-1_8
14. Juričić, V., Stefanec, V., Bosanac, S.: Multilingual plagiarism detection corpus. In: 2012 Proceedings of the 35th International Convention MIPRO, pp. 1310–1314 (2012)

15. Dougherty, M.V.: Translation plagiarism. In: Disguised Academic Plagiarism. REF, vol. 8, pp. 13–36. Springer, Cham (2020). https://doi.org/10.1007/978-3-030-46711-1_2

16. Yankova, D.: On translated plagiarism in academic discourse. Engl. Stud. NBU **6**, 189–200 (2020)

17. Wiwanitkit, V.: How to verify and manage the translational plagiarism? Open Access Macedonian J. Med. Sci. **4** (2016)

18. Pataki, M., Marosi, A.: Searching for translated plagiarism with the help of desktop grids. J. Grid Comput. **11** (2013)

19. Mustofa, K., Sir, Y.A.: Early-detection system for cross-language (translated) plagiarism. In: Mustofa, K., Neuhold, E.J., Tjoa, A.M., Weippl, E., You, I. (eds.) ICT-EurAsia 2013. LNCS, vol. 7804, pp. 21–30. Springer, Heidelberg (2013). https://doi.org/10.1007/978-3-642-36818-9_3

20. Potthast, M., Barrón-Cedeño, A., Stein, B., Rosso, P.: Cross-language plagiarism detection. Knowl.-Based Syst. **45**, 45–62 (2011)

21. Barrón-Cedeño, A., Rosso, P.: Methods for cross-language plagiarism detection. Knowl.-Based Syst. **50**, 211–217 (2013)

22. Alabbas, M., Khudeyer, R.S., Radif, M., Hameed, H.K.: Online multilingual plagiarism detection system using multi search engines. J. Southwest Jiaotong Univ. **54**(6) (2019). https://doi.org/10.35741/issn.0258-2724.54.6.30

23. Anguita, A., Beghelli, A., Creixell, W.: Automatic cross-language plagiarism detection. In: 2011 7th International Conference on Natural Language Processing and Knowledge Engineering, pp. 173–176 (2011)

24. Duong, T.L.: Research on text similarity in Vietnamese and its application to support the assessment of copying electronic articles. Hanoi Open University, Hanoi (2014)

25. Sanderson, M., Zobel, J.: Information retrieval system evaluation: effort, sensitivity, and reliability. In: Proceedings of the 28th Annual International ACM SIGIR Conference on Research and Development in Information Retrieval - SIGIR 2005, pp. 162–169 (2005)

26. Arora, M., Kanjilal, U., Varshney, D.: Evaluation of information retrieval: precision and recall. Int. J. Indian Cult. Bus. Manag. **12**, 224 (2016)

Combine Clasification Algorithm and Centernet Model to Predict Trafic Density

Vu Le Quynh Phuong[1](✉), Nguyen Viet Dong[2], Tran Nguyen Minh Thu[2], and Pham Nguyen Khang[2]

[1] Kien Giang Teachers Training College, Kien Giang, Vietnam
vlqphuong@cdspkg.edu.vn
[2] College of Information & Communication Technology, Can Tho University, Can Tho, Vietnam
dongb1709590@student.ctu.edu.vn, {tnmthu,pnkhang}@ctu.edu.vn

Abstract. Nowadays, the traffic situation is very complicated in Vietnam. Traffic jams happen frequently in densely populated or peak hours. So, it is necessary for an automatic warning system to police officers about traffic status in time and effectively. In this research, the system automatically estimates the vehicle motion rate and the number of vehicles. This system is useful for roads with lots of hard-to-distinguish traffic. The method is based on computer vision such as background subtraction and deep learning such as the CNN network model and the CenterNet object detection model. Experimental data are taken from videos in Vietnam with the view in front of the Kien Giang and Da Nang hospitals. The achieved classification model results can predict with 91.7% accuracy on the test set, the precision of crowded road predictions is 81.9% precision and 70.4% recall. When the CenterNet model is applied to estimate the number of vehicles, the model reached 1.261 MAE. The speed of the system when it is run experimentally on hardware using Nvidia Geforce GTX 1070 GPU reached 4.6 FPS.

Keywords: CenterNet · Object detection · Vehicle counting · Background subtraction

1 Introduction

Traffic congestion is a huge issue in many big cities. Especially, millions of people use the city's infrastructure to move during rush hour. Nowadays, closed-circuit television (CCTV) systems are installed everywhere to counter this problem. The traffic polices observe the monitor. When traffic jams occur, they go to a place that has congestion to control traffic in hope that it could reduce the traffic flow during peak time. This way has proved to be effective in many positive ways. However, this way has got a lot of time, humans, and money. Sometimes, it is not effective. Therefore, they need another way to solve professionally this problem.

In the past, to estimate traffic density, magnetic loop detectors or supersonic wave detectors were used. It would damage the road or block traffic. In recent years, with the rapid development of artificial intelligence and the proposal of efficient algorithms such

T. K. Dang et al. (Eds.): FDSE 2022, CCIS 1688, pp. 588–600, 2022.
https://doi.org/10.1007/978-981-19-8069-5_40

as deep learning, the ability of computer vision to deal with traffic system problems has made a qualitative leap. The traffic management systems utilize images or videos that are collected from CCTV. Video-based traffic density estimation is the most common because of its many advantages: easy and economical to install video, robust, real-time, and intelligent. So, video-based vehicle detection technology is becoming more and more important to ITS.

There are two main approaches to estimating traffic density based on image techniques in the recent literature: microscopic and macroscopic [15]. In microscopic approaches, the vehicles are detected and located exactly. Then, the authors count vehicles and figure out to estimate the traffic density. Some examples of the microscopic are [2, 20]. Another approaches, the vehicles do not need detection or bounding box around the vehicles. They used the local feature vectors over the entire image. Then, they use machine learning or data mining methods to learn [4–6].

Both two approaches are advantages and disadvantages. The macroscopic approaches can estimate only one vehicle type. Meanwhile, there are many kinds of vehicles on the road. In contrast, microscopic approaches can detect or track many types of vehicles. The traffic images have a lot of information. So, it is collected and served ITS purpose. In recent years, there has been a rise in detection methods based on deep learning with good results.

In the microscopic literature, there are many works to solve the problem of traffic monitoring: the frame difference [11], background difference [13], edge detection [7], and deep learning method [16] to detect vehicles. The results of these approaches were bad when the streets are congested or bad weather conditions affect the quality of the input image. Besides, the method based on rate estimation avoids the need to detect and track each vehicle object independently, it solves the case of congested streets.

Background subtraction is a basic technique in Image processing and Computer vision. This is a method of foreground detection, which simply means that we will separate an object in the image from the background behind it, for post-processing purposes such as object recognition, gestures, motion, tracking… Background subtraction is a popular method for isolating the moving parts of a scene by segmenting it into background and foreground. The principle of this algorithm is to subtract the pixels in the current frame and the reference frame. It determines the pixel difference between the two images, then it uses filtering methods to reduce noise and to threshold pixel difference to identify objects or backgrounds [22].

In recent years, there are many different approaches to solving the problem of object detection with deep learning algorithms. The appearance of CNN has promoted the development of the computer vision industry. CNN was developed from an original idea inspired by how the human eye works, breaking down images into convolutions for neurons to process. In 1998, the Convolutional Neural Network was introduced by Bengio, Le Cun, Bottou, and Haffner. Their first model was named LeNet-5 [20]. Chi Kien Huynh et al. proposed a detection method with a CNN model to detect motorbikes [4]. It achieved good results. However, the computation time of CNN is too long. It is not possible to integrate this method into systems with real-time requirements.

In another study, the image object detection models are based on the R-CNN architecture [17–19], also known as two-stage detectors. In this approach, Phuong et al. built a system to estimate traffic monitoring support based on the Faster RCNN model [16]. The system detected vehicles, then counted the number of two-wheels, four-wheels, and priority vehicles to determine traffic conditions. The accuracy of object detection is noted above 75% on the test dataset. However, the detection time is high (1.5–2.8 s for frame). It is not good for real-time detection. When the vehicle is in heavy traffic, the model cannot identify it correctly (cannot detect all vehicles in the area). During traffic jams, it is difficult to recognize vehicles because the image from the video is an overlap vehicle. So, it is not feasible to count vehicles in the area when traffic jams occur. Therefore, it is necessary to change the method of determining traffic density without relying on vehicle counting. It is possible to label each image with the low vehicle, average, crowded, and traffic jam.

To solve the above problem, another approach has been proposed. CenterNet is a fully convolutional neural network with a simple design, but with a good balance of speed and accuracy [21]. The CenterNet model has solved the problem of today's most successful object detection networks. It has not performed computational processes with many discrete steps. Besides that, it is not difficult to optimize for speed like two-stage networks spend a lot of time.

With these successes, we want to employ the usage of image techniques in our problem. We propose a model to estimate the traffic density from the traffic cameras. The input data was taken in front of the Kien Giang hospital's gate and collected from the traffic camera of the DaNang city government. Three models are applied to estimate the traffic. In the first model, the frame is checked by the CNN network: crowded or not. If the scene was crowded, it is classified by the background subtraction algorithm. If the scene was not crowded, we built a second model. This model detects and counts vehicles. There are three labels: the vehicle has two wheels (bike or motorbike); four wheels (vans, cars, buses); the last label is priority vehicles. The system notifies the user: the crowded street (moving normally, moving slowly, and traffic jam); the un-crowded street (medium, low, sparse).

2   Proposed Method

We use a video dataset directly from the traffic camera to estimate the density of traffic. A similar approach was taken in [16] for estimating traffic density. However, this system is not good for crowded streets when the vehicles in the picture overlap. To deal with this problem, we propose a system with 3 steps as Fig. 1.

First, the input video is extracted frame to the image. The output of this classification model is the labels 0 and 1. Label 0 corresponds to the image of the uncrowded street. The 1-label corresponds to a crowded street with a lot of vehicles which can make it impossible for the object detection model to accurately detect objects.

If the result is uncrowded (label 0), the frame will continue to be used as the input of the traffic detection model. The vehicle detection model uses CenterNet architecture for output including parameters: "heatmap", "offset" and "width-height". In this model, we don't need the size of vehicles, so we need only 1 output. Heatmap is used to estimate the location of the center point of the vehicle. The system counts each vehicle in each class. It is based on analyzing the statistical results of the number of each class. Then, it predicts the number of vehicles on the road with labels: sparse, low, or medium.

Conversely, if the result from the road classification model is crowded (label 1), the system will predict traffic conditions on the road by the background subtraction algorithm. Background subtraction is applied to segment vehicles on the road. Based on the analysis of the movement rate of vehicles, it predicts the traffic density on the road: moving normally, moving slowly, and traffic jams.

In this paper, the system detects congestion to give warnings to the traffic police. It will help them control traffic timely and effective.

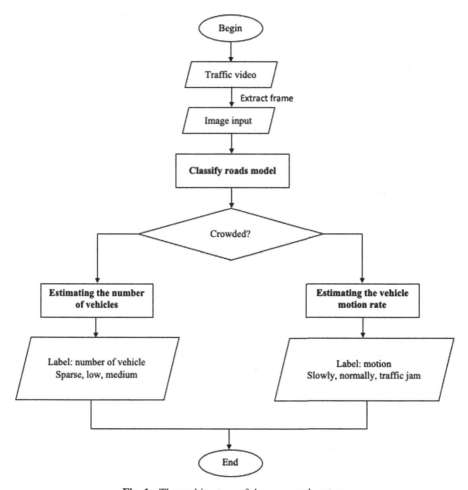

Fig. 1. The architecture of the proposed system

Our system is composed of the following modules:

2.1 Classify Roads Model

The classify roads model is used Convolutional neural networks (CNN). The classification model works with the Keras library. In this paper, based on VGG16, InceptionV3 and ResNet50 models were used to compare the network initialization model with the transfer learning model. Then, we compare and select the effective classification model to use for the system.

The images are cut from the video. Then, we resize the images into 512×512 RGB because they are not a heavy load, and their qualities are good. The convolutional layers will be initialized with weights based on training on the ImageNet dataset [1] and removed the layers at the end. It means, we freeze the convolutional layers, to keep the same feature extractors. Then, we append pre-initialized weights to be suitable for the problem of crowded road classification – 2 classes. First, the output of convolutional layers is flattened one-dimensional. Then, it passes through a cascade with 128 fully connected neurons. The output is activated with the relu function. Finally, the output layer is 1 neuron with a sigmoid activation function because this is a binary classification problem. The output of this model is probability p of 1- label (crowed). So, the 0- label probability is (p-1).

When compiling the model, the model needs a loss function and an optimizer. The loss function is the quantity that will be minimized during training. The optimizer determines how the network will be updated based on the loss function. The optimal algorithm is used: gradient descent with the learning rate of 0.5×10^{-4}; the momentum is 0.9. The loss function of this model is Binary Cross Entropy.

After the classify crowded road model was installed, two models are built. They are the model for estimating the vehicle motion rate and the number of vehicles. The vehicle motion rate is built when the street is uncrowded. On the other hand, the estimated number of vehicles model is built by CenterNet. It is used in the case that the result of the model predicts a crowd of 0 – the road is not crowded.

2.2 Estimating the Number of Vehicles

In the uncrowded-street case, CenterNet model was used to estimate the number of vehicles. Vehicles are divided into 3 types: 2-wheels, 4-wheels, and priority vehicles. The model is built using the "Keras" library. The model input is an RGB image. Its size is 5125×512. The model is trained with the hourglass-52 network which is only one hourglass module. In the CenterNet model used for object detection, the outputs of the feature network are divided into 3 branches corresponding to 3 outputs heatmap, offset, and width-height.

- The first output is a heatmap. A heat map predicts the location of the object, each type of vehicle will have a corresponding heat map,
- The second output is offset. It is the center point. The center point position predicted by the heatmap will be at 128×128 coordinates. When it was converted to 512×512, this offset may have deviated from the actual position. The offset output helps to adjust this error: the two channels are offset width and offset height.
- The third output is bounding box size. It includes width and height.

In our work, the model is used to estimate the number of vehicles through object detection. Therefore, we need only know the number of objects. This problem can be determined through the feature map without parameters such as offset and bounding box. So, we can remove these outputs to increase the speech of the model.

After building the CenterNet model with Hourglass feature network, the next step is to train the model. The Adam optimization algorithm is used in training the CenterNet model. The reduction rate of the loss function when using the Adam optimal function is much faster than SGD and SGD with momentum. Adam is an improved method from Adadelta and RMSprop optimization algorithms. Adam is able to overcome local extremes while still providing rapid gradient descent and fast convergence near the optimal point.

After building and training a model to estimate the number of vehicles, the next step is to design an algorithm to estimate the movement of vehicles. The output of the estimated model is the number of vehicles according to each type of "2-wheel", "4-wheel" and "priority". Next, the density score will be calculated by the formula:

$$Count\ score = w_{2w} \times C_{2w} + w_{4w} \times C_{4w} + w_{pr} \times C_{pr} \tag{1}$$

The count score is the value density, and w is the weight corresponding to the vehicle type. In this paper, we choose the weights (1, 2, 2.5) corresponding to the labels ("2-wheel", "4-wheel", "priority") because of the large vehicle. Then the "count score" value is the threshold. If the "count score" is less than 10 then the road density is predicted as "sparse", if the "count score" is between 10 and 20 then it is predicted to be "low", if the "count score" is greater than 20 then it is predicted as "high density".

2.3 Estimation of the Vehicle Motion Rate

In the crowded-street case, a background subtraction algorithm was applied to estimate the vehicle motion rate. The basic principle of the subtraction algorithm should be divided into two parts: "background modeling" and "background subtraction". "Background modeling" is a background model used to estimate the components of the background. This model exists throughout the operation of the system. It is gradually updated over time when a new image is applied. "Background subtraction" will calculate the difference distance between the current frame and the current "background" estimated by the background model. If it is greater than a given threshold, it will be considered a foreground object; in contrast, it will be considered background.

The system will be used as an input image for the next two steps: "foreground mask" and "difference mask". For the "foreground mask" estimation step, the input image is de-noised by increasing contrast and blurring with a Gaussian Blur filter. Then, it is applied "BackgroundSubtractorMOG2" with a long background learning history enough that the background doesn't update so quickly that a vehicle is mistaken for the background when it suddenly stops moving for a short period of time (less than 1 h) (long term BackgroundSubtractorMOG2). The background is re-learned every 1–2 h. The background is updated relatively well during congestion. When the vehicles are not moving, the model can still detect the vehicles on the road. Based on experimental observations, the selected history length value is 1600 and the selected threshold is 70. These parameters give a relatively good segmentation ability. The output that we get is a segmented mask of the traffic on the road that may still have a little noise. At this time, the Median Blur filter is applied to remove the noise. The result in the "foreground mask" estimation step is the mask of the vehicles on the road.

Simultaneously, we copy the input image that is converted to the grayscale image. It is applied "BackgroundSubtractorMOG2" and the background learning history length is 1. The background is relearned in every frame. When the new frame is applied, it will be subtracted from the background of a close previous frame for the output of the offset segment mask due to vehicle movement.

The ratio between the "difference mask" and the "foreground mask" is calculated by the formula:

$$Moving\ rate = \frac{difference\_mask \times 100}{foreground\ mask}. \tag{2}$$

If the moving rate of vehicles is less than 10%, it will be considered a "traffic jam". If the movement rate is between 10–25%, it will be considered "slowly moving". If the movement rate is more than 25%, it will be considered "normally moving".

2.4 Evaluation Method

In this study, we evaluate three models with different parameters. The scenario of training, evaluation, and testing for each parameter of each model with each test dataset measures the accuracy.

We use the test dataset to evaluate the performance of the model in actual running. The models will be evaluated using the "Precision", "Recall" and "F1" stages. In addition, the time prediction will also be recorded for comparison. In this measure, the IoU ratio is used as a threshold for determining whether a predicted outcome is a true positive or a false positive. If the IoU $\geq$ "threshold" it is counted as "True Positive" (TP), otherwise, it is "False Positive" (FP). There is also a property called "False negative" (FN), which is "ground truth", which was not detected. "Precision" is defined as the number of correct scores in the detected scores, calculated using the formula:

$$Precision = \frac{TP}{TP + FP} = \frac{TP}{\text{all detection}} \tag{3}$$

"Recall" is defined as a number of points true in the "ground truths":

$$Recall = \frac{TP}{TP + FN} = \frac{TP}{\text{all ground truths}}. \tag{4}$$

The classified road model is trained, and the model to estimate the number of vehicles using the CenterNet model was built. The vehicle number estimation model is used to estimate the vehicle density in the case that the result of the model predicts the busy road to be 0 – the road is not crowded. In this study, the output of the CenterNet object detection model has been stripped of some outputs to estimate the number of vehicles. The heat map output is used to estimate the number of traffic vehicles in this model, it can be counted as vehicles. The result of the numerical estimation is a number that can be used to evaluate the effectiveness of the model in estimating the quantity. In this study, the mean absolute error (MAE) is used to evaluate the effectiveness of the model in estimating the number of vehicles.

$$MAE = \frac{1}{N} \sum_{i=1}^{N} |y_i - \hat{y}_i| \qquad (5)$$

The MAE is calculated using the formula (3), the meaning of the MAE is the average difference between the value estimated by the regression model and the true value in the ground truth. In this study, MAE is calculated on the total and each class. For the case of calculating MAE on each class, to obtain a good MAE, we handle one class for a vehicle type. We consider only images containing that vehicle type, and compute MAE on the image set containing this class rather than on the entire dataset because not all images contain the type of vehicle under consideration.

3 Experiment Results and Discussion

3.1 The Datasets

In this paper, we collect datasets in two cities: Kien Giang and Da Nang. All videos are real-time traffic cameras. Frames are cut from videos (Fig. 2, Fig. 3).

Fig. 2. Traffic camera in DaNang

Fig. 3. CAM 3 in Kien Giang

- Dataset 1: It is collected from traffic cameras in Da Nang city. The video data is from a public camera source at the address http://camera.0511.vn/. We use the camera in front of hospital DaNang because this place has many vehicles.
- Dataset 2: It is provided by the police of Vinh Thanh Van ward – Rach Gia city – Kien Giang province. The cameras are located on LeLoi street (opposite the KienGiang hospital). Each video is nearly 1 h. The dataset has 03 camera angles (CAM1, CAM3, CAM5). From 10 AM to 11 AM, the scene was sunny (CAM 1, CAM 3); From 4:30 PM to 5:30 PM, the scene was sunny at first, but after that, it started to rain (CAM 5). The resolution at the angle of CAM1 and CAM5 is 1920 × 1080, FPS is 15 frames/sec and 12 frames/sec, respectively. Particularly, the resolution at the angle of CAM3 is 1280 × 720, FPS: 10 frames/sec.

Because our system has 2 modules, so we have 2 part classify:

Data for Classifying Road Model
The input video will be reviewed and selected. The crowded road sections will be cut using the "Trim" in the "Photos" application on Windows 10. After capturing the crowded road videos, frames were cut from the video (1 frame every second). After cropping the videos, the dataset has 3903 images in jpg format. Images are labeled with two labels "0": for un-crowded roads; "1": for crowded roads. The labeled data have 3.903 images with a label ("0" – 3018, "1" – 885). The labeled data is divided into 3 subsets "train", "valid" and "test" with the respective division ratio is 8:1:1. The dataset division is done manually. First, we arrange the frames in the original dataset according to the timeline as in the original video. Then, we take the first 80% of the images into the "train" folder. The remaining 20% is further divided into 2 equal parts for "valid" and "test". The data in the "train" "test" and "valid" sets come from different periods. The diversity of angles and contexts in the dataset remains constant.

Data for Estimating the Number of Vehicles
All images are labeled with the LabelImg tool. The training dataset has 1.260 images with 3 labels: 2-wheel, 4-wheel, and priority. The valid dataset includes 360 images. And 4 evaluation datasets: test dataset 1 (test1) include 180 images from CAM3; test dataset 2 (test2) has 100 images from CAM1; test dataset 3 (test3) has 100 images from CAM5; Test dataset4 (Test4) has100 images from CAM5 after these images are rotated 15 degrees.

3.2 Experiment Results

The process of training, testing, and evaluating the model was performed on Google Colab Pro with hardware configuration: Intel(R) Xeon(R) CPU @ 2.20 GHz 2 Core, 12 GB RAM, and the Tesla P100-PCIE GPU with 16 GB of RAM.

The combined model receives an input 512×512 image. First, the image will be in the crowded road classification model to classify the current road: crowded or un-crowed. If the road is uncrowded, this image will be in the Estimation of the traffic density model for vehicle detection and speed estimation to predict the vehicle density. The input image is also used to update the background in the background subtraction algorithm. If the road is crowded, the input image will be input to the background subtraction algorithm to compare the difference with the previous frame to determine the movement of the vehicles.

The performance of speed and accuracy of the system is determined by the efficiency of the road classification model and the object detection model. To check the recognition efficiency of the model, the testing process is performed on crowded road classification and Estimation of the traffic density model.

Classify the Road Model
The classified model with different feature networks has been trained and tested on the above dataset in order to choose the model with the best classification ability. The trained backbone networks include InceptionV3, VGG16, and ResNet50. Backbone networks

are initialized with pre-trained weights on the ImageNet dataset, then it is trained to adjust the weights using the training dataset and select the optimal parameters using the valid and test dataset. In the process of training the models using the methods of data augmentation including horizontal and vertical displacement, flipping the image horizontally, rotating the image slightly, zooming the image, and adjusting the brightness. The results are recorded in Table 1.

The results of the evaluation of the models on the validation dataset in Table 1 give information on the accuracy of the three backbones. The classify model using the VGG16 and InceptionV3 networks is a backbone network that gives good results in terms of both accuracy and F1-score. The model using VGG16 and ResNet have the same time. VGG-16 has many more parameters than ResNet, but this does not mean it's faster. Because the inference time depends on many factors: memory access cost and degree of parallelism. The classification model using InceptionV3 gives the best accuracy but the slowest. Therefore, if the user chooses a system for real-time, we propose using backbone VGG16 because time and accuracy are good.

Table 1. Results of the models on the dataset

Network	Valid dataset			Test dataset		
	Accuracy	F1	Time (ms)	Accuracy	F1	Time (ms)
VGG16	**0.907**	0.763	**46.761**	**0.917**	**0.757**	**46.761**
InceptionV3	**0.915**	0.784	58.201	0.912	0.738	58.201
ResNet50	0.835	0.483	**46.620**	0.882	0.566	**46.620**

Estimation of the Traffic Density

The train set and valid set use the data augmentation methods include: flip the image horizontally, shift the image horizontally and vertically, zoom the image, rotate the image, adjust the brightness, tone, sharpness, contrast, and merge with the mosaic method. The CenterNet model was built and trained with the Hourglass-52 model using these data. The results were obtained in Table 2 with the MAE measure.

Table 2. CenterNet Hourglass-52 model MAE results, input size 512 × 512, epoch 6

	Focal loss> = 0.5				Focal loss> = 0.7		
	MAE	2-wh	4-wh	Priority	MAE	2-wh	4-wh	Priority
test1	**1.344**	1.267	0.247	0.207	5.183	4.294	0.916	0.931
test2	1.630	1.820	0.765	N/A	4.220	3.580	1.255	N/A
test3	**4.260**	3.650	0.969	1.000	7.030	6.210	1.266	1.000
test4	2.390	2.040	0.770	1.000	5.670	4.919	1.279	1.000

We can be seen that the MAE error is quite good on test1 and test2 sets with a confidence threshold of 0.5 achieved at about 1.5 MAE. The results of the predicted time by CenterNet models using the Hourglass-52 backbone network is 85.9 ms. It is faster than R-CNN of Phuong et al. [1].

Program
The program is built using "flask" and "flask socket" libraries on the server and Html, CSS, and javascript on the web interface. The program creates a fixed connection between the website and the server. The website will continuously crop the image. Then, it sends the image to the server. In sever, the image will be processed and then it returns the results to the website for display.

The experimental program is run and observed on the device with hardware: Intel(R) Core(TM) i7-6700 CPU @ 3.4 GHz 8 Core, 16 GB RAM memory, and Nvidia Geforce GTX 1070 GPU with 8 GB RAM. When we run experimentally, the system achieved 4.6 FPS. In the road classification model ranges from 8–12 FPS. CenterNet model with Hourglass-52 featured network can work with 4.6 FPS. The estimated speed of movement using the background subtraction algorithm reached over 15 FPS. The program's operation is divided into two parallel operation parts: the model to classify the crowded road and the model to estimate the amount and level of movement. Depending on the results of the classification, will decide what the model used (Fig. 4).

Fig. 4. The estimation moving traffic program

4   Conclusion and Future Work

In this paper, a system has been built to estimate the density and movement of vehicles. We successfully trained and integrated the classification model into the classification of crowded or uncrowded. We edit and train the CenterNet model for estimating the number of vehicles. We apply a background subtraction algorithm to detect the movement of vehicles.

The traffic condition classification model is trained on 3 models using 3 different feature networks, VGG16, InceptionV3, and ResNet50. The classification model that gives the best results is the model using the feature network VGG16 with an overall accuracy of 91.7% on the test set. In which, the system predicts traffic jams achieved 81.9% accuracy. For the estimate of the number of vehicles using the CenterNet model, when we train the model with the data augmentation, the highest number of vehicles obtained MAE 1,261, and the prediction speed is 18 times faster than the Faster R-CNN model.

The speed of the system when we run experimentally reached 4.6 FPS on hardware using Nvidia Geforce GTX 1070 GPU. In which, the road classification model ranged 8–12 FPS. CenterNet model with Hourglass-52 featured network can work with 4.6 FPS. The estimated speed of movement using the background subtraction algorithm reached over 15 FPS.

The accuracy of CenterNet model needs to be further improved in datasets other than rotation angle and location to increase model flexibility. The thresholding of vehicle density based on the number of vehicles and the level of traffic thresholding is only based on experimental methods through visual observation, there is no theoretical basis or testing method to evaluate the effectiveness of thresholding. The program interface does not yet support direct input from the camera and does not yet support many video formats.

Acknowledgment. The authors would like to thank Vinh Thanh Van ward police department in RachGia city (Kien Giang, VietNam) for providing the traffic videos. We would also like to express our gratitude to the police for their help in collecting and publishing the datasets.

References

1. Krizhevsky, A., Sutskever, I., Hinton, G.E.: ImageNet classification with deep convolutional neural networks. Commun. ACM **60**(6), 84–90 (2017)
2. Chan, A.B., Vasconcelos, N.: Counting people with low-level features and Bayesian regression. IEEE Trans. Image Process. **21**(4), 2160–2177 (2012)
3. Szegedy, C., Vanhoucke, V., Ioffe, S., Shlens, J., Wojna, Z.: Rethinking the inception architecture for computer vision. arXiv preprint, arXiv:1512.00567v3, Dec 2015
4. Huynh, C.K., Dang, T.K., Nguyen, C.A.: Motorbike counting in heavily crowded scenes, future data and security engineering. In: 8th International Conference, FDSE 2021, pp. 175–194 (2021)
5. Darwishalzughaibi, A., Ahmed Hakami, H., Chaczko, Z.: Review of human motion detection based on background subtraction techniques. Int. J. Comput. Appl. **122**, 1–5 (2015)
6. Guo, J., et al.: A new moving object detection method based on frame difference and background subtraction. In: Iop Conference, Dec, pp. 242–246. ASME Press (2017)
7. Gui-Ping, B., Yi-Lin, Q.: An adaptive edge-detection method based on Canny algorithm. Electr. Des. Eng. **116**, 886–893 (2017)

8. Law, H., Deng, J.: CornerNet: detecting objects as paired keypoints. arXiv preprint, arXiv: 1808.01244v2 (2018)
9. Redmon, J., Divvala, S., Girshick, R., Farhadi, A.: You only look once: unified, realtime object detection. In: 2016 IEEE Conference on Computer Vision and Pattern Recognition (CVPR), pp. 779–788, 2016. https://doi.org/10.1109/CVPR.2016.91
10. Simonyan, K., Zisserman, A.: Very deep convolutional networks for large-scale image recognition. In: ICLR 2015. arXiv preprint, arXvir:1409.1556v5
11. Duan, K., Bai, S., Xie, L., Qi, H., Huang, Q., Tian, Q.: CenterNet: keypoint triplets for object detection. In: 2019 IEEE/CVF International Conference on Computer Vision (ICCV), 2019, pp. 6568–6577. https://doi.org/10.1109/ICCV.2019.00667
12. He, K., Zhang, X., Ren, S., Sun, J.: Deep Residual learning for image recognition, Dec 2015. arXiv preprint, arXiv:1512.03385v1
13. Law, H., Deng, J.: CornerNet: detecting objects as paired key points. Int. J. Comput. Vision **128**(3), 642–656 (2019). https://doi.org/10.1007/s11263-019-01204-1
14. Liu, W., et al.: SSD: Single Shot MultiBox Detector, vol. 9905, pp. 21–37. https://doi.org/10.1007/978-3-319-46448-0_2 (2016)
15. Asmaa, O., Mokhtar, K., Abdelaziz, O.: Road traffic density estimation using microscopic and macroscopic parameter. Image Vis. Comput. **31**, 887–894 (2013)
16. Phuong, H., Thu, K.: Estimating the traffic density from traffic cameras. In: 8th International Conference, FDSE 2021, pp. 248–263
17. Girshick, R., Donahue, J., Darrell, T., Malik, J.: Rich Feature Hierarchies for Accurate Object Detection and Semantic Segmentation. In: 2014 IEEE Conference on Computer Vision and Pattern Recognition, 2014, pp. 580–587. doi: https://doi.org/10.1109/CVPR.2014.81
18. Girshick, R.: Fast R-CNN. In: 2015 IEEE International Conference on Computer Vision (ICCV), 2015, pp. 1440–1448. https://doi.org/10.1109/ICCV.2015.169
19. Ren, S., He, K., Girshick, R., Sun, J.: Faster R-CNN: towards real-time object detection with region proposal networks. IEEE Trans. Pattern Anal. Machine Intell. **39**(6), 1137–1149 (2017). https://doi.org/10.1109/TPAMI.2016.2577031
20. LeCun, Y., Bottou, L., Bengio, Y., Haffner, P.: Gradient based learning applied to document recognition (1998)
21. Zhou, X., Wang, D., Krähenbühl, P.: Objects as points. arXiv preprint, arXiv:1904.07850v2 (2019)
22. Zang, Y., et al: Vehicles detection in complex urban traffic and counting using linear quadratic estimation technique. In: Int. Conf. on Inventive Systems and Control, Valencia, Spain, pp. 603–607 (2018)

Data Analytics and Healthcare Systems

Comparison of Health Indicators Construction for Concrete Structure Using Acoustic Emission Hit and Kullback-Leibler Divergence

Tuan-Khai Nguyen, Zahoor Ahmad, and Jong-myon Kim[✉]

Department of Electrical, Electronics, and Computer Engineering, University of Ulsan, Ulsan, Republic of Korea
{khaint,cadet.zahoor,jmkim07}@mail.ulsan.ac.kr

Abstract. This paper investigates the construction of health indicators (HIs) for concrete structures using acoustic emission (AE) hit and Kullback-Leibler Divergence (KLD). Health indicator has an important role in the structural health monitoring (SHM) framework through its portrayal of the deterioration process. By harnessing AE nondestructive test, the authors suggest that the HI can be constructed through a deep learning model from the raw data. Prior to the training of the deep neural network (DNN), its parameters are achieved by autoencoder pretraining and fine-tuning. Afterwards, the AE hits and KLD values are extracted from the data to be the training label for two different types of HI. The evaluation of two HIs are done with fitness analysis and remaining useful lifetime (RUL) prognosis, which shows both their capability to present the deterioration process and their drawback in regard to this matter.

Keywords: Acoustic emission · Acoustic emission hit · Concrete structures · Deep neural network · Health indicator · Kullback-Leibler divergence

1 Introduction

Structural health monitoring (SHM) is one of the popular topics in recent years as multiple studies have been proposed by researchers from both the industrial and academic backgrounds in the search for performance improvement solution [1–8]. Among the most concerned specimens in SHM tasks, concrete structures are a familiar sight to both civil and industrial uses. Even though concrete itself has been proven as a material durable enough to withstand extreme environment, the modern utilization of reinforcing rebars can drastically worsen a structure's useful lifetime in exchange for better tensile strength. This is mainly due to the rusting and fracture progression. Through the analysis and prognosis of the structure's health condition, it is possible to identify the damage sustained and upcoming trend of the deterioration process. This information can be greatly of use, as users are allowed time to plan a better maintenance strategy, thus minimizing the safety concerns, financial risks and possibly extend the specimen's remaining useful lifetime (RUL).

© The Author(s), under exclusive license to Springer Nature Singapore Pte Ltd. 2022
T. K. Dang et al. (Eds.): FDSE 2022, CCIS 1688, pp. 603–613, 2022.
https://doi.org/10.1007/978-981-19-8069-5_41

In the SHM framework, health indicator (HI) has a vital role in portraying the deterioration process, especially for prognosis tasks. Following the recent studies [9–13] in this matter, HI construction is often approached in a two-step manner: firstly, the HI-constructing factor(s) (features) are calculated; afterwards, based on this result, HI is constructed.

HI-constructing factor(s) are often extracted from time, frequency or time-frequency domain. Fast and accessible solutions are the criteria that can be expected in time domain approaches [9, 14, 15], which is often centered around statistical computation and impulse analysis. Despite wide application towards different specimens and faults, their performance can be greatly affected by the interferences, to which pre-processing techniques are imperative. Frequency domain approaches [16, 17] are often used when expertise knowledge concerning the system and the fault characteristics have already been attained. In these studies, such knowledge is harnessed for outliners investigation, separating them from a known condition. Frequency domain approaches are known for their efficacy; however, they are often system- or fault-specific and might not be relevant to others. In comparison to the two aforementioned domains, the time-frequency domain [18] is often where the most robust and powerful solutions are proposed, at the cost of much higher computational complexity.

Following the computation of HI-constructing factor(s), they are forwarded to the constructor, which is often built by either a model-based or a data-based method. Proficiency in the system and fault's characteristics is obligatory to the first approach for the imitation of a real-life process through mathematical mean, such as [17, 19, 20] investigating fault-related frequencies or [21] manually choosing relevant features, etc. The knowledge required for such procedure can be extremely difficult to get and implement when the target process is complicated. Unlike model-based methods, the second approach does not focus on a specific system or fault, but mainly explore whatever provided by the data, which allows it to be widely applicable to different scenarios. Multiple studies with this approach have been proposed with promising results of HI construction, such as [16, 22] with statistical projection, [23, 24] with evolutionary computation or [25–27] with deep learning models, etc.

In this paper, two HIs constructed based on acoustic emission (AE) hits and Kullback-Leibler Divergence (KLD) are discussed. Initially, the raw AE data is collected from the specimen in deterioration process and then forwarded to the constructor, where the AE hits and KL-D values are calculated. Since the size of the raw data is huge, its spectrum is extracted and fed to the deep neural network (DNN) as the input, in which the previously computed AE hits and KL-D are used as the training labels for two different HIs. Prior to learning to construct HI, the DNN undergoes pre-training and fine-tuning with a stacked auto-encoder (SAE). Finally, the constructed HIs are evaluated by analyzing their fitness.

2 Health Indicators Construction

2.1 Acoustic Emission Hit Detection

AE is the phenomenon in which elastic waves are released upon the deformation of a solid material. It has been an important asset for non-destructive testing in recent years due to its wide band of frequency, non-directional mean of monitoring and its capability to perform testing without compulsory downtime [28].

In AE testing, there are two important terms: AE event and AE hit. AE event refers to the physical phenomenon that releases of the elastic wave, for example in concrete structures, it can be the appearance of crack. When the AE event is recorded by a sensor, it is called an AE hit. Simply put, an AE hit can be understood as how the sensor "perceive" an event. There are two types of AE hits: burst type, which can be used to analyze the event and continuous type (or AE noise), which is often caused by distorted, overlapped burst hits from far sources. Only the burst-type AE hits are useful and from this point, when we refer to AE hit, this is the type currently being discussed. In this paper, the average constant false alarm rate (ACFAR) is used to detect AE hits.

ACFAR investigates a cell under test (CUT), which is surrounded both in front and back by two guard cells and two training cells. This algorithm checks if there is a hit within the region by estimating the noise power from the neighborhood and establishing a detection threshold as follows:

$$Detection\ threshold = \alpha P_{noise} \tag{1}$$

in which, α is the threshold factor:

$$\alpha = N\left(FAR^{-1/N} - 1\right) \tag{2}$$

and the estimated noise power:

$$P_{noise} = \frac{\sum_{i=1}^{N} x_i}{N} \tag{3}$$

with N being the training cell number, FAR as the false alarm rate and x_i as the training cell sample.

Once the AE hits have been detected, it is essential to ensure that they correctly describe the deterioration process. By theory, only one AE hit can be recorded in a sensor from a specific event. However, in real practice, it can be expected that a single event might register more than a single hit [9, 29], which happens due to specimen's dimension and high AE activity allowing refraction, reflection, hit split, etc. Over time, the detection of abundant hits can greatly exaggerate the deterioration process. Therefore, one-class support vector machine (OC-SVM) by Tax and Duin [30] is employed to remove the anomalous AE hits for a better lifetime representation. The characteristics of an AE hit which are considered for the OC-SVM are: hit arrival time, hit duration, energy, rise time and hit counts.

Since the AE hits are the direct consequence of the damage sustained by a specimen, it can be expected to be a potential candidate for lifetime portrayal. After the removal process is finished, the number of AE hits in each one-second window is counted and then forwarded to the DNN as the training label.

2.2 Kullback-Leibler Divergence

KLD was first proposed by Solomon Kullback and Richard Leibler [31] in the early 1950s, following Harold Jeffreys's work [32] in the previous decade. The initial scope of KLD was for information theory, but then became widely applicable towards multiple contexts, most prominently machine learning's optimization task. Given two probability distribution P and Q, KLD(P,Q) can be perceived as the mean information discrimination, which is calculated as follows:

$$KLD(P, Q) = \sum_{i=1}^{N} P(x_i) log \frac{P(x_i)}{Q(x_i)}$$ (4)

The idea behind using KLD for HI construction is that given a known normal condition probability distribution, it is possible estimate the intensity of AE activity from unknown data, and through that, construct the HI. Since AE has a now-or-never quality, which states that an event cannot be recorded at any when else other than the moment of its occurrence, an AE test must be conducted with the current state of a specimen already known. Therefore, the reference probability distribution can be extracted from a random sensor at the beginning of the test.

Afterwards, the KLD values from all one-second window are forwards to the DNN as the training label for the second type of HI.

2.3 DNN-Based HI Constructor

One of the core ideas for the HI construction presented in this paper is that the whole construction block can build HI from raw input. Since the raw AE data is huge even in one-second window, its spectrum is calculated through Fast Fourier Transform and then fed in size-of-2000 block to the auto-encoder as both input and output for pretraining. The auto-encoder consists of six layers equally divided into an encoder and a decoder. The sizes of the layers are as follows: 1000-200-10-200-1000-2000. The encoder uses Xavier initialization and exponential linear unit (ELU) activation. For the improvement of regularization, dropout layers are applied prior to the dense layers at the rate of 0.1. Auto-encoder training is processed with gradient descent, Adam optimization and noise addition to the input to improve the robustness. Following the completion of pretraining, the DNN reuses the encoder layers with a logistic regression layer on top. In addition, the training process also tries to gain the best parameters by employing checkpoint and early stopping techniques. The normalized AE hit number and KLD values, both within the range from 0 to 1 (representing best condition and expiration of useful lifetime, respectively), are used as training labels for two different types of HI.

3   Experimental Setup

To evaluate the reliability of the two HIs, a four-point bending test scenario was set with three reinforced concrete beams (RCB). Details concerning the test are listed in Table 1:

In addition, the RCBs were marked with grids on the region where crack happened and a linear variable differential transformer was deployed at the bottom center to track vertical displacement. The pictorial of the test setup including sensor placement is presented in Fig. 1.

Each test on a RCB was done in two phases. The first phase tracked the AE activity while the loading was still lower than the RCB's maximum loading capability and so,

Table 1. Test description.

Test description	Detail
Sensors	8 R3I-AST sensors
Sampling frequency	5 MHz
Test time	600, 650 and 620 s
RCB's dimension	0.15 * 0.3 * 2.4 m
RCB's compressive strength	24 MPa
RCB's rebar	D16 (SD400)
Loading velocity	0.001 m/s

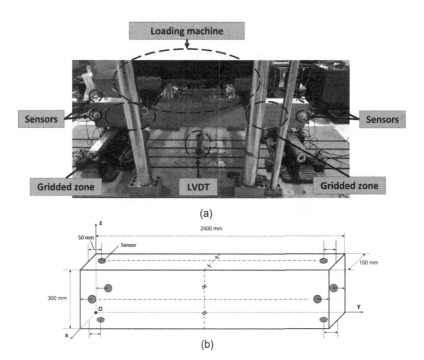

Fig. 1. Experimental setup: (a) Four-point bending test scenario (b) sensor placement

there was an absence of significant AE activity, which implied that no notable deformation happened during this time. The second phase tracked the AE activity while the loading was above the maximum capacity and increasing steadily. Initialization of cracks and their evolution from micro to macro cracks were witnessed during this time, along with intense AE activity in recorded data. Each test ceased when the monitoring team, including our lab members and construction specialists, decided that the specimen had sustained enough damage to render it unusable, without reaching total collapsion.

With the eight-sensor deployment scheme for each of three RCBs, a total of 24 data streams were recorded. By separating four channels' data of each RCB from the rest, two equal sets of data were attained, one for training and one for testing in the evaluation process of this paper.

4 Result and Comparison

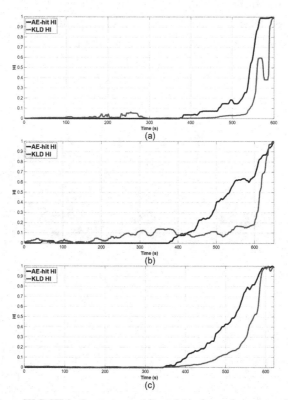

Fig. 2. AE-hit HI versus KLD HI, both constructed from data of a random channel from 3 RCBs.

The reliability of HI construction can be evaluated through appropriate means. Since HI is being investigated in the realm of prognosis tasks, there are generally two ways to determine this: fitness analysis of HI and prognosis capability measurement. The authors divide this part in two subsections: A. Fitness analysis; B. Prognosis capability.

4.1 Fitness Analysis

The aim of HI fitness analysis is to investigate the HI's intrinsic nature. The two most popular metrics for this task are monotonicity and trendability, which measures the HI's monotonic trend and the HI-time correlation, respectively. They can be computed as follows:

$$Monotonicity = absolute\left(\frac{{}^{n}d_{/dx>0} - {}^{n}d_{/dx<0}}{N-1}\right) \quad (5)$$

$$Trendability = \frac{N\sum xt - \sum xt}{\sqrt{\left[N\sum x^2 - \left(\sum x\right)^2\right]\left[N\sum t^2 - \left(\sum t\right)^2\right]}} \quad (6)$$

where N is the observation number, x represents either AE-hit or KLD HI and t is the time index.

Concerning these two parameters, an HI can be considered a good description of deterioration process when it can show a high level of trendability along while its monotonicity is not low, especially towards the end of the specimen's useful lifetime. Table 2 presents in detail the fitness analysis of the two HIs.

Table 2. Fitness analysis of the HIs

Heading level	Fitness analysis metric	
	Monotonicity (average)	Trendability (average)
AE-hit HI	0.6801	0.6788
KLD HI	0.6807	0.6953

From Table 2 and Fig. 2, the fitness analysis of AE-hit HI and KLD HI are seen to be comparable, with both showing the traits of what can be expected from a good HI representation.

4.2 Prognosis Capability Measurement

Since HI construction is irrefutably a vital part of numerous prognosis solutions, it is essential that its prognosis capability should also be tested. A prognosis structure from [33], which uses a long short-term memory recurrent neural network (LSTM-RNN), was implemented for this purpose. Each window of 50 HI sample is fed to the model to predict the sample right after it. By this way, the model is forced to make prediction at each time the window moves by one sample. When given a data series of limited length, it can continue to predict by taking in the value which has just been prognosed as the final value of the next window.

The value of HI ranges from 0 to 1. However, in real-life situations, it sometimes can be difficult for the HI prognosis to absolutely reach 1. Therefore, the threshold when a specimen's useful lifetime expires is chosen at first time that HI reaches 0.95 to avoid complications in prognosis. The time difference between then and the time when prognosis is currently being done is the true RUL. By substituting the predicted HI into the real HI's place, the prognosed RUL can be obtained. The absolute difference between the true RUL and the prognosed RUL is used as the metric to evaluate the prognosability of the two considered HIs.

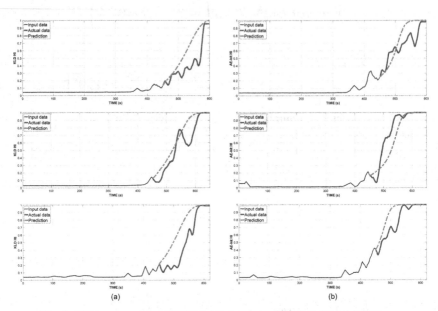

Fig. 3. RUL prognosis on 3 RCBs' AE data using (a) KLD HI (b) AE hit

Generally, a prognosis is not performed at the earlier stage of a nondestructive test. At this time, the specimen's condition is still good or has not degraded enough for a maintenance to be scheduled. Since the second phase of the test, which roughly initiates after around 350 one-second cycles, is when the specimen's loading capacity is exceeded, the authors decided to perform RUL prognosis at the 450th cycle. Approximately at this time of each test, the micro cracks started to evolve into major ones, along with the increase in AE activity which can be witnessed clearly on the data. Figure 3 shows the plots of RUL prognosis for AE-hit HI and KLD HI in comparison to each other.

Table 3. Prognosis capability measurement.

Type of HI	RUL prognosis error		
	RCB 1	RCB 2	RCB 3
AE-hit HI	19 ± 4	31 ± 7	24 ± 3
KLD HI	11 ± 7	18 ± 7	16 ± 5

Unlike in the fitness analysis, the prognosis performance of the two HIs as displayed in Table 3 shows a noticeable difference. The KLD HI outperforms AE-hit HI by 17, 10 and 20 cycles, respectively on three specimens. This, however, does not disqualify the AE-hit HI from being potentially a good HI. This outperformance can be understood and expected because the AE hit extraction is a very sophisticated model-based process and still has many rooms for improvement, especially concerning overlapped hit detection which this study lacks. In real-life scenarios, it is expected that the AE data would be more affected by interference from daily usage, environmental phenomenon, etc. also. The KLD HI would not be able to achieve this level of performance without having an effective noise filtering scheme.

5 Conclusion

In this paper, the authors presented a comparison of two health indicator (HI) constructions for prognosis task based on acoustic emission (AE) hit and Kullback-Leibler Divergence (KLD). Through the help of HI construction from AE nondestructive test, it is possible to predict the future health condition of an in-service specimen without halting any process. The deep neural network (DNN) based constructor undergoes a pretraining and fine-tuning process with autoencoder using the signal spectrum. The AE hits and KLD values are extracted from the raw AE data, which are then used by the DNN as training labels for two different HIs.

Given the scope of prognosis task, two HIs were evaluated through two methods: fitness analysis and prognosis capability measurement. Whilst investigating the intrinsic nature of the HIs in the first method, it was shown that they achieved comparable results, both implicating a good description of deterioration process. Significant performance difference was witnessed as remaining useful lifetime (RUL) prognosis was performed at the 450th cycle of three reinforced concrete beams (RCBs). KLD HI showed a better result of 17, 10 and 20 cycles less in prediction error. Nevertheless, AE-hit HI still has a lot of potential, especially in real-life situations when KLD HI would not be able to achieve such performance with the presence of unaccounted interferences.

Acknowledgements. This work was supported by the Korea Technology and Information Promotion Agency (TIPA) grant funded by the Korea government (SMEs) (No. S3126818). This work was also supported by the Technology Infrastructure Program funded by the Ministry of SMEs and Startups (MSS, Korea).

References

1. Ohtsu, M., Isoda, T., Tomoda, Y.: Acoustic emission techniques standardized for concrete structures. J. Acoust. Emission **25**, 21–32 (2007)
2. Sagar, R.V., Prasad, B.K.R., Kumar, S.S.: An experimental study on cracking evolution in concrete and cement mortar by the b-value analysis of acoustic emission technique. Cem. Concr. Res. **42**(8), 1094–1104 (2012). https://doi.org/10.1016/j.cemconres.2012.05.003
3. Wang, J., Basheer, P.A.M., Nanukuttan, S.V., Long, A.E., Bai, Y.: Influence of service loading and the resulting micro-cracks on chloride resistance of concrete. Constr. Build. Mater. **108**, 56–66 (2016). https://doi.org/10.1016/j.conbuildmat.2016.01.005

4. Han, Q., Yang, G., Xu, J., Fu, Z., Lacidogna, G., Carpinteri, A.: Acoustic emission data analyses based on crumb rubber concrete beam bending tests. Eng. Fract. Mech. **210**, 189–202 (2019). https://doi.org/10.1016/j.engfracmech.2018.05.016
5. Wolf, J., Pirskawetz, S., Zang, A.: Detection of crack propagation in concrete with embedded ultrasonic sensors. Eng. Fract. Mech. **146**, 161–171 (2015). https://doi.org/10.1016/j.engfra cmech.2015.07.058
6. Ohno, K., Ohtsu, M.: Crack classification in concrete based on acoustic emission. Constr. Build. Mater. **24**(12), 2339–2346 (2010). https://doi.org/10.1016/j.conbuildmat.2010.05.004
7. Aggelis, D.G., Mpalaskas, A.C., Matikas, T.E.: Investigation of different fracture modes in cement-based materials by acoustic emission. Cem. Concr. Res. **48**, 1–8 (2013). https://doi. org/10.1016/j.cemconres.2013.02.002
8. Abarkane, C., Rescalvo, F.J., Donaire-Ávila, J., Galé-Lamuela, D., Benavent-Climent, A., Molina, A.G.: Temporal acoustic emission index for damage monitoring of RC structures subjected to bidirectional seismic loadings. Materials **12**(17), 2804 (2019). https://doi.org/ 10.3390/ma12172804
9. Moctezuma, F.P., Prieto, M.D., Martinez, L.R.: Performance analysis of acoustic emission hit detection methods using time features. IEEE Access **7**, 71119–71130 (2019). https://doi. org/10.1109/ACCESS.2019.2919224
10. Nguyen, T.-K., Ahmad, Z., Kim, J.-M.: A scheme with acoustic emission hit removal for the remaining useful life prediction of concrete structures. Sensors **21**(22), 7761 (2021). https:// doi.org/10.3390/s21227761
11. Li, J., Zi, Y., Wang, Y., Yang, Y.: Health indicator construction method of bearings based on Wasserstein dual-domain adversarial networks under normal data only. IEEE Trans. Ind. Electron. **69**(10), 10615–10624 (2022). https://doi.org/10.1109/TIE.2022.3156148
12. González-Muñiz, A., Díaz, I., Cuadrado, A.A., García-Pérez, D.: Health indicator for machine condition monitoring built in the latent space of a deep autoencoder. Reliab. Eng. Syst. Saf. **224**, 108482 (2022). https://doi.org/10.1016/j.ress.2022.108482
13. Wen, P., Zhao, S., Chen, S., Li, Y.: A generalized remaining useful life prediction method for complex systems based on composite health indicator. Reliab. Eng. Syst. Saf. **205**, 107241 (2021). https://doi.org/10.1016/j.ress.2020.107241
14. Shukla, S., Yadav, R.N., Sharma, J., Khare, S.: Analysis of statistical features for fault detection in ball bearing. In: 2015 IEEE International Conference on Computational Intelligence and Computing Research (ICCIC), pp. 1–7 (2015). https://doi.org/10.1109/ICCIC.2015.7435755
15. Mahamad, A.K., Hiyama, T.: Development of artificial neural network based fault diagnosis of induction motor dearing. In: 2008 IEEE 2nd International Power and Energy Conference, pp. 1387–1392 (2008). https://doi.org/10.1109/PECON.2008.4762695
16. Yu, J.: Local and nonlocal preserving projection for bearing defect classification and performance assessment. IEEE Trans. Ind. Electron. **59**(5), 2363–2376 (2012). https://doi.org/10. 1109/TIE.2011.2167893
17. Leite, V.C.M.N., et al.: Detection of localized bearing faults in induction machines by spectral kurtosis and envelope analysis of stator current. IEEE Trans. Ind. Electron. **62**(3), 1855–1865 (2015). https://doi.org/10.1109/TIE.2014.2345330
18. Cui, J., et al.: An improved wavelet transform and multi-block forecast engine based on a novel training mechanism. ISA Trans. **84**, 142–153 (2019). https://doi.org/10.1016/j.isatra. 2018.09.023
19. Xia, M., Li, T., Shu, T., Wan, J., De Silva, C.W., Wang, Z.: A two-stage approach for the remaining useful life prediction of bearings using deep neural networks. IEEE Trans. Ind. Informatics **15**(6), 3703–3711 (2019). https://doi.org/10.1109/TII.2018.2868687
20. Elforjani, M., Shanbr, S.: Prognosis of bearing acoustic emission signals using supervised machine learning. IEEE Trans. Ind. Electron. **65**(7), 5864–5871 (2018). https://doi.org/10. 1109/TIE.2017.2767551

21. Liu, K., Gebraeel, N.Z., Shi, J.: A data-level fusion model for developing composite health indices for degradation modeling and prognostic analysis. IEEE Trans. Autom. Sci. Eng. **10**(3), 652–664 (2013). https://doi.org/10.1109/TASE.2013.2250282
22. Mosallam, A., Medjaher, K., Zerhouni, N.: Data-driven prognostic method based on Bayesian approaches for direct remaining useful life prediction. J. Intell. Manuf. **27**(5), 1037–1048 (2014). https://doi.org/10.1007/s10845-014-0933-4
23. Nguyen, K.T.P., Medjaher, K.: An automated health indicator construction methodology for prognostics based on multi-criteria optimization. ISA Trans. **113**, 81–96 (2021). https://doi.org/10.1016/j.isatra.2020.03.017
24. Liao, L.: Discovering prognostic features using genetic programming in remaining useful life prediction. IEEE Trans. Ind. Electron. **61**(5), 2464–2472 (2014). https://doi.org/10.1109/TIE.2013.2270212
25. Han, T., Liu, C., Yang, W., Jiang, D.: Learning transferable features in deep convolutional neural networks for diagnosing unseen machine conditions. ISA Trans. **93**, 341–353 (2019). https://doi.org/10.1016/j.isatra.2019.03.017
26. Gugulothu, N., Vishnu, T.R., Malhotra, P., Vig, L., Agarwal, P., Shroff, G.M.: Predicting Remaining Useful Life using Time Series Embeddings based on Recurrent Neural Networks. *ArXiv*, vol. abs/1709.0 (2017)
27. Bektas, O., Jones, J.A., Sankararaman, S., Roychoudhury, I., Goebel, K.: A neural network filtering approach for similarity-based remaining useful life estimation. Int. J. Adv. Manuf. Technol. **101**(1–4), 87–103 (2018). https://doi.org/10.1007/s00170-018-2874-0
28. Miller, R.K., Hill, E.K., Moore, P.O.: Third Edition Technical Editors
29. Rodríguez, P., Celestino, T.B.: Application of acoustic emission monitoring and signal analysis to the qualitative and quantitative characterization of the fracturing process in rocks. Eng. Fract. Mech. **210**, 54–69 (2019). https://doi.org/10.1016/j.engfracmech.2018.06.027
30. Tax, D.M.J., Duin, R.P.W.: Support vector data description. Mach. Learn. **54**(1), 45–66 (2004). https://doi.org/10.1023/B:MACH.0000008084.60811.49
31. Kullback, S., Leibler, R.A.: On information and sufficiency. Ann. Math. Stat. **22**(1), 79–86 (1951). https://doi.org/10.1214/aoms/1177729694
32. M.G.K. undefined: Theory of probability. By Harold Jeffreys. Second Edition. Pp. vii, 411. 30s. 1948. (Oxford University Press). Math. Gaz. **32**(302), 304 (1948). https://doi.org/10.2307/3609901
33. Tra, V., Nguyen, T.K., Kim, C.H., Kim, J.M.: Health indicators construction and remaining useful life estimation for concrete structures using deep neural networks. Appl. Sci. **11**(9), 4113 (2021). https://doi.org/10.3390/app11094113

Lung and Colon Tumor Classification Based on Transfer Learning-Based Techniques

Trinh Huy Hoang[1(✉)], Nguyen Thanh Binh[2,3], Vy Van[1], and Nguyen Quang Tan[4]

[1] Ho Chi Minh City University of Education, 280 An Duong Vuong, Ho Chi Minh City, Vietnam
{hoangth,vanv}@hcmue.edu.vn
[2] Department of Information Systems, Faculty of Computer Science and Engineering, Ho Chi Minh City University of Technology (HCMUT), VNU-HCM, 268 Ly Thuong Kiet Street, District 10, Ho Chi Minh City, Vietnam
ntbinh@hcmut.edu.vn
[3] Vietnam National University Ho Chi Minh City, Linh Trung Ward, Thu Duc City, Ho Chi Minh City, Vietnam
[4] Phan Thiet University, 225 Nguyen Thong, Phan Thiet, Vietnam

Abstract. One of the biggest difficulties facing medicine today is cancer. Lung cancer along with colon cancer, stomach cancer and liver cancer, are the four most dangerous cancers. If the disease is detected early and treated properly, it can prolong the patient's life. Today, many tasks in many fields, including medicine, can be resolved by using deep learning techniques. This paper proposes to modify the Deep Neural Network transfer learning for the lung and colon cancer classification based on GoogLeNet. Specifically, the main idea of the inception module of GoogLeNet that is running multiple operations (pooling, convolution) with multiple filter sizes in parallel so that we do not have to face any trade-off. The second advantage of the inception module is dimensionality reduction of feature maps and over parameterization dealing. The output of classification was adjusted to 3 or 2 classes due to the required classes of lung and colon problems. The accuracy of the proposed method is 99.66% and 100% in the lung and colon image dataset, respectively. The results of the proposed method are better than the other methods such as VGG16, Resnet50, NASNetMobile and original GoogLeNet.

Keywords: Lung cancer · Colon cancer · Tumor classification · Transfer learning · GoogLeNet

1 Introduction

In recent decay, cancer is one of the most challenging medical areas. There are nearly 10 million deaths in 2020 for cancer worldwide [1]. Many medical studies detect cancer early to reduce mortality. The medical images are different from regular images, because the information in the image is very important, sometimes the wrong processing will lose the information in the image. We want to process medical images so as to preserve the information in the images, each information in medical images is very valuable in the process of diagnosis and treatment of diseases. The automatic image diagnosis by deep

© The Author(s), under exclusive license to Springer Nature Singapore Pte Ltd. 2022
T. K. Dang et al. (Eds.): FDSE 2022, CCIS 1688, pp. 614–624, 2022.
https://doi.org/10.1007/978-981-19-8069-5_42

learning technology to help medical staff that reduce image diagnostic time by manual method.

Lung cancer was divided into two crucial histological types: adenocarcinoma and squamous cell carcinoma. Invasive adenocarcinoma of the lungs has five major characteristics: lepidic, acinar, micropapillary, papillary and solid. Squamous cell carcinoma of the lungs is one of type malignant epithelial tumors with squamous differentiation or keratinization. The various types of lung cancer are very small for the morphological differences. On the other hand, Lung abnormalities are very small and difficult to distinguish between damaged and healthy cells. So, the cancer diagnosis is not easy for a correct result [2].

Many tasks in many fields can be resolved using deep learning techniques. Deep learning can be used to classify images of benign and malignant conditions in the medical field, such as lung and colon cancer. As the rapid growth of deep learning research, an ImageNet competition for achieving better performance was introduced in [3]. Transfer learning is a method for repurposing and developing a built-in model to a new task. Two common approaches of transfer learning are developing model approach and pre-trained model approach. In this paper, we propose to modify the Deep Neural Network transfer learning for the lung and colon cancer classification based on GoogLeNet. GoogLeNet is built to classify familiar objects such as cat, dog, apple, lemon, etc. Therefore, when we use GoogLeNet to classify Lung and Colon, we cannot reuse network of GoogLeNet, we should train from the beginning to preserve the information in the image.

The rest of the paper is organized as follows: Sect. 2 presents the related works, and Sect. 3 proposed method for lung and colon classification using transfer learning. Section 4 and 5 are the experimental results and conclusions, respectively.

2 Related Work

In recent years, the studies on the detection and classification of lung cancer using Computer - Aided Detection have been conducted in many places with many author groups around the world. There are many proposed deep learning methods by scientists to solve this problem. Asuntha et al. [4] used deep learning to detect and classify cancerous tissues. To extract the lung region, they used artificial bee colony segmentation. To select the most important feature, they used a convolution neural network method based on Fuzzy Particle Swarm Optimization algorithm for reducing the computational complexity of CNN. The average accuracy of this model is 95.62%. Zhuo et al. [5] proposed a method for automatic designing of Lung nodule detection systems. They used a multiscene deep learning framework which contains several steps, and the design of CNN contains a pooling layer, a convolutional layer, and a fully integrated layer. Pragya et al. [6] aggregated the results of more than 40 groups with many methods of detecting and classifying cancer through different types of tomography images with high accuracy from 81.42% to 98.42%.

In recent studies, deep learning models, especially CNN networks, were focused and applied into the 3D input architecture for the lung cancer detection and classification problem. The candidate feature extraction is oriented capabilities and preserving the 3-D structure of the data. With positive results, this approach has many development expectations and has implications in the application and assessment of clinical detection and diagnosis. Tafadzwa et al. [6] proposed a model which can detect adenocarcinoma with higher specificity than sensitivity. It suggests greater potential for assisted diagnosis of the computing and limited value as a screening tool. Furthermore, this model has a deterministic signal by using the histological prediction on an independent and disparate dataset. The ability of noninvasive tumor histology prediction has the potential to enhance the pathologist's accuracy and productivity, providing significant time and cost savings.

Previous studies have demonstrated the utility of CNNs as fixed feature extractors for image classification and analysis tasks, with many tools using outputs from summation layers, integrated or fully connected in the VGG or related models [7–9]. Shrinking the size of the deep radiation feature space benefits performance and avoids overfitting. This model was done with the kNN estimator performing on pair with the original neural network in terms of learned features, while other classifiers including SVM also showed predictive power. The findings suggest dimensionality reduction of CNN-derived feature maps to summarize them by using low-dimensional vectors. It can serve as an efficient multi-step alternative to neural networks that is fully connected. This approach is consistent with similar methods.

Jason et al. [10] proposed a deep learning model to classify major and minor histological patterns on whole-slide images of lung adenocarcinoma. This model consists of a residual cumulative neural network for patch classification combined with a slide-wide communication mechanism to identify major and minor subtypes across the entire slide. The model performed on pair with pathologists in an independent set of tests. This model can be used to classify these histological specimens.

3   Lung and Colon Classification based on Transfer Learning-based Techniques

As present in above section, the information in the medical image is very important, medical image processing must preserve the information in the image. Lung abnormalities, the cells in the spectrum and colon are very small, making it difficult to distinguish between damaged and healthy cells. Therefore, we cannot reuse GoogleNet's network, we should retrain some features to preserve information in the image. In this study, we chose a modified GoogLeNet architecture for lung image classification problems. The GoogLeNet architecture has 22-layer depth and 27 included pooling layers. Besides, 9 inception modules stacked linearly in total as Fig. 1.

The inception module runs multiple operations (pooling, convolution) with multiple filter sizes such as: 3×3, 5×5, etc. in parallel so that the model doesn't need to face any trade-off. The ends of the inception modules are connected to the global average pooling layer to replace a fully connected layer. The global average pooling is more advantageous than the fully connected layers because it is more compatible with

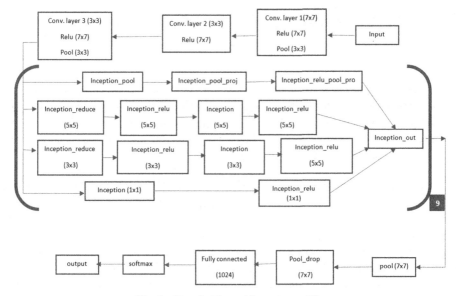

Fig. 1. GoogLeNet architecture modify

the convolution structure by enforcing correspondences between feature maps and categories. GoogLeNet architecture was based on the idea of having filters with multiple sizes that can operate on the same level. It makes the network wider rather than deeper.

In general, there are several layers in a network such as convolutional layer, normalization layer, pooling layer, dropout layer and fully connected layer. The brief explanation as follows:

Convolutional layer applies a convolution operation to the input, passing the result to the next layer. A convolution converts all the pixels in its receptive field into a single value. For example, if an image is applied to a convolution, the image size will be reduced as well as bring all the information in the field together into a single pixel. The final output of the convolutional layer is a vector. The size of the convolution kernel (filter) for our study the convolution operation is performed on inputs with three filter sizes: (1×1), (3×3), and (5×5). Due to time-consuming and expensive cost to train the network, GoogLeNet limits the number of input channels by adding an extra (1×1) convolution before the (3×3) and (5×5) convolutions to reduce the dimensions of the network. It helps to perform the computations faster.

Normalization layer simply estimates the normalization statistics from the summed inputs to the neurons within a hidden layer. The normalization does not introduce any new dependencies between training cases. The normalization normalizes the activations along the feature direction instead of mini-batch direction. In general, normalization layers are added in the model to speed up and stabilize the training process.

An activation function, such as Sigmoid, ReLU, Softmax, works as a filter to get the required values for feeding the next layer. The ReLU activation function is found to be advantageous in terms of speed and accuracy over 'sigmoid' and 'tanh' function [11].

The ReLU function is defined as Eq. (1):

$$f(x) = \begin{cases} x \ if \ x \geq 0 \\ 0 \ if \ x < 0 \end{cases} \tag{1}$$

Softmax layer is normally added in the last layer for classification problems to compute the probability belonging to classes. The Softmax function with multinomial logistic loss is the loss function [12]. The Softmax is a neural transfer function that calculates a layer's output from its net input. For a given feature sample x and its true class N_i, the posterior probability (Pi) is represented as Eq. (2):

$$y_i = P_i(N_i|x) = \frac{exp[a_i^T x + a_{i0}]}{\sum_{j=1}^{k} exp[a_j^T y + a_{j0}]} \tag{2}$$

where, $y(y_1, y_2, ...y_c)$ is the score vector. It calculates the output vectors with elements between 0 and 1; a_0 and a_i are the bias and weights updated by backpropagation; T is stands for the transpose operation

Pooling layers used, after the ReLU activation function, to reduce the dimensions of the feature maps. They reduce the amount of computation performed in the network and the number of parameters to learn. The pooling layer is used to collect the features present in a region of the feature map which is generated by a convolution layer. In this case, almost all the pooling operation is done by max-pooling that picks the maximum value of the sliding window of size $[3 \times 3]$ or $[7 \times 7]$. Moreover, dropout may be added with a pooling layer in a few last steps to prevent overfitting.

The classification phase of GoogLeNet starts from the fully connected layer, which takes the output of the last pooling layer as input. In the process, the neurons in the previous layer remain connected to the neurons in the fully connected layer. To identify the larger patterns, all the features learned by the previous layer are combined in this layer. Fully connected layers are simply, feed forward neural networks. It forms the last few layers in the network.

3.1 Loss Function

The loss function is defined as Eq. (3):

$$L(A) = -Y_g^T ln(y) \tag{3}$$

where, the ground-truth vector $Y_g(Y_{g1}, Y_{g2}, Y_{g3}, Y_{gc})$ and y formulate the loss function that estimates the distance between the present model and the target model. The ground truth function value is 1 for the targeted neuron and 0 for the other neurons. The loss function is minimized by updating the bias and weights. The updated weights are calculated as Eq. (4):

$$a_{new} = a_{old} - \psi \frac{\delta L}{\delta a_{old}} \tag{4}$$

where, 'ψ' is the learning rate based on information accuracy and computational time. In classification algorithm, the cross-entropy loss is calculated as Eq. (5):

$$\varepsilon = -\frac{1}{S} \sum\nolimits_{i=1}^{S} \sum\nolimits_{j=1}^{N} w_j y_{ij}.lnq_{ij} \tag{5}$$

where, S represents the number of samples; N represents the number of classes; w_j is the weight for class number j; q_{ij} is either one indicating whether the sample number i belongs to the class number j else zero; y_{ij} represents the output for sample i and class j obtained from the Softmax function. Here, we set $w_j = 1$ for all classes.

3.2 Evaluation Metrics

For classification problem [15, 16], the accuracy is defined as Eq. (6):

$$accuracy = \frac{N}{T} \times 100 \tag{6}$$

where, N is the number of correct predictions; T is the total number of predictions.

For binary classification, accuracy calculated as Eq. (7):

$$accuracy = \frac{TP + TN}{TP + TN + FP + FN} \times 100 \tag{7}$$

where, TP = True Positives; TN = True Negatives; FP = False Positives; FN = False Negatives.

4 Experimental Results

4.1 Dataset

The experiments were implemented on LC25000 Lung and colon histopathological image dataset [13]. This dataset includes 25000 color images with 5 classes. Every class includes 5000 images. The size of each image is 768 x 768 pixels and is stored as a jpeg file. Colon image sets and lung image sets are two different types of datasets, respectively. Lung_aca has 5000 lung adenocarcinoma images. Lung_scc has 5000 lung squamous cell carcinoma images. And lung n has 5000 lung benign tissue images. A subfolder called colon aca contains 5000 images of colon adenocarcinomas, and a subfolder called colon n contains 5000 images of benign colonic tissues.

This dataset divided 80% for training and 20% for testing. The hyperparameters are set up include Max epoch 30, Learning rate 0.001, Mini-batch size 128, Validation frequency 50, Optimizer Adam. Figure 2 visualizes the training lung and colon image dataset.

For the lung training dataset, the number of lung_aca, lung_n, and lung_scc samples are balanced, each group containing 4000 images present as Fig. 2(a). The characteristic of each group was visualized as Fig. 3. In Fig. 3, the two left images belong to lung_n group, the two right images belong to lung_aca and lung_scc group, respectively.

For the colon training dataset, the number of colon_aca and colon_n samples are also balanced, each group containing 4000 images as Fig. 2(b). The characteristic of each group was visualized in Fig. 4. In Fig. 4, the two left images belong to colon_aca group, the two right images belong to colon_n group, respectively.

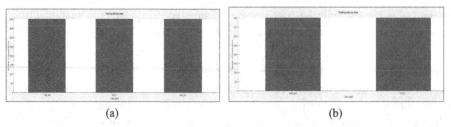

(a)   (b)

Fig. 2. Visualize the training lung and colon image dataset. (a) With lung image dataset (3 classes, each class comprises 4000 lung images). (b) With colon image dataset (2 classes, each class comprises 4000 colon images).

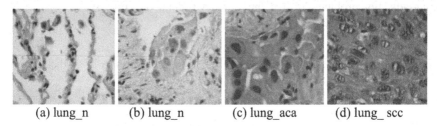

(a) lung_n   (b) lung_n   (c) lung_aca   (d) lung_ scc

Fig. 3. Visualize a few lung images belonging to lung_n, lung_aca or lung_scc class.

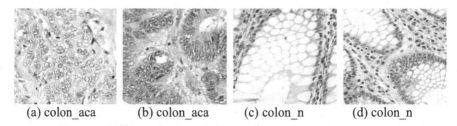

(a) colon_aca   (b) colon_aca   (c) colon_n   (d) colon_n

Fig. 4. Visualize a few colons images belongs to colon_n, or colon_aca class

4.2 Results Evaluation

This section clearly presents results of the proposed method for lung tumor classification. Our experimental programs were developed using the python language on a computer of Intel(R) Core (TM) i7–10700 CPU, 2.90 GHz, 16.0 GB RAM, 64-bit operating system, x64-based processor, Windows 10 Education.

Figure 5 and Fig. 6 present the loss function by using GoogLeNet transfer learning for Lung image and Colon image dataset. These figures obviously show the loss functions of the training and validation process reduce to 0. This means that the GoogLeNet model works efficiently on both Lung and Colon image dataset.

Figure 7 and Fig. 8 presented the accuracy with GoogLeNet transfer learning for lung image and colon image dataset. These figures obviously show the accuracy of the training and validation process are high (accuracy 99.66% for Lung image dataset and accuracy 100% for Colon image dataset). This means that the GoogLeNet model works

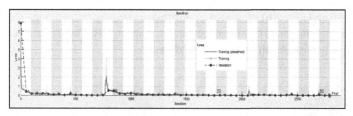

Fig. 5. Loss function by using GoogLeNet transfer learning for Lung image dataset

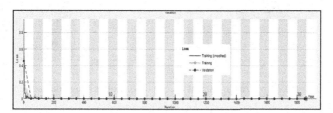

Fig. 6. Loss function by using GoogLeNet transfer learning for Colon image dataset

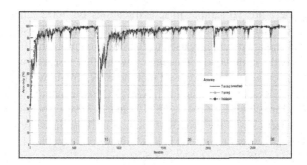

Fig. 7. The accuracy 99.66% with GoogLeNet transfer learning for Lung image dataset

efficiently on the training and validation dataset of Lung and Colon. In other words, GoogLeNet adapts for the Lung and Colon dataset.

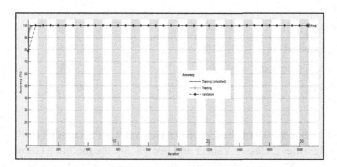

Fig. 8. The accuracy 100% with GoogLeNet transfer learning for Colon image dataset

Figure 9(a) and Fig. 9(b) presented a confusion matrix by using GoogLeNet transfer learning for Lung image and Colon image dataset, respectively. These confusion matrices show the classification result on the testing dataset.

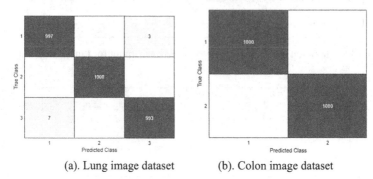

(a). Lung image dataset   (b). Colon image dataset

Fig. 9. Confusion matrix by using GoogLeNet transfer learning for Lung image and Colon image dataset

In Fig. 9(a), there are 10 sample misclassifications on 3000 samples testing. In Fig. 9(b), there are 0 sample misclassifications on 2000 samples testing. The results have high accuracy and are potentially used to classification problems for medical areas.

Table 1 presents the comparison in accuracy with other research work. With Lung image dataset, the accuracy of the proposed method is 99.66% in while the accuracy of VGG16 method [14], Resnet50 method [17], NASNetMobile method [14] and Original GoogLeNet method are 98.45%, 96.84%, 97.71% and 98.34%, respectively. With Colon image dataset, the accuracy of the proposed method is 100% in while the accuracy of VGG16 method [14], Resnet50 method [17], NASNetMobile method [14] and Original GoogLeNet method are 98.71%, 97.92%, 98.53% and 98.97%, respectively.

Table 1. The comparison between GoogLeNet and other networks

Methods	Accuracy for Lung image dataset	Accuracy for Colon image dataset
VGG16 method [14]	98.45%	98.71%
ResNet50 method [17]	96.84%	97.92%
NASNetMobile method [14]	97.71%	98.53%
Original GoogLeNet method	98.34%	98.97%
Proposed method	99.66%	100%

The classification result of the Colon dataset has high accuracy (100%) due to the problem only classifies 2 classes, cancer and benign. So, the modified GoogLeNet easily extracts the features of the cancerous and non-cancerous images. For the lung dataset, the modify GoogLeNet needs to classify 3 classes. There is a confusion between lung_aca (class 1) and lung_scc (class 3) because both 2 classes are the same cancer, so there are some same or overlap characteristics. Since the features can be similar causing confusion, but for non-cancerous images, the network still classifies 1000 samples correctly (class 2) as Fig. 9.

The result of classification target is better than other networks due to the characteristics of GoogLeNet architecture, especially the inception layer. The main idea of the inception module that is running multiple operations (pooling, convolution) with multiple filter sizes in parallel so that we do not have to face any trade-off. The second advantage of the inception module is dimensionality reduction of feature maps and over parameterization dealing. The hyper parameters configuration in this study is shown in Fig. 1. The output of classification was adjusted to 3 or 2 classes due to the required classes of lung and colon problems.

5 Conclusion and Future Work

Tumors in the lung and colon lung are one of the common diseases. The advancement of medicine in surgery, chemotherapy and radiotherapy will help patients to improve survival time and quality of life. Lung metastases are malignant tumors that originates in another organ in the body and spread to the lungs. The lung is one of the second most common sites of cancer metastasis. In this study, we modified the Deep Neural Network transfer learning for the lung and colon cancer classification based on GoogLeNet in the medical field. The LC25000 Lung and Colon Histopathological Image database was used to support our experiments. The results of the proposed method are better than the other methods such as VGG16, Resnet50, NASNetMobile and original GoogLeNet. The outcomes demonstrated the effectiveness of GoogLeNet in solving the lung and colon categorization issue. In future works, we will continue to learn other features of tumor to increase accuracy and improve the quality of tumor classification by applying the other algorithms.

Acknowledgement. We acknowledge the support of time and facilities from Ho Chi Minh City University of Technology (HCMUT), VNU-HCM and Ho Chi Minh city University of Education for this study.

References

1. World Health Organization (WHO). https://www.who.int/news-room/fact-sheets/detail/cancer. Accessed 15 May 2022
2. Chen, C.-L., et al.: An annotation-free whole-slide training approach to pathological classification of lung cancer types using deep learning Nat. Commun., 1–13 (2021). https://doi.org/10.1038/s41467-021-21467-y
3. Canziani, A., Paszke, A., Culurciello, E.: An analysis of deep neural network models for practical applications, pp. 1–7 (2017). https://arxiv.org/pdf/1605.07678.pdf. Accessed 15 May 2022
4. Asuntha, A., Srinivasan, A.: Deep learning for lung Cancer detection and classification. Multimedia Tools Appl. **79**, 7731–7762 (2020). https://doi.org/10.1007/s11042-019-08394-3

5. Liu, Z., Yao, C., Yu, H., Wu, T.: Deep reinforcement learning with its application for lung cancer detection in medical internet of things. Future Gener. Comput. Syst. **97**, 1–9 (2019). https://doi.org/10.1016/j.future.2019.02.068

6. Chaturvedi, P., Jhamb, A., Vanani, M., Nemade, V.: Prediction and classification of lung cancer using machine learning techniques. IOP Conf. Ser. Mater. Sci. Eng., 1–19 (2020). https://doi.org/10.1088/1757-899X/1099/1/012059

7. Ramanjaneyulu, K., Hemanth Kumar, K., Snehith, K., Jyothirmai, G., Venkata Krishna, K.: Detection and classification of lung cancer using VGG-16. In: 2022 International Conference on Electronic Systems and Intelligent Computing, pp. 69–72 (2022). https://doi.org/10.1109/ICESIC53714.2022.9783556

8. Thanzeem Mohamed Sheriff, S., Venkat Kumar, J., Vigneshwaran, S., Jones, A., Anand, J.: Lung cancer detection using VGG NET 16 architecture. In: International Conference on Physics and Energy, pp. 1–8 (2021). https://doi.org/10.1088/1742-6596/2040/1/012001

9. Lu, Y., Liang, H., Shi, S., Fu, X.: Lung cancer detection using a dilated CNN with VGG16. In: 4th International Conference on Signal Processing and Machine Learning, pp. 45–51, (2021). https://doi.org/10.1145/3483207.3483215

10. Wei, J.W., Tafe, L.J., Linnik, Y.A., Vaickus, L.J., Tomita, N., Hassanpour, S.: Pathologist-level classification of histologic patterns on resected lung adenocarcinoma slides with deep neural networks, Sci. Rep., 1–8 (2019). https://doi.org/10.1038/s41598-019-40041-7

11. Szandała, T.: Review and comparison of commonly used activation functions for deep neural networks. In: Bhoi, A.K., Mallick, P.K., Liu, C.-M., Balas, V.E. (eds.) Bio-inspired Neurocomputing. SCI, vol. 903, pp. 203–224. Springer, Singapore (2021). https://doi.org/10.1007/978-981-15-5495-7_11

12. Luo, J., et al.: Improving the performance of multisubject motor imagery-based BCIs using twin cascaded Softmax CNNs. J. Neural Eng. **18**(3) (2021). https://doi.org/10.1088/1741-2552/abe357

13. LC25000 Lung and colon histopathological image dataset. https://www.kaggle.com/datasets/andrewmvd/lung-and-colon-cancer-histopathological-images. Accessed 15 May 2022

14. Garg, S., Garg, S.: Prediction of lung and colon cancer through analysis of histopathological images by utilizing Pre-trained CNN models with visualization of class activation and saliency maps. In: 3rd Artificial Intelligence and Cloud Computing Conference, pp. 38–45 (2020). https://doi.org/10.1145/3442536.3442543

15. Ali, M., Ali, R.: Multi-input dual-stream capsule network for improved lung and colon cancer classification. Diagnostics (8), 1–18 (2021). https://doi.org/10.3390/diagnostics11081485

16. Chehade, A.H., Abdallah, N., Marion, J.-M., Oueidat, M., Chauvet, P.: Lung and colon cancer classification using medical imaging: a feature engineering approach. Phys. Eng. Sci. Med., 1–25 (2022). https://doi.org/10.1007/s13246-022-01139-x

17. Bukhari, S.U.K., Asmara, S., Bokhari, S.K.A., Hussain, S.S., Armaghan, S.U., Shah, S.S.H.: The histological diagnosis of colonic adenocarcinoma by applying partial self supervised learning. medRxiv (2020)

An Enhanced Diabetes Mellitus Prediction Using Feature Selection-Based Type-2 Fuzzy Model

Joseph Bamidele Awotunde[1](✉) (ID), Sanjay Misra[2] (ID), and Quoc Trung Pham[3](✉) (ID)

[1] Department of Computer Science, Faculty of Information and Communication Sciences, University of Ilorin, Ilorin 240003, Kwara State, Nigeria
awotunde.jb@unilorin.edu.ng

[2] Department of Computer Science and Communication, Østfold University College, Halden, Norway
Sanjay.misra@hiof.no

[3] School of Industrial Management, Ho Chi Minh City University of Technology (VNU-HCM), HCMC, Vietnam
pqtrung@hcmut.edu.vn

Abstract. The diabetes mellitus has been known to be a serious illness and revered for its ability to cause high mortality rate. This disease is famous among both youth and adult for its existence in the human body, and very difficult to diagnose, thus, produces an under-diagnosis issue when clinicians try to pinpoint the precise symptoms for disease prediction. The majority of the currently used diagnostic and monitoring methods are designed on type 1 fuzzy logic or ontology, which, as a result of the inconsistent and ambiguous nature of the collected data, is unsatisfactory. Therefore, this paper proposes an enhanced feature selection-based enabled type-2 fuzzy logic (T2FL) model for the prediction of diabetes patients. The proposed model used Particle Swarm Optimization to select the most relevant features from the dataset so as to remove irrelevant features from the data, and T2FL technique was used for the classification of the disease. The model extract precise information and correctly conclude the result. The proposed technique utilizes T2FL to determine the membership values of the clinical information, and the decision-making mechanism properly processes the evidence derived from the crisp values. A comprehensive computer simulation using a diabetes dataset shows that the suggested strategy works noticeably better than the ones already in place based on type-1 fuzzy logic and ontology in terms of determination effectiveness.

Keywords: Diabetes mellitus · Feature selection · Type-2 fuzzy logic · Particle swarm optimization · Diagnosis · Prediction · Mortality rate

1 Introduction

The usage of fuzzy logic systems (FLSs) in a number of various processes and applications includes Network anomaly detection system [1, 2], image processing [3, 4], data analysis [5, 6], internet of things [7, 8], classification problems [9, 10], healthcare data processing [11, 12], among others. Hence, one of the most popular topics in recent

© The Author(s), under exclusive license to Springer Nature Singapore Pte Ltd. 2022
T. K. Dang et al. (Eds.): FDSE 2022, CCIS 1688, pp. 625–639, 2022.
https://doi.org/10.1007/978-981-19-8069-5_43

years has been the study of FLSs. Numerous applications show that type-2 fuzzy logic (T2FL) and general type-2 (GT2) FLSs are superior than type-1 fuzzy logic (T1FL) FLSs like the works in decision making systems [13], fault detection [14], control systems [15], financial services [16], clustering algorithms [17], among others. Medical diagnosis is the process of categorizing the condition that accounts for a person's state as a distinctive sickness [18]. It sometimes has to do with underlying clinical setting. With advancements in technology, many tools could be used to track and gather medical information on a particular ailment [19]. This information could be utilized to determine and make prognosis-related healthcare recommendations in the future and therapy to enhance precision, dependability, and diagnostic efficiency.

One in four individuals over the age of 65 may have diabetes [20]. Over 246 million individuals globally have been afflicted by this condition, according to the World Health Organization, and by 2025, 380 million people are anticipated to be living with diabetes globally [21]. It is well known that some people don't even realize they have this illness. With no cure in sight, diabetes is now considered the sixth most lethal disease globally (REF). When diabetes is discovered early, it can be managed. On the other hand, a delayed diagnosis can lead to serious complications and, eventually, results to various sickness like foot problems, eye issues, heart disease, nerve damage, and renal disease [22]. As artificial intelligence (AI) continues to advance in the fields of healthcare and clinical applications for monitoring, prediction, diagnosis, and treatment, thus, diabetes cases and symptoms can be well-managed and recognized.

AI-based models in the context of medicine refers to the simulation of expert medical knowledge by machines or computers that have been designed to behave in an expert manner, and replicate their methods for making medical diagnoses [23]. AI is frequently used to extract intriguing patterns from healthcare records [24, 25]. Experts analyze diabetes using a variety of AI techniques. Recently, several machine learning, AI-based models, and statistical techniques have been utilized to diagnose diabetes like support vector machine (SVM) [26], artificial neural network (ANN) [27], K-nearest neighbor (KNN) [28], Genetic Algorithms [29], Ant Colony Optimization [30], decision tree [31] among others. Various studies demonstrate the effectiveness of various classification techniques; however, those classifiers produce classification algorithm that use complicated mathematical models; and they are thought to be impenetrable and transparent to humans. These classifiers cannot be used in numerous real-world domains due to this flaw, where accuracy in classification and understandability are both required. Recently, excellent results using fuzzy logic techniques have been achieved in a variety of application sectors, especially in the field of medicine. When building a classification model, fuzzy logic is unable to handle data from a high number of input variables.

To increase FLSs' performance, studies into the creation of novel learning algorithms and FLSs' fundamental changes are ongoing. One of the recent and effective method is the Type-2 Fuzzy Logic (T2FL) model to expand FLSs for huge data issues and to maximize the antecedent factors. The application of the Type-1 Fuzzy Logic (T1FL) model create uncertainty and imprecision especially in disease prediction and classification, thus to weak for disease datasets that are very huge. Based on the available literature, no comprehensive research has been conducted to combine PSO feature selection method and T2FL model for the prediction of diabetes. As a result, the performance of classification and detection accuracy of diabetes has increased due to the transparency and clarity of T2FL with PSO for feature selection and optimization approach. Because of the excessively tiny value of the output's time-derivative with reference to these properties. Additionally, a higher pace of adaption can lead to instability issues. Two solutions have been proposed to address this issue. The application of Particle Swarm Optimization (PSO) and Bio-inspire algorithm for feature selection to remove irrelevant features from the dataset, thus will increase the performance of the model and derivative calculations are not required because all parameters are optimized at the same rate [32, 33].

The following are the layout of the paper: Sect. 2 presents the related work on the application of fuzzy logic and other models. Section 3 discusses the methodology used in the study. Section 4 present the experimental results and analysis of this study, and finally, Sect. 5 concluded the paper with future directions to the study.

2 Related Work

To identify diabetes, a variety of strategies and algorithms regulating several distinct technologies have been employed. Some of these strategies will be discussed and summarized in this section. Starting with ANN-based model, a computational model of the human brain based on the idea of neurons existing in the brain. Since it has cognitive capacities comparable to those of the human brain, diagnosis and prediction are among its main applications. ANNs aid doctors in diagnosing and have a significant impact on their decisions, which boosts their credibility. The ability of ANN can handle data in parallel makes it effective in recognizing complicated patterns [34]. It can be laborious to use ANN for diabetes detection because a single layer network can't produce precise prediction, and so it is essential to combine the non-linear element, which can be done by creating a multi-layer complicated architecture. Time is influenced by this because of heavy processing.

The ML or AI-based algorithms that are utilized in predictive systems sometimes rely on vast amounts of data. Big data analytics now comes into the picture as a result [35]. Big data, as the name suggests, is a system that effectively and successfully manages an abundant amount of data. A significant limitation for ANNs and DL was identified to be the insufficient diabetic datasets, but big data analytics analysis helps in solving this [36]. Big data integrates the chaotic data, making its manipulation relatively simple [37]. Big data struggles with issues like high memory needs and concerns about the confidentiality of patient information [38].

When it comes to data mining, there are several ways to examine vast amounts of data while taking the desired goal into account in order to uncover hidden knowledge [39]. The information is displayed based on the connections between the variables and the degree of their dependence or influence on the result. The repository for the decision-making process is this knowledge base. The discrepancy across various situations and datasets, however, can be detrimental, while data mining leaves no room for ambiguity. On the other hand, fuzzy logic has the distinction of being cheaper to design than the other technologies we previously covered [40]. The disadvantage of utilizing fuzzy logic is that the precision may suffer when fuzzy values are converted to precise real-world values.

A combination of conventional and hybrid methodologies was used by the author [41] to describe the intricate explanation of the predictive method for predicting diabetes. For the diagnosis of diabetes, a fuzzy ontology-based semantic Case Representation and Retrieval (CBR) system has been proposed [42]. Boundary value issues have been solved using fuzzy logic [43]. The author in [44] created a model for the diagnosis of diabetes using a Swarm Optimized Fuzzy Reasoning Model. The data preprocessing employs fuzzy c-means clustering based attribute weight, the classification of the diabetes dataset has been proposed [45] using classifier algorithms like SVM and KNN.

Large knowledge is created through a fuzzy inference system for diabetes prediction. A fuzzy extension criterion was put out by the authors in [46] as a search method to incorporate more adaptable variables into fuzzy space, it enables different features to be taken into account while optimizing. The multi-objective optimization issue is solved using the enhanced version criteria. When a minimum number of features is obtained, this problem arises, thus, lowers the classification's precision. As a result, the research offers new objective functions (such as fuzzy) with considerable flexibility to address the issue of multi-objective extracted features. The sample size (between 178 and 699) and number of features (varying from 9 to 279) of the UCI datasets have been varied when assessing the suggested fuzzy goal functions. For the bulk of the datasets, the suggested fuzzy technique displays strong classification effectiveness.

For the feature selection and classification challenge, authors in [47] used fuzzy similarity measures with a multi-objective genetic algorithm (GA) finding the ideal combination of features (subset). Using datasets from UCI, the effectiveness of this strategy was assessed, and the findings demonstrated that it outperformed correlation-based feature selection techniques. For the classification of diabetes, another approach utilized hybrid ACO and fuzzy logic. The outcome demonstrated that the suggested technique performed better in term of accuracy than the benchmark models. Additionally, this study produced a diabetes detection expert system [48].

The authors in [49] study revealed a classification for customized hypoglycemic drugs used to treat diabetes. The information, which included 21,796 diabetic patients, was taken from the China EHR repository. In this study, a logistic regression classification algorithm was compared to the performance of a hierarchical recurrent neural network. The outcome demonstrated that the suggested method performed better than logistic regression. KNN classification technique was employed on a dataset from Stanford University repository in a work by authors in [50], and the dataset included 11 patient characteristics. Numerous K values were employed in the investigation, and the best outcome was $K = 5$, with an accuracy rate of 75%. For the diagnosis of diabetes, authors in [18] suggested three categorization methods. These techniques included the decision tree, Naive Bayes, and SVM. Using the Naive Bayes classifier, the highest classification accuracy of 76.30% was achieved.

For the purpose of detecting network anomalies, authors in [51] created a multi-criteria fuzzy classifier hybrid with a greedy feature selection technique. The effectiveness of intrusion-detection systems was significantly impacted by this proposed method. The suggested hybrid method decreased the number of selected features to roughly 74% while improving detection rates for various incursion types. Similarly, authors in [52] created FCS-ANTMINER, a swarm intelligence classifier for diabetes diagnosis. To derive a predictive model, the classifier was built using a combination of fuzzy logic and ACO. The classification result was 84.24% when the performance of the classifier was compared to cutting-edge algorithms used in the literature.

3   Materials and Methods

3.1   Data Preprocessing

A diabetes dataset typically contains noise, missing values, maybe in a format that is undesirable and inaccessible to ML-based models. To clean up the data and make it suitable for the prediction model, feature pre-processing is required, thus, improves the efficiency and accuracy of a prediction model [53]. The pre-processing approach provides information about managing zero values, standardization, management of categorical variables, one-hot encoding, and multidimensional predictability.

3.2   Feature Selection

Most frequently, feature pre-processing reveals that some unrelated samples do not support and may significantly reduce the accuracy of the detection. It is a method that is widely used to get rid of unnecessary data attributes and reduce the time complexity of pattern prediction [54]. The dependability of the model is significantly influenced by the input data. When data is gathered utilizing data mining and fuzzy logic techniques, some of the specifics are characterized by having missing values. It also has a high propensity for noise abatement.

Because not enough pertinent characteristics are chosen, neural networks are frequently prone to under- or over-fitting of data. This issue can be reduced by selecting an ideal subset of the currently available features [55]. The terminology "feature selection" refers to this selection of pertinent features. Additionally, the imbalanced nature of the data can have a negative impact on the ML-based models that are built. In test data, it was discovered that these models had larger bias and a higher rate of misclassification of datasets, both of which may be reduced by employing techniques like resampling. Subset of appropriate parameters feature selection can be utilized to further improve accuracy rate [56].

3.3   Particle Swarm Optimization

If the prospective optimization issue solution is thought of as a particle, the particle travels through space constantly, and based on its own experience, the position is modified and the finest person's experience in the process of looking for the greatest job. Initializing the PSO model first yields a collection of random solutions, and then repeats, monitoring the best particles in the current space to discover the best answer. A collection of m particles exists in the multidimensional search space. The position and velocity of the i^{-th} particle in the t^{-th} iteration are $X_{i,t}$ and $V_{i,t}$, respectively. By controlling two ideal solutions, the particle updates its position and speed. The first is the ideal outcome that the particle itself seeks, i.e. the intimate best $pbest_i$. The other is the best option being pursued by the entire group right now, or the global $gbest_t$. Particles modify their speed and new position using the following formula when looking for these two ideal solutions:

$$V_{i,t+1} = w * V_{i,t} + c_1 * rand * (pbest_i - X_{i,t}) + c_2 * rand * (gbest_t - X_{i,t}) \quad (1)$$

$$X_{i,t+1} = X_{i,t} + \lambda * V_{i,t+1} \quad (2)$$

In Eq. (1 and 2), the learning factors are c_1 and c_2, and w is the velocity inertia factor; $rand$ is the chance value between [0, 1], and is the velocity coefficient, which is often equal to $\lambda = 1$.

3.4 The Type-2 Fuzzy Logic Model

The five parts of the T2LF model examine the dataset to ascertain the level of membership: (i) fuzzifier, (ii) T2F rule, (iii) inference engine, (iv) reducer, and (v) defuzzifier. The T2FL function implements the "if-Then" criterion to the crisp input data that was received and fuzzified. The type-reducer completely converted T2FL outcomes to T1FL outputs. The T1FL was further transformed into a crisp value through defuzzification. The defuzzification findings show the average points of the right and left ends of the type-reduced set. Figure 1 shows how data was transformed into a T2FMFs interval and then into a T1Fs interval via fuzzification. The triangle membership function was used to determine the fuzzy membership values for the sensor data, with x, a, b, and c as the membership values for each input.

$$f(x; a, b, c) = \begin{cases} 0, & x \le a \\ \frac{x-a}{b-a} & a \le x \le b \\ \frac{x-c}{b-c} & b \le x \le c \\ 0, & c \le x \end{cases} \quad (3)$$

$$f(x; a, b, c) = max\left(min\left(\frac{x-a}{b-a}, \frac{x-c}{b-c} \right), 0 \right) \quad (4)$$

Four linear functions were used to characterize the Footprint of Uncertainty (FOU), Lower Membership Function (LMF), and Upper Membership Function (UMF), and five points a, b, c, d, and e. Hence, the centroid of the Type-2 fuzzy logic membership function is expressed using the following equations.

$$traigular(x, a, b, c, d, e) = max(0, min(T_1, T_2, e)) \quad (5)$$

$$UMF = T_1(x, a, b, c) \quad (6)$$

$$LMF = T_1(x, d, e, c) \quad (7)$$

$$c = \frac{\sum_{i=1}^{q} \mu(x_i).x_1}{\sum_{i=1}^{q} \mu(x_i).} \quad (8)$$

$$\lfloor c_1, c_2 \rfloor = \left[\frac{\sum_{i=1}^{q} \mu'(x_i).x_1}{\sum_{i=1}^{q} \mu'(x_i).}, \frac{\sum_{i=1}^{q} \mu''(x_i).x_1}{\sum_{i=1}^{q} \mu''(x_i).} \right] \tag{9}$$

The LMF and UMF values for the minimizes and maximizes weighted averages, respectively, were represented by the letters $\mu_{x,i}$ and $\mu''_{x,i}$. The basic data used for diabetes monitoring and prediction includes age (age), blood sugar (BS), weight (wgt), body temperature (BT), and patient health status (PHC). The ranges of the values for the boundary of the uncertainty of UMF and LMF are established by the input variables since all of the variables used as input are uncertain. The membership value of the gathered data was calculated using the T2FL model, and the model's prediction outcomes served as the foundation for the knowledge engine of the proposed system, which used them to represent the membership value of each sensor data and process it for decision-making. To cope with the ambiguity and inconsistent nature of the data from diabetes dataset, the T2FL model was used, and the output of the membership function is converted to a mass value. To arrive at a choice, the rules are combined.

The exhaustive and mutually exclusive finite set is represented as $\Omega = \{\theta_1, \theta_2, \ldots, \theta_n\}$, Ω is the framework for judgment (FoD), 2^{Ω} demonstrates the set of Ω, and the 2^{Ω} element formulations include:
$2^{\Omega} = \{\theta, \{\theta_1\}, \{\theta_2\}, \ldots, \{\theta_n\}, \{\theta_1, \theta_2\}, \ldots, \Omega\}$, the mass function, denoted by the letter m, is a mapping from the power set 2^{Ω} *to the interval of* $[0, 1]$ meets the following prerequisites:

$$\begin{cases} \sum_{A \leq \theta} m(A) = 1 \\ m(\theta) = 0 \end{cases} \tag{10}$$

A focal element happened if $mA > 1$, and mA determines how strongly the signal supports the proposal using the mass function _A. The Basic Probability Assignment (BPA) depicts the focus set and the corresponding mass value called BoE, or Basic Belief Assignment (BBA):

$$(\mathbb{R}, m) = \{A, \langle m \rangle : A \in 2^{\Omega}, m(A) > 0\}, \tag{11}$$

The subset of the set is $\mathbb{R}, 2^{\Omega}, A(\in \mathbb{R})$ each has an associated non-zero mass value $m(A)$.

The BPA can be indicated by the association belief function, Bel, and the Pl (plausibility function), which may be expressed as follows:

$$Bel(A) = \sum_{\varnothing \neq B(\leq A)}^{\cdot} m(B) \tag{12}$$

$$Pl(A) = \sum_{B \cap A \neq \varnothing} m(B) \tag{13}$$

3.5 The Dataset Used for the Evaluation of the Proposed Model

The Pima Indians Diabetes Database dataset was produced by the National Institute of Diabetes, Digestive and Kidney Diseases. Based on a set of predetermined criteria and diagnostic values in the dataset, it was possible to ascertain whether a patient had diabetes or not. The majority of the patients in the sample are girls with Pima Indian origin, who are all at least 21 years old. One outcome variable and several medical predictor factors exist. These factors include, among others, age, BMI, insulin and glucose levels, the number of pregnancies, and others. The dataset contains 8 distinctive features with 768 occurrences, as shown in Table 1.

Table 1. Pima dataset attribute characteristics

Name of the attribute	Categorized value
Age (year)	Age
Plasma glucose level	PGL
Diastolic blood pressure (mm Hg)	DBP
Body mass index (kg/m^2)	BMI
Frequency of pregnancy	Preg
Diabetes pedigree function	DPF
Thickness of triceps skin (mm)	TTS
2-h serum insulin	2HSI
Label class (0 or 1)	Class

4   Results and Discussion

The proposed system was created using Python on a Windows 10 computer with an Intel Core i7-2600 CPU and 8 GB of RAM. The programming language gathers data from diabetes databases to calculate a patient's risk score. Using the Keras Library of the Python programming language, the PIMA diabetes datasets were categorized. k-fold cross-validation techniques were used to divide the dataset into a number of folds for training and testing. The results were compared to the performance of conventional fuzzy logic and T1FL-based models, which proved the effectiveness of the proposed model. The performance metrics results for the proposed model using metrics like accuracy, F1-score, sensitivity, and specificity, respectively are shown in Table 2. The proposed model performs significantly better than existing models based on the performance metrics used to test the proposed model. The patient's diabetes condition is ascertained using each dataset folding.

Table 2. The performance of the diabetes dataset using the four metrics.

	Accuracy	F1-score (%)	Sensitivity (%)	Specificity (%)
2-fold	93%	94%	96%	93%

(continued)

Table 2. (*continued*)

	Accuracy	F1-score (%)	Sensitivity (%)	Specificity (%)
3-fold	95%	94%	98%	93%
4-fold	93%	93%	94%	91%
5-fold	95%	96%	97%	92%
6-fold	97%	96%	96%	94%
7-fold	94%	93%	94%	92%
8-fold	98%	95%	96%	93%
9-fold	95%	95%	98%	92%
10-fold	97%	98%	98%	97%

According to the proposed system's cross-validation findings on the dataset, accuracy is greater than 90% across all folds, the performance metrics employed, etc. The accuracy is 96% at a 10-fold scale, with an F1 score of 98%, and a 98% sensitivity at a 9-fold and 98% specificity at a 10-fold increase. The suggested model performs much better across all measures and cross-validations, with the best sensitivity of 98.1%.

To evaluate the different output metrics, the one trail/run closer to the average classification accuracy value was selected. The overall accuracy of the results rating was 98%. The proposed model performance evaluation metrics for classifying the reduced dataset are shown in Table 2. Table 3 show the comparison of the proposed model with other state-of-the-art models using the same dataset, and the results show that the proposed model accuracy outperformed other models in the literature.

The PSO was used for feature selection to be able to reduce the features to the most relevant features that will add to the classification of the dataset. This also help in deleting samples that were outliers, inconsistent, and noisy, and the data normalization help with the replacement of missing values using mean method. The PSO was utilized as a feature selection approach and its output was given to the T2FL model using a 10-fold cross-validation procedure for the prediction of the dataset. PSO was used to choose various features from the initial set of attributes during each run, and the run-by-run classification accuracy was recorded.

Table 3. The performance of the proposed model

Performance measures	Reduced dataset
Reduced features	**5**
Sensitivity (%)	98.00
Specificity (%)	98.00
F1-score (%)	97.00
Model accuracy (%)	98.00

Table 4 and Fig. 1 show the accuracy of the system's diagnosis of diabetes mellitus. The outcomes demonstrate that the hybridized model outperformed the single approach.

Table 4. The accuracy obtained from the three systems for diagnosis

Performance measures	Reduced dataset
Fuzzy logic accuracy (%)	93.3
T1FL model accuracy (%)	93.7
T2FL accuracy (%)	95.3
T2FL + PSO accuracy (%)	98.0

THE MODELS PERFORMANCE

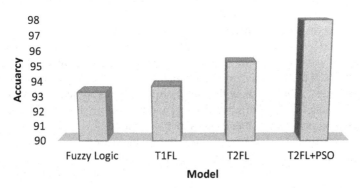

Fig. 1. The performance of the models accuracy compared with the proposed model.

4.1 Comparison of the Proposed Model with Some Existing Work

The proposed framework revealed a better performance when compare with other existing work that used the same dataset with an accuracy of 98.0%. This may be due to the application of PSO feature selection to remove irrelevant features from the dataset. In the study, the accuracy of classification techniques for identifying diabetes mellitus was compared. Using the Pima Indian Diabetes dataset, which is presented in Table 5 from other studies.

Table 5. The comparison of the proposed model with some existing studies

Reference	Model	Accuracy (%)
[57]	Modified Artificial Bee Colony	82.2
[58]	J48graft with Re-RX	83.8
[59]	ANFIS + PCA	89.0
[60]	FNN + ANN	84.2
[61]	Similarity Classifier + Feature Selection	76.0
[62]	Extreme ML model	77.6
[63]	Hierarchical Fuzzy Classification	83.8
Proposed model	T2FL + PSO	98.0

5 Conclusion and Future Direction

Globally, the prediction of diabetes mellitus is a serious medical issue specially to detect the illness in early stage. Consequently, early diabetes diagnosis is crucial for effective treatment. Therefore, this paper proposed a hybrid model for the prediction of diabetes mellitus based on feature selection algorithm and a prediction model. The proposed model comprised of two major stages: (i) the PSO feature selection model, (ii) Type-2 Fuzzy Logic classifier for the prediction of diabetes mellitus using PIMA dataset to test the performance of the proposed model. The proposed system can be used to discovered diabetes problems in earlier stage by using the model to predict the patient in real-time. The suggested classifier also shown the capacity to choose relevant features that increased classification precision. It also illustrated the significance of feature identification in diabetes prediction, and demonstrated that after giving this strategy more thought, the classification's performance improved. For the purpose of validation, the suggested classifier fared better than other cutting-edge classifiers like Fuzzy logic, T1FL, and T2FL models. Future study can still consider the using of other bio-inspire algorithms, stochastic local search classifiers, guided local search and iterated local search for feature selection purposes. This could further improve the accuracy of the prediction model and reduce the error rate of the classifier. The implementation of deep learning algorithms with various feature selection can be used to further improve the diagnosis and prediction of diabetes mellitus patients, and the introduction of Internet of medical of Things will help the diagnosis of patients living with diabetes in real-time and in remote environments.

References

1. Hamamoto, A.H., Carvalho, L.F., Sampaio, L.D.H., Abrão, T., Proença, M.L., Jr.: Network anomaly detection system using genetic algorithm and fuzzy logic. Expert Syst. Appl. **92**, 390–402 (2018)

2. Almseidin, M., Al-Sawwa, J., Alkasassbeh, M.: Anomaly-based intrusion detection system using fuzzy logic. In: 2021 International Conference on Information Technology (ICIT), pp. 290–295. IEEE, July 2021

3. Soltani, A., Battikh, T., Jabri, I., Lakhoua, N.: A new expert system based on fuzzy logic and image processing algorithms for early glaucoma diagnosis. Biomed. Signal Process. Control **40**, 366–377 (2018)

4. Amza, C.G., Cicic, D.T.: Industrial image processing using fuzzy-logic. Procedia Eng. **100**, 492–498 (2015)

5. Arji, G., et al.: Fuzzy logic approach for infectious disease diagnosis: a methodical evaluation, literature and classification. Biocybern. Biomed. Eng. **39**(4), 937–955 (2019)

6. Zaitseva, E., Piestova, I., Rabcan, J., Rusnak, P.: Multiple-valued and fuzzy logics application to remote sensing data analysis. In: 2018 26th Telecommunications Forum (TELFOR), pp. 1–4. IEEE, November 2018

7. Awotunde, J.B., Jimoh, R.G., AbdulRaheem, M., Oladipo, I.D., Folorunso, S.O., Ajamu, G.J.: IoT-based wearable body sensor network for COVID-19 pandemic. In: Hassanien, A.-E., Elghamrawy, S.M., Zelinka, I. (eds.) Advances in data science and intelligent data communication technologies for COVID-19. SSDC, vol. 378, pp. 253–275. Springer, Cham (2022). https://doi.org/10.1007/978-3-030-77302-1_14

8. Awotunde, J.B., Folorunso, S.O., Bhoi, A.K., Adebayo, P.O., Ijaz, M.F.: Disease diagnosis system for IoT-based wearable body sensors with machine learning algorithm. In: Kumar Bhoi, A., Mallick, P.K., Narayana Mohanty, M., de Albuquerque, V.H.C. (eds.) Hybrid Artificial Intelligence and IoT in Healthcare. Intelligent Systems Reference Library, vol. 209, pp. 201–222. Springer, Singapore (2021). https://doi.org/10.1007/978-981-16-2972-3_10

9. Souza, P.V.C.: Regularized fuzzy neural networks for pattern classification problems. Int. J. Appl. Eng. Res. **13**(5), 2985–2991 (2018)

10. Elkano, M., Sanz, J.A., Barrenechea, E., Bustince, H., Galar, M.: CFM-BD: a distributed rule induction algorithm for building compact fuzzy models in big data classification problems. IEEE Trans. Fuzzy Syst. **28**(1), 163–177 (2019)

11. Maheshwari, V., et al.: Nanotechnology-based sensitive biosensors for COVID-19 prediction using fuzzy logic control. J. Nanomater. **2021**, 1–8 (2021)

12. Dubey, S., Verma, D.: Fuzzy logic based intelligent data sensitive security model for big data in healthcare. Int. J. Electron. Telecommun. **68**, 245–250 (2022)

13. Tian, Z.P., Nie, R.X., Wang, J.Q.: Social network analysis-based consensus-supporting framework for large-scale group decision-making with incomplete interval type-2 fuzzy information. Inf. Sci. **502**, 446–471 (2019)

14. Rocha, E.M., et al.: A fuzzy type-2 fault detection methodology to minimize false alarm rate in induction motor monitoring applications. Appl. Soft Comput. **93**, 106373 (2020)

15. Mohammadzadeh, A., Kumbasar, T.: A new fractional-order general type-2 fuzzy predictive control system and its application for glucose level regulation. Appl. Soft Comput. **91**, 106241 (2020)

16. Takahashi, A., Takahashi, S.: A new interval type-2 fuzzy logic system under dynamic environment: application to financial investment. Eng. Appl. Artif. Intell. **100**, 104154 (2021)

17. Tao, Y., Zhang, J., Yang, L.: An unequal clustering algorithm for wireless sensor networks based on interval type-2 TSK fuzzy logic theory. IEEE Access **8**, 197173–197183 (2020)

18. Sisodia, D., Sisodia, D.S.: Prediction of diabetes using classification algorithms. Procedia Comput. Sci. **132**, 1578–1585 (2018)

19. Vitabile, S., et al.: Medical data processing and analysis for remote health and activities monitoring. In: Kołodziej, J., González-Vélez, H. (eds.) High-performance modelling and simulation for big data applications. LNCS, vol. 11400, pp. 186–220. Springer, Cham (2019). https://doi.org/10.1007/978-3-030-16272-6_7

20. Khanal, N., et al.: FootAssure: a multimodal, in-home wound detection device for diabetic peripheral neuropathy. In: 2021 43rd Annual International Conference of the IEEE Engineering in Medicine and Biology Society (EMBC), pp. 4019–4022. IEEE, November 2021

21. Oladipo, I.D., Babatunde, A.O., Awotunde, J.B., Abdulraheem, M.: An improved hybridization in the diagnosis of diabetes mellitus using selected computational intelligence. In: Misra, S., Muhammad-Bello, B. (eds.) ICTA 2020. CCIS, vol. 1350, pp. 272–285. Springer, Cham (2021). https://doi.org/10.1007/978-3-030-69143-1_22

22. Bhatti, J.S., et al.: Oxidative stress in the pathophysiology of type 2 diabetes and related complications: current therapeutics strategies and future perspectives. Free Radic. Biol. Med. **184**, 114–134 (2022)

23. Luxton, D.D.: An introduction to artificial intelligence in behavioral and mental health care. In: Artificial Intelligence in Behavioral and Mental Health Care, pp. 1–26. Academic Press (2016)

24. Mohd Sharif, N.A., et al.: A fuzzy rule-based expert system for asthma severity identification in emergency department. J. Inf. Commun. Technol. (JICT) **18**(4), 415–438 (2019)

25. Ayo, F.E., Folorunso, S.O., Abayomi-Alli, A.A., Adekunle, A.O., Awotunde, J.B.: Network intrusion detection based on deep learning model optimized with rule-based hybrid feature selection. Inf. Secur. J. Glob. Perspect. **29**(6), 267–283 (2020)

26. Mohan, N., Jain, V.: Performance analysis of support vector machine in diabetes prediction. In: 2020 4th International Conference on Electronics, Communication and Aerospace Technology (ICECA), pp. 1–3. IEEE, November 2020

27. Pradhan, N., Rani, G., Dhaka, V.S., Poonia, R.C.: Diabetes prediction using artificial neural network. In: Deep Learning Techniques for Biomedical and Health Informatics, pp. 327–339. Academic Press (2020)

28. Garcia-Carretero, R., Vigil-Medina, L., Mora-Jimenez, I., Soguero-Ruiz, C., Barquero-Perez, O., Ramos-Lopez, J.: Use of a K-nearest neighbors model to predict the development of type 2 diabetes within 2 years in an obese, hypertensive population. Med. Biol. Eng. Comput. **58**(5), 991–1002 (2020). https://doi.org/10.1007/s11517-020-02132-w

29. Abdollahi, J., Nouri-Moghaddam, B.: Hybrid stacked ensemble combined with genetic algorithms for diabetes prediction. Iran J. Comput. Sci. **5**, 205–220 (2022). https://doi.org/10.1007/s42044-022-00100-1

30. Anwar, N.H. K., Saian, R., Bakar, S.A.: An enhanced ant colony optimization with Gini index for predicting type 2 diabetes. In: AIP Conference Proceedings, vol. 2365, no. 1, p. 020004. AIP Publishing LLC, July 2021

31. Hasan, M.K., Alam, M.A., Das, D., Hossain, E., Hasan, M.: Diabetes prediction using ensembling of different machine learning classifiers. IEEE Access **8**, 76516–76531 (2020)

32. Sarabakha, A., Fu, C., Kayacan, E.: Intuit before tuning: Type-1 and type-2 fuzzy logic controllers. Appl. Soft Comput. **81**, 105495 (2019)

33. Alcalá-Fdez, J., Alcalá, R., González, S., Nojima, Y., García, S.: Evolutionary fuzzy rule-based methods for monotonic classification. IEEE Trans. Fuzzy Syst. **25**(6), 1376–1390 (2017)

34. Soltani, Z., Jafarian, A.: A new artificial neural networks approach for diagnosing diabetes disease type II. Int. J. Adv. Comput. Sci. Appl. **7**(6), 89–94 (2016)

35. Awotunde, J.B., Jimoh, R.G., Oladipo, I.D., Abdulraheem, M.: Prediction of malaria fever using long-short-term memory and big data. In: Misra, S., Muhammad-Bello, B. (eds.) ICTA 2020. CCIS, vol. 1350, pp. 41–53. Springer, Cham (2021). https://doi.org/10.1007/978-3-030-69143-1_4

36. Odedra, D., Samanta, S., Vidyarthi, A.S.: Computational intelligence in early diabetes diagnosis: a review. Rev. Diabet. Stud. RDS **7**(4), 252 (2010)

37. Suvarnamukhi, B., Seshashayee, M.: Big data processing system for diabetes prediction using machine learning technique. IJITEE (2019). ISSN 2278-3075

38. Lalmi, F., Adala, L.: Big Data for Healthcare: Opportunities and Challenges. In: Hamdan, A., Hassanien, A.E., Razzaque, A., Alareeni, B. (eds.) The Fourth Industrial Revolution: Implementation of Artificial Intelligence for Growing Business Success. SCI, vol. 935, pp. 217–229. Springer, Cham (2021). https://doi.org/10.1007/978-3-030-62796-6_12

39. Thakkar, H., Shah, V., Yagnik, H., Shah, M.: Comparative anatomization of data mining and fuzzy logic techniques used in diabetes prognosis. Clin. eHealth 4, 12–23 (2021)

40. Al-Behadili, H.N.K., Ku-Mahamud, K.R.: Fuzzy unordered rule using greedy hill climbing feature selection method: an application to diabetes classification. J. Inf. Commun. Technol. 20(3), 391–422 (2021)

41. Jayanthi, N., Babu, B.V., Rao, N.S.: Survey on clinical prediction models for diabetes prediction. J. Big Data 4(1), 1–15 (2017). https://doi.org/10.1186/s40537-017-0082-7

42. El-Sappagh, S., Elmogy, M.: A decision support system for diabetes mellitus management. Diabet. Case Rep 1(102), 2 (2016)

43. Last, M., Kandel, A.: Automated detection of outliers in real-world data. In: Proceedings of the Second International Conference on Intelligent Technologies, pp. 292–301. InTech, November 2001

44. Narita, K., Kitagawa, H.: Outlier detection for transaction databases using association rules. In 2008 The Ninth International Conference on Web-Age Information Management, pp. 373–380. IEEE, July 2008

45. Shahi, A., Atan, R.B., Sulaiman, M.N.: Detecting effectiveness of outliers and noisy data on fuzzy system using FCM. Eur. J. Sci. Res. 36(4), 627–638 (2009)

46. Vieira, S.M., Sousa, J.M., Kaymak, U.: Fuzzy criteria for feature selection. Fuzzy Sets Syst. 189(1), 1–18 (2012)

47. Nosrati Nahook, H., Eftekhari, M.: A new method for feature selection based on fuzzy similarity measures using multi objective genetic algorithm. J. Fuzzy Set Valued Anal. 2014, 1–12 (2014)

48. Mallikarjun, T.N.V., Gundabathina, J.: Fuzzy classification rules generation with ant colony optimization for diabetes diagnosis. Int. J. Emerg. Trends Technol. Comput. Sci 5, 39–44 (2016)

49. Mei, J., et al.: Deep diabetologist: learning to prescribe hypoglycemic medications with recurrent neural networks. Stud. Health Technol. Inform. 245, 1277 (2017)

50. Saxena, K., Khan, Z., Singh, S.: Diagnosis of diabetes mellitus using k nearest neighbor algorithm. Int. J. Comput. Sci. Trends Technol. (IJCST) 2(4), 36–43 (2014)

51. El-Alfy, E.S.M., Al-Obeidat, F.N.: A multicriterion fuzzy classification method with greedy attribute selection for anomaly-based intrusion detection. Procedia Comput. Sci. 34, 55–62 (2014)

52. Ganji, M.F., Abadeh, M.S.: A fuzzy classification system based on Ant Colony Optimization for diabetes disease diagnosis. Expert Syst. Appl. 38(12), 14650–14659 (2011)

53. Awotunde, J.B., Misra, S., Ayeni, F., Maskeliunas, R., Damasevicius, R.: Artificial intelligence based system for bank loan fraud prediction. In: Abraham, A., et al. (eds.) HIS 2021. LNNS, vol. 420, pp. 463–472. Springer, Cham (2022). https://doi.org/10.1007/978-3-030-96305-7_43

54. Adeniyi, E.A., Gbadamosi, B., Awotunde, J.B., Misra, S., Sharma, M.M., Oluranti, J.: Crude oil price prediction using particle swarm optimization and classification algorithms. In: Abraham, A., Gandhi, N., Hanne, T., Hong, TP., Nogueira Rios, T., Ding, W. (eds.) ISDA 2021. LNNS, vol. 418, pp. 1384–1394. Springer, Cham (2022). https://doi.org/10.1007/978-3-030-96308-8_128

55. Awotunde, J.B., Misra, S.: Feature extraction and artificial intelligence-based intrusion detection model for a secure internet of things networks. In: Misra, S., Arumugam, C. (eds.) Illumination of Artificial Intelligence in Cybersecurity and Forensics. LNDECT, vol. 109, pp. 21–44. Springer, Cham (2022). https://doi.org/10.1007/978-3-030-93453-8_2

56. Ali, L., Bukhari, S.A.C.: An approach based on mutually informed neural networks to optimize the generalization capabilities of decision support systems developed for heart failure prediction. IRBM **42**(5), 345–352 (2021)
57. Beloufa, F., Chikh, M.A.: Design of fuzzy classifier for diabetes disease using Modified Artificial Bee Colony algorithm. Comput. Methods Programs Biomed. **112**(1), 92–103 (2013)
58. Hayashi, Y., Yukita, S.: Rule extraction using Recursive-Rule extraction algorithm with J48graft combined with sampling selection techniques for the diagnosis of type 2 diabetes mellitus in the Pima Indian dataset. Inform. Med. Unlock. **2**, 92–104 (2016)
59. Polat, K., Güneş, S.: Artificial immune recognition system with fuzzy resource allocation mechanism classifier, principal component analysis and FFT method based new hybrid automated identification system for classification of EEG signals. Expert Syst. Appl. **34**(3), 2039–2048 (2008)
60. Kahramanli, H., Allahverdi, N.: Design of a hybrid system for the diabetes and heart diseases. Expert Syst. Appl. **35**(1–2), 82–89 (2008)
61. Luukka, P.: Feature selection using fuzzy entropy measures with similarity classifier. Expert Syst. Appl. **38**(4), 4600–4607 (2011)
62. Ding, S., Zhao, H., Zhang, Y., Xu, X., Nie, R.: Extreme learning machine: algorithm, theory and applications. Artif. Intell. Rev. **44**(1), 103–115 (2013). https://doi.org/10.1007/s10462-013-9405-z
63. Feng, T.C., Li, T.H.S., Kuo, P.H.: Variable coded hierarchical fuzzy classification model using DNA coding and evolutionary programming. Appl. Math. Model. **39**(23–24), 7401–7419 (2015)

A Novel Approach of Using Neural Circuit Policies for COVID-19 Classification on CT-Images

Hieu Minh Truong[1] (ID) and Hieu Trung Huynh[2]([✉]) (ID)

[1] Vietnamese – German University, Binh Duong, Vietnam
hieu.tm@vgu.edu.vn
[2] Industrial University of Ho Chi Minh City, Ho Chi Minh City, Germany
hthieu@iuh.edu.vn

Abstract. Fully connected (FC) layers as a classifier to categorize data have been practiced widely by the deep learning community. The dense wiring topology might lead to redundant complexity and overfitting during training. To overcome the disadvantages, we investigate neural circuit policies (NCP) to alternate the FC layers in this paper. NCP networks enable sparse and polarized connections between layers. Neurons within one layer can interact with themselves as well. However, NCP can handle only sequential data. To be compatible with the image classification task, we use sequence modeling techniques to simulate sequential data within the images. The ultimate comparison between NCP and FC models relies on the performance in classifying COVID-19 CT-slides. With our novel modeling technique, Z-NCP, the NCP models obtain the most stable scores. The FC models are comparably good and less resource-demanding. However, they are much less efficient considering the accuracy-complexity trade-off.

Keywords: Image classification based on recurrent neurons · Image sequence modeling using z-axis · Neural circuit policies · COVID-19 diagnosis

1 Introduction

Recently, convolutional neural networks (CNN) have been considered the first choice for image classification tasks [1, 2]. A typical CNN structure has two main parts, including a backbone followed by a head. When receiving an input image, the backbone extract (encode) features using multiple convolutional and pooling blocks. Later on, the head performs classification based on the given features. In our experiments, we focus on the design and efficiency of classification heads.

$$y = f(\mathbf{x} \cdot \mathbf{W} + b), \tag{1}$$

where $\mathbf{x}$ is the input, y is the output, f is an activation function, $\mathbf{W}$ and b are parameters. Conventionally, a CNN head is a combination of densely-connected layers of neurons [1, 2], called fully-connected (FC) layers. As shown in Fig. 1, the layers act as a

T. K. Dang et al. (Eds.): FDSE 2022, CCIS 1688, pp. 640–652, 2022.
https://doi.org/10.1007/978-981-19-8069-5_44

feature filtering system. Each of these layers contains neurons representing the features. Along with the depth, features shrink until reaching a desired number of categories (the classification of the input image). Between any two layers, each neuron of the previous layer connects to all the neurons in the next layer. Mathematically, the implementation of the connections is a matrix multiplication as in Eq. 1, where x and y represent the neurons in the previous and following layers. W and b are learnable matrices.

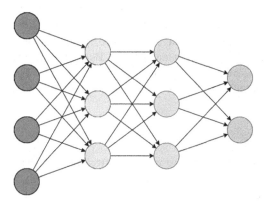

Fig. 1. CNN head - fully-connected layers

In contrast, the neural circuit policies (NCP) network [3, 4] is a biological-inspired neural system with a hierarchical, sparse, compact, and polarized wiring topology. Its effectiveness is demonstrated comprehensively in recent works on controlling autonomous cars using sequential frames from a real-time camera [4]. With only 19 neurons interconnected by 253 synapses, the NCP model outperformed other three times heavier state-of-art models with a much lower number of car crashes.

Motivated by the efficiency, we adopt NCP to CNN head to classify images. In partic-ular, we examine NCP in confirming COVID-19 in computed tomography (CT) slides. Since 2019, COVID-19 has been a deadly global crisis that has caused 548,990,094 cases worldwide[1]. CT imagery is a popular and comprehensive capturing method enabling the investigation inside a human body non-invasively. In detail, each CT scan provides a set of cross-sectional images displaying internal organs, slide by slide. With the captures, doctors can observe the COVID-19 manifestation and its severity inside a patient's lungs. To obtain such information, a part of the process requires the doctors to go through the set to pick out positive slides. The task is repetitive and hence expensive for the experts to perform. Therefore, it has urged for an automatic and accurate approach to classifying the COVID-19 slides for doctors, especially when there has been an explosive number of cases.

However, the classification of COVID-19 images and controlling autonomous cars are two distinct tasks. To drive cars, NCP is designed with liquid time-constant [5] recurrent neurons to capture the changes of frames during the operation time. On the

---

[1] https://covid19.who.int/.

other hand, a CT slide does not exhibit any serialized properties. Therefore, we have to simulate sequences within every input slide for compatibility.

Two modeling techniques, namely Y-NCP and Z-NCP, are investigated. Y-NCP considers the changes of information along the spatial dimension (y-axis) of an image. It has been practiced widely for the educational purpose of using recurrent neural networks for image classification [5–9]. Regarding the Z-NCP, we proposed a novel sequence modeling technique taking the depth dimension (z-axis) to account. Conventionally, an image can have four channels at most, making the data series too short for recurrent learning. To lengthen the sequence, we utilize convolutional layers in the CNN backbone. Through feature enrichment, we adjust the image channel to desired depths.

To inspect the efficiency, we compare the NCP-adopted networks with an equivalent FC network concerning the depth and number of neurons. Performance, network complexity, and resource demands are combined evaluation criteria.

2   Methods

To extract features of a CT slide, we use a lightweight CNN backbone CRNet [10]. The backbone has a relatively simple architecture containing only 506,720 parameters. Compared to other heavy state-of-the-art networks, X. He et al. confirmed the comparable efficiency of CRNet in classifying COVID-19 based on CT images [10]. Utilizing such a simple feature extractor has an advantage in demonstrating the affection of alternating the FC layers with the NCP network in the head.

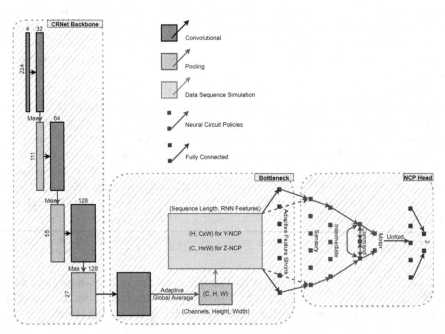

Fig. 2. CRNet with NCP adoption

CRNet encodes information using three repetitions of convolutional-pooling encoding blocks, as depicted in the *CRNet Backbone* block in Fig. 2. Along the path, pooling blocks reduce the spatial size of the input image while convolutional blocks enrich the number of channels. At the bottleneck, the encoded image moves to an additional convolutional and then an adaptive average pooling block for shape adjustment. The output shape is optimized depending on different sequence modeling techniques.

To simulate a data sequence within an image, denoted as tensor (C, H, W), we considered the changes of a set of pixel values along the y-axis and z-axis. Respectively, the techniques are named Y-NCP and Z-NCP. In the tensor denotation, parameters C, H, and W are the channels, height, and width.

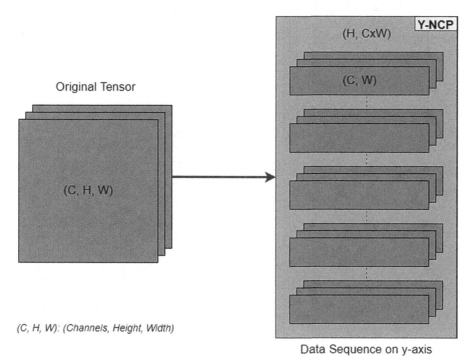

Fig. 3. Y-NCP sequence modeling technique

Regarding the Y-NCP modeling technique, a tensor is split into rows of pixels and connected as in Fig. 3. It forms a sequence of H elements having $C \times W$ features each. As a result, the NCP network monitors the changing behavior of the pixel rows along the image height to indicate its classification. The length H and features $C.W$ are highly-coupled since the image is square ($H = W$). The expansion or shrinkage of the spatial dimensions changes the sequence length and the number of features simultaneously.

Besides the conventional use of the y-axis, a novel usage of Z-NCP serializes pixel values along the z-axis. As depicted in Fig. 4, channel layers are split and connected to make a sequence of length C, while the two remaining dimensions form the sequential features. Each layer brings up $W \times H$ feature values. Compared to the Y-NCP, this

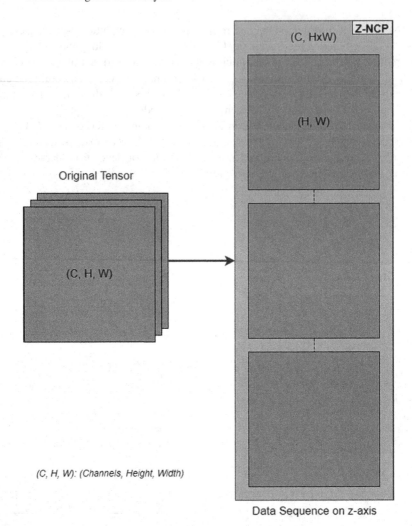

Fig. 4. Z-NCP sequence modeling technique

approach exhibits the length-features uncoupling property where the change of sequential features (number of pixels) does not affect the sequence length (number of channels). As a result, this enables independent learning between sequential instances. In addition, the property helps the backbone encode information more efficiently.

After the sequence modeling operation, an additional FC layer gently adjusts the size of sequential features before feeding them to sensory neurons of the NCP network. NCP is the inspirational design capturing the biological wiring of *C. elegans* nematode. The network hierarchy consists of four functional layers. In order, they are sensory, inter, command, and motor layers. Sensory neurons input outer-environment "stimulus signals" from which inter and command neurons conduct reasonings and issue instructions. Based on that, motor neurons fire the "actions" correspondingly.

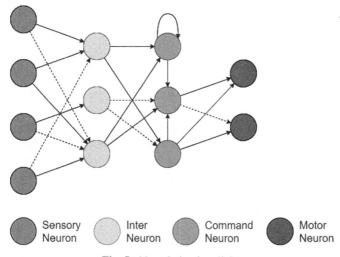

Fig. 5. Neural circuit policies

Figure 5 illustrates a simplified NCP network topology. Unlike FC layers, a neuron from pre-layer connects the ones of the post-layer sparsely with synaptic polarity. Excitatory and inhibitory synapses are denoted respectively by solid arrows and dashed arrows. The polarity of each connection is randomly decided based on Bernoulli distribution with a given probability. To be noted, the neurons within the command layer are enabled to be self-connected.

NCP fundamental units are implemented with liquid time-constant (LTC) neurons [5] to enable the capability of learning sequential changes. In brief, LTC is based on neural ordinary differential equations (ODE) [11] but with an improved time-constant parameter. Mathematically, an LTC neuron uses Eq. 2 to define its hidden state x at time t. In the formula, θ and A are network parameters, τ is time-constant, I is network input, and f is the general expression of the network. With LTC units, the network is recurrent. It computes the changes in neural values $\frac{d\mathbf{x}(t)}{dt}$ recursively using its previous hidden states $x(t)$.

$$\frac{d\mathbf{x}(t)}{dt} = -\frac{\mathbf{x}(t)}{\frac{\tau}{1+\tau f(\mathbf{x}(t),I(t),t,\theta)}} + f(\mathbf{x}(t), \mathbf{I}(t), t, \boldsymbol{\theta})A \quad (2)$$

τ_{sys} in Eq. 3 is the core value of the LTC concept that dynamically defines network transmission speed and neural coupling level. The term varies based on the input $I(t)$ and $\mathbf{x}(t)$, imposing the "liquid" characteristic of the whole system.

$$\tau_{sys} = \frac{\tau}{1 + \tau f(\mathbf{x}(t), \mathbf{I}(t), t, \boldsymbol{\theta})} \quad (3)$$

For every image, the LTC-NCP network processes the simulated sequence element-by-element. As a result, we obtained a series of predictions for one input image. These values need to be unfolded and compressed to two values which indicate the COVID-19 positive and negative scores (classification scores). A whole prediction series are first concatenated together and then flattened to a one-dimensional array. The FC layer at the end (Fig. 2) filters the array to two classification values.

3   Experiment Settings

3.1   Dataset

We used Python programming language with Pytorch machine learning framework [12] to implement our experiments. Source code is available at our git repository[2]. Regarding the hardware, we conducted model training on Nvidia GeForce RTX 2080 Ti and Nvidia GeForce RTX 3090 GPUs. Training time in the result section concerns the experiments on the RTX 3090 GPU. We want to thank the PAN-ASEAN coalition for Epidemic and Outbreak Preparedness (PACE-UP) project for letting us borrow the RTX 3090 GPU.

Table 1. Dataset properties

Dataset	Country	Number of cases	
		COVID	Normal
MosMed COVID-19 Chest CT	Russia	50 patients	–
CT segmentation dataset 1	Italy	100 slides from more than 40 patients	–
CT segmentation dataset 2	Global	829 slices from 9 patients	–
CT segmentation dataset 3	Global	20 cases	–
COVID-CT-MD	Iran	–	76 cases
Total	–	119 cases	76 cases

Regarding the COVID-19 dataset, we utilized a dataset of 15,662 CT slices from [13]. The dataset combines multiple public datasets available at [14]. The specification in Table 1 shows them in detail with origins and number of cases. In total, we worked with 119 cases of COVID-19 and 76 healthy cases globally. Because CT images are three-dimensional (3D) and heterogeneous in origins, we had to split them into 2D slides (quantified in Table 2) and standardize their labels. Among 15,662 collected slides, we obtained 3,100 COVID-19 positives and 12,562 negatives. Regarding the pixel intensity, pixels in Hounsfield Unit (HU) scale were mapped to the conventionally shallower

Table 2. Number of slides of each category

Category	Number of slides
COVID-19 (PNG)	3,100
Healthy (PNG)	12,562

---

[2] https://github.com/minhhieutruong0705/ltc-recurrent-neurons-in-cnn.

255 value scale, denoted as PNG. This low-quality version does not affect the overall performance in classifying COVID-19 [13, 15].

Since the slide distribution is biased towards the negative (healthy) category, the negatives were subsampled as large as the positive set during training, validating, and testing. Furthermore, the following augmentations expose images to random noises to enhance training robustness.

(1) pixel intensity normalization (mean: 0, standard deviation: 1)
(2) image resizing (256 × 256)
(3) random resized crop (224 × 224, scale: 0.8–1.0, probability: 0.5)
(4) random rotation (limit angle: 15, probability: 0.5)
(5) random Gaussian blur (kernel: 5, probability: 0.5)
(6) random contrast and brightness (factor: 0.2, probability: 0.5)

3.2 Hyper-parameters

We evaluated each network based on its performance over seven runs. For each run, we trained the networks and evaluated their models using different image sets. To enable that, we (re-)split the images randomly into three mutually disjoint parts for training, validation, and testing before each run. Their split proportions were 65%, 20%, and 15%, respectively. We used the training set to train the networks. During training, we tuned the performance based on the validation set. The checkpoint having the best validation scores was the model of the run. It then performed classification on the test set (unseen images), and we counted these test scores.

The training of models used Adam optimizer [16] with Kaiming initialization technique [17]. The learning rate was set to 1e−4 and warm-restarted every ten epochs using the Cosine Annealing scheduler [18]. Based on validation tunning, networks achieved optimal scores within 100 dataset loops using 64 image batches.

3.3 Evaluation Metrics and Loss Functions

We evaluated model performance using accuracy and dice similarity coefficient (DSC). Accuracy, Eq. 4, measures the correctness of the predictions in a balanced manner considering true positives (TP) and true negatives (TN) equally. FP and FN stand for false positives and false negatives.

$$acc = \frac{TP + TN}{TP + TN + FP + FN} \tag{4}$$

However, the TP predictions should be more concerned than TN when performing COVID-19 classification. DSC metric, Eq. 3, modifies the accuracy to focus more on TP by removing the contribution of TN.

$$DSC = \frac{TP}{TP + FP + FN} \tag{5}$$

Binary cross-entropy (BCE) and DSC-based loss functions, the respective Eqs. 6 and 7, were used to compute training gradients. In Eq. 6, p and y are respectively the prediction and ground-truth of the input image.

$$loss_{bce} = -(y\log(p) + (1-y)\log(1-p)) = \begin{cases} -log(p), & y = 1 \\ -log(1-p), & y = 0 \end{cases} \quad (6)$$

DSC loss is the remaining value after subtracting the DSC score from one. In the combined loss, we weighted BCE loss by 0.4 and DSC loss by 1.0. The higher weighted DSC loss reduces the concentration on the TN predictions since it is vital to focus on TP and FN rates when confirming COVID-19 infection.

$$loss_{dsc} = 1 - \frac{TP}{TP + FP + FN} \quad (7)$$

4 Results and Discussion

To make a fair comparison, we designed FC wiring similar to NCP topology. The setting allows NCP networks to reach their full potential since they have lower scalability than FC networks. Compared to matrix operations in FC, solving ODEs in NCP costs more hardware computational power. NCP also has a constraint of four-layer architecture, while FC could be freely customized. Therefore, it is required to use NCP as a wiring standard. We expanded the NCP to the maximum setting concerning the RTX 2080 Ti GPU processing capacity.

Networks 1, 2, and 3 illustrate the respective FC, Y-NCP, and Z-NCP network configurations. In the denotation, $Xfc \rightarrow$ means that X neurons of the current layer connect densely (fully connected) to all the neurons in the next layer. $XfoY \rightarrow$ means that each of X neurons of the current layer has Y outgoing (fanning-out) synapses. In contrast, $XfiY \rightarrow$ indicates that each of X neurons of the current layer has Y incoming (fanning-in) synapses. $XrY \rightarrow$ denotes that there are Y inter-connecting (recurrent) synapses among X neurons in this layer.

$$\text{FC: } 21632fc \rightarrow 1024fc \rightarrow 192fc \rightarrow 48fc \rightarrow 2 \qquad (Net.\ 1)$$

$$\text{Y} - \text{NCP: } 2048fc \rightarrow 1024fo96 \rightarrow 192fo32 \rightarrow 48r48 \rightarrow 4fi48 \qquad (Net.\ 2)$$

$$\text{Z} - \text{NCP: } 729fc \rightarrow 1024fo96 \rightarrow 192fo32 \rightarrow 48r48 \rightarrow 4fi48 \qquad (Net.\ 3)$$

Among the three networks, they have significant differences in the first neuron layers because of different features used for learning. The FC network takes into the whole image, which makes 21,632 neurons. Each sequential element of Y-NCP has 2048 features. Regarding Z-NCP, 729 (27×27) is the maximal number of available features. At the end of the CRNet backbone, the encoded image has only 27×27 pixels.

Table 3 shows the network properties in detail. Compared to the two Y-NCP and Z-NCP, FC brings up the most complicated topology with 22,898 neurons and 22,357,088 synapses. The network weight is hence the heaviest among the three investigating

Table 3. Network parameters and resource demands

Model	Neurons	Synapses	Head params	Training time	GPU memory
CRNet-FC	22,898	22,357,088	22,358,354	**24 min 19 s**	**5233 MiB**
CRNet-Y-NCP	3,316	2,201,840	3,338,662	46 min 25 s	11117 MiB
CRNet-Z-NCP	**1,997**	**851,184**	**1,988,006**	46 min 40 s	11083 MiB

heads. However, the cost to train an FC model is the least expensive due to the simple implementation using matrix multiplication.

Regarding the NCP family heads, they demand high computational capacity to handle the ODEs. Although they have a much smaller number of parameters, both training time and GPU memory required by NCP heads are nearly double the needs for FC. Compared to the conventional Y-NCP, Z-NCP has a much simpler network structure. The differences are from their first layers. Z-NCP has only 729 neurons, while Y-NCP more than doubles with 2048 neurons. Brough into comparing same-size networks with fully-connected layers, network sparsity rates of Y-NCP and Z-NCP are 95.6% and 89.36%, respectively.

Table 4 informs the differences in using FC, Y-NCP, and Z-NCP heads to classify COVID-19 CT slices. After seven runs, FC obtained the best score with 92.52(1.72) % DSC. Holding the second place is the lightest Z-NCP with 92.14(1.04) % DSC, only 0.38% lower. Although having more parameters than Z-NCP, Y-NCP performed worse with 91.52(1.38) % DSC.

Table 4. Model performance on COVID-19 classification

Model	Accuracy	DSC
CRNet-FC	**96.05 ± 0.94**	**92.52 ± 1.72**
CRNet-Y-NCP	95.51 ± 0.76	91.52 ± 1.38
CRNet-Z-NCP	95.84 ± 0.57	92.14 ± 1.04

Regarding stability, there is a clear proportional relationship between the score fluctuation and the number of parameters. The advantage of having a sparse and compact network topology helps the training of Z-NCP models robust to overfitting. In both accuracy and DSC statistics, Z-NCP obtained the lowest standard deviation. In contrast, the heaviest FC has the scores fluctuating the most, although its mean scores are the highest.

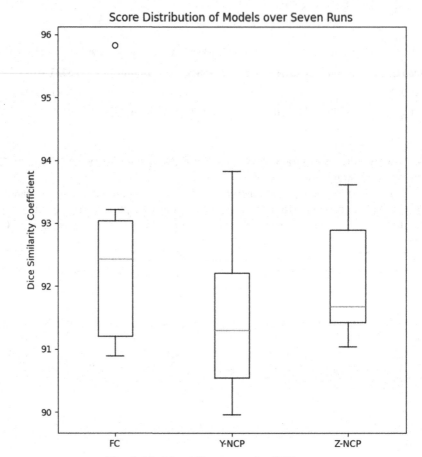

Fig. 6. Model stability concerning DSC scores

The boxplots in Fig. 6 further inform the score distribution of the models over seven runs. Up to this point, it is not surprising that Y-NCP obtained poor performance with low and highly varied scores. Comparing Z-NCP to FC, the diagram shows that FC has a higher median than Z-NCP. However, Z-NCP is more robust since its minimum score is higher than the FC's minimum score, and so is the maximum score regardless of the FC outlier. Z-NCP also has an interquartile range shorter than FC, which shows stability. Regarding the distribution, scores of Z-NCP are a bit low-whiskered, while FC scores tend to concentrate in the two ends of its range.

5   Conclusion

In this work, we investigated LTC-enhanced NCP to classify non-sequential data. In particular, we trained recurrent models to perform COVID-19 classification based on CT images. Besides the conventional consideration of data changes along the y-axis (Y-NCP), we proposed a novel approach Z-NCP to model data sequences along the channel axis of an image. Among FC, Y-NCP, and Z-NCP, Z-NCP was the most efficient model concerning the performance-weight ratio. Compared to the Y-NCP, it obtained higher scores although having a significantly simpler network topology. Z-NCP was comparable with FC, only 0.38% lower in the DSC metric. However, FC required 22,358,354 parameters to get the results, while Z-NCP used only 1,988,006 parameters. Thanks to the lightweight property, Z-NCP obtained the most stable performance. Between FC and Z-NCP, Z-NCP has a bit lower mean scores since FC has an upper outlier. Ultimately, Z-NCP performed better than FC in the maximum, minimum, and interquartile range.

Concerning resource demands, Z-NCP is not scalable since using ODEs to model the neuron behavior. The training for Z-NCP requires ODE solving, demanding almost double the memory usage and time compared to FC. To further improve Z-NCP, more efficient ODE solvers should be used. Moreover, NCP wiring policies is not yet fit non-sequential tasks. We should remove the concept of four-layer architecture (sensory-inter-command-motor) since NCP does not capture motions when classifying images. As a consequence, interconnections should be available in any layer of the network.

References

1. Chen, L., Li, S., Bai, Q., Yang, J., Jiang, S., Miao, Y.: Review of image classification algorithms based on convolutional neural networks. Remote Sens. **22**(13), 4712 (2021)
2. Rawat, W., Wang, Z.: Deep convolutional neural networks for image classification: a comprehensive review. Neural Comput. **29**(9), 2352–2449 (2017)
3. Lechner, M., Hasani, R.M., Grosu, R.: Neuronal circuit policies. arXiv preprint (2018)
4. Lechner, M., Hasani, R., Amini, A., Henzinger, T.A., Rus, D., Grosu, R.: Neural circuit policies enabling auditable autonomy. Nat. Mach. Intell. **2**, 642–652 (2020)
5. Hasani, R., Lechner, M., Amini, A., Rus, D., Grosu, R.: Liquid time-constant networks. arXiv preprint (2020)
6. Zhang, K.: LSTM: an image classification model based on fashion-MNIST dataset. In: ANU Bio-inspired Computing, Canberra, Australia (2018)
7. Visin, F., Kastner, K., Cho, K., Matteucci, M., Courville, A., Bengio, Y.: ReNet: a recurrent neural network based alternative to convolutional networks. arXiv preprint (2015)
8. Munich, T., Germany, H.: Offline handwriting recognition with multidimensional recurrent neural networks. In: The Conference and Workshop on Neural Information Processing Systems (2008)
9. Chandra, B., Sharma, R.K.: On improving recurrent neural network for image classification. In: 2017 International Joint Conference on Neural Networks (IJCNN), pp. 1904–1907 (2017)
10. He, X., et al.: Sample-efficient deep learning for COVID-19 diagnosis based on CT scans, 4 (2020)
11. Chen, R.T.Q., Rubanova, Y., Bettencourt, J., Duvenaud, D.K.: Neural ordinary differential equations. In: Advances in Neural Information Processing Systems 31 (NeurIPS 2018) (2018)
12. PyTorch (2022). https://pytorch.org/docs/stable/index.html. Accessed 17 Apr 2022
13. Truong, H.M., Huynh, H.T.: A novel approach for CT-based COVID-19 classification and lesion segmentation based on deep learning. Comput. J. (2022). https://doi.org/10.1093/com jnl/bxac015
14. COVID-19 imaging datasets. The European Institute for Biomedical Imaging Research (2022). https://www.eibir.org/covid-19-imaging-datasets/. Accessed 05 Apr 2021

15. Yang, X., He, X., Zhao, J., Zhang, Y., Zhang, S., Xie, P.: COVID-CT-dataset: a CT scan dataset about COVID-19, 30 March 2020
16. Kingma, D.P., Ba, J.: Adam: a method for stochastic optimization. arXiv preprint (2014)
17. He, K., Zhang, X., Ren, S., Sun, J.: Delving deep into rectifiers: surpassing human-level performance on ImageNet classification, 6 Febraury 2015
18. Loshchilov, I., Hutter, F.: SGDR: Stochastic gradient descent with warm restarts, 13 August 2016

Lung Lesions Segmentation and Classification with Deep Neural Networks

Thuong-Cang Phan[1]([✉]) [iD], Anh-Cang Phan[2] [iD], Quoc-Thinh Tran[2],
and Thanh-Ngoan Trieu[1,3] [iD]

[1] Can Tho University, Can Tho City, Vietnam
{ptcang,ttngoan}@cit.ctu.edu.vn
[2] Vinh Long University of Technology Education, Vinh Long Province, Vietnam
{cangpa,thinhtq}@vlute.edu.vn
[3] University of Brest, Brest, France

Abstract. The risk of lung disease is immense for many people, especially in developing countries, where billions of people face energy poverty and are dependent on polluting forms of energy. The World Health Organization estimates that more than four million premature deaths occur each year from diseases related to household air pollution, including pneumonia. Radiologists diagnose and detect medical conditions with imaging techniques such as CT, MRI, and X-rays. However, they face many challenges interpreting chest radiographs in high workload conditions, even for highly experienced physicians. A tool for automatically locating and classifying anomalies would be of great value, and a deep learning approach provides several ways to achieve this goal. In this study, we train Faster R-CNN neural network for lung disease classification using the feature extraction networks such as ResNet, CheXnet, and Inception ResNet V2. The experiments are conducted on a dataset of 112,000 images with corresponding labels annotated by experienced radiologists. The experimental results show that the models can identify the exact lesion area for a given chest X-ray and the classification accuracy is up to 95.5%. The Grad-CAM is performed to highlight the lesion area thus reducing stress for physicians while providing patients with a more accurate diagnosis.

Keywords: Lung injury · Lung lesion classification · Faster-RCNN · RetinaNet · 14 classes

1 Introduction

The risk of lung injury is immense for many people, especially in developing countries, where billions of people face energy poverty and are dependent on polluting forms of energy. Pneumonia is the most common cause of death overall in developing countries. Therefore, timely and accurate diagnosis helps patients quickly receive treatment, avoiding adverse effects on human life. One of the

T. K. Dang et al. (Eds.): FDSE 2022, CCIS 1688, pp. 653–664, 2022.
https://doi.org/10.1007/978-981-19-8069-5_45

clinical measures to detect lung disease is a diagnosis based on chest X-rays. The application of advanced information technology will solve two problems at the same time, reducing the doctor's workload and increasing the capacity for medical examination. In this research, we build convolution neural network models to diagnose lung lesions on X-ray images. This will help the clinical examination be simple, quick, and highly accurate.

Rachna Jain et al. [5] detected pneumonia on X-rays using CNN models and transfer a learning approach. VGG16, VGG19, ResNet50, and Inception-V3 are transfer learning models available on Keras that have been trained and tested on the ImageNet dataset. This is the largest dataset for image classification consisting of about 15 million images belonging to 22,000 different categories. They experimented with six models in which the first two models consist of two and three convolutional layers and the other four models are VGG16, VGG19, ResNet50, and Inception-V3. The experimental results showed an accuracy of up to 92.31%. Asnaoui and Chawki [?] provided a comparative study on the use of deep network models (VGG16, VGG19, DenseNet201, Inception ResNet V2, Inception V3, ResNet50, and MobileNet) to deal with the detection and classification of lung lesions caused by Covid-19. The experiments were conducted on chest X-rays/CT consisting of 6,087 images (2,780 images of bacterial pneumonia, 1,493 images of coronavirus, 231 images of Covid-19, and 1,583 normal images). The results showed that Inception ResNet V2 yielded better results than other models with an accuracy of 92.18%. Laboni et al. [9] proposed CheXNet to effectively detect COVID-19 patients. The authors tested the model on a dataset consisting of 13,800 chest radiography images across 13,725 patients. They performed both two-class and three-class classifications and achieved the accuracy of 96.49% and 93.71%, respectively. Nahida et al. [?] used a dataset of 5,856 chest X-ray images of patients aged 1 to 5 years old. They combined CheXNet and VGG19 to extract features and then ensembled the features for classification. The ensembled feature vector is classified using Random Forest, Adaptive Boosting, and K-Nearest Neighbors. Random Forest got better performance providing 98.93% accurate prediction.

The studies mentioned above detected and classified 2 to 4 types of lung lesions and trained on a limited amount of data. Therefore, in this study, we detected and classified 14 types of lung lesions on the dataset of 112,120 X-ray images. The training will combine three neural networks that give the best results from previous related studies, i.e., ResNet-50, CheXNet, and Inception ResNet V2 on the Faster R-CNN network model to localize and classify lung lesions. The rest of the paper is presented as follows. Section 2 presents the basic theoretical background used in this study. Section 3 details the proposed method using deep neural networks to localize and classify lung lesions. Section 4 presents the experiments and evaluates the experimental results. Finally, we draw conclusions in Sect. 5.

2   Background

2.1   Lung Lesions on X-Ray Images

Lung disease is one of the most common diseases that refers to many disorders affecting the lungs, such as asthma, pneumonia, tuberculosis, and lung cancer. Lung disease can be caused by many common causes such as air pollution, smoking, and genetics. Figure 1 presents several types of lung diseases including atelectasis, pleural effusion, infiltration, pneumonia, pneumothorax, cardiomegaly, nodule, and mass.

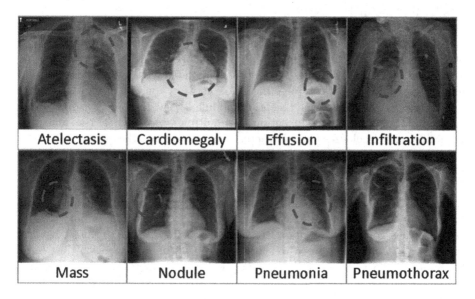

Fig. 1. Chest X-ray images of lung lesions.

Chest X-rays are valuable in the detection and diagnosis of lung diseases, assessment of severity and respiratory complications, and monitoring of response to treatment. However, it must be combined with epidemiological characteristics and clinical manifestations to make a suitable diagnosis.

2.2   Neural Networks for Feature Extraction

2.2.1   ResNet

ResNet [3] becomes the most commonly used architecture at the moment since it has fewer parameters. Networks with a large number of layers can be trained easily without increasing the training error. It is also the earliest architecture to adopt batch normalization. ResNet consists of four different architectures, which are ResNet-34, ResNet-50, ResNet-101 and ResNet-152. ResNet helps in solving the vanishing gradient problem using skip connections. Among the four architectures, ResNet-50 achieved a quite good performance thus we choose this architecture in our experiments.

2.2.2   CheXnet

CheXnet [7] is a 121-layer Dense Convolutional Network (DenseNet) trained on the ChestX-ray14 dataset, which contains 112,120 frontal-view X-rays of 30,805 patients. The weights of CheXnet are initialized with a model pre-trained on the ImageNet dataset. DenseNet [4] controls the amount of information to be added, improves information flow with direct connections, and makes optimization of very deep networks tractable. DenseNet has less than half the parameters of ResNet-50 but has higher accuracy when training on the ImageNet dataset.

2.2.3   Inception ResNet V2

Inception ResNet V2 [10] was developed from the Inception architectures [11] to take advantage of residual networks, improve the accuracy, and convergence speed of the original model. Inception ResNet V2 is more exquisitely designed on the basis of Inception V4. It utilizes residual connections to accelerate the training and improve performance. A complete Inception network consists of multiple Inception modules. The idea of the Inception module is that instead of using a Conv layer with a fixed kernel size, Inception uses multiple Conv layers at the same time with different kernel sizes (1, 3, 5, 7, etc.) and concatenate the outputs.

2.3   Faster R-CNN for Classification

Faster R-CNN [8] is used to train and automatically classify common lung lesions. It is one of the modern and effective methods for object detection and classification. It has gone through many versions such as R-CNN [2] and Fast R-CNN [1]. Faster R-CNN is proposed to solve the problem of the execution time of R-CNN and Fast R-CNN, by training a more efficient model replacing the selective search algorithm, which is inherently slow. Faster R-CNN is rated much faster than the previous R-CNN series. In addition, the network is also commonly used for detection and classification. Therefore, we take Faster R-CNN for the detection and classification of common lung lesions.

2.4   Evaluation Metrics

2.4.1   Loss Values

The Loss function is determined by Classification Loss and Localization Loss as Eqs. 1 and 2.

$$Loss(\{p_i\}, \{t_i\}) = \frac{1}{N_{cls}} \Sigma_i L_{cls}(p_i, p_i^*) + \lambda \frac{1}{N_{reg}} \Sigma_i p_i^* L_{reg}(t_i, t_i^*) \tag{1}$$

$$smooth_{L1}(x, y) = \begin{cases} 0.5(x_i - y_i)^2 & if \mid x_i - y_i \mid < 1 \\ \mid x_i - y_i \mid -0.5 & otherwise \end{cases} \tag{2}$$

where: i is the index of the anchor in mini-batch; p_i is the predicted probability of anchor i being an object; the ground-truth label value p_i^* is 1 if the anchor is positive, and 0 otherwise; t_i is a 4-dimensional vector represents the coordinate values of the predicted bounding box; t_i^* is a 4-dimensional vector represents the coordinate values of the ground-truth box corresponding to the positive anchor; L_{cls} is the log loss of 2 classes (object and non-object); and L_{reg} is calculated based on Eq. 2.

2.4.2 Accuracy

Accuracy calculates the ratio between the number of correctly predicted samples and the total number of samples in the testing dataset. It is calculated based on Eq. 3.

$$Accuracy = \frac{TP + TN}{TP + TN + FP + FN} \tag{3}$$

where: TP is the true positive; TN is the true negative; FP is the false positive; and FN is the false negative.

2.4.3 AUC - Area Under the ROC Curve

A ROC curve (receiver operating characteristic curve) illustrates the performance of a classifier at all classification thresholds. The curve plots two parameters, True Positive Rate (TPR) and False Positive Rate (FPR), calculated based on Eq. 4.

$$TPR = \frac{TP}{TP + FN} \qquad\qquad FPR = \frac{FP}{FP + TN} \tag{4}$$

AUC provides an aggregate measure of performance, which is the capability of distinguishing between classes. AUC ranges in values between 0 and 1 and the higher the AUC, the better the model is (Fig. 2).

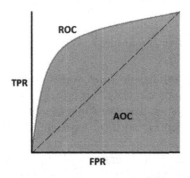

Fig. 2. Illustration of AUC - ROC.

3 Proposed Method

The general model (Fig. 3) consists of two phases, the training phase and the testing phase. The details are described as follows.

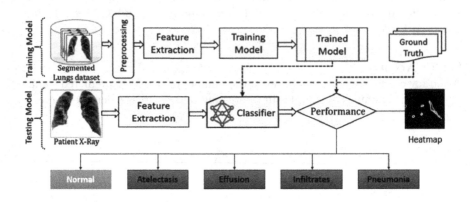

Fig. 3. General model of the proposed method.

3.1 Training Phase

3.1.1 Pre-processing
The pre-processing of X-ray images consists of two different tasks, image enhancement and data enhancement.

Image Enhancement: Various image enhancement techniques are applied to the input X-ray images, such as filter-Gabor, Local binary Pattern, Histogram Equalization, Adaptive Histogram Equalization (AHE), etc. The AHE [6] technique enhances the contrast of the image and performs well in CNN-based feature extraction. The images are resized to 256×256 to train with the requirements of the pre-trained models. Besides, the images are scaled in the range from 0 to 1 to match the input type of the models.

Data Enhancement: Training deep network mo dels requires large amounts of input data. Limited input datasets can create models that perform well on learning data but do not generalize. We apply two data enhancement techniques (random cropping and flipping) to have more input data for training models. Random cropping produces images as random sub-regions of the original inputs. It is useful for generating data diversity to learn knowledge unrelated to the location of the problem. Random flipping creates a mirror image from the origin. Given the intuition that the original image and the mirror image should be recognized equally in a classification task, flipping is an efficient way to double up the dataset without many extra operations.

3.1.2 Feature Extraction

After pre-processing, we perform feature extraction with three network models, ResNet-50, CheXnet, Inception ResNet V2 as described in Sect. 2.2.

3.1.3 Training

At this stage, we trained the dataset on Faster R-CNN. Due to the limitation of the experimental dataset, we use the transfer learning technique [12] to re-use the pre-trained network models. This helps to learn new features faster, shortens the training time, and does not require large datasets. When the loss value is not improved (not reduced), we will stop the training phase and move to the testing phase.

3.2 Testing Phase

The images in the testing dataset after feature extraction will be passed through the trained models to produce lesion classification results. The results include bounding boxes containing the lesions and the labels of the lesions. In this work, we use the GradCAM heat map to accurately identify the area of severe lung injury.

4 Experiments

4.1 Dataset Description and Installation Environment

The experiments are conducted on Kaggle environment with Python programming language. The configuration of the computer is 16 GB RAM and GPU Nvidia Tesla P100. Tensorflow GPU 1.15 is the library used to support training the network models. NIH [?] is the dataset used in the experiments that is publicly available on Kaggle. The dataset consists of 112,000 images, of which 89,600 images are used as the training dataset and 22,400 images are used as the testing dataset, corresponding to the ratio of 80:20 (Fig. 4).

4.2 Scenarios

We propose three scenarios with the training network models and parameters as described in Table 1. In scenarios 1, 2, and 3, we use Faster R-CNN with ResNet-50, CheXnet, and Inception ResNet V2 for feature extraction. All three scenarios have the same learning rate of 0.0001, mAP@IoU of 0.5, and 20 training steps. The number of classes is 14 corresponding to 14 types of lung lesions.

Table 1. Proposed scenarios and training parameters

Senarios	Classification models	Feature extraction	Learning rate	Num_steps	mAP@IoU	Num classes
1	Faster R-CNN	Inception ResNet V2	0.0001	20	0.5	14
2	Faster R-CNN	CheXNet	0.0001	20	0.5	14
3	Faster R-CNN	ResNet-50	0.0001	20	0.5	14

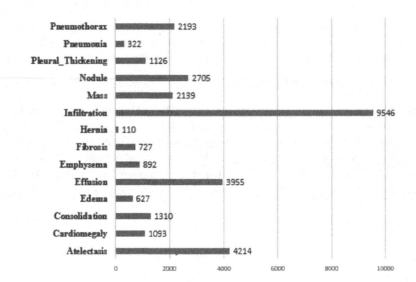

Fig. 4. Input dataset description.

4.3 Results

4.3.1 Loss Value

Figure 5 shows the loss values of the three scenarios. The loss value tends to decrease rapidly at the beginning of the training process. It greatly and evenly decreases in the next learning steps showing that after a long training time, the features are learned effectively. We stop the training process when the loss value no longer decreases. The average loss values of three scenarios 1, 2, and 3 are 0.24, 0.096, and 0.112, respectively. The loss value of scenario 1 is the highest among the three scenarios.

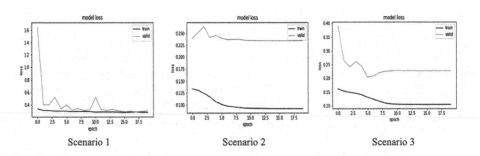

Fig. 5. Loss value of Faster R-CNN in scenarios 1, 2, and 3.

4.3.2   Accuracy

Figure 6 shows that the Inception ResNet V2 in scenario 1 has lower accuracy (88.3%) than the other models and it is unstable between training times. After 15 epochs, the train accuracy of scenario 1 reaches 89% and the validation accuracy fluctuates around 88%. The other two scenarios with CheXnet and ResNet-50 give quite similar and stable results at 95.2% and 95.5%, respectively. In scenario 2, the train and validation accuracy start to be stable after 8 epochs with a small gap (0.4%) between the train accuracy and validation accuracy. Scenario 3 starts to have stable accuracy after 6 epochs with 95.7% train accuracy and 95.1% validation accuracy. Among the three scenarios, the model in scenario 1 receives the lowest accuracy among the three scenarios.

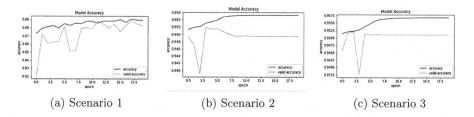

(a) Scenario 1   (b) Scenario 2   (c) Scenario 3

Fig. 6. Accuracy of Faster R-CNN in three scenarios 1, 2, and 3.

4.3.3   AUC

The AUC of scenarios 1, 2, and 3 is shown in Fig. 7. It shows that the Faster R-CNN with Inception ResNet V2 in scenario 1 has unstable accuracy between classes due to the use of modules to reduce the convolution size making the network deeper leading to the loss of information. The largest difference in this scenario belongs to the class Cardiomegaly (AUC: 0.89) and Pneumonia (AUC: 0.62). The other two scenarios show on average a higher AUC than the first scenario. Cardiomegaly is the class with the highest AUC value, which is 0.9 in scenario 2 and 0.87 in scenario 3. Infiltration is the class with the lowest AUC value, which is 0.71 in scenario 2 and 0.69 in scenario 3. The combination of Faster R-CNN and CheXnet in scenario 2 shows a high and uniform accuracy across classes. This is the same with Faster R-CNN ResNet-50 in scenario 3.

4.3.4   Training Time

Faster R-CNN Inception ResNet V2 provides the shortest training time compared to the remaining models. The longest training time is 7.1 h of Faster R-CNN ResNet-50. The training time of the models is shown in Fig. 8.

4.3.5   Illustrations of Classification Results

Some illustrations of lung lesion detection and classification of the four scenarios are presented in Fig. 9. In these results, it is possible to localize the damaged areas of the lung, but it is not possible to determine the most severe area of the

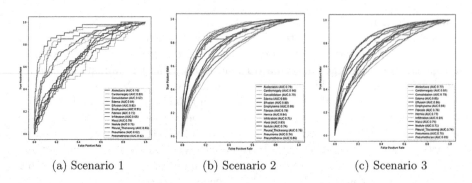

(a) Scenario 1   (b) Scenario 2   (c) Scenario 3

Fig. 7. AUC plot of Faster R-CNN in three scenarios 1, 2, and 3.

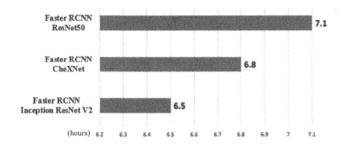

Fig. 8. Training time of the four scenarios.

injury. We applied the GradCam heat map to solve this problem. Some examples are shown in Fig. 10. The first image is the original image and we stack the heat map layers on top of the original image to get the exact lesion location with red color for the most severe damage.

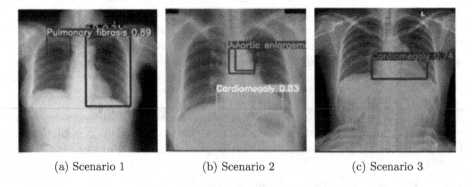

(a) Scenario 1   (b) Scenario 2   (c) Scenario 3

Fig. 9. Illustration of drowsiness detection and prediction on videos for four scenarios

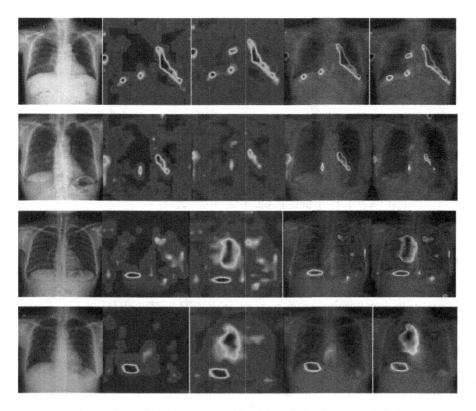

Fig. 10. GradCam heat map on X-rays.

5   Conclusion

The overall pollution levels in upcoming decades are projected to increase strongly, especially in Asia, leading to an increased risk of lung diseases. Automatic segmentation and classification of lung lesions will help physicians to interpret chest X-rays, reduce the workload, and increase the capacity of medical examination. Previous studies only detected and classified 2 to 4 types of lung lesions. In this study, we build deep learning models to diagnose 14 types of lung lesions on chest X-rays using Faster R-CNN with 3 different backbones. The Faster R-CNN network model is trained with the combination of three network models for feature extraction, i.e., ResNet, CheXnet, and Inception ResNet V2. The experiments are conducted on a dataset of 112,000 images publicly available on Kaggle. We perform data enhancement to limit the negative effect of the small dataset. The experimental results show that the Faster R-CNN ResNet-50 model gives the highest results of 95.5%. The possible direction is to apply the transfer learning approach to other well-developed datasets including X-rays that can help the classifier performs better.

References

1. Girshick, R.: Fast r-cnn. In: Proceedings of the IEEE International Conference on Computer Vision, pp. 1440–1448 (2015)
2. Girshick, R., Donahue, J., Darrell, T., Malik, J.: Rich feature hierarchies for accurate object detection and semantic segmentation. In: Proceedings of the IEEE Conference on Computer Vision and Pattern Recognition, pp. 580–587 (2014)
3. He, K., Zhang, X., Ren, S., Sun, J.: Deep residual learning for image recognition. In: Proceedings of the IEEE Conference on Computer Vision and Pattern Recognition, pp. 770–778 (2016)
4. Huang, G., Liu, Z., Van Der Maaten, L., Weinberger, K.Q.: Densely connected convolutional networks. In: Proceedings of the IEEE Conference on Computer Vision and Pattern Recognition, pp. 4700–4708 (2017)
5. Jain, R., Nagrath, P., Kataria, G., Kaushik, V.S., Hemanth, D.J.: Pneumonia detection in chest x-ray images using convolutional neural networks and transfer learning. Measurement 165, 108046 (2020)
6. Pizer, S.M., et al.: Adaptive histogram equalization and its variations. Comput. Vision Graph. Image Process. 39(3), 355–368 (1987)
7. Rajpurkar, P., et al.: Chexnet: radiologist-level pneumonia detection on chest x-rays with deep learning. arXiv preprint arXiv:1711.05225 (2017)
8. Ren, S., He, K., Girshick, R., Sun, J.: Faster r-cnn: towards real-time object detection with region proposal networks. Adv. Neural Inf. Process. Syst. 28 (2015)
9. Sarker, L., Islam, M.M., Hannan, T., Ahmed, Z.: Covid-densenet: a deep learning architecture to detect covid-19 from chest radiology images. Preprint 2020050151 (2020)
10. Szegedy, C., Ioffe, S., Vanhoucke, V., Alemi, A.A.: Inception-v4, inception-resnet and the impact of residual connections on learning. In: Thirty-First AAAI Conference on Artificial Intelligence (2017)
11. Szegedy, C., Vanhoucke, V., Ioffe, S., Shlens, J., Wojna, Z.: Rethinking the inception architecture for computer vision. In: Proceedings of the IEEE Conference on Computer Vision and Pattern Recognition, pp. 2818–2826 (2016)
12. Weiss, K., Khoshgoftaar, T.M., Wang, D.: A survey of transfer learning. J. Big Data 3(1), 1–40 (2016)

Short Papers: Security and Data Engineering

Image Denoising Using Fully Connected Network with Reinforcement Learning

Phuoc-Nguyen Bui[1], Van-Vi Vo[3], Duc-Tai Le[2], and Hyunseung Choo[3(✉)]

[1] Department of Superintelligence, Sungkyunkwan University, Suwon, South Korea
[2] College of Computing and Informatics, Sungkyunkwan University,
Suwon, South Korea
[3] Department of Electrical and Computer Engineering, Sungkyunkwan University,
Suwon, South Korea
choo@skku.edu

Abstract. Deep reinforcement learning (DRL), where an agent learns behaviors in an environment by actions and receiving rewards, has been applied successfully in the robotics area and game controllers at a human level. However, the application of DRL in image processing is still scarce. In this paper, we present a novel approach for image denoising by combining a fully connected network with the gated recurrent unit in an asynchronous advantage actor-critic scheme. The proposed method assigns an agent to every pixel of the input image, and the agent changes the value of each pixel by selecting an action from a predefined list. The goal is to learn an optimal policy to maximize the reward at all pixels of the image. We conduct the denoising experiments on the BSD68 dataset and the results show that the proposed approach produces equivalent or higher PSNR scores compared to several state-of-the-art models based on supervised learning. Our approach is interpretable to humans by showing the agent's actions, which is a significant difference from original CNNs.

Keywords: Asynchronous advantage actor-critic · Deep reinforcement learning · Fully connected network · Gated recurrent unit

1 Introduction

Deep reinforcement learning (DRL) has received a lot of attention with the release of deep Q-Network in 2015, which can perform at a human level in Atari games. Recently, DRL has been studied for a variety of image processing problems including color enhancement [7], and image cropping [6]. However, these methods have a limitation of only performing global steps for the whole image. Therefore, they are confined to basic tasks such as global color improvement and image cropping. Consequently, applications requiring pixel-level manipulations such as image denoising still needs further improvements in DRL algorithms.

To apply DRL for image processing on the pixel-level, we formulate a new problem setting. Following the multi-agent RL (MARL) algorithm, each pixel of the input image is considered an agent. The goal for each agent is to learn

T. K. Dang et al. (Eds.): FDSE 2022, CCIS 1688, pp. 667–673, 2022.
https://doi.org/10.1007/978-981-19-8069-5_46

the optimal order of behaviors for maximizing the mean of the total anticipated rewards at all positions of input image. The value of each pixel is taken into account as the current state and modified repeatedly by actions executed by the agent. However, applying the current techniques of the MARL without any modifications to this problem is computationally impractical due to the huge number of agents. We employ the fully connected network (FCN) to address this problem due to the advantage of adopting CNN is that all the agents of the input image can share the weights and they can learn more efficiently. We summarize the main contributions of this article as follows:

- We propose an effective DRL based framework which combine FCN and GRU to remove noise in gray-scale image, where the current MARL techniques are not applicable.
- The experimental results on BSD68 dataset demonstrate better or equivalent performance when comparing with CNN based methods.
- Our approach is interpretable to humans by showing the agent's actions, which is a significant advantage from conventional CNNs.

2   Related Works

Deep Reinforcement Learning (DRL in short) techniques have recently been applied for some image processing tasks. For example, authors in [2] proposed a DRL based method to generate face images with super-resolution quality. This DRL based method has two steps including selecting a local region by the agents and processing it using a local enhancement network. Particularly, the local low-resolution patch is converted to a high-resolution one by the enhancement network, and then the agent chooses the next patch that should be processed. The method repeats this process until the maximum time step. Consequently, the whole image with high-resolution is produced. Another application of DRL is image cropping by Li *et al.* [6]. The goal is to achieve the highest cropped image's aesthetics score by reshaping the cropping window iteratively.

Image denoising attempts to reconstruct the original image by removing noise from a corrupted one. In literature, there are several methods applied to solve this task and they are separated into two groups: non-learning based approaches such as BM3D [4] and learning based methods including CNN [9]. The former includes many classical approaches which mainly use image processing (*e.g.* dilation and erosion) and filtering techniques (*e.g.* Gaussian filter, medical filter). Dictionary-based techniques are also used in the latter, however convolutional neural networks are increasingly being used to complete image denoising tasks [9]. In general, neural network based methods have outperformed non-leaning-based methods in terms of denoising performance. Comparing our denoising method to other neural network based techniques provides a whole new perspective. The proposed method eliminates noise with a series of straightforward pixel-level manipulations iteratively, in contrast to most other methods that denoise an image by reverting noise or real pixel values from a corrupted image.

3   Methodology

Figure 1 illustrates the proposed framework in detail. Firstly, we extract features of input image using a fully convolutional network (FCN) at each time step. To increase the receptive field, we utilized dilated convolutional layer introduced in [8] for FCN. After that, we employ a Gated Recurrent Unit (GRU) to exploit the relationship between images in two consecutive time steps. GRU is proposed to address the short-term memory limitation of Recurrent Neural Network (RNN). GRU has the same workflow as RNN but the operations inside the GRU unit with two gates (reset gate and update gate) are different. The output of FCN and previous hidden state are fed to GRU before using for π-Net and V-Net. Figure 2 illustrates the architectures of FCN, π-Net, and V-Net.

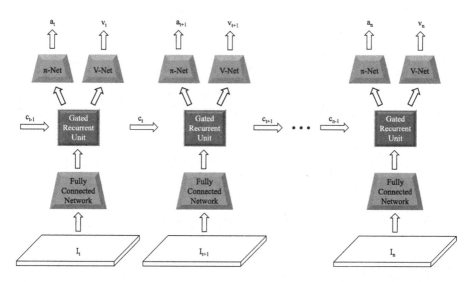

Fig. 1. The proposed framework workflow in detail. The fully connected network, π-Net and V-Net share the same architecture among frames.

Inspired by the idea of multi-agent reinforcement learning algorithm (**MARL** in short), we consider each pixel I_i ($i = 1, ..., N$) of input image as an agent. Therefore, each agent I_i acts based on its policy $\pi_i(a_i^{(t)}|s_i^{(t)})$, where $a_i^{(t)}(\in A)$ is the action and $s_i^{(t)}$ is the state of i-th agent at time step t. We define an action set A in Table 1 and $s_i^{(0)} = I_i$. The agent obtains the next state $s_i^{(t+1)}$ and reward $r_i^{(t+1)}$ from the environment by taking the actions $a_i^{(t)}$ chosen from its policy $\pi_i^{(t)}$. The final goal of the proposed framework is to obtain the highest total mean of the anticipated rewards at all positions of the input image by learning the optimal policies $\boldsymbol{\pi} = (\pi_1, \pi_2, ..., \pi_N)$ as described in Eq. 1.

$$\pi^* = \arg\max_{\boldsymbol{\pi}} E_{\boldsymbol{\pi}} \left(\sum_{t=0}^{\infty} \gamma^t \bar{r}^{(t)} \right). \tag{1}$$

$$\bar{r}^{(t)} = \frac{1}{N} \sum_{i=1}^{N} r_i^{(t)}, \tag{2}$$

where $\bar{r}^{(t)}$ and γ denotes the mean of the anticipated rewards at all pixels and the discount factor, respectively. The reward for each pixel is defined as follows:

$$r_i^{(t)} = (I_i^{target} - s_i^{(t)})^2 - (I_i^{target} - s_i^{(t+1)})^2 \tag{3}$$

where I_i^{target} is the value of i-th pixel in the original image. The reward in Eq. 3 expresses how much the action $a_i^{(t)}$ reduced the squared error on the i-th pixel.

Table 1. Pre-defined action list

Id	Action	Filter size n	Parameters
0	Pixel value $-=1$	5	–
1	Do nothing	5	–
2	Pixel value $+=1$	5	–
3	Gaussian filter	5	$\sigma = 0.5$
4	Bilateral filter	5	$\sigma_c = 0.1$, $\sigma_S = 5.0$
5	Median filter	5	–
6	Gaussian filter	5	$\sigma = 5.0$
7	Bilateral filter	5	$\sigma_c = 1.0$, $\sigma_S = 5.0$
8	Box filter	5	–

4   Performance Evaluation

BSD68 dataset is utilized for the experiments. This dataset includes 432 training and 68 testing images. All images are in gray-scale with varying size, we pre-process all images by cropping them into the size of 70×70. The proposed method is implemented based on Chainer and PyTorch libraries with Python 3.7. We set the length of each episode t_{max} to 5. To train the proposed method, we employed ADAM optimizer, with the learning rate parameter is initialized as $1e-3$ and decayed every episode. We then train the proposed method for 30,000 iterations in nearly 28 h on an NVIDIA A6000 GPU.

We use the peak signal-to-noise ratio (PSNR in short) metric to assess the denoising results of all methods. The higher PSNR value proves the method's effectiveness. The term PSNR is referred to as the ratio between the signal's highest potential value and the distorting noise's power that affects the quality of its representation. The decibel scale calculated using the mean square

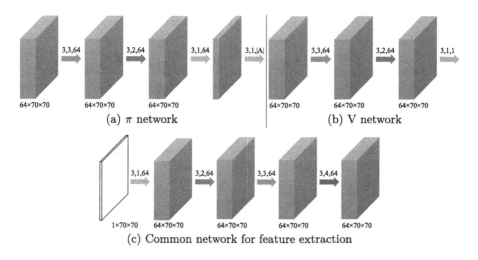

(a) π network   (b) V network

(c) Common network for feature extraction

Fig. 2. Illustration of three convolutional networks: FCN, π-Net, and V-Net.

error (MSE) is typically used to express the PSNR as a logarithmic number as described in Eq. 4. Given an original image with size of $m \times n$ I without noise and its reconstructed version K, MSE is defined as follows:

$$MSE = \frac{1}{m * n} \sum_{i=0}^{m-1} \sum_{i=0}^{n-1} [I(i,j) - K(i,j)]^2 \qquad (4)$$

The PSNR (in dB) is defined as follows:

$$PSNR = 10 \cdot log_{10}(\frac{MAX_I^2}{MSE}) \qquad (5)$$

Table 2. Gaussian denoising PSNR [dB] scores on BSD68 test

Method	$\sigma = 15$	$\sigma = 25$	$\sigma = 50$
BM3D [4]	31.07	28.57	25.62
MLP [1]	-	28.96	**26.03**
WNNM [5]	31.37	28.83	25.87
TNRD [3]	31.42	28.92	25.97
CNN [9]	31.63	29.15	26.19
Ours	**31.50**	**29.01**	25.99

We compare our method with non-learning methods (i.e., BM3D [4] and WNNM [5]) and learning-based ones (i.e., MLP [1], TNRD [3], and CNN [9]). As shown in Table 2, CNN method [9] achieves the best PSNR score. The proposed method obtains the second best results. Their results are highlighted in red and blue, respectively. The reason for this improvement is the agents can get considerably more reward by reducing the noises at their own positions rather than taking into account the neighboring pixels when the noises are strong. Moreover, the actions done by the agents are understandable to human-being, which is a significant improvement above conventional CNNs. By understanding what happened to each pixel of the input image to get the final results, we can improve our algorithm further. We illustrate the output of the proposed method for three cases of σ values, *i.e.*, 15, 25, 50 in Fig. 3. In terms of average running time on a single test image, our method takes 0.44 sec on an A6000 GPU, which is longer than other methods (CNN [9]: 0.038 sec/image; TNRD [3]: 0.032 sec/image) because the proposed method performs the actions sequentially.

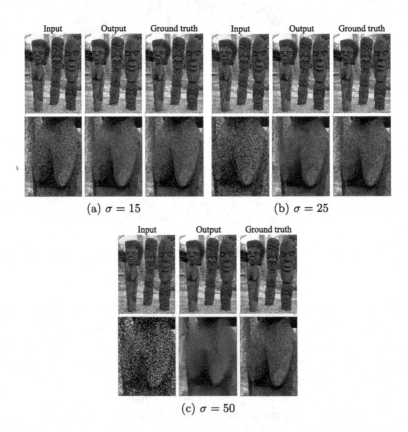

Fig. 3. Results of the proposed method under three Gaussian noise cases.

5   Conclusion and Future Work

In this article, we present a novel deep RL-based method for image denoising by combining a fully connected network with gated recurrent unit in an asynchronous advantage actor-critic algorithm. In our method, each pixel of input image has an agent, and it modifies the pixel value by performing an action from a pre-defined list. The objective of the proposed framework is to obtain the highest total mean of the anticipated rewards at all pixels by learning the optimal policies. The proposed method combines FCN and GRU to remove noise in gray-scale image by learning from the feature map of the previous state. The experimental results on BSD68 dataset show that the proposed method achieves equivalent or outperforms other methods using supervised learning. Our approach is interpretable to humans by showing the agent's actions, which is a significant difference from original CNNs. In future work, we will study the effectiveness and robustness of the proposed approach on other non-Gaussian noise such as salt and pepper noise or apply to other image processing tasks.

Acknowledgements. This research is partially supported by the Ministry of Science and ICT, Korea, under GITRC (IITP-2022-2015-0-00742), ICT Creative Consilience program (IITP-2022-2020-0-01821), and Artificial Intelligence Innovation Hub (No. 2021-0-02068).

References

1. Harold, B., Christian, S., Stefan, H.: Image denoising: can plain neural networks compete with BM3D? In: Proceedings of the IEEE Conference on Computer Vision and Pattern Recognition, pp. 2392–2399. IEEE (2012)
2. Cao, Q., Lin, L., Shi, Y., Liang, X., Li, G.: Attention-aware face hallucination via deep reinforcement learning. In Proceedings of the IEEE Conference on Computer Vision and Pattern Recognition, pp. 690–698. IEEE (2017)
3. Yunjin, C., Thomas, P.: Trainable nonlinear reaction diffusion: a flexible framework for fast and effective image restoration. IEEE Trans. Pattern Anal. Mach. Intell. **6**, 1256–1272 (2016)
4. Kostadin, D., Alessandro, F., Vladimir, K., Karen, E.: Image denoising by sparse 3-D transform-domain collaborative filtering. IEEE Trans. Image Process. **8**, 2080–2095 (2007)
5. Gu, S., Zhang, L., Zuo, W., Feng, X.: Weighted nuclear norm minimization with application to image denoising. In: Proceedings of the IEEE Conference on Computer Vision and Pattern Recognition, pp. 2862–2869. IEEE (2014)
6. Huang, K., Li, D., Wu, H., Zhang, J.: A2-RL: aesthetics aware reinforcement learning for automatic image cropping. In: Proceedings of the IEEE Conference on Computer Vision and Pattern Recognition, pp. 8193–8201. IEEE (2018)
7. Park, J., Lee, J.-Y., Yoo, D., So, K.I.: Distort-and-recover: color enhancement using deep reinforcement learning. In: Proceedings of the IEEE Conference on Computer Vision and Pattern Recognition, pp. 5928–5936. IEEE (2018)
8. Yu, F., Koltun, V.: Multi-scale context aggregation by dilated convolutions. arXiv preprint arXiv:1511.07122 (2015)
9. Zhang, K., Zuo, W., Gu, S., Zhang, L.: Learning deep CNN denoiser prior for image restoration. In: Proceedings of the IEEE Conference on Computer Vision and Pattern Recognition, pp. 3929–3938. IEEE (2017)

Energy Harvesting Aware
for Delay-Efficient Data Aggregation
in Battery-Free IoT Sensors

Van-Vi Vo[1], Phuoc-Nguyen Bui[2], Duc-Tai Le[3], and Hyunseung Choo[1(✉)]

[1] Department of Electrical and Computer Engineering, Sungkyunkwan University,
Suwon, South Korea
choo@skku.edu
[2] Department of Superintelligence Engineering, Sungkyunkwan University, Suwon,
South Korea
[3] College of Computing and Informatics, Sungkyunkwan University,
Suwon, South Korea

Abstract. Battery-Free Wireless Sensor Network (BF-WSN) is a new
energy harvesting technology that has been successfully integrated into
Wireless Sensor Networks (WSNs). It allows sensor batteries to be
charged using renewable energy sources. Sensor nodes in BF-WSNs are
no longer constrained by the equipped batteries, but rather by the
amount of energy harvested from their surroundings. In sensor networks, data aggregation is a fundamental procedure in which sensory
data collected by relay nodes is merged using in-network computation.
The Minimum Latency Aggregation Scheduling (MLAS) problem, which
has been widely studied in battery-powered WSNs, is always a critical issue in WSNs. Modern approaches used in battery-powered WSNs,
on the other hand, are incompatible with the use of BF-WSNs due to
the limited energy harvesting capabilities of battery-free sensor nodes.
In this paper, we investigate the MLAS problem in BF-WSNs. Leveraging the energy harvesting ability of the battery-free sensor nodes, we
propose an approach that assigns more senders to relay nodes having
high energy harvesting rates and schedules nodes whenever are ready for
energy capacity data transmissions. Through extensive simulations, our
proposed scheme surpasses the modern approach at most 40% in terms
of aggregation delay.

Keywords: Internet of things · Wireless sensor network · Data
aggregation · Energy harvesting · Battery-free

1 Introduction

Battery-Free Wireless Sensor Networks (BF-WSNs) are now being developed,
and energy harvesting technologies for charging sensor batteries have been successfully integrated into WSNs. When charged by solar, vibration, wireless
energy transfer, and other renewable energy sources, the lifetime of BF-WSNs

T. K. Dang et al. (Eds.): FDSE 2022, CCIS 1688, pp. 674–681, 2022.
https://doi.org/10.1007/978-981-19-8069-5_47

can be greatly extended [1]. This increases the usefulness of BF-WSNs. However, because of the limited capability of heterogeneous sensor nodes, harvested energy from the environment is limited and highly variable. As a result, there is a growing research interest in how to use harvested energy wisely [2,3].

Data aggregation is a common operation in most WSN applications, where the sink expects a summary of data from the entire network. As a result, aggregation scheduling that is quick and free of conflicts is in high demand. The problem of Minimum Latency Aggregation Scheduling (MLAS) in traditional energy-abundant WSNs has been proven to be NP-hard and has been extensively studied. The MLAS problem is solved in such networks by constructing an efficient aggregation tree and generating a conflict-free schedule. Furthermore, the duty-cycled scheme has been introduced as an efficient way of conserving energy, in which each sensor node alternates between the active and dormant states on a regular basis. For duty-cycled networks, the MLAS problem is solved by accounting for each node's active time slots in order to reduce latency [4–6].

For BF-WSNs, captured energy is still scarce and varies greatly between sensors. Before a node transmit or receive packets, it may need to charge for an extended period of time. As a result, all the known MLAS algorithms are inapplicable to BF-WSNs. In this research, we study the MLAS problem in BF-WSNs. An aggregation scheduling scheme is divided into two phases which are data aggregation tree construction phase and data schedule phase. We propose a data aggregation tree construction approach that leverages the energy harvesting rates of the sensor nodes. The nodes with high energy harvesting rates tend to receive data from more nodes compared to others. From the constructed aggregation tree, a scheduling scheme plans the time as soon as any nodes ready for data transmissions. By this way, the ready nodes will be scheduled first while other nodes can continuously harvest the energy. This approach can further helps to reduce data aggregation latency in the BF-WSNs.

The paper is organized as follows. We formulate the network model and the problem statement in Sect. 2. In Sect. 3, we present our proposed scheme that includes tree construction phase and data scheduling phase. We conduct extensive experiments to verify performance of the proposed scheme in Sect. 4. Finally, we claim our work and plan for our future research in Sect. 5.

2   Preliminaries

A BF-WSN is formulated as an undirected graph $G = (V, E)$ where V is a set of deployed BF sensor nodes and E is a set of communication links between sensor nodes in the network. Every sensor node has a uniform communication range d. Two nodes u and v can communicate to each other, i.e., neighbor relationship, if $(u, v) \in E$. The link (u, v) is calculated as a Euclidean distance between u and v, $dist(u, v) \leq d$. The interference range of a BF sensor node with its neighbors, denoted as d_i, is equal to the communication range, i.e. $d_i = d$. Each BF sensor is equipped with a limited capacitor E_c and we assume that it can harvest the energy from surrounding environment such as the sun, the wind, or radio frequency signal with different harvesting rate h_r. The energy consumed for transmitting and receiving data is denoted as E_t and E_r, respectively. In this paper, we exclude the energy consumed for data processing before transmitting to other intermediate nodes and sensing from surrounding environment.

There are two kinds of data conflicts might happen when sensors transmit/receive data to each other. When two sensor nodes transmit data to a same receiver, a data conflict happens at the common node, this is called primary conflict. A secondary conflict happens when a receiver overhears data from its neighbor (This neighbor node is sending data to another receiver) while receiving data from a sender. These kinds of conflicts are considered as time conflicts. In BF-WSNs, beside time conflicts, sensor nodes transmit or receive data only when they have enough energy in their capacitors. Therefore, allocating proper sender-receiver pairs (child-parent pairs) for data transmission further reduce the total data aggregation time. The conflicts that prevent data transmissions due to insufficient energy capacity at the sensor nodes, are called energy conflicts.

In this paper, we study Minimum Latency Aggregation Scheduling (MLAS) problem in BF-WSNs. The data aggregation completes when sink node s collects data from all other sensor nodes in the network. In other words, all nodes in the network except the sink must be assigned time slots when the scheduling completes to transmit data with conflict-free. The Data aggregation latency is the time needed to aggregate data by the sink from all nodes in the network. The target of MLAS in BF-WSNs is to reduce data aggregation delay while also ensuring that all scheduled transmissions are conflict-free.

3   Proposed Scheme

The proposed scheme is divided into two phases: Data aggregation tree construction phase where parent-child (receiver-sender) pairs are adopted for battery-free sensors; and data scheduling phase based on the constructed tree, the battery-free sensor nodes are assigned the time to send data to the designated receivers (which are determined in the tree construction phase) with collision-free.

Algorithm 1 presents the procedures to construct the aggregation tree (lines 1–14) based on Maximal Independent Set (MIS) and schedule the BF sensor nodes for data transmissions (lines 15–25). The inputs are the communication graph $G(V, E)$; energy harvesting rates of sensor nodes $r(u), u \in \backslash \{s\}$ since the sink s assumes always to have enough energy and be responsible to calculate the schedule for all other nodes in the network; the energy consumed for transmitting and receiving data E_t, E_s, respectively; and a storage capacitor E_c is equipped to each BF sensor node. The algorithm completes when all the BF sensor nodes except the sink are assigned the time for data transmission.

The aggregation tree initially adds the sink s. Based on the hop distance from the BF sensor nodes to the sink, the network is divided into $R + 1$ layer, i.e., $\{L_0, L_1, ..., L_R\}$, where only the sink s is in the layer L_0. The algorithm, then, constructs a maximal independent set (MIS) layer by layer starting from the sink. Nodes in set MIS are non-adjacent and the one at each layer that has highest energy harvesting rate prioritize to be selected first. In the BF-WSNs, beside time collisions, the data scheduling also depends on the residual energy at

---

Algorithm 1: Proposed scheme

Input : $G(V, E)$, Energy harvesting rates of sensor nodes $r(u), u \in V \setminus \{s\}$,
E_t, E_r, E_c

Output: All nodes in the network are scheduled

// Aggregation tree construction phase

1 $V_T \leftarrow \{s\}; E_T \leftarrow \emptyset$

2 Divide the network into $R + 1$ layers based on their hop distance to the sink
$\{L_0, L_1, ..., L_R\}$

3 $MIS \leftarrow$ Set of non-adjacent nodes layer by layer with nodes having high energy
harvesting rates first

4 **for** $i \in [1, L_R]$ **do**

5     $R_i \leftarrow$ Set of nodes at layer i

6   **for** $u \in R_i$ **do**

7   **if** $u \in MIS$ **then**

8           $p(u) \leftarrow v \mid \max\limits_{v \in R_{i-1} \cap N(u)} \{r(v)\}$

9           $C(v) \leftarrow C(v) \cup \{u\}$

10          $V_T \leftarrow V_T \cup \{u\}; E_T \leftarrow E_T \cup \{(u, v)\}$

11   **else**

12          $p(u) \leftarrow v \mid v \in MIS$ and $\min\limits_{v \in R_{i-1} \cap N(u)} \{C(v)\}$

13          $C(v) \leftarrow C(v) \cup \{u\}$

14          $V_T \leftarrow V_T \cup \{u\}; E_T \leftarrow E_T \cup \{(u, v)\}$

// Data scheduling phase

15 Starting scheduling time $t \leftarrow 0$

16 $\bar{S} \leftarrow V \setminus \{s\}$

17 $\gamma \leftarrow \max\limits_{u \in V, |C(u)|=0} \{r(u)\}$

18 $t \leftarrow t + \frac{E_t}{\gamma}$

19 $Q \leftarrow \emptyset$

20 **for** $u \in \bar{S}$ **do**

21    $e_t(u) \leftarrow min\{r(u).\frac{E_t}{\gamma}, E_c\}$

22   **if** $|C(u)| = 0$ and $e_t(u) \geq E_t$ and $e_t(p(u)) \geq E_r$ **then**

23       $Q \leftarrow Q \cup \{u\}$

24 **while** $|\bar{S}| \neq 0$ **do**

25   Apply **DAS Algorithm** [10] to schedule candidate BF sensor nodes in Q,
then update set Q from $\bar{S}$

26 **return** All nodes in the networks are scheduled

---

the sensors. Assigning many child nodes to a node that has low energy harvesting rate create a bottleneck at the parent node, because the child nodes must wait the parent node harvest enough energy to perform the data communication. As a result, the total data aggregation latency becomes larger due to waiting time of child nodes at the low energy harvesting rate parent node. Therefore, the intuitive idea is to assign more child nodes to the sensor that has high energy harvesting rate when constructing the aggregation tree.

The tree construction works in a top-down manner from layer 1 to layer R. Let R_i be a set of nodes in layer L_i (line 5). For each node $u, u \in R_i$, if u is set MIS, u will adopt a neighbor v in upper layer that has highest energy harvesting rate among others as its parent, the aggregation tree is updated by adding u and the transmission link (u, v) (lines 7–10). If node u does not belong to set MIS, it adopts a node v in MIS such that this node is in the previous layer and has smallest number of children at the considering moment. Then v and the transmission link (u, v) are updated into the tree (lines 12–14). At each layer, all BF sensor nodes are added to the aggregation tree one by one, and the process is repeated for every layer until the algorithm reaches the lowest layer L_R. As a result, we obtain a complete aggregation tree.

The data scheduling phase starts when the aggregation tree construction is completed. The scheduling time is initialized as $t = 0$ (line 15. The algorithm takes set $\bar{S}$ to contain non-scheduled nodes except the sink, i.e., $\bar{S} = V \setminus \{s\}$. A metric γ is determined as the highest energy harvesting rate among leaf nodes. At the beginning, the BF sensor nodes do not have enough energy for data communication, so that they need to harvest enough energy for transmitting or receiving data. From obtained γ, the sink computes the time needed for the first transmission $t + \frac{E_t}{\gamma}$ in which t is the initial scheduling time (lines 15–18). At the time that there is a least one BF sensor node ready for the data transmission, all nodes in $\bar{S}$ updated the stored energy in their capacitors as long as the energy does not exceed the capacity of the sensor $min\{r(u).\frac{E_t}{\gamma}, E_c\}, u \in \bar{S}$ (line 21).

A set Q, which is initialized as the empty set, contains candidate BF sensor nodes ready to send data to their parents. A candidate BF sensor node $u, u \in \bar{S}$ are added into set Q when they are satisfied following conditions:

- The BF sensor node is leaf, i.e., $|C(u)| = 0$.
- The stored energy in its capacity is larger or equal to the energy consumed for data transmission, i.e., $e_t(u) \geq E_t$.
- The parent (receiver) node $p(u)$ of the candidate sender u must have enough energy to receive data, i.e., $e_t(p(u)) \geq E_r$.

The scheduling process then follows the same procedures with DAS Algorithm in [10] for all nodes in $\bar{S}$ (lines 24–25). In this process, the candidate set Q will be updated when the candidate BF nodes in the current Q are scheduled. In addition, the scheduled nodes are removed from $\bar{S}$ so that the schedule completes when $\bar{S}$ is empty.

4   Experiment Results

We test performance of the proposed scheme in term of aggregation latency. We check the impact of the network size (number of BF sensor nodes), energy harvesting rate, and energy capacity to the latency and compare the results with Data Aggregation Scheduling scheme (DAS) proposed in [10]. We assume that the sensor nodes harvest the energy from the radio frequency signal, the rate is varied from $1\,\mu J/s$ to $200\,\mu J/s$ as claimed by [8]. The consumed energy for

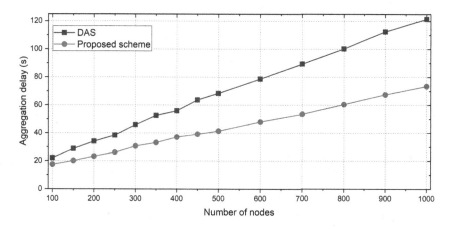

Fig. 1. Aggregation delay affected by number of BF sensor nodes.

transmitting and receiving data of a Mica2dot sensor node are $E_t = 59.2\,\mu\text{J/s}$, and $E_r = 28.6\,\mu\text{J/s}$, respectively, according to [9]. By default, we simulate a BF-WSN consisting of 300 battery-free sensor nodes randomly distributed in an area $100 \times 100\,\text{m}^2$ using Networkx in Python [7]. All BF sensor nodes are equipped with same size capacitor $E_c = 200\,\mu\text{J}$. We assume that a valid data transmission takes the time $\tau = 100\,\text{ms}$. In other words, the energy harvesting rates of BF sensor nodes become varying from $0.1\,\mu\text{J}/\tau$ to $20\,\mu\text{J}/\tau$. The sink node is deployed at the center of the area and responsible for the computation so that it has unlimited power source. Initially, all sensor nodes have no energy in their capacitor at the time they are deployed. The transmission range and interference range of any node are equal $d = 15\,\text{m}$. We simulate 100 BF-WSNs for each parameter, each result presented in Fig. 1 and 2 is the average results of 100 BF-WSNs.

Figure 1 presents the impact of network density on the data aggregation latency. We set the number of BF sensor nodes varied from 100 to 1000 nodes, in each network, the BF sensor nodes are randomly deployed. The energy harvesting rates of sensor nodes are followed triangular distribution, and the average energy harvesting rate is $\bar{r} = \frac{\sum_{u=1}^{N} r(u)}{N} = 100$. The aggregation delay of both schemes increase when the number of BF sensor nodes increases in the same network area. It is because when the number of BF sensor nodes increases, more collisions occur among the sensors. However, our proposed scheme improves at most 40% in high density networks, i.e., from 600 to 1000 BF sensor nodes.

We also evaluate the performance of the proposed scheme by varying the average energy harvesting rates and energy capacity. Herein, we deploy the network of 300 BF sensor nodes, the energy harvesting rates of BF sensor nodes are also followed by triangular distribution within values from $1\,\mu\text{J/s}$ to $200\,\mu\text{J/s}$. The average energy harvesting rates of each network is varying from 40 to $180\,\mu\text{J/s}$. Figure 2a shows that the average energy harvesting rate has little impact on the aggregation delay of our proposed scheme since only nodes having high

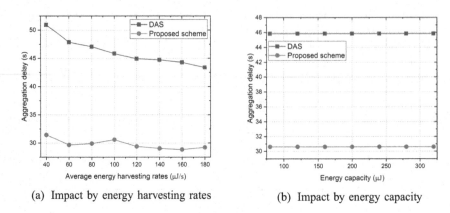

(a) Impact by energy harvesting rates   (b) Impact by energy capacity

Fig. 2. Aggregation delay affected by average energy harvesting rates and energy capacity.

energy harvesting rates receive data from more children. In addition, our proposed scheme can improve up to 38.26% when the average energy harvesting rate $\bar{r}$ is $40\,\mu\mathrm{J/s}$.

Figure 2b presents the impact of energy capacity on the aggregation delay. We fix the average energy harvesting rate as $100\,\mu\mathrm{J/s}$, and vary the energy capacity from 80 to $320\,\mu\mathrm{J}$ with the increment of $40\,\mu\mathrm{J}$. The results show that in this energy capacity region, the energy capacity seems to have no impact on the aggregation delay for both schemes because as long as the BF sensor nodes harvest enough energy, they perform the data communication with others. In addition, nodes in the MIS set have high energy harvesting rates, each time τ they harvest enough energy for one transmission and the node in MIS set can perform only one data communication with one of their neighbors. As a result, the energy capacity does not affect to the aggregation delay as long as its capacity stores enough energy for the data transmission.

5   Conclusion and Future Work

In this paper, we propose a data aggregation scheduling approach that consists of the aggregation tree construction based on the energy harvesting of BF sensor nodes in the top-down manner and nodes scheduling in a bottom-up manner for any BF sensor nodes ready for data communication. The proposed scheme reduces the aggregation delay by assigning more senders for those who have high energy harvesting rates and scheduling nodes as soon as they are ready for data communication. We examine the effectiveness of the proposed scheme through extensive simulations comparing with modern approach. Our proposed scheme outperform the reference approach up to 40% in term of aggregation latency.

Acknowledgement. This work is supported by the Ministry of Education Korea (NRF-2020 R1A2C2008447) and by IITP grant funded by the Korea government (MSIT) under the ICT Creative Consilience program (IITP-2022-2020-0-0182) and Artificial Intelligence Innovation Hub (No.2021-0-02068).

References

1. Yang, S., Tahir, Y., Chen, P., Marshall, A., McCann, J.: Distributed optimization in energy harvesting sensor networks with dynamic in-network data processing. In: IEEE INFOCOM 2016-The 35th Annual IEEE International Conference on Computer Communications, pp. 1–9. IEEE (2016)
2. Chen, K., Gao, H., Cai, Z., Chen, Q., Li, J.: Distributed energy-adaptive aggregation scheduling with coverage guarantee for battery-free wireless sensor networks. In: IEEE INFOCOM 2019-IEEE Conference on Computer Communications, pp. 1018–1026. IEEE (2019)
3. Chen, Q., Gao, H., Cai, Z., Cheng, L., Li, J.: Energy-collision aware data aggregation scheduling for energy harvesting sensor networks. In: IEEE INFOCOM 2018-IEEE Conference on Computer Communications, pp. 117–125. IEEE (2018)
4. Le, D.T., Lee, T., Choo, H.: Delay-aware tree construction and scheduling for data aggregation in duty-cycled wireless sensor network. EURASIP J. Wirel. Commun. Networking **2018**(1), 1–15 (2018)
5. Nguyen, T.-D., Le, D.-T., Vo, V.-V., Kim, M., Choo, H.: Fast sensory data aggregation in IoT networks: collision-resistant dynamic approach. IEEE Internet Things J. **8**(2), 766–777 (2020)
6. Vo, V.-V., Nguyen, T.-D., Le, D.-T., Kim, M., Choo, H.: Link-delay-aware reinforcement scheduling for data aggregation in Massive IoT. IEEE Trans. Commun. **70**, 5353–5367 (2022)
7. Networkx. https://networkx.org/
8. Lu, X., Wang, P., Niyato, D., Kim, D.I., Han, Z.: Wireless networks with RF energy harvesting: a contemporary survey. IEEE Commun. Surv. Tutor. **17**(2), 757–789 (2014)
9. Wander, A.S., Gura, N., Eberle, H., Gupta, V., Shantz, S.C.: Energy analysis of public-key cryptography for wireless sensor networks. In: Third IEEE International Conference on Pervasive Computing and Communications, pp. 324–328. IEEE (2005)
10. Zhu, T., Li, J., Gao, H., Li, Y.: Data aggregation scheduling in battery-free wireless sensor networks. IEEE Trans. Mob. Comput. **21**, 1972–1984 (2020)

Deep Models for Mispronounce Prediction for Vietnamese Learners of English

Trang Phung[1], Duc-Quang Vu[2,3]([✉]), Ha Mai-Tan[4], and Le Thi Nhung[1]

[1] Thai Nguyen University, Thai Nguyen, Vietnam
[2] Thai Nguyen University of Education, Thai Nguyen, Vietnam
[3] National Central University, Taoyuan, Taiwan
quangvd@tnue.edu.vn
[4] National Taiwan University, New Taipei, Taiwan

Abstract. Second language learners' correct and exact pronunciation is one of the important factors that help improve their own communication skills. Therefore, a system for predicting mispronunciation or assessing pronunciation accuracy for second language learners has been proposed and studied for decades. However, the results obtained are still very limited. In this paper, we present two popular deep learning models including Convolutional Neural Network (CNN) and Long Short-term Memory (LSTM) to solve the problem of predicting incorrect pronunciation for Vietnamese learners of English. This has great significance in building systems to help Vietnamese people during their English acquisition, specifically to improve their correct pronunciation of English. The experiment results on the L2-ARCTIC dataset have shown that both models achieve state-of-the-art performance. In addition, we also found that the LSTM model outperforms the CNN model by 6.3% in terms of accuracy due to the memory mechanism at each unit. The source code of our approach can be found at https://github.com/vdquang1991/Mispronounce_Prediction.

Keywords: Deep learning · Predicting english pronunciation · Vietnamese people learning pronunciation · Assessing english pronunciation

1 Introduction

As mobile devices e.g., smartphones, tablets, etc. become increasingly popular, automatic speech recognition (ASR) is found in many kinds of applications. Various applications such as identifying the words a person speaks into the microphone and automatically converting them into readable text. Recent developments in speech-to-text capabilities have encouraged the implementation of ASR in Computer Assisted Language Learning (CALL) and have gained popularity in second language education [4].

Most of the available assessment methods are based on ASR. One simple approach is Words Correctly Recognized Per Minute (WCPM). In addition, careful

T. K. Dang et al. (Eds.): FDSE 2022, CCIS 1688, pp. 682–689, 2022.
https://doi.org/10.1007/978-981-19-8069-5_48

evaluations are usually carried out in three steps including (1) Using the ASR system to segment the speech signal into vocal units, e.g. phones or words; (2) Calculation of local or global features based on segmentation extracted in step 1; (3) Generate proficiency scores from local/global features. The features used can be classified into two categories: phonemic features and prosodic features. Phonemic features indicate the pronunciation quality of individual phone (or word). The most successful phonetic features are the phone-level likelihood or posterior [14], others include phone duration, formants, articulation class, phonetic distance, etc. Prosodic features describe intonation, stress, or fluency. The most common features of Prosodic include sound pitch, sound intensity, speech rate (number of words per minute), silence time [6]. Calculating pronunciation scores from these features can be done by some simple methods, such as averaging if the input features take place under posterior probability at the speech sound level or using Gaussian to evaluate the characteristics of pitch and sound intensity. Witt et al. [27] provided technical to evaluate pronunciation quality.

With the explosion of big data, deep learning methods have achieved great success in solving problems, such as computer vision, sound recognition and natural language processing in recent years. For the ASR problem, the initial methods focused on manual feature extraction and conventional techniques such as Gaussian Mixture Modeling (GMM), Dynamic Time Warping (DTW) algorithms and Hidden Markov Models. Recently, neural networks such as Recurrent Neural Networks (RNNs), Convolutional Neural Networks (CNNs) and Transformers have been applied on ASRs and obtained better performance. However, for the problems of automatic pronunciation assessment or mispronounce prediction, the conventional models such as DNN-HMM [19], GOP [2] still have limitations. It can be explained by the reason of linguistic diversity, that makes the problems more localized or the lack of large standard datasets.

In this paper, we proposed some deep learning models to predict the mistakes in English pronunciation for Vietnamese people. This work has significant contribution to improve the standard of English pronunciation for Vietnamese learners because the pronunciation is the premise for the development of other skills such as listening and speaking. At the same time, to avoid the phenomenon of guessing the sound for the same word, for example, some English words have the same spelling (homographs), but the pronunciation is completely different. Our main contributions can be summarized as follows:

- Propose models based on deep learning techniques to detect and predict the incorrect pronunciation for pepople speaking English in Vietnam.
- The results showed that the LSTM model had the best performance compared to other methods such as CNN.

2   Related Work

There are three types of ASR systems [17,28], distinguished by different levels of training including (1) depends on the speaker; (2) independent of the speaker;

and (3) can adapt to the speaker. Speaker-dependent ASR requires the user to train the speech recognizer with their own speech samples; so the system works just fine for the person who trains it. Speaker-independent ASR does not require the system to train with the speaker before use, so the recognizer is pre-trained during system development with speech samples from different speakers. Therefore, many different speakers will be able to use the same ASR application with relatively good accuracy as long as their speech is within the range of the samples collected. Speaker-adaptable ASR is similar to speaker-independent ASR in that no training with the speaker is required prior to use. However, unlike the speaker-independent ASR system, the speaker-adaptive ASR system is updated during using i.e., the recognizer gradually adapts to the user's voice.

The majority of studies that have investigated the impact of ASR on the acquisition of second language (L2) vocalization have shown that, despite its limitations, the technology still has the potential to be effective. The early discovery work of [3,11] and Mostow et al. [12] indicated that ASR system is still not as accurate as human analysis. Therefore, they have suggested that ASR can be useful for students' practice with only some aspects of pronunciation such as segmentation. However, recent developments in ASR especially for language learning have demonstrated this technology's effectiveness for L2 pronunciation learning (e.g. in [13,18]).

In summary, the available literature suggests that ASR can have positive effects on the acquisition of L2 pronunciation. Although the results obtained are not as good in studies done more than a decade ago. However, with modern machine learning methods such as deep learning, new ASR systems have shown that this technology has made significant progress in detecting non-native speech such as GMM [10], DNN-HMM [19], GOP [2], etc.

3   Proposed Models

3.1   Problem Setup

Given a training dataset with N samples as $\{(x_1, y_1, z_1), (x_2, y_2, z_2), ...(x_N, y_N, z_N)\}$ where $x_i, i \in N$ is the pronunciation speech obtained from recording devices and y_i is the score for the pronunciation speech x_i. This score is assessed based on the accuracy and fluency of the word pronounced, pronouncing the correct stress. The scale (value domain) of y_i is in the set $\{1, 2, 3, 4, 5\}$. In which, 1 is the lowest score i.e., the speech x_i is the incorrect pronunciation meanwhile 5 is the highest score that represents the correct input pronunciation sound like native speakers or native speakers can understand. z_i indicates the standard sound pronounced by native speakers.

3.2   Convolutional Neural Network

CNN is a set of convolution layers and use nonlinear activation functions such as ReLU or Tanh to activate the weights in the nodes. Each layer after applying activation functions is generate more complex information for the next layer. CNN model is one of the popular architecture for image recognition such as image classification [7,21], object detection [5,16], object segmentation [1,9], action recognition [23–26], video prediction [15], etc. However, not only applied to the image domain, CNNs have been also applied to many different types of data e.g., text, and give promising results. For example, Vieira et al. [22] proposed to use the CNN model on many English datasets for sentence classification problem. The results show that the model achieve better performance compared to previous methods such as CRF, SVM or RNN. *Advantage:* Using fewer parameters and lower computational cost than neural networks (NNs), the inference speed of CNNs is usually faster than that of NNs. *Drawback:* There is no memory capacity like RNN or LSTM. For the prediction of mispronouncing by Vietnamese learners of English, we build a CNN network model as shown in Table 1.

Table 1. The CNN architecture for prediction of mispronouncing by Vietnamese learners of English.

No.	Layer	Output size
1	Input	(32000×1)
2	Conv $(11 \times 11,$ stride $= 8)$ BatchNorm, ReLU	(4000×16)
3	Conv $(7 \times 7,$ stride $= 4)$ BatchNorm, ReLU	(1000×16)
4	Conv $(7 \times 7,$ stride $= 4)$ BatchNorm, ReLU	(250×32)
5	ZeroPadding1D (padding $= 3$)	(256×32)
6	Conv $(7 \times 7,$ stride $= 4)$ BatchNorm, ReLU	(64×32)
7	Conv $(7 \times 7,$ stride $= 2)$ BatchNorm, ReLU	(32×64)
8	Conv $(7 \times 7,$ stride $= 2)$ BatchNorm, ReLU	(16×64)
9	Conv $(7 \times 7,$ stride $= 2)$ BatchNorm, ReLU	(8×128)
10	Flatten	$(1024, 1)$
11	Dropout (drop rate=0.5)	$(1024, 1)$
12	FC (softmax)	$(5, 1)$

3.3 Long-Short Term Memory

Long Short Term Memory Networks, commonly known as LSTMs - is a special type of Recurrent Neural Network (RNN) that can capable of learning long-term dependencies. LSTM was first introduced by Hochreiter and Schmidhuber [8] and then it has been refined and popularized in recent years. It works extremely well on many different problems with different data types such as audio/speech [20].

Because of the ability to be capable of learning long-term dependencies, LSTM models offer impressive performance on many tasks compared to RNNs. Moreover, remembering information for a long time is their default property, we do not need to manipulate it to be able to remember it. That means it can be memorized by itself without any intervention [8].

The LSTM is capable of removing or adding information necessary for the cell state, which is carefully regulated by the gates (e.g., Input gate, forget gate). Currently, there are many variants of LSTM proposed such as: Bi-LSTM, GRU, etc. *Advantage:* Usually applied to text or audio domain because of their good memorization ability. *Drawback:* More complex than RNN, so the speed is slower.

Table 2 describes the LSTM model for the prediction of mispronouncing by Vietnamese learners of English. In this problem, the input and output of the LSTM network is set up similarly to the CNN network.

Table 2. The LSTM architecture for prediction of mispronouncing by Vietnamese learners of English.

No.	Layer	Output size
1	Input	(32000×1)
2	Conv (11×11, stride = 4) BatchNorm, ReLU	(8000×32)
3	Bi-LSTM (16 units)	(8000×32)
4	MaxPool (stride = 4)	(2000×32)
5	Bi-LSTM (32 units)	(2000×64)
6	MaxPool (stride = 4)	(500×64)
7	Bi-LSTM (64 units)	(500×128)
8	MaxPool (stride = 4)	(125×128)
9	Bi-LSTM (128 units)	(125×256)
10	GlobalAvgPool1D	$(256, 1)$
11	Dropout (drop rate = 0.5)	$(256, 1)$
12	FC (softmax)	$(5, 1)$

4 Experiment

4.1 Datasets and Implementation

We implement our experiments on the L2-ARCTIC [29] non-native English corpus for mispronunciation detection, voice conversion and accent conversion studies. Corpus was recorded from 24 speakers whose first languages (L1) were Hindi, Korean, Mandarin, Spanish, Arabic and Vietnamese. Each speaker contributes approximately one hour reading the speech annotated with 150 pronunciation errors of three types: substitution, deletion, and addition.

We hold out 4 folders containing Vietnamese pronunciation including HQTV, PNV, TLV, and THV for our experiments. In each folder, there are 150 audio files of the reading speeches along with files marking the start and end times of each word. The words extracted from the audio files are normalized to the same size of 2 s with an audio frequency of 16KHz (i.e. the input will be an array of size (32,000,1)). We also collect the corresponding standard pronunciation segments from Google with British and American accents and label them with the values of 5, 4, 3, 2, 1 with respective accuracy above 80%, above 60%, above 40%, above 20% and the remainder, equal to or less than 20%. We divide the data into two subsets, 90% for training and 10% for validating.

We train both models for 200 epochs using the Adam optimizer and an initial learning rate of 0.002. The learning rate will be reduced by 10 times if validation loss is not improved for 10 consecutive epochs. All experiments are conducted using python language and on a 2080Ti GPU.

4.2 Benchmark Results

The results of the CNN and LSTM models for detecting English pronunciation errors in speakers whose native language is Vietnamese are presented in Table 3. The results show that the CNN and LSTM models achieved the accuracy of 68.5% and 74.8%, respectively. The LSTM model performed better than the CNN model with higher accuracy of 6.3% because the LSTM model has a memory mechanism through memory cells.

Table 3. The results of CNN and LSTM models for mispronunciation detection.

Model	Accuracy
CNN	68.5%
LSTM	74.8%

Figure 1 presents the results of the training process of both models, in which, the CNN model converges after 50 epochs, whereas the LSTM model converges after 85 epochs. The LSTM model converges slower than the CNN model because the LSTM model has a higher complexity than the CNN model.

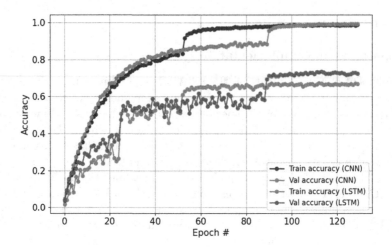

Fig. 1. Accuracy of training and testing phases of the CNN and LSTM.

5   Conclusion

This paper presents two popular deep learning models including CNN and LSTM to address the mispronouncing prediction problem for Vietnamese people during learning a second language (English). Both models have been conducted on the L2-ARCTIC dataset. The experiment results have shown that both models gave a positive performance. Besides of having the memory mechanism, the LSTM model outperforms 6.3% compared to the CNN model. In the future, we will continue to delve into the exploitation of more advanced datasets and models (such as the Transformer) to solve the problem with higher results.

References

1. Chen, X., Girshick, R., He, K., Dollár, P.: Tensormask: a foundation for dense object segmentation. In: ICCV, pp. 2061–2069 (2019)
2. Cheng, S., Liu, Z., Li, L., Tang, Z., Wang, D., Zheng, T.F.: Asr-free pronunciation assessment. arXiv preprint arXiv:2005.11902 (2020)
3. Dalby, J., Kewley-Port, D.: Explicit pronunciation training using automatic speech recognition technology. CALICO J. **16**, 425–445 (1999)
4. Eskenazi, M.: An overview of spoken language technology for education. Speech Commun. **51**(10), 832–844 (2009)
5. Girshick, R.: Fast R-CNN. In: ICCV, pp. 1440–1448 (2015)
6. Graham, C., Nolan, F.: Articulation rate as a metric in spoken language assessment. In: INTERSPEECH (2019)
7. He, K., Zhang, X., Ren, S., Sun, J.: Deep residual learning for image recognition. In: CVPR, pp. 770–778 (2016)
8. Hochreiter, S., Schmidhuber, J.: Long short-term memory. Neural Comput. **9**(8), 1735–1780 (1997)

9. Huang, H., et al.: Unet 3+: a full-scale connected unet for medical image segmentation. In: ICASSP, pp. 1055–1059. IEEE (2020)
10. Knill, K., Gales, M., et al.: Automatically grading learners' English using a gaussian process. In: ISCA (2015)
11. LaRocca, C.S.A., et al.: On the path to 2x learning: exploring the possibilities of advanced speech recognition. CALICO J. **16**, 295–310 (1999)
12. Mostow, J., Aist, G.: Giving help and praise in a reading tutor with imperfect listening-because automated speech recognition means never being able to say you're certain. CALICO J. **16**, 407–424 (1999)
13. Neri, A., Mich, O., Gerosa, M., Giuliani, D.: The effectiveness of computer assisted pronunciation training for foreign language learning by children. Comput. Assist. Lang. Learn. **21**(5), 393–408 (2008)
14. Neumeyer, L., et al.: Automatic text-independent pronunciation scoring of foreign language student speech. In: ICSLP 1996, vol. 3, pp. 1457–1460. IEEE (1996)
15. Phung, T., Nguyen, V.T., Ma, T.H.T., Duc, Q.V.: A (2+1)D attention convolutional neural network for video prediction. In: Dang, N.H.T., Zhang, Y.D., Tavares, J.M.R.S., Chen, B.H. (eds.) Artificial Intelligence in Data and Big Data Processing. ICABDE 2021. Lecture Notes on Data Engineering and Communications Technologies, vol. 124, pp. 395–406. Springer, Cham (2022). https://doi.org/10.1007/978-3-030-97610-1_31
16. Redmon, J., Divvala, S., Girshick, R., Farhadi, A.: You only look once: unified, real-time object detection. In: CVPR, pp. 779–788 (2016)
17. Rosen, K., Yampolsky, S.: Automatic speech recognition and a review of its functioning with dysarthric speech. Augment. Altern. Commun. **16**(1), 48–60 (2000)
18. Strik, H., et al.: Comparing different approaches for automatic pronunciation error detection. Speech Commun. **51**(10), 845–852 (2009)
19. Sudhakara, S., et al.: An improved goodness of pronunciation (gop) measure for pronunciation evaluation with DNN-hmm system considering hmm transition probabilities. In: INTERSPEECH, pp. 954–958 (2019)
20. Tan, H.M., et al.: Selective mutual learning: an efficient approach for single channel speech separation. In: ICASSP, pp. 3678–3682. IEEE (2022)
21. Tan, M., Le, Q.: Efficientnet: rethinking model scaling for convolutional neural networks. In: ICML, pp. 6105–6114. PMLR (2019)
22. Vieira, J.P.A., Moura, R.S.: An analysis of convolutional neural networks for sentence classification. In: CLEI, pp. 1–5. IEEE (2017)
23. Vu, D.Q., Le, N., Wang, J.C.: Teaching yourself: a self-knowledge distillation approach to action recognition. IEEE Access **9**, 105711–105723 (2021)
24. Vu, D.Q., Le, N.T., Wang, J.C.: Self-supervised learning via multi-transformation classification for action recognition. arXiv preprint arXiv:2102.10378 (2021)
25. Vu, D.Q., Le, N.T., Wang, J.C.: (2+1)d distilled shufflenet: a lightweight unsupervised distillation network for human action recognition. In: ICPR. IEEE (2022)
26. Vu, D.Q., et al.: A novel self-knowledge distillation approach with SIAMESE representation learning for action recognition. In: VCIP, pp. 1–5. IEEE (2021)
27. Witt, S.M.: Automatic error detection in pronunciation training: where we are and where we need to go. In: International Symposium on Automatic Detection on Errors in Pronunciation Training, pp. 1–8 (2012)
28. Young, V., Mihailidis, A.: Difficulties in automatic speech recognition of dysarthric speakers and implications for speech-based applications used by the elderly: a literature review. Assist. Technol. **22**(2), 99–112 (2010)
29. Zhao, G., et al.: L2-arctic: a non-native English speech corpus. In: INTERSPEECH, pp. 2783–2787 (2018)

An Approach to Hummed-tune and Song Sequences Matching

Bao Loc Pham[✉], Huong Hoang Luong[✉], Thien Phu Tran,
Hoang Phuc Ngo, Hoang Vi Nguyen, and Thinh Nguyen

IT Department, FPT University, Nguyen Van Cu, Can Tho 90000, Vietnam
phambaoloc163@gmail.com, huonghoangluong@gmail.com

Abstract. Melody stuck in your head, also known as "earworm", is tough to get rid of, unless you listen to it again or sing it out loud. But what if you can not find the name of that song? It must be an intolerable feeling. Recognizing a song name base on humming sound is not an easy task for a human being and should be done by machines. However, there is no research paper published about hum tune recognition. Adapting from Hum2Song Zalo AI Challenge 2021 - a competition about querying the name of a song by user's giving humming tune, which is similar to Google's Hum to Search. This paper covers details about the pre-processed data from the original type (mp3) to usable form for training and inference. In training an embedding model for the feature extraction phase, we ran experiments with some states of the art, such as ResNet, VGG, AlexNet, MobileNetV2. And for the inference phase, we use the Faiss module to effectively search for a song that matched the sequence of humming sound. The result comes at nearly 94% in MRR@10 metric on the public test set, along with the top 1 result on the public leaderboard.

Keywords: Humming sound recognition · Deep learning · Faiss module · Sound preprocessinng

1 Introduction

Recently, with the development of multimedia on the advance of mobile technology, people listen to music more than ever. People spend most of their time listening to music, while shopping, driving, or studying. As music is listened to more often, we have more "earworm" than ever. What if you want to listen to "that song" again, how can you find it when you do not know the song's name? To address that issue with current on-the-market products, we got Shazam [23] and Google's Hum to search [22].

Shazam, released in 2002, is an application that allows you to search for a song's name by letting it listen to music sequences. Nevertheless, Shazam [23]

H. H. Luong, T. P. Tran, H. P. Ngo, H. V. Nguyen, T. Nguyen—These authors contributed equally to this work.

T. K. Dang et al. (Eds.): FDSE 2022, CCIS 1688, pp. 690–697, 2022.
https://doi.org/10.1007/978-981-19-8069-5_49

has a drawback: it can only search by receiving a song recorded from the studio. With other variants such as remix songs or covers, Shazam does not always guarantee having relative accuracy as the original recorded song, which means when coming to human's humming sound, the program cannot return a correct result.

Google's Hum to search [22], released in 2020, has the ability to return some of the matching songs that come from user's hummed tunes. It returns some of the most likely songs to the humming tune. All popular songs from the 80s to now trending music have really good accuracy.

All those mentioned products do not work with Vietnamese songs because the popularity of music genres on the internet is mostly written in English, Spanish, Korean, or Japanese. As a result, Vietnamese people need a search engine for their music, which still can not be fulfilled by Shazam or Google's Hum to search. Fortunately, Zalo - the most popular cross-platform instant messaging application in Vietnam, hosted The Zalo AI Challenge 2021 [20]. In that contest, there was a challenge named Hum2Song, which asked the candidates to develop a Machine Learning model to look for a song using a humming tune. Our purpose for this paper is to present the methodology for solving a music matching problem with the Hum2Song [20] challenge's data.

There are some researches for Vietnamese data: [16–19], etc. All of them focus on the classification, in this paper, we will cover about the Vietnamese music searching pipeline.

This paper consists of 5 sections. The next section is about Related works 2. The Methodology Sect. 3 will cover the details of the data preprocessing, training and inference pipeline. The Experiments Sect. 4 will list all our experiment results. Finally, in the Conclusion Sect. 5, we conclude our paper and summarize other ways to improve or further research for better results.

2   Related Works

There already some researches for specific tasks in music. There are music classification: [9–11]. And cover songs identification: [12–14], etc. Most of them are supervised learning, but labeling data is a time-consuming job. Thankfully, there are many other methods, such as "contrastive learning methods to train neural networks" [15]. "The idea is to make the distance of sequences from the same song close to each other, and sequences from different songs must be far apart." [15]

There is already a well-known software for music searching - Shazam [23], their method was introduced in "An Industrial Strength Audio Search Algorithm" [8]. This software can search for a song, which means it listens to a song sequence and then returns the most related song to that sequence. The query sequences have to be audio recorded songs, which also works with some of the remixes and covers. Shazam [23] "listens" to a song, but does not perform very well on hummed tunes.

"Hum to Search" is a feature in Google search whose methodology was introduced in a blog [22] in 2020. This search feature allows you to hum your tune and returns the top likely options based on the tune, and then you can choose what matches the best for you (like a recommended system). However, as mentioned in the Introduction 1, they cannot return accurate results when searching for a Vietnamese song.

The research is take place from Zalo AI Challenge 2021 [20]'s first prize solution, the solution was created and published by Wano (a three-member team consisting of Mr Vo Van Phuc, Mr Nguyen Van Thieu, and Mr Lam Ba Thinh) on a Github repository named hum2song [21].

3 Methodology

The methodology includes 3 parts: data preprocessing, training embedding model, and inference. The preprocessing of all data for training and inference is only done once. The training embedding models phase is experimented with various state of the arts to find the most sufficient backbone for the task. The inference phase is handled by using Faiss [2] module.

3.1 Data Preprocessing

Observation about the Data

The data consists of 3 sets. The training set has 1000 unique song sequences with their unique id within 2901 song sequences along with 2901 hummed tunes, totals of 1.3 GB. The public test used for evaluating on the public leader board has 419 song sequences and 500 hummed tunes, totals of 539 MB. The private test used for the final leader board standing has 10153 song sequences and 1067 hummed tune, totals of 12.5 GB. You can request the data at Zalo AI Challenge website [20].

Convert Data from Mp3 to Mel-Spectrogram

As the data is original in mp3 format, in order to use it, we process all of it into mel-spectrogram and store it in numpy array format for easy training and inference. We convert data to float32 and normalize the sound by dividing by the largest absolute value in the sound. Next, we convert to mel-spectrogram using config of filter length: 1024, hop-length: 256, win-length: 1024. Finally, we saved all preprocessed file to numpy array. The pipeline is illustrated in Fig. 1.

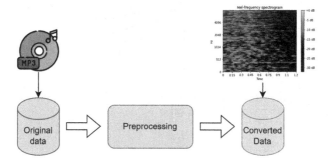

Fig. 1. Preprocessing data pipeline

3.2   Training

■ **Hyperparameters**: All of the backbones were trained on 100 epochs, batch size of 32, the convergence of models vary depends on backbone architecture. The loss function used for this training pipeline is ArcFace, which was introduced in "ArcFace: Additive Angular Margin Loss for Deep Face Recognition" [1]. The optimizer is Stochastic gradient descent with a learning rate of 1e–2, learning rate decay of 0.5 and a weight decay of 1e–1.

3.3   Inference

The inference part contains 3 steps, illustrated in Fig. 2:

- Step 1: Extract all features from both song sequences.
- Step 2: Add song sequences' features to Faiss [2] module to create a vector space of original song sequences.
- Step 3: Extract features from the hummed tune and use the Faiss [?] module to query the closest song sequence to the hummed tune.

The Faiss [2] module using IndexFlatL2 [2] measures the L2 (or Euclidean) distance between all given points between our query vector, and the vectors loaded into the index.

4   Experiments

After done preprocssing data, We tried on some State of the Art backbones in order to select some of the best candidate for embeddings model based on their performance on public test set and their training time. As the Zalo company's policy, the truth label and the results were only based on the public test, which was only used for the public leader board. Please note that all of the experiments use the same configuration. The metric used for evaluating models' performance is the same as the Zalo AI Challenge, which uses MRR@10 (mean reciprocal rank).

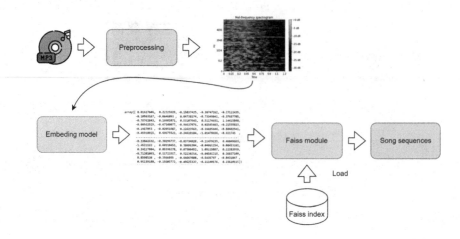

Fig. 2. Inference pipeline

4.1   Compare Results on Different Backbones and ResNet

Table 1. Some Training results on some backbones

Model	Training hours	Loss	Accuracy	MRR	Public test
Resnet18	10.6	0.2736880779	0.8125	0.9982826187	0.9318246032
Alexnet	2.017	1.482195854	0.71875	0.91776315067	0.8409246032
Vgg11 bn	6.75	0.005311204121	0.96875	0.9983863532	0.9063388889
Mobilenetv2	3.167	1.437324166	0.65625	0.9135797438	0.8921666667

Those are results on some backbones. AlexNet [7] and Mobilenetv2 [6] have the lowest training time, but the score on the public test is not as good as ResNet [3] and VGG [4]. All further experiments only focus on ResNet [3] and VGG [4] (Table 1).

Table 2. Training results on Resnet

Model	Training hours	Loss	Accuracy	MRR	Public test
Resnet18	10.6	0.2736880779	0.8125	0.9982826187	0.9318246032
Resnet34	23.6	0.4746982753	0.84375	0.9983287229	0.9423634921

The experiments show that ResNet [3] returned the best score on the public test, but the architecture like ResNet34 [3] took nearly a day for training (Table 2).

Table 3. Training results on modified resnet

Model	Training hours	Loss	Accuracy	MRR	Public test
Resnet18	15.25	0.08737678826	0.90625	0.9983114338	0.9407992063
Resnet34	22.9	0.02092118189	0.9375	0.9981961734	0.9457190476

The highlight ResNet34 is the final model for using in our pipeline because of its performance. The training on ResNet [3] took a lot of time, our team tried to change the architecture of ResNet [3] for better training time and better at creating embeddings. Instead of using the same block in pytorch model hub implementation, the experiments running on ResNet [3] which use variants from the paper Additive Angular Margin Loss for Deep Face Detection [1] increase the training hours but the accuracy increased 9, 10% and the public test score increased 1% at the ResNet18 [3] (Tables 3 and 4).

4.2 Compare Results on VGG

Table 4. Training results on Vgg

Model	Training hours	Loss	Accuracy	MRR	Public test
VGG11	6.75	0.0053112041	0.96875	0.9983863532	0.9063388889
VGG13	8.233	0.0047464803	0.9375	0.998340249	0.9183611111
VGG16	11.1	0.0047137937	0.96875	0.9982249885	0.9229555556

4.3 Evaluation

ResNet [3] variants have more training time and As the results shown on the tables above, based on score and training hours trade-off, if it about the mean reciprocal rank or accuracy, ResNet [3] variants and other big networks which create much better feature extraction are recommended. But as the speed of training, which also provides an acceptable score, VGG [4] variants are recommended.

VGG [4] variants have gradients vanishing problem. To solve that, ResNet [3] variants have "short cut connection", and instead of learning the mapping from x → F(x), the network learns the mapping from x → F(x)+G(x), showed in Fig. 3.

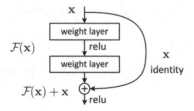

Fig. 3. Residual Block - Image is taken from the original paper

5   Conclusion

In this paper, we presented our pipeline for preprocessing song sequences and hummed tunes, training embedding models, and using Faiss module to optimize searching for the candidate for a hummed tune. The result on the public leader board is about 90%.

There are environmental and human factors in the hummed tune, such as the hummed tune contains noises or depends on the human's memory. In the preprocessing and augmentation phases, you can try to modify the hyperparameters, like increasing the sampling rate, max wav value, etc.

In the searching candidate phase, Faiss module also provides ways to optimize searching. We suggest trying partitioning the index to increase the speed. When the dataset is huge and we store all features in original shapes or vectors as full (e.g. Flat), Product Quantization is also supported by Faiss module.

References

1. Jiankang, D.: ArcFace: additive angular margin loss for deep face recognition. arXiv.Org, 23 January 2018. https://arxiv.org/abs/1801.07698
2. Jeff, J., et al.: Billion-0 Gpus. ArXiv.org, 28 February 2017. https://arxiv.org/abs/1702.08734
3. Kaiming, H., et al.: Deep residual learning for image recognition. ArXiv.org. 10 December 2015. https://arxiv.org/abs/1512.03385
4. Karen, S., Zisserman, A.: Very deep convolutional networks for large-scale image recognition.' ArXiv.org. 10 April 2015. https://arxiv.org/abs/1409.1556
5. Deng, J., Dong, W., Socher, R., Li, L.-J., Li, K., Fei-Fei, L.: ImageNet: a large-scale hierarchical image database. In: 2009 IEEE Conference on Computer Vision and Pattern Recognition, pp. 248–255 (2009). https://ieeexplore.ieee.org/document/5206848
6. Mark, S., et al.: MobileNetV2: inverted residuals and linear bottlenecks. ArXiv.org. 21 March 2019. https://arxiv.org/abs/1801.04381
7. Alex, K.: ImageNet classification with deep convolutional neural networks. In: Proceedings. Neurips.Cc (2012). https://proceedings.neurips.cc/paper/2012/hash/c399862d3b9d6b76c8436e924a68c45b-Abstract.html
8. Avery, W.: An industrial strength audio search algorithm. An Industrial Strength Audio Search Algorithm. https://www.researchgate.net/publication/220723446_An_Industrial_Strength_Audio_Search_Algorithm

9. Keunwoo, C., et al.: Automatic tagging using deep convolutional neural networks. ArXiv.org. 1 June 2016. https://arxiv.org/abs/1606.00298
10. Jongpil, L., et al.: Sample-level deep convolutional neural networks for music auto-tagging using raw waveforms. ArXiv.org, 22 May 2017. https://arxiv.org/abs/1703.01789
11. Jordi, P., Serra, X.: Musicnn: pre-trained convolutional neural networks for music audio tagging. ArXiv.org, 14 September 2019. https://arxiv.org/abs/1909.06654
12. Jiang, C., et al.: Similarity learning for cover song identification using cross-similarity matrices of multi-level deep sequences. IEEE Xplore, 15 May 2020. https://ieeexplore.ieee.org/document/9053257
13. Xiaoshuo, X., et al.: Key-invariant convolutional neural network toward efficient cover song identification. IEEE Xplore, 11 October 2018. https://ieeexplore.ieee.org/document/8486531
14. Zhesong, Y., et al.: Learning a representation for cover song identification using convolutional neural network. ArXiv.org, 1 November 2019. https://arxiv.org/abs/1911.00334
15. Dong, Y., et al.: Contrastive learning with positive-negative frame mask for music representation. ArXiv.org, 3 April 2022. https://arxiv.org/abs/2203.09129
16. Quynh Nhut, N., et al.: Movie recommender systems made through tag interpolation. In: Proceedings of the 4th International Conference on Machine Learning and Soft Computing. ACM Other Conferences, 1 January 2020. https://dl.acm.org/doi/10.1145/3380688.3380712
17. Hao Tuan, H., et al.: Automatic keywords-based classification of vietnamese texts. In: 2020 RIVF International Conference on Computing and Communication Technologies (RIVF), IEEE (2020)
18. Quynh Nhut, N., et al.: Movie recommender systems made through tag interpolation. In: Proceedings of the 4th International Conference on Machine Learning and Soft Computing (2020)
19. Nghia, D.-T., et al.: Genres and actors/actresses as interpolated tags for improving movie recommender systems. Int. J. Adv. Comput. Sci. Appl. 11(2) (2020)
20. Zalo AI Challenge. https://challenge.zalo.ai/
21. Vovanphuc. VOVANPHUC/hum2song: Top 1 Zalo AI Challenge 2021 Task Hum to Song. GitHub. https://github.com/vovanphuc/hum2song
22. Krishna, K.: Song Stuck in Your Head? Just Hum to Search. Google, Google, 15 October 2020. https://blog.google/products/search/hum-to-search/
23. Shazam. https://www.shazam.com/

84 Birds Classification Using Transfer Learning and EfficientNetB2

Hoa Le Duc$^{(\boxtimes)}$, Tin Tang Minh, Khanh Vo Hong, and Huong Luong Hoang

Information Technology Department, FPT University, Can Tho, Vietnam
{hoaldce140469,tintmce130438,khanhvh}@fpt.edu.vn

Abstract. Nowadays, global warming, wildfires, and air pollution have caused significant effects and seriously threatened the life and diversity of animals in common and birds in particular. Therefore, the conservation of birds is very urgent. Identify and classify them for statistics on the number of species, and distribution, and as a way to come up with reasonable conservation measures from scientists who study the environment and animals. In this research, we propose a new approach to classify birds using the EfficientNetB2 model, transfer learning techniques, and customizing the model's hyperparameters. Model trained on the original dataset with the highest accuracy of 93% on both the validation and the testing set.

Keywords: EfficientNetB2 · Transfer learning · Birds classification

1 Introduction

Habitat loss and climate change are seriously affecting the balance of ecosystems and species around the world. Birds not only have a beautiful effect, but they are also very beneficial to our environment.

Almost birds often live in natural environments such as fields, high treetops, or hidden in hollows, so identifying and classifying them is relatively hard due to their small shape and color are easily confused with the environment. There are certain similarities between birds of the same family but different species. It is also challenging the research the classification of birds without being confused between species or birds and the environment.

Our research was divided into five sections. Section 1 presents the introduction of this research. Section 2 will present homologous research by scientists around the world. Section 3 will present research methods and the proposed method for classifying 84 species of birds. Section four talks about the experiment results of the research. The last section will conclude this research.

2 Related Work

In recent years, there has been much research related to the classification of animals and birds that achieved high accuracy from authors around the world. The research identified six animals using CNN with VGG16 Architecture [1] and achieved results of 87%.

© The Author(s), under exclusive license to Springer Nature Singapore Pte Ltd. 2022
T. K. Dang et al. (Eds.): FDSE 2022, CCIS 1688, pp. 698–705, 2022.
https://doi.org/10.1007/978-981-19-8069-5_50

Using IoT devices to collect sounds and identify animals through audio using a CNN model based on TensorFlow achieved a relatively high accuracy of 91.3% for 10 animal species [2]. The animal classification research for Captcha decoding is presented in the paper Animal classification using Deep learning [3], using Dense-SIFT features, using SVM on the learned features and the final result is 94%. In the animal classification research based on Light Convolutional Network Neural Network [4], using AWA datasets of 50 animals and the top-1 accuracy of the model was 85.6%. Research on Similar Animal Classification Based on CNN Algorithm [5] achieved 96.67% accuracy, dataset is constructed by python crawler, with 800 and 200 images for each class respectively as train data and test data.

Our research will overcome the disadvantages of the above papers and apply their advantages to improve the results of our research, after the training process, the model must be compared with other models for a more accurate assessment of its effectiveness.

3   Materials and Proposed Methods

3.1   Convolutional Neural Network

The main components to building the CNN architecture are different types of layers such as a convolutional layer, pooling layer, activation function, and fully-connected layer. Several filters (kernels, weights) of each convolution layer can output the same number of the feature maps by sliding through the filters of the previous layers' feature maps. Pooling layers will conduct subsamples along the spatial dimensions of feature maps and reduce the size of feature maps using average or max pooling [6]. These activation functions will decide whether the input of the network is important or not in the prediction process by performing simple math operations. Fully-connected layers will follow convolutional and pooling layers to constitute some final layers [7]. Figure 1 will simulate the basic architecture of a CNN model.

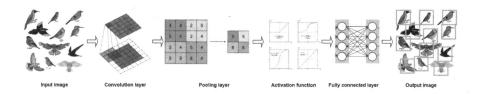

Fig. 1. The basic architecture of a CNN model. [7]

3.2   EfficientNet

EfficientNets is a group of deep convolutional networks that have achieved state-of-the-art accuracy in different classifications with up to 10x better performance and are called smaller and faster. This architecture has shown its novelty through the latest achievement of AutoML, especially the intelligent and controlled expansion of the 3 dimensions (width, depth, resolution) of the neural network using the use of compound coefficients. EfficientNets solves the problem by increasing dimensions and applying grid search according to a fixed resources constraint instead of changing the dimensions.

In EfficientNets, EfficientNetB2 will be used to demonstrate state-of-the-art accuracy to demonstrate the tagline faster and smaller in convolutional neural networks (Fig. 2).

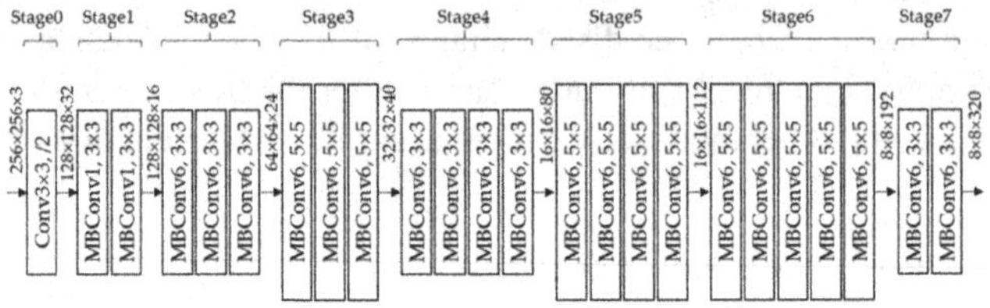

Fig. 2. Architecture of EfficientNetB2 [10]

3.3 Transfer Learning Method

This is a very effective training method for small datasets, the idea of which is to re-leverage the training of previous pre-train models [11] to increase the accuracy of the new model. The EfficientNetB2 model is trained with an ImageNet dataset with 1000 classes and millions of images, including animals, birds, fish, plants, etc (Fig. 3).

Fig. 3. Simulation of transfer learning [11]

3.4 Data Gathering

The data we collected from Kaggle [12], from the Animal Dataset dataset of 398 animal species, each consisting of 1300 images, we separated into 84 species. Of which the majority are birds and a small number of species can fly, about 1300 images each. The total amount of data that we collect and train is more than 100000 images.

3.5   Pre-processing with Histograms of Oriented Gradients (HOG)

The Histogram of Oriented Gradient [13] is a feature used to extract features and remove unhelpful pieces of information by describing the distribution of spatial directions in all image regions. The essence of the HOG method is to exploit the appearance of local objects in the image through fairly good characterization by the distribution of local intensity gradients or edge directions. It will divide the image into small spatial regions, for each region they will calculate a histogram of the gradient magnitude (histogram bin weight/contribution) and the gradient direction [14] in the region. After performing normalization we will get a feature vector that is more invariant [15] for changes in light conditions.

3.6   Split Dataset

About the data used for the training process, we divide the data into three sets including the training set - 60%, validation set - 20%, and testing set 20%.

3.7   Proposed Methods - Classification Model

Our research uses experiments and customizes the hyperparameters to find the best model (Fig. 4).

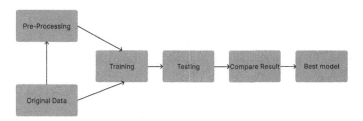

Fig. 4. Process of choosing the best model

The hyperparameters that we have customizes during the training are learning rate 0.001, 3e-4, 3e-5, 3e-6, patience, stop patience, threshold=0.9, dwell=True, momentum=0.99, epsilon=0.001, Dropout(rate=.45, seed=123), kernel_regularizer (l = 0.016), activity_regularizer(0.006), bias_regularizer(0.006), optimizer using Adamax, activation using softmax, batch size are 8, 16, 32, 64, 128, 512, 1024.

The dewell parameter is used for improve the accuracy on each epoch, if the accuracy does not improve on this epoch, the model will use the model weights of the previous epoch.

4   Experiment

4.1   Experiment 1: Classification of the Original Data Set

In this experiment, the model was trained with the original dataset, the hyperparameters selected for establish were as follows: learning rate 0.001, batch_size = 32, threshold

= 0.9, dwell = True, momentum = 0.99, epsilon = 0.001, Dropout(rate = .45, seed = 123), kernel_regularizer (l = 0.016), activity_regularizer(0.006), bias_regularizer(0.006), optimizer uses Adamax, activation uses softmax. The best results in the 100 epochs will be shown in the table below (Table 1 and Figs. 5 and 6).

Table 1. Results of experiment 1

Model	Acc	Loss	Val_acc	Val_loss	Test_Acc	F1-score
Vgg16	0.91	0.21	0.89	0.79	0.89	0.89
DenseNet201	0.94	0.17	0.89	0.43	0.88	0.88
EfficientNetB2	0.99	0.17	0.93	0.49	0.93	0.93

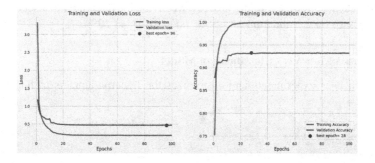

Fig. 5. Comparison of the results of experiment 1

Fig. 6. Confusion matrix on original data, view confusion matrix on github.

4.2   Experiment 2: Classification of the HOG Data Set

In this experiment, the model was trained with a preprocessed dataset using the HOG method as mentioned above, the hyperparameters selected for establish were as follows: learning rate 0.001, batch_size = 32, threshold = 0.9, dwell = True, momentum = 0.99, epsilon = 0.001, Dropout(rate = .45, seed = 123), kernel_regularizer (l = 0.016), activity regularizer(0.006), bias_regularizer(0.006), optimizer using Adamax, activation using softmax. The best results in the 100 epochs will be shown in the table below (Table 2 and Figs. 7 and 8).

Table 2. Results of experiment 2

Model	Acc	Loss	Val_acc	Val_loss	Test_Acc	F1-score
Vgg16	0.67	0.52	0.62	0.63	0.62	0.62
DenseNet201	0.74	0.45	0.68	0.53	0.69	0.69
EfficientNetB2	0.98	0.36	0.81	1.02	0.81	0.81

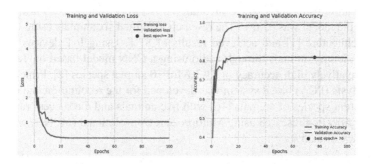

Fig. 7. Comparison of the results of experiment 2

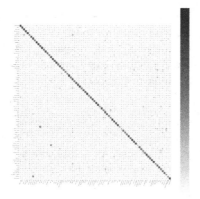

Fig. 8. Confusion matrix on processed data, view confusion matrix on github.

4.3 Evaluation of Test Results

The best results were 93% on the validation set and the testing set after the training process consisted of 100 epochs. During training, we base on the F1 score to decide whether to continue training the model or stop to change the parameters.

Experiment 1 is highly accurate due to the smaller, faster, less complex model, customize with reasonable hyperparameters. Specifically, The EfficientNetB2 model has 8 million parameters compared to the 14.7 million parameters of the VGG16 model and 18.8 million parameters of the DenseNet201 model. In addition, during the training of the dwell parameter promotes the advantage of using the epoch's model weights better than the previous one instead of using the current epoch's model weights.

Experiment 2 has a lower accuracy than experiment 1 due to several reasons: the data we collect includes object and background, so it is easy to confuse them with each other; the implementation of image preprocessing using the HOG method due to the deviation between the object and the background, so the extraction results are not highly accurate. Then continue to train the EfficientNetB2 model with this dataset that will make the training model inefficient.

Besides, our research has higher accuracy than research in the same field as animal classification using the Light Convolutional Network Neuron Network, the top 1 accuracy of the model was 85.6%. The research identified six animals using CNN with VGG16 Architecture [1] and achieved results of 87%. Using IoT devices to collect sounds and identify animals through audio using a CNN model based on TensorFlow achieved a relatively high accuracy of 91.3% for 10 animal species [2]. Principal Component Analysis (PCA) based system was developed for the recognition and classification of different species of animals [16] with five animals and the success rate is 92%. Animal identification research using Multiprocess Convolutional (MPNet) reached the top 1 accuracy of 87.5%.

5   Conclusion

The EfficientNetB2 model we propose is well-trained based on a bird dataset of 84 bird species, from which we can devise measures to better conserve endangered birds. The model is demonstrated through training and comparing with highly complex models such as VGG16 and DenseNet201, shown experimentally 1, with the highest accuracy on the validation set at 93% and the testing set at 93%.

References

1. Khan, S., Singh, S., Almas, S., Razzaque, A.: Animal classification using CNN with VGG-16 architecture. Int. J. Adv. Res. Sci. Commun. Technol. 85–192 (2022). https://doi.org/10.48175/IJARSCT-3240
2. Vithakshana, L.G.C., Samankula, W.G.D.M.: IoT based animal classification system using convolutional neural network. In: 2020 International Research Conference on Smart Computing and Systems Engineering (SCSE), Colombo, Sri Lanka, pp. 90–95, September 2020. https://doi.org/10.1109/SCSE49731.2020.9313018
3. Suryawanshi, S., Jogdande, V., Mane, A.: Animal classification using deep learning. Int. J. Eng. Appl. Sci. Technol. 04(11), 305–307 (2020). https://doi.org/10.33564/IJEAST.2020.v04i11.055
4. Jiang, B., Huang, W., Tu, W., Yang, C.: An animal classification based on light convolutional network neural network. In: 2019 International Conference on Intelligent Computing and its Emerging Applications (ICEA), Tainan, Taiwan, pp. 45–50, August 2019. https://doi.org/10.1109/ICEA.2019.8858309
5. Zeng, P.: Research on similar animal classification based on CNN algorithm. J. Phys. Conf. Ser. 2132(1), 012001 (2021). https://doi.org/10.1088/1742-6596/2132/1/012001
6. Hossain, M.A., Alam Sajib, M.S.: Classification of image using convolutional neural network (CNN). Glob. J. Comput. Sci. Technol. 13–18 (2019). https://doi.org/10.34257/GJCSTDVOL19IS2PG13

7. Bhatt, D., et al.: CNN variants for computer vision: history, architecture, application, challenges and future scope. Electronics **10**(20), 2470 (2021). https://doi.org/10.3390/electronics10202470

8. Tan, M., Le, Q.V.: EfficientNet: rethinking model scaling for convolutional neural networks. arXiv, 11 September 2020. http://arxiv.org/abs/1905.11946

9. Kallipolitis, A., Revelos, K., Maglogiannis, I.: Ensembling EfficientNets for the classification and interpretation of histopathology images. Algorithms **14**(10), 278 (2021). https://doi.org/10.3390/a14100278

10. Jie, Y., et al.: Combined multi-layer feature fusion and edge detection method for distributed photovoltaic power station identification. Energies **13**(24), 6742 (2020). https://doi.org/10.3390/en13246742

11. Hong, K.V., Minh, T.T., Duc, H.L., Nhat, N.T., Hoang, H.L.: 104 fruits classification using transfer learning and DenseNet201 fine-tuning. In: Barolli, L. (eds.) Complex, Intelligent and Software Intensive Systems, vol. 497, pp. 160–170. Springer, Cham (2022). https://doi.org/10.1007/978-3-031-08812-4_16

12. Animal Dataset "Animal Dataset." https://www.kaggle.com/datasets/goelyash/animal-dataset

13. Sancho, C.R., Ahlberg, J., Markuš, N., Salembier, P.: Pedestrian detection using a boosted cascade of histogram of oriented gradients, p. 67 (2014)

14. Kelly, C., Siddiqui, F.M., Bardak, B., Woods, R.: Histogram of oriented gradients front end processing: an FPGA based processor approach. In: 2014 IEEE Workshop on Signal Processing Systems (SiPS), Belfast, United Kingdom, pp. 1–6, October 2014. https://doi.org/10.1109/SiPS.2014.6986093

15. Cheon, M.-K., Lee, W.-J., Hyun, C.-H., Park, M.: Rotation Invariant Histogram of Oriented Gradients. Int. J. Fuzzy Log. Intell. Syst. **11**(4), 293–298 (2011). https://doi.org/10.5391/IJFIS.2011.11.4.293

16. Dandil, E., Polattimur, R.: PCA-based animal classification system. In: 2018 2nd International Symposium on Multidisciplinary Studies and Innovative Technologies (ISMSIT), Ankara, pp. 1–5, October 2018. https://doi.org/10.1109/ISMSIT.2018.8567256

A Session-Based Recommender System for Learning Resources

Nguyen Thai-Nghe[1(✉)] and Pham Hong Sang[2]

[1] Can Tho University, Can Tho, Vietnam
ntnghe@cit.ctu.edu.vn
[2] Tra Vinh Univesity, Tra Vinh, Vietnam

Abstract. Learning resource recommendation systems can help learners find suitable resources (e.g., books, journals, …) for learning and research. In particular, in the context of online learning due to the impact of the COVID-19 pandemic, the learning resource recommendation is very necessary. In this study, we propose using session-based recommendation systems to suggest the learning resources to the learners. Experiments are performed on a learning resource dataset collected at a local university and a public dataset. After preprocessing the data to convert it to session form, the Neural Attentive Session-based Recommendation (NARM) and Recurrent Neural Networks (GRU4Rec) models were used for training, testing, and comparison. The results show that recommending learning resources according to the NARM model is more effective than that of the GRU4Rec model, and thus, using the session-based recommendation system would be a promising approach for learning resource recommendation.

Keywords: Learning resource recommendation · Session-based recommender system · NARM · GRU4Rec

1 Introduction

In the context of online learning due to the impact of the COVID-19 pandemic, learning resource recommendation systems can help learners find suitable resources (e.g., books, journals, …) for learning and research. Thus, the learning resource recommendation is very necessary [2].

For recommending learning resources/books, several works have been done [5]. However, most of them have used the collaborative filtering approach. Reading books or news is a sequence of actions where the next action would be dependent on the previous actions. This context is probably matched with the idea of session-based recommendation systems [1] where the task is to predict the user's next behavior based on the user's behavior sequence, without relying on any user profile information.

This study will propose an approach for learning resources (e.g. books) recommendation using Session-Based Recommendation System (SBRS) techniques to suggest the learning resources to the learners. Based on the user's reading sessions, the system can introduce relevant documents to the users, thus, helping the users find appropriate documents of their interest.

2   Related Work

There are several works on the topic of using recommender systems for learning resources (books, articles, etc.). In [2], the authors presented a deep matrix factorization model extended from standard matrix decomposition to recommend learning resources based on learners' abilities and requirements. Experiments have revealed promising results compared to the baselines. The authors in [3] proposed an effective system for recommending books for online users that rated a book using the clustering method and then found a similarity of that book to suggest a new book. They used the K-means to find the similarity between the books. Their result concludes that recommendations, based on a particular book, are more accurately effective than a user-based recommendation system.

In the work of [4], the authors described an effective hybrid technique for book recommendation with the use of Ontology for user profiling to increase system efficiency. Other works can be found in [5] which presented a survey of recommender systems in the domain of books. The authors have categorized the systems into six classes and highlighted the main trends, issues, evaluation approaches, and datasets. In addition, [6] presents a review of SBRSs by exploring in depth the SBRS sessions, behaviours, and their properties. The authors propose a general problem statement of SBRSs, summarize the diversified data characteristics and challenges of SBRSs, and define a taxonomy to categorize the representative SBRS research. They also discuss new research opportunities in this exciting and vibrant area.

In [8], the authors proposed a deep learning model for news recommender systems. This architecture is composed of two modules, the first responsible to learn news articles representations, based on their text and metadata, and the second module aimed to provide session-based recommendations using Recurrent Neural Networks. Experiments obtained a significant relative improvement in top-n accuracy and ranking metrics. Other works can be found in [10, 11].

In this study, we propose using techniques in session-based recommendation systems to suggest the learning resources (e.g., books) to the learners.

3   Proposed Method

3.1   Problem Statement

On the websites of libraries or learning resource centers, when users need to search for documents for study and research, they select the documents according to their requirements by clicking and viewing. The information about a user's document click constitutes a session sequence. The system will store the entire process of selecting documents and session data. Based on history sessions, the system can predict documents that might be suitable for the next time click or read.

Figure 1 is an example of user A's book selection history. What will the system recommend to user A next? To solve this problem, the author will consider user A's recent browsing history as a session. Formally, a session consists of many user interactions that occur together over a continuous or recent period. The goal is to predict the next documents from user A's interactive session.

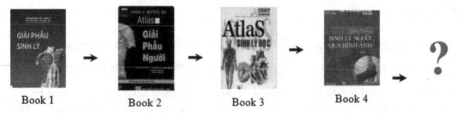

| Book 1 | Book 2 | Book 3 | Book 4 |

Fig. 1. Based on the browsing/reading history of user A, the model will predict the next book that the user may choose

3.2 Proposed Model

As presented above, we would like to predict a list of documents that the user is likely to click or select during the browsing process. To do this, we need to save the browsing sessions of all users to the system. These browsing sessions are stored in chronological order of documents clicked, embedding these sessions in the data set to perform the training. The proposed model is presented in Fig. 2.

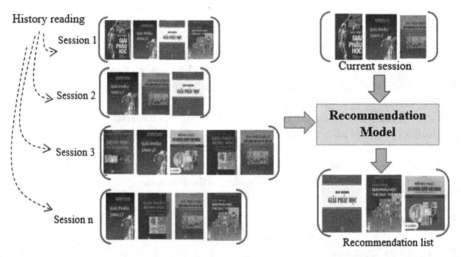

Fig. 2. Proposed book recommendation model using the session-based approach

We propose using the Neural Attentive Session-based Recommendation model (NARM) [1] to train and predict the session data for learning resources (e.g. book) recommendation. The architecture of the NARM model is presented in Fig. 3, where $x = [x_1, x_2 \ldots, x_{t-1}, x_t]$ is a session including input items by a user and $y = [y_1, y_2 \ldots, y_m]$ is the prediction items.

$$\mathbf{y} = [y_1, y_2, ..., y_{m-1}, y_m]$$

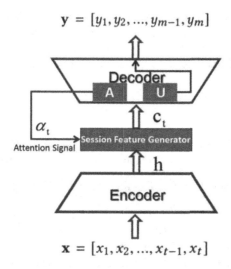

Fig. 3. Using the NARM model [1] for learning resources recommendation

4 Experiments

4.1 Datasets for Experiment

Dataset 1. The first dataset was collected from borrowed books at the Learning Resource Center of Tra Vinh University, Vietnam. These loan histories recorded transactions for each user, the information of the documents, and how long the documents were borrowed in each transaction. The transactions are sequentially borrowed/read by the users. After pre-processing, this dataset has 98614 records and 5 attributes including:

- Session ID: Identifier of the session (session)
- Datetime: Date of the event click/read
- Timestamp: Time of the event click/read
- Item ID: Identifier of the document
- Category: Group of documents list

In this dataset, we consider a session as the user's full borrowing/reading history (all documents read/borrowed in each transaction) in the dataset. For a sequence containing n interactions, we use the first $(n - 1)$ items in that sequence for the training set and the nth item for the test set.

This dataset was filtered out all the itemIds which are less than 3 occurrences and filtered out the sessions with less than 2 itemIds. The input to the model is a list of $(n - 1)$ itemIds in the past, and the prediction is the itemId of the (n) position.

Dataset 2. We also used another dataset which is the YOOCHOOSE[1] for evaluation and comparison. This dataset contains a collection of sessions from a retailer, where each session is encapsulating the click events that the user performed in the session. However, this dataset is too big, so we just selected the first quarter of it.

4.2 Evaluation Methods

In this work, we used the Recall and the Mean Reciprocal Rank (MRR) for evaluating the accuracy of the model [9]. They are calculated as in the following

$$Recall = \frac{number\ of\ correct\ recommended\ learning\ resource}{Number\ of\ selected\ learning\ resources\ by\ the\ user}$$

For example, if the Recall@20 = 10%, it means that if the model is applied to suggest 20 books to the users, the probability that they will click/select those books is 10%.

On the other hand, the MRR index is used to evaluate the ranking position. The MRR is an indicator of ranking awareness. It indicates the ranking position in the suggested list to the user. The smaller its position, the higher the accuracy. MMR@k is the inversed position (rank) of the first relevant document among the first k documents. Therefore, the larger the MRR@k, the better the model quality. MRR is calculated as in the following

$$MRR = \frac{1}{|Q|} \sum_{i=1}^{|Q|} \frac{1}{rank_i}$$

where Q is the query document and $rank_i$ refers to the ranking position of the first relevant document for the ith query.

4.3 Experimental Results

We have also used another session-recommended model to evaluate and compare the model which is the session-based recommendations with Recurrent Neural Networks (GRU4Rec) [7].

---

[1] https://www.kaggle.com/datasets/chadgostopp/recsys-challenge-2015.

Figures 4 and 5 present the experimental results on dataset 1 using the Recall and MRR indicators. On this session dataset, results show that the NARM model has better accuracy than the GRU4Rec for the book recommendation.

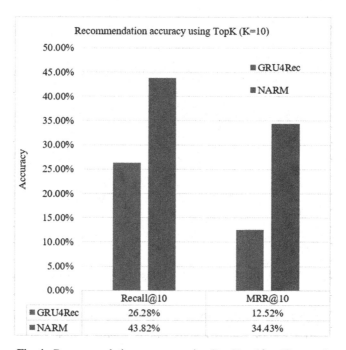

Fig. 4. Recommendation accuracy using Top K = 10 on Dataset 1

Table 1 presents the experimental results on both datasets. This shows that the session-based document recommendation method using the NARM model brings higher accuracy than the GRU4Rec model. The measure of Recall and MRR is still not high on dataset1 since this dataset is a bit small thus it has not had enough data for the model to learn. However, when the application is put into practice with a larger number of stored sessions, the accuracy would be higher. Having more data, we believe that the proposed approach can be applied in practice.

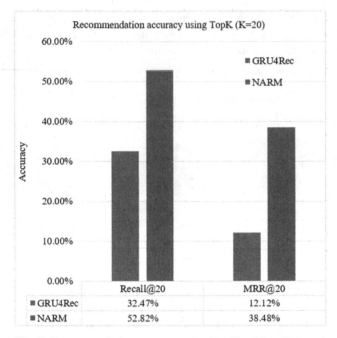

Fig. 5. Recommendation accuracy using Top K = 20 on Dataset 1

Table 1. Recommendation accuracy using Top K = 20 on Dataset 1 and Dataset 2

Model	Dataset 1		Dataset 2	
	Recall@20	MRR@20	Recall@20	MRR@20
GRU4Rec	32.47%	12.12%	59.53%	22.60%
NARM	**52.82%**	**38.48%**	**69.73%**	**29.23%**

5   Conclusion

This work proposes using session-based recommendation systems to recommend the learning resources to the learners. Experiments are performed on a learning resource dataset collected at a local university and a public dataset. After preprocessing the data to convert it to session form, the Neural Attentive Session-based Recommendation (NARM) was used for training, testing, and comparison. Experimental results show that recommending learning resources according to the NARM model is more effective than that of the GRU4Rec model, and thus, using the session-based recommendation system would be a promising approach for learning resource recommendation.

We will continue to collect the data and retrain the model for accuracy improvement.

References

1. Li, J., Ren, P., Chen, Z., Ren, Z., Ma, J.: Neural attentive session-based recommendation. arXiv e-prints, arXiv:1711.04725, November 2017
2. Dien, T.T., Thanh-Hai, N., Thai-Nghe, N.: An approach for learning resource recommendation using deep matrix factorization. J. Inf. Telecommun. (2022). https://doi.org/10.1080/247 51839.2022.2058250
3. Sarma, D., Mittra, T., Hossain, M.S.: Personalized book recommendation system using machine learning algorithm. Int. J. Adv. Comput. Sci. Appl. (IJACSA) 12(1) (2021). https:// doi.org/10.14569/IJACSA.2021.0120126
4. Chandak, M., Girase, S., Mukhopadhyay, D.: Introducing hybrid technique for optimization of book recommender system. Procedia Comput. Sci. 45, 23–31 (2015). https://doi.org/10. 1016/j.procs.2015.03.075
5. Alharthi, H., Inkpen, D., Szpakowicz, S.: A survey of book recommender systems. J. Intell. Inf. Syst. 51(1), 139–160 (2017). https://doi.org/10.1007/s10844-017-0489-9
6. Wang, S., Cao, L., Wang, Y., Sheng, Q.Z., Orgun, M.A., Lian, D.: A survey on session-based recommender systems. ACM Comput. Surv. 54, 7 (2021). https://doi.org/10.1145/3465401. Article 154, 38 pages
7. Hidasi, B., Karatzoglou, A., Baltrunas, L., Tikk, D.: Session-based recommendations with recurrent neural networks. arXiv (2015)
8. de Souza Pereira Moreira, G., Ferreira, F., da Cunha, A.M.: News session-based recommendations using deep neural networks. In: Proceedings of the 3rd Workshop on Deep Learning for Recommender Systems. ACM (2018). https://doi.org/10.1145/3270323.3270328
9. Ludewig, M., Jannach, D.: Evaluation of session-based recommendation algorithms. User Model. User Adap. Inter. 28(4–5), 331–390 (2018). https://doi.org/10.1007/s11257-018-9209-6
10. Hidasi, B., Karatzoglou, A.: Recurrent neural networks with top-k gains for session-based recommendations. In: Proceedings of the 27th ACM International Conference on Information and Knowledge Management. ACM (2018)
11. Quadrana, M., Karatzoglou, A., Hidasi, B., Cremonesi, P.: Personalizing session-based recommendations with hierarchical recurrent neural networks. In: Proceedings of the Eleventh ACM Conference on Recommender Systems (RecSys 2017), pp. 130–137. Association for Computing Machinery, New York (2017). https://doi.org/10.1145/3109859.3109896

A Drowsiness Detection System Based on Eye Landmarks Using IoT

Khang Nhut Lam[1](✉), Vinh Phuoc Mai[1], Gia-Binh Quach Dang[1],
Quoc-Bao Hong Ngo[1], Nhat-Hao Quan Huynh[1], Mai Phuc Lieu[1],
and Jugal Kalita[2]

[1] Can Tho University, Can Tho, Vietnam
lnkhang@ctu.edu.vn
[2] University of Colorado, Colorado Springs, USA
jkalita@uccs.edu

Abstract. Drowsiness is one of the major causes of traffic accidents. This paper presents a simple and effective drowsiness detection system using IoT by locating the eyes from driving images and detecting drowsiness based on the eye aspect ratio obtained from the eye landmarks extracted. We conduct experiments under a variety of circumstances, such as adjusting the distance between the driver and the camera, wearing different accessories, and varying the driver's head movement. Our system can detect eye landmarks well even when the driver covers most of his face with a mask and glasses or a hat and glasses.

Keywords: Drowsiness detection · Eye landmark detection · Facial recognition · IoT

1 Introduction

Driving in an abnormal state, such as being sleepy, tired, or having alcohol concentration above the legal limit, can result in accidents, personal injuries, and property damage. With the explosive development of technology in recent years, several studies have been carried out to detect abnormal states of drivers and provide alerts. Alcohol concentration is usually measured using alcohol detection sensors [5], or a combination of breath-based and touch-based sensors to measure the alcohol and carbon dioxide CO_2 levels, and the chemical properties on the skin [19], respectively. Most existing methods for drowsiness detection observe the action of drivers by tracking their eyes [10,11], measuring the curves of eyelids [18], analyzing the mouth and yawns [1,12,14], recognizing facial expressions [2,7,8], and movement of their heads [16,17]. Car manufacturers have launched driver assistance systems, such as Driver Attention Monitor of Honda and Driver Alert System of Ford. The Attention Assist of Mercedes-Benz helps identify drowsiness by analyzing driving style, road conditions, and crosswinds. This assistant is activated at the speed range from 60 km/h to 200 km/h,

This study is funded in part by the Can Tho University, Code: THS2020-65.

T. K. Dang et al. (Eds.): FDSE 2022, CCIS 1688, pp. 714–722, 2022.
https://doi.org/10.1007/978-981-19-8069-5_52

and after 30 min of continuous driving[1]. Some alert devices for driving safely are the Anti-Sleep Alarm of StopSleep[2], Fatigue Driving Warning device of Mascot, and LGI Driver Fatigue Alarm.

Our goal is to integrate a facial recognition model, an eye landmark detection model, to build a drowsiness prediction model on Raspberry devices and Django server. We conduct experiments under various circumstances, including changing the distance between the driver and the camera, wearing different accessories, and varying the driver's head movement. The rest of this paper is as follows. Section 2 describes the drowsiness detection system. Experiments and discussion are presented in Sect. 3. The study is concluded in Sect. 4.

2   Drowsiness Detection System

This section presents the drowsiness detection system, which includes the overall system, the architecture of the drowsiness detection system and the application.

2.1   Facial Landmark and Drowsiness Detection Models

The drowsiness detection system consists of a facial landmark recognition model, and a drowsiness prediction model, as presented in Fig. 1. Overall, an image of a driver is fed to the face detector to detect face, which is then fed to the facial landmark detection model to locate the facial landmarks on the image. Then, the drowsiness detection model determines whether or not drowsiness sign is present on the facial landmarks extracted. The model provides alerts to the driver if it cannot locate the driver's face, or if drowsiness is detected.

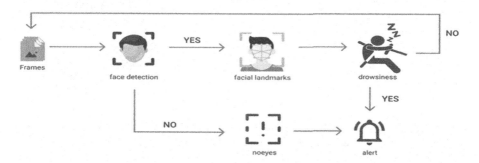

Fig. 1. The overall system with facial landmark and drowsiness detection models.

In particular, the given images are converted to gray-scale with a size of 500×500 pixels. Then, the dlib[3] library with Histogram of Oriented Gradients and a linear SVM face detector is used to recognize faces in images. Next, the

---

[1]   https://www.mersec.net/115/attention_assist.html.

[2]   https://www.stopsleep.co.uk/.

[3]   http://dlib.net/.

Ensemble of Regression Trees algorithm [9] is used to detect facial landmarks. If signs of drowsiness are detected from the facial landmarks extracted, the system triggers a series of alert activities to the driver consisting of making auditory alerts, displaying messages, and recording a series of driving images.

We perform experiments on 11,511 labeled images of the iBUG 300-W dataset [13], including 85% for training and 15% for testing, to identify 68 points of a facial landmark. Each point is labeled with a pair (x, y) of coordinates on a face contour. We observe that some drivers, especially female drivers in Vietnam, can wear masks while driving to protect their health or skin on sunny days. We also observe that the drowsiness of human which mainly manifests at the eyes. Therefore, we focus on the landmark locations of eyes, which are labeled from 37 to 42 for the left eye and from 43 to 48 for the right eye. The Eye Aspect Ratio (EAR) [4] is obtained on the landmarks of eyes to detect drowsiness:

$$EAR = \frac{||p_2 - p_6|| + ||p_3 - p_5||}{2 \times ||p_1 - p_4||}, \tag{1}$$

where p_i is represented in on the right side of Fig. 2. Soukupová and Čech [4] state that a closed eye has an EAR value near zero, whereas an open eye has an EAR value around 0.25. To provide timely and meaningful alerts, if the EAR value is less than a threshold (which is 0.15 in our experiments), our system considers this eye is not in a normal state. In addition, to avoid being sidetracked by blinking, we observe a collection of consecutive frames with EAR values less than a threshold to determine if a driver is drowsy.

Fig. 2. The 68 points of a facial landmark from iBUG300-W (left side), an open eye landmark (top right), and a closed eye landmark (bottom right) [4].

2.2   The Architecture of the Drowsiness Detection System

The drowsiness detection system follows the client-server architecture. Each client is installed on a specific vehicle. To analyze data and provide timely sound alerts, the data need to be transmitted between the client and the server in real-time. In our system, the Raspberry Pi 3 B+[4] is the main processing circuit.

---

[4] https://www.raspberrypi.com/products/raspberry-pi-3-model-b-plus/.

This device provides wireless connection and plays the primary communication role in sending requests and receiving responses between the server and the client. In addition, the Raspberry Pi Camera Module V2[5] is used to collect driving images of drivers, which are inputs for the facial landmark and drowsiness detection models.

The next step is to integrate the facial recognition model, the facial landmark detection model, and the drowsiness detection model into the Raspberry devices and Django server to create the final drowsiness detection system, as shown in Fig. 3. The Raspberry Pi is responsible for collecting driving images, which are inputs of the prediction model to detect drowsiness. When a drowsiness state is detected, images captured while driving are saved by the Raspberry Pi. A shared room is established between the Raspberry Pi and the Django server in order to communicate in real time. The information exchanged are as follows.

- Raspberry Pi sends signal online/offline,
- Raspberry Pi sends time and signal of drowsiness detected,
- Raspberry Pi sends and receives images on requests, and
- The server establishes a connection to Raspberry Pi.

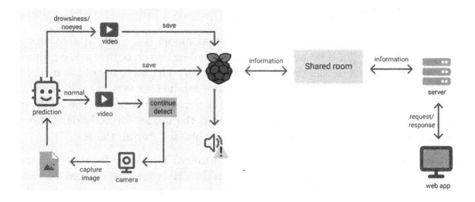

Fig. 3. The architecture of the drowsiness detection system.

2.3   Drowsiness Detection Application

The client is installed on a specific vehicle with a unique registration number, and has a unique identity (ID) and a password to log in. When the vehicle moves, the system generates a trip card comprising basic information about the journey, such as depart time, vehicle name, registration number, equipment status (inactive or active). The system updates the driver's state based on the drowsiness detection results (a normal state or a drowsiness state) as well as some other information, such as the duration of driving and time of driving.

---

[5] https://ecadio.com/jual-modul-camera-raspberry-pi.

If a state of drowsiness is detected, the system creates an audible alert, displays a message, and starts recording a sequence of images of the driver while driving. That driver can view images recorded and provide feedback. If the driver confirms that these images show normal state, the system records it and does not perform any drowsiness warning action; otherwise, the system saves all images and generates continuous display and audible alerts. In short, the system recognizes the face and detects eyes of the driver to predict drowsiness. A driver may be in one of the two following states:

- Normal state: The system is able to recognize the face and the eyes of the driver, and the EAR values of eyes are greater than or equal to a threshold. The system performs nothing special.
- Drowsy state: A driver is considered in a drowsy state if one of these following condition happens. (i) The system is able to recognize the face and the eyes of the driver, and the EAR values of eyes are less than a threshold. (ii) The system is unable to recognize the face or the eyes of the driver. It is possible that the driver is not focusing on driving. If the system determines that the driver is in a drowsy state, it performs actions as discussed above.

3   Experimental Results

First, we evaluate the eye landmark detection model using the 10-fold cross-validation method [3]. The average Mean Absolute Error between the ground truth and landmarks on the predicted eyes is 7.107. The accuracy of the model's prediction is quite high, about 92%. Besides, we conduct some tests under various conditions to evaluate the model. Each test is performed 3 times. The result in each case is ratio of the number of frames that the model correctly detects eye landmarks out of the total number of frames obtained during the test.

Distance between the Driver and the Camera: The driver faces the camera for 1–2 min. We change the distance between the driver and the camera for each case of testing as presented in Table 1. The results show that the model works well when the distance between the driver and the camera is less than or equal to

Table 1. Evaluating the impact of the distance between the driver and the camera on the eye landmark detection model.

Distance	1st test	2nd test	3rd test
0.2 m	1,869/1,869 (100%)	1,293/1,293 (100%)	1,583/1,583 (100%)
0.4 m	1,560/1,560 (100%)	1,328/1,328 (100%)	1,195/1,195 (100%)
0.6 m	1,361/1,361 (100%)	1,102/1,102 (100%)	1,920/1,920 (100%)
1.0 m	1,161/1,170 (92.23%)	1,373/1,373 (100%)	1,247/1,253 (99.52%)
1.2 m	6/1,312 (0.46%)	9/1,104 (0.82%)	1/1,695 (0.06%)

0.6m, which matches well the usual distance between the driver and the steering wheel, around 0.3 m (∼12 inches) [15] or at least 0.25 m (∼10 in.)[6].

Wearing Accessories: The driver wears accessories such as a mask, a hat, and glasses. The driver sits in front of the camera within a distance of 0.6 m for 1–2 min. We change the accessories for each case of testing, as presented in Table 2. The "glasses" and "hats" in these experiments are clear glasses and sun hats, respectively.

Table 2. Evaluating the impact of accessories on the eye landmark detection model.

Accessories	1st test	2nd test	3rd test
No accessories	900/900 (100%)	1,073/1,073 (100%)	996/996 (100%)
Mask	1,120/1,227 (91.28%)	860/926 (92.87%)	1,609/1,714 (93.87%)
Hat	913/993 (91.94%)	1,513/1,531 (97.58%)	59/1,981 (97.02%)
Glasses	1,001/1,002 (99.90%)	1,114/1,114 (100%)	1,400/1,400 (100%)
Glasses and mask	848/931 (91.08%)	1,212/1,267 (95.66%)	1,293/1,318 (98.10%)
Hat and glasses	922/985 (93.60%)	919/1,011 (90.90%)	1,640/1,746 (93.93%)
Hat, mask, and glasses	433/2,666 (16.24%)	264/1,820 (14.51%)	251/1,452 (17.28%)

The model detects eye landmarks well even if the driver wears a hat, a mask, or clear glasses. If the driver wears a mask and clear glasses, the eye landmarks are also correctly detected. The model cannot detect eyes when the driver wears sunglasses or dark glasses. In addition, wearing a hat, a mask and glasses at the same time may hide most of features of the driver's face. As a result, the model can detect faces and eye landmarks correctly only in about 15% of the total frames in such a case. Some images of a user wearing accessories with high coverage is shown in Fig. 4.

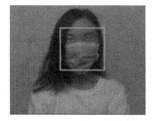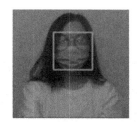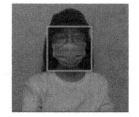

Fig. 4. A user wearing accessories with high coverage: wearing a mask (left side); wearing a mask and glasses (middle); wearing a mask, a hat and glasses (right side).

---

[6] https://thriv.virginia.edu/researchers-find-optimal-distance-to-sit-from-steering-wheel-to-stay-safe-in-crashes/.

Head Movement: The driver wears glasses, faces the camera within a distance of 0.6m for 1–2 minutes, and moves his/her head. For each test, the driver changes the face angle by tilting the head, as presented in Table 3. The face angle of the driver significantly affects the results of this eye landmark detection model. Through experimental observations, sometimes the model detects the bounding box around the face correctly, but it cannot locate the eyes well, and can deviate quite a bit from reality.

Table 3. Evaluating the impact of driver's face angle on the eye landmark detection model.

Description	1st test	2nd test	3rd test
Face the camera	1,160/1,160 (100%)	1,224/1,224 (100%)	1,187/1,187 (100%)
Tilt left/right	515/1,084 (47.51%)	784/1,472 (53.26%)	9,32/1,669 (55.84%)
Face angle 1/4	882/1,076 (81.97%)	1,050/1,358 (77.32%)	1028/1,166 (88.16%)
Face angle 1/3	402/1,439 (27.93%)	629/1,480 (42.50%)	895/1,947 (45.97%)
Face angle 1/2	17/1,920 (0.89%)	21/1,937 (1.08%)	0/1,463 (0.00%)
Look up	314/1,496 (20.99%)	168/1,278 (13.15%)	105/1,151 (9.12%)
Look down	0/1,297 (0.00%)	11/1,736 (0.63%)	24/1,279 (1.88%)

Table 4. Evaluation results of the drowsiness detection model.

k	Predicted	Ground truth		Precision	Recall
		Drowsiness	Normal		
0	Drowsiness	26	7	0.788	0.500
	Normal	26	53		
1	Drowsiness	36	7	0.837	0.692
	Normal	16	53		
2	Drowsiness	40	8	0.833	0.769
	Normal	12	52		
3	Drowsiness	30	7	0.811	0.577
	Normal	22	53		
4	Drowsiness	36	10	0.783	0.692
	Normal	16	50		
Average				0.810	0.646

Based on the experimental results of the impact of different conditions on the eye landmark detection model, we recommend installing the Raspberry Pi Camera facing the driver's face within a distance around 0.6 m.

Table 5. The number of frames in videos that the system detected correctly.

Test case	Time (in second)	Total frames	Frames with drowsiness detected correctly
1	167,46671	2,252	1,689(75,00%)
2	111,19010	1,456	861 (59,13%)
3	195,97789	2,638	1,693 (64,18%)
4	505,82991	6,746	2,813 (41,70%)
5	172,26528	2,216	1,635 (73,78%)

Next, the drowsiness detection system is evaluated on the UTA Real-Life Drowsiness dataset[7] [6], including 180 videos assigned labels of "alertness", "low vigilance", or "drowsiness". Our goal is to detect drowsiness; therefore, we evaluate the drowsiness detection model on a set of 112 videos with labels of "alert" and "drowsiness" from this dataset, consisting of 52 drowsy driving videos and 60 normal (or alertness) driving videos. The drowsiness detection model receives a video and predicts drowsiness in that video. We also evaluate the model using the k-fold method, $k = 5$. Table 4 presents precision and recall of the drowsiness detection model. The number of frames in videos that the drowsiness detection system detects correctly is shown in Table 5. The precision of the drowsiness detection system based on EAR values is about 62.76%.

4   Conclusion

We have constructed a simple and cheap drowsiness detection system for drivers based on IoT. Currently, we are experimenting with neural network approaches to improve the detection model. For future work, we will integrate an alcohol sensor Module-MQ3 into the system to measure the alcohol concentrations of drivers. In addition, an eye detection model and a drowsiness detection model based on deep learning methods will be used to increase the accuracy of the detection models. A reinforcement learning method will also be considered to improve the models. Besides, the system should have an optional function to automatically send a warning message to a registered phone number, which is different from the phone number of the driver, so that there is someone to assist the driver immediately.

References

1. Abtahi, S., Hariri, B., Shirmohammadi, S.: Driver drowsiness monitoring based on yawning detection. In: 2011 IEEE International Instrumentation and Measurement Technology Conference, pp. 1–4. IEEE (2011)
2. Assari, M.A., Rahmati, M.: Driver drowsiness detection using face expression recognition. In: 2011 IEEE International Conference on Signal and Image Processing Applications (ICSIPA), pp. 337–341. IEEE (2011)

---

[7] https://sites.google.com/view/utarldd/home.

3. Browne, M.W.: Cross-validation methods. J. Math. Psychol. **44**(1), 108–132 (2000)
4. Cech, J., Soukupova, T.: Real-time eye blink detection using facial landmarks. Cent. Mach. Perception, Dep. Cybern. Fac. Electr. Eng. Czech Tech. Univ. Prague 1–8 (2016)
5. Charniya, N.N., Nair, V.R.: Drunk driving and drowsiness detection. In: 2017 International Conference on Intelligent Computing and Control (I2C2), pp. 1–6. IEEE (2017)
6. Ghoddoosian, R., Galib, M., Athitsos, V.: A realistic dataset and baseline temporal model for early drowsiness detection. In: Proceedings of the IEEE/CVF Conference on Computer Vision and Pattern Recognition Workshops, pp. 178–187 (2019)
7. Jeong, M., Ko, B.C.: Driver's facial expression recognition in real-time for safe driving. Sensors **18**(12), 4270 (2018)
8. Kavitha, K., Lakshmi, S.V., Reddy, P.B.K., Reddy, N.S., Chandrasekhar, P., Sisindri, Y.: Driver drowsiness detection using face expression recognition. Ann. Rom. Soc. Cell Biol. **25**, 2785–2789 (2021)
9. Kazemi, V., Sullivan, J.: One millisecond face alignment with an ensemble of regression trees. In: Proceedings of the IEEE Conference on Computer Vision and Pattern Recognition, pp. 1867–1874 (2014)
10. Klaib, A.F., Alsrehin, N.O., Melhem, W.Y., Bashtawi, H.O., Magableh, A.A.: Eye tracking algorithms, techniques, tools, and applications with an emphasis on machine learning and internet of things technologies. Exp. Syst. Appl. **166**, 114037 (2021)
11. Nguyen, T., Chew, M.T., Demidenko, S.: Eye tracking system to detect driver drowsiness. In: 2015 6th International Conference on Automation, Robotics and Applications (ICARA), pp. 472–477. IEEE (2015)
12. Omidyeganeh, M., et al.: Yawning detection using embedded smart cameras. IEEE Trans. Instrum. Measur. **65**(3), 570–582 (2016)
13. Sagonas, C., Tzimiropoulos, G., Zafeiriou, S., Pantic, M.: A semi-automatic methodology for facial landmark annotation. In: Proceedings of the IEEE Conference on Computer Vision and Pattern Recognition Workshops, pp. 896–903 (2013)
14. Saradadevi, M., Bajaj, P.: Driver fatigue detection using mouth and yawning analysis. Int. J. Comput. Sci. Netw. Secur. **8**(6), 183–188 (2008)
15. Segui-Gomez, M., Levy, J., Roman, H., Thompson, K.M., McCabe, K., Graham, J.D.: Driver distance from the steering wheel: perception and objective measurement. Am. J. Public Health **89**(7), 1109–1111 (1999)
16. Son, N.M., Van Binh, N., Lam, N.N.: Designing driver drowsiness detection system. Sci. Technol. Dev. J. Nat. Sci. **2**(6), 23–31 (2018)
17. Teyeb, I., Jemai, O., Zaied, M., Amar, C.B.: A novel approach for drowsy driver detection using head posture estimation and eyes recognition system based on wavelet network. In: IISA 2014, The 5th International Conference on Information, Intelligence, Systems and Applications, pp. 379–384. IEEE (2014)
18. Truong, D.Q., Nguyen, Q.D.: Driver drowsiness detection system. Can Tho Univ. J. Sci. **2015**, 160–167 (2015)
19. Willis, M., et al.: Driver alcohol detection system for safety (DADSS)-pilot field operational tests (PFOT) vehicle instrumentation and integration of DADSS technology. In: 26th International Technical Conference on the Enhanced Safety of Vehicles (ESV): Technology: Enabling a Safer TomorrowNational Highway Traffic Safety Administration, No. 19–0262 (2019)

A Novel Approach for Vietnamese Speech Recognition Using Conformer

Nguyen Van Anh Tuan, Nguyen Thi Thanh Hoa, Nguyen Thanh Dat,
Pham Minh Tuan, Dao Duy Truong, and Dang Thi Phuc[✉]

Faculty of Information Technology, Industrial University of Ho Chi Minh City,
Ho Chi Minh City, Vietnam
phucdt@iuh.edu.vn

Abstract. Research on speech recognition has existed for a long time, but there is very little research on applying deep learning to Vietnamese language speech recognition. In this paper, we solve the Vietnamese speech recognition problem by deep learning speech recognition frameworks including CTC and Joint CTC/Attention combined with encoder architectures Conformer. Experimental results achieved moderate accuracy using over 115 h of training data of VLSP and Vivos. Compared with the other models, the training results show that the Conformer model trained on CTC achieved good results with a WER value of 20%. Training on big data gives remarkable results and is the basis for us to continue improving the model and increasing accuracy in the future.

Keywords: Deep learning · CTC Joint CTC/Attention · Conformer · Vietnamese speech recognition

1 Introduction

Automatic Speech Recognition is a problem that helps machines understand human speech. In principle, this technique using AI model to automatically recognize and convert to string form of characters or words which is mostly close to the voice segment. Speech recognition is a long-standing problem. Models for this purpose have been developed from Hidden Markov Model (HMM), incorporating Gaussian Mixture Model (GMM), Deep Neural Network (DNN) until end-to- end speech recognition system using deep learning only. [1]. The recognition results have been gradually improved from a hybrid system to end-to-end systems. An end-to-end speech recognition system is important to align the audio feature with the label sequence. Nowadays, there are alignment methods that achieve good results such as Connectionist Temporal Classification (CTC) [2], Attention-based Encoder-Decoder (AED) [3], Recurrent Neural Network Transducer (RNN-Transducer) [4] or a combination of both CTC and AED is Joint CTC/Attention [5]. These architectures have achieved good results in speech recognition with non-Vietnamese data sets such as Deep Speech 2 using CTC [6], Listen Attend and Spell using AED [3], ContextNet and Conformer with RNN-T [7,8]. In the above end-to-end systems, the important part is the encoder

T. K. Dang et al. (Eds.): FDSE 2022, CCIS 1688, pp. 723–730, 2022.
https://doi.org/10.1007/978-981-19-8069-5_53

and decoder architectures to make up the internals of the end-to-end systems. In which, LSTM [2,3,11] VGG [9], Transformer [10], and Conformer [8] are often used for encoder and LSTM [5] Transformer [10] for decoder. There are also some studies on applying the end-to-end system and achieving positive results for Vietnamese Speech Recognition. The paper [12] applies LSTM and Time Delay Deep Neural Network (TDNN) using the CTC model and was evaluated on VLSP 2018 dataset 2 h and FPT 20 h, trained on 2036 h hours of speech data with WER results on TDNN + The LSTM is 0.971 on the VLSP 2018 dataset and 0.1441 on the FPT dataset both using a 3-gram language model trained on a large amount of text data. Vais [13] studied a speech recognition system that combines HMM-DNN with a language model trained on labeled sciencific articles and conversations, with the best result being 0.0485 WER on our test set. VLSP 2018 and 0.1509 on VLSP 2019, but this system is a hybrid speech recognition system but have not yet applied to end-to-end system.

In this paper, we present end-to-end speech recognition systems combined with different encoders and decoders trained on the VLSP 2019 100 h and Vivos 15 h datasets (it means we use 115 h of training data in total) and evaluate using 0.45h of data from Vivos dataset. Section 2 covers the methods used including the end-to-end systems and encoder architectures. Section 3 presents the experiment setup and results of training the models. Section 4 summarizes and suggests a future research direction. The source code of ASR Toolkit is located at this link: https://github.com/tuanio/asr-toolkit.

2   Research Methods

2.1   Conformer

Recently, models based on Transformer and Convolution Neural Network (CNN) have shown results in speech recognition that are superior to those using Recurrent Neural Network (RNN). The Transformer [10] architecture has an excellent global information capture capability because of a self-attention mechanism, while CNN has a good local information capture capability by using convolution. Recent studies have shown that combining convolution and self-attention helps the model capture both types of information effectively, improving performance significantly compared to using each part individually.

In the paper [8], the authors proposed an architecture that combines self-attention and convolution, and its name is Conformer (convolution-augmented transformer). This deep learning architecture achieved the most advanced results in the LibriSpeech evaluation dataset in 2020. A conformer block consists of four modules stacked on top of each other: the first will be a feed-forward, followed by a self-attention module, a convolution module, and finally, a feed-forward module. Figure 1 shows the Conformer single-encoder architecture.

Multi-headed Self-Attention Module: The relative positional encoding allows the self-attention module better generalizing on different input lengths. Thus, the Conformer encoder can work better on the variance of the utterance length.

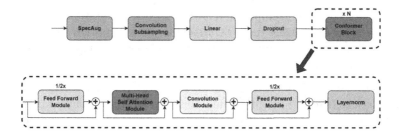

Fig. 1. Conformer encoder architecture

Convolution Module: The convolution module contains a pointwise convolution with an expansion factor of 2, projecting the number of channels with a GLU activation layer, followed by a 1-D depth-wise convolution. The 1-D depth-wise convolution is followed by a Batchnorm and then a swish activation layer.

Feed Forward Module: Feed-forward architecture in Conformer Block adopts feed-forward architecture in Transformer [10], which structure is also adopted by Transformer ASR models [14,15]. The Feed-Forward module applies layer normalization on the input before the first linear layer. We also use swish activation and dropout, which helps regularize the network. Instead of a single feed-forward module post the attention blocks as in the Transformer models, the Conformer block has a pair of macaron-like feed-forward modules sandwiching the self-attention and convolution modules [8].

Conformer Block: The conformer comprises two macaron-like feed-forward layers with half-step residual connections sandwiching the multi-headed self-attention and convolution modules followed by a post-layer norm. Mathematically, for each of the conformer blocks, we will get as follows:

$$\tilde{\mathbf{x}}_{\mathbf{i}} = x_i + \frac{1}{2}FFN(x_i) \tag{1}$$

$$x'_i = \tilde{\mathbf{x}}_{\mathbf{i}} + MHSA(\tilde{\mathbf{x}}_{\mathbf{i}}) \tag{2}$$

$$x''_i = x'_i + Conv(x'_i) \tag{3}$$

$$y_i = Layernorm(x''_i + \frac{1}{2}FFN(x''_i)) \tag{4}$$

2.2 End-to-end Models

Connectionist Temporal Classification (CTC). Model CTC for Speech Recognition task is designed to convert speech utterance input to character string output. Because the output character length is smaller than the input speech utterance, many empty labels will be inserted between the output character string and the input speech utterance many times to form the output with the same length as the input speech utterance. As CTC is the elementary technique and can simultaneously receive speech utterances and output continuous characters, it is common in empirical real-time speech recognition. One disadvantage people note when using the CTC model is the assumption that the output characters of the speech input are independent of each other [2].

Joint CTC/Attention. Kim at el. [5] uses CTC objective function as the auxiliary task to train the attention model encoder within the multi-task learning (MTL) framework. Where the encoder is collaborative with CTC and attention models. The CTC model can enforce monotonic alignment between speech and label sequences, whereas the attention model cannot. Another advantage of using CTC as an auxiliary task is that the network is learned quickly.

3   Results and Discussions

ASR toolkit developed by us and based on the PyTorch Lightning framework provides a template to manage the speech recognition models used in this study to facilitate the research. Support various types of encoders, decoders, and frameworks for the speech recognition task. However, this paper uses only the CTC Model and the Joint CTC/Attention model. Here is the GitHub direct link to the ASR Toolkit: https://github.com/tuanio/asr-toolkit.

3.1   Dataset

In this paper, we use two datasets which are the VIVOS dataset and the VLSP 2020 ASR Corpus. Details are detailed below.

Vivos Dataset: Vivos is a free Vietnamese speech corpus comprising 15 h of recording speech prepared for the Automatic Speech Recognition task. The corpus has been prepared by AILAB, a computer science lab of VNUHCM - the University of Science, with Prof. Vu Hai Quan as the head. [16].

VLSP 2020 ASR Corpus: One of the two datasets shared by VinBigdata is the speech corpus for the automatic speech recognition task in VLSP-2020. A small speech training dataset of 100 h as VinBigdata-VLSP2020-100h created for Task-01 belongs to the international workshop VLSP-2020. The one that we use for the experiment was shown in this paper [17].

3.2   Experiments and Results

We used the free Kaggle GPU and the free Google Colab GPU to train the models and test the results. However, because it is free, it is impossible to experiment too much, leading to poor results. We are training models on the 115 h speech training dataset (100h VLSP 2020 + 15 h Vivos trainset) and the two validating and testing tasks on the Vivos testing dataset (0.45 h). We train across many kinds of encoders, decoders, and frameworks. The encoder is Conformer, and the decoder is a Transformer model. The framework is CTC and Joint CTC/Attention.

After many attempts, we found that the Conformer - CTC and Conformer - Transformer - Joint CTC/Attention acquire the highest result. The encoder-dimension is 144, encoder-layer is 8, attention-head is 1, We use SpecAugment with mask $F = 27$ and 10 mask with max time-mask is $p_s = 0.05$. The Transformer decoder has 144 parameter for d_{model}, the number of attention head is 1, number of layers feed-forward-dimension is 32 and 0.1 dropout. We use CTC loss for L_{CTC} and Cross Entropy loss for $L_{Attention}$ in Pytorch. Both loss functions use a same learning rate of 0.001 and batch size of 4 for all models. The information on the training task is presented in Table 1.

Table 1. Information on training models.

Model	No. Parameters	Minutes/Epoch	No. Epochs
Conformer - CTC	4.7M	36	90
Conformer - Transformer - Joint CTC/Attention	4.9M	41	55

From Fig. 2 and Fig. 3, we can see that both models significantly vary in training loss. Maybe this is because we use the batch size of 4 due to limitation of GPU resources. Validation WER of Conformer - CTC and Conformer -

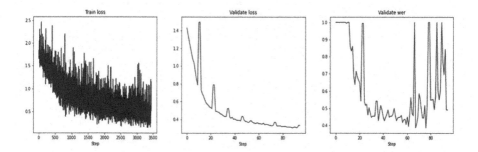

Fig. 2. Conformer - CTC train loss, validation loss, and validation WER over time.

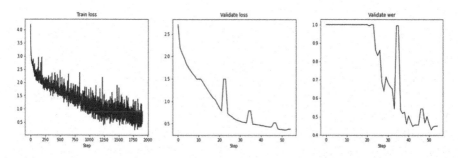

Fig. 3. Conformer - transformer - joint CTC/attention train loss, Validation loss, and validation WER over time.

Transformer - Joint CTC/Attention has high volatility sometimes (jump value between low and high level). We trained until near convergence, but due to insufficient resources, we ended the training early (up to 100 epochs, not 1000 epochs as initially planned).

The prediction results show that Conformer - CTC get better recognization (Table 2). Model using CTC architecture may have character errors when recognizing (adhesive words repeating characters redundant characters) because CTC is a monotonic model with each character being recognized separately regardless of context. The Conformer - Transformer - Joint CTC/Attention model only has the word error because this architecture has an Attention mechanism to investigate the context in the sentence while recognizing. The context that influences the prediction should have a more accurate identification. This model can be recognized much better if the training has enough time and resources.

Table 2. Prediction sample after model training. The meaning of prediction samples: (1) and when I saw that I was still steadfast in replying, (2) the brother was then allowed to bid to build the canal but did not proceed, (3) I am afraid of losing him, but I feel insulted, (4) can heal without leaving a scar.

Model	Ground Truth	Predict
Conformer - CTC	(1) và khi thấy tôi vẫn kiên định trả lời trớt quớt	và khi thấy tôi vẫn kiên định trả lời trớt **quốc**
	(2) người anh sau đó được phép thầu xây kênh này nhưng không tiến hành	người anh sau đó được phép thầu **say kên** này nhưng không **tế hàn**
	(3) em sợ mất anh ấy nhưng lại cảm thấy mình bị xúc phạm	em **sờm mấn** anh ấy nhưng là cảm **thá** mình bị xúc phạm
	(4) có thể lành lặn mà không để lại vết sẹo	có thể **làng lạng** mà không **bể** lại **đết** sẹo
Conformer - Transformer - Joint CTC/Attention	(1) và khi thấy tôi vẫn kiên định trả lời trớt quớt	và khi thấy tôi vẫn kiên định trả lời trớt **quốc**
	(2) người anh sau đó được phép thầu xây kênh này nhưng không tiến hành	người anh sau đó được **phiếp** thầu **phay kên** này nhưng không **tiếng** hành
	(3) em sợ mất anh ấy nhưng lại cảm thấy mình bị xúc phạm	em sợ mất anh ấy nhưng là cảm **thái** mình bị xúc **phải**
	(4) có thể lành lặn mà không để lại vết sẹo	có thể **làng lặng** mà không **bệt sẻo**

Table 3. Compare the results of the research team with other research on Vietnamese

Model	Test dataset	WER(%)
Conformer - CTC (**us**)	Vivos	20
Conformer - Transformer - Joint CTC/Attention (**us**)		44
Wave2vec 2.0 [18]	Vivos	6.15
Google [19]	News	22.41
Data Augmentation [20]	Realistic voice	10.3
TDNN + LSTM (E2E Model) [12]	VLSP2018 + FPT	9.71

The comparison results in Table 3 show that the Conformer - CTC model get best WER value after 90 epochs. Conformer - Transformer - Joint CTC/Attention model also achieved pretty good results after training 55 epochs (only 55 epochs due to limited hardware). This table also shows some comparisons with other researches. Because those papers [12,19,20] do not publicize evaluation data, we do not have specific data to evaluate and compare. Wav2vec 2.0 [18], the model is pre-trained 13k hours, a fine-tuned 250 h data set, and a good GPU for training. Meanwhile, we trained for 115 h with free GPU Google Colab and Kaggle. The highlight of this paper is that we use a Conformer model that no paper uses this architect for the Vietnamese dataset and has a positive result.

4 Conclusion

In this paper, we solve the problem of Vietnamese speech recognition with deep learning models Conformer with CTC and Conformer - Transformer with Joint CTC/ Attention. These models had trained on the Vivos and VLSP 2020 ASR dataset for 115 h. The results show that the Conformer model with the appropriate network architecture trained on the CTC platform has achieved better results than the Conformer - Transformer model with Joint CTC/ Attention on the test dataset. However, with a large amount of data to ensure accuracy in speech recognition, it is necessary to invest more in hardware power and training time. In the upcoming development, we will further improve the network architecture and model optimization and increase the training time to achieve the desired results.

Acknowledgement. We thank the R&D team of EduplaX - WeAi for giving us the time to do a more in-depth study of speech recognition and experiment with the results of this article.

References

1. Li, J.: Recent advances in end-to-end automatic speech recognition. ArXiv arXiv:2111.01690 (2022)
2. Graves, A., Fernández, S., Gomez, F., Schmidhuber, J.: Connectionist temporal classification: labelling unsegmented sequence data with recurrent neural 'networks. In: ICML - Proceedings of the 23rd International Conference on Machine Learning, vol. 2006, pp. 369–376, New York (2006). https://doi.org/10.1145/1143844.1143891
3. Chan, W., Jaitly, N., Le, Q., Vinyals, O.: Listen, attend and spell: a neural network for large vocabulary conversational speech recognition. In: IEEE International Conference on Acoustics, Speech and Signal Processing (ICASSP), pp. 4960–4964 (2016). https://doi.org/10.1109/ICASSP.2016.7472621
4. Graves, A.: Sequence transduction with recurrent neural networks. In: CoRR. (2012). ArXiv arXiv:1211.3711

5. Kim, S., Hori, T., Watanabe, S.: Joint CTC-attention based end-to-end speech recognition using multi-task learning. In: 2017 IEEE International Conference on Acoustics, Speech and Signal Processing (ICASSP), pp. 4835–4839 (2017)
6. Amodei, D., et al.: Deep speech 2: end-to-end speech recognition in english and mandarin (2015). ArXiv arXiv:1512.02595
7. Han, W., et al.: ContextNet: improving convolutional neural networks for automatic speech recognition with global context (2020). ArXiv arXiv:2005.03191
8. Gulati, A., et al.: Conformer: convolution-augmented transformer for speech recognition (2020). ArXiv arXiv:2005.08100
9. Beckmann, P., Kegler, M., Saltini, H., Cerňak, M.: Speech-VGG: a deep feature extractor for speech processing (2019)
10. Vaswani, A., et al.: Attention is all you need (2017). ArXiv arXiv:1706.03762
11. Graves, A., Mohamed, A., Hinton, G.: Speech Recognition with Deep Recurrent Neural Networks, (2013). ArXiv arXiv:1303.5778
12. Nguyen V.H.: an end-to-end model for vietnamese speech recognition. In: 2019 IEEE-RIVF International Conference on Computing and Communication Technologies (RIVF), pp. 1–6 (2019). https://doi.org/10.1109/RIVF.2019.8713758
13. Nguyen, Q.M., Nguyen, T.B., Pham, N.P., Nguyen, T.L.: VAIS ASR: building a conversational speech recognition system using language model combination (2019). ArXiv arXiv:1910.05603
14. Zhang, Q., et al.: Transformer transducer: a streamable speech recognition model with transformer encoders and RNN-T Loss (2020). ArXiv arXiv:2002.02562
15. Dong, L., Xu, S., Xu, B.: Speech-transformer: a no-recurrence sequence-to-sequence model for speech recognition. In: 2018 IEEE International Conference on Acoustics, Speech and Signal Processing (ICASSP), pp. 5884–5888 (2018). https://doi.org/10.1109/ICASSP.2018.8462506
16. Luong, H., T., Vu, H., Q.: A non-expert Kaldi recipe for Vietnamese speech recognition system. In: Proceedings of the Third International Workshop on Worldwide Language Service Infrastructure and Second Workshop on Open Infrastructures and Analysis Frameworks for Human Language Technologies (WLSI/OIAF4HLT2016), Osaka, Japan, The COLING 2016 Organizing Committee, pp. 51–55 (2016)
17. Institute VinBigdata Homepage. https://institute.vinbigdata.org/en/events/vinbigdata-shares-100-hour-data-for-the-community. Accessed 5 June 2022
18. Nguyen, B.: Vietnamese end-to-end speech recognition using wav2vec 2.0. (2021). https://doi.org/10.5281/zenodo.5356039
19. Thanh, N.T.M., Dung, P.X., Hay, N.N., Bich, L.N., Quy, Đ.X.: Đánh giá các he thong nhan dạng giọng nói tieng Viet (Vais, Viettel, Zalo, Fpt và Google) trong ban tin. In: Tạp Chí Khoa Học Giáo Dục Kỹ Thuat, Vietnamese. vol. 63 (2021)
20. Nguyen, Q.B., Mai, V.T., Le, Q.T., Dam, B.Q., Do, V.H.: Development of a Vietnamese large vocabulary continuous speech recognition system under noisy conditions. In Proceedings of the Ninth International Symposium on Information and Communication Technology (SoICT 2018), pp. 222–226. Association for Computing Machinery, New York (2018). https://doi.org/10.1145/3287921.3287938

Enhancing Obfuscated Malware Detection with Machine Learning Techniques

Quang-Vinh Dang[(⊠)][iD]

Industrial University of Ho Chi Minh City, Ho Chi Minh City, Vietnam
dangquangvinh@iuh.edu.vn

Abstract. Obfuscated malware is malware that tries to be hidden from malware detection software. While there are some advances in the malware detection research community in recent years, modern malware uses multiple techniques to avoid being detected by the anti-malware system. In this research, we aim to improve the detection quality of malware by using state-of-the-art machine learning algorithms. The experimental results show that our proposed methods outperform state-of-the-art research studies.

Keywords: Obfuscated malware · Malware detection · Machine learning

1 Introduction

Malware detection is one of the most important research topics of cybersecurity [3]. Despite many efforts in last four decades to fighting against malware, malware is still a severe threat to Internet security according to Global Threat Landscape Report for 2H2021 of FortiGuard [12]. Furthermore, modern malware applied obfuscation techniques to hide themselves against the malware detector. Obfuscation is defined as "a technique that makes programs harder to understand" [22], hence traditional static analysis techniques might not be able to cope with this kind of malware.

As static analyzer is expensive to update to catch up with the evolving speed of the malware, different learning systems are designed to automatically adapt with new malware [9,17]. The main difference of the algorithms are the features feed to the algorithms as they will determine the characteristic of the model, such as a model might prefer speed over accuracy. However, due to the rapid growth of machine learning research and the optimization from implementation details, at the moment we can perform many complex models with less running time than before.

There are different ways to analyze a software to detect if it is a malware [20]. We will review some of them in Sect. 2. In this study we follow the approach of memory analysis [3]. Our approach follows the dynamic analysis approach [20] that analyzes a software dynamically based on their behavior.

T. K. Dang et al. (Eds.): FDSE 2022, CCIS 1688, pp. 731–738, 2022.
https://doi.org/10.1007/978-981-19-8069-5_54

We evaluate our proposed method using a state-of-the-art real-world dataset presented by [3]. The experimental results let us claim that our method outperforms other published method in detecting malware.

Our contributions are:

- We present a different algorithm that outperforms state-of-the-art research works.
- We extend the recent research work from binary classification to multi-class classification.

The paper is organized as follows. We review relevant literature in Sect. 2. We then describe our method in Sect. 3. The experimental results are discussed in Sect. 4. Last we conclude our paper and draw some future research ideas in Sect. 5.

2   Related Works

2.1   Malware Obfuscation Techniques

There are several methods for malware to hide themselves from the detectors.

The most simple way is using encryption technique [18]. By that, a malware encrypted itself to a coded content, hence a manual analyzer might not be able to understand its nature. However, the encrypted content is being constant then can be detected by signature matching technique [11].

An early dynamic obfuscation technique is called dead code insertion [13]. In the dead-code insertion approach, a malware inserted to itself some unused code, hence keep the behavior same but look different.

Other techniques are register reassignment or subroutine reordering [22]. By using these techniques, registers or subroutines are swap in a random order so the malware will have a completely different outlook.

There are other techniques such as code obfuscation to make the code be unreadable. One example is presented in Fig. 1.

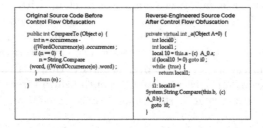

Fig. 1. An example of code obfuscation

2.2 Malware Detection Techniques

We quickly review some relevant malware detection techniques. We refer the audience to other comprehensive review papers [1, 23] for further details.

A common detection method is signature-based detection. A list of signatures will be extracted from malware then stored in a signature database. Then, a list of rules will be designed to determine if a software is malware. A similar technique is being applied to detect intrusion in computer networks [5]. This approach belongs to static analysis approach, as they do not need to observe the behavior of the applications.

Another approach is to dynamically analyse the behavior of the malware. In this approach, the malware detector monitor the behavior of the applications. The detector might monitor:

- File changes [21]
- Network transmission [2]
- API call [8, 15, 19]
- Memory change [3]
- Behavior in a sandbox [21]

In recent years, machine learning has dominated research in malware detection [16]. The authors of [3] has evaluated several popular machine learning algorithms such as Random Forest, Decision Tree and Support Vector Machine (SVM) in malware detection. We will compare our proposed approach with these algorithms as well.

A relevant line of research of malware detection is intrusion detection [5]. The authors of [5] evaluated multiple machine learning algorithms in intrusion detection and claim that the gradient boosting algorithms achieve the highest performance. According to more recent research studies [6, 7], CatBoost [10] is the best algorithm in both running speed and predictive accuracy.

3 Methods

We use CatBoost as our main classification algorithm. CatBoost [10] is a gradient boosting machine learning algorithm, similar to xgboost [4] and LightGBM [14]. The reason of choosing catboost is based on the recent works of [6] where the authors proved that catboost have a superior performance compared to other classification techniques.

CatBoost belongs to gradient boosting learning family. CatBoost is built as multiple decision trees. The next tree will recover the prediction error made by previous tree.

4 Results

4.1 Dataset

We utilize the dataset CIC-MalMem-2022 that is available at https://www.unb.ca/cic/datasets/malmem-2022.html. The dataset is presented in the paper of [3].

Table 1. Breakdown of malware distribution in the dataset

Malware category	Malware families	Count
Trojan Horse	• Zeus	• 195
	• Emotet	• 196
	• Refroso	• 200
	• scar	• 200
	• Reconyc	• 157
Spyware	• 180Solutions	• 200
	• Coolwebsearch	• 200
	• Gator	• 200
	• Transponder	• 241
	• TIBS	• 141
Ransomware	• Conti	• 200
	• MAZE	• 195
	• Pysa	• 171
	• Ako	• 200
	• Shade	• 220

The dataset contains 29,298 memory dumps of benign software and 29,298 memory dumps of malware. The malware number breakdown is presented in Table 1.

In total there are 55 features presented in the dataset. The features include number of commit charges, number of protection, number of mutant handles, etc.

We divide the dataset intro train:validation:test set with the ratio of 60:20:20. All the experimental results are reported based on the evaluation on the test set.

4.2   Results

Binary Classification. In this experiment we perform binary classification, similar to the work of [3]. It means that we only try to classify if a software is malware or benign.

The result of the binary prediction is presented in Fig. 2.

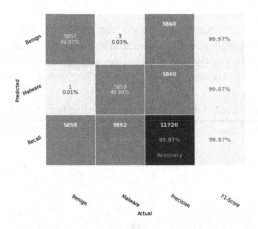

Fig. 2. Confusion matrix in binary prediction setting

We see that the performance is better than state-of-the-art [3]. we show the comparison in Table 2.

Table 2. Comparison with other published methods. We selected only the best models from published papers to present here.

Algorithm	Precision	Recall	F1	Accuracy
CatBoost (this paper)	0.9998	0.9998	0.9997	0.9997
Random Forest [3]	0.98	0.97	0.97	0.97
Naive Bayes + Random Forest + Decision Tree [3]	0.99	0.99	0.99	0.99

It takes 16ms to perform the prediction for 11, 720 samples.

Multi Classification. We extend the work of [3] by performing the multi-class classification. The confusion matrix is presented in Fig. 3. We present the feature importance in Fig. 4.

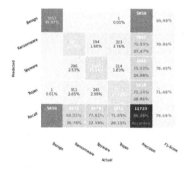

Fig. 3. Confusion matrix in case of multi classification

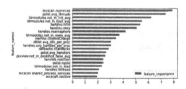

Fig. 4. Feature importance in multi classification

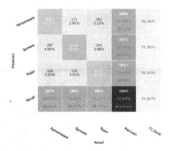

Fig. 5. Confusion matrix in classifying malware only

We observe that the model still perform very well in classifying malware and benign software. However, it is not quite good in classifying the exact type of malware. To verify the assumption, we build another model to classify malware only and present the confusion matrix in Fig. 5. The phenomenon can be explained by the overlapping nature of malware.

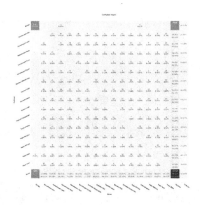

Fig. 6. Confusion matrix in classifying subclass of malware

Furthermore, as we can see in Fig. 6, classifying subclass of malware in fact does not yield a worse performance compared to 3-class classification case. Hence, the ambiguous lies on the difference of classes but not sub-classes.

5   Conclusions

In this paper we study the obfuscated malware detection problem. We propose new models to deal with malware detection. The experimental results showed that our model perform better state-of-the-art models. In binary setting, our model perform at near-perfect level. In the future works we will improve the performance of the model in case of multi-classification.

References

1. Aslan, Ö.A., Samet, R.: A comprehensive review on malware detection approaches. IEEE Access **8**, 6249–6271 (2020)
2. Bekerman, D., Shapira, B., Rokach, L., Bar, A.: Unknown malware detection using network traffic classification. In: 2015 IEEE Conference on Communications and Network Security (CNS), pp. 134–142. IEEE (2015)
3. Carrier., T., Victor., P., Tekeoglu., A., Lashkari., A.: Detecting obfuscated malware using memory feature engineering. In: ICISSP, pp. 177–188. INSTICC, SciTePress (2022). https://doi.org/10.5220/0010908200003120
4. Chen, T., Guestrin, C.: Xgboost: a scalable tree boosting system. In: KDD, pp. 785–794 (2016)
5. Dang, Q.-V.: Studying machine learning techniques for intrusion detection systems. In: Dang, T.K., Küng, J., Takizawa, M., Bui, S.H. (eds.) FDSE 2019. LNCS, vol. 11814, pp. 411–426. Springer, Cham (2019). https://doi.org/10.1007/978-3-030-35653-8_28
6. Dang, Q.-V.: Intrusion detection in software-defined networks. In: Dang, T.K., Küng, J., Chung, T.M., Takizawa, M. (eds.) FDSE 2021. LNCS, vol. 13076, pp. 356–371. Springer, Cham (2021). https://doi.org/10.1007/978-3-030-91387-8_23
7. Dang, Q.-V.: Studying the attack detection problem using the dataset CIDDS-001. In: Antipova, T. (ed.) DSIC 2021. LNNS, vol. 381, pp. 525–532. Springer, Cham (2022). https://doi.org/10.1007/978-3-030-93677-8_46
8. Das, S., Liu, Y., Zhang, W., Chandramohan, M.: Semantics-based online malware detection: towards efficient real-time protection against malware. IEEE Trans. Inf. Forensics Secur. **11**(2), 289–302 (2015)
9. Dhanya, K.A., Dheesha, O.K., Gireesh Kumar, T., Vinod, P.: Detection of obfuscated mobile malware with machine learning and deep learning models. In: Thampi, S.M., Piramuthu, S., Li, K.-C., Berretti, S., Wozniak, M., Singh, D. (eds.) SoMMA 2020. CCIS, vol. 1366, pp. 221–231. Springer, Singapore (2021). https://doi.org/10.1007/978-981-16-0419-5_18
10. Dorogush, A.V., Ershov, V., Gulin, A.: Catboost: gradient boosting with categorical features support. arXiv preprint arXiv:1810.11363 (2018)
11. Elhadi, A.A., Maarof, M.A., Osman, A.H.: Malware detection based on hybrid signature behaviour application programming interface call graph. Am. J. Appl. Sci. **9**(3), 283 (2012)
12. FortiGuard Labs: global threat landscape report (2022). https://visionayrlive.com/tp/ss_at/wat/0wfgigj72/report-q1-2022-threat-landscape.pdf
13. Huidobro, C.B., Cordero, D., Cubillos, C., Cid, H.A., Barragán, C.C.: Obfuscation procedure based on the insertion of the dead code in the crypter by binary search. In: ICCCC, pp. 183–192. IEEE (2018)
14. Ke, G., et al.: LightGBM: a highly efficient gradient boosting decision tree. Advances in Neural Information Processing Systems 30 (NIPS 2017)
15. Ki, Y., Kim, E., Kim, H.K.: A novel approach to detect malware based on API call sequence analysis. Int. J. Distrib. Sens. Netw. **11**(6), 659101 (2015)
16. Kouliaridis, V., Kambourakis, G.: A comprehensive survey on machine learning techniques for android malware detection. Information **12**(5), 185 (2021)
17. Nath, H.V., Mehtre, B.M.: Static malware analysis using machine learning methods. In: Martínez Pérez, G., Thampi, S.M., Ko, R., Shu, L. (eds.) SNDS 2014. CCIS, vol. 420, pp. 440–450. Springer, Heidelberg (2014). https://doi.org/10.1007/978-3-642-54525-2_39

18. Sahay, S.K., Sharma, A., Rathore, H.: Evolution of malware and its detection techniques. In: Tuba, M., Akashe, S., Joshi, A. (eds.) Information and Communication Technology for Sustainable Development. AISC, vol. 933, pp. 139–150. Springer, Singapore (2020). https://doi.org/10.1007/978-981-13-7166-0_14

19. Sai, K.N., Thanudas, B., Sreelal, S., Chakraborty, A., Manoj, B.: MACA-I: a malware detection technique using memory management API call mining. In: TENCON 2019, IEEE Region 10 Conference (TENCON), pp. 527–532. IEEE (2019)

20. Sihwail, R., Omar, K., Ariffin, K.Z.: A survey on malware analysis techniques: static, dynamic, hybrid and memory analysis. Int. J. Adv. Sci. Eng. Inf. Technol. 8(4–2), 1662–1671 (2018)

21. Sikorski, M., Honig, A.: Practical malware analysis: the hands-on guide to dissecting malicious software. No Starch Press (2012)

22. You, I., Yim, K.: Malware obfuscation techniques: a brief survey. In: International Conference on Broadband, Wireless Computing, Communication and Applications, pp. 297–300. IEEE (2010)

23. Zhang, X., Breitinger, F., Luechinger, E., O'Shaughnessy, S.: Android application forensics: A survey of obfuscation, obfuscation detection and deobfuscation techniques and their impact on investigations. Forensic Sci. Int. Digit. Investig. **39**, 301285 (2021)

Detecting Intrusion Using Multiple Datasets in Software-Defined Networks

Quang-Vinh Dang[(✉)] 🆔

Industrial University of Ho Chi Minh City, Ho Chi Minh City, Vietnam
dangquangvinh@iuh.edu.vn

Abstract. Software-defined network (SDN) is an emerging technology that is being used widely to reduce the complexity of programming network functions. However, by splitting the control and data layers, the SDN architecture also attracts different types of attacks such as Distributed Denial of Service (DDoS). In recent years, several research studies addressed the security problem by introducing open datasets and classification techniques to detect attacks on SDN. The state-of-the-art techniques perform very well in a single dataset, i.e. when the training and testing datasets are from the same source. However, their performance reduces significantly in the presence of concept drift, i.e. if the testing dataset is collected from a different source than the training dataset. In this paper, we address this cross-dataset predictive issue by several concept drift detection techniques. The experimental results show that our techniques can improve performance in the cross-dataset scenario.

Keywords: Intrusion detection system · Machine learning · Classification · Software-defined network

1 Introduction

In typical computer networks, the network functions are distributed all over the network. It raises a lot of security issues due to the scale of the network [1]. To deal with this scalability problem, the software-defined network (SDN) is introduced. The main idea of the SDN is to centralize the network control and separate the data and control layers [11]. SDN is claimed to be effective to deal with modern requirements of the network today [22].

In SDN architecture, three layers are presented including data plane, control plane and application plane [17] as visualized in Fig. 1.

Business requirements are implemented in the application plane. The applications connect with the controller in the control plane via the northbound interface. The control plane takes care of the control logic including monitoring service. The data and control planes are connected by the southbound interface. The data plane contains the network devices, such as routers, switches, and other devices that are responsible to transfer data over the network.

However, SDN itself cannot be invulnerable against attacks. Multiple attack types have been discovered in recent years aimed at the SDN [1,11]. As a consequence, many researchers studied the defense techniques to protect the SDN.

T. K. Dang et al. (Eds.): FDSE 2022, CCIS 1688, pp. 739–746, 2022.
https://doi.org/10.1007/978-981-19-8069-5_55

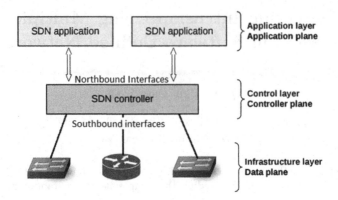

Fig. 1. SDN Architecture

Several open datasets have been introduced that allow the researchers to evaluate their techniques [11]. Some recent studies [7] showed that machine learning classification algorithms can achieve very high accuracy in classifying attacks, given that the attacks come from the same source as known attacks before. However, if the attacks come from a related but different data source, the predictive performance will drop dramatically.

In reality, we cannot expect that the attacks will come from the same data source as the training data. In fact, a crucial problem of cyber-security systems is preventing unknown attacks.

In this paper, we study the problem of intrusion detection in the SDN environment. We evaluate our proposal in the context of multiple data sources using the recent intrusion dataset generated for the SDN context [11]. Our contributions are:

– We extend the recent research study on the multi-data source IDS problem.
– We propose to add another model before the existing model to classify the data source.

We review the related studies in Sect. 2. We describe in detail the dataset in Sect. 3 and present our methodology and the results in Sect. 4. We conclude our paper and discuss some further research directions in Sect. 5.

2   Related Works

In this section, we analyze related studies regarding intrusion detection topics in literature.

The task of detecting intrusion from outside of a network is deployed at an intrusion detection system (IDS). An IDS will perform some classification tasks to decide if traffic is benign or malicious, then let it pass or stop them. In recent years, due to the fast development of machine learning techniques, many studies have utilized the power of state-of-the-art machine learning algorithms to empower the classification task [3,8].

The authors of [3] evaluated many classification algorithms such as logistic regression, naive Bayes and ensemble methods like random forest and xgboost using the CICIDS dataset [21]. The authors claimed that the algorithm xgboost achieved the best predictive accuracy. In the work of [2] the authors also claimed that the ensemble methods can achieve a near-perfect prediction on the testing set. The authors of [7] showed that CatBoost [20] can outperform xgboost for the task of intrusion detection.

As IDS is usually deployed on network devices such as routers, and one of its crucial requirements is the near real-time processing speed, it is important to keep an IDS to lightweight and fast. Several studies focused on feature selection to reduce the complexity of a machine learning algorithm implemented at an IDS. In the work of [13], the authors evaluated multiple feature selection criteria, such as information gain or relief to select the best feature subset. On the other hand, the authors of [5,6] look at the explainability perspective of the features to do the feature selection step. The authors of [4] have a different approach. Instead of reducing the number of features, the authors tried to reduce the number of training samples by using the active learning technique. The core idea of active learning is that, by starting with a small subset of the training dataset, we then evaluate which data point - if labeled - will most likely improve the predictive performance of the model.

Besides the tabular-based machine learning approaches, the text content of the attacks might give us a different look to the problem. The authors of [9] studied the problem of classifying attacks by utilizing some attack knowledge base like CAPEC [18] or CWE [16]. We refer the audience to the review of [14] for further details.

Another approach to detecting cyber threats is applying the knowledge of game theory [10,19]. By that, we model the behavior of attackers and defenders [12,15] with corresponding rewards, then try to find the optimal strategies for each player.

Regarding specifically SDN, the authors of [11] presented the InSDN dataset. The dataset is studied in the work of [7]. We will recall the experimental results of the work of [7] in Sect. 4, but to be short the authors suggested that classification algorithms that are widely used in literature such as xgboost is effective in predicting the known attacks, i.e. when the testing set and the training set are drawn from the same data source. However, if we train the model on a dataset and then predict using a different dataset, the performance will drop significantly.

3 The InSDN Dataset

In this paper we use the dataset InSDN [11], similar with the previous work of [7].

The dataset contains three subsets: normal data that contains benign traffic only, and OVS and mealsplotable data that contain attacking traffic only. The distribution of the traffic class is presented below:

- The normal traffic includes 68, 424 instances.
- The attack traffics targeting the mealsplotable 2 servers that include 136, 743 instances with the following attacks as described in Fig. 2.

Attack type	Number of instances
DoS	1,145
DDoS	73,529
Probe	61,757
BFA	295
U2R	17

Fig. 2. Attack distribution targeting the mealsplotable servers

- The attack traffics targeting the Open vSwitch (OVS) machine that includes 138, 722 instances with the following attacks as described in Fig. 3.

Attack type	Number of instances
DoS	52,471
DDoS	48,413
Probe	36,372
BFA	1,110
Web-Attack	192
BOTNET	164

Fig. 3. Attack distribution targeting the OVS servers

There is in total 83 features are presented in the dataset. We consider two main scenarios: one is when we try to perform the binary classification, i.e. we only need to detect whether traffic is benign or attack, and the second one is when we try to detect not only if traffic is an attack or not but also what attack type of this traffic is.

4   Methods and Experimental Results

For all the predictions presented in this section, we will use Catboost model [20].

First of all, we reproduce the work presented in the work of [7] as we use the training and testing set from the same data source. We present the confusion matrix of the prediction in Figs. 4 and 5 with the data come from the OVS and mealsplotable dataset respectively. We can see that the prediction is very good,

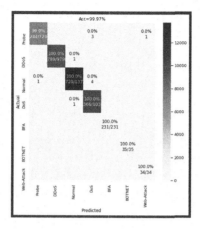

Fig. 4. Confusion matrix when the training and testing set are both from OVS data.

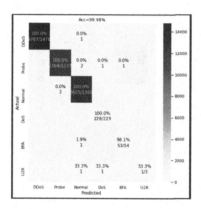

Fig. 5. Confusion matrix when the training and testing set are both from mealsplotable data.

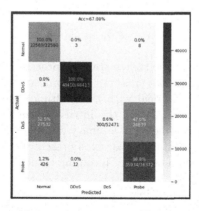

Fig. 6. Confusion matrix when the training is from mealsplotable data and the testing set is from OVS data.

Table 1. A small part of the dataset.

	Flow ID	Src IP	Src Port	Dst IP	Dst Port	Protocol	Timestamp	Flow Duration	Tot Fwd Pkts	Tot Bwd Pkts	TotLen Fwd Pkts	TotLen Bwd Pkts	Fwd Pkt Len Max
0	185.127.17.56-192.168.20.133-443-53648-6	185.127.17.56	443	192.168.20.133	53648	6	5/2/2020 13:58	245230	44	40	124937.0	1071.0	9100
1	185.127.17.56-192.168.20.133-443-53650-6	192.168.20.133	53650	185.127.17.56	443	6	5/2/2020 13:58	1605449	107	149	1071.0	439537.0	517
2	192.168.20.133-192.168.20.2-35108-53-6	192.168.20.133	35108	192.168.20.2	53	6	5/2/2020 13:58	53078	5	5	66.0	758.0	66
3	192.168.20.133-192.168.20.2-35108-53-6	192.168.20.2	53	192.168.20.133	35108	6	5/2/2020 13:58	6975	1	1	0.0	0.0	0
4	154.59.122.74-192.168.20.133-443-60900-6	192.168.20.133	60900	154.59.122.74	443	6	5/2/2020 13:58	190141	13	16	780.0	11085.0	427

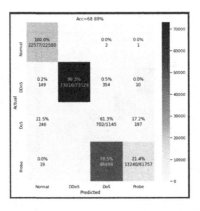

Fig. 7. Confusion matrix when the training is from OVS data and the testing set is from mealsplotable data.

consistent with the results of [7]. Furthermore, when we use the cross-dataset for training and testing, the performance drops significantly, as presented in Figs. 6 and 7.

So we realize that the same-source training process can achieve a very high predictive performance, but the cross-training process cannot. The observation leads us to a simple idea to deal with the multiple data source issue. Before applying a trained model to detect the intrusion, we have another model to detect the data source. The model is a binary-classifier to classify where does a package come from. The confusion matrix is presented in Fig. 8. Hence, we can predict with high precision a source of incoming traffic. Then, we can apply the corresponding predictor.

So we solve the issue of multiple data source by adding one more layer inside the IDS.

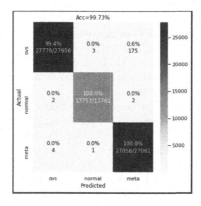

Fig. 8. Confusion matrix we predict the data source of an incoming traffic

5 Conclusions

In this paper, we studied the problem of intrusion detection in multiple data source scenario. Multiple data source is a critical issue that has a lot of impact both in research and practice. We resolve the issue of multiple data source by adding one more classifier before the intrusion classifier, hence we can predict the data source before calling the corresponding classifier. In the future, we will study the problem when we don't have enough training data yet to recognize the incoming class.

References

1. Ahmad, A.A., Boukari, S., Bello, A.M., Muhammad, M.A.: A survey of intrusion detection techniques on software defined networking (SDN). In: International Journal of Innovative Science and Research Technology (2021)
2. Alhowaide, A., Alsmadi, I., Tang, J.: Ensemble detection model for IoT IDS. Internet Things **16**, 100435 (2021)
3. Dang, Q.-V.: Studying machine learning techniques for intrusion detection systems. In: Dang, T.K., Küng, J., Takizawa, M., Bui, S.H. (eds.) FDSE 2019. LNCS, vol. 11814, pp. 411–426. Springer, Cham (2019). https://doi.org/10.1007/978-3-030-35653-8_28
4. Dang, Q.V.: Active learning for intrusion detection systems. In: IEEE, RIVF (2020)
5. Dang, Q.-V.: Understanding the decision of machine learning based intrusion detection systems. In: Dang, T.K., Küng, J., Takizawa, M., Chung, T.M. (eds.) FDSE 2020. LNCS, vol. 12466, pp. 379–396. Springer, Cham (2020). https://doi.org/10.1007/978-3-030-63924-2_22
6. Dang, Q.V.: Improving the performance of the intrusion detection systems by the machine learning explainability. In: IJWIS (2021)
7. Dang, Q.-V.: Intrusion detection in software-defined networks. In: Dang, T.K., Küng, J., Chung, T.M., Takizawa, M. (eds.) FDSE 2021. LNCS, vol. 13076, pp. 356–371. Springer, Cham (2021). https://doi.org/10.1007/978-3-030-91387-8_23

8. Dang, Q.V.: Machine learning for intrusion detection systems: recent developments and future challenges. In: Real-Time Applications of Machine Learning in Cyber-Physical Systems, pp. 93–118 (2022)

9. Dang, Q.V., François, J.: Utilizing attack enumerations to study sdn/nfv vulnerabilities. In: 2018 4th IEEE Conference on Network Softwarization and Workshops (NetSoft), pp. 356–361. IEEE (2018)

10. Dang, Q.V., Ignat, C.L.: Computational trust model for repeated trust games. In: 2016 IEEE Trustcom/BigDataSE/ISPA, pp. 34–41. IEEE (2016)

11. Elsayed, M.S., Le-Khac, N.A., Jurcut, A.D.: InSDN: a novel SDN intrusion dataset. IEEE Access **8**, 165263–165284 (2020)

12. Ferguson-Walter, K., Fugate, S., Mauger, J., Major, M.: Game theory for adaptive defensive cyber deception. In: Proceedings of the 6th Annual Symposium on Hot Topics in the Science of Security, pp. 1–8 (2019)

13. Herrera-Semenets, V., Bustio-Martínez, L., Hernández-León, R., van den Berg, J.: A multi-measure feature selection algorithm for efficacious intrusion detection. Knowl.-Based Syst. **227**, 107264 (2021)

14. Ignaczak, L., Goldschmidt, G., Costa, C.A.D., Righi, R.D.R.: Text mining in cybersecurity: a systematic literature review. ACM Comput. Surv. (CSUR) **54**(7), 1–36 (2021)

15. Ignat, C., Dang, Q., Shalin, V.L.: The influence of trust score on cooperative behavior. ACM Trans. Internet Technol. **19**(4), 1–22 (2019)

16. Martin, R.A., Barnum, S.: Common weakness enumeration (cwe) status update. ACM SIGAda Ada Lett. **28**(1), 88–91 (2008)

17. Mittal, S.: Performance evaluation of openflow SDN controllers. In: Abraham, A., Muhuri, P.K., Muda, A.K., Gandhi, N. (eds.) ISDA 2017. AISC, vol. 736, pp. 913–923. Springer, Cham (2018). https://doi.org/10.1007/978-3-319-76348-4_87

18. Nielsen, T.L., Abildskov, J., Harper, P.M., Papaeconomou, I., Gani, R.: The CAPEC database. J. Chem. Eng. Data **46**(5), 1041–1044 (2001)

19. Pawlick, J., Zhu, Q.: Game Theory for Cyber Deception. SDGTFA, Springer, Cham (2021). https://doi.org/10.1007/978-3-030-66065-9

20. Prokhorenkova, L., Gusev, G., Vorobev, A., Dorogush, A.V., Gulin, A.: CatBoost: unbiased boosting with categorical features. In: Advances in Neural Information Processing Systems, pp. 6638–6648 (2018)

21. Sharafaldin, I., Lashkari, A.H., Ghorbani, A.A.: Toward generating a new intrusion detection dataset and intrusion traffic characterization. In: ICISSP, pp. 108–116 (2018)

22. Stallings, W.: Foundations of modern networking: SDN, NFV. IoT, and Cloud. Addison-Wesley Professional, QoE (2015)

Detecting Exams Fraud Using Transfer Learning and Fine-Tuning for ResNet50

Huong Hoang Luong$^{(\boxtimes)}$, Toan Tran Khanh, Minh Doan Ngoc, Minh Ho Kha, Khang Thuong Duy, and Tho Tieu Anh

IT Department, FPT University,, Nguyen Van Cu 900000 Can Tho, Vietnam
{toantkce150269,minhdnce150022,minhhkce150582,
khangtdce150004,thotace150019}@fpt.edu.vn

Abstract. Online examinations gradually become popular due to Covid 19 pandemic. Environmentally friendly, saving money, and convenient,... are some of the advantages when taking exams online. Besides its major benefits, online examinations also have some serious adversities, especially integrity and cheating. There are some existing proctoring systems that support anti-cheating, but most of them have a low probability of predicting fraud based on students' gestures and posture. As a result, our article will introduce an online examination called ExamEdu that supports integrity, in which the accuracy of detecting cheating behaviors is 96.09% using transfer learning and fine-tuning for ResNet50 Convolutional Neural Network.

Keywords: Online exam · Cheating · Online proctoring · Head pose

1 Introduction

Since the appearance of the COVID-19 virus in late 2019, it has spread throughout the world at an unprecedented rate, causing a pandemic affecting the lives of almost everyone on Earth. The virus's rapid spread was due to its capability to spread through airborne droplets [1]. This allowed COVID-19 to spread easily in crowded places. Because of this, physical distancing was enacted, mandating everyone to keep a distance of at least 6 ft away from each other and to avoid crowded places. Due to this enactment, many businesses, and factories had to close down. This had greatly affected educational institutions all around the world.

By mid-April of 2020, less than half a year after the spread of the corona virus, 94% of learners around the world from across levels of education were affected by the pandemic [2]. This urgency forced schools to quickly switch from face-to-face teaching to online teaching through various means.

The abrupt change from offline teaching to online teaching has brought with it numerous problems [3]. One of those problems lies in the process of conducting the examination. Before the pandemic, examinations were conducted in a physical space, this allows proctors to closely monitor students' behavior,

© The Author(s), under exclusive license to Springer Nature Singapore Pte Ltd. 2022
T. K. Dang et al. (Eds.): FDSE 2022, CCIS 1688, pp. 747–754, 2022.
https://doi.org/10.1007/978-981-19-8069-5_56

thus preventing them from cheating. However, with the examination environment shifting from concentrated classrooms to individual student rooms over the internet, this task has gotten considerably harder. Maintaining an exam's integrity over the internet is highly difficult due to a number of reasons, some of the reasons are as follow: a) involvement of parents or siblings in the process of taking the exam. b) Limited camera view preventing the proctor from closely monitoring the student. These limitations prompt the need for a more secure way to conduct examinations through a digital platform.

We propose a new approach for cheating detection in online exams using deep learning by estimating the head pose of the student. Machine learning has helped human in many aspects of life, such as recommending movies [4,5], classifying texts [6]. It can also help in detecting misconduct during examinations. Our system works by taking a picture of the student's camera feed every 10 s and running it through a convolution neural network to determine whether the student is engaging in suspicious activities or not. The system will then alert the proctor about which student is under suspicion of misconduct. Our model is based on the ResNet50 model [7], and is evaluated using the augmented images of the head pose image database [8].

This paper comprises 5 sections. Section 1 is the introduction, problem and background of our research. In Sect. 2 of this paper, related works on preventing online examination misconduct will be presented. Then, we will detail our proposed method in Sect. 3. Section 4 will include the results and analysis of our experiments. And finally, Sect. 5 will end our paper with the conclusions.

2   Related Works

Online examination is beneficial for students and teachers. Because of the lack of physical presence, monitoring students during exam time is a big challenge for the teacher and the examination system [9]. This is why a good deal of research on cheating behaviors has been conducted in recent years. With Jadi approach [10], provide a whole new setup of software tools for students to use on their laptop/personal computer. El Kohli [11], suggests using an object detection system to detect, and identify prohibited items and notify the moderators using technology based on 3D convolutional neural network (3D CNN). In [12], suggested using fingerprint reader authenticator and eye tribe tracker to determine where the user is looking on the screen. Despite the published result, each method still has some limitations considering it does not reveal all kinds of fraud that students may produce, and it needs students to install a new setup of software tools on their computer to take the exam.

Other related approaches [9–12] proposed a genuine method to enforce fairness during exams.

With the use of the deep learning method, defrauding students will be identified by their head pose. A convolutional neural network (CNN) based system was used to classify the still image as "Cheating" or "Not Cheating." which will help the proctors to identify any fraud at the time of online exams. In this section, we described some related methods and solutions; we will propose and provide a positive solution to solve the problem in online learning systems.

3 Proposed Method

3.1 Training Model

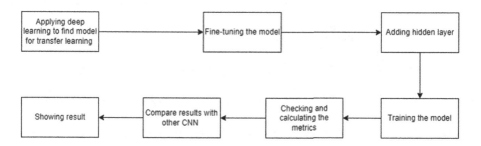

Fig. 1. Training model flowchart

In order to find the best model for our purpose, we performed a number of tests on a set of deep learning models. These models were configured with the same hyperparameters such as epoch from 30 to 50, batch size from 8 to 64 and learning rate: 1e−4, 1e−5. Then they were trained on the same subset of training data and then evaluated on one subset of testing images.

For our training phase, we used the pre-trained model's weights. The models were fitted on the ImageNet data set consisting of 1,28 million images of 1000 classes [13], thus by using transfer learning we utilize these weights without having to fit the model on a large data set. This also allows us to increase the accuracy of our prediction while having a small amount of input data. We then replace the fully-connected layer and the output layer of the original models with a new fully-connected layer and an output layer with activation softmax function for 2 classes *cheating* and *not cheating*. An example transfer learning model is described in Fig. 2.

The training process is separated into two phases, we denote them as Phase A and Phase B. During Phase A, we disable learning for the original neural network and only train the new fully connected layers. As for phase B, we re-enable learning for the original layers and train all layers on our data collection.

After training, we measure the model's accuracy by testing the subset and calculating the necessary metrics to contrast with other architectures later. Using the calculated metrics, we compare the result of these CNN together. As the model and contrasts have been completed, we will display all the tables and graphs for comparison.

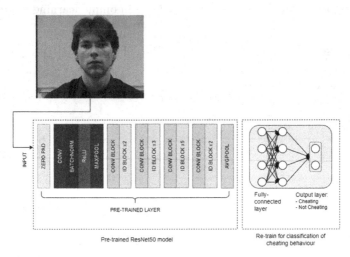

Fig. 2. Transfer learning model

3.2   Applying Model to ExamEdu System

We have developed a video call system for the students when taking the exam. Students and proctors will be in an online meeting room, so the proctors can observe and examine if the students are cheating or not. Our model is applied to support proctors in checking fraud during the examination. The system will capture an image every 5 s from the video call of the student and use it to detect misconduct. If violations are found, warning notifications will be informed to the proctors so they can warn the exam attendees or take necessary measures.

4   Experiment

4.1   Data Set

To detect exam frauds, we use head pose images of 15 persons with variations of face orientation for model training [8]. The database contains images of people with and without glasses and having various skin colors [8]. All images are in JPEG format and the size is 384×288 [8]. The head pose images are divided into cheating and not cheating categories. The data set is distributed to 2520 photographs for cheating head pose and 300 photographs for not cheating head pose. We use the on-the-fly data augmentation method to enlarge the data set for training from 1692 images to 84600 images. Figure 3 gives out an example of the two categories in the data set.

Cheating   Not cheating

Fig. 3. Example of two categories of head pose images in the data set

4.2 Evaluating Method and Comparison

This inquiry separates the data set into training, validation and testing subsets with a 60-20-20 ratio. Compare the findings with MobileNet [14], Inception V3 [15] and DenseNet121 [16] using the accuracy metrics (accuracy - acc) and the F1-score. The research was performed in the following sequence: Firstly, we get all images from two categories: cheating and not cheating. Then, we conduct training, evaluating and testing on the ResNet50 model with transfer learning (A) and fine-tuning (B). Finally, we compare the result of ResNet50 to other CNN architectures.

All models are run under the same hyperparameter: the number of epochs is 50, the batch size is 16, and the learning rate is 0.00001. We added three new layers, including a global average pooling 2D layer, a dense layer with a depth of 1024, and another dense layer consisting of 2 nodes for prediction. The outcome of training and testing are shown in Table 1.

This experiment shows that the ResNet50 model gives the most noticeable results with the accuracy on the test set of 96.09% and the F1-score of 95.98%. Figure 4 illustrates the accuracy and loss during training of ResNet50. The confusion matrix is illustrated in Fig. 5.

Table 1. Results comparison

Phase	Model	train_acc	val_acc	train_loss	val_loss	test_acc	test_F1
A	ResNet50	0.9674	1.0000	0.1325	0.0992	0.8954	0.8477
	MobileNet	0.9688	0.9687	0.1443	0.1142	0.8936	0.8434
	Inception V3	0.9375	0.9688	0.2010	0.0745	0.8794	0.8392
	DenseNet121	0.9479	0.9688	0.1937	0.1487	0.8936	0.8434
B	ResNet50	0.9792	1.0000	0.0762	0.0087	0.9609	0.9598
	MobileNet	0.9896	1.0000	0.0883	0.05342	0.9450	0.9470
	Inception V3	1.0000	1.0000	0.0257	0.0124	0.9539	0.9497
	DenseNet121	0.9896	1.0000	0.0802	0.0182	0.9539	0.9542

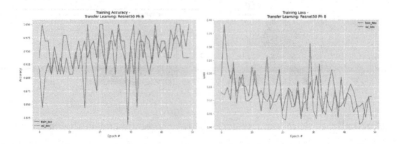

Fig. 4. Training accuracy and loss graph of the ResNet50 model

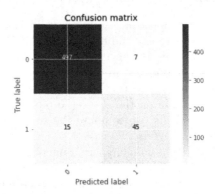

Fig. 5. Confusion matrix illustration

4.3   Evaluating Experiment Result

The experimental findings indicate promising results when using transfer learning with fine-tuned ResNet50 model for detecting fraud based on students' head posture. For instance, the ResNet50 model predicts two classes with 96.09% accuracy, while the F1-score on the testing set is 95.98%.

In addition, the results are also relatively positive compared to [11] with an accuracy of 95%, and in [17] with an accuracy 95.01%.

5   Conclusion

During COVID-19, 94% of learners worldwide from all levels of education were affected [2]. This situation forced schools to switch from face-to-face teaching to online teaching. Taking the exam, an irreplaceable part of online education has shown its weakness in maintaining an exam's integrity over the internet. A tool for supporting proctors in invigilating online exams is crucial. This paper proposes a new approach for cheating detection in online exams using deep learning by estimating the head pose of students using ResNet50 as a transfer learning model and fine-tuning to detect cheating behavior. The model has been trained and tested by a data set containing images of 15 persons with variations in skin color, head pose, and eye accessories. By customizing the original ResNet50 model and finding suitable hyperparameters in the fine-tuning phase, the accuracy of detecting cheating behavior has improved to 96.09%.

References

1. Morawska, L., Cao, J.: Airborne transmission of sars-cov-2: the world should face the reality. Environ. Int. **139**, 105730 (2020)
2. Nations, U.: Policy brief: Education during covid-19 and beyond. United Nations (2020)
3. Hermanto, Y.B., Srimulyani, V.A.: The challenges of online learning during the covid-19 pandemic. Jurnal Pendidikan dan Pengajaran **54**(1), 46–57 (2021)
4. Nguyen, Q.N., Duong-Trung, N., Le Ha, D.N., Ha, X.S., Phan, T.T., Pham, H.X., Huynh, H.X.: Movie recommender systems made through tag interpolation. In: Proceedings of the 4th International Conference on Machine Learning and Soft Computing. ICMLSC 2020, pp. 154–158. Association for Computing Machinery, New York (2020)
5. Huynh, H.T., Duong-Trung, N., Ha, X.S., Quynh Thi Tang, N., Huynh, H.X., Quoc Truong, D.: Automatic keywords-based classification of Vietnamese texts. In: 2020 RIVF International Conference on Computing and Communication Technologies (RIVF), pp. 1–3 (2020)
6. Duong-Trung, N., Nguyen, Q.N., Ha, D.N.L., Ha, X.S., Phan, T.T., Huynh, H.X.: Genres and actors/actresses as interpolated tags for improving movie recommender systems. Int. J. Adv. Comput. Sci. Appl. **11**(2), 67–74 (2020)
7. He, K., Zhang, X., Ren, S., Sun, J.: Deep residual learning for image recognition, pp. 770–778 (2016)
8. Gourier, N., Crowley, J.: Estimating face orientation from robust detection of salient facial structures. FG Net Workshop on Visual Observation of Deictic Gestures (2004)
9. Ahmad, I., AlQurashi, F., Abozinadah, E., Mehmood, R.: A novel deep learning-based online proctoring system using face recognition, eye blinking, and object detection techniques. Int. J. Adv. Comput. Sci. Appl. **12**(10), 847–854 (2021)
10. Jadi, A.: New Detection Cheating Method of Online-Exams during COVID-19 Pandemic. Int. J. Comput. Sci. Network Secur. **21**(4), 123–130 (2021)
11. El Kohli, S., Jannaj, Y., Maanan, M., Rhinane, H.: Deep learning: new approach for detecting scholar exams fraud. Int. Arch. Photogramm. Remote. Sens. Spat. Inf. Sci. **46**(4), 103–107 (2021)
12. Bawarith, R., Basuhail, D.A., Fattouh, D.A., Gamalel-Din, P.D.S.: Exam cheating detection system. Int. J. Adv. Comput. Sci. Appl. **8**(4), 176–181 (2017)
13. Deng, J., Dong, W., Socher, R., Li, L.-J., Li, K., Fei-Fei, L.: Imagenet: a large-scale hierarchical image database. In: 2009 IEEE Conference on Computer Vision and Pattern Recognition, pp. 248–255 (2009)
14. Howard, A.G., Zhu, M., Chen, B., Kalenichenko, D., Wang, W., Weyand, T., Andreetto, M., Adam, H.: MobileNets: efficient Convolutional Neural Networks for Mobile Vision Applications. arXiv (2017)

15. Szegedy, C., Vanhoucke, V., Ioffe, S., Shlens, J., Wojna, Z.: Rethinking the inception architecture for computer vision. CoRR abs/1512.00567 (2015)
16. Huang, G., Liu, Z., Weinberger, K.Q.: Densely connected convolutional networks. CoRR abs/1608.06993 (2016)
17. Behera, A., Gidney, A.G., Wharton, Z., Robinson, D., Quinn, K.: A CNN model for head pose recognition using wholes and regions. In: 2019 14th IEEE International Conference on Automatic Face &Gesture Recognition (FG 2019), pp. 1–2 (2019)

Shape of Pill Recognition Using Mask R-CNN

Nguyen Hoang An, Le Nhi Lam Thuy, and Pham The Bao[✉]

Information Science Faculty, Sai Gon University, Ho Chi Minh City, Vietnam
{thuylnl,ptbao}@sgu.edu.vn

Abstract. Convolutional Neural Networks (CNNs) architecture are widely used in machine learning and deep learning, but its application in pill shape detection and recognition is still a challenge. This paper proposes a method to detect and recognize the shape of a pill with the Mask R-CNN network. Through experimenting and checking the results on some traditional and proposed methods to evaluate the efficiency of the construction model. The CURE dataset was used to both train and test. The proposed method achieved 94.13% IoU score.

Keywords: Pill detection · Pill segmentation · Pill recognition · Mask R-CNN

1 Introduction

Currently, the types of pills on the market are truly diverse, ordinary people, especially the elderly, often have many difficulties in distinguishing or identifying pills without labels, so the rate of hospitalizations or problems with medication misuse is relatively high [1, 2]. The problem of drug classification in general and pill shape recognition has been ordered by many medical centers, nursing homes, companies, and businesses aimed at improving the quality of patient care, preventing risks from the misuse of drugs, especially targeting those with memory problems and lack of clarity such as the elderly in nursing homes. Especially in the Computer vision, many studies have proposed a pipeline for an automatic pill shape recognition system by computer vision, machine learning, and deep learning approach which can use computer power [3, 4]. However, the pill shape recognition system in real-world scenarios still a heavy challenge due to variations in illumination, lighting conditions, complex background. It can cause significant differences and variations in the obtained image parameter values and is the fundamental challenge of this problem in the wild.

Pill shape recognition systems are not effective such as WebMD, Pillbox, RxList, Drugs.com… require users to provide input information describing the characteristics of the pill, for example: colors, shapes, imprints, etc. automatic recognition systems using CNNs. However, Mask R-CNN networks is a method can solve the problem more effectively. CNNs model can extract more general features from various input data. Along with the growth of computational resources like GPU, Mask R-CNN networks has fast speed and high accuracy in object detection tasks, classification problems [5].

T. K. Dang et al. (Eds.): FDSE 2022, CCIS 1688, pp. 755–762, 2022.
https://doi.org/10.1007/978-981-19-8069-5_57

2   Related Works

June 2020, Alphonso Woodbury build a dataset of 15 pill classes with 490 images from the NIH dataset to conduct experiments through transfer learning from the VGG-16 model of pill recognition [6], the accuracy of up to 93% on the test dataset and approximately 50% on the real background dataset. August 2020, Suiyi Ling et al. uses multithreaded convolutional neural network method to identify the shape of a pill with a W2-net network model built on a simple U-net architecture. The system is tested on the CURE dataset containing 8,973 images of 196 classes of pills and the results obtained an IoU accuracy of 94% [7].

On a dataset consists of 13,000 pill images (224 × 224 pixels, data enhancement: rotate and change the viewing angle) belonging to 9,804 classes (two "front-back" faces for 4,902 different pills, in which, the actual user capture is 960 classes) from the NIH dataset, September 2020, Naoto Usuyama et al. built a transfer learning model from Resnet 152 and DenseNet using B-CNN and BCP in the final step to classify pills [8]. Experimental results of 85% mAP and 82% gAP on data are images of tablets with both sides, Fig. 1.

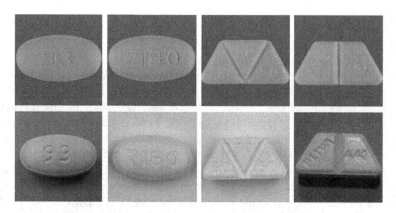

Fig. 1. Pill recognition using B-CNN and BCP model [8]

Next, Suwat Tangwattananuwat et al. used dataset of 3,074 images of 28 drugs applying transfer learning from models VGG16, Inception-Resnet-V2 and Xception [9]. The experimental results of all 3 models VGG16, Inception-Resnet-V2 and Xception give 100% accuracy of the test dataset and respectively 71.42%, 82.14% and 77.38% of evaluation dataset. However, because the authors do not make the dataset public, it is difficult to compare the results.

In addition, Yu and Chen proposed a technique that used the characteristics of the color, shape and imprint to identify the pill and achieved an accuracy of 97.1% on image dataset undisclosed pills include 2,500 pills [10]. The data was enhanced by randomly changing the brightness, contrast, rotation… of each pill image creating an image dataset with a total of 12,500 pill images. Neto et al. proposed a pill feature extraction machine to classify drugs based on the shape and color of the pill; the feature extractor was evaluated using the KNN, SVM and Bayes classifiers [11]. To extract features, they used two datasets PILL BR and NIH NLM PIR and achieved an accuracy of 99.85% and 99.82%. Wang et al. introduced the Highlighted Deep Learning - HDL technique to identify the blister pack, the segmentation and descriptor features can be extracted by the HDL technique [12]. This technique used CNN to properly classify the blister type and is invariant to light rotation and change; archived 100% accuracy on a database of 272 blister packs.

3 Methodology

We have researched and experimented with several popular techniques and modern methods; in which, focusing on 02 main approaches to solve the problem of pill's shape recognition are: (1) Segmentation and pill detection by traditional techniques, in which, images processing and edges detection are performed; and (2) Detecting pills based on machine learning, deep learning techniques.

With the traditional method, before recognition, image features need to be enhanced by methods of preprocessing, clarification, intensity adjustment, which helps to increase the efficiency of object segmentation. Some typical methods such as: Thresholding, Edge Based, Region-Based, Watershed, etc. [13, 14]. The results obtained are objects with closed edges, which are the basis for evaluating and classifying the shape of pills. After image segmentation, it is necessary to identify the pills from each bounding box. There are two common techniques: one is to use the edge or vertex geometry of the object; the second is the technique of matching samples with sample pills.

However, due to the influence of natural conditions (light, luminance, shadow, contrast, etc.) on pill images, traditional methods are often unable to fully detect edges in some drugs or wrongly detect interferences. Solving the difficulties from the above methods, Mask R-CNN, one of CNNs model, can extract features, predicting both bounding box and pill mask accurate to pixels, Fig. 2.

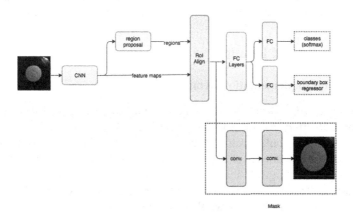

Fig. 2. Model architecture proposed

3.1   Model Initialization

To train the Mask R-CNN model on the pill images dataset, it is indispensable to configure the main information of the network architecture and initialize the data set to store pill images information. Where number_class is the number of drug image classes, min_confidence is the smallest threshold value to determine whether an object is a pill shape type or not, and some values related to the backbone architecture (Resnet50, Resnet101) and the learning rate of the network.

3.2   Pill Detection and Prediction

Region Proposal Network - RPN: To generate RPN targets, Mask R-CNN starts with a grid of anchors covering the entire image at different scales, then computes the inter-section value of the pill bounding boxes (IoU) of the anchors with real pills. Positive anchors are boxes with IoU >= 0.7 with any real pill, and negative anchors are boxes that do not cover any pill by more than 0.3 IoU. Anchor in the middle (that is, covering an object by IoU >= 0.3 but <0.7) is considered neutral and is excluded from training. To train the RPN regressor, also compute the size change needed to make the anchor completely cover the real pill. ROI Align refinement is another major contribution of Mask R-CNN, which solves the calculation of suggested regions that may not have the same size and brings them back to the same size to apply interpolation to calculate better feature map values, thereby increasing the accuracy of Mask R-CNN [15].

In the second phase, in addition to predict class and pill bounding box, Mask R-CNN also outputs a binary mask for each RoI. The mask branch has a dimensional $K\_(m^2)$ output for each RoI, which encodes K binary masks of m × m resolution for each K classes. To apply this technique, it is necessary to apply the sigmoid function on each pixel and define LMask as the mean binary cross-entropy loss. For a RoI associated with the background image layer (grouth-truth) k, the LMask is figured out only on the corresponding k-mask (the non-zero mask output does not contribute to the loss function value). So, the system calculates the error function value of the mask when predicting the pill, which is an especially important result in pill-to-pixel segmentation.

4   Experiments and Results

4.1   Dataset and Implementation Details

We trained and tested on the CURE dataset containing 8,973 images of 196 pills, which is divided into 09 different shapes including: 'Capsule', 'Double_round', 'Heart', 'Modified_rectangle', 'Octagon', 'Oval', 'Pentagon', 'Round', 'Triangle'. We grouped and annotated nearly 1,700 images of the above 09 classes (the unlabeled pills are mainly 02 types of Round and Capsule shapes that have been annotated with a large amount of these 02 classes, so the annotating more will not increase the efficiency of the model).

Moreover, from [7, 8], it is shown that dividing the data at the rate of 80% for the training dataset and 20% for the test dataset helps to supply enough data for model building and testing, evaluate to update the set of weights. Therefore, applying to the problem, we divide the sample data set into 02 training data sets (1,284 images) and

Table 1. Number of labeled pill images of the training set

Class	Images	Class	Images
Capsule	320	Double_round	34
Heart	30	Modified_rectangle	67
Octagon	90	Oval	228
Pentagon	23	Round	828
Triangle	9		

Table 2. Number of labeled pill images of the validation set

Class	Images	Class	Images
Capsule	80	Double_round	8
Heart	8	Modified_rectangle	17
Octagon	22	Oval	57
Pentagon	6	Round	207
Triangle	3		

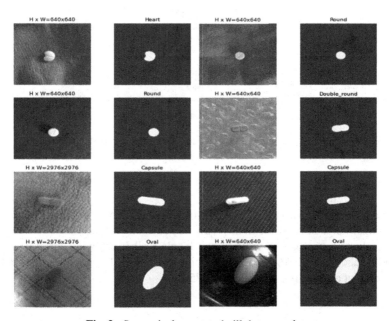

Fig. 3. Some pixel-annotated pill data samples

test (414 images) with the respective proportions of 80% and 20% shown in Table 1 and Table 2; some pill images of the training dataset are presented in Fig. 3.

On Google Colab pro environment, we used the transfer learning technique with pre-trained weights on the above COCO dataset to bring efficiency to the construction system, helping to initialize the weights more reasonably, increasing the extraction the pill features efficiency. For the optimizer method, we evaluated on some algorithm as: the stochastic gradient descent (SGD), Adam, RmsProp... After compare results, we chose SGD algorithm with 0.001 learning rate and 80 epochs.

4.2   Results

Through the experimental results on the evaluation dataset, we obtained results when predicting the IoU score of the pill mask reached 94.13%, the classification accuracy reached 100% higher than when applying the other methods such as: OpenCV, ORB + BoW + KMeans, OpenCV + RandomForest; shown in the form of graphs in the graphs Fig. 4 and Fig. 5. In which, to evaluate the results, the experimental program on 02 architectures is Resnet50, Resnet101 and hybrid.

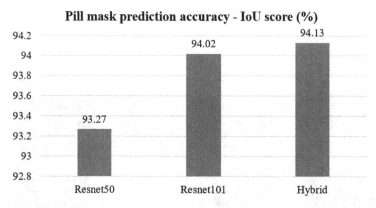

Fig. 4. Pill mask prediction accuracy with 2 different backbone architectures.

We compare our proposed approach result with state-of-the-art methods on the testing set of the CURE dataset, Table 3.

Table 3 shows that Mask R-CNN can work more effectively in the problem of pill shape recognition than other methods [7, 16, 17].

We evaluate our proposed method on Google Collab pro with one A100-SXM4 40 GB GPU and 32 GB RAM. Time for training Mask R-CNN model is around 8 h, and time for predict a single image is around 1.75 s.

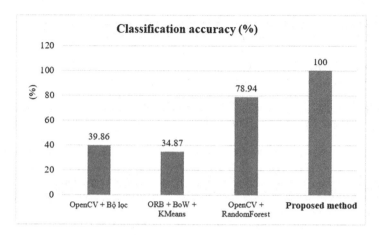

Fig. 5. The results compare the accuracy of the proposed method with the traditional method.

Table 3. Comparison of segmentation results with modern methods - IoU score

Method	Segmentation accuracy (%)
Espnetv2 [16]	78
U-net [17]	90
W2-net [7]	94
Proposed method	**94.13**

5 Conclusion

In this paper, we presented the problem of recognizing the shape of pills; in which, focus on techniques to solve the problem, such as: pill segmentation by boundary finding method; segmentation and pill shape recognition by deep learning model. From there, we proposed to build an experimental program using Mask R-CNN model, training model on around 1,700 pill images of 09 different shapes, thereby obtaining the identity accuracy confirmation reached approximately 94.13%.

For further work, and using the proposed schema, we can consider new deep CNNs model to extract features of pills to achieve more potential results on "shape of pill recognition" in the real world.

References

1. Tariq, R.A., Vashisht, R., Sinha, A., Scherbak, Y.: Medication dispensing errors and prevention. NCBI, January 2021
2. Zirpe, K.G., Seta, B., Gholap, S.: Incidence of medication error in critical care unit of a tertiary care hospital: where do we stand? PMC (2020)
3. Szegedy, C., et al.: Going deeper with convolutions. In: CVPR (2015)

4. Wong, Y.F., et al.: Development of fine-grained pill identification algorithm using deep convolutional network. J. Biomed. Inform. **74**, 130–136 (2017)
5. Dalai, R., Senapati, K.K.: Comparison of various RCNN techniques for classification of object from image. Int. Res. J. Eng. Technolo. (IRJET) **04**(07), 3147–3150 (2017)
6. Woodbury, A.: Increasing medication safety with deep learning image recognition. RxVision (2020)
7. Ling, S., et al.: Few-shot pill recognition. In: IEEE/CVF Conference on Computer Vision and Pattern Recognition (CVPR), pp. 9786–9795 (2020). https://doi.org/10.1109/CVPR42600.2020.00981
8. Usuyama, N., Naoto, L.: ePillID dataset: a low-shot fine-grained benchmark for pill identification. arXiv (2020)
9. Tangwattananuwat, S.: The identification of pill images using convolutional (2020)
10. Yu, J., Chen, Z., Kamata, S.I., Yang, J.: Accurate system for automatic pill recognition using imprint information. IET Image Process. **9**, 1039–1047 (2015)
11. Neto, M.A.V., de Souza, J.W.M., Reboucas Filho, P.P., Antonio, W.D.O.: CoforDes: an invariant feature extractor for the drug pill identification. In: IEEE 31st International Symposium on Computer-Based Medical Systems (CBMS), Karlstad (2018)
12. Wang, J.S., Ambikapathi, A., Han, Y., Chung, S.L., Ting, H.W., Chen, C.F.: Highlighted deep learning-based identification of pharmaceutical blister packages. In: IEEE 23rd International Conference on Emerging Technologies and Factory Automation (ETFA), Turin (2018)
13. Afandi, A., Isa, I.S., Sulaiman, S.N., Marzuki, N.N.M., Karim, N.K.A.: Comparison of different image segmentation techniques on MRI image. In: Zhang, Y.-D., Mandal, J.K., So-In, C., Thakur, N.V. (eds.) Smart Trends in Computing and Communications. Springer, Singapore (2020). https://doi.org/10.1007/978-981-15-0077-0_1
14. Lalitha, K.V., Amrutha, R., Michahial, S.: Implementation of Watershed Segmentation. IJARCCE **5**, 196–199 (2016)
15. He, K., Gkioxari, G., Dollár, P., Girshick, R.: Mask R-CNN. In: Facebook AI Research (FAIR) (2018)
16. Mehta, S., Rastegari, M., Shapiro, L., Hajishirzi, H.: ESPNetv2: a light-weight, power efficient, and general purpose convolutional neural network. In; Proceedings of the IEEE Conference on Computer Vision and Pattern Recognition, pp. 9190–9200 (2019)
17. Ronneberger, O., Fischer, P., Brox, T.: U-Net: convolutional networks for biomedical image segmentation. In: Navab, N., Hornegger, J., Wells, W.M., Frangi, A.F. (eds.) MICCAI 2015. LNCS, vol. 9351, pp. 234–241. Springer, Cham (2015). https://doi.org/10.1007/978-3-319-24574-4_28

Author Index

Printed in the United States
by Baker & Taylor Publisher Services